Artificial Intelligence

Artificial Intelligence

ELA KUMAR

Asst. Professor
Dept. of Computer Engineering
YMCA Institute of Engineering
Faridabad, Haryana

TECHSAR™

NEW DELHI

Published and Printed by

TechSar Pvt. Ltd.
4435-36/7, Ansari Road, Daryaganj
New Delhi–110 002 (India)
E-mail: tech_info@techsarworld.com
Website: www.techsarworld.com

ISBN: 978-81-906566-6-5

Reprint 2025

Dedicated to
Late (Smt.) Sita Devi
my mother-in-law

Preface

Artificial intelligence (AI) is one of the most exciting fields of computer engineering today. AI, as it is known popularly, is the science and technique used to make a machine intelligent. The idea of making a machine intelligent, so that it can function intelligently as we human beings do, is itself fascinating on one hand and challenging on the other. Human beings are considered most intelligent among all the living species around us. If we have to make an intelligent machine at all, first of all, we will have to understand why and how we humans are intelligent. The mechanism of human intelligence is a complex phenomenon. Our ancient philosophers have tried to explain this mechanism in their own way. We are unable to say whether their philosophy is scientific and can be modeled using available modern techniques, but it definitely can be a major guiding force to fulfill the dream of our researchers and scientists who are working day and night to accomplish the task on their hands.

If we talk of philosophy, what can be better than our own four *Vedas*! Vedas are full of thoughts regarding ancient Hindu philosophy. It is not surprising that lot of thoughts regarding human intelligence, its source, its relation with other senses and various aspects of human intelligence etc. have been dealt with in more than one way in this ancient philosophy. Our body is made of many organs. Each organ has distinct function. All human actions and emotions are performed and governed by these organs, individually and collectively, depending upon the situation. The five organs of perception— those of hearing, touching, seeing, tasting and smelling— are produced respectively from the *sattva*, i.e. five elements of *akash* (the sky), *vayu* (the air), *agni* (the fire), *jal* (the water) and *prithvi* (the earth). By an organ, it means not the outer instrument, but something subtle, made of finer matter, which functions through the physical instrument. Thus, the organ of seeing does not mean the outer eyes, but an organ made of intangible, finer matter, which is one of the constituents of subtle body.

The mind or *manas*, is the function of inner organ, *antahkaran*, which considers the pros and cons of a situation. The *buddhi*, i.e., the intellect or intelligence, which is determinative faculty, is a second function of the same organ, by which doubts are resolved and one comes to conclusion regarding the real nature of an object. Hence, philosophically, intelligence is the good work of *antahkaran* and is related to mind. According to Vedanta, the mind is material in nature, because it is produced from the five material elements.

Prakriti, or primordial matter includes everything – inorganic, organic and psychic. Consciousness or *Brahman*, which is self-luminous is utterly different from it. The five organs of perception and the inner organ are endowed with luminosity, i.e., they are capable of illuminating or expressing an object. Nevertheless, it must be remembered that this luminosity of *manas* and *buddhi* is derived from the self-luminous *Atman* or Soul, because they themselves being material are non-luminous by nature. Hence, intelligence derives its strength from *Atman* and not the body.

Atman is inner-self or Self and body is the home of *atman*. Thus, body is non-self. Vedanta analyses the non-self into five *kosa*s or sheaths. These are gross physical sheath (*annamayakosa*), the sheath of *prana* or the vital force (*pranamayakosa*), the sheath of the mind (*manomayakosa*), the sheath of the *buddhi* or intelligence (*vijnanamayakosa*) and the sheath of bliss (*anandamayakosa*). They are called sheaths because, like sheaths, they conceal *Atman*. The *vijnanmayakosa* or *buddhi*, the sheath of intelligence is like mind, a function of inner organ. Though insentient by nature, it appears intelligent and conscious because it reflects *Cit* or pure intelligence. This reflection of pure consciousness in *buddhi* is called the *jiva* or individualized soul. The opposite of intelligence is ignorance. The individual soul, after the attainment of knowledge, realizes that it is the same as *Brahman*. Thus, knowledge removes ignorance and illuminates intelligence. The following *Shloka*, from one of the four Vedas, has explicitly described this fact:

$$\text{अविरोधितया कर्म नाविद्यां विनिवर्तयेत्।}$$
$$\text{विद्याविद्यां निहन्त्येव तेजस्तिमिरसङ्घवत्।।}$$

(Action cannot destroy ignorance. For it is not in conflict with ignorance. Knowledge alone destroys ignorance, as light destroys dense darkness.)

It is the power of knowledge, which makes one intelligent, a fact discovered by our philosophers thousands of years back but realized by researchers of AI much later. There are many facets of human intelligence like learning, thinking, remembering and capability of reasoning etc., which together form a mechanism. This mechanism helps us perform various functions intelligently. However, it is knowledge, which provides life to this mechanism. Our organs perform various functions like knowledge acquisition, knowledge refinement, knowledge storage, inferencing, reasoning etc. for solving a given problem intelligently. These functions are performed naturally and effortlessly most of the time as soon as the *Atman* acquires a shape.

If a machine has to show intelligence, it will have to perform all the functions mentioned above, and many more, with the same ease and efficiency with which human beings perform. For example, learning is one of the most important activities performed by human beings naturally and with utmost ease. Human beings are supposed to be excellent learners. We not only learn new things quickly, adapt to new situations easily, but also perform same task in a better way next time. There is a story in The *Mahabharata*. Abhimanyu, when he was inside his mother's womb, one day, his father Arjuna was telling a story to his mother regarding the art used in the battle called art of *Chakravyuh*. Abhimanyu learnt that art listening to his father through the sense organs of his mother even before his birth, and used the same art while battling with Kauravas in the famous battle of *Mahabharata*. This is the degree of learning ability we possess! Can a machine acquire such degree of learning ability artificially as described above? It must, if it has to act intelligently!

Intelligence is too complex a phenomenon and it is difficult to describe it in a single theory. Philosophers and researchers have devised many theories. However, whatever be the theory, the basic aim is to understand and explore the mechanism of 'mind' that enables intelligent thoughts and actions. The activities like thinking, reasoning, understanding and reacting to a given situation are governed by mind. Our overall behavior is guided by our mind.

In the process to explore and understand the complexities of mind, researchers have recently been able to identify the area and activity hub of the brain that help guide thinking and behavior. In a report published in the English daily *Times of India* in early July, 2008, it has been claimed by the scientists that the outer layer of the brain, the reasoning, planning and self-aware region known as the cerebral cortex, has a central clearing house of activity below the crown of head that is widely connected to more specialized regions in a large network similar to a subway map.

This report provides the most complete rough draft to date of the cortex's electrical architecture, the cluster of interconnected nodes and hubs that help guide thinking and behaviour. The study also provides a striking demonstration of how new imaging techniques focused on the brain's white matter, i.e. the connections between cells, rater than the neurons themselves— are filling in a dimension of human brain function that has been all but dark.

This study has been conducted by a group of scientists from the University of Lausanne in Switzerland, Harvard and Indiana University. They studied the brains of five healthy male volunteers using a new technique called diffusion spectrum imaging. Many more scientists and researchers worldwide are busy in decoding and unfurling the human mind.

Researchers, after working over the years, at least have come to the conclusion, that intelligence is not exclusively attached to humans and have started believing that intelligence can be imparted to machines artificially. All the aspects of intelligence have been explored by engineers and scientists working in the field of AI. Whatever has been done till now, some part of that forms my scope of work. The book in your hands has been divided into twelve chapters to cover the same:

Chapter 1:   First chapter is devoted to introduce AI to readers. Apart from defining AI, a thorough account has been given to development of AI. Emphasis has also been given to the role of knowledge in developing intelligent systems.

Chapter 2:   The role of AI is to develop intelligent machines to solve real-world problems. Chapter 2 takes into account the basic nature of AI problems and the standard methodologies adopted to solve them.

Chapter 3:   In this chapter, various search techniques are described for reaching from start state of a problem to goal state. Alternatively, in simple terms, for solving a problem, there is a path moving along which, we are likely to get the solution. Search techniques are applied to find that path which is most suitable for a particular problem. Readers would get a detailed account of many such techniques in this chapter.

Chapter 4:   Chapter 4 is dedicated to the study of knowledge. Starting with the definition of knowledge to types and use of knowledge, some issues related to knowledge acquisition and representation techniques etc. have been discussed in this chapter.

Chapter 5:   We should always remember that knowledge is backbone of AI. This knowledge is to be acquired and formally represented before it is used by machines, for problem solving. There are numerous methods to represent knowledge. The basic and very popular technique is using logic. Chapter 5 presents the concepts of logic, namely prepositional logic and predicate logic along with introductory concepts, the basic terminology, and syntax of predicate and propositional logic. Lot of solved examples are included in this chapter, not only to make the readers conversant with the theory behind the concept, but also to help them in answering the questions asked in various level examinations.

Chapter 6:   This chapter discusses some of the advanced techniques used for representing knowledge. Knowledge representation is one of the most important issues related with developing intelligent systems. Lot of research has been done in this area and we have tried to give a through account of knowledge representation techniques in this chapter based on that.

Chapter 7:   We all understand this very important fact that computers understand only a definite language designed for a particular purpose. Hence, for the purpose of representing knowledge, we needed to develop languages which computer could understand. In this chapter, some programming languages, specially PROLOG and LISP, have been dealt with in detail. Again, number of solved examples have been given for understanding the use of these languages.

Chapter 8:   Handling Uncertainties is something we do almost daily and throughout our life, easily and effectively. It is very important activity involved in the process of reasoning. Every intelligent agent is required to perform reasoning while handling real life situations, and handling uncertainty is a necessary activity for dealing with such reasoning. Various techniques adopted for handling with uncertain situations have been discussed in detail in this chapter. Lot of real life examples have been taken for clarifying intricate concepts. At the end of the chapter, number of solved examples are included to help the readers attempt the problems asked in competitive examinations.

Chapter 9: Natural language Processing is other very important aspect of computer engineering. Computers understand only the languages designed and developed for a particular task. They are not able to converse in natural languages as we all do in our day-to-day life. Until it is possible for computers in particular, and intelligent machines in general to understand and follow the instructions in natural languages, the task of building a universal intelligent system will remain a dream for the scientists and engineers working in this area. In this chapter, we have discussed some of the techniques used for making the machines to analyze and understand natural languages.

Chapter 10: As mentioned earlier in this presentation, learning is one of the many natural capabilities we possess and they contribute substantially in making us intelligent. Any intelligent system needs to possess the abilities of learning to match the human intelligence. Similarly, understanding is another facet possessed by human beings, which is part and partial of actions performed by human mind. Every intelligent system is expected to possess some form and degree of understanding. Planning is important for the reason that all the actions required to solve a problem need to be planned before their application, for achieving the desired result. All these aspects related with intelligence have been discussed in this chapter.

Chapter 11: In this chapter, we have discussed some of the Applications of AI in complex phenomenon like, neural networks, vision and pattern matching. In fact, an intelligent agent has to perform number of activities of varying nature and stature. First of all, it is extremely difficult to recognize these, and once we are able to do so, it is more difficult to analyze and model these. Even though, researchers have put their best efforts and are still continuing with the same, we are far away from the ultimate goal!

Chapter 12: The primary aim of Artificial Intelligence is to develop Expert systems for solving real-world problems, effectively and economically. Expert systems are noting but the intelligent systems working in a limited domain. In this chapter devoted for expert systems, we have discussed various issues involved with the development of expert systems.

Sincere efforts have been made from our side to keep the language of the book as simple as possible, so that readers are easily able to understand the literal meaning of the language used. As mentioned earlier, the phenomenon of Artificial Intelligence are truly complex and thorough understanding is required to grasp those. Efforts have been made to use real-life examples wherever required to clarify these intricate concepts. In between, and also at the end of the chapters, **solved examples** have been included to help the readers not only to understand the concepts discussed, but also to attempt the numerical problems asked in various examinations. This is one of the unique features of the book presented before the readers, specially, students of undergraduate and post-graduate levels, with the hope that it will serve the purpose for which it has been written. However, observations and comments, from any-body associated in any way with the book after its publication, are always welcome.

At the end, I would like to confess solemnly, that AI is a task intended to challenge the supremacy of the *Siva*, i.e. the nature. Intelligence, like many other unique and special characteristics, is bestowed in us by the nature and it has full command in these. Nature is governed by its own rules and regulations. All the creatures are expected to follow these rules for their survival. However, we, as human beings, have always broken these rules of nature for our advantage, but the consequences are always ignored by us. Although, we are paying the price, but are still not learning the very fact, that nature is supreme and any encroachment made in its supremacy by any living or non-living specie has resulted in its extinction! I am afraid, whether I am part of any such human endeavor! If yes, I would like the *God* or the *Siva* to forgive me for the same! Because, I am fully devoted to the fact mentioned in the following *Shloka*, that the ultimate truth is *Siva*! Neither I, nor You and nor the Intelligent System we are planning to develop!

ॐ मनोबुद्ध्यहङ्कारचिन्तानि नाहं नच
श्रोत्रह्वि न च घ्राणनेत्रे।
न च व्योम भूमिर्न तेजो न वायु श्चदानन्दरूप:
शिवोऽहं शिवोऽहं।।

(Om, I am neither the mind, intelligence, ego nor *citta*,
Neither the ears nor the tongue, nor the senses of smell and sight;
Neither ether nor air, nor fire, nor water, nor earth;
I am Eternal Bliss and Awareness
- I am Siva! I am Siva!)

May God bless you and all!

Ela Kumar

Acknowledgements

First of all, I would like to thank almighty God, the source of all positive energy, for bestowing me the spirit of writing this book.

It is obvious that writing a book of this nature involves enormous task, and in this endeavor, many people have lent their helping hand for the successful completion of the project. It is difficult to name each and every individual here, however, I acknowledge all the persons who have put their direct or indirect efforts in completing this task.

I express my deep sense of gratitude to Dr. Ashok Kumar, Director and Prof A. K. Sharma, Head of department (Computer Engineering), YMCA Institute of Engineering, for their continuous support and encouragement. I cannot forget to express my whole-hearted gratitude to my Ph.D. supervisors Prof J.R.P Gupta, and Prof R. C. Sharma, both professors in Delhi University, for cultivating much needed confidence in me. In fact, during my doctoral work, I got so fascinated with the power of Artificial Intelligence that I could not stop the temptation to pen a book on AI. Hence, a special acknowledgement is due to them. I am also thankful to my other colleagues of Computer Engineering Department, YMCAIE, specially Dr. C.K. Nagpal, Mr. J.P. Sharma, Mr. Dharamveer, and Mr. Mukesh Garg.

I would like to thank my parents for inculcating in me the habit of doing everything sincerely, honestly, finishing that in a timely fashion and making time for maintaining health. I thank them for encouraging me and allowing me to follow what seemed like an odd path at one time. I convey my gratitude to my in-laws, specially my father-in-law, for his blessings. I also want to acknowledge my sisters, brother and other family members. Finally, I would like to express my deep appreciation to my husband Milind, for never failing to encourage me for the accomplishment of this task. I am indebted to my son, Kumar Adwet, who used to sit beside me without disturbing while I was busy doing this work.

ELA KUMAR

Contents

1

Introduction

Artificial intelligence is a rapidly evolving field of engineering with an ultimate objective to build machines capable of acting and thinking like human beings. The early phase of AI was concerned with developing programs for theorem proving and game playing. Modern AI encompasses various tools and techniques for humanlike reasoning, learning, planning, language and pattern recognition. Artificial intelligence is probably one of the most successful branches of a broad area of computing. The credit may be given to the media hype created for the area of AI. In the beginning, the field the AI promised to be the most exciting area and though out of shear overconfidence, at times even threatened to replace the human beings. In the historic Darthmoth conference, scientists predicted that by 1970's they would be able to build intelligent systems that could equal grand masters at chess game, understand spoken language and even compose classical music.

However, the process involved in building intelligent systems is not a fish that can be caught easily, as it would have been imagined by the early researchers, rather it is one of the most intricate, complex and in one way or other, most challenging job ever taken by human beings on their hands, willingly or unwillingly! Knowingly or unknowingly! We are calling it most challenging job ever, since human is trying to prototype his own mind. Yes!, astonishing but true! AI is in one way, an endeavour to prototype human mind. It could only be man who could think of building something about which he hardly had enough knowledge initially, because it is only the man who since inventing fire among the first things invented by him thousands of years back upto inventing his own prototype Robot till today, can boast of inventing so many great and wonderful things in-between, that he has developed confidence to do anything he could think about! Consciously or unconsciously! In reality or in dreams!

The most challenging job in taking up the challenge mentioned above is the study of the complexity of human mind. As we already know that it is our mind which governs our body and whatever intelligence we possess is because our mind enables us to function intelligently. Apart from human mind, there are many other complicated areas which are required to be studied and researched before and alongwith the process of developing intelligent systems. It is just like a dream of man to develop a system which can think and act like him not only efficiently but also, intelligently. Lot of work has been done, remaining is in progress. What has been achieved and how, and what more is required to be accomplished and how, is what, that has been dealt with in this book on your hands. Starting with a simple definition of intelligence, upto the process of building and functioning of a live intelligent system, many other aspects in-between the two which are necessary ingredients and part and partial of the process of building an intelligent system have been discussed, with the hope that whatever could not be achieved till date would be ultimately achieved, if not sooner, than later!

1.1 ARTIFICIAL INTELLIGENCE: CONCEPT AND DEFINITION

Before putting thought to Artificial Intelligence (referred as AI hereinafter), we would try to understand the meaning of *intelligence*. Human beings possess many characteristics like beauty, patriotism, love, hatred, wisdom etc. but it is very difficult to define these. Different people have different ways to define these parameters based on their own thinking and understanding. Intelligence also is a parameter that is abstract in nature and hence, is difficult to define. We can see an act or a behavior and term that as intelligent, but we find it hard enough a task when we try to define intelligence. One thing should be made clear before we proceed further that the *'intelligence'* we are discussing here is the intelligence possessed by living organisms in general, and human being in particular. Human beings acquire this intelligence by gaining knowledge by interaction, studying, learning and experience acquired over the years. This knowledge is stored in mind and mind embodies the knowledge into action. We can sense the existence of intelligence by action and behavior of a human. We can distinguish between an intelligent person and an unintelligent person by the response we get from them about a given situation or the solution we get from them of a particular problem. Different people apply their knowledge to a particular situation in different ways, analyze a problem differently, learn a new thing in different ways and in varying time and hence, they can be termed having different intelligence level. Being able to understand this, we can now dare to define intelligence that has been an arduous task for the scientists and philosophers. To begin with, we will define intelligence in a very simple way based on what we have discussed and understood until now, like:

> *"Intelligence is the ability to learn, to deal with different situations, to acquire, understand and apply knowledge and to analyze and reason."*

We do not know the exact definition of intelligence but we definitely know that intelligence is much more than the one stated in the above definition. Whatever be the definition of intelligence, one thing is sure that intelligence requires possession of knowledge. For example, if we select two persons and ask following questions to them:
1.   What will happen if a cat sees a mouse?
2.   What is the house address of the President of India?
3.   What were the educational degrees possessed by Lord Rama?

First person gives the answer of first question as mouse will run away and the second person says cat will catch the mouse and eat it. You may say that both the answers are correct and hence both the persons can be termed as intelligent. For the answer of second question, both the persons are unaware but try to find out from the record and then come out with the answer as Rashtrapati Bhawan, Rayaseena hills, New Delhi. You may again term both as intelligent as they have ability and required knowledge to find out the answer of a particular question. Regarding third question, first person is unaware and tries to find out the answer, takes lot of time and still keeps on with the exercise, whereas second person immediately says 'Lord Rama possessed no educational degrees'. Here you may call second person as intelligent but first person not, because he does not possess the knowledge that educational degrees like B.Sc., B.Tech., M.B.A. etc. were not awarded at the time of Ramayana and nothing is available on the record about such type of degrees. The educational system was different and education was provided on 'Gurukuls' not in schools and colleges as is provided now in our times.

Hence, it can be concluded from the above discussion that knowledge is basic and most important ingredient for possession of intelligence. It is nothing but the power of knowledge that makes us intelligent, imparts the capacity on us to reason, analyze, manipulate and act in a given situation. We will now look forward to define intelligence in more precise and practical way. The earliest three definitions of intelligence which were mostly accepted are:

"Intelligence is a state grasping the truth, involving reason, concerned with action about what is good or bad for human being...."

"The ability to learn or understand from experience, the ability to acquire and retain knowledge and the ability to respond quickly and successfully to a new situation, use of the faculty of reason in solving problems, directing the conduct effectively."

"The test of a first rate intelligence is the ability to hold two opposite ideas in the mind at the same time and still retain ability to function."

After learning the concepts of intelligence, we may now focus on artificial intelligence. Artificial is, what is not real or natural. We may term intelligence possessed by human beings as real intelligence because human beings develop this intelligence on their own. Hence, artificial intelligence is the intelligence which is created by human beings by applying various scientific and engineering techniques. Since ages, man always used his mind and capacity to make others around him his slaves. Human endeavours were directed towards making his tasks simpler by using other means and developing techniques which replace him from performing his duties which required labour and time. In achieving this feat, man developed many machines to assist him in not only performing routine tasks but also in the intricate areas of problem solving; effectively, efficiently and economically not only to match his own capabilities but to exceed the abilities of his own and others. For example, it was not possible for man to fly like birds. But seeing the birds fly made the man to think and develop some means to assist him in flying. It was this thought which led to the invention of aeroplanes. Now, a migratory bird takes weeks to fly from America to India whereas man can fly the same distance only in hours.

In the same way, many other machines were developed and also computers, which changed the human life and brought a revolution in many areas which required lot of labour, expertise and time in solving problems otherwise by employing other means. It is not at all difficult to imagine, that after developing computer and using it successfully over the years, the innovative mind of man would have thought about many questions such as:

1. Can a computer think like man?
2. Can computer be intelligent like human beings? etc.

Mere thinking about something new is different but if you go through the history, you will believe that man had always tried to embody his thoughts, dreams and ideas, some times unsuccessfully but most of the times, successfully. It is this nature of quest and zeal of man that made not only the animals but even machines his slaves. Hence, it can not be a point of any contention that man ultimately tried to make most sophisticated and most precise tool on his hand, computer, his slave. A slave is supposed not only to obey you but to perform the tasks given by you the way you yourself perform or in some better way. Hence, when above questions came to the mind of man, he started making computer intelligent so that it can think and act intelligently the same way as he himself acts by imparting intelligence in to it. Thus, in simple terms, developing a machine which can act intelligently is the scope of AI. Since, perhaps the intelligence possessed by machines is not real, i.e. not developed by themselves naturally of their own like humans, it is artificial. The term Artificial Intelligence was first used by John McCarthy in 1956 and we are not very sure whether it is the right term used for the purpose and the process but it is used unanimously and widely by all the scientists, engineers and researchers worldwide.

Earlier, when the idea to develop intelligent computer came to the mind of man, as always, two different schools of thought started functioning. There is the one which applied positive approach and believed that human intelligence is computational in nature and therefore can be reproduced in machines. The other school of thought took a negative approach and opined that replicating human intelligence is not possible and role of computers is limited up to assisting and testing the tasks performed by human beings using intelligence. We will discuss these schools of thought in more detail later on in this chapter.

Such types of differences result in confusion and sometimes lead to problems of greater degree, however, we should always welcome such type of discussions.

It is this difference of opinion that has caused most of the big things to happen on this earth. Here also, difference of opinion brought another set of people into arena who devised a middle path and view AI as a process to develop systems which reflect human intelligence in their approach within a limited domain. They are happy as long as computers fulfil their interest and can be applied to solve particular set of problems. It is not necessary for them to worry for a computer exhibiting general intelligence and development of a universal intelligent system. Hence, for majority of people,

"AI is the branch of engineering employed for the creation of computers that possess some form of intelligence and can be used to solve real world problems and function within a limited domain."

We can not claim whether this is the appropriate definition of AI. Different researchers have proposed different definitions of AI based of their own study and understanding of the subject. Some of these are given below:

"AI is the automation of activities that we associate with human thinking, activities such as decision making, problem solving, learning……."

- Bellman, 1978

"AI is concerned with designing intelligent computer systems which exhibit the characteristics we associate with intelligence in human behiviour."

- Barr and Feignenbaum, 1981

"AI is the exciting new effort to make computers think……machines with minds, in the full and literal sense."

- Haugeland, 1985

"AI is the study of mental faculties through the use of computational models"

- Charniak and McDermott, 1985

"AI is the art of creating machines that perform functions that require intelligence when performed by people."

- Kurzwell, 1990

"AI is the study of how to make computers do things at which, at the moment, people are better."

- Rich and Knight, 1991

"AI is the study of the combinations that make it possible to perceive, reason and act."

- Winston, 1992

> *"Computational intelligence is the study of the design of intelligent agents."*
>
> **- Poole et al., 1998**

> *"AI.....is concerned with intelligent behavior in artifacts."*
>
> **- Nilsson, 1998**

We have mentioned several definitions of AI proposed by different scientists and researchers at different times. There can still be many more definitions of AI. Hence, as stated earlier, because of the abstract nature, it is difficult to define intelligence or Artificial Intelligence and it can be concluded that there is no standardize definition of AI as such, yet it has been accepted that whichever system exhibits the following characteristics/behaviour can be considered as intelligent:

1. learning
2. understanding ambiguity
3. handling the complexity
4. responding quickly
5. reasoning
6. inferencing
7. having vision
8. maintaining knowledge regarding a particular task
9. drawing conclusions from knowledge

In other words what people usually associate with thinking includes several facets of intelligence. Thus, a working definition of AI can be:

> *"To program computers to carry out tasks that would require intelligence if carried out by human beings."*

This definition is relevant to a particular era, e.g. many years ago when the first computer that printed the payroll slip would have been considered intelligent because at that time a human being was preparing the payroll, but in today's context it is not an intelligent task.

After gaining sufficient understanding of AI, many questions would be coming to your mind, such as:

1. How does human mind function? What is the mechanism involved in process of thinking?
2. How much knowledge is required for making a computer intelligent?
3. How can knowledge be acquired?
4. How can knowledge be coded and represented?
5. What type of language is required for interacting with intelligent computer?
6. How can computers be made to learn and think?

There can be many such type of questions and it is answering of these questions that forms the scope of this book. In different chapters of this book, we would try to find out the answers of the above questions. In the chapter devoted to Expert Systems, we would study the process of developing knowledge based systems, already existing and working systems, achievements in the field of developing expert systems and goals yet to be achieved.

Before ending our discussion on the subject on hand, we should not forget the importance of the *backbone* of AI. We have already mentioned earlier that it is the power of knowledge that makes us intelligent. Howsoever intelligent a person may be, if he is not able to respond properly, efficiently and timely to a given situation and can not solve a problem precisely and quickly, can not be termed as intelligent scientifically and technically; and it the knowledge which provides us required ability and strength to act intelligently. You might have heard the story of *Tarzen* who reached in the *Jungle*(forest) somehow in his child hood and was brought up by animals. Because he was grown up in the forest among the animals, he could speak the languages spoken by different animals, could interact with them, ate same food that animals ate and had almost all the characteristics of an animal. If one of such type of Tarzen comes before you and you ask him a very simple question, "what is your name?", he will not be able to answer this even after doing his best efforts because he does not possess the required knowledge and does not understand the language you speak, hence, in spite of being a human, he would not be considered as intelligent by you. Hence, we are not intelligent because we are human beings, we are intelligent because we possess something that Tarzen does not.

The purpose of this discussion is not to tell you the story of Tarzen, but to make it clear that we are intelligent because we possess the knowledge about the problem domain, we also have capacity to acquire more and more knowledge, to analyze, to manipulate, to reason and to do so many other things which collectively make us, perhaps, the most intelligent among the species present across the globe! Thus, the word *backbone* mentioned above refers to nothing but knowledge. Knowledge is the backbone of AI. In present era the programs which use knowledge of the relevant field are considered as intelligent. What distinguishes AI program from a normal computer program is the presence of knowledge component on it. Hence, apart from devoting a full chapter for the study of knowledge, many other chapters and sections of other chapters have been devoted for the study of techniques required for knowledge acquisition, knowledge representation etc. and major emphasis is given in analysis and treatment of knowledge.

1.2 HISTORY OF AI

The origins of AI can be seen in Turing's work in his paper on intelligent machines published in 1950. Whilst working at Bletchley part, Turing formulated the first "paper models" of game playing programs. Some date the origins of AI to McCarthy's invention of the LISP programming language in the 1950s. This was the first language designed for solving symbolic problems rather than numerical ones. Newell and Simon's GPS, showed how general search knowledge could be used to solve a range of problems such as the missionaries and cannibals problem. In the 1970s, expert systems were developed which embodied as a set of rules the knowledge of an expert. The most famous of these was the MYCIN medical expert system. At the same time systems were developed to understand language, of which the most famous was Winograd's SHRDLU system. The 1980s saw the development of neural networks as a method of learning examples. We can view the chronological development of AI in the following diagram:

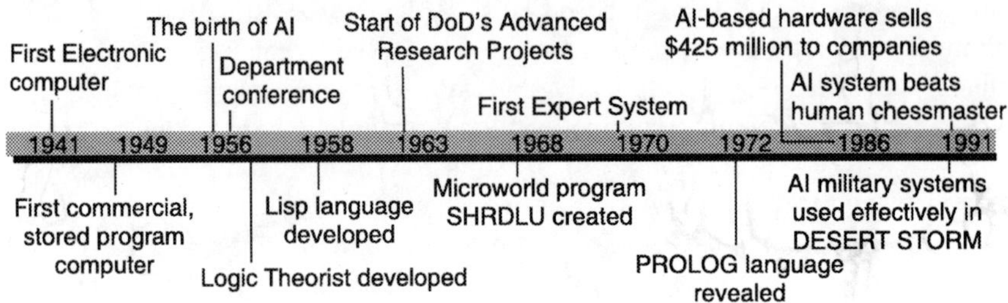

Timeline of major AI events

AI is good around 65 years old now. We can divide the developments taken place during its lifetime, since its inception way back in 1940s, till date, into various groups as mentioned subsequently for getting an account of the history of AI which will not only provide us an information about what all has already been done, how and by whom, but also will help us to form guidelines for future scope of work in the field of AI in particular, and other related fields in general.

1.2.1 Conception of AI (1943-1955)

Warren McCulloch and Walter Pitts proposed a model of artificial neurons way back in 1943. This is the first work that is considered as AI. McCulloch, after acquiring medical degree began his research in epilepsy, head injuries and the central nervous systems. In their work, McCulloch and Pitts showed that any computable function could be computed by some network of neurons and that all the connectives used in framing sentences like, and, or, not etc. are computational in nature. In their study, they were guided by basic physiology, analysis of propositional logic and Turing's theory of computation. They also suggested that suitably defined networks could learn.

Marvin Minsky and Dean Edmonds, two students of Princeton mathematics department built the first neural network computer in 1951 which is known as SNARC. Their work though, did not get early recognition, Minsky later on proved influencing theorems showing the limitations of neural network research.

There were many such types of early works which could be recognised as AI, but it was Alan Turing who is given credit for evolving and exhibiting complete vision of AI in his article published in 1950, 'Computing Machinery and Intelligence.' After this only he introduced his famous **"Turing Test"**.

1.2.2 The Birth of AI (1956)

Another important and influential figure in the field of AI was John McCarthy, who joined Dartmouth College after graduation. He made it convenient to organize a two month long workshop along with Minsky and others which involved U.S. researchers also who were interested in automata theory, neural nets and the study of intelligence. The workshop was organized in the summers of 1956 at Dartmouth which ultimately became the official birthplace of AI.

Though there were ten attendees in the workshop, Allen Newell and Herbert Simon, two researchers from Carnegie Tech overtook the scene because they already had a reasoning program called 'Logic Theorist' that could boast of thinking and solving the mind-body problem. Although, others also had their own ideas and some program for particular applications, the work of Newell and Simon was far more advance.

Though Dartmouth conference did not come out with something substantial and new, it at least provided researchers from different institutes working in different areas a common platform to interact with one another and it is not surprising that for the next 20 years or so, the field of AI was dominated by these people and their students. We can imagine that perhaps none discussed or inferred topics or issues on the said conference would be lasting till date, but one thing which came out of the conference and turned everlasting was the consensus to adopt new name for the field given by McCarthy as **artificial intelligence.**

1.2.3 Adolescence of AI (1952-1969)

Few years earlier before people started thinking to use computer as an intelligent machine, it was acting as mere a calculator that could do arithmetic and nothing more. Hence, in the beginning, there was lot of enthusiasm among the researchers and they started considering each and every thing little clever and unconventional as AI. Alan Turing listed following things which were considered taboo for machines:

> *"Be kind, resourceful, beautiful, friendly, have initiative, have a sense of humour, tell right from wrong, make mistakes, fall in love, enjoy strawberries and cream, make someone fall in love with it, learn with experience, use words properly, be the subject of its own thought, have as much diversity of behaviour as man, do something really new."*

If we view the above mentioned things closely, we would believe that all those are typically associated with living beings or man and are abstract in nature. It would have been very difficult for someone to imagine that machines could possess any of those. Hence, whenever computers performed some new task and the researchers tend to believe that as AI, others were there to mention any of the above mentioned things to contradict their point of view. Thus, early years of 1950s were full of controversies, actions and counteractions in spite of being full of enthusiasm.

As stated earlier, Newell and Simon developed a reasoning program called *Logic Theorist* that was able to prove 38 out of 52 theorems of chapter 2 of *Principia Mathematica*. This program was expanded later on into a problem solving program called *General Problem Solver* or GPS in 1963. This program was designed from the start to imitate human problem solving protocols. Though, it could solve limited class of puzzles, the order in which the program considered sub-goals and approached possible actions was similar to that in which humans approached the same problems. GPS thus may be considered as the first program to embody the thinking abilities of humans. The success of GPS and other subsequent developments led Newell and Simon to devise their famous ***physical symbol system hypothesis*** in 1976. This hypothesis stated that a physical symbol system has the necessary and sufficient means for general intelligent action, and meant in general that any system that exhibits intelligence must operate by manipulating data structures composed of symbols. We will discuss this hypothesis in detail later on in this chapter.

1958 became historic year in the field of AI because of crucial contributions by McCarthy while working at MIT. First, he developed the high-power language **LISP** which became dominant programming language and is the second oldest language still in use. Secondly, McCarthy in the same year published a paper entitled '*programs with common sense*'. In this paper he described a hypothetical program called *Advice Taker* that can be considered as first complete AI program. Marvin Minsky also moved to MIT in 1958. He along with McCarthy started working at MIT and their association, though not very long produced some notable works.

Parallel works were done at IBM also by Rochester and his colleagues who produced some of the early AI programs. In 1959, Herbert Gelernter built the Geometry Theorem Prover that could prove theorems which were difficult and tedious for students of mathematics. Arthur Samuel wrote many programs for checkers starting from 1952 which learned to play like a professional player and later on could achieve degree of proficiency of the level that surpassed even that of its creator.

1.2.4 Youthfulness of AI (1969-1979)

As has been mentioned earlier, during the early stage of the research in the field of AI, even small clever things computer did were considered as intelligent. Out of shear enthusiasm, Simon predicted that within 10 years computer would become a chess champion and machine would be able to prove mathematical theorem considered difficult even for humans. These predictions were made during 1955 and today we know that they became reality but only after around 40 years from the date those were made. Such type of overconfidence of the likes of Simon was not undesired because the response of the computer in solving small problems was highly encouraging, but when the same systems were tested for extended versions of the problems or for varying nature of problems, they failed miserably.

When earlier intelligent systems faced reality, they could not perform satisfactorily because they contained very less or almost nil knowledge of the area in which they functioned. It was then when the importance of knowledge was really felt in developing an intelligent system. Almost a decade of the early research was inclined to find out complete solutions of the problems by trying out different permutations and combinations of the steps involved. This method was termed as *weak method* because, though the method was intended to generalize the system, they were unable to produces systems that could handle difficult problems. This is when need arose to build systems that could handle almost all the problems of a particular area using a powerful knowledge base in a limited domain. This approach was termed as **strong method** and became very successful in building intelligent programs having human like expertise in a particular application area.

One such program was **DANDRAL** developed at Stanford in 1969 by Ed Feigenbaum, Bruce Buchanan and Joshua Lederberg during their experiment to infer molecular structure from the information provided by mass spectrometer. This program will be discussed in detail in one of the following chapters of this book, but here it is worth mentioning that this was the first successful *knowledge-based program* and such type of programs subsequently were famously referred as *expert systems* by the scientists and engineers associated with the field of AI. Other noteworthy development was in the field of medical diagnosis. Feigenbaum, Buchanan and Edward Shortliffe again at Stanford built a program known as **MYCIN** which could match the performance of human experts working in the area. This program was different than DANDRAL in two aspects. First, the difference was in the method and means adopted for *knowledge acquisition* for building *knowledge-base* for two programs and second, in case of MYCIN, the inference rules had to reflect the uncertainty associated with medical knowledge. To take into account this uncertainty, MYCIN incorporated a calculus called *certainty factors*. This concept is discussed later on in one of the chapters.

Research was done in the area of *'natural language understanding'* also. This had always been a fascinating area among the scientists because it was felt that having a computer being able to talk to you in your language will not only remove the complicacies involved in the process of building an intelligent system but also make it viable for even a lay man to converse with the computer. Earlier some programs were developed to translate Russian to English and the exercise was considered very simple as it was thought that simple syntactic transformations based on the grammars of Russian and English and word replacements using an electronic dictionary was all that needed to do the job, but when applied for the actual translation work, the program failed and came out with some funny results. This led the researchers to believe again that knowledge was vital for any system to perform satisfactorily and effectively and several researchers including Eugene Charniak at MIT suggested that robust natural language understanding would require general knowledge about the world and a general method for using that knowledge. However, **SHRDLU** system of Winograd enjoys merit and reputation of being one among the earlier systems built to understand language. Though, it depended more on syntactic analysis and caused some of the problems similar to that of machine translation work, yet it could understand pronoun references.

If we are asked to identify one important outcome of this era, it would definitely be the realization of the fact that knowledge was of utmost importance and it would be wiser to go for intelligent systems that could function within a restricted problem domain using knowledge-base consisting knowledge of a particular area for which the program was developed. Once this was realized, programs were developed to solve real world problems and this increased the demand for workable knowledge acquisition and knowledge representation schemes. A large number of representation and reasoning languages were developed including **PROLOG**.

1.2.5 Maturity and Commercialization of AI (1980-present)

Once AI attained required level of maturity, commercial applications of AI started in form of building expert systems to solve real world problems. The first commercial system successful in its aim was RI that started operations in 1882. By the year 1988, the AI department of Digital Equipment Corporation was able to develop about 40 expert systems. Every major U.S. Corporation had its own AI group which was associated in research and development works related to AI. Japanese announced 'Fifth Generation' project in 1981 to build expert systems running prolog. During the same period, U.S. formed the Microelectronics and Computer Technology Corporation (MCC) as a research establishment keeping AI as part of broad effort that included design and manufacturing of chips.

As mentioned earlier, the conception of AI took shape in the form of research in the field of neural networks, but somehow, the area lost its way in late 1970s because of the likely reason that weak methods were overtaken by strong methods and scientists diverted their attention from developing general purpose systems to intelligent systems that could work within limited domain and solve real world problems. However, psychologists including David Rumelhart and Geoff Hinton continued the study of neural-net models of memory but real revival happened or rebirth of the field took place in mid 1980s when four different groups reinvented the back propagation learning algorithm first born in 1969 by the efforts of Bryson and Ho. More information about the research done in the field of neural networks and other related areas is discussed in detail in the chapter dealing with **neurology**. Lot of work has been done but the field is largely unexplored and still mind and functions of brain remain like a puzzle for man requiring appropriate solution.

Theory of probability formed the base of reasoning process since beginning and Judea Pearl's paper in 'Probabilistic Reasoning in Intelligent Systems' published in 1988 opened a new door for accepting the role of probability and decision theory in AI. An important aspect in development of intelligent systems has been dealing with uncertainties. Theory of probability was used for this during 1960s and 1970s but earlier probabilistic reasoning systems faced may problems. The Bayesian network formalism was invented to allow efficient representation of uncertain knowledge which now dominates the AI research on uncertain reasoning and expert systems.

The earlier developments and concepts of the field of AI might not be relevant today and the approach as well as the process has undergone a sea change over the years especially during last 20 years or so. Many exciting and interesting innovations have occurred in the fields of knowledge representation, robotics and computer vision. With the advancements made in the field of AI and increased association of more and more researchers, scientists and engineers to the field, it has become possible to understand the problems and their complexities in a better way. Use of technology and knowledge of divergent fields led to application of vigorous methods and workable research agendas. Today, the field has become so big and diversified that it has been divided into different specializations and the areas such as vision and robotics etc. have been isolated form the main stream AI.

1.3 RELATED CONCEPTS ABOUT AI

During the presentation of the history of AI, we have used many keywords and names that require elaboration and detailed discussion for their better understanding. In this section we would not only deal with those but many other general and related concepts about the field of Artificial Intelligence.

1.3.1 General Artificial Intelligence

There is one research group that claims to develop the concepts exhibiting artificial intelligence in general domain. It is called general artificial intelligence. General artificial intelligence research aims to create AI that can replicate humans intelligence completely, often called an *Artificial General Intelligence* (AGI) to distinguish it from less ambitious AI projects. As yet, researchers have devoted little attention to AGI, many claiming intelligence is too complex to be completely replicated.

1.3.2 The AI and Consciousness

Efforts have been made to develop a relationship between the concepts of Artificial Intelligence and human consciousness. It is analyzed that whether a machine can be developed giving the attention toward a particular problem like a human being. Even a machine that passed the Turing test would not necessarily be conscious in its efforts like the human being are. The supporters of strong AI claim that machine can really develop the human consciousness equal to human being. The truth of Strong AI depends upon whether information processing machines can include all the properties of minds such as consciousness. However, Weak AI is independent of the Strong AI problem and there can be no doubt that many of the features of modern computers such as multiplication or database searching might have been considered 'intelligent' only a century ago.

1.3.3 Weak and Strong AI

There are two themes of thoughts in Artificial intelligence, namely *weak AI* and *strong AI*. The strong AI line of thinking is very enthusiastic about AI and makes a bold claim that computers can be made to think almost equal to the level of human being and they can possibly be conscious about themselves. Hence if asked whether computers be intelligent, the strong AI says yes, just wait for the faster computers. The weak AI is however not so enthusiastic about the outcomes of AI and it simply says that some thinking like features can be added to computers to make them more useful tools. It says that computers can not be made intelligent equal to human being, unless constructed significantly differently. Weak AI simply states that some "thinking-like" features can be added to computers to make them more useful tools (witness expert systems, drive-by-wire cars and speech recognition software).

Strong AI is the supposition that some forms of artificial intelligence can truly reason and solve problems; strong AI supposes that it is possible for machines to become sapient, or self-aware, but may or may not exhibit humanlike thought processes. The term strong AI was originally coined by John Searle, who writes:

> *"according to strong AI, the computer is not merely a tool in the study of the mind; rather, the appropriately programmed computer really is a mind"*

In contrast to strong AI, **weak AI** refers to the use of software to study or accomplish specific *problem solving* or *reasoning* tasks that do not encompass (or in some cases, are completely outside of) the full range of human cognitive abilities. An example of weak AI software would be a *chess* program such as *Deep Blue*. Unlike strong AI, a weak AI does not achieve self-awareness or demonstrate a wide range of human-level cognitive abilities, and at its finest is merely an intelligent, more specific problem-solver.

Some argue that weak AI programs cannot be called "intelligent" because they cannot really *think*.

1.3.4 Turing Test

Turing test is considered as the basic test for intelligence. It is said that a machine passing this test can be considered as intelligent. In 1950 famous mathematician Alan Turing proposed this test. He proposed to consider the question "Can machines think?" This should begin with definitions of the meaning of the terms "machine" and "think."

Turing Test is meant to determine if a computer program has intelligence. Quoting Turing, the original imitation game can be described as follows:

The new form of the problem can be described in terms of a game which we call the "imitation game." It is played with three people, a man (A), a woman (B), and an interrogator (C) who may be of either sex. The interrogator stays in a room apart from the other two. The object of the game for the interrogator is to determine which of the other two is the man and which is the woman. He knows them by labels X and Y, and at the end of the game he says either "X is A and Y is B" or "X is B and Y is A." The interrogator is allowed to put questions to A and B.

When talking about the Turing Test today what is generally understood is the following: The interrogator is connected to one person and one machine via a terminal, therefore can't see her counterparts. Her task is to find out which of the two candidates is the machine, and which is the human only by asking them questions. If the machine can "fool" the interrogator, it is intelligent.

In order to keep the test simple, conversation is limited to text channel only.

Though the Turing test is considered as the basic test for considering a machine as intelligent, it faced lot of criticism subsequently. Some of the points criticizing it are mentioned below:

1. People said befooling somebody is not intelligence. Rather intelligence should be defined in a positive sense because doing the assigned work properly and more efficiently is intelligence.
2. Computer, as a machine possesses more memory than human being does, so it should be better at tasks that require memory. Comparing it equal to human being is itself a faulty definition of intelligence.
3. The speed of solving a task from computer should be faster than human being. The Turing test did not talk anything about the speed.

Besides the criticisms and many modifications in the basic definitions of intelligence, the Turing test is still considered as basic test of intelligence.

1.4 PHYSICAL SYMBOL SYSTEM HYPOTHESIS

As discussed above the AI has philosophical, mathematical, and sociological roots. The modern AI also contributes to these fields e.g., the questions Turing posed about the intelligent programs also reflect back on our understanding of intelligence itself.

The area of AI requires answering basic questions like:
 (i) What is intelligence?
 (ii) What is the nature of knowledge?
(iii) Can knowledge be represented?
 (iv) What is skill?
 (v) How does knowledge in an application area relate to problem solving skill in that domain? etc.

Newell and Simon in 1976 proposed a stronger model for intelligence with their physical symbol system hypothesis. This hypothesis states that:

> *"The necessary and sufficient condition for a physical system to exhibit general intelligent action is that it be a physical symbol system."*

Sufficient means that intelligence can be achieved by any appropriately organized physical symbol system.

Necessary means that any agent that exhibits general intelligence must be an instance of a physical symbol system. The necessity of the physical symbol system hypothesis requires that any intelligent agent, whether human, space alien, or computer, achieve intelligence through the physical implementation of operations on symbol structures.

General intelligent action means the same scope of action seen in human action. Within physical limits, the system exhibits behavior appropriate to its ends and adaptive to the demands of its environment.

Newell and Simon have summarized the arguments for the necessity and sufficiency of this hypothesis. In later years, both the AI and cognitive sciences explored their territory by this hypothesis.

The physical symbol hypothesis leads to following three methodological commitments:

(i)   The use of symbols and systems of symbols as a medium to describe the world.

(ii) The design of search mechanism, especially heuristic search, to explore the space of potential inferences those symbol systems could support.

(iii) The disembodiment of cognitive architecture, by which it is meant that an appropriately designed symbol system could provide a full causal account of intelligence, regardless of its medium of implementation.

The tokens of a language are referred to as symbols and these are used to denote or refer something other than them. This corresponds to the verbal tokens of the natural language. As verbal tokens in natural language refer the most fundamental concept of that language, the symbols refer the basic concepts in the world of an intelligent agent.

The physical symbol hypothesis defines a representation language that is used to represent all forms of knowledge, skill, intention and causality. This ability to formalize symbolic models is essential to the modeling of intelligence as a running computer program and it can be added to the formal systems.

The second component of AI problem solution is search. (The first component being representation). Search is the systematic examination of instances within the representational framework looking for solutions, sub problem goals or any other aspect of problem that is under consideration.

The third component is heuristics, along with representation and search of symbol based AI. A heuristic is a mechanism for organizing search across the alternatives offered by a particular representation. Heuristics search techniques are designed to overcome the complexity of exhaustive search which acts as barrier to useful solutions for many classes of interesting problems.

There are many deep philosophical issues related with AI e.g., in what sense can we say that a computer can understand natural language expression? The language is constructed by symbols. It is not sufficient to be able to say that a string is well formed. The mechanism devised for understanding the natural language input should be able to understand the symbols in context. What is meaning? What is interpretation? In what sense does interpretation requires responsibility? Similar philosophical issues emerge from many AI application areas whether they may be building an expert system to cooperate with human problem solvers, designing computer vision systems, or designing algorithms for machine learning.

The basic physical symbol system hypothesis assumes that intelligent behavior, either in human or machine, is achieved using:

- symbol pattern, to represent significant aspects of a problem domain,
- operations on these patterns to generate potential solutions to problems, and
- search to select a solution from among these possibilities.

The physical symbol system hypothesis implicitly distinguishes between the patterns formed by an arrangement of symbols and the medium used to implement them. If intelligence is derived only from the structure of a symbol system, then any medium that successfully implements the correct patterns and processes will achieve intelligence regardless of whether it is composed of neurons, logic circuits or Tinkertoys (an object used for basic AI application building). The concept of a machine passing the Turing test depends on this distinction. According to the Church – Turing thesis (Machtey and Young 1979), computers are capable of implementing any effectively described symbolic process.

The physical symbol system hypothesis also outlines the major foci of AI research and application development. It defines the symbol structures and operations necessary for intelligent problem solving and developing strategies to efficiently and correctly search the potential solutions generated by these operations and structures. These are the core issues of a very important dimension of AI called knowledge representation and search and could be regarded as the heart of modern research in Artificial intelligence.

The physical symbol hypothesis was criticized by Searle (1980), Winograd and flores (1986). They argued that intelligence is inherently biological and existential, and can not be captured symbolically. These arguments provide a well considered challenge to the dominant direction of AI research, and have influenced the direction of research in the neural networks, genetic algorithms and agent based approaches. Most of the criticism of physical symbol hypothesis is based on the issue of semantic representation of understanding. Defining the concept of meaning (or semantics) in traditional sense is very difficult. However researchers worked on developing a more mathematics based semantic representation e.g. the Tarskian possible worlds approach is based on this principle. The grounding of meaning (or loss of meaning) is an issue that has forever frustrated both the proponents and critics of the AI and cognitive science enterprises. Searle performed a famous experiment called *"Chinese room experiment"* in this regard. It is discussed later in this chapter. In the area of human language understanding Lakeoff and Johnson (1999) argue that in content of linguistic expression the ability to create, use, exchange, and interpret meaning, the symbols come from social context human's. Our current generation of AI tools and techniques are indeed very far away from being able to encode and utilize any equivalent meaning system.

In spite of these challenges, the assumptions of physical symbol system hypothesis are relevantly applicable in almost all theoretical and practical work in expert systems, planning and natural language understanding.

In AI problem solving methodology, it is required to choose a representation scheme to capture essential features of a problem domain and make that information accessible to problem solving procedure. Obviously, the representation language must allow the programmer to express that knowledge. *Abstraction*, the representation of only that information needed for a given purpose, is an essential tool for managing complexity. It is also important that the resulting program be computationally efficient. In all real time applications, the result is required within few minutes or even in lesser time after the application of the input. For example, in case of a process control managed by using neural network, the output should be available within few milliseconds. *Expressiveness* and *efficiency* are major dimensions for evaluating knowledge representation languages. Some highly expressive representations are too inefficient for use in certain classes of problems. Sometimes expressiveness must be sacrificed to improve efficiency. This must be done without limiting the ability of representations to capture essential problem solving knowledge. Performing the optimization between efficiency and expressiveness is a major task for designers of intelligent systems.

To meet the requirement of symbolic computing, artificial intelligence has developed representation languages such as predicate calculus, semantic networks, frames and objects. LISP and PROLOG are major languages used for implementing the AI problems.

1.5 COMPARISON OF HUMAN AND COMPUTER SKILLS

The Artificial intelligence is the area of making the computers able to do the works now done by humans. Hence, it is must to understand deeply the skills of human and computers.

There are certain tasks computers can perform better than human beings. These are:

  (i) Problems requiring big numerical computation
 (ii) Problems requiring large amount of information storage
(iii) Problems requiring a task to be performed repeatedly.

It is a well-known fact that computers do not get bored, to repeat the same process everyday. Hence, the jobs where a task is to be repeated periodically the computers outperform their creator, the human being.

Unlike above points, there are many activities and skills where even now the humans outperform the computers. These are the activities involving intelligence. Because humans do not just process the information, they understand it, make sense out of what is seen and heard and give innovative ideas.

Humans use common sense to make our way through a world, which seemingly sometimes appears highly illogical. The possession and use of common sense knowledge is very positive aspect of human being over computers. It includes finding the solution in very limited number of steps. It also includes knowing what we know vaguely and what we know clearly. Possessing the intelligence requires the possession of following characteristics:

(i) Flexibly reacting in any situation

(ii) Drawing the conclusion and making sense out of ambiguous or contradictory messages

(iii) To attach relative importance to different elements of a situation.

(iv) To find similarities between situations despite differences which may separate them.

(v) To find the differences between situations despite similarities which may link them. The two situations may look similar on the surface, yet we are able to note the difference and hence adjust our reaction.

The list of skills where, humans outperform the computers is long. In fact, the activities involving cognitive skills are performed better by human beings.

1.6 AI PUT TO TEST

Systems possessing intelligence are being built and several types of these are out to perform. AI has been through a long journey, enthusiastic as well as absorbing! Whatever has been achieved over the years is now used for accessing its capabilities, means AI is being tested to really believe that whatever is still left is not unachievable.

The military put AI based hardware to the test in war during Desert Storm. AI-based technologies are used in missile systems, heads-up-displays, and other advancements. AI has also made the transition to our homes. With the popularity of the computer having intelligence growing, the interest of the man has also grown. Applications for the Apple Macintosh and IBM compatible computer, such as voice and character recognition have become available. In addition, AI technology has made steadying camcorders simple using fuzzy logic. Use of expert system in automobile industries and others is increasing day-by-day for increasing efficiency and economy. With a greater demand for AI-related technology, new advancements are becoming available. Inevitably, Artificial Intelligence has, and will continue affecting our lives.

1.7 PRACTICAL SYSTEMS BASED ON AI

Some of the systems based on AI and used practically are:

- *Autonomous vehicles*: A DARPA-funded *onboard computer system from Carnegie Mellon University* drove a van all but 52 of the 2849 miles from Washington, DC to San Diego, averaging 63 miles per hour day and night, rain or shine;

- *Computer chess: Deep Blue*, a chess computer built by IBM researchers, defeated world champion Gary Kasparov in a landmark performance;

- ***Mathematical theorem proving***: A *computer system at Argonne National Laboratories* proved a long-standing mathematical conjecture about algebra using a method that would be considered creative if done by humans;
- ***Advanced user interfaces***: *PEGASUS* is a spoken language interface connected to the American Airlines EAASY SABRE reservation system, which allows subscribers to obtain flight information and make flight reservations via a large, on-line, dynamic database, accessed through their personal computer over the telephone.

1.8 THE DEVELOPMENT OF LOGIC

In the seventeenth century, Gottfried Wilhelm von Leibniz, with his Calculus Philosophicus, introduced the first system of formal logic as well constructed the machine for automating its calculation. In eighteenth century, Euler, with his analysis for the connectedness of the bridges joining the river bank and islands of the city of Konigsberg, introduced the study of representation that abstractly capture the structure of relationship in the world.

The formalization of graph theory also afforded the possibility of state space search which was later used as a major tool for AI problem representation. The graphs are also used to represent to model the deeper structure of a problem. By describing the entire space of problem solution, state space graphs provide a powerful tool for measuring the structure and complexity of problem and analyzing the efficiency, correctness and generality of solution strategies.

The 19th century Charles Babbage, who is considered as originator of the science of operation research, also has contributed a lot in the area of artificial intelligence. Babbage's "difference engine" was a special purpose machine for computing the value of certain polynomial functions and is considered as a pioneer of analytical engine. The analytical engine designed but not successfully constructed during his lifetime was a general purpose programmable computing machine that possessed many of the architectural assumptions underlying the modern computer.

Babbage's desire was to apply the technology of his day to provide relief to humans from the drudgery of making arithmetic calculations. His analytical engine used the concept of separation of memory and processor, which Babbage called "store" and "mill". The concept of a digital rather than analog machine and its programmability was based on the execution of a series of operation encoded on punched cards.

Another 19th century mathematician George Booole contributed a lot by developing formal languages. Later on, these logic based languages were popularly used for the implementation of AI problems. Though he made contributions to number of areas of mathematics, his best known work was in the mathematical formalization of the laws of the logic, an accomplishment that forms the very heart of modern computer science. In the 1st chapter of his book named "*an investigation of the laws of thought*", based on which are founded the mathematical theories of logic and probabilities, Boole has mentioned his goal as:

"to investigate the fundamental laws of those operations of the mind by which reasoning is performed: to give expression to them in the symbolic language of a calculus and upon this foundation to establish the science of logic and instruct its method;..... and finally to collect from the various elements of truth brought to view in the course of these enquiries some probable intimations concerning the nature and constitution of the human mind"

The Boole's work has devised three operations " AND, OR, NOT" which formed the centrepoints of his logical calculus. These operations have remained the basis of all subsequent developments in formal logic, including the design of modern computer. Gottlob Freg, in his *'foundations of Arithmetic'* (Frege, 1879) created a mathematical specification language for describing the basis of arithmetic in a clear and precise fashion. With this language he formalized many of the issues first addressed by *Aristotle's logic*. His language is now called *first order predicate calculus*. It offered a tool for describing the propositions and truth value assignments that make up the elements of mathematical reasoning and described the axiomatic basis of meaning for these expressions.

Russel's and Whitehead (1950) developed the mathematics through formal operations. He created it as a collection of axioms. Although many mathematical systems have been constructed from basic axioms, the most significant contribution of his work is creation of mathematics as pure formal system. This means that axioms and theorems would be treated solely as strings of characters: proofs would proceed solely through the applications of well defined rules for manipulating these strings. There would be no reliance or meaning or the intuition or the meaning of the theorems as a basis of proof. Every step of a proof is followed from the strict application of formal syntactic rules to either axioms or previously proven theorems. This treatment of mathematical reasoning in purely formal terms provided an essential basis for automation on physical computers. The logical syntax and formal rules of inference developed by Russell and Whitehead are still a basis for automatic theorem proving systems. The work of Russell and whitehead was modified by Alfred Tarski to include the semantics component into it. By this inclusion the formal logics are related with the real world events.

Though in the eighteenth, nineteenth and twentieth century the development of logic was done in a big way, it was not until in twentieth century the introduction of digital computers, AI became the viable scientific field. By the end of 1940 the digital computers were available in well developed form to have memory and processing power required by intelligent programs. With this development it became possible to implement formal reasoning system on a computer and to empirically test their ability for exhibiting intelligence.

1.9 COMPONENTS OF AI

1.9.1 Theoretical Components

The theory of Artificial Intelligence consists of following components:

1. *Problem solving through heuristics techniques*: this involves the solutions of those problems which requires some sort of knowledge for solution. This makes the different kinds of problems to be solved in the AI.
2. *Knowledge representation:* it includes various mechanisms to code the real world phenomenons into form that can be suitably represented and stored in computers memory. In addition to simple storage, we should also be able to draw some inferences from this knowledge.
3. *Handling uncertain situations*: real world is full of situations which are uncertain. The humans have excellent capacity to use their perception to handle the uncertain situation. The development of a machine, if claimed to exhibit intelligence, will not be complete if it is not able to deal with the uncertain situations.
4. *Theorem proving:* this area of AI deals with using the mathematical formalizations, to prove the existing theorems. It developed certain methodologies to solve the resolutions and prove their validity.
5. *Game playing:* this is an interesting component of AI which analyzes the concepts behind game playing. It develops automated computer programs which can play certain games which are normally considered as a brain games.
6. *Natural language processing*: this involves the study, understanding, and processing of natural languages so as to provide natural language interlace to information systems, etc.
7. *Expert systems*: these are the computer programs that can exhibit intelligence like experts in a narrow domain.
8. *Computer vision*: this entails the ability to recognize shapes, features etc. automatically and in turn produce automation through robots.
9. *Dealing philosophical issues*: as the intelligence is a term primarily defined for human being, the Artificial intelligence theories encounter the problem of dealing with philosophical and psychological issues also. For example, if a medical diagnosis system is developed, the system should also be able to psychologically satisfy the patient about the prescription.

1.9.2 Hardware/Software Components of AI

1.9.2.1 Software

The software, which takes part in AI software systems, is:
  (i) Machine language
  (ii) Assembly language

 (iii) High level language
 (iv) LISP language
  (v) 4th generation language
 (vi) Object oriented language
(vii) Distributed language
(viii) Natural language

1.9.2.2 Architecture

  (i) Uniprocessor
 (ii) Multiprocessor
(iii) Special purpose processor
 (iv) Array processor
  (v) Vector processor
 (vi) Parallel processor
(vii) Distributed processor

1.9.2.3 AI Components

  (i) Symbolic processing
 (ii) Numeric processing
(iii) Pattern matching
 (iv) Problem / puzzle solving
  (v) Logic representation
 (vi) Heuristic search
(vii) Natural language processing
(viii) Knowledge representation
 (ix) Expert system
  (x) Neural networks
 (xi) Learning
(xii) Planning

1.10 THE MIND BODY PROBLEM

The validity and development of the field of AI always remained a point of discussion among philosophers. The mind body problem asks how many mental states and processes are related to bodily (typically brain) states and processes. This analysis is done to find out the possibility of developing machines that can think. The "mind–body" relationship is considered as a problem, because philosophers (like Rene –Descartes) said mind is different than soul (dualist theory). He said, immortal soul interacts with the body and mind is only an intermediate state. On the other hand, the monist theory, often called materialism, states that there are no such things as immaterial soul, only material objects and mental states, such as pain, knowing that one is climbing a ladder are brain states. John Searle called the idea with the slogan as "Brains cause minds".

The materialist's world faces two problems:

(i) *Free will*: we know that our mind has liberty to have free will, means it is free to think in its own way. Now, as per materialist theory, if there is no soul, how can it be that purely physical mind (thus laws of physics) governs the will and every transformation of mind?

(ii) *Consciousness issue*: it says that " why is it that it feels like something to have certain brain states, whereas presumably does not feel like anything to have other physical states." Means, mind remains in action mode and possesses consciousness even when it is actually idle.

These problems cause a big hurdle in the representation of mental states. In AI applications wherever the understanding is required, the mental state needs to be represented. The modeling of belief system is also a derived problem, which arises whenever some AI expert system tries replacing human being.

To understand the contribution of mind in human functioning, a typical experiment called "***brain in a vat***" experiment was done. It imagines that the brain has been removed from the body at the berth and the body is allowed to develop. The brain is kept in sophisticated vat, and all the signals (electronically engineered) are fed to the brain. However as body is not   there, it will not feel the hunger, pain , taste etc. It will not pay any extra attention towards most tasty meal. In this case would it be the same mental state, as one held by a brain in the body?

One way to resolve the dilemma, is to say that the contents of mental state can be interpreted from two different points of view:

(i) Wide content point of view, interprets it from the point of view of an omniscient outside observer with access to the whole situation who can distinguish differences in the world. So under wide content the brain in a vat beliefs are different from those of a normal person.

(ii) Narrow content considers only the internal subjective point of view, and under this view, the beliefs would all be the same.

1.11 THE CHINESE ROOM EXPERIMENT

This experiment is most famous among the other philosophical experiments. John Searle (1980) performed this experiment to exhibit the fact that a system running and passing the Turing test may not have understanding.

He described a hypothetical system, which consists of a human who can understand only English, a rule book and blank papers. The system is inside a room with a small opening on the outside. Through the opening the slip of the paper with indecipherable symbols is passed to the human. The human finds matching symbols in the rule book, and follows the instruction. The instructions may include writing the symbols in the new slip of the paper, finding symbols in the stack, rearranging the stack and so on. Eventually the instructions will cause one or more symbols to be transcribed onto a piece of paper that is passed back to the outside world. From outside world the input is taken in form of Chinese sentences and answers are generated in Chinese. This exercise should be considered as intelligent according to "Turing Test". The Searle argues as follows: the person in the room does not understand Chinese, the rule book and the stack of paper, obviously do not understand Chinese, therefore, there is no understanding of Chinese developing through this experiment. Hence, according to Searle, running the right program does not necessarily generate understanding and is not a sufficient condition for having a mind. Based on this experiment Searle gave following axioms:

  (i) Computer programs are formal systems.
 (ii) Mind have mental contents.
(iii) Syntax by itself is not sufficient for semantics.
 (iv) Brains cause minds.

From the first three axioms, he concluded that something running a program could be mind but it would not be a mind only because of having capacity to run a program. From the fourth axiom he concludes that "any other system capable of causing minds would have to have causal power equivalent to those of brains." Thus it can be inferred as any artificial brain would have to duplicate the causal powers of brain, not just the capacity to run a particular program, and the human brains do not produce mental phenomenon only by running a program.

1.12 PARALLEL AND DISTRIBUTED AI

With the advent of parallel computing, a widened new dimension of AI has evolved which can make use of high speed computing. There are three main areas in which parallel and distributed architecture contribute to the study of intelligent systems. These are:
* Psychological modeling
* Improving efficiency, and
* Organizing systems in modular fashion.

We will discuss these in brief.

(i) Psychological modeling

This system was proposed as model of human information processing and modeling the psychological behavior. Some production system models stress the sequential nature of production system. Other models stress on parallel aspects.

One such system is SOAR. It was developed in 1987. It has dual mission. On one side, it is intended as architecture for building integrated AI systems. On the other side, it models human intelligence. SOAR incorporates both sequential and parallel aspects of production systems. It has two phases. One is 'elaboration phase' and another is 'decision phase'. In elaboration phase, production fire in parallel. In decision phase, operators and states are chosen and working memory is modified. By trying these phases to particular timings SOAR accounts for a number of psychological phenomenon.

There is another approach of modeling the psychological aspect. That is using neural networks. It draws inspiration from the physical organization of human brain itself. It consists of neurons. The human neurons are quite slow compared to digital computer circuits but in brain, they are large in number. Vast number of these richly interconnected components operate concurrently.

(ii) Parallel reasoning systems

AI programs consume significant time and space resources. A reasoning system of actual expert system may require using several thousand rules. Thus the use of parallel architecture algorithm in this regard will improve the efficiency. The following sources are identified which increase speed using parallel architecture in production systems:

1.13 CONCLUSION

The first thought to make a machine intelligent might have come from the philosophical thinking that human mind is like a machine which operates on knowledge encoded in some internal language. It is this thought that could have inspired the early researchers that if mind is like a machine, why cannot machine be a mind! What happened after that is what that has been presented and discussed in the last pages. After going through all that, it can be concluded that though, in some aspects, AI systems have performed better than human beings can, but in the applications involving human cognitive skills, it has not been possible to develop a universal intelligent system, which possesses some of the basic abilities of even a five year old child.

In spite of stringent and sincere efforts, human mind is still an unsolved puzzle for us. How do we think? What is the process involved in thinking? Is thinking a mechanical process or biological phenomena? Is it only mind that is involved in thinking or is mind guided by soul? It is these and several other questions like these, which are baffling scientists over the years. Some of these have been answered, but many still elude us of proper and logical answer. Until we are capable of understanding the mechanism involved in the thinking process of our mind, it would not be possible to transform an intelligent system into a thinking system.

One more aspect related to human reaction about a particular situation is emotions. We as living species are governed by emotions most of the time. Our interaction with other human is always guided by our emotions at smaller or larger degree, depending upon the subject matter of discussion. Similarly, an intelligent machine emulating a human action must have power to emulate emotions also. A team of European researchers is working in this area and very recent development evolved in the world arena is that scientists are all set to build '*emotional machine*' (Times of India, April 2008). Roddy Cowie, coordinator of the EU-funded Humaine project says, "*As our interactions with machines get more and more pervasive, it becomes harder and harder to ignore the emotional element. Taking it into account will become a routine part of computer science courses and computer development."*

Machines that feel and converse may no longer be confined to the realm of science fiction. Led by DFKI, the German Centre for Research on Artificial Intelligence, experts are developing a computer system that can interact with a human being by reacting to the signals such as tone of voice. They plan to build a Sensitive Artificial Listener system, which will observe a user's facial expression and voice and then connect with him. Looking into the pace of the developments in the field of AI, we should always feel optimistic that an intelligent, emotional and thinking machine is very much possible.

However, the basic idea of making a thinking machine is in itself fascinating. If this theoretical concept in future could be implemented in its true spirit, and intelligently thinking machines could be built, the world would really change.

EXERCISES

1. Explain the basic differences between natural intelligence and artificial intelligence. List the similarities and dissimilarities between the two.
2. Suggest your own dimension of AI. Give reasons and examples in support of this.
3. You have read conventional mind body problem. Answer the following based on this.
   (i)   are the mind and body distinct entities, interacting somehow with each other ?
   (ii) is body an expression of physical processes?
   (iii) is body just an illusion of rational mind?
4. Describe the Turing test and write the criticism it faced.
5. Write the differences between conventional computing and intelligent computing.
6. Though computing is a relatively new discipline , philosophers and mathematicians have been thinking about the issues of automated problem solving for thousand of years. What is your opinion about the relevance of these philosophical issues in the development of intelligent machines.
7. Pick one problem area of your choice to estimate the energy required to design an expert system. Spell the problem out in some detail based on your intuition, which aspect of this solution should be most difficult to automate.
8. Take some new topic within the scope of AI and write an essay on the state of art development in this field.
9. List the similarities and differences between intelligent agent and human agent.
10. List and discuss two potentially negative effects on society of the developments of artificial intelligence techniques.

2

Problem Solving Through AI

2.1 INTRODUCTION

In the last chapter, we have tried to explain that Artificial Intelligence is the science and technology applied to make machines intelligent. The ultimate aim of researchers is to develop universal intelligent system to match the intelligence capabilities of human beings. In this regard, lot of progress has been made and considerable amount of success has been achieved, although, universal intelligent system is still a dream. Scientists have developed techniques to use AI in a limited domain and have successfully developed many AI systems, which work in a problem specific domain and show expertise not only matching those of human experts, but also exceeding those in many ways and in many applications. It should be kept in mind that for the time being, the most important application of AI is to develop intelligent systems to solve real world problems, which otherwise take considerable amount of time and human efforts, and hence, become uneconomical as well as inefficient at times. Hence, problem solving becomes major area of study, which involves methods and various techniques used in problem solving using AI.

In this chapter, we will discuss the methods of solving real world problems using Artificial Intelligence (AI) techniques. In real world, there are different types of problems. We will try to explain various characteristics of problems and their solution methodologies.

The method of solving problem through AI involves the process of defining the search space, deciding start and goal states and then finding the path from start state to goal state through search space. The movement from start state to goal state is guided by set of rules specifically designed for that particular problem (sometimes called production rules). The production rules are nothing but valid moves described by the problems.

Let us first discuss some terms related with AI problem solution methodology:

Problem	It is the question which is to be solved. For solving a problem it needs to be precisely defined. The definition means, defining the start state, goal state, other valid states and transitions.

Search space:	It is the complete set of states including start and goal states, where the answer of the problem is to be searched.
Search:	It is the process of finding the solution in search space. The input to search space algorithm is problem and output is solution in form of action sequence.
Well defined problem:	A problem description has three major components. Initial state, final state, space including transition function or path function. A path cost function assigns some numeric value to each path that indicates the goodness of that path. Sometimes a problem may have additional component in form of heuristic information.
Solution of the problem:	A solution of the problem is a path from initial state to goal state. The movement from start states to goal states is guided by transition rules. Among all the solutions, whichever solution has least path cost is called optimal solution.

Hence, it is evident that the method of solving problem through AI techniques involves the process of defining the search space, deciding about start and goal state and then finding a path from start state to goal state through search space. The movement from start state to goal state is guided by transition rules or production rules. After designing the search space involving different start states, goal states and transition arcs, the solution needs to be searched. The search techniques are the methods which are used to find a way from start to goal state.

Thus, to build an AI computational system to solve a particular problem the following activities are needed to be performed:

1. Define the problem precisely. This definition must include precise specifications of initial states and final states of the problem.
2. Analyze the problem. This phase abstracts the salient features of the problem that can have an immense impact on the appropriateness of various possible techniques used for solving the problem.
3. Isolate and represent the task knowledge that is necessary to solve the problem.
4. Choose the best problem solving technique and apply it to the particular problem.

Now let us discuss these steps in detail.

2.1.1 Defining Problem as State Space Search

In AI, the representation and definition of problem plays a key role. The representation of the problem requires selection about state representation, and corresponding knowledge representation. The representation is guided by specific conventions, which also judge its suitability from the computational viewpoint.

The good representations support explicit constraint exposing description. Every practical problem has certain constraints or limitations. The representation should clearly highlight these constraints. For representation of some problems, one should look for desired data and should avoid irrelevant details. Some features of good representation are given below:

1. Good representation captures the important features and relations between them completely.
2. They expose natural constraint. It should be able to express the relations between different objects.
3. They bring objects and relations together.
4. They suppress irrelevant details of the problem. The rarely used details are kept out of sight, but one should be able to get them when necessary.
5. They are transparent. That is, one can understand the salient features represented by them immediately.
6. They are complete. They should be able to represent all aspects of the problem.
7. They are concise. That means, they efficiently and concretely should say whatever is to be specified.
8. They should be suitable from computational viewpoint. They should allow fast storage and retrieval of information.
9. Their storage should consume minimum memory.
10. They should be computable, i.e. one should be able to create them with an existing procedure.

2.1.2 Analyzing the Problem

This activity requires analyzing the problem in detail and capturing, its salient features, e.g., in the game playing type of problems, the solution or the selection of winning move must include visualizing the opponent's move also; or in the path finding problems, it should see the cost of each path etc. Besides this, the natural language processing applications include the analysis of syntactic and semantic details of the input. Hence, the analysis phase performs complete analysis of the problem.

2.1.3 Isolating the Task Oriented Knowledge

As is mentioned earlier, the solution of a problem requires the availability of related knowledge. Hence for solving a problem the knowledge related to problem field is isolated and represented in a suitable format. As the nature of AI applications varies widely, accordingly so, the types of knowledge and there representation techniques, e.g., a 8 queens problem will require storage of only position of queens on the board, whereas a natural language understanding application will require storing the syntactic and semantic details of the words/grammars etc. Further, the medical diagnosis application will require storage of large amount of medical symptoms and corresponding diagnosis. Various knowledge representation (KR) techniques are devised for this phase. These KR methodologies have their respective advantages and disadvantages, and specific techniques are suitable for specific applications. Various KR techniques are described in detail in following chapters.

2.1.4 Finding the Solution

After representation of the problem and related knowledge in the suitable format, the appropriate methodology is chosen which uses the knowledge and transforms the start state to goal state. The techniques of finding the solution are called search techniques. Various search techniques are developed for this purpose. They are dealt-with in detail in one of the following sections and also in next chapter.

2.2 REPRESENTATION OF AI PROBLEMS

In this section, we would learn the technical aspects of problem representation required from computational perspective. From this orientation, the representation of AI problems can be covered in following four parts:

1. *A lexical part*: that determines which symbols are allowed in the representations of the problem. Like the normal meaning of the lexicon, this part abstracts all fundamental features of the problem.
2. *A structural part*: that describes constraints on how the symbols can be arranged. This corresponds to finding out possibilities required for joining these symbols and generating higher structural unit.
3. *A procedural part*: that specifies access procedures that enable to create descriptions, to modify them, and to answer questions using them.
4. *A semantic part*: that establishes a way of associating meaning with the descriptions.

Let us understand these steps by an example presented below:

We are given the problem of "playing chess". To define the problem, we should specify the starting position of chess board, the rules that define the legal moves and the board positions that represent a win for one side or the others. Here, the:

1. Lexical part contains the board position, which may be an 8 x 8 array where each position contains a symbol indicating an appropriate chess piece in the official chess opening position. The goal is any board position in which opponent does not have a legal move and his king in under attack.
2. The structural part describes the legal moves. The legal moves provide the way of getting from an initial state to a goal state. They are described as set of rules consisting of a left hand side that serves as a pattern to be matched against the current board position and a right hand side that describes changes to be made to board position to reflect the move.
3. The procedural part will be methods for applying appropriate rule for winning the game. It will include representing the "set of winning moves"

of standard chess playing. Out of all legal moves, only those moves, which bring the board position to a winning position of respective player are captured and stored in procedural part.

However, in chess the total *'legal moves'* are of the order of 10^{120}. Such a large number of moves are difficult to be written, so only *'useful moves'* are written. It should be noted that there is a difference between legal moves and useful moves. The legal moves are all those moves which are permissible according to game rules and useful moves will be those legal moves which bring the game in a winning position. Hence the 'useful moves' will be a subset of 'legal moves'. The state space is total valid states possible in a problem and finding a problem solution is "starting at an initial state, using a set of rules to move from one state to another and attempting to end up in one of a set of final states."

4. The semantic part is not required in "chess game" because, there is no hidden meaning associated with any piece and all the move meanings are explicit. However in natural language processing type of applications, where there is "meaning" associated with words and "complete message" associated with sentence, the semantic part captures and stores, the meaning of words and message conveyed by sentence.

Thus, in AI, to design a program for solution, the first step is the creation of a formal and manipulable description of problem itself. This includes performing following activities:

1. Define a state space that contains all the possible configurations of the relevant objects.
2. Specify one or more states within that space, which describe possible situations from which problem solving process may start. These are called initial states.
3. Specify one or more states that would be acceptable as solutions to the problem. These are called goal states.
4. Specify a set of rules that describes the action (operators) available.

2.3 PRODUCTION SYSTEM

In the above section, we have discussed basic aspects of AI problem solution. An AI system developed for solution of any problem is called production system. Once the problem is defined, analyzed and represented in a suitable formalism, the production system is used for application of rules and obtaining the solution. A production system consists of following components:

1. *A set of production rules*, which are of the form $P \rightarrow Q$. Each rule consists of a left hand side constituent that represents the current problem state and a right hand side that represents a result or generated output state. A rule is applicable if its left hand side matches with the current problem state. Thus, the left side of the rule determines the applicability of the rule and the right side that describes the output, if rule is applied. It is important to note

that there may be multiple constituents on the left hand side of a rule (i.e. $P1_\wedge P2_\wedge....P_n \rightarrow Q$). In this situation, all constituents of left hand side should be satisfied for applying the rule. After applying the rule, the left hand side of the rule becomes the current state.

2. *One or more knowledge/data bases,* that contain all the appropriate information for the particular task. Some parts of the database may be permanent while some part of this may pertain only to the solution of current problem. The information in these databases may be structured in an appropriate way.

3. *A control strategy* that specifies order in which the rules will be compared to the database of rules and a way of resolving the conflicts that arise when several rules match simultaneously.

4. *A rule applier,* which checks the applicability of rule by matching the current state with the left hand side of the rule and finds the appropriate rule from the database of rules.

2.3.1 Salient Features of Production Rules

As mentioned above, a set of rules is applied for finding appropriate solution of a problem. These rules are important part of production system. Some of the main features of production rules are described as follows:

1. *Expressiveness and intuitiveness*: In real world, many times a situation is encountered, which says *if this happens – I will do this, if this is so – then this should happen.* The production rules essentially tell us what to do in a given situation. This type of situation can be coded in 'IF–THEN' form of structures. The representing and coding of rules in IF-THEN type of structures is quite common in AI applications and the rules of almost all types of expert systems and rule-based systems are coded in this way.

2. *Simplicity*: The uniform structure of 'IF- THEN- ELSE' coding structure of rule based system provides simplicity in knowledge representation. This feature improves the readability of production rules and communication between various parts of a single program.

3. *Modularity and modifiability*: Modularity means, production rules code the knowledge available in discrete pieces. In real world, the knowledge is available in discrete pieces hence, their coding in modular form suits very much. Information can be treated as a collection of independent facts which may be added or deleted from the system with essentially no deleterious side effects. Modifiability stands for the facility of modifying the rule. The modular and modifiable features allow the development of production rules in a block or skeletal form first and then it is "fine tuned" to suit a specific application. In case of similar expert systems having a large number of production rules, the basic production rules can be borrowed or copied and they can be molded in a tailor-made fashion to suit to another application. Hence, it will reduce the amount of efforts required to develop a new database.

4. *Knowledge intensive*: The knowledge base of production system stores extensive and pure knowledge. This part contains no control or programming information. The problem of semantics is resolved by representing the knowledge in proper structure.

5. *Opacity*: Along with the advantages, there are certain disadvantages also associated with production systems. Opacity is the problem generated by combination of production rules. Though, the individual production rules may be models of clarity, the combined operation and effects of control program may be opaque. The opacity is generated because of less prioritization of rules.

6. *Inefficiency*: Sometimes, several of the rules become active during execution. A well devised control strategy reduces this problem. As the rules of production system are large in number and they are hardly written in hierarchical manner, it requires exhaustive search through all the production rules for each cycle of control program. It makes the functioning inefficient.

7. *Absence of learning*: The simple rule based production system does not store the results of computations for later use. Hence, it does not exhibit any type of learning capabilities.

8. *Conflict Resolution*: The rules in ideal production system should not have any type of conflict. The new rule whenever added in the database should ensure that it does not have any conflict with the existing rules. Besides this, there may be more than one number of rules that can be applied (typically called *fired*) in one situation. While choosing the rule also, the conflict should not happen. If conflict is found, it should be resolved in following ways:

    (i)   Assign priority to the rules and fire the rule with the highest priority. This method is used in many expert systems. Its virtue lies in its simplicity, and by ordering the rules in the approximate order of their firing frequency. This can be made using a relatively efficient strategy.

    (ii) Use a longest matching strategy. This means that fire a rule having largest number of matching constraints. Its advantage is that the discrimination power of a strict condition is greater than of a more general condition. A rule with more constraints provides more knowledge.

    (iii) Choose most recently used rule for firing. Its advantage is that it represents a depth first search, which follows the path of greatest activity.

2.3.2 Characteristics of Production System

Now let us describe some of the main characteristics of production system from the aspect of their storage in computer system. The production systems can be of various types, but the most popular production system is monotonic system. A monotonic production system is a production system in which the application of one rule never prevents the later application of another rule. The characteristics of production systems are presented below:

1. ***Data structure***: After defining the problem, it will be required to be represented in a suitable data structure. The data structures best suited for traditional AI problems are graphs and trees. Nodes in the graph correspond to problem state and arcs between nodes correspond to valid transitions, e.g., in an 8-puzzle problem, various different states derived from a single state will be put as children of that state. While searching for the solution, the graph sometimes needs to be converted into tree. The directed graph cannot always be converted into tree. There is a special type of tree representation called AND – Or graph which is used in AI problem. It will be described in detail later on in this chapter.

   To apply the AI problem solving algorithms, the representation of problem/data is done in problem representation, and application of operator is done using various control strategies. The following section discusses these control strategies.

2. ***Control Strategies***: These are also called search strategies. Control strategies are adopted for applying the rules and searching the problem solution in search space. It is already mentioned earlier that the control strategy is responsible for obtaining the solution of the problem. Hence, if the wrong control strategy is applied, it may be possible that a solution is never obtained, even if it exists. The salient characteristics of control strategies are described below:

   (i) The first requirement of good control strategy is that it should cause motion. It means that whenever we apply a rule the movement of the problem should be in the direction of obtaining the solution. In real practice, there is a cost or effort associated with application of a rule. In case the application of the rule does not cause motion, the efforts will go as waste. To check whether the application of an operator moves the problem in the direction of the solution, it is checked that the operator should not generate the output state as any previously generated states. Otherwise, it will create a cycle, e.g., in a water-jug problem, if we choose operator for filling 4 gallon jug and then emptying 4 gallon jug. Next time also we choose same sequence of operator, it will create cycle and will never generate the solution. Again, some sequence of operator always start with filling 4 gallon jug first, and applying the first applicable operator on it, we will never obtain the solution.

   (ii) It should be systematic. That means there should be systematic method to select a rule for application.

There are various control strategies. These are described in detail, in one of the coming sections, known as "search strategies".

2.4 ALGORITHM OF PROBLEM SOLVING

Although, the nature of AI problems varies widely, and accordingly, their solution methodologies are of varying types. Hence, any one algorithm for problem solution is not applicable over all types of problems. However, in a very crude and elementary format, the algorithm for problem solving can be represented as follows:

Algorithm: "problem name"

1. Choose data about start state, goal state and production rules from initial database.
2. Until the goal state is achieved (or solution can not be achieved and operators are exhausted), do the following:
3. Begin
4. Select some rule from the set of rules that can be applied to data.
5. Note new state generated after the application of the rule. Make this as current state.
6. End.

2.5 EXAMPLES OF AI PROBLEMS

This section discusses some common AI problems. Though we present large number of problems here, it should be noted that the applications of AI are not limited to only these problems and there may be many other problems where AI can be applied. Some of the popular problems are discussed in the following subsections:

2.5.1 Tic-Tac-Toe

Tic-Tac-Toe is a game involving two players. It is played by putting 'X' or 'O' alternately by two players, in any one of the 9 board positions shown as follows. Playing means making the mark of 'X' or 'O' in any one square. The player who is able to make his marks in horizontal, vertical, or diagonal straight line first, is declared as winner.

From AI viewpoint, the problem of playing Tic-Tac-Toe will be formulated as follows:

The start state is all blank squares out of 9 squares. Player 1 can play in any one square. As the game proceeds, blank squares remain the choice, which can be marked by the players. The data structure used to represent the board is a 9-element vector, with element positions shown in Fig 2.1:

1	2	3
4	5	6
7	8	9

Fig 2.1: Element positions of TIC-TAC-TOE

Board position: = {1,2,3,4,5,6,7,8,9}

An element contains the value 0, if the corresponding square is blank; 1, if it is filled with "O" and 2, if it is filled with "X".

Hence starting state is {0,0,0,0,0,0,0,0,0}

The goal state or winning combination will be board position having "O" or "X" separately in the combination of ({1,2,3}, {4,5,6}, {7,8,9},{1,4,7},{2,5,8}, {3,6,9}, {1,5,9}, { 3,5,7}) element values. Hence two goal states can be {2,0,1,1,2,0,0,0,2} and {2,2,2,0,1,0,1,0,0}. These values correspond to the goal states shown in the figure.

The start and goal state are shown in Fig. 2.2.

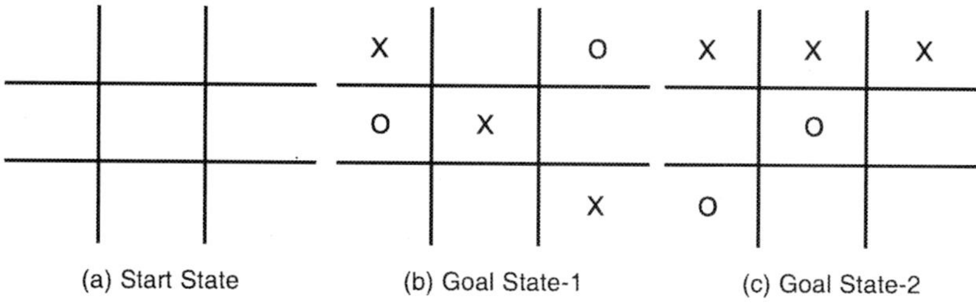

Fig 2.2: Start and goal states of TIC-TAC-TOE

Any board position satisfying this condition would be declared as win for corresponding player. The valid transitions of this problem are simply putting '1' or '2' in any of the element position containing 0.

In practice, all the valid moves are defined and stored. While selecting a move it is taken from this store. In this game, valid transition table will be a vector (having 3^9 entries), having 9 elements in each.

2.5.2 Water-Jug Problem

This problem is defined as:

> *"We are given two water jugs having no measuring marks on these. The capacities of jugs are 3 liter and 4 liter. It is required to fill the bigger jug with exactly 2 liter of water. The water can be filled in a jug from a tap".*

In this problem, the start state is that both jugs are empty and the final state is that 4-liter jug has exactly 2 liters of water. The production rules involve filling a jug with some amount of water, filing the water from one jug to other or emptying the jug. The search will be finding the sequence of production rules which transform the initial state to final state.

Part of search tree of water jug problem is shown in Fig. 2.3.

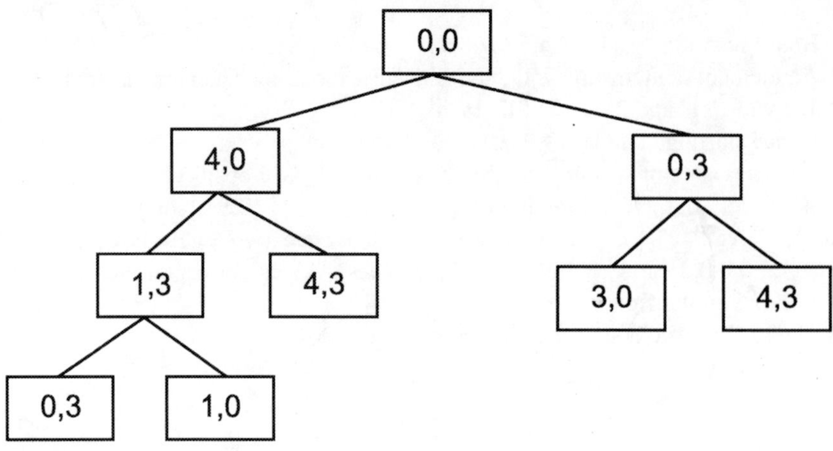

Fig 2.3: Partial search tree of water jug problem

The state space for this problem can be described by set of ordered pairs of two variables (x, y) where, variable x represents the water in the 4-liter jug, and y represents the water in the 3-liter jug. Variable x can take the value 0, 1, 2, 3, 4 and variable y can take the value 0, 1, 2, 3. The start state is (0, 0) and the goal state is (2, 0). The production rules are formulated as follows:

Rule 1 : $(x, y) \rightarrow (4, y)$	(fill the 4-liter jug, applicable if x<4)
Rule 2 : $(x, y) \rightarrow (x, 3)$	(fill the 3-liter jug, applicable if y< 3)
Rule 3 : $(x, y) \rightarrow (x{-}x1, y)$	(pour some water out from 4-liter jug)
Rule 4 : $(x, y) \rightarrow (x, y{-}x1)$	(pour some water out from 3-liter jug)
Rule 5 : $(x, y) \rightarrow (0, y)$	(empty the 4-liter jug)
Rule 6 : $(x, y) \rightarrow (x, 0)$	(empty the 3-liter jug)
Rule 7 : $(x, y) \rightarrow (4, y - (4{-}x))$	(fill the 4-liter jug by pouring some water from 3liter jug)
Rule 8 : $(x, y) \rightarrow (x - (3 - y), 3)$	(fill the 3-liter jug by pouring some water from 4-liter jug)
Rule 9 : $(x, y) \rightarrow (x{+} y, 0)$	(empty 3-liter jug by pouring all its water in to 4-liter jug)
Rule 10: $(x, y) \rightarrow (0, x{+}y)$	(empty 4-liter jug by pouring all its water in to 3-liter jug)
Rule 11: $(0, 2) \rightarrow (2, 0)$	(pour the 2 liters from 3-liter jug into 4- liter jug)
Rule 12: $(2, y) \rightarrow (0, y)$	(empty the 2 liters in the 4-liter jug on the ground)

These are set of rules, which can be applied to solve water-jug problem. Solution of the problem will include applying appropriate rules in the specific sequence to transform the start state to goal state. One solution is applying the rules in the sequence 2, 9, 2, 7, 5, 9. The solution is presented in the following Table 2.1.

Table 2.1: Production rules applied in Water-Jug problem

Rule applied	Water in 4-liter jug	Water in 3-liter jug
Start state	0	0
2	0	3
9	3	0
2	3	3
7	4	2
5	0	2
9	2	0

2.5.3 8-Puzzle Problem

The 8-puzzle problem belongs to the category of "sliding-block puzzle" types of problems. It is described as follows:

"It has set of a 3x3 board having 9 block spaces out of which, 8 blocks are having tiles bearing number from 1 to 8. One space is left blank. The tile adjacent to blank space can move into it. We have to arrange the tiles in a sequence."

The start state is any situation of tiles, and goal state is tiles arranged in a specific sequence. Solution of this problem is reporting of "movement of tiles" in order to reach the goal state. The transition function or legal move is any one tile movement by one space in any direction (i.e. towards left or right or up or down) if that space is blank. It is shown in following Fig. 2.4:

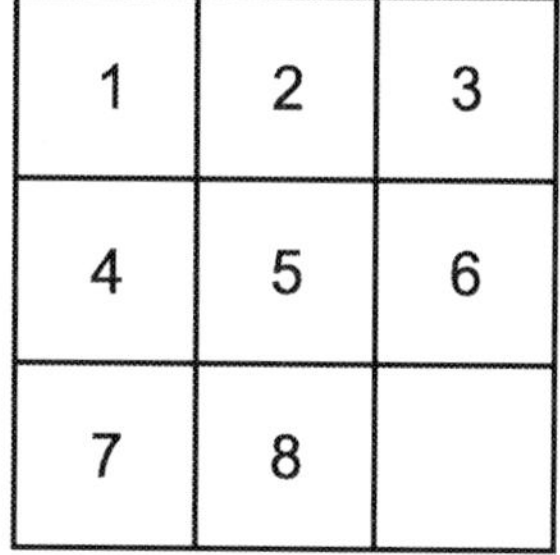

(a) Start state   (b) Goal state

Fig. 2.4: Start and Goal states of 8 puzzle problem

Here the data structure to represent the states can be 9-element vector indicating the tiles in each board position. Hence, a starting state corresponding to above configuration will be {1, blank, 4, 6, 5, 8, 2, 3, 7} (there can be various different start positions). The goal state is {1, 2, 3, 4, 5, 6, 7, 8, blank}. Here, the possible movement outcomes after applying a move can be many. They are represented as tree. This tree is called state space tree. The depth of the tree will depend upon the number of steps in the solution. The part of state space tree of 8-puzzle is shown in Fig 2.5.

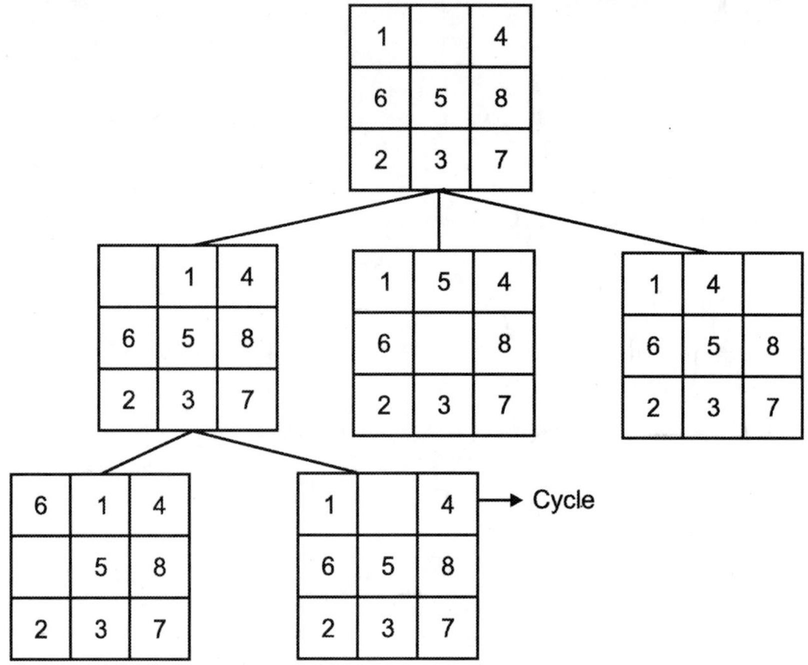

Fig 2.5: Partial search tree of 8-puzzle problem

2.5.4 8-Queens Problem

This problem is presented as follows:

> *"We have 8 queens and a 8 x 8 chessboard having alternate black and white squares. The queens are placed on the chessboard. Any queen can attack any another queen placed on same row, or column, or diagonal. We have to find the proper placement of queens on the chessboard in such a way that no queen attacks other queen".*

The 8-queen problem is shown in following diagram:

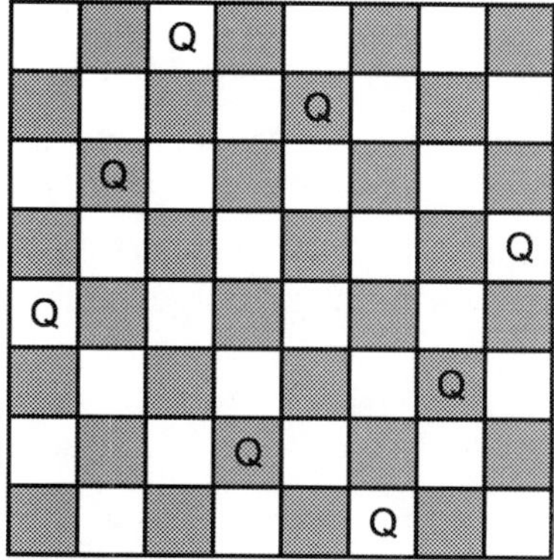

Fig 2.6: A possible board configuration of 8 queens problem

2.5.5 Chess Problem

It is a normal chess game. In a chess game problem, the start state is the initial configuration of chessboard. The final or goal state is any board configuration, which is a winning position for any player (clearly, there may be multiple final positions and each board configuration can be thought of as representing a state of the game). Whenever any player moves any piece, it leads to different state of game.

It is estimated that the chess game has more than 10^{120} possible states. The game playing would mean finding (or searching) a sequence of valid moves which bring the board from start state to any of the possible final states.

The start state of chess game is shown in Fig 2.7.

2.5.6 Missionaries and Cannibals Problem

The problem is stated as follows:

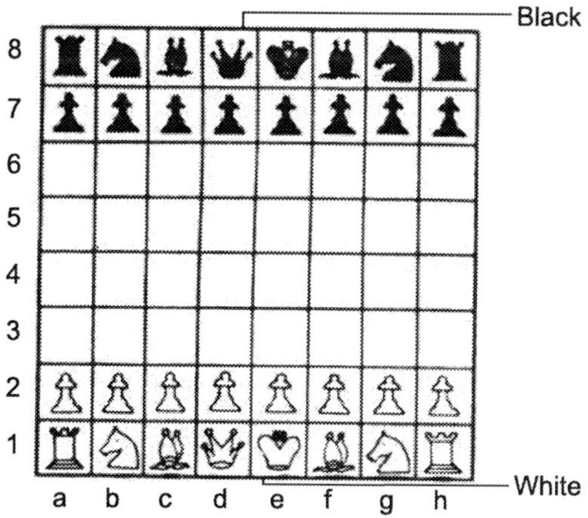

Fig 2.7: Start state of chess game

"Three missionaries and three cannibals are present at one side of a river and need to cross the river. There is only one boat available. At any point of time, the number of cannibals should not outnumber the number of missionaries at that bank. It is also known that only two persons can occupy the boat available at a time."

The objective of the solution is to find the sequence of their transfer from one bank of river to other using the boat sailing through the river satisfying these constraints.

We can form various production rules as presented in water-jug problem. Let Missionary is denoted by 'M' and Cannibal, by 'C'. These rules are described below:

Rule 1 :   (0, M)   :   One missionary sailing the boat from bank-1 to bank-2
Rule 2 :   (M, 0)   :   One missionary sailing the boat from bank-2 to bank-1
Rule 3 :   (M, M)   :   Two missionaries sailing the boat from bank-1 to bank-2
Rule 4 :   (M, M)   :   Two missionaries sailing the boat from bank-2 to bank-1
Rule 5 :   (M, C)   :   One missionary and one Cannibal sailing the boat from bank-1 to bank-2
Rule 6 :   (C, M)   :   One missionary and one Cannibal sailing the boat from bank-2 to bank-1
Rule 7 :   (C, C)   :   Two Cannibals sailing the boat from bank-1 to bank-2
Rule 8 :   (C, C)   :   Two Cannibals sailing the boat from bank-2 to bank-1
Rule 9 :   (0, C)   :   One Cannibal sailing the boat from bank-1 to bank-2
Rule 10 :   (C, 0)   :   One Cannibal sailing the boat from bank-2 to bank-1

All or some of these production rules will have to be used in a particular sequence to find the solution of the problem. The rules applied and their sequence is presented in the following Table 2.2.

Table 2.2: Rules applied and their sequence in Missionaries and Cannibals problem

After application of rule	persons in the river bank-1	persons in the river bank-2	boat position
Start state	M, M, M, C, C, C	0	bank-1
5	M, M, C, C	M, C	bank-2
2	M, M, C, C, M	C	bank-1
7	M, M, M	C, C, C	bank-2
10	M, M, M, C	C, C	bank-1
3	M, C	C, C, M, M	bank-2
6	M, C, C, M	C, M	bank-1
3	C, C	C, M, M, M	bank-2
10	C, C, C	M, M, M	bank-1
7	C	M, M, M, C, C	bank-2
10	C, C	M, M, M, C	bank-1
7	0	M, M, M, C, C, C	bank-2

2.5.7 Tower of Hanoi Problem

This is a historic problem. It can be described as follows:

> *"Near the city of 'Hanoi', there is a monastery. There are three tall posts in the courtyard of the monastery. One of these posts is having sixty-four disks, all having a hole in the centre and are of different diameters, placed one over the other in such a way that always a smaller disk is placed over the bigger disk. The monks of the monastery are busy in the task of shifting the disks from one post to some other, in such a way that at no point of time, a bigger disk is placed above smaller disk. Only one disk can be removed at a time. Moreover, at every point of time during the process, all other disks than the one removed, should be on one of the posts. The third post can be used as a temporary resting place for the disks. We have to help the monks in finding the easiest and quickest way to do so".*

Can we really help the monks? Before indulging ourselves in finding the solution of this problem, let us realize that even the quickest method to solve this problem might take longer time than the time left for the whole world to finish! Are you still interested in attempting the problem?

64-disk configuration is shown in Fig 2.8.

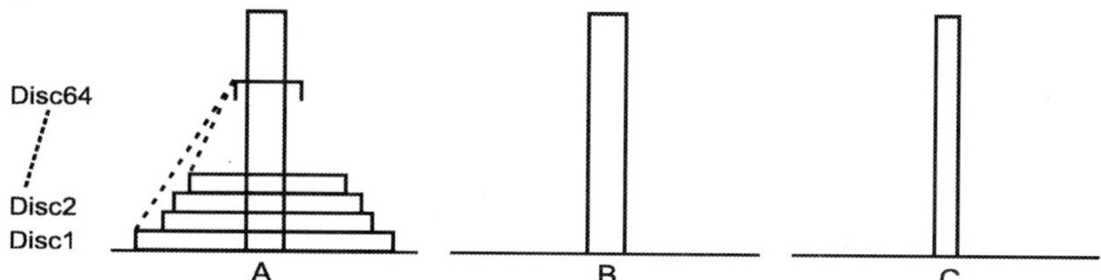

Fig 2.8: Tower of Hanoi problem

2.5.8 Traveling Salesperson Problem

This problem falls in the category of path finding problems. The problem is defined as follows:

> *"Given 'n' cities connected by roads, and distances between each pair of cities. A sales person is required to travel each of the cities exactly once. We are required to find the route of salesperson so that by covering minimum distance, he can travel all the cities and come back to the city from where the journey was started".*

Diagrammatically, it is shown in Fig 2.9.

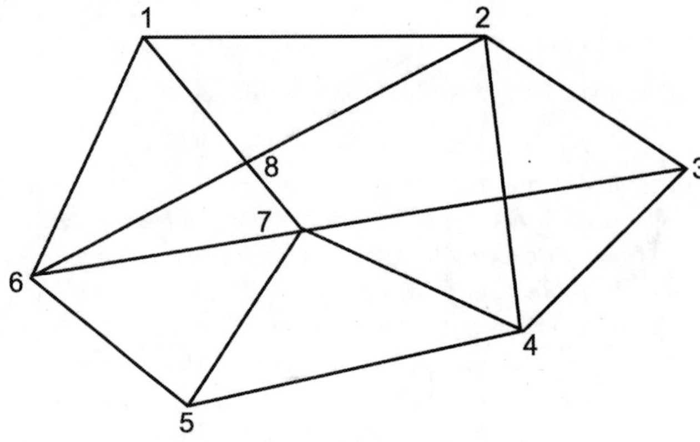

Fig 2.9: Cities and paths connecting these

The basic travelling salesperson problem comprises of computing the shortest route through a given set of cities.

Following Table 2.3 shows number of cities and the possible routes mentioned against them.

Table 2.3: Possible routes of travelling salesperson problem

Number of cities	Possible Routes
1	1
2	1 -2-1
3	1 -2 -3 1
	1 -3 -2 1
4	1- 2- 3- 4-1
	1- 2- 4- 3- 1
	1- 3- 2- 4- 1
	1- 3- 4- 2- 1
	1- 4- 2- 3-1
	1- 4- 3- 2- 1

We can notice from here that the number of routes between cities is proportional to the factorial of the (number of cities – 1), i.e., for three cities, the number of routes will be equal to !2 (2x1), and for four cities, !3 (3x2x1).

While there are !9 = 362880 routes for 10 cities, there are !29 = 8.8 E30 possible routes for 30 cities. The travelling salesperson problem is a classic example of ***combinatorial explosion***, because the number of routes increases so rapidly that there are no practical solutions for realistic number of cities. If it takes 1 hour of a mainframe CPU time to solve for 30 cities, it will take 30 hours for 31 cities and 330 hours for 32 cities. Practically, the actual application of such type of problem is for routing a data packet on computer networks. It requires managing thousands of cities. Hence for this much large amount of data the required problem solution time will be unaffordable.

The solution of this problem is done using neural network. The neural network can solve the 10 city case just as fast as the 30 city case whereas a conventional computer takes much longer time for these.

2.5.9 Magic Square

The problem is represented as follows:

"We are given a square of same number of rows and columns, where consecutive numbers are filled in blank spaces of each row and column such that numbers in each row, column and two diagonals, add up to the same number. The numbers have to be consecutive and one number can be used only once".

Therefore, the 3×3 square and 4×4 square would require any set of 9 and 16 consecutive numbers respectively. The problem is finding out the placement of numbers. The magic squares of order 3×3, where numbers from 1 to 9 are filled, is shown in Fig 2.10. It should be noted that there could be multiple solutions of magic square problem.

6	7	2
1	5	9
8	3	4

Fig. 2.10: A 3×3 magic square configuration

Let us describe the manual process of solving 3×3 magic square by filling numbers from 1 to 9. The steps required to attempt the problem are presented as follows:

Step 1: The sum of the numbers in each row and column can be predetermined as:

$$\text{Sum of numbers in each row, column and diagonal} = \frac{\text{Sum of numbers used}}{\text{Number of rows or columns}}$$

In our case, this figure is equal to 45/3, i.e. 15. (Sum of numbers from 1 to 9 divided by 3)

Step 2: Suppose the numbers to be filled in each blank space are x_1 to x_9. The magic square then will look like:

x_1	x_2	x_3
x_4	x_5	x_6
x_7	x_8	x_9

Now, since we know the sum of numbers in each row, column and diagonals is 15, we can form following equations:

$$x_1 + x_2 + x_3 = 15 \qquad \ldots\ldots (1)$$
$$x_4 + x_5 + x_6 = 15 \qquad \ldots\ldots (2)$$
$$x_7 + x_8 + x_9 = 15 \qquad \ldots\ldots (3)$$
$$x_1 + x_4 + x_7 = 15 \qquad \ldots\ldots (4)$$
$$x_2 + x_5 + x_8 = 15 \qquad \ldots\ldots (5)$$
$$x_3 + x_6 + x_9 = 15 \qquad \ldots\ldots (6)$$
$$x_1 + x_5 + x_9 = 15 \qquad \ldots\ldots (7)$$
$$x_3 + x_5 + x_7 = 15 \qquad \ldots\ldots (8)$$

Step 3: We will have to solve the above equations for finding the values of numbers. You may notice that number x_5 comes in most of the equations hence; we should try to find the value of x_5 first.

Add the equations (5), (7) and (8), to get:

$$x_2 + x_5 + x_8 + x_1 + x_5 + x_9 + x_3 + x_5 + x_7 = 45$$

Putting values from equations (1) and (3), we get,

$$3\,x_5 = 15 \Rightarrow x_5 = 5.$$

Step 4: Put the value of x_5 in the equations where it appears, we get,

$$x_4 + x_6 = 10 \qquad \ldots\ldots (9)$$
$$x_2 + x_8 = 10 \qquad \ldots\ldots (10)$$
$$x_1 + x_9 = 10 \qquad \ldots\ldots (11)$$
$$x_3 + x_7 = 10 \qquad \ldots\ldots (12)$$

Step 5: Assume $x_1 = 1$, hence $x_9 = 9$ [from equation (11)]

After getting three values, our magic square will look like:

1	x_2	x_3
x_4	5	x_6
x_7	x_8	9

Now, try to find the location of number 2. Any number out of x_2, x_3, x_4, and x_7 cannot be 2, because in that case remaining number will be 12 to make the sum as 15, which is not permissible. Hence, either x_6 or x_8 will be 2. But, it is also not possible, because in that case, x_3 or x_7 will be 4 and x_2 or x_4 will become 10, which is again not possible. Therefore, x_1 cannot be 1. Revise this step with another assumption.

Step 6: Assume $x_2 = 1$, hence $x_8 = 9$ [from equation (10)].

After getting three values, our magic square will look like drawn ahead.

x_1	1	x_3
x_4	5	x_6
x_7	9	x_9

Now, any number out of x_1 and x_3 cannot be 2, because of the reason mentioned in the above step, hence one number out of x_4, x_6, x_7 and x_9 will be equal to 2. Assume $x_4 = 2$, hence $x_6 = 8$ [from equation (9)]. Notice that 3 can not come in the same row, column or diagonal in which either 1 or 2 comes, because then, the remaining number will be either 11 or 10, which is not possible. Hence, for $x_4 = 2$, x_1, x_3, and x_7 cannot be 3, resulting in $x_9 = 3$. However, this is also not possible, because number 3 cannot come with 9 since the remaining number in that case will also be 3, which cannot be. Therefore, x_2 or x_4 cannot be 2. Try another assumption.

Step 7: Assume x_7 or $x_9 = 2$, resulting in x_3 or $x_1 = 8$ [from equations (12) and (11)].

After getting one more number, our magic square will look like:

x_1	1	x_3		x_1	1	x_3
x_4	5	x_6		x_4	5	x_6
2	9	x_9		x_7	9	2

From the above squares, we can calculate the remaining numbers as, $x_9 = 4$, $x_1 = 6$, $x_3 = 8$, $x_6 = 3$ and $x_4 = 7$ for the first square; and $x_7 = 4$, $x_3 = 6$, $x_1 = 8$, $x_4 = 3$ and $x_6 = 7$ for the second square; and the solutions for the magic square will be:

<table>
<tr><td>6</td><td>1</td><td>8</td></tr>
<tr><td>7</td><td>5</td><td>3</td></tr>
<tr><td>2</td><td>9</td><td>4</td></tr>
</table>

<table>
<tr><td>8</td><td>1</td><td>6</td></tr>
<tr><td>3</td><td>5</td><td>7</td></tr>
<tr><td>4</td><td>9</td><td>2</td></tr>
</table>

As mentioned earlier, there can be several solutions to the magic square depending upon which number you assume as 1 to start with in the step 5.

Similarly, we can solve magic square of the order 4×4. A typical solution is given as follows in the Fig 2.11 :

7	13	12	2
10	4	5	15
1	11	13	8
16	6	3	9

Figure 2.11: Magic square of the order 4 x 4

2.5.10 Language Understanding Problems

This type of problems include the understanding of natural languages, conversion of one language to another language, language comprehension, design of intelligent natural language interfaces etc. It also includes answering of a query using a database. More regarding such type of problems and other various issues involved in natural language understanding are deal with in another chapter of this book.

2.5.11 Monkey and Banana Problem

This problem is described as follows:

"A monkey and a bunch of banana are present in a room. The bananas are hanging from the ceiling. The monkey cannot reach the bananas directly. However, in the room there is one chair and a stick. The monkey can reach the banana standing on the chair. We have to find the sequence of events by which monkey can reach the bananas".

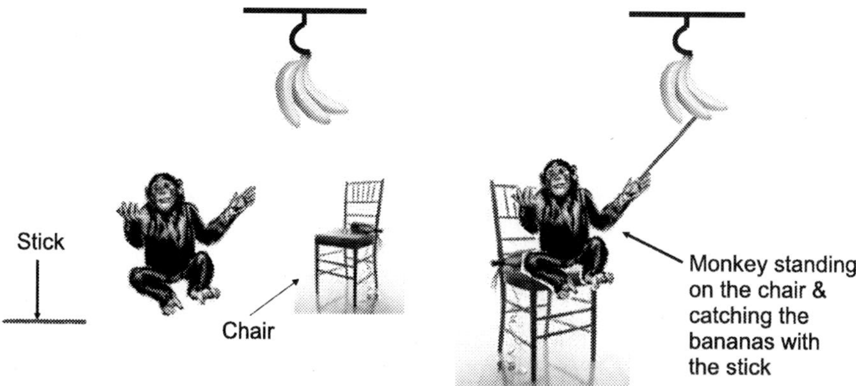

Fig 2.12: Monkey and banana problem

Solution of this problem means finding the sequence of actions for the monkey to reach the banana. It is much simpler than the problems of water and jug or Missionaries and Cannibals discussed above, hence, we leave it for the readers to formulate the set of production rules and to find the appropriate sequence of the actions required for the solution. The problem is pictorially represented in Fig 2.12.

2.5.12 Cryptarithmatic Puzzle

It is a puzzle involving decoding of digit represented by a character. It is in the form of some arithmetic equation where digits are distinctly represented by some characters. The problem requires finding of the digit represented by each character. One such problem is shown in Fig. 2.13.

$$
\begin{array}{r}
R\ I\ N\ G \\
+\ D\ O\ O\ R \\
\hline
B\ E\ L\ L
\end{array}
$$

Fig. 2.13: A cryptarithmatic problem

These types of problems require constraint satisfaction. Constraints are that all the laws of arithmetic must hold good and any letter should represent same digit wherever it comes in the puzzle. Also, no two different letters can be represented by same digit. For example, in the puzzle shown above, the laws of summation of two given numbers must hold good and digit R, which comes at two different places must be represented by same digit. Similarly, letter O and L must be represented by same digit, however, R, O and L, together with other letters, must be represented by different digits. The process involved in solving these puzzles is described in detail in the next chapter of this book.

2.5.13 Block World Problems

The problem can be represented as follows:

> *"There are some cubic blocks, out of which, each is placed either on the table or on other block forming a particular configuration. We have to move the blocks to arrange them to form some other given configuration by applying minimum number of moves. The requirement of moving a block is that only the top block from a group can be shifted in a move. It can be placed either on the table or on top of any other block."*

The live application of this type of problem can be seen in a container depot where lot of containers are placed one over the other in several groups. A crane or a robot is used to arrange these containers in different groups for loading in trains and ships. The start and goal states of a typical block world problem are shown in Fig 2.14.

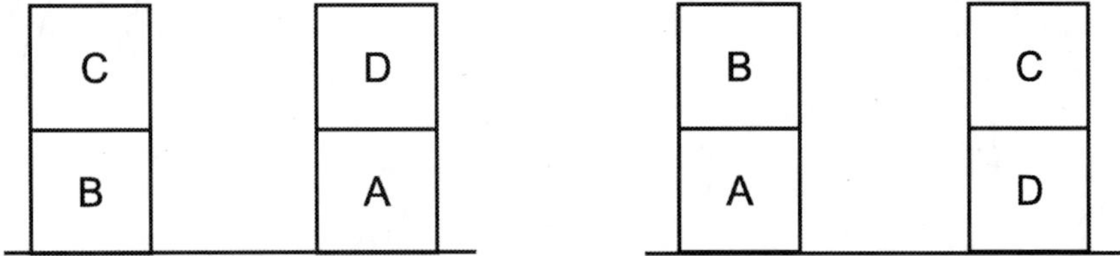

Fig. 2.14: The start and goal configuration of block world problem

Detailed account of this problem is given in the section of *Planning* of chapter -11 of this book.

2.6 NATURE OF AI PROBLEMS

In this section, we will highlight the nature of real world AI problems. As mentioned earlier, problems can be of several types and solution of a particular problem depends upon the nature of the problem. We may categorize problems based on their nature in the manner discussed hereunder:

2.6.1 Path Finding Problems

In this type of problems, the solution involves reporting of path (or sequence of steps used to obtain the solution). The traveling salesperson problem discussed above is an example of this kind of problem.

2.6.2 Decomposable Problems

In this type of problems, the problem can be broken into small subproblems and the solution of the main problem is obtained by joining the solutions of small subproblems, e.g. in mathematical equation, if the expression involves the solution of various components then these components can be solved independently, and the complete answer can be obtained by joining the solutions of subproblems. However, all the real world problems are not decomposable problems.

Consider following arithmetic equation:

$$\int (x^3 + 3x^2 + \sin^2 x + \cos^2 x)\ dx = 0$$

If we want to solve this equation, we can find the solution of different integrals separately and then join the results to get complete solution. Hence, above problem is broken into four problems, i.e. (i) $\int x^3\ dx$, (ii) $\int 3x^2\ dx$, (iii) $\int \sin^2 x\ dx$, (iv) $\int \cos^2 x\ dx$.

2.6.3 Recoverable Problems

There are certain types of problems, where the application of operator can be reverted if required, and on the initial state, a new operator can be applied. Such types of problems are called recoverable problems. 8-puzzle problem is an example of this kind because if you apply a move and find that it is wrong or not worth, you may revert to the original position and apply another move. The recoverability of a problem plays an important role in determining the control structure necessary for problem solution. There is another type of problems like "theorem proving" where the steps can be ignored. These are called ignorable problems. These can be solved using simple control structures, which are easy to implement. But there are certain types of problems like medical diagnosis problems where if an operator is applied, it cannot be reverted to original state. In such types of problems, the selection of operator is very critical because if a wrong operator is applied, it may be possible that a solution is never obtained even if it exists. Such types of problems are called '**irrecoverable**' problems. Chess playing is another irrecoverable problem where once you apply a move, you are not allowed to revert. The recoverable problems require little complex control structure, which checks the outcomes of every move and in case the move is found to be wrong, it is reverted and initial state is restored back. The control structure of irrecoverable problems is difficult because it will involve a system that expands a great deal of effort in exploring each decision, since the decisions once chosen must be final.

2.6.4 Predictable Problems

These are the types of problems where all the outcomes of a particular move can be judged with definiteness. For example, consider the 8-puzzle problem where the outcomes after applying a certain move can be easily predicted because all the numbers and their positions are open before you. Hence, while deciding about a move, the suitability of these outcomes can be judged and planning the entire sequence of moves is possible. Whereas in card games like bridge or game where all the cards are not open, it cannot be decided in advance that what will be the effect of a particular move because your next move depends entirely upon the move of other players involved, hence planning a sequence of moves is not possible. Similar situation will be there in a game involving two players. One player can not judge the move played by other player. In such situations, multiple moves are considered for suitability and a probabilistic approach is applied to decide about the best move.

2.6.5 Problems Affecting the Quality of Solution

There are certain types of AI problems where the process of finding solution stops by just finding one solution and there is no need to ensure the validity of this solution by finding the other solutions, e.g., the database query applications. In query applications, whenever the query is answered, the other possible answers are not checked. However, in route finding problems (like traveling salesperson problem) once a route from source to destination is obtained, still other possibilities need to be checked to judge whether it is the shortest path or not (optimal solution). Thus, we can say that there are certain types of problems where any one solution is enough and in other types of problems where to accept a solution all the possible solutions need to be checked.

2.6.6 State Finding Problem

In this type of AI problems, the answer is reporting of a state instead of path. The examples of such type of problems are natural language understanding applications. In such type of applications the interpretation of a particular sentence is required and it is not important how the solution is obtained. As far as the interpretation of the input sentence is correct, the steps used in obtaining the solution can be ignored. However, there are another kinds of problems where the solution demands the reporting of state as well as path. These are the problems requiring justification, e.g., medical diagnosis problems using expert system. Here, besides the name of the medicine, the patient requires explanation about the process or the path applied for finding that particular medicine.   Thus, it involves the 'belief' of user as well. To satisfy him, the process of obtaining the solution (i.e. the path) and the solution (i.e. the state) both need to be stored. Hence, the types of problems, which involve human belief, fall in the category of problems where state and path both should be reported.

2.6.7 Problems Requiring Interaction

This is the kind of problems, which require asking some questions from the user or interacting with the user. There are many AI programs already built which interact with the user very frequently to provide additional input to the program and to provide additional reassurance to the user. In the situations where computer is generating some advice for a particular problem, it is always advisable to take the views of user at regular interval. Doing this will help providing the output in the form suitable to the user.

2.6.8 Knowledge Intensive Problems

These are kinds of AI problems, which require large amount of knowledge for their solution. Consider the tic-tac-toe game. Here, to play the game, the required amount of knowledge is only about legal moves and other player's moves. This is little amount of knowledge. Whereas in chess game, the number of legal moves are more, and to decide a particular move, more future moves of opponent and those of oneself in *"look ahead manner"* (technically called *ply*) are visualized. Hence, the amount of knowledge required to play a chess game is more as compared to tic-tac-toe game. Further, if we consider the medical expert system, the amount of knowledge required is enormous. Such types of AI applications are called knowledge intensive applications. Similarly, in the application of a data query, the knowledge required is only about the database and query language whereas if it is a natural language understanding program, then it will require vast amount of knowledge comprising of syntactic, semantic and pragmatic knowledge. Hence, the amount of knowledge and role of knowledge varies in different AI problems.

From the above discussion, it is evident that the nature of various AI problems is widely different and in order to choose the most appropriate method for solving a particular problem, the nature of problem needs to be analyzed. The problem characteristics can be summarized as follows:

1. If the problem is decomposable into independent smaller or easier sub problems.
2. Is backtracking possible or not.
3. Is the problem's universe predictable.
4. Is a good solution to the problem obvious without comparison to all other possible solutions.
5. Is the desired solution a state or a path.
6. Is a large amount of knowledge absolutely required to solve the problem or is knowledge important only to constrain the search.

2.7 SEARCH TECHNIQUES

As stated earlier, the process of the solution of AI problem searches the path from start state to goal state. This is very important aspect of problem solving because search techniques not only help in finding most viable path to reach the goal state, but also make the entire process efficient and economical. In this section, we discuss basic search techniques adopted for finding the solution of AI problems. Broadly, the search is of two types:

(i) *Blind (or unguided or uninformed) search*: The uninformed or blind search is the search methodology having no additional information about states beyond that provided in the problem definitions. In this search total search space is looked for solution.

(ii) *Heuristic (or guided or informed) search*: These are the search techniques where additional information about the problem is provided in order to guide the search in a specific direction.

In this chapter, we will discuss the unguided search techniques and the guided search techniques will be dealt with in the next chapter. Following search techniques comes under the category of unguided search techniques:

(i)   Breadth-First search (BFS)
(ii) Depth-First search (DFS)
(iii) Depth-Limited search (DLS)
(iv) Bidirectional search

2.7.1 Breadth-First Search

In this type of search, the state space is represented in form of a tree. In addition, the solution is obtained by traversing through the tree. The nodes of tree represent start state, various intermediate states and the goal state. While searching for the solution, the root node is expanded first, then all the successors of the root node are expanded, and in next step all successors of every node are expanded. The process continues till goal state is achieved, e.g., in the tree shown in following Fig. 2.15, the nodes will be explored in order A, B, C, D, E, F, G, H, I, J, K, L:

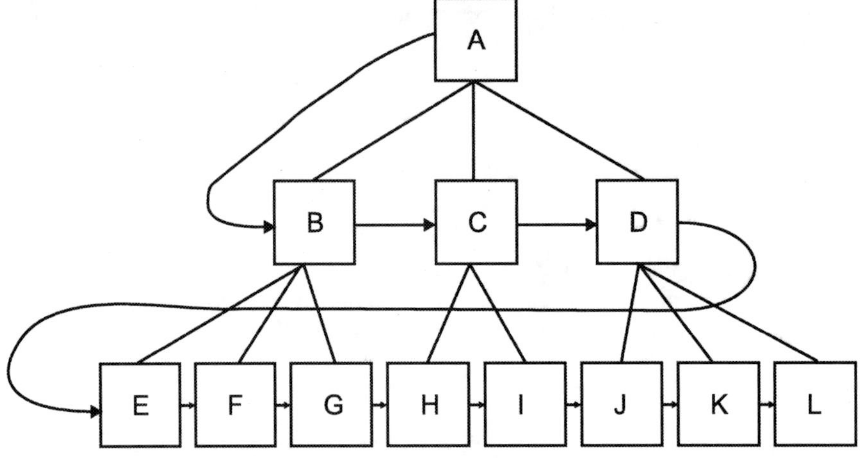

Fig. 2.15: Breadth-First Search Tree

In breadth-first search, the space complexity is more critical as compared to time complexity. Analysis shows that the time and memory requirement of the problem of depth 8 and 10 are 31 hours, 1 terabyte and 129 days, 101 terabyte respectively. Fortunately, there are other strategies taking lesser time in performing the search. In general, the problems involving search of exponential complexity (like chess game) cannot be solved by uninformed methods for the simple reason, the size of the data being too big. The data structure used for breadth first search is First In First Out (FIFO).

Algorithm for breadth first search is described as follows:

(i)   Create a variable called Node-List and set it to initial state.
(ii) Until a goal state is found or Node-List is empty do:
   (a)   Remove the first element from node-list and call it E. If node-list was empty, quit.
   (b)   For each way that each rule can match the state described in E do:
      (i)   Apply the rule to generate a new state.
      (ii)   If new state is a goal state, quit and return this state.
      (iii) Otherwise, add new state to the end of node-list.

2.7.1.1 *Advantages of Breadth First Search (BFS)*

The breadth first search is not caught in a blind alley. This means that, it will not follow a single unfruitful path for very long time or forever, before the path actually terminates in a state that has no successors. In the situations where solution exists, the breadth first search is guaranteed to find it. Besides this, in the situations where there are multiple solutions, the BFS finds the minimal solution. The minimal solution is one that requires the minimum number of steps. This is because of the fact that in breadth first search, the longer paths are never explored until all shorter ones have already been examined. Thus, if the goal state is found during the search of shorter paths, longer paths would not be required to be searched, saving time and efforts.

Traveling sales person problem discussed above can be solved using Breadth-First Search technique. It will simply explore all the paths possible in the tree and will ultimately come out with the shortest path desired. However, this strategy works well only if the number of cities is less. If we have large number of cities in the list, it fails miserably because number of paths and hence the time taken to perform the search become too big to be controlled by this method efficiently.

2.7.2 Depth First Search

There can be another type of search strategy than the one described above. In this type of approach, instead of probing the width, we can explore one branch of a tree until the solution is found or we decide to terminate the search because either a dead end is met, some previous state is encountered or the process becomes longer than the set time limit. If any of the above situations is encountered and the process is terminated, a backtracking occurs. A fresh search will be done on some other branch of the tree, and the process will be repeated until goal state is reached. This type of technique is known as Depth-First Search technique.

It generates the left most successor of root node and expands it, until dead end is reached. The search proceeds immediately to the deepest level of search tree, or until the goal is encountered. The sequence of explored nodes in the previous tree will be A, B, E, F, C, G, H, K, L, D, I, J. The search is shown in Fig 2.16 below:

The DFS has lesser space complexity, because at a time it needs to store only single path from root to leaf node. The data structure used for DFS is Last-In-

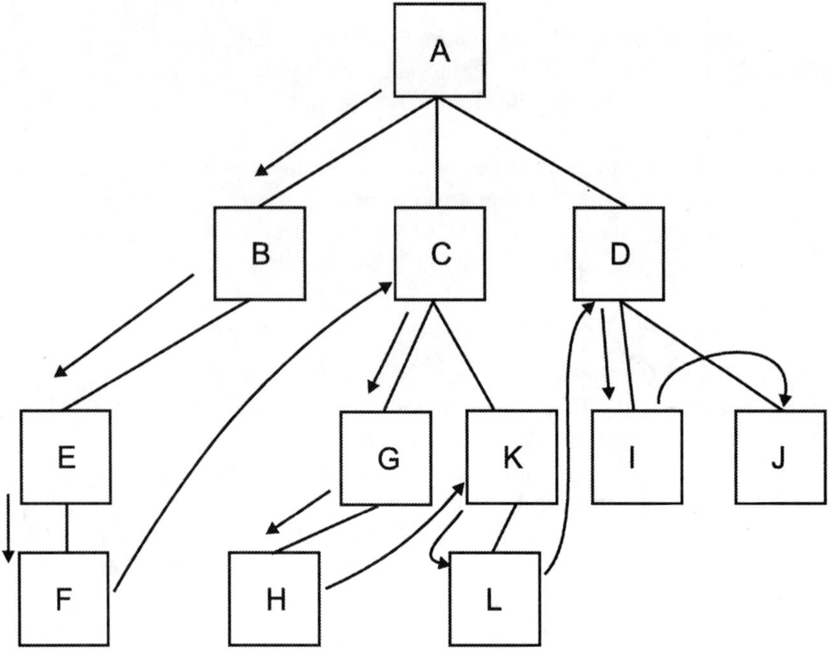

Fig 2.16: Depth First search tree

First-Out (LIFO).

Algorithm for Depth First Search is described as follows:

1. If initial state is a goal state, quit and return success.
2. Otherwise, do the following until success or failure is reported:
    (a)   Generate a successor E of the initial state. If there are no more successors signal failure.
    (b)   Call Depth-First Search with E as initial state.
    (c)   If success is obtained, return success, otherwise continue in this loop.

The procedure to perform DFS for tree of node 'n' is given below:

Procedure: unbounded DFS for tree of node n, [DFS1(n)].

Start

If n is a goal node then

Start

Solution : = n;

Exit;

End;

For each successor ni of n do

If ni is not an ancestor of n then

P1(ni);

Return;
End;

Algorithm :
Depth first branch and bound

Unbounded depth branch and bound search [BBS(n)]
Start
If f(n) > cost (solution) then return;
If n is a goal node then
Solution := superior (m, n);
For each ni of n do
BBS (ni);
Return;
End;

2.7.2.1 *Advantage of depth-first search*

Depth-First Search strategy has following advantages:
(1) Requires less space and hence, less memory, since nodes on the current path are stored.
(2) It may find a solution without examining much of search space, because we may get the desired solution in the very first go. Hence, for the problems, which have only one solution or one solution is considered sufficient, this technique is advantageous.

Out of the two most elementary search techniques described until now, the depth-first search has some problems as compared to breadth-first search. The DFS, unlike BFS may follow a single unfruitful path for a very long time. Theoretically, in the situation when there are no successors, only then it will stop searching. In the problems, where production rules form a loop, it is probable that DFS may be stuck up in the loop. For example, in the water-jug problem discussed above, there are number of production rules and problem can be solved by applying some rules in a particular sequence. Suppose, the DFS technique is applied to find the correct path and the solution of the problem. In the tree, it starts searching a branch having rules 1, 8 and 5. By applying these rules, 4-liter jug will be filled, some water from 4-liter jug will be filled into 3-liter jug and 4-liter jug will be emptied. The process will be repeated and we will never get a solution. Also, the DFS does not guarantee to find an optimal solution because as soon as a solution is found, it will stop the search and this solution may not be the optimal one. It may find the answer in more number of steps by unnecessary exploring the wrong paths.

On the other hand, BFS technique takes lot of time and becomes unmanageable if number of paths is large. It is more suitable if the problem has more than one solution and we have to find optimal solution. However, for the problems having single solution, it may take unnecessary time in exploring all the paths in spite of getting a solution early.

Hence, a better approach would be to devise the search strategies that combine the advantages of both DFS and BFS. Some of these strategies are described in detail in the following section.

2.7.3 Depth-Limited Search

It is a combination of BFS and DFS. In this, node at certain level (say l) is considered as having no successor. Up to the considered depth, the tree is explored by DFS method and the rest of the tree is explored by BFS method. Depth-First Search method is a typical Depth-Limited Search method with depth equal to infinity. The algorithm of DFS can be modified to perform the search up to a certain depth (d). The procedure of DFS of limited depth is given below:

Procedure:
depth (d) bounded DFS of n nodes [DDFS1(n, d)].
Start
If d is , then return;
If n is a goal node then
Start
Solution := n;
Exit;
End;
For each successor n_i of n do
If n_i is not an ancestor of n then
DDFS1 (n_i, d-1);
Return;
End;

2.7.3.1 Depth First Iterative Deepening

Sometimes the depth of the considered search tree in depth-limited search is dynamically changed according to problem to get best depth limit. It is called iterative deepening search. It actually increases the limit to 0, 1, 2 until a goal is found. In the situation where the search space is more and depth of solution is not known in advance, the iterative deepening is preferred as search method. The algorithm for depth first iterative deepening is presented below:

Algorithm:
Start
d:= 0;
repeat
d := d +1;

DDFS (root, d);
Until success;
End;

2.7.4 Bidirectional Search

As the name indicates, it is search in two directions. In the search methods discussed above, the search proceeds only from start to goal, unlike in bidirectional search, where two simultaneous searches are done. One search proceeds in forward direction (i.e. starting from start node towards goal node) and another search proceeds in the backward direction (i.e. starting from goal node towards start node). Wherever two searches meet, the process stops. The bidirectional search is advantageous then unidirectional search, because for a tree of depth 'd' and branching factor 'b', the unidirectional search requires b^d number of comparisons but bidirectional search requires $b^{d/2}$ comparisons in each direction. As $b^{d/2} + b^{d/2} < b^d$, the bidirectional search has lesser time complexity. However, it is applicable to only on those situations where search tree is completely defined, i.e. all actions in state space are reversible. A bidirectional search is shown in Fig 2.17.

Here A, B, C, E, F are cities to be traveled and the distance between each pair of cities is mentioned in the graph. In the solution of this problem, the location of cities can be represented in graph by nodes indicating the cities. The starting state

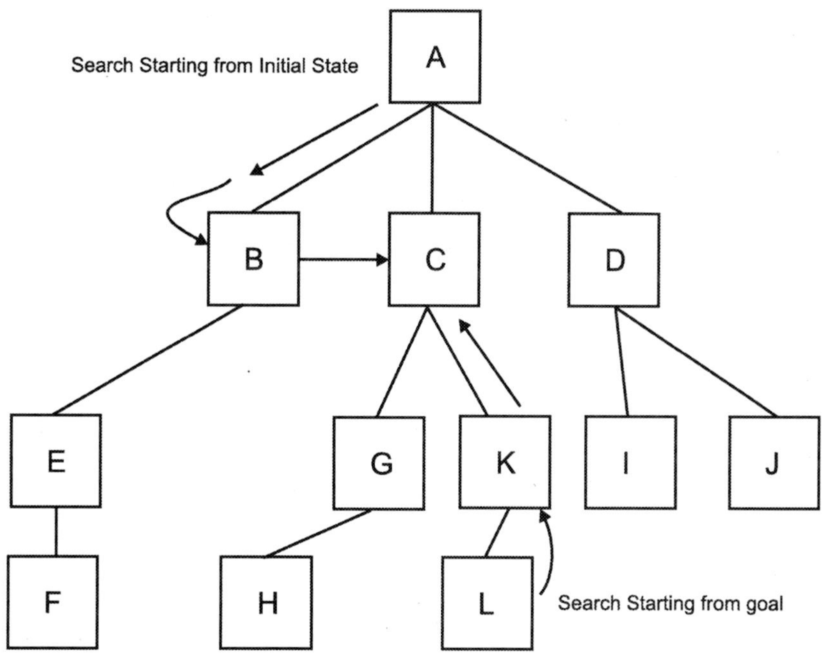

Fig. 2.17: Example of Bidirectional search

of this problem can be any node and objective is to find the shortest path covering all cities. Route finding algorithms are used in a variety of applications like routing in computer network, military operations planning etc.

Finding the solution of AI problems using blind search techniques is applicable only in very specific problems of very limited size. In the problems having large number of production rules, using such techniques implies mere wastage of efforts. The actual real world problems require application of large number of production rules, on the large amount of data. There is another category of search techniques called guided search techniques, which reduce the search space based on additional information provided regarding the problem. These guided search techniques are discussed in next chapter.

EXERCISES

1. What are the basic components of AI problem solving methodology. Describe them in detail.
2. Think of a new problem other than described in this chapter. State the important requirement of its solution and write the algorithm to solve it. Devise the production rules and its state space.
3. Write the algorithm for breadth first and depth first search.
4. Write a recursive algorithm using open and closed lists to implement breadth first search. Does recursion allows the omission of open list when implementing breadth first search.
5. Repeat the solution of water jug problem with the capacity of two jugs as (i) 3 and 5 liters (ii) 3 and 7 liters (iii) 6 and 8 liters. Devise all the production rules and write the algorithm.
6. Give the graph representation of farmer, wolf, goat and cabbage problem. Let the nodes represent state of the world, e.g. farmer and the goat are on the west bank and the wolf and the cabbage on the east. Discuss the advantages of bread the first and depth first for searching this space.
7. Explain various types of AI problems. Determine whether goal driven or data driven search would be preferable for solving each of the following problem. Justify your answer:
   (i)   diagnosing mechanical problems in an automobile.
   (ii) A person giving a common ancestor's name " Ramdada" claims to be your distant cousin. You want to verify her claim.
      (a) another person claims to be your distant cousin. He does not know common ancestor's name, but knows that it was no more than 6 generations back. You would like to find either this ancestor or determine that she did not exist.
      (b) A theorem prover for geometrical applications.
      (c) A program for examining sonar readings and interpreting them such as telling a large submarine, from a small submarine.

8. What are the important characteristics of control strategies. How does the control strategies lead to combinational explosion. What is the way out to solve the problem in such a case.

9. What is meant by production system characteristics. Explain its each component in detail.

10. A Hamiltonian path is a path that visits every node of a graph exactly once. What conditions are necessary for such a path to exist.

11. Find the optimal route for traveling salesperson, who has to visit 5 cities joined as follows.

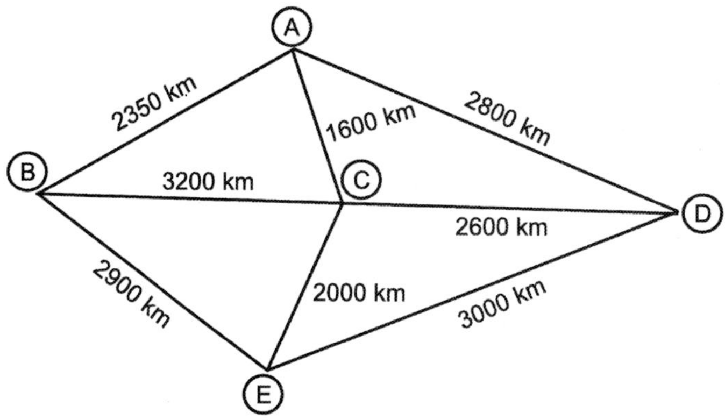

12. Write the algorithm for breadth first and depth first search.

13. Write a recursive algorithm using open and closed lists to implement breadth first search. Does recursion allows the omission of open list when implementing breadth first search.

3

Heuristic Search

3.1 INTRODUCTION

The literal meaning of heuristic is '*serving to find out*'. Hence, '*heuristic search*' means '*search techniques applied to find out*'. The word heuristic is derived from the Greek word '*eurisco*', which means 'I discover'. We have discussed in the last chapter that our aim is to find out the solution of problems using AI. For this purpose, search techniques are required to find the path from start state to goal state. *Heuristics* basically, are formal rules applied to find those branches in a state space that are most likely to lead to an acceptable and viable solution of a given problem.

In a given state space search, once we start search, we may find the solution ultimately without the application of any specialized methodology, but that search might take lot of time and efforts, and could become inefficient and unacceptable. On the other hand, heuristic search might reduce the time and efforts considerably in finding the solution of the same problem. We normally apply heuristics in the situations described as:

1. The problem on hands does not have any exact solution because of inherent ambiguities in the problem statement or the data available. For example, in the problem of medical diagnosis, the symptoms collected from patients might lead to utter confusion in the mind of the doctor indicating towards many possible diseases exactly in contrast. In such type of situation, doctors use heuristics to select most likely disease and accordingly plan the treatment.

2. A problem is having exact solution, but the cost of finding that solution is unbearable. As discussed in the previous chapter, in many problems, the state space grows exponentially with number of states increasing factorially with the depth of the search. For example, in chess game, the number of possible states are huge and the search techniques described in the last chapter, i.e. breadth-first and depth-first search techniques might find it difficult to get the solution in acceptable time limit. Heuristic search techniques handle such types of problems by guiding the search in the most promising direction by eliminating the unpromising states form the search space.

It should be understood before proceeding further that heuristics is nothing but an *informed guess* of the next step to be taken in attempting the solution of a problem. It is similar to the situation when you are attempting a problem of which four alternative answers are given. You are not sure of the answer but based on whatever knowledge you have about the problem, you attempt the problem and apply your guessing power to find the solution. That solution might be right or wrong. Similarly, in heuristic search, many times the search might lead to suboptimal solution or we might not get any solution at all. This is an inherent limitation of heuristic search.

Two of the oldest applications of artificial intelligence have been game playing and theorem proving. Both of these require heuristics to explore the state space for searching proper solution. Hence, heuristic search techniques have been core of AI research since long. However, recent developments in the field of expert systems have further strengthen the role of heuristics in problem solving. When a human expert solves a problem, he or she definitely applies heuristics at some stage of the process. Thumb rules used frequently by experts are also heuristic in nature. These heuristics are extracted, coded and represented by expert system designers to be used in developing intelligent expert systems for various real-world applications.

In the last chapter we mentioned that there are two types of search techniques:
(i)   Uninformed (also called blind or unguided) search techniques
(ii) Informed (also called heuristic or guided) search techniques

The blind search techniques are breadth-first search and depth-first search etc. These are discussed in previous chapter. In this chapter, we would discuss heuristic search techniques.

3.2 BASIC CONCEPT OF HEURISTIC SEARCH

Heuristic search is also called guided search because in this, the search is guided in a specific direction. In normal blind search techniques discussed in the last chapter, the search space is defined by only production rules, and in the problem definition, besides the production rules, any other information is not included. In absence of any additional information regarding the problem, the search proceeds by blindly expanding any node randomly. In heuristic search, besides normal production rules, additional information or knowledge about the problems is given in form of clue. The additional information or clue is called '*heuristics*'. This additional information or clue restricts the expansion of only promising nodes in search tree and guides the search in a specific direction towards the goal. Thus, it reduces the search space and the solution of problem is obtained efficiently. Heuristics help to guide a search process and they improve the quality of the paths that are explored. The additional information is given for search in terms of *heuristic function*. This additional task domain knowledge is called *heuristic knowledge*. Because of the presence of additional information, heuristic search is also called *informed search*. To understand the functioning of heuristic, go through following example:

Consider a situation in which, one wants to search a particular house in a city. If the available information about the house, is only address of the house, then searching the house will require seeing the address of all houses till the required house is found. This is an example of blind search. Now, if an additional information or clue regarding the house is also given that "the house under search is a pink-colored building". Then finding the house will require checking only pink-colored buildings. All houses which do not match this criteria of color are straight away rejected. This reduces the search space. If further more information regarding the house is given as "it is pink-colored double story building", in this case the search space is further reduced and limited to searching only pink-colored double story buildings.

This is the case of heuristic search. The additional clue (here information about color and number of stories in the building) is called heuristic information (or simply *'heuristics'* and corresponding knowledge *'heuristic knowledge'*). During search process, the additional clues discard the possibilities of certain states to become goal state and thus reduce the search space. Hence, in search process, these states are not explored further. As the search space is reduced, the solution is obtained in lesser number of steps. For applying the heuristic search techniques, while defining the problems, the additional information is given in terms of a mathematical function, called *'heuristic function'*. In blind search techniques, a node is selected for expansion without any preference. That means, any node, which comes on top according to BFS or DFS is selected for expansion. But in guided search, the selection of a node for expansion is done according to its value of heuristic function.

3.3 CONCEPT OF HEURISTIC KNOWLEDGE

The heuristic knowledge is a problem/task specific knowledge. It is obtained by consulting experts of concerned fields. The use of heuristics is common in human being also. A human expert of a particular field gains heuristic knowledge with experience. Consider the case of a medical practitioner. Until he is new in the field, he takes time to understand and analyze the patient's symptoms and suggest a medicine. But slowly and with passage of time, as he gains experience, he takes lesser time for solving the same problem. This is because of the fact that by handling the similar problem again-and-again, the solution strikes quicker to his mind. Similarly, an experienced teacher can understand the student's problem more quickly and effectively as compared to a new teacher. In all these situations, the difference between an expert and a layman is the presence of heuristic knowledge they posses. The human expert with experience gains the heuristic knowledge, and it is the amount of heuristic knowledge that converts a normal practitioner into an expert practitioner. In some problems (like informing the color of building) the heuristic is definite, and it is guaranteed to return the correct solution in lesser number of steps. However, in some problems like medical diagnosis where the heuristic can be considered as making the guesswork about the solution, it might be possible that the heuristic search fail to obtain the solution. A heuristic is a technique that improves the efficiency of a search process, possibly by sacrificing claims of completeness.

Heuristic knowledge plays an important role in the designing of the expert systems. While designing the practical computational AI systems, this domain specific heuristic knowledge is incorporated into a rule base of search procedure. There are two major ways of doing this. These are mentioned below:

(i) The heuristic knowledge is incorporated in the rules themselves, e.g., the rules for a chess playing system might describe not simply the set of legal moves but rather a set of 'sensible and useful' moves as determined by rule writer. It means, use of these rules will not be only a mechanical phenomena, but would guide the process to lead to the most viable and efficient solution, because of heuristic knowledge associated with them.

(ii) The heuristic knowledge is also incorporated in and as a heuristic function that evaluates individual problem state and determines how desirable they are.

A heuristic function maps the desirability of a problem state from descriptive to quantitative numbers. In the normal problem state identification, each state has only descriptive definition and any numerical value is not associated with it. The heuristic functions attach a numerical value with each state. The heuristic function considers important aspects of problem state, evaluates those aspects and gives weights to individual aspects in such a way that heuristic function at a given node in a search process gives an estimate of whether that node is on the desired path to a solution. The purpose of heuristic function is to guide the search process in the most profitable search direction by suggesting which path to follow first, when more than one search paths are available.

In certain types of AI problems, without the use of heuristic knowledge the solution is not possible. Consider the example of 'chess game'. It is estimated that a normal chess game has more than 10^{120} possible states. Hence the chess game playing would mean finding (or searching) a sequence of valid moves which bring the goal state from start state to any final state. But as it has more than 10^{120} possible states, while applying the search techniques the number of states grow at exponential rate. This situation is termed as problem of, ***combinatorial explosion***. In this problem, the number of states grow exponentially with the number of basic elements. In such types of AI problems, the solution is obtained by reducing search space to manageable limits using heuristics. In chess game, the heuristics is obtained by getting information about winning moves. Hence, while selecting a move only those possibilities of moves are explored which bring the chess board in winning state. This reduces the number of moves to be considered in the search to a large extent.

3.4 DESIGNING OF HEURISTIC FUNCTION

The designing of heuristic function is a critical task. In the problems where start and goal states are known, the heuristic function somehow relates the current search state with the desired goal state. However, there are certain states where the goal state is not known. In that case, heuristic function is designed based on other criterion. Hence, it continuously indicates that whether the search is moving in the right direction or not. In the actual AI problems, there is certain associated cost with the expansion of every node. The cost should be viewed in terms of the related efforts required to expand the nodes. It may or may not be the monetary cost.

Consider the example of "traveling of a person to a specific city". Here, "trying a possibility" (i.e., first going to any intermediate city and if not required then coming back) involves monetary cost, time and energy. The "trying of a possibility without any analysis" corresponds to a "blind node expansion". In this case, if the move is not found suitable then backtracking will be done. In this problem, backtracking means going back to original city and starting the travel again. Here, performing the backtracking will mean wastage of time, energy and money. Though, it is not advisable to waste such efforts, somehow it could be considered as affordable. Unlike this, in most of the AI problems, backtracking is not allowed, and the cost of wrong selection and expansion of node may be infinite, and it is also possible in certain situations that the solution   is never obtained, even if it exists.

Consider another problem of medical diagnosis. In this, the "node expansion" means "choices to select a particular medicine out of possible medicines". Here, the choices may be considered as nodes of decision tree, and opening a wrong node would correspond to wrong diagnosis according to symptoms, which may cost even patient's life. It means, in the problems where backtracking is not possible, the cost of opening a wrong node becomes infinite and the search may follow a wrong path, ultimately giving wrong decision about the problem. In context of medical diagnosis problem, a wrong diagnosis means prescription of wrong medicine. This will have associated cost of life and that is unaffordable. In the situations, where heuristic functions are used for selecting the node expansion, the suitability of a node would be judged by the value of heuristic function of that node in addition to the cost of opening a node. One more point regarding heuristic search which must also be noted is, that heuristic is a technique that improves the efficiency of search process by sacrificing claims of completeness. Thus, providing wrong heuristic information (or, if the heuristic becomes wrong), it may be possible that the solution is never obtained even if it exists. This reveals the criticality of designing of heuristic function, e.g., in above example of house search, if by mistake it is told that the house is "red", the search for the house would be limited to only to red-colored houses and the solution (requiring pink-colored houses) will never be obtained. But, practically this situation is very rare and heuristic search works well in most of the situations. Moreover, the decision about how many states will be terminated will depend upon, how good the heuristic function is. The designing of heuristic function is done in such a way that it provides best mathematical value of a move.

Let us design the heuristic function of 8-puzzle problem. Assume the board configuration as shown in Fig 3.1.

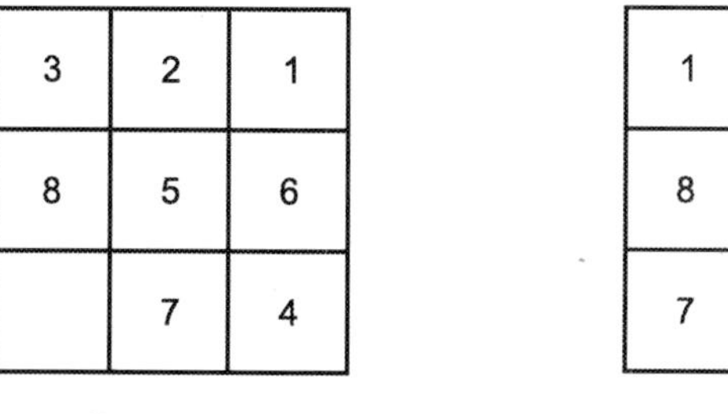

Start state   Goal state

Fig 3.1: 8 puzzle configuration

The average branching factor of 8-puzzle problem is 3, because for the middle tile it is 4, for the corner tiles it is 2, otherwise it is 3. To design the heuristic function for this puzzle, we take the sum of distances of every tile in any board position from the corresponding tile in the standard goal position. Then we calculate sum of horizontal and vertical position. Here for above configuration it is:

$$h = 2 + 0 + 2 + 1 + 2 + 2 + 1 + 0 = 10$$

Whenever a move (to displace the tile) is considered, the move, which minimizes the value of heuristic function, should be chosen.

There exist multiple heuristic functions for the same problem. In such situations, function which brings the solution in minimum number of steps is considered best.

3.5 TYPES OF HEURISTIC SEARCH TECHNIQUES

Various Heuristic search techniques are listed below:
  (i)   Generate-and-test
 (ii)   Best-first search
(iii)   Problem reduction
 (iv)   Hill-climbing search
  (v)   Constraint satisfaction
 (vi)   Means ends analysis
(vii)   Mini-max search

We shall describe these methods in detail in the following sections.

3.5.1 Generate and Test

As the name indicates, this approach simply is to generate the result and test whether it is the desired solution of the given problem. It is the simplest of all the approaches we have named above. Application of this strategy involves following steps:

Algorithm: "Generate-and-test"

Do the following until a satisfactory solution is obtained or no more solutions can be generated.

1.   Generate a possible solution
2.   Test to see if this is a solution.
3.   If a solution has been found, quit, otherwise return to step 1

The generate-and-test approach can be compared with dept-first search technique because we would have to generate a complete solution of the problem before it can be tested. There can be two methods to complete generate-and-test process. The first method could be to generate a random solution and test it. If found wrong, create another solution and test it again. This method might give you a solution on the first trial, however, there are chances, rather better chances that the solution is never found!

In the second method, systematic approach of generating a solution is applied and we are sure of ultimately getting the right solution if it exists. But, the difficulty with this method could be that it might take lot of time if problem space is large. Hence, what to do when 'random' as well as 'systematic', both the methods are not serving the purpose? Adopt a middle path, i.e., proceed the search process systematically, but discard some paths in-between which are not likely to provide the solution.

For simple problem having limited problem space, generate-and-test technique can be successfully deployed to do exhaustive search, however, for the problems having bigger space, this method proves inefficient. But the technique could be very effective when combined with other techniques by restricting the search space. For example, an AI program developed in 1980 and known as DANDRAL uses a strategy called *plan-generate-test*, in which planning part uses constraint satisfaction techniques (described later in this chapter) to create lists of recommended substructures, and generate-and-test method then uses these lists to explore only limited set of structures. Thus, in such types of combined uses, generate-and-test approach has proved to be very effective.

3.5.2 Best-First Search

It is a general heuristic based search technique. In best first search, in the graph of problem representation, one *evaluation function* (which corresponds to heuristic function) is attached with every node. The value of evaluation function may depend upon cost or distance of current node from goal node. The decision of which node to be expanded depends on the value of this evaluation function. The best first can be understood from following tree. In the tree, the attached value with nodes indicates utility value. The expansion of nodes according to best first search is illustrated in Fig 3.2

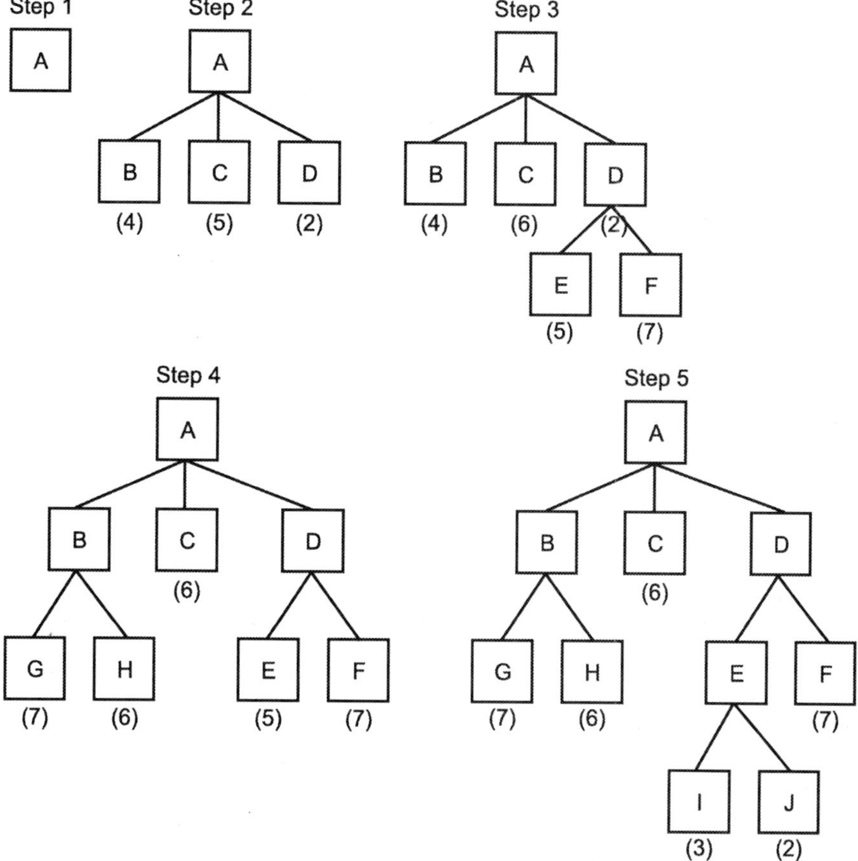

Fig 3.2: Tree indicating expansion according to best-first search

Here, at any step, the most promising node having least value of utility function is chosen for expansion.

In the tree shown above, best-first search technique is applied, however, it is beneficial sometimes to search a graph instead of tree to avoid the searching of duplicate paths. In the process to do so, searching is done in a direct graph in which each node represents a point in the problem space. This graph is known as *OR-graph*. Each of the branches of an OR-graph represents an alternative problem solving path.

Two lists of nodes are used to implement a graph search procedure discussed above. These are:

1. *OPEN*: these are the nodes that have been generated and have had the heuristic function applied to them but have not been examined yet.
2. *CLOSED*: these are the nodes that have already been examined. These nodes are kept in the memory if we want to search a graph rather then a

tree because whenever a new node will be generated, we will have to check whether it has been generated earlier.

The best-first search is a way of combining the advantages of both depth-first and breath-first search. The depth-first search is good because it allows a solution to be found without all competing branches having to be expanded. Breadth-first search is good because it does not get trapped on dead ends of paths. The way of combining this is to follow a single path at a time but switches between paths whenever some competing path looks more promising than current one does. Hence, at each step of best-first search process, we select most promising node out of successor nodes that have been generated so far.

The functioning of best-first search is summarized in the following steps:

(i)   It maintains a list *'open'* containing just the initial state.

(ii) Until a goal is found or there are no nodes left in open list, do:

    (a)   Pick the best node from open,

    (b)   Generate its successors, and for each successor:

        (i)   Check, and if it has not been generated before, evaluate it and add it to open and record its parent.

        (ii) If it has been generated before, and new path is better than the previous parent then change the parent.

The algorithm for best-first search is given as follows:

Algorithm: "Best-first search"

1.   Put the initial node on a list, say 'OPEN'.
2.   If (OPEN = EMPTY   or   OPEN = GOAL) terminate search, else
3.   Remove the first node from open. (say node is a)
4.   If (a = GOAL) terminate search with success, else
5.   Generate all the successors of node 'a'. Send node 'a' to a list called 'CLOSED'. Find out the value of heuristic function of all nodes. Sort all the children generated so far on the basis of their utility value. Select the node of minimum heuristic value for further expansion.
6.   Go back to step 2.

The best-first search can be implemented using priority queue. There are variations of best-first search. Example of these are, greedy best first, A* and recursive best first search.

3.5.2.1 *Greedy best-first search*

The greedy best first search technique expands the node which is closest to goal. The node expansion is purely based on distance from goal. It is used in route finding problems. This technique has the limitation that it is not optimal and it is incomplete as it can start on an infinite path and never return to other possibilities.

3.5.2.2 *Optimal search and A**

The A* algorithm is a specialization of best-first search. It is most widely known form of best-first search. It provides general guidelines about how to estimate goal distances for general search graphs. At each node along a path to the goal node, the A* algorithm generates all successor nodes and computes an estimate of the distance (cost) from the start node to a goal node through each of the successors. It then chooses the successor with the shortest estimated distance for expansion. It calculates the heuristic function based on distance of current node from start state and distance of current node to goal node.

The form of the heuristic estimation function for A* is defined as follows:

$$f(n) = g(n) + h(n)$$

where, $f(n)$ =   evaluation function
         $g(n)$ =   cost (or distance) of current node from start node
         $h(n)$ =   cost of current node from goal node

In A* algorithm, the most promising node is chosen for expansion. The promising node is decided based on the value of heuristic function. Normally the node having lowest value of $f(n)$ is chosen for expansion. We must note that the goodness of a move depends upon the nature of problem, in some problems the node having least value of heuristic function would be most promising node, whereas in some situations, the node having maximum value of heuristic function is chosen for expansion. A* algorithm maintains two lists. One stores the list of open nodes and other maintains the list of already expanded nodes. A* algorithm is an example of optimal search algorithm. A search algorithm is optimal if it has admissible heuristics. An algorithm has admissible heuristics if its heuristic function $h(n)$ never overestimates the cost to reach the goal. Admissible heuristics are always optimistic because in them, the cost of solving the problem is less than what actually is. The A* algorithm works as follows:

A* algorithm:

1. Place the starting node 's' on 'OPEN' list.
2. If 'OPEN' is empty, stop and return failure.
3. Remove from OPEN the node 'n' that has the smallest value of f* (n). If node 'n' is goal node, return success and stop otherwise.
4. Expand 'n' generating all of its successors 'n' and place 'n' on CLOSED. For every successor 'n' if 'n' is not already OPEN, attach a back pointer to 'n'. Compute f*(n) and place it on CLOSED.
5. Each 'n' that is already on OPEN or CLOSED should be attached to back pointers which reflect the lowest f*(n) path. If 'n' was on CLOSED and its pointer was changed, remove it and place it on OPEN.
6. Return to step 2.

3.5.2.3 Recursive Best First Search

It is a simple recursive algorithm, which is a combination of standard best-first search and recursive depth-first search. The difference of it from standard algorithm is that it uses only linear space. Like recursive depth-first search, it expands the nodes towards depth but for further expansion of any node, it follows the pattern of best-first search.

3.5.3 Problem Reduction

We have learnt search strategies for OR-graphs in the previous section. In these methods, a single path is found from node to goal state. There is another technique discussed in the following subsection known as AND-OR graph which is a problem reduction technique.

3.5.3.1 AND – OR graphs

There are certain types of AI problems which can be decomposed into smaller problems. 'And- Or' graph is useful for finding the solution of such problems. The problems are solved by breaking the problem into a set of smaller sub problems, all of which must be solved in order to solve the complete problem. In the tree representation of state space search, such sub problems generated from a main problem create 'AND' arc. One arc may point to any number of successor nodes, all of which must be solved in order to get the complete solution. Similarly, there may be situations where the problem can be broken into small problem, in such a way that solution of any one subproblem works as solution of complete problem. Representation of such problem is done using OR graph.

The functioning of AND-OR graph is illustrated in following example.

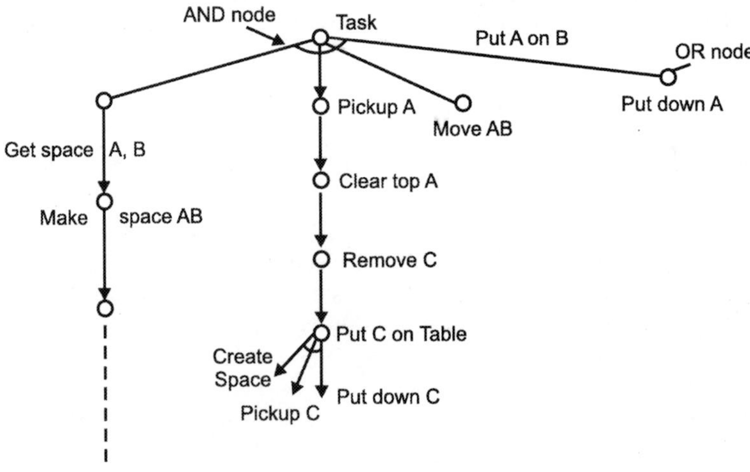

Fig. 3.3: The AND-Or problem reduction

The AND-OR graph is also applicable for parse tree generation in English language. Consider following simple English Grammar.

   (i) S ↔ Np Vp
  (ii) Np ↔ N
 (iii) Np ↔ art N
  (iv) Vp ↔ V
   (v) Vp ↔ V Np
  (vi) art ↔ a
 (vii) art ↔ the
(viii) N ↔ man
  (ix) N ↔ dog
   (x) V ↔ likes
  (xi) V ↔ bites

Its AND-OR graph is shown in Fig 3.4.

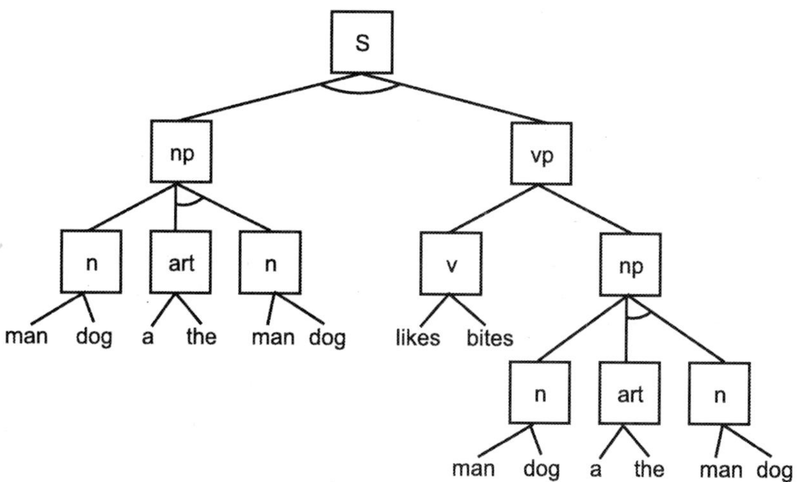

Fig. 3.4: AND – OR graph of English Grammar

The method of finding a solution using AND-OR problem reduction is AO* algorithm. It is similar to A* algorithm. But as AO* algorithm works for AND – OR graphs, and to identify all the subtrees required to be solved, it labels traversed node in the tree as *solved or unsolved* . To account for AND node arcs in the solution process, which requires solutions to all successor nodes, the leveling of nodes is required. The solution of problem is found when the start node is labeled as solved. The AO* algorithm is presented as follows.

3.5.3.2 The AO algorithm*

1.   Place start node 's' on open list.
2.   Using the search tree constructed so far, compute most promising solution.
3.   Select a node n and remove n from open and place it on closed.
4.   If n is a terminal goal node, label n as solved if solution of n results in any of n's ancestors being solved. Label all the ancestors as solved if start node s is solved. Exit with success. Remove from open all nodes with a solved ancestor.

Before moving further for studying remaining heuristic search techniques, there are many important issues related to whatever has been discussed so far, and whatever is to be discussed ahead, for better understanding of the subject matter under consideration. We would try to learn these issues in the following sections before taking up matter related to advanced heuristic search techniques such as hill-climbing, constraint satisfaction, means-end analysis and mini-max search.

3.5.4 Local Search Algorithm

The search techniques discussed so far are designed to explore search spaces systematically by keeping one or more path in memory and by recording alternatives already explored at each point along the path and also paths unexplored. When a goal is found, the path of that goal constitutes a solution to the problem also. However, in many problems, the path to the goal is irrelevant. For example, in 8-queen problem discussed in the previous chapter, the order in which queens are added to get the final acceptable configuration is irrelevant. What matters is the final solution. This type of approach where path to reach goal state is not a matter of concern is used in many applications such as integrated circuit design, automatic programming, telecommunication network optimization, vehicle routing and portfolio management.

Thus, for the search where path does not matter, a different kind of algorithm is used. Local search algorithms are one such type of algorithms, which operate by using a single current state and generally move only to neighbors of that state. In the process used in applying these algorithms, the paths followed by the search are not retained. In spite of not being systematic, the local search algorithm have two key advantage:

1.   Memory requirement is less (as total search space is not searched) than normal blind search.
2.   They normally find reasonably fast solution in big search space.

The general search methodology of local search algorithm can be summarized as follows:

Algorithm: "Local Search Technique"

(1) Start with initial state. If it is not a goal state, go to step two

(2) Repeat the following till either goal state is reached or applicable operators are over:

(i)   Select yet unapplied operator, apply it to produce new state, which moves in the direction of increasing value of evaluation function.

(ii)   Evaluate new state. If it is goal state or no operator generates state having value of objective function more than previous one, then terminate.

3.5.5 Branch and Bound Search

This is a type of local search algorithm. It applies to problems having a graph search space where more than one alternate path exists between two nodes. The example of such type of problem is traveling salesperson problem. It is called branch and bound search as each move in this search process generates one path at a time, keeping track of the best circuit or closed path generated so far. It stores this value as '*bound*' for future use. If the algorithm determines that the best possible extension to the branch will have greater cost than bound, it eliminates the partial · paths and all of its extensions. It reduces search space from N! to 1.26^N. Hence, this strategy saves all path lengths (or costs) from a node to all generated node and chooses the shortest path for further expansion. It then compares the new path lengths with all old ones and again chooses the shortest path for expansion. Thus, any path to a goal state is certain to be minimal length path. The typical algorithm of this type of search is presented below:

Algorithm: "Branch and bound search"

1.   Place the start node of zero path length on the queue.
2.   Until the queue is empty or a goal state has been found:
   (i)   Determine if the first path in the queue contains a goal node
   (ii)   If the first path contains a goal node exit with success
   (iii) If the first path does not contain a goal node, remove the path and form new paths by extending removed path by one step
   (iv)   Compute the cost of new paths and add them to the queue
   (v)   Sort the path or the queue
3.   Otherwise exit with failure.

3.5.6 Memory Bounded Heuristic Search

In the memory bounded heuristic search, the decision to cut off the expansion of a node is based on memory requirement. It reduces the memory requirement of A* algorithm by adopting the criteria of iterative deepening method. In this, the decision to cut off a node is based on cost (g + h), i.e., the addition of distance of current node from start and goal node, instead of the depth at each iteration. The cut off value of any node expansion is the smallest cost of any node, which exceeds the cost of that node expansion.

3.5.7 Local Beam Search

In the algorithms discussed earlier, one successor of current state was considered at a time for further processing because of memory limitations. However, if we set aside the criticalities associated with memory requirement, there are algorithms, which work well and at a faster pace for most of the applications. The local search beam algorithm is one such algorithm. This algorithm considers k current states rather than just one current state at a time. It sets k states as initial states and at each step, all successors of all the k states are generated. If any state is found to be goal state, the algorithm stops, otherwise, it selects k best successors from the complete list and continues.

On lighter viewing of this strategy, one might consider it nothing more than running k random restarts in parallel, instead of in sequence. However, two approaches are entirely different. In local beam search strategy, useful information is passed among k parallel search threads. The advantage of this is that whenever one state generates several good successors and remaining k-1 states generate bad successors, the algorithm abandons unfruitful searches and moves its resources to fruitful searches. A variant of local beam search is *stochastic beam* search. In this, instead of choosing the best k from the pool of successor candidates, stochastic beam chooses k successors at random, where probability of choosing a given successor is an increasing function of value.

Before discussing other heuristic techniques, let us discuss some properties of heuristic search algorithms first.

3.5.8 Properties of Heuristic Search Algorithms

In one of the sections above, we have described various categories of AI problems. According to the nature of problems, there exist different search algorithms. For a single problem also, there can be many algorithms. Obviously, it is necessary to compare these algorithms. The performance matrix analyses the performance of these algorithms. These matrix and properties of these algorithms are discussed in the following section:

1. *Admissibility condition* – Any algorithm is called admissible if it is guaranteed to return an optimal solution when one exists. A solution is optimal if it generates the solution in minimum number of steps. A* is admissible algorithm. An algorithm will be admissible if it has a heuristic function that does not overestimate. That means, if any AI heuristic function has admissible heuristics, then it will provide optimal solution. The admissible heuristics is optimistic because they assume the cost of solving a problem is less than the actual cost. Optimality is the property, which identifies that whether the algorithm gives the optimal solution.

2. *Completeness condition*– An algorithm, say A* algorithm, is complete if it always terminates with a solution when one exists.

3. *Dominance property*– The dominance property compares multiple algorithms created for solution of same problem. Let A*1 and A*2 be admissible algorithm with heuristic estimation functions h1* and h2* respectively. A*1 is said to dominate A*2 whenever h1*(n)> h2*(n) for all n. A*1 also said to be more informed than A*2. The dominance property indicates that how good a heuristic function is. A heuristic function that reaches at solution in

least number of steps is considered best. The function where maximum clue or additional information regarding the problem is given, will reach the solution in least number of steps. The algorithm, which uses such heuristic function will be called more informed. Hence, for two A* heuristics h1 and h2 if $h1(n)^3 h2(n)$, for all states n in search space , heuristic h1 is said to be more informed than h2.

4. ***Consistent heuristics-*** A heuristics is said to be consistent if, for every node n and its successor n¢ (generated by action a), the estimated cost of reaching the goal from n is not greater then the step cost of getting to n¢ plus estimated cost of reaching goal from n¢ i.e.,

$$h(n) \leq c\ (n,\ a,\ n') + h\ (n')$$

The property of consistent heuristic is also known as 'monotonicity'. This property indicates that search space is everywhere locally consistent with the heuristics employed. The difference between the heuristic measure for a state and any one of its successor is bound by the actual cost of going between that state and its successor. This is to say that heuristics is everywhere admissible, and it reaches at each state along the shortest path from its ancestors. The monotonicity property is mathematically defined as follows:

A heuristic function 'h' is monotone, if it satisfies following two properties:

(i)   For all states n_i and n_j, where n_j is descendent of n_i

$$h(n_i) - h(n_j) \leq \text{Cost}(n_i,\ n_j)$$

where, cost $(n_i,\ n_j)$) is actual cost of going from state n_i to n_j in term of number of moves.

(ii)   The heuristic evaluation of goal state is zero, or $h(goal) = 0$

5. ***Time and space complexities:*** Time complexity indicates how much time an algorithm takes to solve a problem. Time complexities are defined in terms of their best-case performance, worst-case performance and average-case performance. Space complexity indicates how much memory an algorithm takes to solve a problem.

Algorithms having lesser value of time and space complexities are considered as better algorithms. Time and space complexities are decided based on state space graph size, because the graph is the actual data structure given as input to algorithm. In terms of AI problem representation, the size can be in terms of the number of problem states, the number input characters, which specify the problem or some other term defined in the similar manner. The algorithm is said to have linear time complexity, if it is of $O(n)$, quadratic if $O(n^2)$ and exponential if it is $O(n^k)$, where 'n' is the size of the problem.

The time and space complexities are dependent on following factors:

(i)   Branching factor: which indicates maximum number of successors of any node

   (ii)   The depth of shallowest goal node, and

   (iii) Maximum length of any path in state space.

3.5.9 Overestimation and Underestimation of Heuristic Function

We have mentioned earlier that the heuristics provide a guess about the solution of the problem and if a wrong heuristics is provided, it may never obtain the solution. Besides this, if heuristics is perfect estimation of problem, then it will provide the solution in least number of steps and the A* algorithm will converge immediately to the goal. However, if the heuristic function h¢ overestimates or underestimates the ideal (hypothetical) value of h, it may take longer time to find the solution.

The underestimation of heuristic function is explained below:

Consider a graph situation shown in Fig 3.5.

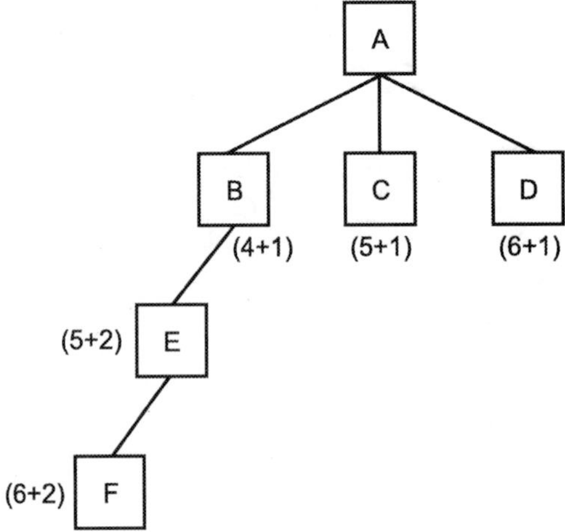

Fig. 3.5: Graph indicating underestimation of heuristic function

Here the heuristic function value $(4 + 1)$ corresponds to the components $f = h + g$ (i.e. utility value of node + cost of opening the node). Hence, at level 1 of successor, it will be 1, at level 2 it will be 2 and so on. Here, for simplicity we have assumed the cost of all arcs as 1. Here node B has least value of f, so it will be expanded first. Assume it has one successor, which is 3 moves away from goal. Now, if f'(E) and f'(C), the node E and C both becomes equally promising for further expansion. Let us assume we resolve this in favor of path we are currently following and we expand E next. It also has one successor and that is 3 moves away from goal. It makes f' (F) and f' (D) equally promising. We are making up moves without any progress. But f' (E) > f'(C), so we will expand C first, and leave the path currently being followed. Here, it is evident that by underestimating h(B) we have wasted effort.

The overestimation of heuristic function is explained as follows. Consider a particular instance of above graph (Fig 3.5) with corresponding utility values as shown in Fig 3.6.

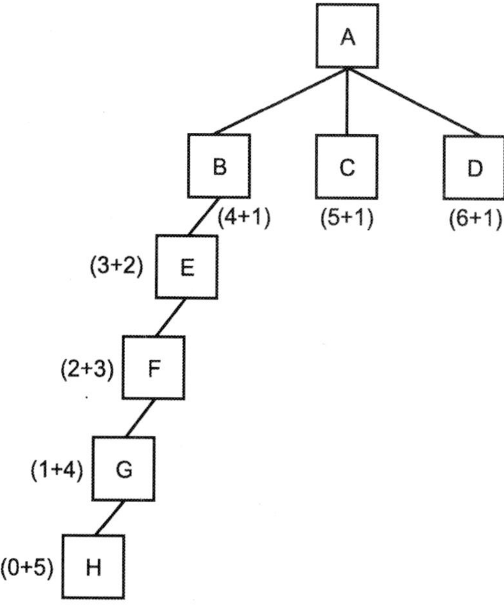

Fig. 3.6: Overestimation of heuristic function

Here we expand B, then E, F, G, H and we get solution after five expansions. It has the cost of nodes expansion (5). If there exists a direct path from D to a solution giving path length 2, we would never explore it. Thus by overestimating the $h'(D)$, we make D look so bad that we are ready to take some worse solution instead of expanding D. In general, if h' might overestimate h, we cannot be guaranteed of finding the cheapest path solution unless we expand the entire graph until all paths are longer than the best solution.

3.5.10 Hill-Climbing Search

The 'Hill-climbing search' falls in the category of local search algorithm discussed above. The problem solving techniques discussed so far, explore the search space and report the path as solution. There is another category of problems where the path reporting is not important and only reporting of final state is important. This category of applications include, job-shop scheduling, automatic programming, circuit designing, vehicle routing and portfolio management. For such types of applications, another problem solving technique called hill-climbing technique is useful. As it works on the principle of local search algorithm, it operates using a single current state and it contains a loop that continuously moves in the direction of increasing value of objective function.

The name hill-climbing is derived from simulating the situation of a person climbing the hill. The person makes every move towards the top of hill. His movement stops when it reaches at the peak of hill, and no peak has higher value of heuristic function than this. The Hill-climbing is a variant of generate-and-test in which feedback from the test procedure is used in deciding in which direction the search should proceed. At each point in the search path, a successor node that appears to reach most quickly to the top of hill (goal) is selected for exploration. As mentioned earlier, the hill climbing technique is useful for AI problems where knowledge of the path is not important, so in obtaining the problem solution, it is not recorded. It does not maintain a search tree and the current node data structure requires recording of only state and its objective function value. It does not look ahead beyond its immediate neighbor. The hill-climbing technique is useful in pure optimization problems, where objective is to find the best state according to objective function. The functioning of Hill-climbing search technique is explained in following algorithm:

Algorithm: "Hill-climbing search"

1. Evaluate the initial state. If it is also a goal state then return it and quit, otherwise continue with initial state as the current state.

2. Loop :

    Until a solution is found, or until there are no new operators left to be applied in current state:

    (a)   Select an operator that has not been applied to current state and apply it to produce a new state.

    (b)   Evaluate the new state:

        (i)   If it is a goal state then return and quit

        (ii)   If it is not a goal state but it is better than the current state, then make it the current state.

        (iii)   If it is not better than the current state then continue in the loop.

The functioning of hill-climbing search is illustrated in following example: Consider 8-puzzle problem in configuration shown in figure 3.7 (a) and (b):

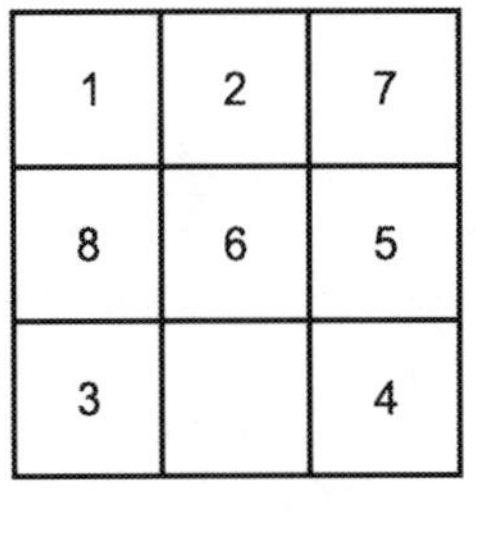

(a)

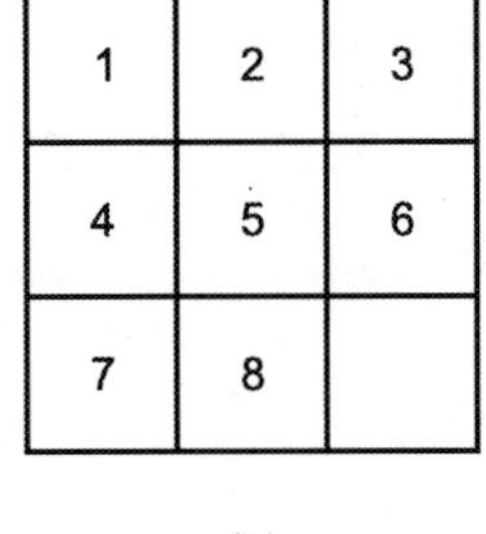

(b)

Fig. 3.7: 8 puzzle configuration (a) start state, (b) goal state

As discussed earlier that the heuristic function of this problem is a 'number', which indicates the displacement of each tile from standard (or goal) configuration.

1ˢᵗ move:

Here, in first move there are three possibilities (i) move tile numbered 3 towards right, (ii) move tile numbered 6, toward down (iii) move 4 towards right.

(i) move 3 towards right, it will make the value of h as

$$h = 0 + 0 + 3 + 3 + 1 + 1 + 4 + 2 = 14$$

it generates the configuration shown in Fig 3.8

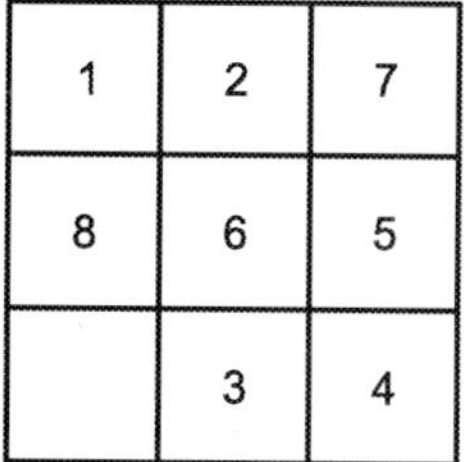

Fig 3.8:

(ii) move 6 downwards , it will make the value of h as

$$h = 0 + 0 + 4 + 3 + 1 + 2 + 4 + 2 = 16$$

it generates the configuration shown in Fig 3.9

Fig 3.9:

(iii) move 4 towards right , it will make the value of h as

$$h = 0 + 0 + 4 + 2 + 1 + 1 + 4 + 2 = 14$$

it generates the configuration shown in Fig 3.10

<table>
<tr><td>1</td><td>2</td><td>7</td></tr>
<tr><td>8</td><td>6</td><td>5</td></tr>
<tr><td>3</td><td>4</td><td></td></tr>
</table>

Fig. 3.10:

here 1st and 3rd possibilities are most promising (lowest values of h) but out of these both h values are same , hence both possibilities equally promising. Let us assume we randomly choose option 3 in first move,

2nd move

In second move there are two possibilities. (i) move 5 downwards , (ii) move 4 towards left.

(i) move 5 downwards:
$$h = 0 + 0 + 4 + 2 + 2 + 1 + 4 + 2 = 15$$
see Fig 3.11

<table>
<tr><td>1</td><td>2</td><td>7</td></tr>
<tr><td>8</td><td>6</td><td></td></tr>
<tr><td>3</td><td>4</td><td>5</td></tr>
</table>

Fig. 3.11:

(ii) move 4 towards left: it will generate a cycle, and it will correspond to simple backtracking. Hence, it will not be done.

Similarly , we can proceed further.

The linear state space of hill climbing problem is represented in Fig 3.12

In this evaluation corresponds to objective function and aim to find goal state (point A). In the problem where objective function represent cost, a global minimum (point B) is to be found.

3.5.10.1 Limitations of hill-climbing search

There are three problems encountered in hill climbing technique:

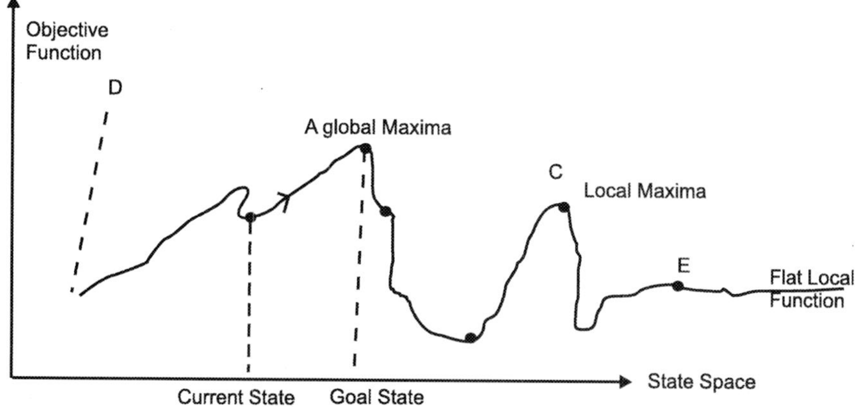

Fig. 3.12: State space of hill climbing

(1) *Local maxima*: It is a peak, which is higher than local suberb but less than global maxima (point C). In this situation once point C is reached, as the next calculation of objective function will move towards down the hill, they will not be followed and point C will be reported as solution. Which is actually not global maximum and a distant peak having higher height or higher value of objective function is available.

(2) *Ridge*: It is a special kind of local maxima having very steep slope which is difficult to be traced in one calculation of objective function (like point D).

(3) *Plateau*: It is a flat area in state space (like point E), where next move does not give better solution then present state. So, it becomes difficult to decide where to move. A hill-climbing search might be unable to find its way off the plateau

These limitations are illustrated in Fig. 3.13:

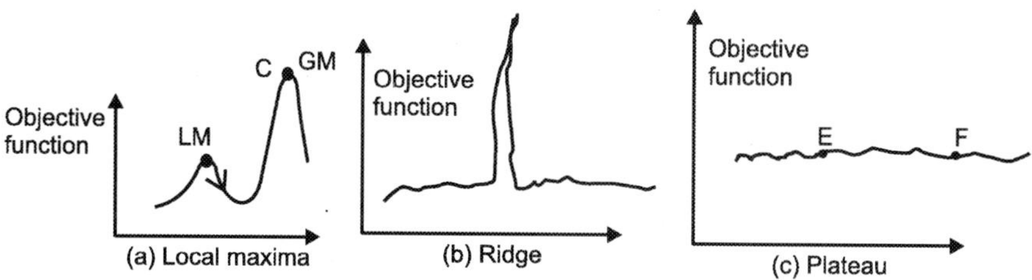

Fig. 3.13: Limitations of hill climbing

The limitations of hill-climbing search are illustrated in following example. Consider the 8-puzzle problem again. Assume board configuration of Fig. 3.14.

1	2	3
8	5	6
4	7	

Fig 3.14: (a) start configuration

1	2	3
4	5	6
7	8	

(b) goal configuration

Here $h = 0 + 0 + 0 + 1 + 0 + 0 + 1 + 2 = 4$

1ˢᵗ move

Here in first move there are two possibilities (i) move tile numbered 7 towards left, (ii) move tile numbered 6, toward down.

If we move 7 towards left, it will make the value of h as

$$h = 0+0+0+1+0+1+1+2 = 5$$

it generates the configuration shown in Fig 3.15

1	2	3
8	5	6
4		7

Fig. 3.15:

However if we move 6 downwards , it will make the value of h as

$$h = 0+0+0+1+0+1+1+2 = 5$$

it generates the configuration shown in Fig 3.16

1	2	3
8	5	
4	7	6

Fig. 3.16: Configuration of 8 puzzle

here both h values are same , hence both moves are equally promising.

Let us choose to follow first option and tries goes for next stage of moving the tile.

2nd move

in second move there are three possibilities. (i) move 4 towards right , (ii) move 5 downwards, (iii) move 7 leftwards

out of these three possibilities , the third possibility is just reverse of 1st stage move. It is a simple backtracking and it will generate cycle. Such moves are normally avoided.

The heuristic function and corresponding configuration of two possibilities is shown below.

(i) move 4 towards right:

$$h = 0 + 0 + 0 + 2 + 0 + 0 + 2 + 2 = 6$$

1	2	3
8	5	6
	4	7

Fig. 3.17:

(ii) over 5 downwards:

$$h = 0 + 0 + 0 + 1 + 1 + 0 + 2 + 2 = 6$$

in second move also the heuristic value comes out to be same. Hence, again it is required to make a blind guess about the next move.

This problem where visibly no move appears to be promising is the problem of plateau.

1	2	3
8		6
4	5	7

Fig 3.18:

3.5.11 Simulated Annealing Search

The problem of local maxima has been overcome in simulated annealing search. In normal hill-climbing search, the movements towards downhill are never made. In such algorithms the search may stuck up at local maximum. Thus, this search cannot guarantee complete solution. In contrast, a random search (or movement) towards successor chosen randomly from the set of successor will be complete, but it will be extremely inefficient. The combination of hill-climbing and random search, which yields both efficiency and completeness, is called simulated annealing.

The simulated annealing method was originally developed for the physical process of annealing. That is how the name simulated annealing was found and restored. In simulated annealing search algorithm, instead of picking the best move, a random move is picked. The standard simulated annealing uses term *objective function* instead of *heuristic function*. If the move improves the situation, it is accepted, otherwise algorithm accepts the move with some probability less than 1. This probability is

$$P = e^{-\Delta E/kt}$$

Where ΔE is positive charge in energy level, t is temperature and k is Boltzman constant. As indicated by the equation, the probability decreases with badness of the move (evaluation gets worsened by amount ΔE). The rate at which ΔE is cooled is called annealing schedule. The proper annealing schedule is maintained to monitor T.

This process has following differences from hill-climbing search:

  (i) The annealing schedule is maintained.

 (ii) Moves to worse states are also accepted.

(iii) In addition to current state, the best state record is also maintained.

The algorithm of simulated Annealing is presented as follows:
Algorithm: "Simulated annealing"

1. Evaluate initial state. Mark it as current state. Till current state is not a goal state, initialize best state to current state. If the initial state is best state, return it and quit.

2. Initialize T according to annealing schedule.

3. Repeat the following until a solution is obtained or operators are not left:
   - (a) Apply yet unapplied operator to produce new state
   - (b) for new state compute $\ddot{A}E$ = value of current state – value of new state
     If, new state is goal state then stop, or if it is better than current state, make it current state and record as best state.
   - (c) If c is not better than current state, then make it current state with probability P
   - (d) Revise T according to annealing schedule

4. Return best state as answer.

3.5.12 Constraint Satisfaction

Constraint satisfaction is a problem solving method, which is applicable to different categories of problems. There are many problems in AI in which the goal state is not specified in the problem and it requires to be discovered according to some specific constraint. Problems like cryptarithmatic puzzle, design tasks in which design must be created within fixed limits of time, cost and material etc., fall in this category, where the constraint satisfaction technique is applicable.

Formally, a constraint satisfaction problem (CSP) is described by set of variables X1, X2, X3.....Xn, and a set of constraints C1, C2, ...Cn. Each variable Xi has some possible value Vi. Each constraint allows specific variable to accept only specific value. A state of the problem is defined by an assignment of values to some or all variables. (e.g. Xi = Vi, Xj = Vj) Assignment is based on the criterion that do not violate any constraint solution. In complete assignment, all variables are assigned a specific value. Solution to CSP is one that finds out the values of all variables that satisfy all constraints.

Consider the example of map-coloring problem. The problem is to color different regions of a map in such a way that no two neighboring regions have same color. For example, the graph of figure 3.19 has seven regions, which are to be filled with three colors say, red, green and blue. Thus, the problem formulation of CSP will be as follows:

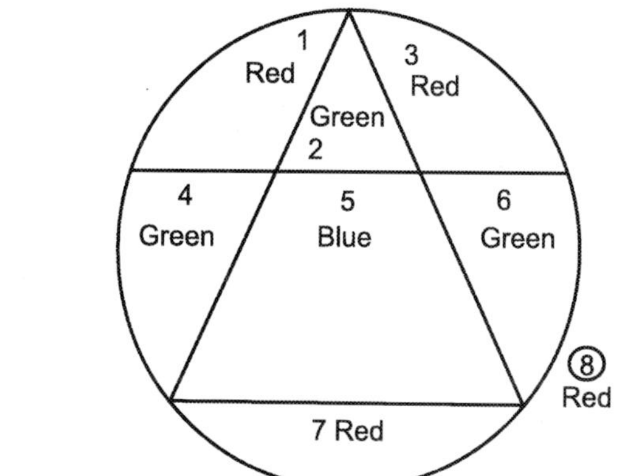

Fig: 3.19a: The map coloring problem

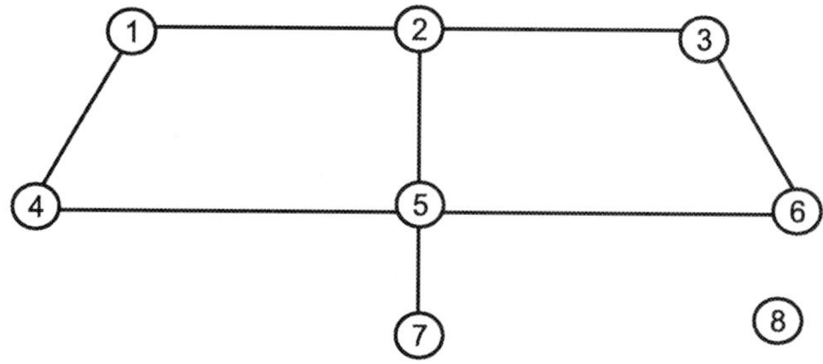

Fig: 3.19b: Constraint Graph for map coloring problem

It has seven variables; domain of each variable is red, green or blue. The constraint requires that neighboring regions should have different colors. For solution purpose, the CSP should be visualized as *constraint graph*, where each node corresponds to variable and arcs to constraints. The constraint graph of above problem would be as shown in Fig. 3.19 (b).

The map-coloring problem is the simplest type of problem having variables that are discrete and have finite domains. The 8-queen problem also falls in this category, which has 8 variables (i.e. queen positions in each column Q1, Q2, Q8, and domain {1,2,....8}.

Another category of problem can have infinite domain (like set of integers or strings). The domain can be continuous   instead of discreet, like scheduling of time of experiments in space telescope requires very precise timing observations. So, start and finish time of each observation can be considered as continuous variable.

3.5.12.1 Types of constraints

The constraints can be of various types. Some of the varieties of constraints are mentioned as follows:

(i) *Unary constraint*, which is applicable on only one variable, e.g. Indians dislike red color. Here, constraint is about liking of a particular color and is applicable only on one variable, i.e. Indians, since Pakistanis, Americans or citizens of any other country might not be averse of red color, and hence, this particular constraint is not applicable on them.

(ii) *Binary constraint*, which is related to two variables, e.g. India $\neq$ Nepal is a binary constraint because it imposes constraint on India as well as on Nepal.

(iii) *Higher order constraints*, which involve three or more variables, like cryptarithmetic puzzles described in the following section.

3.5.12.2 Cryptarithmetic problem

In this problem, some equation in the form of hidden digit is given, and the solution is to identify the digit representing each letter. Consider following puzzle. Here each letter O, N, E, T, W and I represent a unique digit from 0 to 9. The decoding of these letters is required as solution of this problem. Obviously, the solution must satisfy the basic principles of mathematical addition.

$$
\begin{array}{r}
O\ N\ E \\
+\ T\ W\ O \\
\hline
WI\ T\ T
\end{array}
$$

To solve such types of problems, first the variables and constraints are defined. In this case, variables are O, N, E, T, W, I. Every letter represents a different digit. Here, one set of constraints is, that O $\neq$ T $\neq$ E......,

Other set of constraints are:

$E + O = T + 10\ C1$

$N + W + C1 = T + 10C2$

$O + T + C2 = I + 10\ C3$

$C3 = W$

Here, $C_1,\ C2\ C3$ are auxiliary variable (i.e. variables that are intermediately generated or additionally introduced. Here they correspond to carry of different states). The carry generated from first stage (which is passed to second stage) is called C1. According to normal mathematical rules, these variables can take the value 0 or 1, because in decimal number system the *carry* generated by two digits addition can not be more than 1. Constraint satisfaction is a two-step process. In one step, constraints are discovered and propagated and in second step, if solution is not found then search is done. Some initial guess about the solutions is made, and according to these guess, new constraints are obtained. Let us further discuss the above example.

```
    O N E
  + T W O
  ---------
    WI  T T
```

The basic sets of constraints are described above. Some additionally derived constraints based on these constraints are:

(i) $W = 1$ as addition of two digits can not generate carry more than 1.

(ii) $O + T + C_2 > 9$, to generate a carry.

The complete solution using this method is shown in following example:

Example 1: Consider following cryptarithmetic puzzle and find the solution?

```
    C3  C2  C1
     T   W   O
  +  T   W   O
  --------------
  F  O   U   R
```

Answer:

Step 1: C3=1 since two single digit numbers plus a carry can not be more than 19, hence, F=1.

Step 2: $T + T + C2 > 9$ (to generate a carry and C2 can be 0 or 1, depending upon if the previous column is generating a carry or not)

Assume C2 = 1

$2T > 8$

$T > 4$

Hence, T can be 5 or 6 or 7 or 8 or 9. Let us start the solution by assuming T = 5

Step 3: If T = 5,

T + T + C2 = 11, means, O = 1, but O can't be 1, as F = 1
Thus T = 5 can not generate the solution.
Go to step 2.
Step 4: Assume T = 6
If T = 6, O=3 (T+T+C2=13)
From right most column of the puzzle, O+O=R
Hence, for O = 3, R=6 and C1=0 (no carry is generated)
But, R cannot be 6, as T=6, hence, T=6 can't generate a solution.
Go to step 2.
Step 5: Assume T=7, hence O=5. (from T+T+C2=15)
For O=5, R=0 and C1=1. (from O+O=R)
Step 6: We have middle column of the puzzle as W+W + C1 = U
But, W can not be 0 and 1 (as F =1, and R=0).
Further, since we have already assumed C2=1, hence, W+W must
generate a carry,
Hence, W $\geq$ 5 (to generate a carry as C2)
Step 7: Assume W=5, means U=1 (because, for W =5, W+W+C1=11)
But U can't be 1 as F =1. Hence, W cannot be 5.
Repeat step 7.
Step 8: Assume W=6, means U=3 (from W+W+C1=13)

Thus we get the values of different variables as : T= 7, W =6, O = 5, U = 3,
R = 0, F =1, and the puzzle would look like:

$$\begin{array}{r} 7\ 6\ 5 \\ +\ 7\ 6\ 5 \\ \hline 1\ 5\ 3\ 0 \\ \hline \end{array}$$

[In step 2 mentioned in the solution of the above puzzle, we have assumed
C2=1. However, C2 can be 0 also, if no carry is generated from previous column,
i.e., W+W=O. Readers are suggested to assume C2=0 in the step2 and see what
happens! We are happy to tell you in advance that if remaining steps are applied
accordingly and correctly, you will get another valid solution of this puzzle as
presented below:

$$\begin{array}{r} 7\ 3\ 4 \\ +\ 7\ 3\ 4 \\ \hline 1\ 4\ 6\ 8 \\ \hline \end{array}$$

However, this does not happen always, and most of the puzzles have a unique
solution.]
Let us consider one more example, slightly bigger and tougher one.

Example 2: Solve the following cryptarithmetic puzzle:

$$
\begin{array}{r}
C\ R\ O\ S\ S \\
+\ R\ O\ A\ D\ S \\
\hline
D\ A\ N\ G\ E\ R \\
\hline
\end{array}
$$

Answer

Here also it has been assumed that the carry generated from the right most column (say, first column) and passed on to second column is C1, from second column and passed to third one is C2, and similarly, generated from fifth and last column and passed to next column is C5. The steps of the solution are as follows:

Step 1: Looking into puzzle, it is evident that the last column is generating a carry, which is D. Since two single digit numbers when added can't generate a carry more than 1, hence C5 = **D=1**

Step 2: We have constraints as C+ R+C4 = A +10C5

And, C + R+ C4 >9 (to generate a carry, which is D)

C4 can be 0 or 1 (depending upon whether a carry is generated from the previous column)

Assume C4 =0 ⇒ C+R > 9

Assume **C=9** ⇒ R > 0

Value of R will depend upon first column, hence explore that before moving ahead.

Step 3: S + S = R + 10C1 (from first column)

Notice here, that R can only be an even number, because sum of two same numbers is always an even number.

Let R =2 ⇒ S=1, but S can't be 1 (because D = 1)

Repeat step3.

Step 4: Replace R by 4 ⇒ S=2 and C1=0 (since no carry is generated)

From second column, we have

S+D+C1 = E + 10C2

We have D=1, S=2 ⇒ C2 =0 (because no carry will be generated for S=2 and D=1)

⇒ E = 3

R comes in the fifth column also, hence explore that before finalizing the value of R.

Step 5: C+R +C4 = A + 10C5 (from fifth column)

We already have, C=9, R=4, C4=0 and C5=1

Putting these values, we get

A=3, but A can't be 3 as E =3

Go to step4.

Step 6: Replace R by 6 ⇒ **S=3** and C1= 0 (because no carry will be generated)

Further, we have S+D+C1=E+10C2 (from second column)

We have D=1, S=3 $\Rightarrow$ C2=0 (because no carry will be generated for S=3 and D=1)

$\Rightarrow$ **E = 4**

Go to step5.

Step 7: C+R +C4 = A + 10C5 (from fifth column) .

We already have, C=9, **R=6**, C4=0 and C5=1

Putting these values, we get

A=5.

R appears in fourth column also, hence explore that before finalizing the value of R.

Step 8: R+ O+ C3   =N +10C4 (from fourth column)

We have R=6 and C4=0.

$\Rightarrow$ 6 + O + C3 = N

Also, R + O+ C3 $\le$ 9 (for C4 to be 0, i.e. no carry should be generated from this column)

C3 could be 0 or 1 (depending upon whether a carry is generated from third column)

For C3 = 0, 6 + O + 0 $\le$ 9 $\Rightarrow$ O $\le$ 3

For C3 = 1, 6 + O + 1 $\le$ 9 $\Rightarrow$ O $\le$ 2

But O can't be 3, because S = 3

Hence, assume O = 2 (which is true for both the values of C3)

For C3 = 0, 6 + 2 + 0 = N + 0 $\Rightarrow$ N = 8 (for already assumed C4=0)

For C3 = 1, 6 + 2 + 1 = N + 0 $\Rightarrow$ N = 9

But, N can't be 9 since C = 9 (assumed earlier and still holding)

Hence, **N = 8** and C3 = 0.

Step 9: O + A + C2 = G +10C3 (from column three)

We already have, O = 2, A = 5, C2 = 0 and C3 = 0

Hence, 2 + 5 + 0 = G + 0

$\Rightarrow$ **G = 7**

Hence the values of the various variables as found from above process are A =5, C= 9, D=1, E= 4, G = 7, S=3, O=2, N=8, S=3 and R=6, and the puzzle would look like:

$$
\begin{array}{r}
9\ 6\ 2\ 3\ 3 \\
+\ 6\ 2\ 5\ 1\ 3 \\
\hline
1\ 5\ 8\ 7\ 4\ 6 \\
\hline
\end{array}
$$

[Many more such types of puzzles are given in the section of exercises of this chapter. Answers are also given to ascertain the validity of the puzzles and to help you in solving them. So, go ahead and enjoy the challenge and fun associated in solving these puzzles!]

Another example involving constraint satisfaction is problem of magic square. Consider a magic square of three rows and three columns, commonly called 3x3-magic square. We are required to fill nine consecutive numbers in the nine blank squares of the magic square in such a way that the sum of numbers in all the rows, columns and two diagonals is same. Also, no number should be repeated. A magic square of this kind will be as presented below:

<table>
<tr><td>x_1</td><td>x_2</td><td>x_3</td></tr>
<tr><td>x_4</td><td>x_5</td><td>x_6</td></tr>
<tr><td>x_7</td><td>x_8</td><td>x_9</td></tr>
</table>

Fig. 3.20 : 3 x 3 - magic square

Let us assume we have to fill numbers from 1 to 9 in this magic square. The sum of numbers of all the rows, columns and diagonals in this case will be 15 (45 divided by 3).

The constraints for this problem are given below:

(i) $x_1 + x_2 + x_3 = 15$
(ii) $x_4 + x_5 + x_6 = 15$
(iii) $x_7 + x_8 + x_9 = 15$
(iv) $x_1 + x_4 + x_7 = 15$
(v) $x_2 + x_5 + x_8 = 15$
(vi) $x_3 + x_6 + x_9 = 15$
(vii) $x_1 + x_5 + x_9 = 15$
(viii) $x_3 + x_5 + x_7 = 15$

We are required to solve these equations using constraint satisfaction algorithm to find the solution of the magic square. Complete methodology adopted in solving these constraints is mentioned in the previous chapter.

3.5.13 Means Ends Analysis

The solution finding strategies discussed so far apply search only in one direction. Based on the nature of the problem, they proceed either in forward direction or in backward direction. As mentioned earlier, the forward search starts from the start state and proceeds towards goal state, and backward search starts from goal state and proceeds towards start state. In some situations, a bidirectional search or a mixed search is useful, where the parts of the problem are independently solved using forward search and backward search simultaneously and then sub problem solutions are joined to obtain complete solution. The means ends analysis is a technique, which uses bidirectional search. The means ends analysis solves problem in parts and then finds the final solution of the problem by combining part-solutions. The means ends analysis detects the differences between the current state and goal state and once such a difference is identified, an operator that can reduce the difference must be found. We apply backward chaining in which, operators are selected and then sub-goals are set up to establish preconditions of the operator. This is called *operator subgoaling*.

In case the existing operator cannot be applied on the current state, the operator which will bring the current state in the state where that operator is applicable is applied first. By repeatedly applying the operators, which reduces the difference between start and the goal state, the problem solution is found. Like other problem solving techniques, the means ends analysis has set of operators that can transform the states. There are certain typical initial conditions, on which these rules or operators can be applied, these are called *preconditions,* And the newly generated states after the rules are applied are called *postconditions*. To keep track of the difference between current state and goal state a table is maintained. This is called *difference table*.

The method of means ends analysis can be understood by the following example:

Assume one has to move from place 'A' in the city of Delhi, to place 'B' in the city of Mumbai. The available means of transport are walking, self-driving, taking a bus, taking a cab, taking a train or flying.

Here the operators (i.e. means of transport) that will be utilized to take an action will be:

  (i) Walking
 (ii) Driving by own car
(iii) Taking a bus
(iv) Taking a train, and
 (v) Taking a flight

The multiple operators can also be applied in appropriate sequence. There are certain preconditions associated with every operator, e.g., for catching a flight one must reach airport first. Similarly, after application of every operator the new conditions or post conditions are generated. The available operators along with their preconditions and post conditions are listed below:

Operators

Let source loc = starting location of movement,
dest loc = destination location
dis = distance between the starting location and destination location,
We can define various operators as:
(i) Walk(source loc, dest loc)
     precondition at (person, source loc) $\wedge$ dis ($<$ 3 Km)
     postcondition at (person, bus stop)

  (ii) drive (source loc, dest loc)
       precondition at (person, source loc) $\wedge$ dis (< 300 km)
       postcondition at (person, airport)
 (iii) takebus (source loc, dest loc)
       precondition at (person, bus stop) $\wedge$ dis (< 300 km)
       postcondition at (person, airport)
 (iv) fly (source loc, dest loc)
       precondition at (person, airport) $\wedge$ dis (> 300 km)
       postcondition at (person, airport)
  (v) takecab (source loc, dest loc)
       precondition at (person, airport)
       postcondition at (person, hotel)

Here, while designing the operator, it is assumed that a person normally can not walk beyond 3 km. The amicable distance to be traveled by car is less than 300 km, and aeroplane is normally available for distances beyond 300 km. Let us assume that the starting position in city 'A' is a house 2.5 km away from the local bus stop. The distance between bus stop and airport in Delhi is 40 km. The distance between Delhi and Mumbai is 3200 km. Further, the distance of bus stop for place B in Mumbai is 60 km from airport and location of 'B', say some hotel at Mumbai is 30 km from bus stop. The locations of various spots between A and B are shown in the following diagram:

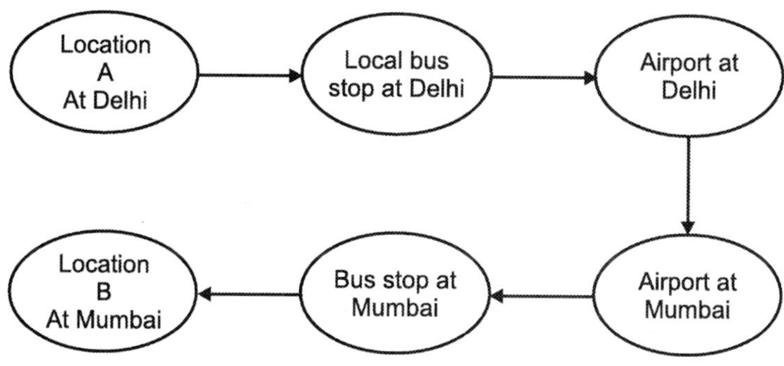

In this case, means ends analysis can be applied to plan this travel. Seeing the distance of Delhi and Mumbai, it is decided to apply operator 'FLY'. But this operator has preconditions at (person, airport) $\wedge$ distance > 300 km. (that means, person should be present at airport and distance from source to destination should be more than 300 km.) Out of these preconditions, the second condition is satisfied but first condition is not yet satisfied because the person is at present standing at A, which is not the airport. In order to apply operator 'FLY', first some other operator should be applied which brings the person to airport. The appropriate operator is 'TAKEBUS', which has a post condition at (person, airport), that means after applying this operator the person will be at airport. Hence, before applying operator 'FLY', operator 'TAKEBUS' should be applied. Operator 'TAKEBUS' has a precondition at (person, bus stop) and distance less than 300 km. Out of these two preconditions, the second precondition is satisfied but the first is not, because the person is not at the bus stop. Hence to satisfy first precondition, any operator which generates postcondition at (person, bus stop) should be chosen. 'WALK' is the appropriate operator. So, before applying 'TAKEBUS' operator, 'WALK' should be applied. Similarly, at Mumbai airport, operator 'TAKECAB' can be applied which brings the person directly to the hotel from the airport. Here, you need not to follow the route from airport to Mumbai bus stop and from bus stop to hotel because the distance can be covered using single operator. The sequence of application of operators would be:

  (i) FLY
 (ii) TAKEBUS, FLY
(iii) WALK, TAKEBUS, FLY
(iv) WALK, TAKEBUS, FLY, TAKECAB

This example presents an oversimplified description of means ends analysis and omits many details for the purpose of understanding, e.g., the order in which operators are applied is important. Normally the operators are applied, which reduce significant differences, otherwise most of the energy would be wasted in finding out the operators which reduce small differences.

The steps followed in the means ends analysis problem solution technique are summarized below:

1. Compare current state and goal state. If they are not same then compute the difference 'dig ' between them.
2. An operator 'Ok' is selected to reduce the difference *dig*.
3. Check whether the selected operator Ok is applicable on the present conditions (that means, the preconditions of Ok matches with the present conditions) if possible. If operator is applicable then apply it and make the new post conditions as present conditions and select a new operator, which is applicable on these conditions. If operator is not applicable on current conditions then the current state is saved as subgoal and means ends analysis is applied recursively to solve this subgoal.

The general procedure of means ends analysis approach is presented below:

3.5.13.1 *Procedure of Means Ends Analysis: (c_state , g_state)*

1. If c_state = g_state, means there is no difference between these states and goal is achieved. Hence, stop.
2. Otherwise, find the difference between g_state and c_state, repeat the following till the difference becomes zero:

(i)   Apply yet unapplied operator which reduces this difference by maximum amount. Check pre condition of that operator. If the c_state is not the same as precondition, choose some other operator Ok′, which has postcondition same as required precondition. If no such operator exists, report failure.

(ii)   Otherwise, apply Ok′ and change c_state to state generated by precondition.

3.5.14 Mini-Max Search

The search techniques discussed so far consider only single *'agent'*. In the language of AI, an agent is defined as something that perceives and acts in an environment. In simple language, it can be said as whosoever is performing the activity, is an agent, e.g., the agent playing a crossword game involves a single person, so it is called single agent environment, whereas in a chess game, two players are involved and in a card game, there may be multiple players playing the game. The situation where more than one agent is in picture is called *'multi agent environment'*. The different agents working in a system may work in cooperation with each other like a team of senior scientists and junior scientists working on a problem. Otherwise, it may be competitive environment like two players playing chess game where each player will try to win the game by increasing his performance and decreasing others performance. Hence, their interests will be contradictory.

Problems involving game playing, i.e., having competitive environment, is generally solved using a search technique called *'adversial search'*. Mini-max search procedure is a type of search technique used in game playing.

3.5.14.1 *Theory of game playing*

Let us discuss in brief some basics of theory of game playing from the view point of AI. Game playing was one of the first tasks undertaken in AI. The development of chess game program started in 1950. The AI games are usually considered as deterministic (i.e. deriving some conclusion) and fully observable, in which there are two agents and there actions alternate. In this case, the utility values (like objective function), which have some mathematical value determining goodness of a move, are equal and opposite, e.g. if player A in chess gains 1 point, player B loses 1 point. The name adversial search is derived because of this adverse situation created by A and B. Multiplayer games, non-zero sum games, and stochastic games come under this category. In the game playing strategy, one player tries to maximize his points and minimize other player's points. Because of alternate maximization and minimization of objective function by players, this search strategy is also called *'mini-max'* search.

Formally, a game is defined as a kind of search problem with:

(i)   *Initial state*: It includes starting state (board position), and identifies the player to apply a move.

(ii) *An operator selector*: which selects an 'operator' from valid list of operators; and returns a (move, state) pair, each indicating a legal move and the resulting state.

(iii) *Final state or terminal state*: which determines when the game is over.

(iv) *Objective function*: also called utility function, which associates some numeric value with a move to decide which move should be taken in the situation when multiple moves are simultaneously valid. In the game of chess, the outcome is a win, loss or draw. These are given values +1, -1 or 0. Some games have wider variety of possible outcomes, e.g. the payoffs in backgammon range from +192 to -192.

Various moves of a game are represented by game tree. It has the root that represents the initial state and children of root represent various other states. The partial game tree of tic- tac- toe game is shown in Chapter 2.

In a normal search problem, the optimal solution is found by a sequence of valid moves leading to goal state, but in game playing search, the moves alternate between two players and each player while deciding his move, pays attention to following two points:

(i) win his game

(ii) stop the opponent from winning

Accordingly, the moves alternately try to maximize the utility function and minimize the utility function. Moreover, the strategies are contingent, means, while deciding next move every player will check his own move also.

3.5.14.2 *Mini-Max search procedure*

Now, let us discuss the procedure of mini-max search. It is a depth first, depth limited search procedure. To decide one move, it explores the possibilities of winning by looking ahead to more than one step. This is called ply. Thus in a two ply search, to decide the current move, game tree would be explored two levels farther. Consider the tree shown in the following Fig. 3.21.

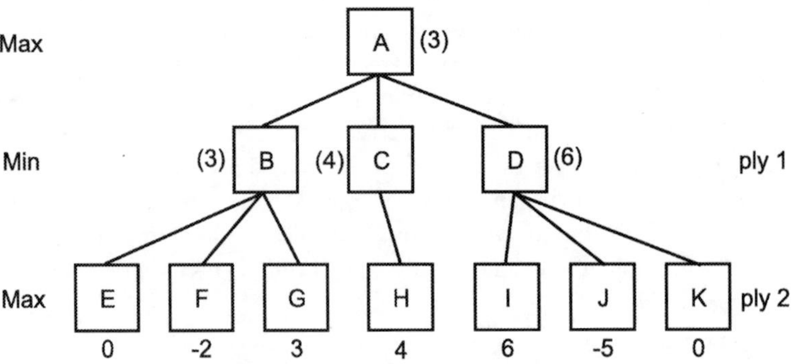

Fig. 3.21: Tree showing two-ply search

In this tree, node A represents current state of any game and nodes B, C and D represent three possible valid moves from state A. Similarly, E, F and G represent possible moves from B, and so on. To decide which move to be taken from A, the different possibilities are explored to two next steps. As mentioned earlier, the number of levels to which the look ahead is performed to decide one move is called *ply*. Fig. 3.21 shows two plies of tree. Numbers 0, -2, 3, 4, 6, -5, 0 represent utility values of respective move. They indicate goodness of a move. The utility value is back propagated to ancestor node, according to a situation whether it is Max ply or Min ply. As mentioned earlier, in a two-player game, the utility value is alternately maximized and minimized. Here as second player's move is maximizing, so maximum value of all children of one node will be back propagated to node. Thus B, C, D get values 3, 4, 6. Again as ply 1 is minimizing, so minimum value out of these (i.e. 3) is propagated to A. From A, move will be taken to B.

3.5.15 Alpha-Beta Pruning

In MINIMAX search, number of game state increases exponentially. To reduce the search, the pruning is done. Alpha – beta is one such pruning technique. It maintains two threshold values one is called alpha (or 'α') and other beta ('β'). These threshold values are defined as follows:

α = Lower bound on maximum value of utility function. It is the least acceptable value of utility function in maximizing ply.

β = Upper bound on minimum value of utility function. It is the highest acceptable value of utility function in case on minimizing ply.

In searching the game tree in mini-max search, the part of tree having utility value less than α indicates that this particular move will not at all be useful. Hence, part of tree having utility value less than alpha will be pruned. That means, in future all the nodes below it will never be explored. Similarly, if utility value comes out to be more than beta in case of minimizing ply, it will indicate that this move is at all not useful and that sub tree will be pruned on similar ground. Let us consider an example (see Fig 3.22).

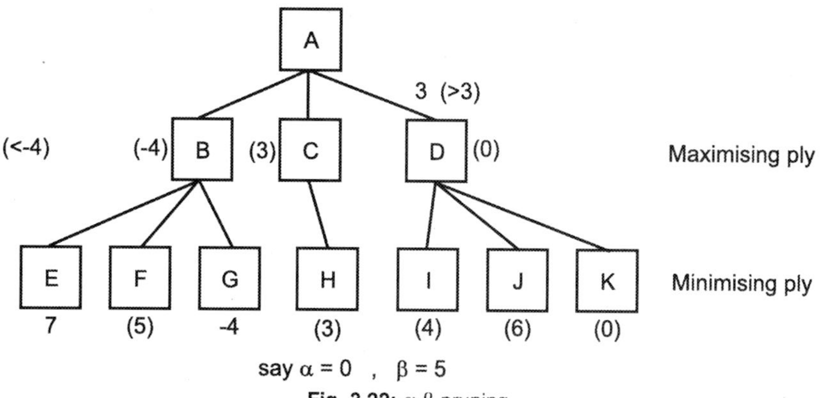

Fig. 3.22: α-β pruning

Here the possibilities are considered up to 2 ply. At min ply, the best value from three nodes is -4, 3, 0. These will be back propagated towards root and a maximizing move 3 will be taken. Now node E having utility value 7 is far more, then accepted. (as it is minimizing ply). So further node E will not be explored. In the situation when more plies are considered, whole sub tree below E will be pruned.

Similarly if alpha = 0 and beta = 5, all nodes and related sub trees having value of utility function less than 0 at maximizing ply and more than 5 at minimizing ply will be pruned. The procedure for minimax search is as follows.

Procedure MINIMAX A, B (Position)

{Procedure Minimax (Position, Depth, Player)

1. If reached last ply (Position, Depth)

then return the structure VALUE = STATIC (Position, Player)

2a Path = nil

2. Otherwise, generate one more ply of the tree and set SUCCESSOR to the list, it returns.

3. If SUCCESSOR is empty, then return the same structure.

4. Otherwise, examine each element and find best one.

5. After examining all the nodes, return the structure

VALUE = BEST-SCORE

PATH = BEST-PATH}

The worthiness of α, β pruning depends upon the order in which paths are examined. If the worst successor is generated first then no cut offs will occur. Kunth and Moore (1975) have analyzed that for a search tree of branching factor b and depth d, the α - β search needs examining only $b^{d/2}$ nodes to pick up best move, instead of b^d for mini-max. That means, effective branching factor becomes vb instead of b. For a chess game, where the value of 'b' is 35, with alpha beta pruning the effective branching factor will become 6. This indicates a significant amount of saving in search.

3.5.16 Horizon Effect

It is a phenomenon that arises when a program is facing a move by opponent that causes wide damage and is unavoidable. To overcome this problem, a double check is applied to choose the move to make sure that a hidden pit fall does not exist a few moves ahead. To do this, if normal moves are decided using four ply, some moves may be explored further that is up to six or seven plies. This is also considered as *'secondary search'*. That is, if a primary search is applied on main search tree up to 4 plies, then on part of the tree, a search up to 6 plies will be performed.

3.6 POPULAR GAME PLAYING THEORIES

Game playing has been most sought after avenue for AI scientists since its inception and from the very beginning when AI was just at introductory phase. AI has been successfully applied to even chess game, one of the most mind-boggling game requiring lot of thinking and expertise. Search techniques described in this chapter so far are applied in one way or the other in almost all the theories devised for the purpose of game playing. We would discuss some of the popular games and theories applied in playing them.

3.6.1 Card Games

Card games are most popular among the games played by computers. In normal card games, cards are dealt randomly and distributed to players. Any player can see his own card. Player to take first move is decided by some mutual scheme or by toss. Winner of a particular move initiates next move. Let us explain the process by selecting one of the simplest card playing game. Assume two players A and B having following cards:

A: (H) 7   (D) 7   (C) 10   (C) 8
B: (H) 4   (S) 2   (C) J   (C) 5

Where,
   H: Heart
   D: Diamond
   S: Spade
   C: Club

Let player A starts the game, so he will try to maximize his move and minimize B's move. If A plays (C) 10, B will play card of same suit, either (C) J or (C) 5. Let us say B plays (C) J and wins. Next B plays (S) 2, A does not have spade, so it must throw some card. The correct choice is (D) 7. So, it throws it and B wins. Now whichever card B plays, A will win next both the tricks. Thus, game is tied at 2:2. By exploring various possibilities. By mathematical analysis it can be proved that A's move 'c' is an optimal choice.

In general, for playing a move, player will evaluate a given course of action:
* by first computing mini-max value of particular action for each possible deal of cards, when there are unseen cards,
* then, computing the expected value of overall deals using probability of each deal.

3.6.2 Chess

Program for chess game, known as '*deep blue*', was developed by Murray Campbell etc. at IBM. The machine used was parallel computer with thirty IBMRS

– 6000 processors. Deep blue searches 126 million nodes per second on an average. It generated up to 30 billion positions per move, reaching depth 14 routinely. The game used iterative deepening ***alpha-beta search*** with a transposition table, though key to its success was its ability to generate extensions beyond depth limit for some moves. It is this program, which defeated world champion Gary Kasparov in a six game exhibition match. One another quite famous chess program was "***Deep Thought***". Deep thought is the name of general game developed for playing chess. It used to play the actual chess and to the surprise of many experts, an extremely good chess game can be played by a search based chess program, as long as the program can search deeply enough. The best of such programs is deep thought. It uses a sophisticated special purpose computer and uses alpha beta procedure. Deep thought usually is able to search down to about 10 ply.

Using the singular extension heuristics, deep thought usually goes much further still shocking some human opponents with its ability to penetrate complicated situations. Deep thought's static evaluator considers piece count, piece placement, pawn structure, passed pawns and the arrangement of pawns and rooks on columns, which are called files in the chess vernacular.

Interestingly, the playing strength of several generations of search oriented chess programs seem proportional to the number of ply that the program can search. The relation between depth in ply and program rating, as measured by the US chess federation on its own developed rating scale is shown in following Fig. 3.23.

A successor to deep thought, projected to be 1000 times faster, is under development. Given a real branching factor of 35 to 40 for chess, the effective branching factor is about 6. Thus, 1000 times more speed should enable Deep thought's successor to search to about 14 ply. If the relation between ply and rating continues to hold, this next generation machine should have a rating in the

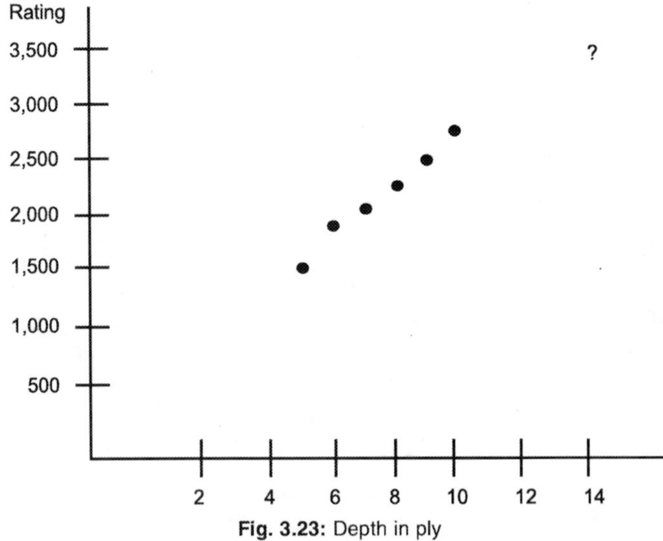

Fig. 3.23: Depth in ply

vicinity of 3400, which is well above the 2900 rating of Gary Kasparov or of Vishvanathan Anand, the present world chess champion.

3.6.3 Checkers

Arthur Samuel of IBM in 1952 developed a program for playing checkers, which had good capacity of learning. It could learn from its own evaluation function by playing with itself. It exhibited so good learning capabilities, that after playing thousands of times and by self-learning, it was able to ultimately beat its own creator. Computing equipment of Samuel was IBM 704 and had 10,000 words of main memory, magnetic tape for long term storage and a 0.000001 GHz processor.

3.6.4 Bridge

It is a game of imperfect information (i.e. unlike chess or tic-tac-toe, where other player's moves are visible, in bridge other player's cards are hidden). Bridge is also a multiplayer game with 4 players instead of 2. The optimal play in bridge includes, elements of information gathering communication, bluffing, and careful weighing of probabilities. A popular bridge program ***Bridge Baron***^{tm} (smith et. al., 1998) won 1998 computer championship.

EXERCISES

1. Explain the difference between blind search and heuristic search techniques. When does blind search become better than heuristic search?
2. What is meant by Hill-climbing search technique? What are various problems encountered in it?
3. Consider the following tree:

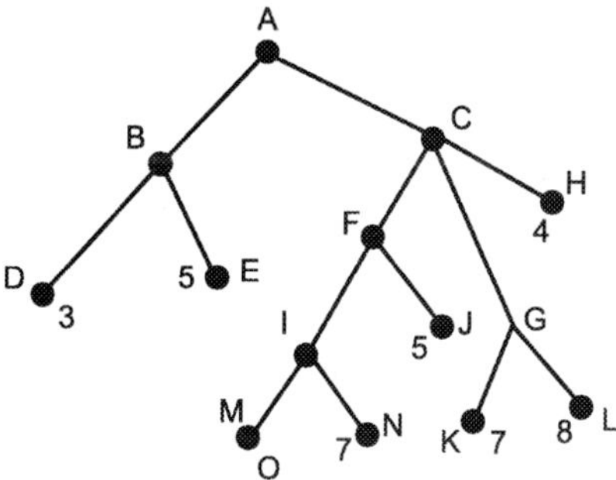

   Now, in above tree, the heuristic value of every node is written. Trace the path of the goal L.
4. Consider the following tree:
   In this figure, the nodes are expanded according to heuristic value written with the nodes. Write node expansion sequence for goal (i) J (ii) m (iii) I.

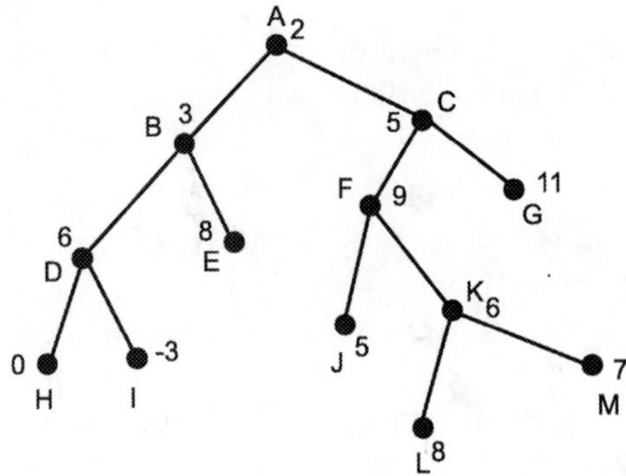

5. Suggest a good heuristic function for 8-puzzle problem and chess problem.
6. List the difference between hill-climbing and simulated annealing. Give examples of applications where they are used.
7. Differentiate between depth-first search, breadth-search and uniform cost search.
8. Design a heuristic function that a block stacking program must use to solve the problems of the form "stack block X on block Y". Is it admissible? Is it monotonic?
9. Consider a new puzzle called sliding block puzzle. It has 3 red tiles, 3 green tiles and one tile space arranged as follows:

R	R	R		G	G	G

The goal is to swap the position of all tiles. It has two legal moves:
(a)   A tile can move into an adjacent empty location with cost 1.
(b)   It can jump over one or two other tiles into empty position. This has a cost equal to the number of tiles jumped over.
   (i)   Analyze the state space with respect to complexity and looping.
   (ii)   Propose a heuristic for solving this problem and analyze it with respect to admissibility, monotonicity and informedness.
10. Prove that A* is admissible by showing that it fulfils following conditions:
   (i)   A* search will terminate.
   (ii)   During its execution, there is always a node on open that lies on an optimal path to the goal.
   (iii)   If there is a path to the goal, A* will terminate by finding the optimal path.
11. Solve the following cryptoarithmatic puzzles:
   (i)   P U S H   Answer: 3 7 8 6
         +   D O O R   + 2 1 1 4
         ____________   ____________
             B E L L   5 9 0 0
         ____________   ____________

(ii)

	G I V E	Answer:	1 4 0 7
	+ T H E M		+ 2 3 7 9
	H E L P		3 7 8 6

(iii)

	S O M E	Answer:	1 9 3 4
	+ T I M E		+ 8 5 3 4
	S P E N T		1 0 4 6 8

(iv)

	C A T	Answer:	7 1 5
	+ R U N		+ 6 0 4
	A W A Y		1 3 1 9

(v)

	F O U R	Answer:	1 0 8 2
	+ M I C E		+ 9 7 6 3
	F O U N D		1 0 8 4 5

4

Introduction to Knowledge

4.1 INTRODUCTION

In modern era of fast development and rapid advancement where competition is growing among individuals and organizations with equal pace, the increase in efficiency and productivity has become need of the hour to sustain and to acquire desired benefits, and to enhance productivity, experts systems are used. **Expert Systems** are AI based systems, which make the task of diagnosis, analysis, querying and suggesting appropriate solutions to real-world problems of the quality at par with the quality of human being.

The most important use of AI is to develop expert systems to help human beings for solving real world problems easily, effectively, efficiently and economically. Expert systems are developed using **knowledge** and are a kind of **knowledge-based system** which are designed to match the expertise of an expert practitioner of a particular field. Various techniques are used for **Knowledge Acquisition** and **Knowledge Representation** for acquiring and representing knowledge for using in the development of expert systems. Knowledge based systems are used by **knowledge engineers** and the process of development, building and maintaining knowledge –based systems is the domain of **Knowledge Engineering.**

In the present chapter we will discuss the key words used above and many more in detail to understand the concepts of knowledge, its representation and its use.

Knowledge plays an important role in building AI systems. It is the core aspect of Artificial Intelligence. It is the presence of knowledge that differentiates ordinary human from an expert. An expert of any field possesses more knowledge of that field. In a layman's language knowledge can be defined as the body of facts and principles accumulated by human being, or act or state of knowing. In addition of these basic aspects, knowledge has familiarity with language, concepts, procedures, rules, ideas, abstraction, places, customs, facts, and associations coupled with the ability to use these notions effectively in modeling different aspects of the world. Without this ability these concepts and aspects are worthless. Knowledge is related with the intelligence by the fact that intelligence requires possession and access of knowledge.

Now we will try to define knowledge. The basic components of knowledge are:

- A set of data
- A form of belief or hypothesis
- A kind of information

Basically, knowledge is one or all of the above but, in different form.

Knowledge is different from data. Data is raw form of observations. *Knowledge is organized form of data and procedures which can be used for some useful purposes,* e.g., a physician treating a patient uses both knowledge and data. The data is patient's record, symptoms, history etc. Knowledge is what the physician has learnt in school and with experience. Knowledge consists of facts, beliefs, and heuristics. Knowledge requires use of data and information. It combines relationships, correlations, dependencies with data and information.

Knowledge is also different from belief and hypothesis. Belief is any meaningful coherent expression that can be expressed. Thus belief may be true or false. Hypothesis is a belief that is not known to be true. Thus a hypothesis is a belief that is backed with some supporting evidence but it may still be false. *Knowledge is true justified belief.* There are two more related terms, epistemology and meta knowledge. Epistemology is the study of nature of knowledge and meta knowledge is knowledge about knowledge (knowledge about what we know).

Information can be distinguished from the knowledge in a way that information is data plus meaning of the same. If information is limited up to data and their meaning, it is only information, and when information is capable of creating more information and can become part of some action, then it can fall in the category of knowledge. Information only increases the volume of data possessed by an expert, whereas knowledge supplements the thoughts and subsequently enhances the power of an expert to alter the things. Thus, *knowledge is information about objects, concepts and relationships that are assumed to exist in a particular area of interest.* Hence, we can define knowledge as information and processing of the same for the purpose of changing something or somebody as well as for creating new knowledge based on existing knowledge using logical reasoning.

Thus, knowledge is richer, more structured and more contextual form of information that is required to perform the task of problem solving. The salient points to be noted in context of knowledge are:

(i) Use or understand knowledge
(ii) Use knowledge for decision making
(iii) Recognize objects through vision
(iv) Interpret situations
(v) Plan Strategies

4.2 TYPES OF KNOWLEDGE

Knowledge can be of various types like:
1. Declarative Knowledge
2. Procedural knowledge
3. Inheritable knowledge
4. Inferential knowledge
5. Relational knowledge
6. Heuristic knowledge
7. Common sense knowledge
8. Explicit knowledge
9. Implicit knowledge
10. Uncertain knowledge

4.2.1 Declarative Knowledge

It is the knowledge, which gives the simple facts about any organization or phenomenon. Declarative knowledge means representation of facts or assertions. This tells 'what' about a situation, e.g., the facts about the college like its building, its courses, location, organizational setup consist of declarative knowledge. The facts may be static facts, or dynamic facts. The static facts do not change with time whereas the dynamic facts changes with time, e.g., in the college, it may be possible that the location of college is permanent, then it will become static fact, however, the new courses may be added in curriculum pattern of college, then it will become dynamic fact. The frame representation method can be used to represents static knowledge, i.e., it gives the information about existing things.

4.2.2 Procedural Knowledge

The declarative knowledge does not tell anything regarding functioning of the concerned object. In context of college, it does not tell anything about running of the college. It does not tell how a student is examined, how syllabus is framed, how fees deposit is made etc. The procedural knowledge represents the functioning of organization. It describes dynamic attributes using production rules, e.g., following rules may give information regarding operation of a college-

> If: student has deposited fees and
> student has opted a course and
> student has attended 90% classes and
> student has passed the examination
>
> Then: declare the student pass.

Or

> If: student has scored distinction in all subjects and
> student has good communication skills and
> student has participated in extra curricular activities

Then: student is the best student.

Similarly, procedures regarding other operations of a college may be declared. The procedural knowledge in AI program is represented as production rules. These rules can be easily coded in lisp structures.

4.2.3 Inheritable Knowledge

In real world, there are many situations where general concepts regarding some event, thing or activity are already known, and object of that particular type inherits all features of that event, e.g., consider the word "college". A "college" has certain features like it will have classrooms, teachers, a playground, building, students, office etc. Further, the classrooms will have a blackboard, cupboard, furniture, students etc. Besides these, there will be some general concepts regarding the functioning of the college, like it will have time table for each class, a fee deposit plan, examination pattern, course module, cultural activity, etc. Similarly, it can have many more deep concepts like promotional scheme of its staff, placement of its student etc. Now, if we say "X is a college", then X will automatically inherit all the features of the college. It may be possible that X has some additional features. Those additional details may be separately given; for example, X may be a girl's college, this information may be given as sex= female. The inheritable knowledge is diagrammatically represented in Fig 4.1.

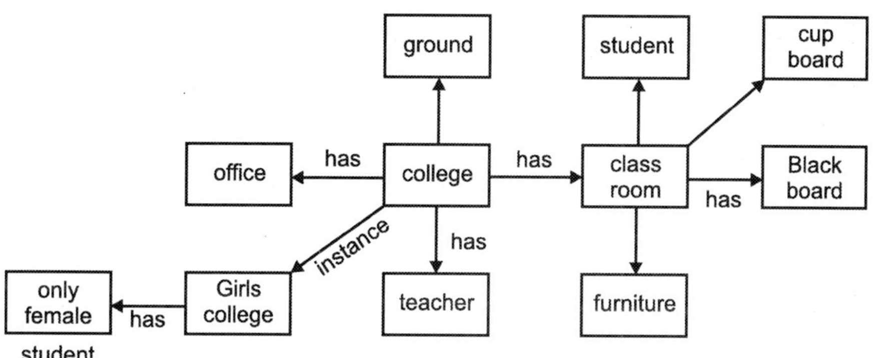

Fig. 4.1: College attribute representation

Here, the relationship 'has' indicates the salient features (or property called attributes) and 'is a' represents the variable (or instance, here X) of that type. X inherits all the properties of college and has one additional feature of having only female students. This is called property inheritance. To support property inheritance, objects must be organized into classes. This knowledge representation is implemented using frames. When these frames store semantic information, the structure is called semantic net. From the implementation point of view, individual frames may be considered as data structure, similar in many aspects like a record that contains information relevant to stereo typed entities. The frame contains information about:

- Frame identification.
- Relationship of this frame to other frames, e.g., X is an instance of college
- Attributes of a frame: These are the characteristics of the frame.
- Procedural information on use of structure described. An important feature of frame is the ability to attach procedural code to a slot.
- Default information: These represent characteristics of a frame. When no contrary information is found this default information is taken, e.g., chair has four legs, telephone has push buttons etc.
- New instance information: some frame slots are left vacant to accommodate the expansions.

4.2.4 Inferential Knowledge

The knowledge representation method, which can use inference mechanism to use this knowledge is called inferential knowledge. The property inheritance, which is discussed above is a powerful form of inferential knowledge representation. Besides this, predicate logic representation is also used to represent inferential knowledge. Example of this type of knowledge is given below:

(i) $\forall$x: Ball(x) $\wedge$ Fly(x) $\wedge$ Fair(x) $\wedge$ Infield_catchable(x) $\wedge$ occupied base (First) $\wedge$ Occupied base (Second) $\wedge$ (outs $<$ 2) $\neg$[line_drive (x) $\vee$ attempted_B(x)] $\rightarrow$ Infield_fly (x)

(ii) $\forall$x, y : Batter(x) $\wedge$ Batted (x, y) $\wedge$ Infield_fly(y) $\rightarrow$ Infield_fly (x)

The inferential knowledge requires an inference mechanism for the purpose of exploiting it. The inference procedures implement the standard logic rules of inference. There are many inference procedures discussed earlier. The forward inference moves from start state to goal state, and backward inference starts from goal towards start state. Resolution is one such procedure. This form of knowledge is powerful knowledge structure, which describes relationships among values.

4.2.5 Relational Knowledge

In this type of knowledge, the facts are represented as set of relations in a tabular form. The table stores salient attributes of object, e.g., the knowledge regarding students may be represented as mentioned in Fig. 4.2.

Player	Height	Weight	Bats
A	6 - 0	180	Left
B	5 - 10	170	Right
C	6 - 2	215	
D	6 - 3	205	

Fig. 4.2: Knowledge about student

This representation is the simplest and can be used in database systems. It can be used to answer simplest questions like "who is the tallest boy, "whose marks are maximum", "who is worst in communication skills", but this representation is very simple and can not store any semantic information, e.g., from this representation, it can not answer the queries like "is Adwet a good boy?".

4.2.6 Heuristic Knowledge

This type of knowledge can be defined as experimental, rarely discussed and individualistic knowledge. This is more of a judgmental knowledge of any performance. For example, knowledge of good guessing is heuristic knowledge. Such type of knowledge can not be acquired from books; rather it comes from within the individual and differs from individual to individual.

For example, if it is asked that how many runs the Indian Cricket team would score in a particular one-day international match against Australia, different people will give different answers based on the knowledge they possess about the cricket match using heuristics. The answers might be 120, 278, 347, 86 etc. The individual answers this question based on the heuristic knowledge he or she possesses about the match in question. The answer would be based on various factors such as past performances, average total scored at that particular ground, weather conditions etc. Obviously, if somebody gives the answers such as 10 or 1024, it would be inferred that those individuals do not have the knowledge regarding the problem.

4.2.7 Common sense Knowledge

It is general contextual knowledge about any phenomenon. It is gained by our experience. Unlike other knowledge, it is domain independent knowledge. Though this is theoretically true, still the commonsense knowledge about the globe is enormous. Thus commonsense knowledge can be considered as domain independent knowledge of a particular context, e.g., regarding the inheritable knowledge of college, the additional knowledge like the concept of preliminary school education, general idea about the concept of education, its social and ethical impact, its contribution in the development of human being etc. can be viewed as commonsense knowledge. The presence of commonsense knowledge plays vital role in differentiating human from other animals. A person gains this knowledge, knowingly or unknowingly throughout his life. It is the knowledge, which is most difficult to represent and code. The size of this cannot be judged and it is a mixture of almost all types of knowledge. The reasoning performed by this knowledge is called commonsense reasoning. The storage of commonsense knowledge is a major shortcoming of AI systems as compared to human beings.

If we compare computers and human beings, the computers are capable of performing some amazing feats. They can effortlessly store vast quantities of information. Their circuits operate in nanoseconds. They can perform arithmetic calculations without error. Humans can not approach these capabilities. On the other hand, humans routinely perform 'simple tasks such as walking, talking, and commonsense reasoning. Current AI systems can not do any of these things better than human. One reason of this may be that brain is suited to these tasks, but not suited to tasks such as high speed arithmetic calculation.

4.2.8 Explicit Knowledge

Explicit knowledge is the one which an individual holds explicitly and which remains in ones conscious. This knowledge can be expressed clearly into formal language including mathematical expressions, grammatical statements, specifications, manuals etc. For example, the knowledge that if two is multiplied by two, it becomes four, is a kind of explicit knowledge.

Explicit knowledge is communicable to others, verbally or in stored form. Also, it can be processed by computers, can be stored and transferred electronically.

4.2.9 Tacit Knowledge

Literal meaning of tacit knowledge is one that is understood or not expressed in any conventional form. The form of knowledge an individual possesses about which he or she may or may not be aware of, is tacit knowledge. This kind of knowledge is acquired by experience and involves intangible factors such as personal beliefs, perspective and the value system. Tacit knowledge is often subconscious and internalized and is difficult to be expressed in the form of formal language. It contains intuitions and subjective insights. Tacit knowledge can not be transmitted before it is converted into words, models or numbers that can be understood.

Tacit knowledge can be represented in two dimensions:

4.2.9.1 Technical Dimension

Highly subjective and personal insights, intuitions and inspirations derived from long experience fall into the category of technical dimension of tacit knowledge. For example, a craftsman has enormous amount of expertise in his field which he acquires from years long experience but he is hardly able to express the technical and scientific principles involved in his expertise. Hence, the expertise of a craftsman falls in the category of tacit knowledge and the science and technology involved in his expertise is the technical dimension of tacit knowledge.

4.2.9.2 Cognitive Dimension

There are things, which are so deeply associated with us that we seldom acknowledge those as knowledge, but they are part of knowledge with the help of that we perceive the world around us. The dimensions such as beliefs, ideals, principles, values and emotions fall in the category of cognitive dimensions of tacit knowledge. For example, 'we should respect our elders', is a kind of tacit knowledge, which almost all of us possess and use in day-to-day life but seldom acknowledge this as knowledge.

4.2.10 Uncertain Knowledge

There is one more property of Knowledge, that is, it is uncertain and usually incomplete. Though we have defined various types of knowledge above, but still it is crude fact that regarding any organization / phenomenon / problem the complete knowledge can not be provided. What we provide, is the information which is known to us. Hence we can say that we provide knowledge complete to the best of our capacity, but that is never absolutely complete. Moreover, the knowledge is uncertain also. The real world phenomenon are highly uncertain. The kind of knowledge required to represent this is uncertain knowledge. It provides the methods to deal with uncertain situations. The set of methods for using uncertain data in the form of uncertain knowledge in the reasoning process is called reasoning with uncertainty. An important subclass of methods adopted for reasoning with uncertainty are by using probabilistic techniques or "fuzzy logic", and the systems that use such methods are called "fuzzy systems".

4.3 KNOWLEDGE REPRESENTATION

We have understood until now, that the basic task of AI is to help in building expert systems. Expert systems require huge amount of knowledge to perform at par with the human experts. This knowledge is to be represented in usable form using different knowledge representation techniques. The basic knowledge representation of facts is illustrated through Fig. 4.3.

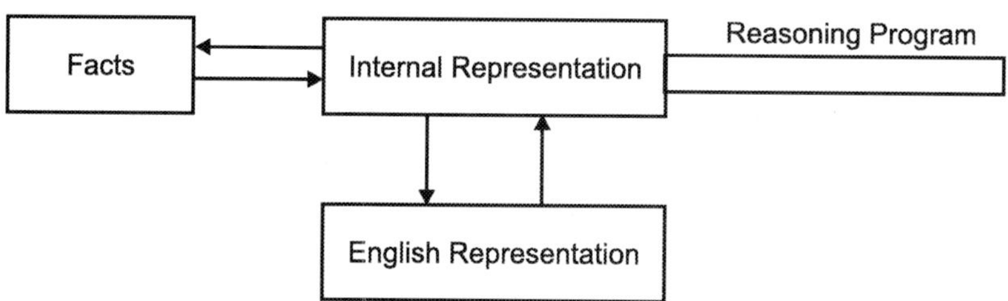

Fig. 4.3: Basic knowledge representation of facts

The nature of AI problems is widely different. Like; in natural language question answering type of application, the understanding of meaning is required. In puzzle solution problem, sometimes the goal is to be reported (e.g. 8 queen problem) and sometime the path is to be reported (like in traveling salesperson). In medical diagnosis or expert system type of application, the inferencing is required and some conclusion needs to be drawn. In few applications, simple search is performed over solution space to find the answer.

Since the nature of problems related to AI are different, different types of knowledge is required for finding their solutions, accordingly the knowledge representation techniques are different. Some issues in knowledge representation are of general concern, e.g.,

- What are the attributes of objects that should be captured and what relationship does exist between the attributes?
- What is the granularity of representation? This is an important aspect in knowledge representation. Granularity means the depth of detail. If every minute detail of event is captured, that would be called fine grain. If fewer details are captured, that would be called coarse grain. The granularity will decide size of knowledge base. As more and more information is stored, the size of knowledge base grows. In the applications like natural language inferencing and medical diagnosis, in- depth knowledge is required.
- What is the inferencing mechanism used? Inferencing means drawing conclusions or finding the solution of some problem with the help of stored knowledge. Normally a large amount of knowledge remains stored in database and the inferencing decides how can relevant parts be accessed when they are needed.

The knowledge representation should also address the issue of how to code the knowledge from the storage point of view. The salient features that are to be considered while representing the knowledge are:

- Important attributes of a particular phenomenon or object that needs a special consideration and should be captured for representation point of view.
- Relationship among the attributes. It will decide the suitable representation methodology.
- Choosing granularity among the representation. The granularity indicates the quantum of details in which we want to represent the attributes. The more details will mean more accurate information, but from storage point of view it will increase the size of knowledge base. However, if fewer details are stored the decisions requiring more depth can not be generated.

Thus, knowledge representation formalizes and organizes the knowledge. One example of representation is *production rule* or simply *rule*. A rule consists of condition and an action, means IF part (condition) and THEN part (an action). The IF part lists a set of conditions in logical form. If IF part is satisfied, the THEN part can be concluded or problem solving action can be taken. If the knowledge is represented in rule form, then expert systems using such knowledge are called *rule-based systems*.

A computational system can be made artificially intelligent if we are able to supply it the same amounts of knowledge as human being possess. Thus to store the knowledge, it requires analysis / treatment like,   how to define it, how to represent it, how to code it in a machine compatible manner, how to store it and finally how to use this to derive conclusions like human being do. To handle these aspects of knowledge treatment we simultaneously require analyzing in detail how this is done in human beings.

In human brain, the knowledge is stored in the form of neurons. In computer, knowledge can be stored as symbolic structures. Knowledge representation has two entities:

- **Facts**: these are the observations about some event in real world. These are the entities, we want to represent.
- **Representation of fact**: The facts should be mapped to some suitable formalism for the purpose of storage in computer's memory. The representation should be suitable so that we can manipulate them according to our requirement. The representation of facts is very difficult, because in real world, there are some entities, which are physically visible but some are conceptual phenomenon, which are not physically visible. Representations of conceptual activities are difficult.

4.4 KNOWLEDGE STORAGE

For using the knowledge for any specific purpose, it has to be collected and stored properly in communicable form. As a collected and stored data is called data base, a collected and stored knowledge is called knowledge base.

Thus, a knowledge base is a set of files that stores the knowledge for knowledge management. There are two major categories of knowledge base:

- **Machine-readable knowledge base**- these knowledge bases store knowledge in computer-readable form. They contain set of data often in form of rules that describe the knowledge in a logically consistent manner.
- **Human-readable knowledge base**- these knowledge bases contain knowledge, which can be used by people primarily for training purposes. Explicit knowledge of an organization such as, articles, papers, user manuals etc., stored in a manner in which that can be referred by people during need and for training purposes falls in the category of human-readable knowledge base.

The main benefit of such a knowledge base is that it provides solution to problems which have already known solutions that can be applied again and again for same kind of problems.

A knowledge base contains different types of information. Hence, the most important aspect of knowledge base is the quality of information it contains. A knowledge base is considered best, if it has:

- Carefully written articles that are updated regularly.
- Excellent search engine for easier accessibility.
- A carefully designed content format and classification structure for better understanding.

Structure (entity types and relationships) is an important aspect of a knowledge base. Ontology may be used by a knowledge base to specify its structure. An ontology is a formal representation of knowledge in a domain. Thus, knowledge base is an ontology plus a set of examples of its classes.

A knowledge base contains what type of information and where that information resides in a knowledge base is determined by the processes that support the system. These processes help to locate information contained in a knowledge base. A vigorous process structure is the backbone of a successful knowledge base.

Expert systems are artificially intelligent programs that achieve expert-level competence in problem solving by acquiring knowledge about specific task. In other words, an expert system is an intelligent knowledge-based system that matches the knowledge and reasoning capabilities of a human expert.

Every expert system consists of two principal parts: the knowledge base and the reasoning or inference engine.

The knowledge base of an expert system contains two types of knowledge:

*   **Factual knowledge**- the knowledge of task domain that is found in text books, papers and journals, widely shared and is agreed upon by the experts of a particular field.
*   **Heuristic knowledge**- as defined above.

From the above, we may conclude that an expert system requires a knowledge base. A knowledge base requires knowledge and that knowledge is to be stored systematically and represented in proper form in knowledge base. Hence, a technique of *knowledge representation* is to be adopted for properly representing the knowledge.

Another part of expert systems is inference engine. Inference engines are program modules that manipulate and use knowledge in knowledge base to form a line of reasoning. Program modules of inference engines contain problem solving methods. Thus, problem solving model or paradigm organizes and controls the steps taken to solve the problem. The chaining of IF-THEN rule to form a line of reasoning is one such common paradigm. If the chaining starts from IF, means a set of conditions, and moves towards THEN, means a conclusion, then it is called *forward chaining*. Sometimes the conclusion is known means, a goal to be achieved is known but the path to achieve that conclusion is not known then we have to move backwards from 'THEN' to 'IF' and the chaining is called *backward chaining*. Thus, object of inference engine is to decide the path and basis of solving a problem as well as to manipulate the use of knowledge.

An expert system requires a large amount of knowledge to be acquired from experts using various knowledge acquisition techniques. The area of human intellectual capabilities to be acquired by an expert system is called the task domain. Task refers to some goal oriented problem-solving activity such as diagnosis, planning, scheduling, configuration and designing. Domain refers to area within which task is to be performed. The power and capacity of an expert system depends upon knowledge they contain about task domain. Knowledge representation and reasoning methods are continuously explored by researchers in the field of AI and more and more techniques are added every day. As knowledge is most important ingredient in any expert system, and because current knowledge acquisition methods are slow and tedious, the future of expert systems depends upon breaking the bottleneck of knowledge acquisition.

A more comprehensive account of the expert systems is given in a separate chapter.

4.5 KNOWLEDGE ACQUISITION

The gathering of knowledge from various sources is called knowledge acquisition. The human beings gather knowledge from various sources like books, journals, magazines, media, newspapers, schools, parents, interaction with the people etc. The knowledge acquisition is a continuous process and is spread over entire lifetime. As far as the knowledge acquisition for an AI system is concerned, it is done by gathering knowledge from various sources like consulting the experts, collecting from books, and other media.

The early years of knowledge acquisition were full of problems. To acquire enough high quality knowledge to build an expert system was a very long and expensive activity. As such, knowledge acquisition was considered and identified as the bottleneck in building an expert system. This made knowledge acquisition major area of research within knowledge engineering.

Knowledge acquisition, normally denoted as KA, is acquiring the knowledge from various experts to form a knowledge base that can be used to build an expert system. It includes elicitation, collection, analysis, modeling and validation of knowledge.

4.5.1 Issue of Knowledge Acquisition

The aim of knowledge acquisition is to develop methods and tools that make the difficult task of capturing and validating the knowledge of an expert easier. While developing such methods and tools, many issues are to be taken care of and some of the issues involved in knowledge acquisition are:
- Most knowledge is in the heads of experts.
- Experts have vast amount of knowledge.
- Experts are busy people.
- Experts possess lot of tacit knowledge.
- They do not know all that they know and use.
- Tacit knowledge is difficult to describe.
- Each expert doesn't know everything.

4.5.2 Requirements for KA Techniques

While developing KA techniques, above issues are to be dealt with properly. Hence, to deal with these issues, techniques are required which:
- Allow non experts to understand the knowledge.
- Focus on the essential part of knowledge.
- Can capture tacit knowledge.
- Allow knowledge to be collected from different experts.
- Allow knowledge to be manipulated and validated.

4.5.3 Knowledge Creation or Conversion

Knowledge creation is a part of knowledge acquisition. We already know that knowledge can be of two types: explicit knowledge and tacit knowledge. To fulfill the above requirements of knowledge acquisition techniques, sometimes one form of knowledge is to be converted into other form for collection and analysis and hence for its acquisition. The modes of knowledge creation or conversion are:

*   ***From tacit to tacit*** (Socialization)- means sharing experiences to create tacit knowledge since tacit knowledge is mainly in the form of experiences.
*   ***From explicit to tacit*** (Internalization)- means written form of knowledge into ones head. Knowledge is verbalized into documents or oral stories to tacit knowledge.
*   ***From tacit to explicit*** (Externalization)- means articulating knowledge in the head into communicable form through concepts, hypothesis or models.
*   ***From explicit to explicit*** (Combination)- means transferring knowledge through documents, meetings and conversation. Reconfiguration of information by sorting, combining and categorizing.

4.5.4 KA Techniques

Many techniques have been developed to deduce knowledge from an expert. These are referred to as knowledge acquisition techniques. Some techniques used for acquiring, analyzing and modeling knowledge are mentioned below:

*   ***Protocol-Generation techniques*- these include various types of unstructured and structured interviews, reporting techniques and observational techniques.
*   ***Protocol-Analysis techniques*- these are analyzing techniques to identify types of knowledge such as goals, decisions, relationships and attributes from transcripts of interviews or other text based information.
*   ***Hierarchy-Generation techniques*- such techniques are used to build hierarchical structures such as goal trees decision networks.
*   ***Matrix-Based techniques*- these involve the construction of grids indicting such things as problems encountered against possible solutions.
*   ***Sorting techniques*** - these are used for capturing the methods by which people compare and order concepts.
*   ***Diagram-Based techniques*- these include the generation and use of concept maps, event diagrams and process maps. The use of these techniques is mainly important in capturing "why, when, who, how and where" features of tasks and events.

4.5.5 Use of KA Techniques

In this section we would try to emphasize how and when are the above techniques used in a knowledge acquisition project. This general process is illustrated by a simple method. This method starts using natural techniques and moves to use more developed techniques.

The process is summarized as follows-

- To conduct an interview with the expert in order to decide the type of knowledge to be acquired, the purpose for which knowledge is to be used, gain some understanding of technology and to build some rapport with the expert.
- To analyze the above interview, in order to create a concept ladder of the resulting knowledge. This should aim to provide a broad representation of the knowledge in the domain. The concept ladder thus created is used to develop a question bank that covers the essential issues across the domain and in tern, serves the knowledge acquisition project.
- To conduct a semi-structured interview with the expert using above prepared question bank.
- To analyze the resulting protocol from above interview for getting an idea about the types of knowledge present. Typically, this exercise would give the information about concepts, attributes, values, relationships, tasks and rules.
- To represent the knowledge elements derived from above using the most appropriate knowledge models, e.g., ladders, network diagrams, grids etc.
- To use the knowledge models formed above and structured text with developed techniques such as lettering and repertory grid to allow the expert to modify and expand on the knowledge already captured.
- To ascertain that experts and knowledge engineers feel satisfied about the goals to be realized for the project.
- To validate the knowledge thus acquired with other experts and to make modifications wherever necessary.

This is very brief coverage of what actually happens. Here it has been assumed that no previous knowledge has been gathered. However, in reality, the aim is to reuse as much previously acquired knowledge as possible. As the reuse of knowledge is the essence of making the knowledge acquisition process more efficient and effective, techniques have been developed to assist the process of reusing previously acquired knowledge such as use of ontologies and problem solving models.

Knowledge acquisition is an incessant process. A number of recent developments are continuing to improve the efficiency of the knowledge acquisition process.

4.6 KNOWLEDGE ORGANIZATION AND MANAGEMENT

In earlier sections we have discussed many aspects of knowledge. This section discusses the organization and management of knowledge. It is already mentioned that the knowledge based systems tend to require large amount of knowledge. To access this knowledge effectively, the appropriate structuring of knowledge is must. As knowledge of real world continuously changes, hence the memory organization of knowledge base should not be static one. The dynamic memory organization can accommodate the continuously changing knowledge of world. For this, the continuous reorganization of knowledge, addition of new knowledge and deletion of knowledge is required. As the knowledge base (KB) increases in size and complexity, the access of required knowledge becomes more difficult. The time to search, test, select, and retrieve a minimal amount of requisite knowledge from large amount of knowledge can be very time consuming, if knowledge is poorly organized. The human memory also exhibit remarkable dynamic properties. We are able to adapt to varied changes in the environment and still improve our performance. In our memory, new knowledge is continuously added and existing knowledge is continuously being revised. That means a continuous reorganization of knowledge takes place. This process leads to improved memory performance through most of the span of our lives.

The efficient manipulation of KB is dependent on representation. Beside knowledge representation, the search program should also be able to locate and retrieve the appropriate knowledge in an efficient manner. The most simple but least effective search is exhaustive search. More effective retrieval is accomplished through indexing or grouping the knowledge.

In AI applications, a normal expert system is expected to have thousands or even tens of thousands of rules in its KB, e.g., A XCON system has a rapidly growing KB, which at present time consists of more than 12000 production rules. Large number of rules are needed in the system like this which deal with complex reasoning tasks. If each rule contained about four to five conditions in its antecedent part, then the required searches would be 40000 – 50000. Clearly, time required to perform this number of tests is intolerable. Hence, some form of memory management is needed. The salient features of effective memory organization are as follows:

  (i) It should always be able to accept new knowledge.

  (ii) The organization of knowledge should be such that it should be possible to locate any stored item of knowledge efficiently.

  (iii) The addition of new knowledge should be consistent from the previous one.

  (iv) The organization of knowledge should be in clustered format. This is essential for reasoning and learning functions.

  (v) The organization should facilitate the process of consolidating recurrent incidents and forgetting knowledge when it is no longer needed.

4.6.1 Indexed Organization of Knowledge

As discussed above, it is always advisable to organize the knowledge in the form of clusters. The related clusters should be grouped together in close proximity to each other and be linked to similar concepts through associative relations. The concept of keeping the similar clusters together is called indexing. Access to any given cluster should be possible through either direct or indirect links such as concept pointers indexed by meaning.

The knowledge in practical systems is stored in auxiliary storage. Storage and retrieval of information in secondary storage is performed in terms of equal sized blocks consisting of between 256 and 4096 bytes. The block behaves as minimum unit of data transfer. Clearly, the grouping of related knowledge reduces the number of block transfers and hence total access time.

The indexed organization of clusters greatly reduces the time to determine the storage location of an item. The indexing is done by segregating knowledge into two or more groups and storing the location of the knowledge for each group in smaller index file. The index stores sorted records according to some key. The key can be any unique field of record. Each physical block of main file results in one entry in index file. The following diagram shows indexed file organization.

	Index File		KB File	
	(k, b)		b	k
	007, 100		100	009
	140, 250		100	110
	....			
	....		200	138
Key Value	....		....	....
379	375, 900		200	165
	410, 950		......	......
			900	375
b = block address of record			900	377
k = key			900	379

Fig. 4.4: Index file organization

An index file contains a list of entry pairs (k, b) where the values k are the keys of first record in each block whose starting address is b.

For large indexed file, a binary search can be used to speed up the index file search. A binary search will significantly reduce the search time over linear search when the number of items is not too small. When a file contains n records, the average time for a linear search is proportional to n/2 compared to a binary search time of the order of $\ln_2(n)$.

When the total number of records in a knowledge base file is n with r records stored per block giving a total of b blocks (n = r * b), the average search time for a non indexed sequential search is b/2 block axes time plus n/2 record tests. For indexed organization, search time is b/2 index tests, one block access, and r/2 record tests. A binary index search would require only $\ln_2(b)$ index tests, one block access, r/2 record tests. Thus, for large n and medium r the time saving using binary indexed access is substantial.

The indexing in LISP is implemented with property lists.

4.6.1.1 Human Associative Memory System (HAM)

The HAM is one of the earliest computer models of memory. This memory is organized as a network of propositional binary trees, e.g., the statement, "in a park a hippie touched a debutante" is shown in following Fig. 4.5.

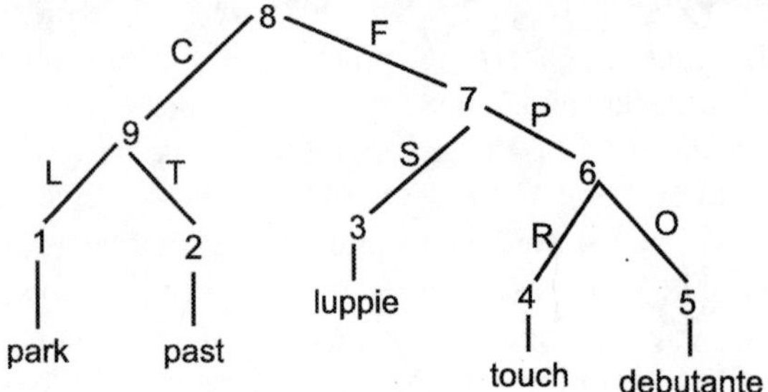

Fig. 4.5: Propositional binary tree for the given sentence

Nodes in the tree are assigned unique numbers and the link labels have following meaning:

C: context for tree facts
e: set membership
F: a fact
L: a location
O: object
P: predicate
R: relation
S: subject
T: time

When HAM is given new sentences, they are parsed into similar tree like memory structure and stored in knowledge base. When HAM is posed with a query, it is formed into a tree structure. This structure is then matched against existing memory structures for the best match. The structure with the closest match is used to formulate and answer to the query.

4.7 BASIC CONCEPTS OF KNOWLEDGE ENGINEERING

This section discusses the basic concepts about an emerging field in Artificial Intelligence called knowledge engineering. Keeping in view what we have learnt so far, knowledge engineering can be defined as *"the art of designing and building knowledge based systems"*, and this art is practiced by knowledge engineers. Knowledge engineering is an applied part of Artificial Intelligence, which, in turn, is a part of computer science. Thus, knowledge engineering is a field within AI that develops knowledge-based systems. Basically, such systems are computer programs. The main ingredients of these programs are: knowledge and reasoning mechanisms to provide solutions to real-world problems and the main objectives of knowledge engineering are building, maintaining and developing knowledge-based systems. Theoretically, then, knowledge engineering is computer science that develops and implements programs that incorporate AI techniques.

4.7.1 Knowledge Engineering Techniques

Various activities of knowledge engineering involved in the development of knowledge-based systems are:
*   Assessment of problem.
*   Acquisition of knowledge and specific preferences.
*   Implementation of structured knowledge into knowledge-base.
*   Testing and validation of inserted knowledge.
*   Development of structured knowledge-based system.
*   Integration and maintenance of the system.
*   Revision and evaluation of the system.

The above list projects the job as straightforward and simple, but knowledge engineering being more art than engineering, things do not work as neatly as shown above. While applying the above activities in practice, phases may overlap, process may be iterative and many challenges could appear.

4.7.2 Knowledge Engineering Principles

As has been described earlier, knowledge acquisition is one of the most important activities of the process to build an expert system. Knowledge engineers have developed number of principles, methods and tools to improve the process of knowledge acquisition. Some of the key principles are stated below:
*   It is known that knowledge is of different types and right approach and technique should be adopted for acquiring desired knowledge.
*   It is also acknowledged that experts are of different types and so is their expertise. Hence, appropriate methods should be adopted.
*   Knowledge engineers recognize that ways to represent knowledge are different.
*   The ways of using knowledge are different; hence, knowledge acquisition process should be selected to meet the aim of the project.
*   Structured methods are used by knowledge engineers to increase the efficiency of the acquisition process.

4.7.3 Views of Knowledge Engineering

There are two main views of knowledge engineering:
*   **Transfer view**- this is the traditional view. Here, human knowledge is transferred into Artificial Intelligence system using conventional knowledge engineering techniques.
*   **Modeling view**- this is the alternative view. Here, attempts are made to model the knowledge and problem-solving techniques into AI system.

4.7.4 Knowledge Engineering Methodologies

A number of developments are continuing to improve the efficiency of knowledge acquisition process. One of these developments is introduction of methodologies. Some of the methodologies to assist the development of knowledge-based systems are:
- CommonKADS
- SPEDE
- MOKA

4.7.4.1 CommonKADS

Many methodologies have been introduced to provide framework to help and guide knowledge acquisition activities. One of such leading methodology is commonKADS. CommonKADS is based on the notion that knowledge acquisition project should be model-driven. CommonKADS advises use of six models: the organization model, the task model, the agent model, the expertise model, the communication model and the design model. It supports most aspects of knowledge based system development project, such as:
- Project management
- Organizational analysis including problem identification
- Knowledge analysis and modeling
- Acquisition of user requirements
- Analysis of system integration issues
- Knowledge-based system design

There are two main perspectives for knowledge-based system development as described by commonKADS:
- **Result perspective**- in this, different aspects of knowledge-based system are modeled and these are continuously improved during the life cycle of a project.
- **Project management perspective**- in this, a risk driven life-cycle model prepared that can be configured into a process suited to a particular project

4.7.4.2 SPEDE

SPEDE methodology was developed under the guidance of Rolles-Royce plc involving staff from Epistemics as consultants. The SPEDE is also a methodology and is a combination of principles, techniques and tools taken from knowledge engineering and applied for use in knowledge management. It provides an effective means to capture, validate and communicate vital knowledge to provide desired benefits.

SPEDE has been specifically developed to act as a training course for knowledge engineers or those assisting a knowledge management activity. The main outcome of most SPEDE projects is an intranet website. However, many projects have delivered quality procedures, process improvement information and expert systems also. Projects using SPEDE methodology follow a set of procedure coordinated by experienced staff. All projects have a coach who coordinates the activities of one or more knowledge engineers.

All SPEDE projects have to pass through a number of checkpoints during the entire span of the project development. These checkpoints are basically meetings held among the experts and knowledge management personnel to assess the results of the present phase and to give "go/no go" signal for moving/not moving to the next stage. Each checkpoint consists of a definite well-defined criterion to ensure that the project is on track to meet the objectives and identify any problems and the actions to be taken. There are in general five checkpoints: project launch review, scoping review, technical review, delivery review and post-delivery review.

4.7.4.3 MOKA

Companies need to continuously improve their business processes mainly to reduce time, to find new solutions, to make *correct first time* and to retain best practices. For this purpose, the knowledge has to be managed and reused. The use of knowledge-based systems (KBS) in aeronautical and automobile industries has increased many folds in recent times because of the above-mentioned reasons. Experience has shown that adopting a systematic methodology and use of knowledge-based systems reduces long term risk and makes the functioning easy and smooth and hence becomes a cost-effective solution to increase productivity. The project called MOKA is intended to satisfy the need of developing KBS by providing both a methodology and supporting software tool.

Methodology and tools Oriented to Knowledge-based engineering Applications (MOKA) is thus, a methodology for developing knowledge-based engineering applications i.e. systems that support knowledge engineers. While it can not be denied that use of KBS provide great support and huge benefits can be derived by using KBS, the lack of a recognized methodology has resulted in a significant risk when developing and maintaining KBS applications. In addition, development and maintenance of knowledge based software tools is a complex and expensive activity. The aim of MOKA is to provide such a methodology, that:

- Reduces lead time and associated cost of developing KBS by 20 – 25%
- Provides a consistent way of developing and maintaining KBS
- Will match international standards
- Makes use of a software tool to support the use of the methodology.

EXERCISES

1. How knowledge is important in making human being intelligent. Explain the importance of knowledge in day to day life.
2. What are various types of knowledge. Explain them giving example of each.
3. What is meant by knowledge acquisition. What are various sources from where knowledge can be gathered.
4. Explain the process of knowledge organization and management with the help of suitable diagram.
5. What important knowledge products are currently being marketed like other commodities. What are some new knowledge products likely to come in future.

5
Logic

5.1 INTRODUCTION

The functioning of human mind had always been a challenging but fascinating area for early philosophers and researchers. No matter "Artificial Intelligence" got its name much later, actual work started thousands of years back, which could well be called artificial intelligence. As we already know, knowledge forms the basis of all the intelligence possessed by human beings. Human mind applies some reasoning process to infer and apply knowledge for problem solving. Although our history is full of thoughts and concepts related to cultural, moral, ethical as well as intellectual aspects of artificial intelligence, we are mainly concerned with intellectual aspect of AI in this part of our scope.

One more phenomenon of human mind which is a very important aspect of intelligence is "thinking". Process of thinking is intricate and complex phenomenon. To understand this, philosophers gave different views and regarded thinking as a form of computation. Thinking could be a process mathematical in nature, which uses computations much like mathematical computations that involve some mechanism. In mathematics, we use operators to perform calculations and using these operators, we come out with results. There is a definite formal language to represent these mathematical calculations. Similarly, thinking results in thoughts. There must be some mechanism and operators involved in process of thinking and evolution of thoughts. The logical starting of such a philosophy is found in the works of Aristotle. Aristotle compiled together the insights, wonders and fears of the early Greek society with the careful analysis and disciplined thought that became the standard for modern science.

For Aristotle, the most fascinating aspect of nature was change. In his *Physics*, he defined "Philosophy of nature" as the study of things that change. He introduced two separate entities as *matter* and *form* for all things. Matter changes into form and form transforms into matter. For example, when *brass* is molded into a sculpture of some *human*, matter brass changes into form human. The matter/form distinction provides a philosophical basis for modern notions such as symbolic computing and data abstraction. In computing, even with numbers, we are actually manipulating patterns that are the forms, with the aspect of solution process that is matter. Identifying and abstracting forms from the medium of its representation not only allows these forms to be manipulated computationally but also provides basis for the theory of data structure which is the heart of modern computer science.

Like *"change"* which is integral part of nature, there are things that never change. Aristotle in his *Metaphysics* developed a science of things that never change. However, we are more concerned about Aristotle's epistemology that is *'science of knowing'*, discussed in his *logic*. Aristotle referred to his logic as the *'instrument'* and investigated whether certain propositions can be said to be 'true' because they are related to other things that are known to be true. For example, if we know, "all men are mortal" and that "Socrates is a man", then we can conclude, "Socrates is mortal." This argument is what Aristotle referred to as a syllogism using the deductive form *modus ponens*. The process of drawing conclusion in the above example is known as *reasoning* in the language of computer science. Reasoning is construction, organization and manipulation of statements to arrive at new conclusions. And, In simple terms, the mechanism involved in the process of reasoning is called logic. Thus, though the formal recognition and axiomatization of reasoning took around two thousand years for its full utilization in the works of Gottlob, Frege, Bertrand Russel, Kurt Godel, Alan Turing, Alfred Tarski and others, its roots may be traced to Aristotle.

Once philosophers started considering thinking as a form of computation, the next step had to be, and was the formalization and mechanization of the process of thinking. In the seventeenth century, Gottfried Wilhelm von Leibniz, with his *Calculus Philosophicus* introduced the first system of formal logic and also, constructed a machine for automating its calculation.

From the above presentation, it is apparent that the idea of formal logic can be traced back to the philosophers of ancient Greece, but its mathematical development really begin with the work of Goerge Boole (1815-1864). Although, Boole made contributions to a number of areas of mathematics, he is best known for his work in mathematical formalization of the laws of logic, a work that forms the very heart of modern computer science. The goal of Boole in developing his system seems quite close to that of contemporary AI researchers. In the first chapter of *"An investigation of the laws of thought"* on which, mathematical concepts of logic and probability are based, Boole described his goal as:

> *"to investigate the fundamental laws of those operations of the mind by which reasoning is performed: to give expression to them in the symbolical language of a calculus, and upon this foundation to establish the science of logic and instruct its method"*

The interpretation of above mentioned goal of Boole will give rise the definition of logic which is hidden in the same. Hence, in one sense, we can define logic as:

> *"Logic is the expression given to the reasoning process performed by mind in the form of symbolic language of a calculus."*

The greatness of Boole's accomplishment lies in the extraordinary power and simplicity of the system he devised. Basically, three operations, "AND" (denoted by * or ∧), "OR" (denoted by + or ∨) and "NOT" (denoted by ¬) formed the heart of his logical calculus. These operations formed the basis of all the subsequent developments in formal logic including the design of modern computers. Boole's language not only provided the basis of binary arithmetic but also demonstrated that an extremely simple formal system was adequate to capture the full power of logic. The system developed by Boole formed the basis of all modern facets of formalized logic, from Russell and Whitehead's *Principia Mathematica*, through the work of Turing and Godel up to modern automated reasoning systems.

In *Foundation of Arithmetic* by Gottlob Frege, a mathematical specification language was created for describing the basis of Arithmetic in a clear and precise manner. With this language, Frege formalized many of the issues first addressed by Aristotle's *logic*. Frege'd language, now called *first-order predicate calculus* presents a tool for describing the propositions and truth values that make up the elements of mathematical reasoning. The first-order predicate calculus offers the tools necessary for automated reasoning and a logical calculus for inferring new expressions.

Another mathematician whose work is important for laying the foundation of modern AI is Alfred Tarski. Tarski created a *theory of reference* wherein the *well-formed formulae* of Frege can be said to be referring to the physical world. Tarski also described his theory of reference and truth-value relationship in one of his papers.

After introduction of digital computers in twentieth century, AI became a viable scientific discipline. By the end of 1940s, digital computers had demonstrated their potential to exhibit intelligence component in programs. Once AI research gathered momentum, importance of knowledge was felt and techniques required to acquire and represent knowledge in formal language became need of the hour. Most AI programs represent knowledge in some formal language that is then manipulated by algorithms. Like graph theory plays an important role in the analysis of problem spaces as well as providing basis for semantic networks, formal logic has emerged as an important representational tool for AI research. Thus, another way to define logic could be as:

"Logic is a language used to represent facts."

There are many knowledge representation techniques, but the use of logic for fact representation has come out as most popular and appropriate method for many applications. Hence, logic is popularly used for designing of knowledge base for AI based programming. The elementary knowledge representation methodologies are:

 (i) Representation using binary numbers

 (ii) Representation as set of pixels

(iii) Representation in graphical form

(iv) Representation in prepositional logic

 (v) Representation in predicate logic

(vi) Representation through semantic net

(vii) Representation using conceptual dependency structures

Out of above methodologies, the first three techniques are elementary knowledge representation techniques. However, from AI viewpoint, most used techniques are from (iv) to (vii) mentioned above.

Generally, a knowledge representation technique should have following characteristics:

 (i) It should be adequate to express all the necessary information.

 (ii) It should provide natural scheme for expressing the required knowledge.

(iii) It should support efficient execution for inferencing purpose.

As mentioned above, logic is a formal language used to represent knowledge and facts. There are two types of logic used to do the good in the field of AI: the *propositional logic* or *propositional calculus* and *predicate calculus*. These are attractive knowledge representation techniques most acknowledged and widely used. These are methods used to represent the real world facts in the form of a language, which uses words, phrases and sentences to represent and reason about properties and relationships in the word. We will study these methods in detail in the subsequent sections.

5.2 PROPOSITIONAL CALCULUS

Propositions are statements used in mathematics. A proposition or sentence is classified as declarative sentence whose value is either 'true' or 'false'. Consider the following sentences in English:

1. New Delhi is the capital of India
2. The square root of 4 is 2.
3. India will be superpower by 2020 AD.
4. Mathematical logic is a difficult subject.
5. No, thank you!
6. This statement is false.

Here the statements 1 and 2 are propositions. They both are 'true'. The outcome of sentence 3 cannot be said as 'true' or 'false', but definitely it cannot be 'both'. Hence statement 3 is a proposition. Sentence 4 is a proposition. Statement 5 is an assertion, so we cannot assign true or false with it. Hence, this cannot be a proposition. Sentence 6 has either 'true' value or 'false'. Hence, it is a proposition.

Propositions are of two types: *atomic propositions* and *molecular propositions* or *complex propositions*. Atomic propositions are single propositions. Like the ones mentioned above are all atomic propositions. Molecular propositions are formed by combining two or more atomic propositions. For example,

"Sachin Tendulkar is a cricketer and Steffi Graf is a tennis player."

This is molecular proposition that is a combination of two atomic propositions "Sachin Tendulkar is a cricketer" and "Steffi Graf is a tennis player".

After understanding the meaning and types of propositions, let us come back to our main area of interest, i.e. propositional calculus. Propositional logic or propositional calculus is basically a language to represent propositions using well defined symbols. If we have to learn English language, we will have to learn its alphabets first. Similarly, in mathematics, basic symbols like '+', '-', 'x' etc. will have to be learnt for performing computations. Hence, first step to describe any language is to understand the 'symbols' used in it. We, thus start with the introduction of formal syntax of propositional calculus.

5.2.1 Syntax of Propositional Calculus

Propositional symbols comprise of *propositions* or statements and *connectives* to combine these propositions. Various symbols used in propositional calculus are defined as follows:

5.2.1.1 Atomic symbol

Atomic symbol is most elementary logic or proposition. It is also called as **literal**. Propositions can represent any phenomenon of the real world. These can be true or false. Any symbol that is a proposition and can be true or false is atomic symbol. Uppercase letters are used to denote the atomic symbols like P, Q, R, and so on. As mentioned earlier, each P, Q, R can be separately true or false. There are two special propositions with fixed meaning. These are 'true' and 'false'. 'True' represents always-true proposition and 'false' represents always-false proposition. Every propositional symbol and truth symbol is a sentence. For example,

true, P, Q and R are sentences.

5.2.1.2 Logical connectives

The connectives are used to join atomic prepositions to form complex structures. These propositions joined with connectives make well-formed formula. These well formed formulas (WFF) are used to represent complex world phenomenon.

Valid connectives used to combine atomic propositions in propositional calculus are defined as follows:

- **not (¬ or negation)** : Any sentence ¬P is called negation of P. Any atomic proposition is either positive or negative. If literal P is true, ¬ P will be false. The negation of a literal or sentence is a sentence, i.e.
  ¬P and ¬false are sentences
- **Conjunction (represented by 'AND' or ∧)**: A sentence whose main connective is 'AND' or '∧' is called conjunction, e.g., P∧Q. The parts P and Q of conjunction are called conjuncts. P∧Q, that is, the value of logic 'P AND Q' will be true if both P and Q are separately true. In case of 'n' number of propositions, their conjunction will be true if all conjuncts are

separately true. The conjunction of two or more sentences is also a sentence, i.e.

P∧¬Q is a sentence

- **Disjunction (represented by 'OR' or ∨):** A sentence whose main connective is 'OR' or '∨' is called disjunction, e.g., P∨Q. The sentences P and Q are called *disjuncts*. P OR Q, that is the value of logic 'P OR Q' will be true if either P or Q or both are true. In case of 'n' number of propositions, the disjunction of these will be true, if any one or more number of disjuncts are true. The disjunction of two or more sentences is also a sentence, i.e. *P∨¬Q is a sentence.*

- **Implication (read as implies, represented as →):** A sentence such as P→Q means P implies Q. That means if P is true, Q is true and if P is false then Q is false. Here P is called premise or antecedent and Q is called conclusion or consequent.

- **Biconditional (read as 'if and only if' and represented as →):** Two sentences P and Q are Biconditional if and only if both are same i.e. P→Q.

- **Equivalence (represented as '≡'):** Equivalence of two sentences P and Q is defined as P ≡ Q and is also a sentence.

In propositional calculus sentences, some more symbols like ( ) and [ ] are also used to group symbols into sub-expressions and hence, to control their order of evaluation and meaning. For example, (P ∨ Q) ≡ R is quite different from P ∨ (Q ≡ R).

5.2.2 The Semantics of Propositional Calculus

In the previous section, we have discussed syntax of propositional calculus by defining some set of rules for producing legal sentences or WFFs. In the present section, we take up the *semantics* or *meaning* of these sentences. The meaning of a propositional sentence is just the value true or false, i.e., it is an assignment of truth-value to the sentence. It is important here to note that the truth of the conclusion of a WFF depends upon the truth of the sentences forming the WFF.

As mentioned earlier, a proposition symbol corresponds to a statement about the world. For example, P may denote a complete sentence as "I am working." A proposition may be either true or false in a particular circumstance. The truth-value assignment to a propositional sentence is called *interpretation*, which is an assertion about its truthness. Alternatively, in simple terms, interpretation determines the truth-value of a statement. For example, consider a statement (P∧Q). One interpretation I_1 assigns 'true' to P and 'false' to Q, whereas, another interpretation I_2 assigns 'true' to P and Q both. Hence statement (P∧Q) will have different truth-values depending upon the truth-values assigned by different interpretations to P and Q.

As mentioned in the previous section, **true** and **false** are parts of the set of well formed sentences of the propositional calculus, hence, it is necessary to differentiate between these and the truth-value assignments. To enforce this distinction, the symbols **T** and **F** are used for truth-value assignments.

Like syntax, we will now define semantics of propositional calculus as follows:

An interpretation of a set of propositions is the assignment of truth-value in the form of T or F to each propositional symbol. The interpretation of truth value for sentences is determined by:

The *truth assignment of negation*, ¬P, where P is any propositional symbol is F, if the assignment to P is T; and T, if assignment to P is F.

The *truth assignment to conjunction*, ∧, is T only when both the conjuncts have the truth-value T; otherwise it is F.

The *truth assignment of disjunction*, ∨, is F only when both the disjuncts have truth-value F; otherwise it is T.

The *truth assignment of implication*, →, is F, only when the symbol before the implication, i.e. premise is T and the symbol after the implication, i.e. the consequent is F; otherwise, it is T.

The *truth assignment of Biconditional*, ↔, is T, only when symbols on both the sides are either T or F; otherwise it is F.

The truth assignments of compound propositions are often described by truth tables. A truth table lists all possible truth-value assignments to the atomic propositions of an expression and gives the truth-value of the expression for each assignment. A truth table, thus, enumerates all the possible worlds of interpretations that may be assigned to an expression. The truth table of sentences formed by using connectives described above is shown below:

Table 5.1: Truth-value of literals using various connectives

P	Q	¬P	P∧Q	P∨Q	P→Q	P→Q
F	F	T	F	F	T	T
F	T	T	F	T	T	F
T	F	F	F	T	F	F
T	T	F	T	T	T	T

Let us consider one real world example to understand the semantics of propositional calculus. Consider, in terms of real world knowledge, the proposition P denotes the phenomenon, "it is cloudy" and Q denotes the phenomenon "it is raining". Then the meaning of various complex propositions will be as follows:

¬P	:	It is not cloudy
¬Q	:	It is not raining
P ∨ Q	:	It is cloudy OR it is raining.
P ∧ Q	:	it is cloudy AND it is raining

P → Q :   it is cloudy indicates, it is raining
P ↔ Q :   it is cloudy indicates, it is raining and it is raining indicates that it is cloudy

There can be further complex structures or WFFs like:

(P ∨ ¬Q) ∧ (P → Q)   :   it is cloudy OR it is not raining AND it is cloudy indicates that it is raining

(¬P ∧ ¬Q) ∨ (P∧Q)   :   it is not cloudy OR it is not raining OR it is cloudy AND it is raining.

Here we do not check the semantics of these formulas like "whether it is practically possible to have rain without clouds or not". These WFFs are only the representations of these phenomenon. The other aspects of well-formed formulae are discussed in proceeding section.

Refer examples 1 to 3 for understanding whatever has been discussed until now.

5.2.3 Well Formed Formula

We have seen that the propositions P ∧ Q and Q ∧ P have same truth-values irrespective of any proposition in place of P and Q. Based on this, the concept of propositional variable and well-formed formula is derived. A propositional variable is a symbol representing any proposition. Note that a real variable is represented by the symbol x. This means that x is not a real number but can take real value. Similarly, a propositional variable is not a proposition, but can be replaced by a proposition.

In practice, there are two methods to define an object:
(i) In terms of the properties possessed by that mathematical object and,
(ii) Using recursion, in which initially some objects are declared and others are recursively defined using basic definition.

Based on the above concept, in logic, the well-formed formula is defined as:

"Well formed formulae consist of atomic symbols joined with connectives."

Hence, P, P∧¬P, P∧Q, P∨Q, P→Q, P↔Q are well-formed formulae. A well-formed Formula (WFF) is defined recursively as:
(i) If P is a propositional variable then it is a WFF.
(ii) If P is a WFF, then ¬ P is a WFF.
(iii) If P and Q are well-formed formulae, then (P ∨ Q), (P ∧ Q), (P → Q) and (P ↔ Q) are well-formed formulae.
(iv) A string of symbols is a WFF if and only if, it is obtained by a finite number of applications of (i) – (iii).

We should note here that:

(i)   A WFF is not a proposition, but if we substitute a proposition in place of a propositional variable, we get a proposition, e.g. $\neg (P \vee Q) \wedge (\neg Q \wedge R) \rightarrow (\neg Q \wedge R)$ is a WFF.

(ii) The parenthesis can be dropped where there is no ambiguity

(iii) The WFF is conveniently also called formula.

(iv) The well formed formulae are conveniently represented as truth table

(v)   A well formed formula for all true entries is called **tautology**

(vi) Two WFFs α and β in propositional variable P1, P2, ... Pn are equivalent if the formula $\alpha \leftrightarrow \beta$ is a tautology. The equivalent statements are represented as $\alpha \equiv \beta$.

(vii) There is a difference between $\alpha \leftrightarrow \beta$ and $\alpha \equiv \beta$. The former is a formula whereas the later is not a formula but it denotes a relation between α and β.

Few laws related to propositional knowledge are stated below:

(i)	Idempotency	:	$P \vee P = P$
		:	$P \wedge P = P$
(ii)	Commutative law	:	$P \vee Q = Q \vee P$
		:	$P \wedge Q = Q \wedge P$
		:	$P \leftrightarrow Q = Q \leftrightarrow P$
(iii)	Associative law	:	$(P \vee Q) \vee R = P \vee (Q \vee R)$
		:	$(P \wedge Q) \wedge R = P \wedge (Q \wedge R)$
(iv)	Distributive law	:	$P \wedge (Q \vee R) = (P \wedge Q) \vee (P \wedge R)$
		:	$P \vee (Q \wedge R) = (P \vee Q) \wedge (P \vee R)$
(v)	De Morgan's rule	:	$\sim (P \vee Q) = \sim P \wedge \sim Q$
		:	$\sim (P \wedge Q) = \sim P \vee \sim Q$
(vi)	Implication removal	:	$P \leftrightarrow Q = \sim P \vee Q$
(vii)	Biconditional elimination	:	$P \rightarrow Q = (P \rightarrow Q) \wedge (Q \rightarrow P)$
(viii)	Absorption law	:	$P \vee (P \wedge Q) \equiv P,\ P \wedge (P \vee Q) \equiv P$
(ix)	Contrapositive	:	$P \Rightarrow Q \equiv \neg Q \Rightarrow \neg P$
(x)	Double negation	:	$P \equiv \neg (\neg P)$
(xi)	Fundamental identities	:	(a) $P \vee \neg P \equiv T$
			(b) $P \wedge \neg P \equiv F$
			(c) $P \vee T \equiv T$
			(d) $P \vee T \equiv P$
			(e) $P \vee F \equiv P$
			(f) $P \vee F \equiv F$
			(g) $(P \Rightarrow Q) \wedge (P \Rightarrow \neg Q) \equiv \neg P$
			(h) $P \Rightarrow Q \equiv (\neg P \vee Q)$

Refer examples 5 to 7 for understanding formation of truth tables.

5.2.4 Properties of Statements

Before moving ahead, let us discusses some properties of propositional calculus statements or WFFs described as follows:

(i) ***Valid***: A sentence is valid, if it is true for all values of inputs or for every interpretation. An all true statement is also called tautology. For example, $P \vee \neg P$ is valid since every interpretation of P results in a true value for $P \vee \neg P$.

(ii) ***Satisfiable***: A statement having at least one interpretation for which it is true, is called Satisfiable. For example, if statement P is Satisfiable, it will have at least one interpretation of P for which the value of P is true. However, P will not necessarily be valid because it is not true for every interpretation of P i.e., a value F for P will result in a value F for sentence P.

(iii) ***Unsatisfiable*** (or ***contradiction***): A statement or preposition is called Unsatisfiable if there is no interpretation for which it is true. For example, $P \wedge \neg P$ is unsatisfiable because it is false for every interpretation of P.

(iv) ***Equivalence***: Two statements s_1 and s_2 are equivalent if for every interpretation they have the same truth-value. For example, two statements P and $\neg (\neg P)$ are equivalent since both have the same truth-value for every interpretation of P.

(v) ***Logical consequence***: Statement s_2 is said to be logical consequence of s_1, if it is satisfied by all interpretations which satisfy s_1. For example, out of given two sentences P and $P \wedge Q$, P is said to be logical consequence of $P \wedge Q$ because for every interpretation for which $P \wedge Q$ is true, P is also true.

These properties of statements are used to derive new statements in the process of inferencing. The technique to find logical consequence provides method for valid inferencing.

The propositional calculus has certain limitations. In this, each atomic symbol is denoted by different proposition. Hence, two propositions "Ram is a student" and "Shyam is a student" are considered as different propositions. However, we know that they share the common property of being students. Similarly, we can't express some facts like, when we move block X from one place to another, it is same that block X is now on block Y (i.e. making assertion ON_X_Y true). In propositional calculus, atoms have no internal structures. Moreover every phenomenon is represented by a separate proposition. Hence, if in the same statement the variable is different, it will be considered as different proposition, e.g., ON_X_Y, and ON_A_B are entirely different in propositional calculus.

5.2.5 Inferencing in Propositional Logic

In logical reasoning, certain number of propositions are assumed to be true, and based on that assumption, some other propositions are derived. This is called inferencing. Logical inference means given a new proposition, find out whether according to facts of knowledge base it is true or not. The propositions that are assumed to be true are called *hypotheses* or *premises*. The proposition derived by using the rule of inference is called *conclusion*. In context of Artificial Intelligence, the propositions are basically facts representing some real world knowledge. It is already mentioned that to model any system, the facts are identified and stored in knowledge base in terms of if – then – else rules. In the inferencing process, the rules are applied in succession (called chaining) till a situation arrives that there is no rule which is applicable. A rule is said to be applicable if the left hand side of rule matches with the proposition. Thus we can say that inferencing is used to perform logical deduction. Formally the inferencing can be defined as: given a set of statements S={S1,S2….Sn} are true, prove a new statement as true or not. The given set of statements are called 'premises' and new statement is called 'conclusion'. One method for drawing the conclusion is using truth table. Other method is inferencing or deduction.

The rules of inference can be simple tautologies in the form of implication. (i.e., $P \rightarrow Q$). For example, $P \rightarrow (P \vee Q)$ is a simple tautology, and it is a rule of inference. This is:

written in the form $\dfrac{P}{P \vee Q}$. Here P denotes a premise. The proposition

below the line is $(P \vee Q)$. This is called conclusion. Presented below are the rules for deriving conclusions:

- **Addition**: From a given statement P, infer $P \vee Q$, where Q can be any other statement. This is also written as:

$$\frac{P}{\therefore (P \vee Q)}$$

For example,

Given   : Adwet is an obedient boy
Conclude   : Adwet is an obedient boy or Sushant is a lazy boy

This rule can be represented in implication form as $P \rightarrow (P \vee Q)$.

- **Conjunction**: From given two sentences or statements P and Q, infer $P \wedge Q$, or:

$$\frac{\begin{array}{c} P \\ Q \end{array}}{\therefore (P \wedge Q)}$$

For example,

Given   : Vishal is an intelligent student
And   : Shyam is a good player
Conclude   : Vishal is an intelligent student and Shyam is a good player

Implication form of this rule is represented as $P \wedge Q \to (P \wedge Q)$.

- **Simplification**: From given sentence $P \wedge Q$, infer P, or:

$$\frac{P \wedge Q}{\therefore P}$$

For example,

Given   : Kate is a beautiful woman and John is an ugly man
Conclude : Kate is a beautiful woman

This rule can be represented in implication form as $(P \wedge Q) \to P$.

- **Modus Ponens**: From given two statements P and $P \to Q$, infer Q. This is also written as:

$$\frac{\begin{array}{c}P\\P \to Q\end{array}}{\therefore Q}$$

For example:

given   : Adwet is intelligent
and   : Adwet is intelligent $\to$ Adwet tops the class
conclude   : Adwet tops the class

This rule is written in implication form as $(P \wedge (P \to Q)) \to Q$.

- **Modus tollens:** From the two given statements $\neg Q$ and $(P \to Q)$, infer $\neg P$, or:

$$\frac{\begin{array}{c}\neg Q\\P \to Q\end{array}}{\therefore \neg P}$$

For example,

Given   : Justin is not a religious person
And   : Justin goes to church daily implies Justin is a religious person
Conclude : Justin does not go to church daily

Implication form of this rule is represented as $(\neg Q \wedge (P \to Q)) \to \neg P$.

- **Chain rule or Hypothetical Syllogism**: From $(P \to Q)$ and $(Q \to R)$, infer $(P \to R)$, or

$$\frac{\begin{array}{c}P \to Q\\Q \to R\end{array}}{\therefore (P \to R)}$$

For example,

Given   : India has natural resources $\to$ India can generate energy
And   : India can generate energy $\to$ India is prosperous country
Conclude : India is prosperous country

This rule is represented in implication form as $((P \to Q) \wedge (Q \to R)) \to (P \to R)$.

- **Disjunctive syllogism**: From two given sentences ¬P and (P ∨ Q), infer Q, or:

$$\neg P$$
$$P \vee Q$$
$$\overline{\qquad\qquad}$$
$$\therefore Q$$

For example,

Given   : Mohit is not a laborious boy
And   : Mohit is a laborious boy or Suchi is an honest girl
Conclude   : Suchi is an honest girl

Implication form of this rule is written as (¬P∧(P ∨ Q))→Q.

- **Constructive dilemma**: From given two sentences ((P→Q)∧(R→S)) and (P∨R), infer (Q∨S), or:

$$(P{\to}Q)\wedge(R{\to}S)$$
$$P\vee R$$
$$\overline{\qquad\qquad}$$
$$\therefore (Q\vee S)$$

For example,

Given   : (Bret loves Kate implies Kate loves Bret) and (Jash hates Sushi implies Sushi hates Jash)
And   : Bret loves Kate or Jash hates Sushi
Conclude   : Kate loves Bret or Sushi hates Jash

This rule is represented in implication form as (((P→Q)∧(R→S))∧(P∨R))→(Q∨S).

- **Destructive dilemma**: From given two sentences ((P→Q)∧(R→S)) and (¬Q∨¬S), infer (P∨R), or:

$$(P{\to}Q)\wedge(R{\to}S)$$
$$\neg Q\vee\neg S$$
$$\overline{\qquad\qquad}$$
$$\therefore (P\vee R)$$

For example,

Given   : Albart scored 85% marks implies Albart is an intelligent student and Steffi scored 54% marks implies Steffi is a weak student
and   : Albart is not an intelligent student or Steffi is not a weak student
conclude   : Albart scored 85% marks or Steffi scored 54% marks

Implication form of this rule is written as $((P{\rightarrow}Q){\wedge}(R{\rightarrow}S)){\wedge}(\neg Q{\vee}\neg S)$ $\rightarrow(P{\vee}R)$.

Refer examples 7 and 8 given ahead for understanding use of these inference rules.

5.2.6 Solved Examples on Propositional Calculus

Example 1:   Find the truth value of following propositions:
    (i)   If 2 is not an integer, then ½ is an integer.
    (ii)   If 2 is an integer, then ½ is an integer.

Solution: Assume propositions P and Q be '2 is an integer' and '1/2 is an integer'. Then in (i) P is false and Q is false, that means $P \rightarrow Q$ is true. In (ii) P is true and Q is false, hence $P \rightarrow Q$ is false.

The above statement indicates that we can prove anything if we start with a false assumption.

Example 2:   Translate the following sentences into propositional forms:
    (a)   If it is not raining and I have time, then I will go to a movie.
    (b)   If it is raining and I will not go to a movie.
    (c)   It is not raining.
    (d)   I will not go to a movie.
    (e)   I will not go to a movie only if it is not raining.

Solution: Consider the following assumptions:
Let P represents the predicate "it is raining".
Q represents the predicate "I have the time".
R represents the predicate "I will go to movie".

Then the above statements can be written as:
    (i) $(\neg P \wedge Q) \rightarrow R$
    (ii) $P \wedge \neg R$
    (iii) $\neg P$
    (iv) $\neg R$
    (v) $R \rightarrow \neg P$

Example 3:   If P, Q, R are the propositions, defined as above. Write the sentences in English corresponding to the following propositional forms:
    (i) $(\neg P \wedge Q) \leftrightarrow R$
    (ii) $(Q \rightarrow R) \wedge (R \rightarrow Q)$
    (iii) $\neg (Q \vee R)$
    (iv) $R \rightarrow \neg P \wedge Q$

Solution:

    (i)   I will go to a movie, if and only if it is not raining and I will have the time.

    (ii)   I will go to a movie, if and only if I have the time.

    (iii)   It is not the case that I have time or I will go to movie.

    (iv)   I will go to a movie if it is not raining or I have time.

Example 4:   Construct the truth table for:

$$A = (P \vee Q) \rightarrow ((P \vee R) \rightarrow (R \vee Q)).$$

Solution: The truth table is given as:

P	Q	R	$P \vee R$	$R \vee Q$	$(P \vee R) \Rightarrow (R \vee Q)$	$(P \vee Q)$	A
T	T	T	T	T	T	T	T
T	T	F	T	T	T	T	T
T	F	T	T	T	T	T	T
T	F	F	T	F	F	T	F
F	T	T	T	T	T	T	T
F	T	F	F	T	T	T	T
F	F	T	T	T	T	F	T
F	F	F	F	F	T	F	T

Example 5:   Show that $A = (P \rightarrow (Q \rightarrow R)) \rightarrow ((P \rightarrow Q) \rightarrow (P \rightarrow R))$ is a tautology.

Solution:

P	Q	R	$Q \Rightarrow R$	$P \Rightarrow (Q \Rightarrow R)$	$P \Rightarrow Q$	$(P \Rightarrow Q) \Rightarrow (P \Rightarrow R)$	A
T	T	T	T	T	T	T	T
T	T	F	F	F	T	F	F
T	F	T	T	T	F	T	T
T	F	F	T	T	F	F	T
F	T	T	T	T	T	T	T
F	T	F	F	T	T	T	T
F	F	T	T	T	T	T	T
F	F	F	T	T	T	T	T

Example 6:   Show that $(P \rightarrow (Q \vee R)) = ((P \rightarrow Q) \vee (P \rightarrow R))$.

Solution:

P	Q	R	Q ∨ R	P⇒R∨Q	P ⇒ Q	(P⇒Q)	(P⇒Q)∨(P⇒R)
T	T	T	T	T	T	T	T
T	T	F	T	T	T	F	T
T	F	T	T	T	F	T	T
T	F	F	F	F	F	F	F
F	T	T	T	T	T	T	T
F	T	F	T	T	T	T	T
F	F	T	T	T	T	T	T
F	F	F	F	F	T	T	T

Example 7:   Derive S from the following premises using a valid argument.
(i) $P \Rightarrow Q$ (ii) $Q \Rightarrow \neg R$ (iii) $P \vee S$ (iv) R

Solution: The following are the steps of the proof.
   (i) $P \Rightarrow Q$ premise (i)
   (ii) $Q \Rightarrow \neg R$ premise (ii)
   (iii) $P \Rightarrow \neg R$ lines 1 and 2 and hypothetical syllogism
   (iv)   R premise (iv)
   (v) $\neg(\neg R)$ using law of double negation
   (vi) $\neg P$ using lines (iii) and (v) and rule of Modus Tollen
  (vii) $P \vee S$ Premise (iii)
 (viii)   S using lines (vi) and (vii) and rule of disjunctive syllogism

Example 8:   Test the validity of following argument:
"If milk is black, then every cow is white. If every cow is white then, it has four legs. If every cow has four legs, then every buffalo is white and brisk. The milk is black. Therefore, the buffalo is white".

Solution: Assume following propositions:
P : 'The milk is black'
Q : 'Every cow is white'
R : 'Every cow has four legs'
S : 'Every buffalo is white'
T : 'Every buffalo is brisk'

The given premises are

(i) $P \rightarrow Q$

(ii) $Q \rightarrow R$

(iii) $R \rightarrow S \wedge T$

(iv) P

The conclusion is

1. P : premise (iv)
2. $P \Rightarrow Q$: premise (i)
3. Q : using rule of modus ponens
4. $Q \Rightarrow R$: premise (ii)
5. R : using lines 4 and 5 and rule of modus ponens
6. $R \Rightarrow S \wedge T$: premise (iii)
7. $S \wedge T$: using modus ponens in lines 5 and 6
8. S : using rule of simplification

5.3 PREDICATE LOGIC

Predicate logic is another logic representation scheme, which is more suited to represent real world phenomenon. We have discussed the limitations of propositional logic earlier. The predicate logic overcomes those limitations. It represents the phenomenon by creating the symbols called predicates, directly from the phenomenon. Hence, it is a representation that is more realistic. The predicate is a declarative part of sentence describing the properties of an object or relation among the objects, e.g. in the sentence "Ram is a student", "*is a student*" is defined as predicate.

Sentences involving the predicates, that describe the property of objects are denoted by $P(x)$, where P denotes the predicate and x is a variable denoting any object, e.g., $P(x)$ can denote "x is a student'. In this sentence, x is a variable and P denotes the predicate "is a student'.

The sentence "x is a father of y" also involves a predicate 'is father of'. Here the predicates describe the relation between two persons. This can be written as $F(x, y)$. Similarly, $2x + 3y = 4z$ can be described by $S(x, y, z)$.

We should note that $P(x)$ looks like a proposition, but actually, it is not a proposition. As $P(x)$ involves a variable x, we cannot assign a truth value to $P(x)$. However, if we replace x by an individual object, we get a proposition, e.g., if we replace x by "Ram" in $P(x)$, we get a proposition.

The predicate logic has following characteristics:

(i) It has sound theoretical foundation.

(ii) Inferencing can be applied in predicate logic.

(iii) It allows accurate representation of real world facts.

(iv) It is commonly used for program design.

(v) If the truth-value for two different interpretations are same under every interpretation, they are said to be equivalent.

(vi) A predicate that has no variable is called a ground atom.

It is important to note here that the predicate calculus we are studying is *first order predicate logic*, popularly known as **FOPL**. First order predicate calculus allows quantified variables to refer to objects in the domain of discourse and not to predicate or functions. There are higher order predicate calculi also. Some researchers have used higher order languages to represent knowledge in natural language understanding programs however; FOPL is most suited and widely used for representing knowledge in almost all the application areas of AI.

5.3.1 The Syntax of Predicate Calculus

Like in propositional calculus, we will understand the syntax, i.e. the symbols used in predicate calculus. Before defining the syntax of correct expressions in the predicate calculus, we will define an alphabet and grammar for creating the symbols of the language. Predicate calculus symbols, like the tokens in programming language, are irreducible syntactic elements, i.e. they cannot be broken into their component parts by the operations of the language.

5.3.1.1 Predicate Calculus Symbols

In this section, we will discuss basic terminology of Predicate logic comprising of strings of letters and digits beginning with a letter. Blanks and non-alphanumeric characters cannot appear within the string. Underscore may be used to improve readability. The alphabets that make up the symbols of the predicate calculus are presented below:
(i)   The set of letters both uppercase and lowercase of the English alphabet.
(ii) The set of digits 0 to 9.
(iii) The underscore _.

Special characters like #, $, *, / , ", are not included.
Valid predicate calculus symbols are: George, weather, XXXX, son_of, Father_of.
The invalid symbols are: 3milind, xy%ab, ***&32.
Symbols are used to denote objects, or properties or relations in a real world of discourse. The symbols are generally given names which indicate appropriate meaning. Thus, though l(g, k) and likes(Gaurav, Suresh) are formally equivalent, but second formalism represents the meaning more explicitly.
Parentheses, commas and *periods* are used to construct well formed structure and do not denote objects or relations in the world. These are called improper symbols.
Predicate calculus symbols may represent *variables, constants, functions* or *predicates.*

Constants

Constants represent specific objects or properties of real world. Constant symbols must begin with a lowercase letter. Thus, adwet, 5, -25, bag, red, train_2432 or tree, are examples of well-formed constant symbols.

Variables

Variable symbols are used to represent general classes of objects or properties in the world. Variables can assume different values over a given domain. Variables are represented by symbols beginning with an uppercase letter. Thus, Rohit, Dorthy, KAte are examples of legal variables whereas, moHIT, blue and jOY are not the variable symbols.

Functions

Predicate calculus also consists of symbols called functions on objects in the world of discourse. Functional symbols, like constants, also begin with a lowercase letter. Functions denote a mapping of one or more elements of a *domain* into the elements of *range*. Elements of domain and range are objects in the world of discourse. Thus, f, g, h or father_of, student_of are some of the examples of function symbols.

Every functional symbol has an associated *arity* with it. Arity denotes the number of elements in the domain mapped onto each element of the range. Thus, father could denote a function of arity 1 that maps people onto their male parent, i.e. father. Similarly, plus could be a function of arity 2 that maps two numbers onto their arithmetic sum. For example,

father (adwet) and plus(4,5)

The function symbols of any arity, are a string of alphanumeric characters indicating the functionality of predicate, e.g., mother_of, distance between etc. Thus, an n-arity function can be represented as:

$$f(t_1, t_2, t_3, \ldots\ldots t_n).$$

The above function is also called *function expression*, where f is function symbol and $t_1, t_2, t_3, \ldots\ldots t_n$ are called its arguments. The arguments are elements from the domain of the function. The number of arguments is equal to the arity of the function. Thus,

$f(x, y)$
father (Adwet)
age_of (Ravi)
plus (3,6),

are examples of well-formed function expressions.

The last expression is of arity 2 and its value is integer 9. The act of replacing a function expression with its value is known as *evaluation*. A zero arity function is a constant.

If we summarize whatever has been discussed in the above section, we get that predicate calculus symbols consist of:

1. *Truth symbols* **true** and **false**.
2. *Constant symbols,* which are symbol expressions of fixed-value terms having the first character lowercase.
3. *Variable symbols,* which assume different values and are symbol expressions having first character uppercase.
4. *Function symbols,* which denote relations defined on a given domain and are symbol expressions having the first character lowercase. Functions have an attached arity indicating the number of elements of the domain mapped onto each element of the range.

Terms

Consider an example of function expression mentioned above:

$$f(t_1, t_2, t_3, \ldots\ldots t_n).$$

The above function expression consists of a function constant f of arity n, followed by its n arguments, $t_1, t_2, t_3, \ldots\ldots t_n$, enclosed in parentheses and separated by commas. These arguments are known as ***terms.***

A *term* in the language of predicate calculus is any, out of a constant, variable or function expression. A term may be used to denote objects and properties in a problem domain. For example, consider the following expression:

Father (father(Adwet), Jyoti)

Here, who is father of Adwet is unknown, however, it is certain that he is a person. Since father is a function and father (Adwet) is function expression, it is a term in predicate logic. Other examples of term are:

mouse

A

red

ravi

mother(smriti)

Predicates

Predicate symbols represent relations or functional mappings from the elements of domain D to the values true or false. Like functional symbols, predicate symbols are also attached with its arguments called arity. A predicate symbol begins with a lowercase letter. Predicate denotes relation among its arguments. For example,

loves (john, sushi)

likes (arti, mukul)

helps (rohit, shyam)

friends(father_of(adwet),father_of(sushma)

In above examples, predicates *loves, likes, helps* and *friends* indicate the relationship between their respective elements or arguments. Like functions, predicates may also have n number of arguments. For example,

$$P(t_1, t_2, t_3, \ldots\ldots t_n),$$

where P is a predicate and $t_1, t_2, t_3, \ldots\ldots t_n$ are its arguments. Here n is called arity of predicate P. A 'zero-arity' predicate is a constant predicate or a proposition.

Connectives

Like in propositional calculus, predicate calculus uses following five connective symbols:
- *Conjunction* : denoted by AND or $\wedge$
- *Disjunction* : denoted by OR or $\vee$
- *Negation*   : denoted by NOT or $\neg$
- *Implication* : denoted by $\rightarrow$
- *Equivalence* : denoted by $\equiv$

Quantifiers

There are two types of quantifier symbols:
(i) $\exists$, known as existential quantifier, where $(\exists x)$ means for some x or there is an x, and
(ii) $\forall$, known as universal quantifier, where $(\forall x)$ means for all x.

5.3.1.2 Predicate Calculus Sentences

An atomic sentence is a predicate constant of arity n followed by n terms t_1, t_2, $t_3, \ldots\ldots t_n$, enclosed in a parenthesis and separated by commas. Every atomic sentence is a sentence. Predicate calculus sentences are defined as:
1. The truth values 'true' and 'false' are atomic sentences.
2. If **s** is a sentence then its negation $\neg$**s** is also a sentence.
3. If s_1 and s_2 are sentences then their conjunction $s_1 \wedge s_2$ is also a sentence.
4. If s_1 and s_2 are sentences then their disjunction $s_1 \vee s_2$ is also a sentence.
5. If s_1 and s_2 are sentences then their implication $s_1 \rightarrow s_2$ is also a sentence.
6. If s_1 and s_2 are sentences then their equivalence $s_1 \equiv s_2$ is also a sentence.
7. If **X** is a variable and **s** is a sentence then $\exists$**Xs** is also a sentence.
8. If **X** is a variable and **s** is a sentence then $\forall$**Xs** is also a sentence.

As mentioned earlier, atomic sentence is predicate constant of arity n. For example, let **plus** is a function symbol and **equal** is predicate symbol then,

plus(7,3) is a function expression and not an atomic sentence.

equal (plus (7,3),10) is an atomic sentence.

5.3.2 Semantics of Predicate Logic

The semantics defines the rules for determining the *truth- value* of a sentence in context of a particular model. As we have learnt above, the propositional logic simply fixes value *true* or *false* with every propositional symbol. However, normally the real world events cannot be satisfactorily represented by just two values as true or false. Hence, for the designing of practical AI system the use of predicate logic is preferred. As mentioned earlier, in predicate logic the symbols are chosen according to the meaning of symbols in terms of objects, properties and relations in the world. Predicate calculus semantics provide a formal basis for determining the truth value of well-formed expressions. The truth of a predicate sentence depends upon the mapping of the constants, variables, predicates and functions into objects and relations in the domain of discourse. The truth of the relationship in the domain determines the truth of the corresponding expression. For example, information about a person Adwet and his friends Gaurav and Piyush may be represented by:

friends(adwet, gaurav)
friends(adwet, piyush)

If the relationship between adwet and his friends is true, the above expressions will have truth value T. If gaurav is the friend of Adwet but piyush is not, the second expression will have a truth value F.

5.3.2.1 Interpretation

An interpretation over D, where d is a nonempty set, is defined as an assignment of the entities of D to each of the constant, variable, predicate and function symbol of a predicate calculus expression, such that:

1. Each constant is assigned an element of D.
2. Each variable is assigned to a nonempty subset of D.
3. Each predicate p of an arity n arguments from D and defines a mapping from D^n into $\{T,F\}$.
4. Each function f of arity m is defined on m arguments of D and defines a mapping from D^m into D.

The meaning of a predicate expression is a truth-value assignment over the interpretation for a given interpretation.

5.3.2.2 Truth value of predicate calculus expressions

Let us given an expression E and an interpretation I for E over a nonempty set D. In this case, the truth-value for E is determined as:

1. The truth -value of symbol 'true' is T and that of 'false' is F.
2. The value of an atomic sentence is either T or F depending upon interpretation I.
3. The value of negation of a predicate sentence is T if the value of the sentence is F, and is F if the value of the sentence is T.
4. The truth-value of the conjunction of two sentences is T if value of both sentences is T, and is F otherwise.

5. The truth-value of disjunction of two sentences is T if value of both sentences is T, otherwise it is F.

6. The truth value of implication is F only when the sentence before the implication is T and the truth value of the sentence after the implication is F; otherwise it is T.

7. The truth-value of equivalence is T only when both the sentences have the same truth assignments for interpretation I; otherwise it is F.

8. The truth-value of $\forall$Xs is T if s is T for all assignments to X for I, and is F otherwise.

9. The truth-value of $\exists$Xs is T if there is an assignment to X in the interpretation for which s is T; otherwise it is F.

5.3.2.3 Use of quantifiers

Sometimes the facts are represented using some quantifiers. It means they somehow use numbers by using 'nobody', 'some people', 'somebody', 'all' type of phrases in representation. In predicate calculus to represent such types of facts which indicate some numerical quantity, '*quantifiers*' are used. There are two types of quantifiers:

(i) *Universal Quantifier*: It is used to represent the phrase 'for all'. It indicates the true value of sentence for all values of variables. It is symbolically represented by $\forall$, e.g.,

    (a)   All Indians love India.

    (b) $\forall$x: likes (x, ice cream) (that means for all values of x, x likes ice cream. Which effectively means that everybody likes ice cream)

    (c)   'for all x, $x^2 = (-x)^2$ is written as $\forall$ x Q (x), where $Q(x) = x^2$

(ii) *Existential quantifier*: It is used to represent the phrase 'there exist'. It indicates that variable value is true for at least one interpretation. It is symbolically represented by $\exists$, e.g.,

    (a) $\exists$ y: bestfriend (y, Adwet). That means there is one value of y, which is a best friend of Adwet. This effectively means that Adwet has one best friend.

    (b)   The sentence 'There exists x such that $x^2 = 5$" is written as $\exists$x: R(x), where R(x) is $x^2 = 5$.

Refer examples 9 for understanding representation of sentences in symbolic form.

5.3.3 Representing the Facts using FOPL

Let us discuss how real world facts are represented in predicate logic.

See following real world facts and their representation.

Facts	Representation
(i) Vishwant is a boy	boy(vishwant)
(ii) Adwet is intelligent boy	intelligentboy(adwet)
(iii) Vidushi is girl	girl(vidushi)
(iv) It is evening	evening
(v) If it is night, then it is not a day	night $\rightarrow \neg$day
(vi) It is my house	Myhouse
(vii) The color of my house is brown	colormyhouse(brown)
(viii) Snow is white	snow(white) or colorsnow(white)
(ix) We live on earth	live(earth)
(x) It is raining	raining
(xi) Sun rises in the east	sunrises(east)

Here, boy, intelligent boy, girl etc. are predicates. The predicates are chosen in such a way that they represent the main theme of statement. Here evening, raining, myhouse etc. are main meaning of the sentence. In predicate logic, the real world facts are represented using wffs made by predicate. The facts represented above are simple and single wffs. Compound predicate statements are formed by using logical connectives described earlier.

Following are some examples of compound sentences:

1.   If it is raining, then sky will be cloudy.
       raining $\rightarrow$ cloudy(sky)

2.   If it is raining then weather will be humid.
       raining $\rightarrow$ weather (humid)

3.   If it is raining then it will not be dry.
       raining $\rightarrow \neg$dry

4.   If you will work hard, you would succeed.
       workhard $\rightarrow$ succeed

The predicates may also be defined on multiple arguments, e.g., for a sentence like "it is rained on Tuesday", can be represented by creating a predicate weather, which indicates the relationship between a day and its weather e.g., weather(tuesday, rain).

Example of some more predicates are:

Statement	Representation
(i) Rajesh is a tall boy.	tallboy(rajesh)
(ii) Manmohan singh is prime minister of India	primeminister(manmohansingh, India)
(iii) Weather is cold in Himalayas	weather (cold, Himalayas)
(iv) John is a father of Bob	father(john, bob)
(v) Roses are red and violets are blue	red(roses)∧blue(violets)
(vi) Every elephant has a trunk	$\forall x$: elephant (x) →hastrunk(x)
(vii) Every chicken hatched from an egg	$\forall x$: chicken (x) → hatched_from_an_egg
(viii) All dogs are mammals	$\forall x$: dog(x)→mammal(x)
(ix) No dog is an elephant	$\forall x$: dog(x) →¬ elephant(x)
(x) Some programs have bugs	$\exists x$: program(x)→ have_bugs(x)
(xi) None of my programs have bugs	$\forall x$: program(x) ∧ created_by(x, me) → ¬have_bugs(x)
(xii) All of your programs have bugs	$\forall x$: program(x) ∧ created_by(x, you) → have_bugs(x)
(xiii) Anyone with two or more spouses is a bigamist	$\exists x$: two_or_more_spouse(x)→ bigamist(x)
(xiv) Some language is spoken by every person in this room	$\forall x,\exists x$: Person_this_room(x) ∧ language(y) →speak(x, y)
(xv) The coat of cupboard belongs to Reena	$\forall x$: coat(x) ∧ cupboard(x) → belongs (x, reena)
(xvi) One of the coat in the cupboard belong to Sarah	$\exists x$: coat (x) ∧ cupboard (x) → belongs (x, Sarah)
(xvii) Pratibha only likes easy games	likes (pratibha, easygames)
(xviii) Boxing is hard	hard(boxing)
(xix) All the indoor games are easy	$\forall x$: indoorgame(x) → easy(x)
(xx) Chess is an indoor game	indoorgame(chess)

5.3.4 Inferencing in Predicate Calculus

Before discussing the rules for inference, it should be noted that:

(i) The proposition formulas are also predicate formulas.

(ii) The predicate formulas where all the variables are quantified are proposition formulas. Therefore, all the rules of inference for the proposition formulas are applicable to predicate calculus wherever necessary.

For predicate sentences not involving connectives, e.g., A(x), P(x, y), we can get equivalences and rules of inference similar to those for propositional calculus described in sections 5.2.3 and 5.2.4. We will have to replace propositional variables by predicate variables only.

Some necessary equivalence involving two quantifiers and valid implications are given below:

(i) $\exists x\ (P(x) \vee Q(x)) \equiv \exists x\ P(x) \vee \exists x\ Q(x)$
$\exists x\ (P \vee Q(x)) \equiv P \vee (\exists x\ Q(x))$

(ii) $\forall x\ (P(X) \wedge Q(x)) \equiv \forall x\ P(x) \wedge \forall x\ (x)$
$\forall x\ (P \wedge Q(x)) \equiv P \wedge (\forall x\ Q(x))$

(iii) $\neg\ (\exists x\ P(x)) \equiv \forall x\ \neg\ (P(x))$

(iv) $\neg\ (\exists x\ P(x)) \equiv \exists x\ \neg\ P(x))$

(v) $\exists x\ (P \wedge Q(x)) \equiv P \wedge (\exists x\ Q(x))$

(vi) $\forall x\ (P \vee Q(x)) \equiv P \vee (\forall x\ Q(x))$

(vii) $\forall x\ P(x) \Rightarrow \exists x\ P(x)$

(viii) $\forall x\ P(x) \vee \forall x\ Q(x) \Rightarrow \forall x\ P(x) \vee Q(x)$

(ix) $\exists x\ (P(x) \wedge Q(x)) \Rightarrow \exists x\ P(x) \wedge \exists x\ Q(x)$

Refer examples 10 to 13 given ahead on use of rules of inference.

5.3.5 Summary of Predicate Logic

Based on the above discussion, we can recapitulate that predicate logic language consists of the following:

(i)   Alphabet:
-   a set of constant terms
-   a set of variables
-   a set of predicate, each taking a specified number of arguments
-   a set of functions, each taking a specified number of arguments
-   the connectives 'if', 'and', 'or', and 'not'
-   the quantifiers 'exists' and 'for all'

(ii)   The terms of the language are:
-   the constant terms
-   variants
-   functions applied to the correct number of terms.

(iii)   The formulas of language are:
-   A predicate applied to the correct number of terms
-   If p and q are formulas, then (if p q), (and p q), (or p q), and (not p) are formulas.
-   If x is a variable, and p is a formula, then (exists (x), p) and (for all (x), p)

(iv)   Vocabulary of logic:

(i)   A world's objects are terms.

(ii)   Variables ranging over a world's object are terms

(iii)   Functions are terms. The arguments to functions and the value returned are terms. Terms are the only thing that appear as arguments to predicates.

(iv)   Atomic formulas are individual predicates together with arguments.

(v)   Literals are atomic formulas and negated atomic formulas.

(vi) Well formed formulas are defined recursively, i.e.

    (a) Literal are wffs.

    (b) Wffs that are connected together by valid connectives are wffs.

    (c) Wffs surrounded by quantifiers are also wffs.

5.3.6 Solved Examples on Predicate Calculus

Example 9:   Express the following sentences involving predicates in symbolic form:

1. All students are clever
2. Some students are not successful
3. Every clever student is successful
4. There are some successful students who are not clever
5. Some students are clever and successful

Answer: As quantifiers are involved, we have to specify, the universe of discourse. We can take the universe of discourse as the set of all students.

      Let c(x) denote 'x is clever'

      Let s(x) denote 's is successful'

      Then sentence l can be written as "x C(x).

      Sentences 2-5 can be written as :—

$\exists x \, (\neg \, S(x))$

$\forall x \, (c(x) \Rightarrow S\,(x))$

$\exists x \, (\, S(x) \wedge \neg \, (c(x))$

$\exists x \, (c(x) \neg \, S\,(x))$

Example 10:   Discuss the validity of following argument:

      All graduates are educated.

      Jack is a graduate.

      Therefore, Jack is Educated

Answer: Let the notations are:

      (i) G(x) : 'x is a graduate'

      (ii) E(x): 'x is educated'

      (iii) J : 'Jack'

Hence, given premises are

      (i) $\forall(G(x) \Rightarrow E(x))$ and

      (ii) G (J)

the conclusion is E(J)

$\forall(G(x) \Rightarrow E(x))$ premise (i)

$G(J) \Rightarrow E(J)$ universal instantiation

$G(J)$ premise (ii)

$\therefore E(J)$

Example 11: Find out whether argument is true or not.

All graduates can read and write.

Ram can read and write

Therefore Ram is a graduate

Answer: Let G(x) denote 'x is a graduate'

Let L(x) denote 'x can read and write'

Let R denote 'Ram'

The premises are $\forall x\ (G(x) \Rightarrow L(x))$ and $L(R)$

The conclusion is $G(R)$

$((G(R) \Rightarrow L(R)) \wedge L(R) \Rightarrow G(R)$ is not a tautology. Hence, we can not derive $G(R)$.

Example 12: State, the converse, opposite and Contrapositive to the following statements:

(a) If a triangle is isosceles, then two of its sides are equal.

(b) If there is no unemployment in INDIA, then the Indians won't go to the USA for employment.

Answer: If $P \Rightarrow Q$ is a statement, then its converse, opposite, and Contrapositive, statements are $Q \Rightarrow P$, $\neg P \Rightarrow \neg Q$, $\neg Q \Rightarrow \neg P$ respectively.

(a) Converse: If two of the sides of a triangle are equal, then the triangle is isosceles.

Opposite: if the triangle is not isosceles , then two of its sides are not equal.

Contrapositive: if two of the sides of a triangle are not equal, then the triangle is not isosceles.

(b) Converse: if the Indians won't go to USA for employment then, there is no unemployment in INDIA.

Opposite: if there is unemployment in INDIA, then the Indian's will go USA for employment.

Contrapositive: If the Indians go to the USA for employment, then there is unemployment in INDIA.

5.4 RESOLUTION

One practical application of Artificial Intelligence is theorem proving. The method to prove theorem is to use proof procedure. Proof procedures use manipulations known as '*sound rules of inference*', that produce new expressions from old expressions such that new models are guaranteed to be models of the new ones. The most straightforward proof procedure is to apply sound rules of inference to the axioms, and to the results of applying sound rules of inference, until the desired theorem appears.

Resolution is one procedure used for theorem proving. Resolution works on the principle of mechanical inferencing using symbolic FOPL expressions. Basic principle of resolution is:

> *If there is an axiom of the form $E_1 \vee E_2$ and there is another axiom of the form $\neg E_2 \vee E_3$, then E_2 and $\neg E_2$ being identical and opposite to each other, get cancelled, and after their cancellation, with these two axioms $E_1 \vee E_3$ logically follows.*

Mathematically, the resolution is defined as:

> Given two clauses C_1 and C_2 with no variables in common, if there is a literal L_1 in C_1, which is complement of a literal L_2 in C_2, both L_1 and L_2 are deleted and a disjuncted C is formed from the remaining reduced clauses. The new clause C is known as *resolvent* of C_1 and C_2.

Hence, resolution is the process of generating these resolvents from a set of clauses. Resolution based theorem proving works on the technique of *'refutation'*. That means, initially it presumes that statement to be proved is not true, and then it proves that whatever we have assumed is not true, and hence the original statement is true. Resolution with factoring is *complete* in the sense that it will always generate the empty clause from a set of Unsatisfiable clauses. For example,

Suppose we have a set of clauses or axioms C_1, C_2, ... C_n and we wish to deduce or prove the clause D, that is, to show that D is a logical consequence of C_1 & C_2 & ...& C_n. First we negate D and generate a clause $\neg$D, then this newly generated clause is added to the set of clauses C_1, C_2, ... C_n. Then using resolution principle [i.e. $(\neg P \vee Q)$ and, $(\neg Q \vee R)$ is replaced by $(\neg P \vee R)$] together we show that the set is *unsatisfiable* by deducing a contradiction. In the similar manner, in the big system where there are multiple clauses, all pairs of resolvable clauses are identified and resolved.

The resolution of clauses $(\neg P \vee Q)$ and $(\neg Q \vee R)$ is written as:

$$\frac{(\neg P \vee Q), \ (\neg Q \vee R)}{(\neg P \vee R)}$$

The resolution procedure is summarized as:
 (i) Assume that the negation of the theorem, which is to be proved, is true.
 (ii) Show that the axioms and the assumed negation of the theorem together cannot be true.
(iii) Conclude that the assumed negation of the theorem cannot be true, because it leads to contradiction.
(iv) Conclude that the theorem must be true as the assumed negation of the theorem is not true.

Resolution is applicable only on the facts represented in clausal form. Let us first understand what clausal form is and how to represent a propositional fact to clausal form. Clause is a representation of fact where different literals have disjunctive relation. A clause having no variable is called '*ground clause*'. A clause having at the most one positive literal is '*horn clause*'.

The conversion of propositional formulae to clausal form is done through following steps:

(i) Eliminate the implication.
(ii) Move the negation down to atomic formulas
(iii) Eliminate the existential quantifier
(iv) Rename the variables, if necessary.
(v) Move the universal quantifiers to the left.
(vi) Move the disjunction down to the literals
(vii) Eliminate the conjunctions.
(viii) Rename the variables, if necessary.
(ix) Eliminate the universal quantifiers.

The conversion is elaborated as follows:

Step 1: Eliminate implication and equivalence using replacement. $P \rightarrow Q$ is replaced by $\neg P \vee Q$ and $P \leftrightarrow Q$ is replaced by $(\neg P \vee Q) \wedge (\neg Q \vee P)$.

Step 2: Move all negations to immediately precede an atom i.e., replace $\neg(\neg P)$ by P and use De Morgan's laws for other replacements i.e., $\neg(a \wedge b) = \neg a \vee \neg b$ and $\neg(a \vee b) = \neg a \wedge \neg b$. Replace $\exists x: P(x)$ by $\forall x: \neg P(x)$ and $\neg(\forall x: P(x)) = \exists x: \neg P(x)$ i.e., use existential quantifier for removing negative literal and universal quantifier.

Step 3: Introduce dummy variable to segregate binding of variables, e.g., the expression $\forall x: P(x) \rightarrow (\exists x (Q(x))$ is rewritten using a new variable as $\forall x: P(x) \rightarrow (\exists y(Q(y))$. Perform the introduction of new variable throughout in the FOPL statement.

Step 4: Eliminate existential quantifiers by introducing new constants. Conceptually existential quantifier indicates the presence of one specific value for some FOPL. This is replaced by a constant, e.g., statement $(\exists y(\text{principal}(y))$ is transformed to statement principal (name), where variable holds the value of the real name of the principal. This process of removing existential quantifier is called as skolemisation. If the existential quantifier falls in the scope of universal quantifier then value that satisfies predicate depends upon the value of universal variable, e.g.,

$$\forall x: \exists y : \text{student}(y, x)$$

That means for all student x there will be one teacher y. The same concept can also be written as $\forall x:$ student (teacher(x), x).

Teacher (x) is newly introduced predicate, which means teacher of x. as for every student a teacher is must, and for every student there will be a unique teacher, so instead of calling that variable 'x' directly, call it teacher(x). The newly introduced predicate is called *skolem function*. Variables are removed using skolem function.

Step 5:   Remove all universal quantifiers and bring the expression in conjunctive normal form. That is remove 'OR' by using theorem a∨(b∨c) = (a∨b)∨c and remove 'AND' by using distributive property i.e. (a∧b)∨c = (a∨c)∧(b∨c)

The algorithm of resolution in propositional logic is represented as follows:

5.4.1 Resolution Algorithm

Algorithm in Propositional Logic

1. Convert all the propositions of input function F to clause form.
2. Assume the negation of the literal is true (say ¬ P). Convert this to clause form and add it to the set of clauses of step 1.
3. Repeat following steps, either a contradiction is found or no progress can be made:
   (i) Select two clauses and call them parent.
   (ii) Resolve them together, if possible. The resulting clause   is called 'Resolvent.'
   (iii) If the Resolvent is empty clause then a contradiction will be found. If it is not, then add it to the set of clauses available to the procedures.

Algorithm in Predicate Logic

1. Convert all statements of F to clause form.
2. Assume ¬ P is true and add the clausal form of result, to existing set of clauses.
3. Repeat the following steps until either result is obtained or no progress can be made:
   (i) Select two clauses called 'parent' clauses.
   (ii) Resolve them together. The Resolvent will be disjunction of all literals of both parent clauses with appropriate substitution performed.
   (iii) If Resolvent is empty clause, then a contradiction will be found. If it is not, then add it to the set of clauses available to the procedure.

5.4.2 Skolemisation

In predicate logic, the existential and universal quantifiers are used. As discussed earlier that Skolemisation (after the name of logician Thoraf Skolem) is the process of managing these quantifiers. In the process of skolemisation, for universal quantifiers nothing changes and such variables are always turned into pattern matching variables. The universal quantification becomes implicit in the fact that such a variable will match anything.

The removal of existential variable is trickier. Every existential variable, whose arguments are the universal variable, must be turned into a function term from quantifiers, whose scope include that of existential quantifier. This term than replaces every occurrence of variable.

The Skolemisation is summarized as:

(i)   Determine which variables are existential and which are universal.

(ii) Replace each existentially quantified variable by a function. The arguments of that function are universally quantified variables, which include the existential in their scope.

(iii) If two different universally quantified variables have same name, rename one of them.

(iv) Replace each universally quantified variable 'v' by simply v, i.e., $\forall x{:}v(x)$ is replaced by v.

Refer examples 13 to 16 for better understanding of resolution principles.

5.4.3 Types of Resolution

Resolution can be of several types depending upon the number and types of parents. Some of them are discussed below:

Unit Resolution

A number of clauses are resolved simultaneously to produce a unit clause. All except one of the clauses are the unit clauses, and that one clause has exactly one more literal than the total number of unit clauses, e.g., resolving the set,

$$\{\neg married\ (x, y) \vee \neg mother\ (x, z) \vee father\ (y, z),$$
$$married\ (sushma, gaurav), \neg father\ (gaurav, mukesh)\},$$

where the substitution $\beta = \{\ sushma\ /x, gaurav/y, mukesh/z\}$ is used, results in the unit clause

$$\neg MOTHER\ (sushma, mukesh)$$

Binary Resolution

Two clauses having complementary literals are combined as disjuncts to produce a single clause after deleting the complimentary literals, e.g., the binary resolvent of :

$$\neg P(x, a) \vee Q(x)\ and\ \neg Q\ (b) \vee R(x)$$
$$is\ \neg P(b, a) \vee R(b)$$

The substitution $\{b/x\}$ was made in two parent clauses to produce the complimentary literals $Q(b)$ and $\neg Q(b)$ which were then deleted from the disjunction of the two parent clauses.

Linear Resolution

When each resolved clause C_i is a parent to the clause C_{i+1} (i = 1, 2,.......n-1), the process is called linear resolution, e.g., given the set S of clauses with C_0 Í S, C_n, is derived by a sequence of resolutions, C_0 with some clause B_0 to get C_1, then C_1 with some clause B_1 to get C_2 , and so on until C_n has been derived.

The resolution gives us technique to implement the concept of automated reasoning. But unless some further refinements are done, the resolution can be intolerably inefficient. Randomly resolving clauses in a large set can result in inefficient or impossible proofs. For bigger problems the curse of combinatorial explosion occurs.

When attempting a proof by resolution, the ideal situation is to generate a minimally unsatisfiable set of clauses, which includes the conjectured clauses. A *minimally unsatisfiable set* is defined as a set, which is *Satisfiable* when any member of the set is omitted. The reason for creating this set is to avoid the irrelevant clauses, which are not needed in the proof. They contribute nothing towards the proof. Indeed, they can sidetrack the search direction resulting in a dead end and loss of resources. Of course, the set must be Unsatisfiable otherwise, a proof is impossible.

A minimally Unsatisfiable set is ideal in the sense that all clauses are essential and no others are needed. Thus if we wish to prove B, we would like to do so with a set of clauses S = {A_1, A_2, ... A_k} which becomes minimally Satisfiable with the addition of ¬B.

Choosing the order in which clauses are resolved depends upon search strategy. Though there are many search strategies, the "set- of- support strategy" is most important for the purpose of resolution.

Set- of- support strategy

The set-of- support strategy is formally defined as:

Let S be an Unsatisfiable set of clauses and T be a subset of S. Then T is a set of support for S if 'S – T' is Satisfiable. A set of support resolution is a resolution of two clauses not both from 'S–T'. This means that given an Unsatisfiable set {A_1, A_2, ... A_k}, resolution should not be performed directly for theorem proving applications.

5.5 UNIFICATION

As discussed earlier, for merging two or more predicates, either the predicates should have constants or they should have same value of variable. The predicates having an argument as one value of variable and another argument as different value of that variable cannot be merged (or resolved). For example bigcity (x) and ¬ bigcity (gurgaon) can not be merged, because there may be various values of variable x. Similarly predicate man and ¬man(geeta) can not be merged (or resolved), as first predicate does not have variable and second predicate has variable. On the similar ground P(x) and ¬P can not be resolved.

Unification is a technique where the predicates having variables are merged. In this process, we check whether by performing some substitution for variables, the predicates can be made identical. The substitutions for the variables are tried to generate identical and opposite predicate sets such that they can be combined. To carry out the process of unification, we first determine that whether the predicates are same or not. If they are same then the substitutions for the variable are tried. Unification identifies complementary literals in two clauses and deletes them, thereby forming a new literal. Whenever two identical and opposite literals are obtained they are merged (or called resolved). The above procedure is valid for clauses having no variables. When the literals have variables, the process becomes complicated and in such situations substitutions are made. There are three types of substitutions:

1.   Substitution of a variable by a constant.
2.   Substitution of a variable by another variable.
3.   Substitution of a variable by a function that does not contain the same variable.

In propositional logic, because it does not contain variables, it is easy to find out that two literals cannot be true simultaneously. In predicate logic, as discussed above, the matching process is more complicated as the arguments need to be considered, e.g., goodboy(adwet) and ¬goodboy(adwet) is a contradiction. But goodboy(ram) and ¬goodboy (sohan) is not a contradiction. Moreover, goodboy(ram) and ¬ boy(ram) is not a contradiction , as the predicates are different.

For example, let us try to unify P(x, x) and ¬P (y, z). First, check the predicate. These are same and opposite. Now, we check the arguments. Let us check first argument, it is x in first literal and y in second literal. These can be made similar, if we substitute x in place of y in both predicates. It may be noted that because x and y are variables hence these substitutions are possible. In the situation where one predicate has variable and another predicate has constant, then only variable can be replaced by the constant. The constant cannot be replaced by variable. One more point must be noted that the replacements of one variable by another should be done throughout all occurrences of that variable in all predicates. The replacement of y by x is denoted by x/y. After doing this replacement the literals become P(x, x) and P(x, z). Now, to match the second argument x should be replaced by z, but we can not do this as the substitution of x by y and z both are not possible in one set of problem. Hence these two literals can not be unified. However, if the above predicates are P(x, x) and ¬P (y, y). After the substitution x/y, they become P(x, x) and ¬P (x, x) and they can be unified.

In Artificial Intelligence system, the LISP language is used for storage of facts. The LISP stores them in terms of list. Unification is popularly used for unifying the axioms in inferencing mechanism. In context of list representation, it can be said that the unification is a process in which two arbitrary lists containing constants and variables are unified by generating a set of bindings for the variables in the lists so that they become identical. Binding refers to substitution of variable.

Besides LISP, another popular language used for AI system implementation is PROLOG. In context of PROLOG representation, the unification of prolog statements is thought in terms of matching. The PROLOG identifiers will match only with themselves, but variables are matched against some value. Normally the variables can take any value unless they have already been matched against something and are therefore bound to some value. This unification operation is very useful in natural language processing for construction of syntactic structures. In natural languages, the knowledge is given in terms of rules and facts which are stored in databases in form of lists to prove various facts.

5.5.1 Unification Algorithm

The algorithm for performing the unification is as follows:

Consider X and Y as literals to be unified. The steps of algorithm will be as follows:

1. if X and Y are identical then return nil.
2. else, if P is a variable, then if X occurs in Y then return FAIL, else return (Y/X)
3. if Y is a variable and if Y occurs in X, then return FAIL else return (X/Y).
4. else return FAIL.
5. if the initial predicate symbols in X and Y are not identical, then return FAIL.
6. if the X and Y have different number of arguments then return FAIL.
7. set *substitution* list to nil. (This list contains the substitutions made for performing the unification).
8. for i = 1 to number of arguments in X:
   8.1   call unify with arguments of X and the ith argument of Y , putting result in S.
   8.2   if S contains FAIL then return (FAIL).
   8.3   if S is not equal to nil then
   8.4   Apply S to remainder of both X and Y.
   8.5   *Substitution* := APPEND (S, *substitution)*.
9. return *Substitution.*

5.5.2 Solved Examples on Resolution and Unification

Example 13: Show the operation of resolution using following predicates.

$$\begin{array}{lll} A & : & P \vee Q \vee R \\ B & : & {\sim}P \vee R \\ C & : & {\sim}Q \\ D & : & {\sim}R \end{array}$$

Answer: The resolution procedure is shown below:

$$\begin{array}{lll} A & : & P \vee Q \vee R \\ B & : & {\sim}P \vee R \end{array}$$

```
X  :   Q∨ R
Y  :   R
D  :   ~R
Z  :   NIL
```

The deduction tree is

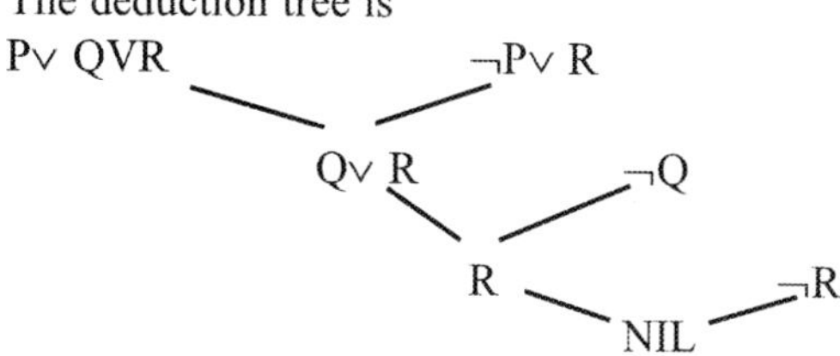

Example 14: Given the predicates P∨ ¬ Q and Q∨R, are true. Show P∨R is also true.

If P and ¬ Q are true, and Q ∨ R are also true , then as Q and ¬Q can not be simultaneously true , so they will be merged (called resolved, i.e. $Q \wedge \neg Q = F$)

Hence,

$$\frac{P\vee \neg Q, \; Q\vee R}{P\vee R}$$

Example 15:   Convert the following wff to clause form
$$\forall x \, [P(x) \Rightarrow P(x)]$$

Answer: $\forall x: \; [\neg P(x) \vee P(x)]$
$\neg P \vee P$
This is the required clause from.

Example 16:   Consider following figure:

<table>
<tr><td>B</td></tr>
<tr><td>A</td></tr>
</table>

The axioms are on (B, A)
on (A, table)
These axioms are already in clausal form. Show that B is above the table, i.e., above (B, table)

Answer: To prove this let us represent these as quantified expressions
$\forall x: \forall y \, [On \, (x, y) \rightarrow Above \, (x, y)]$
$\forall x: \forall y: \forall z \, [Above \, (x, y) \, \& \, Above \, (y, z) \rightarrow Above \, (x, z)]$

After resolving to clause from these axioms become:

¬on (u, v) ∨above (u, v)
¬above (x, y) ∨ ¬above (y, z) ∨above (x, z)
Assume that the expression to be proved is:
¬above (B, table)

The resolution goes as follows:

$\neg$on (u, v) $\vee$above(u, v)   (1)

$\neg$above (x, y) $\vee\neg$above (y, z) $\vee$above (x, z)   (2)

on (B, A)   (3)

on (A, table)   (4)

$\neg$above (B, table)   (5)

Resolving clause 2 and clause 5 gives: (by replacing x to B and z to table)

$\neg$above (B, y) $\vee\neg$above (y, table) $\vee$above (B, table)

$\neg$above (B, table)

$\neg$above (B, y) $\vee$ $\neg$above (y, table)   (6)

Resolving clause (1) and 6 by replacing u with y and special v to Table, gives:

$\neg$on (y, table) $\vee$above(y, table)

$\neg$above (B, y) $\vee\neg$ above (y, table)

$\neg$on (y, table) $\vee$ $\neg$above(B, y)   (7)

Resolving 1 and 7 by replacing u by B and v by y:

$\neg$on (B, y) $\vee$above(B, y)

$\neg$on (y, table) $\vee$ $\neg$above(B, y)

$\neg$on (B, y) $\vee\neg$on (y, table)   (8)

Resolving clause 3 and clause 8, specializing y to A

on (B, A)

 $\neg$on (B, A) $\vee\neg$on (A, table)

on (A, table)   (9)

Resolving clause 4 and clause 9 , we get

on (A, table)

on (A, table)

nil

It means we have reached to contradiction, so the negation of the theorem $\neg$above (B, table) must be false. Hence the theorem, above (B, table) must be true.

Example 17:   Give a substitution sequence to unify following two clauses.

P (x, f(z), mary) and $\neg$P (x, y, z)

Solution:

Substitute z / mary, we get

P (x, f (mary), mary), $\neg$ P(x, y, mary)

Again substitute, y /f(mary), we get

P (x, f(mary), mary) and $\neg$ P (x, f(mary), mary)
Now, they posses same set of arguments, hence they can be unified. Thus the sequence of substitution is z / Mary, y / f(Mary).

5.6 LIMITATIONS OF LOGIC

This section discusses the limitations of logic. The logic works well on certain types of applications but it is not suitable for certain other types of applications. People tried to use logic for various types of difficult problems like theorem proving. Nevertheless, logic is not suitable for major categories of AI problems. This is because of the fact that the logic has certain inherent limitations. These limitations are presented and described below:

   (i) Theorem prover may take too long a time. The complete theorem prover requires search, and the search is inherently sequential. Moreover, theorem prover may not help to solve practical problems, even if they do their work instantaneously.

  (ii) Logic is weak as a representation language for certain kinds of knowledge. Logic cannot represent facts, which have multiple values. You should recall that the logic could only represent the facts taking value 'true' or 'false'. For example, in the sentence "it is very cold today", how can the relative degrees of heat be represented? i.e., meaning of the terms like 'very cold' depends upon one's own perception. The temperature, which is 'very cold' for one person may not be so for the other. Hence, it is not possible to assign 'true' or 'false' to above mentioned sentence.

 (iii) The logic cannot represent the uncertain situations, e.g., in sentence 'Blonde haired people often have blue eyes', how can the amount of certainty be represented?

 (iv) In the sentence "if there is no evidence to the contrary, assume that any adult you meet knows how to read". How can we represent that one fact should be inferred from the absence of another?

  (v) The heuristic information cannot be represented by logic, e.g. "it is better, to have more pieces on the board than the opponent has". In the representation of this sentence as the number of pieces of opponent is not known in advance, so this type of heuristic information cannot be represented by logic.

 (vi) The knowledge involving user's belief can not be represented using logic. Consider sentence "I know, Suresh thinks the giants will win, but I think they are going to loose". This type of belief system cannot be represented by logic.

Hence, from above discussion it is evident that though logic is a powerful language, but for representing actual real world facts, it is not suitable. For representing knowledge required for AI systems, more powerful knowledge representation techniques have been devised. These are discussed in next chapter.

5.7 LOGIC PROGRAMMING

Until now, in this chapter we have discussed the length and width of logics, their meaning and their representation. This section discusses the use of logic in designing of knowledge base of AI based systems. The propositional and predicate logics are widely used to encode knowledge of rule-based systems. The rule-based knowledge base consists of two categories of representation:

(1) *A Declarative Representation*: It consists of facts and the logical assertions about the problem. The set of logical assertions can be combined with resolution theorem prover to give a complete program for solving problems.

(2) *A Procedural Representation*: It is one in which the control information that is necessary to use the knowledge is considered to be embedded in knowledge itself.

Abstracting, representing and coding of the appropriate facts corresponding to a task in a rule based system is done through logic programming. Logic programming is a programming language paradigm in which logical assertions are viewed as programs. Most popular logic programming system is PROLOG. A PROLOG program is described as a series of logical assertions, each of which is a '*Horn Clause*'. A 'Horn Clause' is a clause having at most one positive literal. Hence, p, $\neg p \lor q$, and p$\rightarrow$q are all Horn clauses.

The PROLOG interpreter accepts input for the goal to be proved. Backward reasoning is applied to try to prove the goal given the assertions in the program. The program is read top to bottom, left to right and search is performed depth first with backtracking.

Corresponding to declarative and procedural knowledge the PROLOG program consists of facts and rules. Facts represent statements about specific objects. Rules represent statements about classes of objects.

Thus, it is clear that the logic programming include coding of facts and procedures in AI programming languages like PROLOG and LISP. There are few differences between the logic and PROLOG representation. These are:

1. In logic, variables are explicitly quantified. In PROLOG quantification is provided implicitly by the way variables are interpreted.

2. Logic use connections in their representation. PROLOG uses symbols for and ( ), but there is none for 'or'. The disjunction should be represented as a list of alternative statements, any of which may provide the base for a conclusion.

3. Unlike logic, the implication in PROLOG is written backward.

5.7.1 Forward Reasoning and Backward Reasoning

As mentioned in earlier chapter that prime objective of AI problem solving is to devise a search procedure which discovers a path in problem's search space from initial state to goal state. The forward and backward reasoning are techniques of implementing these search procedures. These are also called forward and backward chaining respectively. The forward chaining starts from start state, and proceeds towards the goal state. The backward chaining starts from goal state and proceeds towards start state. It may be noted here that PROLOG only searches from goal state. So if the rules are implemented in PROLOG, then only backward reasoning is applicable.

In general, the decision about which reasoning is suited in a particular application depends widely upon the nature of problem. However, following factors influence the direction of reasoning process.

(1) Number of start and goal states- The Reasoning is chosen in the direction from smaller set of states to lager set of states.

(2) Direction of branching factor- The branching factor is defined as the average number of nodes that are generated from a single node The reasoning is performed in the direction of lower branching factor.

(3) Requirement of problem- in certain AI applications, like medical diagnosis, the justification of the solution is also required. Hence, it is found out that in a certain application "Is it required to justify reasoning process?" If so, it is important to choose the reasoning in the direction that corresponds more closely with the way the user think.

The process of forward chaining and backward chaining are explained below.

5.7.1.1 Forward Chaining

It is already mentioned that the rules are stored in knowledge base in form of atomic formula represented in propositional or predicate logic. Each formula has one or more clauses in the left hand side and one or more clauses in the right hand side. In the process of forward chaining the left side of rules is instantiated and the rules are executed from left to right. In this the left part of the sentence is matched with existing expression and if match occurs, it is replaced by right part of rule. Next time, this right side of previous rule is considered as left side of present rule to find applicability of a rule. The finding of the rules becomes as sub goals to be fulfilled. These subgoals may in turn cause new subgoals to be established and so on until facts are found to match the lowest subgoal conditions. Whenever the goal is achieved, the search process stops. The forward chaining is also known as data driven inference as input data is used to guide the direction of inference process.

The algorithm of forward chaining can be summarized as follows:

Algorithm : forward chaining

(i) Repeat until no rule produces a new assertion
  (a) for each rule, match the first antecedent with an exciting assertion. Create a new binding set with variable bindings established with the match.

(b)   using a exciting variable bindings , try to match the next antecedent with an exciting assertion. If any new variable appears in this antecedent augment the exciting variable bindings.

(c)   Repeat the previous step for each antecedent , accumulating variable bindings as you go until.

(d)   There is no match with an exciting assertion using the binding set established so far. in such situation backup to a previous match of an antecedent to an assertion looking for an alternative match that produces an alternative workable binding set.

(e)   There are no more antecedent to be matched, in this case use the binding set in hand to instantiate the consequent.

(f)   Determine if the instantiated consequent is already asserted. if not, assert it.

(g)   Backup to the most recent match with unexplored bindings. look for an alternative match that produces the workable binding set.

(h)   There are no more alternative matches to be explored at any level.

5.7.1.2 Backward chaining

The backward chaining is said as **goal driven search**. It starts from the goal and moves towards the start state. In a rule it matches the existing state with the right hand part of rule , and if match occurs it is replaced by left hand side of rule.

The backward chaining procedure is summarized below.

a.   Find a rule whose consequent matches the hypothesis and create a binding set (or argument) in the existing binding set.

b.   Using the existing binding set, look for a way to deal with the first antecedent.

c.   Try to match the antecedent with an existing assertion.

d.   Treat the antecedent as a hypothesis and try to support it by backward chaining through other rules using the existing binding set.

e.   Repeat the previous step for each antecedent, accumulating variable bindings until.

f.   There is no match with any existing assertion or rule consequent using the binding set established so far. In this case backup to the most recent match with unexplored bindings, looking for an alternative match that produces a workable binding set.

g.   There are no more antecedents to be matched. In this case the binding set in hand supports the original hypothesis. If all possible binding is desired', report the current binding set and quit.

h.   There are no more alternative matches to be explored at any level.

The combination of forward search and backward search is bidirectional search. Many practical and successful AI systems have been developed using a combination of forward and backward reasoning., and most AI programming environments provide explicit support for such hybrid reasoning.

Although , the same set of rules can be used for both forward and backward reasoning , in practice, it has proved useful to define two classes of rules, each of which encode a particular kind of knowledge.

(i) Forward rules: The forward rules encode about how to respond to certain input configuration.

(ii) Backward rules: these encode knowledge about how to achieve a particular goal.

To find out whether it is possible to use the same rule for both forward and backward reasoning, the rule form is checked. If both left side and right side contain pure assertion then forward chaining can match assertion on the left side of a rule and add to the state description of assertion on the right hand side. But if arbitrary procedures are allowed as the right side of the rule, then the rules will not be reversible. Some production languages allow only reversible rule, others do not. When , irreversible rules are used, then a commitment to the direction of search must be made at the time the rules are written.

5.7.1.3 *Combining forward and backward chaining*

In certain type of situation the backward chaining is more preferable and in another type of situation forward chaining is more preferable e.g. in medical diagnosis problem, normally the forward chaining is most suitable. In certain situation it might accept thirty or more facts about the patients data then apply forward chaining based on that data. Now suppose at some point the left hand side of rule is nearly satisfied. It might be effective to apply backward chaining for rest of rules.

Whether it is possible to use same rules for both forward and backward reasoning, also depend upon the form of rules. If both left hand side and right hand side contain assertion , then forward chaining can match assertion on the left side of a rule and add to the state description of assertion on the right hand side. On the contrary, a rule will not be reversible, if arbitrary procedures are allowed at right in the rule. Some production language allow only reversible rules, others do not. When irreversible rules are used, then a commitment to the direction of search must be made, at the time the rules are written.

5.8 MATCHING

It is mentioned earlier that the knowledge is stored in knowledge base in form of rules and to solve a particular problem appropriate rule need to be applied. These rules applied to individual problem state generates new states. The new rules are applied to new states to further generate new states.

To find which rules are applicable, the current state of the problem and its preconditions are matched with left hand side of the rule. This is done using matching.

One way to select applicable rule is simply searching through all rules. In the process of matching the left hand side of rule is compared with the input and all rules that match are extracted. The difficulties of this simple search techniques are:

(i) In big problems large number of rules are used. Scanning through all of these rules at every step of the search would be hopelessly inefficient.

(ii) It is not clearly visible to find out which condition will be satisfied.

Some of the matching techniques are described below:

1. *Indexing:* To overcome above problems indexing is used. In this, instead of searching all the rules the current state is used as index into the rules, and select the matching rules immediately e.g. Consider the chess game playing. Here, the set of valid moves is very large. To reduce the size of this set only useful moves are identified. At the time of playing the game , the next move will very much depend upon the current move. As the game is going on , there will be only 'few' moves which are applicable in next move. Hence, it will be a wasteful effort to check the applicability of all moves. Rather, the important and valid legal moves are directly stored as rules and through indexing the applicable rules are found. Here, the indexing will store the current board position .The indexing makes the matching process easy, at the cost of lack of generality in the statement rules. Practically there is a trade off between the ease of writing rules and simplicity of matching process. The indexing technique is not very well suited for the rule base where rules are written in high level predicates. In PROLOG and many theorem proving systems, rules are indexed by predicates they contain. Hence all the applicable rules can be indexed quickly.

2. *Matching with variable:* In the rule base if the preconditions are not stated as exact descriptions of particular situation, the indexing technique does not work well. In certain situations they describe properties that the situation must have. In the situations where single condition is matched against a single element in state description, the unification procedure can be used. However in practical situation it is required to match complete set of rules that match the current state. In forward and backward chaining system , the depth first search technique is used to select the individual rule. In the situations where multiple rules are applicable, conflict resolution technique is used to choose   appropriate applicable rule. In case of the situations requiring multiple match, the unification can be applied recursively, but a more efficient method is to use RETE matching algorithm.

3. *Complex matching variable:* A more complex matching process is required when preconditions of a rule specify required properties that are not stated explicitly in the description of current state. However the real world is full of uncertainties and sometimes practically it is not possible to define the rule in exact fashion. The matching process becomes more complicated in the situation where preconditions approximately match the current situations e.g a speech understanding program must contain the rules that map from a description of a physical wave form to phones. Because of the presence of noise the signal becomes so variable that there will be only approximate match between the rules that describe

an ideal sound and the input that describes that unideal world. Approximate matching is particularly difficult to deal with, because as we increase the tolerance allowed in the match the new rules need to be written and it will increase number of rules. It will increase the size of main search process. But approximate matching is nevertheless superior to exact matching in situations such as speech understanding, where exact matching may result in no rule being matched and the search process coming to a grinding halt.

5.9 CONFLICT RESOLUTION

In the ideal production system, all rules are continuously checked in the global database and a rule fires instantaneously as soon as its 'IF' part matches with the left hand side of the rule. However, in practical production system, the firing of one rule may change activation of another rule. Hence the control structure allows only one rule to fire in one cycle. If more than one rules are found to be applicable in one cycle, then a situation called '*conflict*' occurs. All the applicable rules generate '*conflict set*'. In the situation of conflict, the control structure must determine which rule to fire from this conflict set of active rules. This selection is called '*conflict resolution*'.

The following policies are used for conflict resolution.

(i) Priority based: in this policy the rules are ranked according to some assigned priority. And from the applicable rules, whichever rule has highest priority is fired first. This, combined with redundancy avoidance was the strategy used in many expert systems. The strength of this scheme lies in its simplicity, and by ordering the rules in the approximate order of their firing frequency this can be made relatively efficient strategy.

(ii) Based on maximum number of matched condition: this is also known as longest matching strategy. In this strategy, from the conflict set the rule with most strict condition is chosen for firing. Its advantage is that the discrimination power of a strict condition is greater than of a more general condition. A rule with a strict condition "effectively injects more knowledge into the database" when it is fired.

(iii) Most recently used: This policy chooses the most recently used rule from conflict set for firing. Its advantage is that it represents a depth first search which follows the path of greatest activity in generating new knowledge base. A variant of this scheme is choose the rule from the conflict set with the most recently used variable. This strategy is possible as long as firing the rule did not contribute redundant information.

(iv) Most recently added: This policy selects the rule which is most recently added in the set of rules. This policy works only for dynamic knowledge. In dynamic knowledge base the production rules are added, deleted, or modified automatically during execution. This scheme provides greater efficiency by enhancing the depth first search. Though this is an attractive policy but such system exhibit much higher level of abstraction and complexity.

(v) Execution time based: this scheme computes the execution time priority and fire the rule with the highest priority.

(vi) Random selection: this rule randomly selects a rule for firing. In some situations it simply fires all rules from the conflict set which are applicable.

The policies discussed above are normal conflict resolution strategies. In practice, sometimes mixed strategies are also used. The intelligent design of conflict resolution strategies is one of the current areas of research in AI. The particular choice of strategy affects both the *sensitivity* of the production system and its *stability*. The sensitivity is the ability of respond quickly to changes in the database, and the stability is the ability to carry out long sequences of actions.

EXERCISES

1. Translate, each of the following sentences into predicate calculus, conceptual dependencies, and conceptual graphs.
    (i)   Gaurav gave Sushil an ice cream cone.
    (ii)   Basketball players are tall.
    (iii)   Paul cut down the tree with an axe.
    (iv)   place all the ingredients in a bowl and mix thoroughly.
2. Show that
    (i) $(P \rightarrow Q) = \neg P \vee V\ Q$ ($\equiv$ represent equivalence)
    (ii) $(P \rightarrow Q) = (P \rightarrow Q) \wedge\wedge (Q \rightarrow P)$
3. Find the value of
    (i) $(\exists z)(\forall x)[P(x) \rightarrow Q(z)]$
    (ii) $(\exists z)[(\exists x)(P(x) \rightarrow Q(z)]$
4. Prove that clauses $(\neg P_1 \vee P_2 \ldots\ldots\ldots \vee P_n \vee Q)$ and $P_1 \wedge P_m \rightarrow Q$ are equivalent.
5. Prove following assertions.
    (i) $P \subseteq Q$ is valid, if and only if the sentence $P \rightarrow Q$ is valid.
    (ii) $P \equiv Q$ is true, if sentence $P \leftrightarrow Q$ is valid.
    (iii) $\neg P \vee Q \wedge R \rightarrow S$
6. Prove that every clause regardless of number of positive literals can be written in the form
$$(P_1 \wedge P_2 \ldots\ldots\ldots \wedge P_m) \rightarrow (Q_1 \vee \ldots\ldots \vee Q_m)$$
    where P_m and Q_m are propositional symbols. A knowledge base consisting of literals in these forms are in implicative normal from. Write down the full resolution rule of sentences in implicative normal form.
7. Perform the following Conversion.
    (I) $(X \rightarrow ((Y \wedge Z) \rightarrow P))$ into disjunctive normal form.
    (j) $(X \rightarrow Y) \rightarrow Z$ into conjunctive normal form.
8. Explain the process of Skolemisation. For what purpose it is used? Convert following formulas into Skolem form.
    (i) $P = \exists q\ \forall r\ \exists s\ \exists t\ (A(q, r) \rightarrow B(s, t))$
    (ii) $\exists x\ \forall y\ \exists z\ \exists a\ \exists b\ Q (x, y, z, a, b)$

9. Write down the full resolution rules for sentences in implicative normal form.

10. Write predicate calculus equivalent of following sentences.
    (i)   every city has a dog catcher who has been bitten by every dog in the town.
    (ii) All squares on the top of squares that have been moved or that are attached to squares that have been moved, have also been moved.

11. Define 'Well Formed Formula' (wff). Find whether the following expressions are wff's or not.
    (i) $\exists x \{ \forall y [P (x, y) \land Q(y, x) \rightarrow R(x)]\}$
    (ii) $\neg P [A, g (A, B, A)]$
    (iii) $\neg f(A)$
    (iv) $f(P,A)$

12. Consider the facts 'a' and 'b' are given
    (a) $\forall x [engineer (x) \rightarrow knows \rightarrow drawing(x)]$
    (b) engineer [Akash]
    prove the assertion knows_drawing (Akash) using (i) Modus Ponen (ii) Resolution
    Comment upon the relative merits of the two methods.

13. What is meant by free and bound variable. In the wff $\forall x P(x) \rightarrow Q(x, y)$ identify free variable and bound variable. also verify that to evaluate the expression all variables must be bound in the wff.

14. Differentiate between propositional logic and predicate logic. Represent the following statements in logic.
    (i)   All government employees earning Rs 4 lac or more in a year pay taxes.
    (ii) Some employees are sick today.
    (iii) No employee earns more than the president of India.

15. Perform the unification on the following
    (i)   Knows (John, x), knows (John, Jane)
    (ii) Knows (John, x), knows (y, Bill)
    (iii) Knows (John, x), Knows (y, Mother(y))
    (iv) Knows (John, x), Knows (x, Elizabeth)
    Also mention the case where Unification fails.

6

Advanced Knowledge Representation Techniques

6.1 INTRODUCTION

We have discussed some conceptual aspects regarding knowledge in chapter 4. The discussion was primarily focused on types of knowledge, their expressiveness, dimensions, validity of knowledge and other related aspects including knowledge representation and knowledge acquisition. A basic knowledge representation technique is logic-based representation, also known as propositional and predicate calculus. This is discussed in detail in previous chapter. In this chapter we would discuss some advanced knowledge representation techniques. These are frames, semantic network, conceptual graphs, conceptual dependencies and scripts, CYC, and object oriented representation. But before that, let us put some emphasis on knowledge representation itself, not only to understand the need of knowledge representation and its importance in building AI systems, but also to know why do we need advanced techniques and are these sufficient to serve the purpose.

The logic based representation techniques discussed earlier focused primarily on expressiveness, consistency, inference methods etc. They hardly gave consideration to the way in which knowledge is structured or the type of data structure that should be used. Also, These methods failed to consider the methods adopted for organizing knowledge structure in memory. These issues are of utmost importance for addressing the issues related with knowledge representation to make it effective for use in developing knowledge-based systems.

The need of knowledge representation was felt as early as the idea to develop intelligent systems. With the hope that readers are well conversant with the fact by now, that intelligence requires possession of knowledge and that knowledge is acquired by us by various means and stored in the memory using some representation techniques, we can make out that knowledge representation is simply, capturing critical aspect of intelligence activity for use on a computer. Putting in another way, knowledge representation is one of the many critical aspects, which are required for making a computer behave intelligently. Realizing the importance of this aspect, the research related to issues addressing knowledge representation started as early as in 1950s.

Here, some of the early works done by Newell and Simon deserve mention. In late 1950s and early 1960s, Newell and Simon developed several programs to test the intelligent behavior resulting from heuristic search. The *Logic Theorist*, developed by J.C. Shaw based on the concepts of Newell and Simon proved theorems using *logic*, an elementary method of knowledge representation. Later on, in *General Problem Solver* or GPS, Newell and Simon continued their efforts to find general principles of intelligent problem solving. The GPS was able to solve problems formulated as state space search. GPS used means-end analysis for conducting search. This approach has been discussed in a chapter earlier in this book. The earlier methods adopted for problem solving are termed as *weak problem-solving methods*.

The second phase (1980s) of developments in the area of knowledge representation and problem solving, used *strong methods* for problem solving. In strong methods, problem solvers made certain assumptions about the nature of intelligent systems. These assumptions were formulated by Brian Smith (1985), in the form of *knowledge representation hypothesis*. The important theme of this hypothesis included the assumption that the knowledge would be represented *propositionally*. Propositional representation means, representing the knowledge explicitly, so that the same could be observed and accessed by any outside observer; and this knowledge appears to him as natural.

The last theme of knowledge representation is described as *agent-based problem solving*. In this approach, problem solving is considered as distributed, with different agents performing different tasks in domain of their context. The problem solving task is viewed as works done by individual agents with little or no coordination among them. For example, in interactive game playing, the agent would address a local issue, e.g., defending a move, without any general concern for the overall problem handling. Many researchers, including Brooks, Jennings and Wooldridge have done considerable amount of work using this approach. Several researchers in the area of robotics have built agent based systems.

We have tried to give a brief account of the work done so far in different phases by various researchers in the area of problem solving and knowledge representation. We would discuss some of the important methodologies adopted for representing knowledge in the following sections.

6.2 FRAMES

Frames were introduced by Marvin Minsky in 1975 in his book on computer vision. It is a method to represent conceptual and commonsense knowledge. Frames are used to represent a mental model of a stereotypical situation like shopping in a market, driving a car, attending a meeting, eating in a restaurant, or educating in a university. It is used to represent the activities associated with conceptual events taking place in supermarket, theatre, college, university etc. The Minsky proposed the organization of knowledge in form of small packets called frames. The knowledge about these conceptual events are created in the frame like structure and stored in the knowledge base. The contents of the frame are slots, which have certain values. All slots of a given frame contain information such as attribute-value pair, default value condition for filling a slot, pointers to other related frames and procedures that are activated when needed for default purposes. The slots may be of any type and any size. Slots typically have names and values or subfields called facets. Facets may also have names and any number of values. Whenever a new similar situation is encountered, an appropriate frame is selected from the memory for use in reasoning about the situation.

To understand the concept of a frame, let us take an example of a university computer science department. The department has certain infrastructure like faculty rooms, computer laboratories, equipments like computers, printers, furniture, teachers, students, supporting staff etc. Besides these, there may be many more things present in the department. If we have seen a department then we have its certain picture in mind. Out of all objects present in the department, there are certain thing which are common to all departments like faculty room, furniture etc. whereas some objects may be department specific like computer laboratory or chemical laboratory etc. This knowledge about the department can be coded into a frame, then whenever a situation of a department is given, it will give a general idea about the department, and for new department, the additions can be incorporated.

Thus, *a frame is a data structure that has slots for various objects and these slots contain some values.* The example of frame of a university department is shown in Fig. 6.1.

```
(department

(FACULTY         (Number (VALUE 8))
                 (Education (VALUE  Ph.D.))

(CLASSROOM       (Number (VALUE 10))
                 (Capacity (VALUE 60))

(LABORATORY      (Number (VALUE 2))
                 (Type (VALUE Chemistry))

(COLLEGE         (VALUE YMCAIE))

(UNIVERSITY      (VALUE MDU))))
```

Fig. 6.1: The frame structure of a department

The frame discussed above consists only descriptive type of knowledge, hence, it is called *declarative frame*. Besides declarative knowledge, a frame may consists of knowledge about the actions or procedures. These are called *procedural frames*. A normal frame typically consists of slots for:

(i) *actor* – which holds the information about who is performing the activity,

(ii) *object* – giving the information about the item to be operated on,

(iii) *source slot* – it holds the information from where the action has to begin,

(iv) *destination slot*- holds the information about the place where action has to end.

The general frame structure is shown in Fig. 6.2.

```
(<frame name >
        (<slot1>        (facet1 < value1> .....<value k>)
                        (facet2 < value1> .....<value k>)
                        (facet3  <value1> .....<value k>)

                        ......

                        ......

                        ........

                        (facet n  <value1> .....<value k>)
```

Fig. 6.2: A general frame structure

6.2.1 Reasoning with Frames

The frames can be attached with another frame and can create a network of frames. The main task of action frame is to provide the facility for procedural attachment and help in reasoning process. Reasoning using frames is done by instantiation. Instantiation process begins, when the given situation is matched with frames that are already in existence. The reasoning process tries to match the current problem state with the frame slot and assigns them values. The values assigned to the slots depict a particular situation and by this, the reasoning process moves towards a goal. The reasoning process can be defined as filling slot values in frames. Generally, if a given slot characteristics is not present, the slot provides a default value for that characteristic. It has been observed that the problem situation is generally not static. If there is any deviation in the characteristic, the values of the corresponding slots are updated so that it conforms to the current situation.

6.2.2 Frame Based Representation Language

Due to popularity of frame representation, special frame based languages were developed. These are primarily LISP based languages. They have built in procedures to create, access, modify, update, and display frames. Functions to define a frame might be:

$$(f \; define \; f\_ name < parents> < slots>)$$

where, f defines frame definition function, 'f_ name' is name of frame, < parents> is list of parents, and < slots> is a list of names of slots and the initial values. A frame for the car is shown in Fig. 6.3.

```
CAR
    (Manufacturer      (Cheve          (Brand Spare))
                       (Country        (Germany))
                       Year            (Value 2008))
    (Color             (Body           (Value Red))
                       Bumper          (Value Black))
    (Running)          (Fuel           (Value Petrol))
                       (Average        ( Value 16 km/it)))
```

Fig. 6.3: Frame Representation of 'car'

6.3 SEMANTIC NETWORK

A semantic network is a graphical knowledge representation technique. This knowledge representation system is primarily on network structure. The semantic networks were basically developed to model human memory. But, now their use is diversified to other fields also, including neural networks and expert systems.

A semantic net consists of nodes connected by arcs. The objects under consideration serve as nodes and the relationships between nodes are given by arcs. The nodes represent objects, concepts or events. The arcs are defined in a variety of ways, depending upon the kind of knowledge being represented. Most common arc types are: *is-a* and *has part*. Some examples of network is shown in the Fig. 6.4 (a), and (b).

The nodes can be of various types like *generic node*, which represents a general class like canine or dog, or it can be *individual or instance node* like 'Pomerian' or 'Doberman', which indicates a specific instance (or type) of dog. There may be many instances of one particular type of generic node. Similarly, there can be

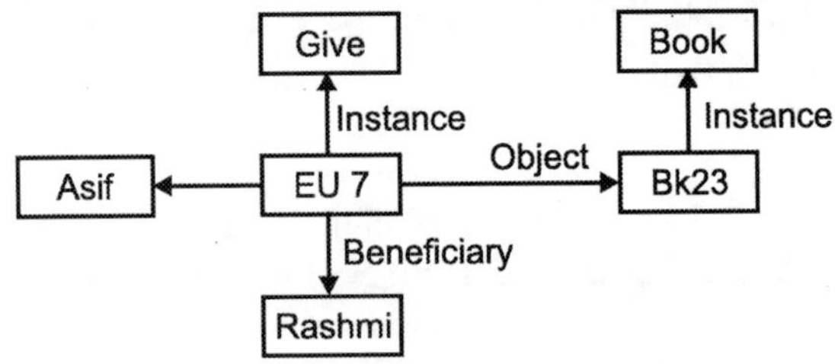

Fig. 6.4 (a): Semantic Network representation of "Asif gave a book to Rashmi."

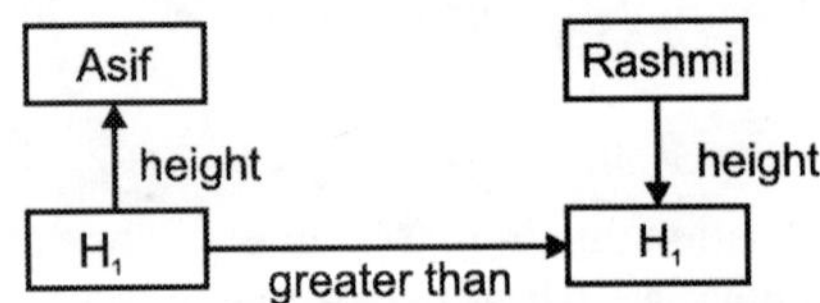

Fig. 6.4 (b): Semantic Network representation of "Asif is taller than Rashmi"

many types of arcs like is-a, has-no, tail, owns etc. These arc types indicate the relationship between nodes. Out of all these links, the link *is-a* is the most important and it links a generic node to generic node.

In earlier chapter, we have discussed the concept of inheritable knowledge. Semantic nets can easily represent this type of knowledge. The concept of inheriting a property is termed as 'property inheritance'. In this, the element of a subclass inherits the properties of its class. Consider the example of *"Dog world"*. The Dog world is a typical example cited for AI applications. The Dog world assumes that all the facts about the dog are stored in the database of the system. Using the dog world, following facts can be derived *"Great Ribu has a tail and is carnivorous"*, where, Ribu is name of the dog, from the facts that a dog has a tail and a canine is carnivorous, respectively. However, the properties of a subclass can be modified and can be given different values. In that case they will possess their own defined values. Using semantic net, the links can be developed between various domains. This activity can be performed by developing the association between various domains. These nets are called *'associated semantic nets'*.

The semantic network based knowledge representation mechanism is useful where an object or concept is associated with many attributes and where relationships between objects are important. Semantic nets have also been used in natural language research to represent complex sentences expressed in English. The semantic representation is useful because it provides a standard way of analyzing the meaning of sentence.

Consider one example of English sentence:
"Vishwant gave Vidushi a flower."
Its semantic net representation is given in Fig. 6.5.
The arcs define the relationship between the predicate (GIVE) and the concepts, such as Vidushi and Gift, associated with that predicate.

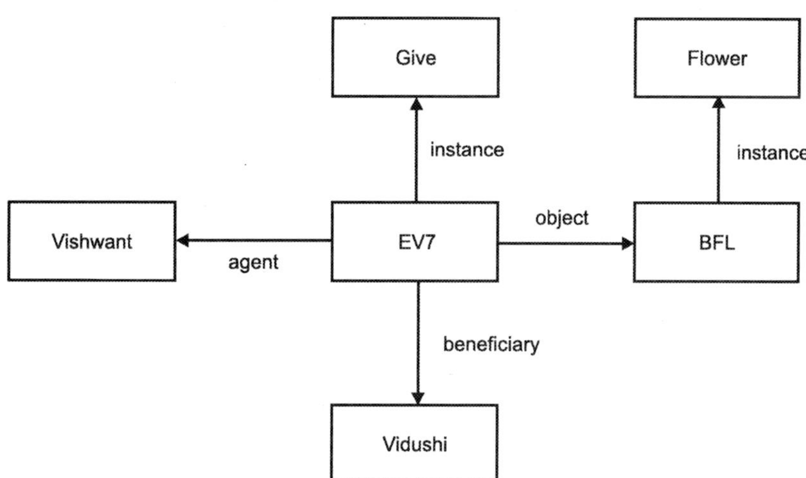

Fig. 6.5: Semantic network of "Vishwant gave Vidushi a flower"

A semantic network of a more complicated sentence "John told Bobby that he gave Vidushi a gift" is presented in Fig. 6.6.

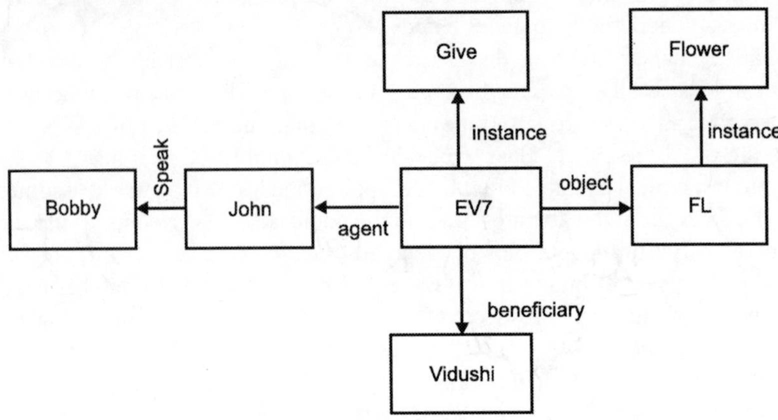

Fig. 6.6: Semantic net representation of sentence "John told Bobby that he gave Vidushi a gift".

The following examples illustrate some more semantic network representation.

***Example 1*:**   Give a semantic net representation of following:
(i)   is a circus_elephant elephant

(ii)   has part elephant head

(iii)   has part head mouth

(iv)   is a elephant animal

(v)   has part animal heart

(vi)   is a circus elephant performer

(vii) is a costumes cloth

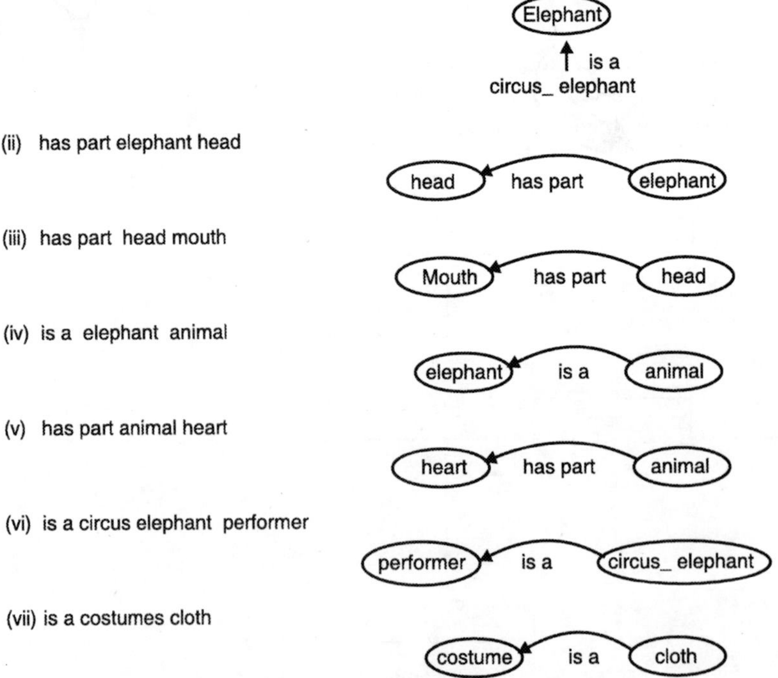

Example 2:   Give Semantic Net representation for "all dogs have bitten a postman."

Answer:

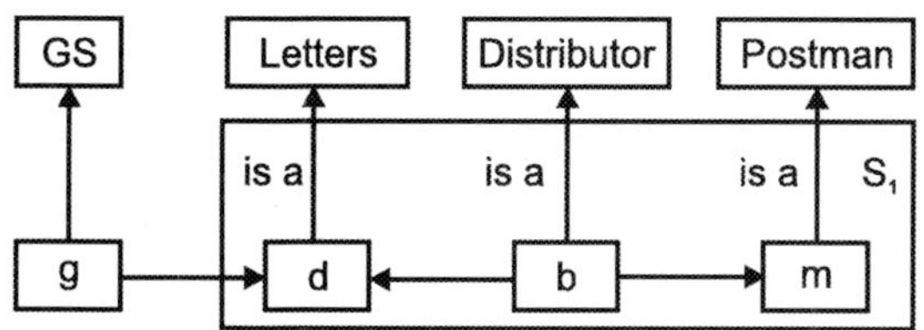

Example 3:   Construct a semantic net representation for the following:
(i) Pompian (Marcus), Blacksmith (Marcus)

Answer:

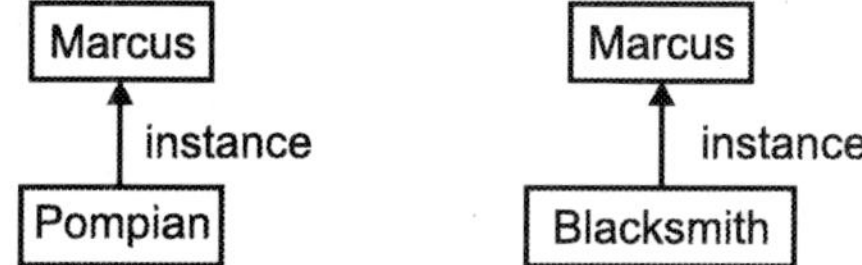

Example 4:   Mary gave the green flowered vase to his favorite cousin.

Answer:

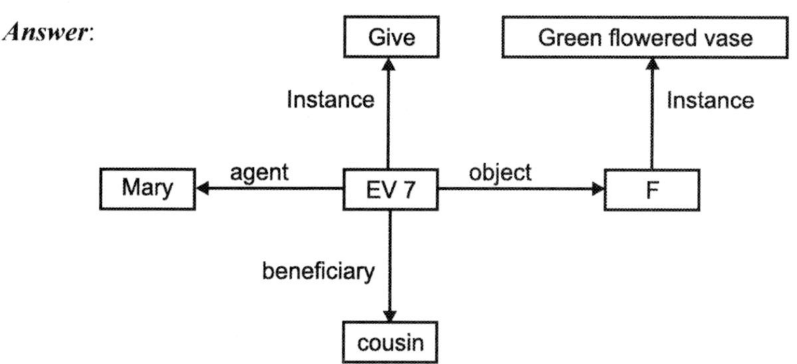

Example 5:   Construct semantic net for,
(i) Every batter hit a ball.
(ii) All the batters like the pitcher

Answer:
(i)

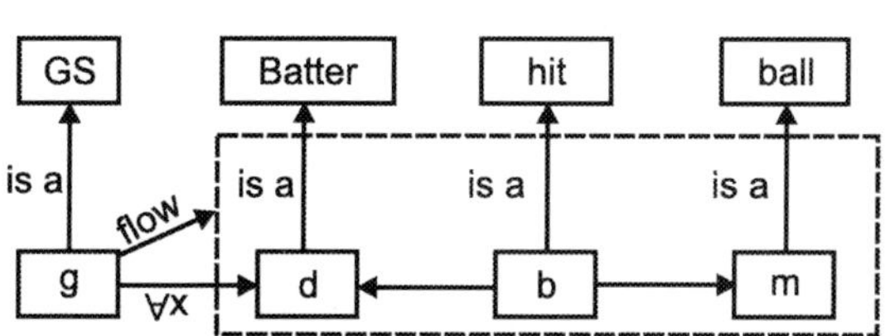

(ii)

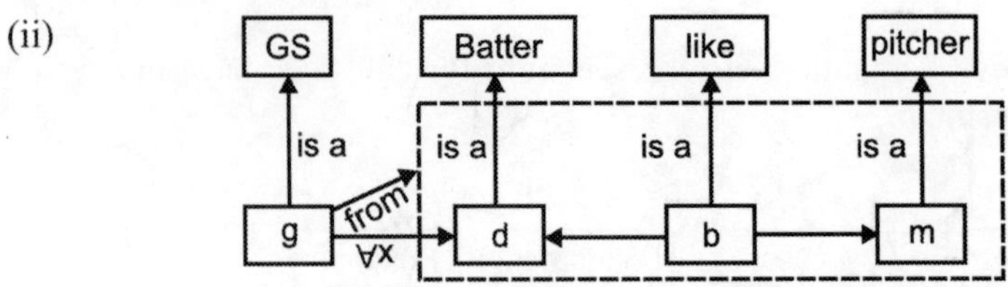

Example 6:   Make semantic network representation of following database:

Atom	Property	
	Is a	**has part**
Circus _elephant	elephant performer	
Elephant	(animal)	(head trunk)
Head		mouth
Animal performer		heart
Costume	cloth	button

Answer:

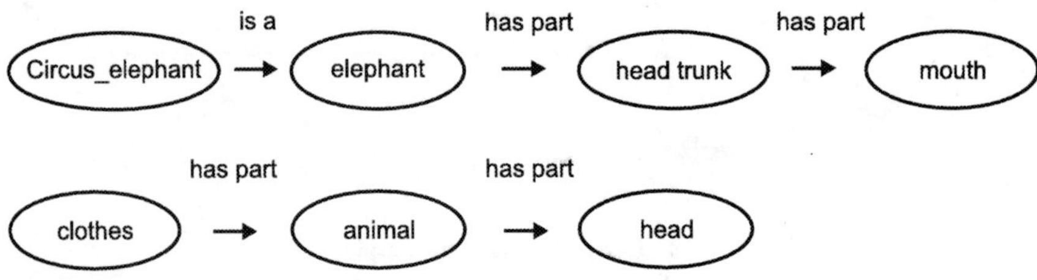

6.4 CONCEPTUAL GRAPHS

Conceptual graph is another method of knowledge representation. As the name indicates, it tries to capture the concepts about the events and represents them in the form of a graph. It is a basic building block for associative network. John Sowa and his colleagues primarily did the development of conceptual graph. It is a graphical portrayal of mental perception of primitive concepts and the relationships that exist between the concepts. Concepts like AGENT, OBJECT, INSTRUMENT, and PART are obtained from a collection of standard concepts. New concepts and relations can be defined from these basic ones. These are also basic building block for associative network. A linear conceptual graph is an elementary form of this structure. These can be clubbed together in a coherent way to form a more complex knowledge structure. The conceptual graph for "Rashmi is eating ice-cream with spoon." is shown in Fig. 6.7.

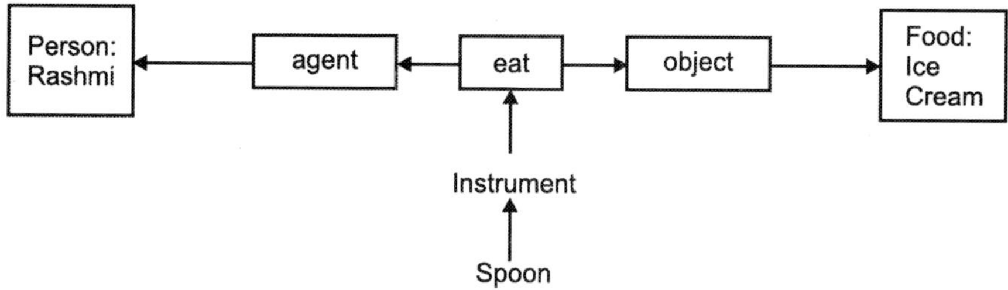

Fig. 6.7: Conceptual graph for "Rashmi is eating ice-cream with spoon"

The above sentence can also be represented in a text format of conceptual graph. The textual format is easy to represent. The linear equivalent form of above sentence is given below:

[person : Rashmi] ¬ (AGENT) ¬ [EAT] ¬ (OBJECT) →FOOD : ice-cream]
(INSTRUMENT) →[SPOON]

Where, square brackets have replaced concept boxes and parenthesis have replaced relation circles.

The basic alphabets of conceptual graph consist of alphabet, boxes, circles, directed arcs, special characters including: -,?, !, #, @, α, ∧, ", : ,[,], (,), {,}

Out of these symbols, some symbols are used to exhibit the structure of graph, while others are used to determine referents. Meanings of some of the symbols are mentioned below:

 (i) **Dash** signifies continuation of linear graph on next line.
 (ii) **Question mark** signifies a query about the concept. When placed in referent field, e.g., [FLOWER:?] means which flower.
 (iii) **Exclamation mark** is used for emphasis to draw attention to a concept.
 (iv) **Asterisk** indicates variable or unspecified object.
 (v) **Pound** signifies a definite article known to the speaker, e.g., FLOWER: # Rose refers to a specified flower.
 (vi) **@** relates to quantification, e.g., [FLOWER :@n] means n flowers.
(vii) ∀ signifies every or all. It is used in the meaning similar to FOPL.
(viii) ¬ Indicates negation.
 (ix) "delimits literal string.

The conceptual graph can be converted to equivalent FOPL statement, and inferring can be applied on it. By modifying and combining graph through the use of operator and basic graph inference rules. Some graph formation operators are:

 (i) **COPY**: It produces a duplicate copy of Conceptual Graph.
 (ii) **RESTRICT**: It modifies a graph by replacing a type level of a concept with a subtype or specialization from generic to individual by inserting a referent of same concept type.
(iii) **JOIN**: It combines two identical graphs C_1 and C_2 by attaching all relation arcs from C_2 to C_1 and then erasing C_2.

(iv) **SIMPLIFY**: It eliminates one or two identical relations in a conceptual graph when all connecting arcs are also the same.

The inference rules for the conceptual graph are defined as follows:

(i) *Erasure*: Any conceptual graph enclosed by an even number of negation may be erased.

(ii) *Insertion*: Any conceptual graph may be inserted into another graph context, which is enclosed by an odd number of assertions.

(iii) *Iteration*: A copy of conceptual graph C may be inserted into a graph context in which C occurs or in which C is dominated by another concept.

(iv) *De-iteration*: Any conceptual graph, which could be the result of iteration may be erased from a conceptual graph context.

(v) *Double negation*: A double negation may be erased before any conceptual graph or set of graphs.

As an example of some of the above rules, any graph **b** may be erased from consequent of implication, i.e., ¬ [**a** ¬ [**b c**]] will derive ¬ [**a** ¬ [**c**]]. Any graph **b** may be inserted in the consequent of implication, i.e., ¬ [**a** ¬ [**c**]] will derive ¬ [**a** ¬ [**b c**]].

Example 7:   Give a conceptual graph representation for the sentence "Mary drive her car to market".

Answer:

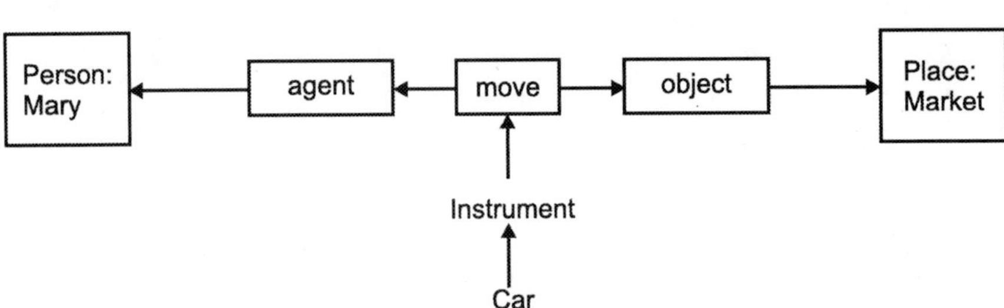

6.5 CONCEPTUAL DEPENDENCIES

These are the formal methods to represent the knowledge about abstract concepts. The conceptual dependency structures were originally developed by Roger C. Schank (1977). These conceptualizations are used to represent the semantic structure of a sentence. Conceptual dependency (CD) based knowledge representation methodology was primarily developed to understand and represent natural language structures. It offers many advantages. As it captures the semantics of natural language, the problem of ambiguity is reduced. Consider following sentences:

(i)   I hit the boy with the girl with long hair with a hammer with vengeance.
(ii) John's love for Mary was Harmful.
(iii) John's can of beans was edible.
(iv) Time flies like an arrow.

In sentence (i), the syntactic structure will not be enough illustrative to provide complete meaning of the sentence. That is, if we need to capture information from this sentence that the hammer hit the boy, we would have to do it by more sophisticated methods then simple syntactic analysis. In sentences (ii) and (iii), the main message conveyed by the sentence is of abstract or conceptual type. Moreover, in sentence (iv), a concept is metaphorically mentioned.

If a computer program is to be developed that can understand wide phenomenon represented by natural languages, the knowledge representation should be powerful enough to represent these concepts. The conceptual dependency representation captures maximum concepts to provide canonical form of meaning of sentences. Thus, all sentences which have same semantics (i.e. their meaning is same) will be represented internally by syntactically identical form. That means, the conceptual structures are required to represent the meaning of natural language utterances in unambiguous way. Hence, any two utterances, which mean the same thing, whether they are in the same or different languages, should be characterized only in one way by the conceptual structures. This effectively means that the conceptual aspects of an utterance should be interlingual and as neutral as possible. In devising a knowledge representation, it is not kept in mind that, whether it is possible to say something in a given language or not. Whereas the attention is paid towards the fact that once something is said, a representation should account for the meaning of that utterance in an unambiguous way; and one that can be transformed back into that utterance or back into any other utterance that have the same meaning. A sentence has two visible levels namely syntactic and semantic. In addition to these, it has a level above it, and that is *conceptual*. At this level, the complete concept conveyed by the sentence is understood. In terms of knowledge representation, the construction of this level is called *conceptualization*. A conceptualization consists of basic concepts and certain relations among these concepts.

The salient motivating factors for developing the conceptual dependency theory are represented as follows:

(i)   To develop computer programs capable of understanding abstract concept conveyed by natural languages.
(ii) To make inference from the statements, and also, to identify conditions in which two sentences have similar meaning.
(iii) To develop language conversion packages.
(iv) To provide a means of representation, which are language independent.

To represent knowledge in conceptual dependency form, certain primitive actions have been defined. These primitive actions and their meaning are given below in Table 6.1.

Table 6.1: Primitive actions

CD primitive action		Explanation
1. ATRANS	:	transfer of abstract relationship like give, accept, take
2. PTRANS	:	transfer of physical location of an object like go, come, run, walk
3. PROPEL	:	Application of physical force to an object like push, pull, throw
4. MOVE	:	movement of a body part from some animate like kick
5. GRASP	:	Grasping of an object by an actor like hold
6. INGEST	:	taking some object inside like eat, drink etc.
7. EXPEL	:	Expel from an animals body (cry)
8. MTRANS	:	Transfer mental information (tell)
9. MBUILD	:	Mentally make new information (decide)
10. CONC	:	Conceptualize or think about an idea (think)
11. SPEAK	:	Produce sound (say)
12. ATTEND	:	Focus sense organ (listen)

Apart from primitive actions, the object categories are defined as:

(i)   PP : Picture producers

(ii) ACT : Actions are done by an actor to an object

(iii) LOCs : Indicates the location of the action

(iv) Ts : Indicates the time of action

(v)   AAs : Action aiders, these serve as modifiers of action like PROPEL has a speed action associated with it.

(vi) PAs : Picture Aides that serve as aides of picture producers.

In the theory of Conceptual Dependency, some basic conceptual dependency rules are defined. These are given as follows in Table 6.2:

Table 6.2: Conceptual Dependency rules

	Conceptual dependency Rule	Example
1.	PP $\Leftrightarrow$ ACT	John $\Leftrightarrow$ hit
2.	PP $<\equiv>$ PA	John $<\equiv>$ tall
3.	PP $\equiv$ PP	John $\equiv$ doctor
4.	PP $\uparrow$ PA	John $\uparrow$ tall
5.	PP $\uparrow\uparrow$ PPs	man $\uparrow\uparrow$ loc Delhi
6.	ACT $\uparrow$ o PP	

In above rules:

? : indicates the direction of dependency, and

ó : indicates two-way link between actor and action.

The main goal of CD representation is to capture the implicit concept of a sentence and make it explicit. In normal representation of the concepts, besides actor and object, other concepts of time, location, source and destination are also mentioned. Following conceptual tenses are used in CD representation:

(i)	o	:	object case relationship
(ii)	r	:	recipient case relationship
(iii)	p	:	past
(iv)	f	:	future
(v)	t	:	transition
(vi)	Ts	:	start transition
(vii)	Tf	:	finisher transition
(viii)	k	:	continuing
(ix)	?	:	interrogative
(x)	/	:	negative
(xi)	nil	:	present
(xii)	delta	:	timeless
(xiii)	c	:	conditional

CD brought forward the notion of "language independence" knowledge representation methodology, because all ACTs are language independent primitives. These primitives are used to represent the concepts of sentence. The conceptual dependency structure of some sentences are given below:

(i) Vishwant gives Vidushi a book.

$$\text{Vishwant} \Leftrightarrow \text{ATRANS} \xleftarrow{\ o\ } \text{book} \longleftarrow \begin{cases} \to \text{Vidushi} \\ \to \text{Vishwant} \end{cases}$$

Here, the arrow indicates direction of dependency. The basic activity conveyed by this sentence is "giving". Thus, ATRANS is the "primitive" to describe this event. As 'giving' activity requires, one agent (here Vishwant), one object (here gift) and one recipient (here Vidushi). In its representation, O represents object and R represents recipient.

(ii) The man took a shirt.

$$\text{Man} \overset{p}{\Leftrightarrow} \text{ATRANS} \xleftarrow{\ o\ } \text{book}$$

Here, man is the actor and shirt is the object of the action took.

(iii) I gave the man a dictionary.

$$\text{Jatin} \overset{p}{\Leftrightarrow} \text{ATRANS} \xleftarrow{\;o\;} \text{book} \longleftarrow \begin{cases} \rightarrow \text{Jatin} \\ \rightarrow \text{Man} \end{cases}$$

(ii) Adwet pushed the block.

$$\text{Adwet} \overset{p}{\Leftrightarrow} \text{PROPEL} \xleftarrow{\;o\;} \text{book}$$

Here, p indicates the past tense.

(iii) My grandmother told me a story.

$$\text{Grandmother} \overset{p}{\Leftrightarrow} \text{MTRANS} \xleftarrow{\;o\;} \text{story}$$

Grandmother   MTRANS   story

(iv) Prakhar eats ice cream.

$$\text{John} \Leftrightarrow \text{INGEST} \xleftarrow{\;o\;} \text{ice cream}$$

Prakhar   INGEST   ice cream

$$\text{John} \overset{p}{\Leftrightarrow} \text{INGEST} \xleftarrow{\;o\;} \text{ice cream}$$

(vi) Jatin bagged Meeta for a pencil.

$$\text{Jatin} \Leftrightarrow \text{SPEAK} \xleftarrow{\;o\;} \text{pencil} \longleftarrow \begin{cases} \rightarrow \text{Meeta} \\ \rightarrow \text{Jatin} \end{cases}$$

6.6 SCRIPT

We would present here one more method of knowledge representation called Scripts. It uses a frame like structure to represent the commonly occurring experiences like going to the movies, eating in a restaurant, shopping in a supermarket or visiting an ophthalmologist. The scripts structures are described in terms of the frames where different slots are used to store the field representing various activities.

An example script of 'visiting a doctor' is given in Fig. 6.8

```
SCRIPT–NAME:        Visiting a doctor
PLACE:              clinic
ROLES:              attendant
```

	Nurse
	Chemist
	Gatekeeper
	Counter clerk
	Receptionist
	Patient
	Sitting bench
	Stature
	Other specialist doctors like Anesthesia specialist, orthopedist, Pediatrician etc.
ENTRY CONDITION:	Patient need consultation
	Visiting time on
PROPS:	Medicines
	Doctor's table having thermometer, stethoscope, writing pad, torch
	OPD table having flood light on it
	Patient sitting chair
	Prescription
	Cashier
	Money
SCENE 1:	Patient enters clinic
	Patient sits on chair
SCENE 2:	Doctor examines the patient
	Doctor asks for the blood test, urine test
SCENE3:	Patient gives blood sample at collection room
	Patient gives urine sample at collection centre.
SCENE4:	Patient collects the examination reports
	Patient shows the report to doctor
SCENE5:	Doctor examines the report
	Doctor suggest the medicine
SCENE 6:	Patient pays the doctor's fees
	Patient collects the medicine
	Patient leaves the clinic
RESULTS:	Patient has less money
	Patient has prescription and medicine

Fig. 6.8: A script structure of visiting to a doctor

To perform reasoning using scripts, a script with partially filled fields is created to meet the current situation. Next, a known script, which matches with the current situation is recalled from memory. The script name, preconditions, or other keywords provide index value, which is used to search the current script. Inference is accomplished by filling a slot with inherited and default values that satisfy certain conditions. Scripts have now been used in a number of language understanding systems at YALE University by Schank and his team. One such system is Script Applier Mechanism, which reads and reasons with text to demonstrate an understanding of stories, that were script based.

6.7 CYC

CYC is a project, which was basically developed with the aim of capturing and storing commonsense knowledge. It was started in 1990. A big proportion of credit to human intelligence goes to possession of commonsense knowledge. This type of knowledge is virtually gathered in a complete lifetime of a person. The goal of CYC is to encode a large amount of knowledge that is so obvious that it is easy to state it explicitly. The commonsense knowledge is coded and stored in a separate knowledge base. Such a knowledge base could then be combined with specialized knowledge bases to produce systems that are less brittle than most of the ones available today. The CYC represents a specific theory of how to describe world. It is widely used in AI applications like natural language understanding. It is like conceptual dependency knowledge representation technique, but unlike CD, CYC is more comprehensive. The CD provides a specific theory of representation for events whereas CYC contains a more generalized representation of events, objects, attitudes etc. The CYC is used to create a very large knowledge base that usually contains millions of objects. The decision to create large database is because of following reasons:

1. *Brittleness*: Specialized knowledge base systems are brittle. They cannot handle novel situations and their program degradation is not graceful. Normally, the programs designed to handle deep commonsense knowledge about the world should have firmer and flexible knowledge bases.
2. *Form and content*: The knowledge representation techniques discussed earlier are suitable for specific applications. These techniques may or may not be sufficient for general purpose AI applications. These specific KR techniques aim primarily at form of knowledge representation as compared to the content of knowledge. Whereas, a more practical approach should aim at content of knowledge base as compared to form of knowledge representation.
3. *Shared Knowledge*: Small knowledge base systems must make simplifying assumption about how to represent things like space, time, motion and structure. If these things can be represented at a very high level than domain specific systems can gain leverage easily.

To design a big and central knowledge base having immense knowledge, one possibility is to create it from scratch, which is costly activity in terms of time and money. Other possibility is to use methods that automatically gather knowledge. The second possibility is more appealing. It can be performed using two methods:

1. ***Machine Learning***: Through automated learning, the data of solved problems is kept back for future use. However, the current techniques of learning permit only modest extensions of a program's knowledge. In order for a system to learn a great deal, it must already know more. The system with more knowledge will be able to employ powerful analogical reasoning.

2. ***Natural Language Understanding***: As mentioned earlier, human gains knowledge by reading book and talking with other humans. With the evolution of internet we have online version of encyclopedias and dictionaries, these can be directly fed to an AI program and all information can automatically be gathered, for example, if we hear the sentence:

> *"Sushil went to bank to deposit rupees one thousand",*

we easily interpret the meaning of bank as financial institution and not river bank or blood bank or sperm bank. To do this we apply deep knowledge about what a financial institution is, what is meant to deposit and rupee is a kind of money etc.

The approach adopted by CYC to code knowledge is to hand code millions of facts that makeup commonsense knowledge.

6.7.1 CYCL

The knowledge of CYC is encoded in a representation language called CYCL. It is frame-based system that incorporates most of the techniques of multiple inheritance, slot and full-fledged objects, relationships like transfer through mutually disjoint CYC. CYCL generalizes the notion of inheritance so that properties can be inherited along any link not just as a and instance. An example CYC representation is given as follows:

```
                 Mary
                       Likes: ???
              Constraints: (lisp constraint)
      Lispconstraint
                  Slotconstrint: (likes)
           Slotvalue subsumes:
```

Besides frames, CYCL contains a constraint language that allows the expression of arbitrary first order logical expressions, e.g., in above frame, indicating "Mary likes people who program solely in lisp." Mary had a constraint called lisp constraint, which restricts the value of her likes slot. The slot value subsumes attribute of lisp constraint ensures that Mary's likes slot will be filled with at least those individuals that satisfy logical condition namely that they program in lisp language and no others.

The constraint language allows for the expression of facts as arbitrary logical expression. Though first order logic is more powerful than CYC's frame language, still CYC maintains both because frame based inference is very efficient while general logical reasoning is computationally hard. CYC actually supports 20 types of efficient inference mechanisms, each with its truth maintenance facility.

The constraint language allows for the expression of facts that are too complex for any of these mechanisms to handle.

6.8 OBJECT ORIENTED REPRESENTATION

In the previous chapter, it has been mentioned that there are two types of knowledge namely declarative knowledge and procedural knowledge. The declarative knowledge represents the facts and the procedural knowledge represents the functions. The object oriented knowledge representation techniques groups the knowledge and related procedures into one cohesive unit. The grouping of facts and procedures is advisable for easy retrieval of knowledge as well as from human cognitive point of view. In human brain, the knowledge required for a given cognitive task is usually quite limited in domain and scope. Therefore, accessing and processing can be made more efficient by grouping or partitioning related knowledge, together. Analyzing the computational aspect of procedural programming languages like FORTRAN and Pascal, we find that a program consists of a procedural part and a data part. The procedural part consists of set of program instructions and the data part stores number of string and characters that are manipulated by the instruction. Program typically contains several modules of instructions that perform computation on the same data set. The updations done in one module should be reflected in all modules for the same variable. This poses heavy burden on the software maintenance process and makes these programs more prone to errors. This problem is reduced in object oriented systems (OOS). In OOS, the emphasis between data and procedures is reversed. In this, data becomes the primary object and the procedures the secondary. That is, for OOS, everything in the universe is considered as object and objects are inaccessible to outside procedures. This form of structuring is called encapsulation.

With encapsulation, the objects are associated with their own procedures and as such, are responsible for their own actions. Hence, when some change is required in data or procedure, only the changed object need be modified. Other objects are not affected and therefore require no modification. The object oriented system design is a well known design principle which makes design more modular and robust. In OOS terminology everything is considered as object, e.g., a 'car' is an object, consisting of many interacting components.

The object is defined as having a name, a class characterization, several distinguishing attributes and a set of operations, e.g., the 'car' entity will store everything about the 'car'. Hence, whenever some change is to be made in the 'car', only this object need to be called. Thus, we can say that the basic idea behind an OOS is the notion of classes of objects interacting with each other to accomplish some set of task. The objects have well defined behavior. They interact with each other through the use of messages. When a task needs to be performed on an object, a message is passed, which specifies the task requirement. The receiving object then takes appropriate action in response to the message and responds by returning a message to the sender. In performing the task, if the object needs to interact with other objects then it passes messages to other objects. In general, a task may consist of any definable operation, such as, changing an object position, loading a cargo, manipulating a character string, or popping up a prompt window. A complete program would then be a sequence of basic tasks such as the simulated movement of ships into and out of the seaport after discharging and taking on cargo.

Now let us define the basic concepts of OOS like object, class, message, methods, and class hierarchies.

6.8.1 Object

This is the most fundamental unit of Object Oriented System. All entities except parts of a message, comments and certain punctuation symbols are objects. The objects consist of data and procedures. The examples of objects are numbers like; 10, 567, 23, strings like; "India", "Rose", arrays such as; # [23, "this is my college"] , some graphic objects defined in LOGO, real world objects like flower, car, cup, tree, garden, etc. Objects are characterized by attributes and by the way, they behave when messages are sent to them. All objects belong to some class. They are created by declaring them as instances of an existing class and instantiating instance variables.

6.8.2 Message

Messages are like functions or procedures called in other languages. The actions are performed in an OOS by sending message to an object. The format of a message is

$$< object> < selector> < arg\ 1, arg2, ...arg\ n>$$

where, object is the receiver object, selector is the message selector, and arg 1,......arg n, is the sequence of arguments. Messages may also be given in place of an argument, since a message always elicits an object as response. When an object receives a valid message, it responds by taking appropriate actions like executing a procedure or sending message to other objects and then, returning a result.

The messages can be of following types:
1. *Unary message*: A unary message requires no argument.

   e.g., 7 sign,

   15 factorial,

   #(a b c) reversed,

   65 as character.

In each of these examples, the first item in the message is the receiver object and the second item is selector. The first message returns the sign of number 7, which will be 1, indicating a positive integer. The second message will return the factorial of 15. The third example returns #(c b a), the fourth example returns A, which is ASCII equivalent of number 65.

2. ***Binary message***: These are the messages that take one argument. Arithmetic operations are typically of binary types of messages. In this, the first operand is receiver, the selector is arithmetic operation to be performed and the second operand is the argument. Examples of binary messages are:

19+ 30	"an addition message"
19 – 6	"A subtraction message"
22*22	"multiplication message"
# (a b c), # (d e f)	"the comma concatenates two arrays"
7 < 9	"relational test message"
9 @ 14	"an X-Y coordinate point reference"

here, The message returned by first three examples will be their arithmetic value, the fourth message combines two arrays into one, fifth is a Boolean relational test, and last is the creation of graphical coordinate point at column 9 row 14 respectively.

3. ***Keyword Message***: These are the most general types of messages. These messages have selectors, which consist of one or more keyword identifiers, where each is followed by a colon and an argument. The argument can be an object or any message. In OOS program, the comments may be placed anywhere using double quotation mark. Example of keyword messages are:

5 between: 4 and: 10	"a Boolean test"
'aecdb' copy from: 4 to: 7	"copies position 4 of the string to position 7"
#(a b c x) at: 4 put: # (d e)	"the elements of #(d e) replace x in array"
set 1 add: (i+1)	"add new elements to set 1"

The execution of a message takes place from left to right. Regarding operators, the unary messages take precedence followed by binary and then keyword.

6.8.3 Method

In the terminology of OOS, the procedures are called methods. They determine the behavior of an object when a message is sent to the object. Methods are sequence of instructions executed by an object, e.g., in order to respond to the message 6 + 8, the object 6 must initiate the method to find the sum of integer numbers 6 and 8.

Methods are written in programming languages. The constructs used to build higher level methods are defined in terms of a number of primitive operations and basic methods provided as part of the OOS. The primitives of an OOS are coded in some host language such as an assembler language or C. A typical OOS may have as many as, a few hundred predefined primitives and basic methods combined.

6.8.4 Class and Hierarchies

A class is a general object that defines a set of individual instances of objects, which share common characteristics. For example, the class of rabbits contain many individual rabbit objects, each with four legs, long ears, whiskers and short bushy tails. All objects are instances of some class and class hierarchies. The classes are subclasses of some higher class, except for a most general root class. The root class for an OOS is the class named object.

Classes permit the formation of hierarchies of objects, which can be depicted as a tree. Objects of same class have same variable and the same method. They also respond to the same set of messages called protocol of the class. Each class in the hierarchy inherits the variables and methods of all of its parents or super class of the class.

When a message is sent to the object, first it is checked that the method of the message belongs to same class or not. If it is not so, the method of nearest super class is checked. If they are not adequate, the search process continues up the hierarchy recursively until methods have been found or the end of a chain has been reached. If the concerned method is not obtained an error message is printed.

One important feature of object oriented knowledge representation is polymorphism. Polymorphism is the capability for different objects to respond to the same message protocols but exhibit their own unique behavior in response, e.g., a selector move forward could invoke the forward movement of a ship as well as advancing a piece in a game such as checkers. Both classes use the same message template but respond differently. The only requirement is that the message protocol for the classes be implemented as required for a given class.

6.8.5 Object Oriented Languages

This section discusses some object oriented languages. There are many object oriented languages like extended LISP, various versions of Small talk and many more. Here we discuss extended LISP in brief.

6.8.5.1 OOS with LISP extension

One language based on LISP, developed primarily for OOS is FLAVORS. In FLAVORS, classes are created with deflavor form, and methods are created with defmethod. An instance of a flavor is created with a make-instance type of function.

For example, to create a new flavor class of ships with instance variables x-position, y-position, x-velocity, y-velocity, and cargo capacity, the following expression is evaluated:

```
(deflavor ship( x-position y-position x-velocity y-velocity cargo capacity))
```

Methods are written for ship flavor in a similar manner with a defmethod, say for ship's speed, as:

```
(defmethod (ship: speed)( )
(sqrt (+ (* x-velocity x-velocity)
(* y-velocity y-velocity))))
```

Values for the ship instance variable can now be assigned either with a message or when the instance of the ship is created.

(send ship-42: set-cargo- capacity 22.5)

or

(setf ship42 (make- instance'ship: x-position 5.0

: y-position 8.0))

Variable assignments can be examined with the describe method, one of the base methods provided with the system

(describe ship42)

#< SHIP 1234567>, an object of flavor ship,

has instance variable values:

x-position   5.0

y-position   8.0

x-velocity   unbound

y-velocity   unbound

Cargo Capacity   22.5

Besides the extensions of LISP, there are some special purpose languages for OOS systems. A typical special purpose OOS language is ROSS developed by Rand Corporation for military battle simulation. Messages are sent to objects in ROSS with an "ask" form having the following structure:

(ask <object><message>)

For example, to send a message to a fighter base requesting that a fighter be sent to intercept a penetrator, the following message might be sent:

(ask fighter- base1 send fighter2 guided by radar3 to penetrator 2)

in response to this message, a method associated with the fighter base class would be evaluated and appropriate actions would be initiated through direct computations and embedded message transmissions to other objects.

EXERCISES

1. What are main differences between frame structures and scripts.
2. Transform the following FOPL statements into equivalent conceptual graph.
   (a) " x NORMAL(x) & GROWN(x) ® WALK (x)
   (b) " x, y MARRIED (x, y) ® MARRIED (y, x).
   (c) " x HASWINGS(x) & LAYEGGS(x) ® ISBIRD(x)
3. Express the following sentences into equivalent conceptual dependency structures.
   (a) Bill is a programmer
   (b) Sam gave Mary a box of candy
   (c) Charlie drove the pickup fast.
4. Consider following conceptual graph:
   person :   Sajid
   agent   eat

object   soup
instrument
part   hand
translate this conceptual graph into predicate calculus.

5. Give evidence from your own experience that suggests a frame like organization of human memory.

6. Define a script for
    (i)   fast food restaurant
    (ii) interacting with a usual car salesperson
    (iii) going to the opera.

7. Construct a hierarchy of subtypes for concept vehicle, e.g., the subtype may be two wheeler and 4 wheeler. They can have further subtypes. Is this best represented as tree, lattice or general graph. Do the same for the concept " move" and" angry".

7

Programming Languages

7.1 INTRODUCTION

We have understood by now that AI problem solving requires use of knowledge and that knowledge has to be coded in a form suitable from computational aspects. Various programming techniques have been developed for this purpose. The basic aim of programming language is to implement the representation and control structure required for intelligent problem solving. The need of these structures to a large extent determines the features of required AI implementation language. In this chapter we will discuss the programming languages named PROLOG and LISP used for AI problem solving. These two are the most frequently used languages in artificial intelligence. The most acknowledgeable advantage of these languages is that their syntactic and semantic features devise powerful ways of thinking about problems and their solutions. Over the years, these languages have had powerful influence on the historical development of AI. The ability of these languages to function as "tools for thinking" is vivid reflection of their strength as programming languages. These languages are well used in areas like:

- Maintaining a big knowledge base
- For building inference engine
- For building natural language interface
- For dynamic knowledge acquisition

7.1.1 Prolog

In chapter 5, it is discussed that one most popular logic based Knowledge representation technique is use of predicate and propositional logic. The programming language which is used for this purpose is PROLOG (**PRO**gramming in **LOG**ic). The logic programming is essential part of AI problem solving and its contribution in this regard is significant. These contributions are its declarative semantics, a means of directly expressing problem relationships in AI as well as built in unification, some techniques for pattern matching and search.

The use of PROLOG as AI implementation language has its roots in research on theorem proving by J.A. Robinson. Robinson designed *resolution procedure* for theorem proving. Prolog is quite useful in solving the problems related with automatic code generation, program verification and design of high level specification language.

The prolog was first written in Masseille in 1970s as part of project in natural language understanding. The major development of Prolog language was carried out from 1975 to 1979 at department of Artificial Intelligence of University of Edinburgh. They produced first prolog interpreter robust enough for delivery to the general computing community. This system was built on DEC system-10 and could operate in both interpretive and compiled modes. Prolog is quite important language and is used in many research projects.

The basic syntax of prolog consists of rules and facts. The fact is a statement of truth or belief in one's world. The collection of facts gives rise to knowledge. The facts can be represented by defining suitable predicates. Some facts are as given below:

- My *name* is "Adwet."
- My *"age"* is "10" years.
- My *country* is "India."
- "Babbar" was *father* of "Humayun."
- "India" is a *"cricket" playing* nation.
- Dial *"101"* in case of fire.
- "Carbon" is an *element and its symbol* is "C."
- "Shyam" is a *bachelor* aged "30", is a *"graduate"* and is working as manager in "State Bank of India."
- "Mother" *likes* "Son."
- "Das" is an *operating system*.

7.1.2 Lisp

LISP has derived its name from **LISt** Processing. The list is the basis of both programs and data structures in LISP. LISP was first proposed by John McCarthy in the late 1950s. Originally, the language was intended to alternative model of computation based on the theory of recursive functions. In the beginning, the aim of McCarthy was to create a language for symbolic rather than numeric computations, to implement a model of computation based on the theory of recursive functions, to provide a clear definition of the syntax and semantics of the language and to formally demonstrate completeness of this computational model. Though LISP is one of the oldest computing languages still in existence, the thought process given to its original design and the extensions and modifications made to it throughout its life time have kept the language alive among the bunch of programming languages. In fact, this programming model have proved to be so effective that a number of other languages have derived roots from the concept of functional programming, e.g., SCHEME, ML, and FP.

LISP was originally designed as a compact language consisting of functions for constructing and accessing lists, defining new functions and evaluating expressions. A single condition and recursion were the only means to control the program. Whenever needed, more complicated functions were defined in terms of these primitives. With the time, these new functions became part of the language itself. This process of extending the language by adding new functions led to the development of several dialects of LISP. These dialects act as a vehicle riding on which, LISP, from a simple model of computing, has evolved into a rich and powerful tool for building large intelligent systems.

7.1.3 Declarative v/s Procedural Language

In procedural programming (in languages like Pascal, basic etc.) we tell the computer what to do and exactly how to do it. This is done through specific instructions given to the machine in the program. A typical example of procedural approach is:

```
J:= 1;
For 1: = 1 to 10
Begin
J:=  (J * 1) /1;
Write ( J)
End;
```

In procedural languages, we specify the iterations, the calculation and the variable assignments through each iteration.

Unlike this, in declarative languages like Prolog, we merely describe or declare the problem and it is up to the computer to find the solution. What is implied here that it is actually the language which takes care of telling the computer how to find a solution or perform a task. In the following sections, you will find that a prolog program looks like:

```
Like (John,  football)
Likes ( bill , cricket)
Likes Mary (x) if likes (x, football) – (rule)
```

Here program will infer from the given facts and rules that Mary likes John, though we did not tell Prolog what and how to do it. Declarative programming emphasizes static facts and rules and the procedural details are hidden in the inference mechanism. It should be noted here that there is a trade off between the two styles of programming. in the programming in these different language the efficiency is achieved at the cost of reliability. By telling a computer how to obtain a solution, we introduce complexities in the program, thereby reducing the reliability of the result. Which out of the two approaches i.e. declarative or procedural should be selected, depends a lot upon the situation on hands. However, Prolog is not a pure declarative language, though it leans more towards declarative side.

7.1.4 Still Prolog and Lisp?

Year after year, the field of Artificial Intelligence has developed and matured considerably demonstrating its utility and applicability to wide range of practical problems. Because of this, the dependence of AI on PROLOG and LISP has also diminished. The varying needs and standards in the field of software development and artificial intelligence programming have led to the development of AI systems in various languages such as C, C++, Smalltalk and Java, still PROLOG and LISP continue to enjoy the importance given to them by AI programmers because of their prototyping abilities and power to act as thinking tools.

Also, these languages have provided ground for development of features which are incorporated into modern programming languages. The best example to illustrate this is Java language, which uses and derives benefits from the features, such as dynamic binding, automatic memory management and other, of AI programming languages.

7.2 PROGRAMMING IN PROLOG

PROLOG has made enormous contribution to problem solving in AI. As mentioned earlier, PROLOG is an implementation of logic programming. A logic program is a set of specifications in formal logic. PROLOG makes use of first order predicate calculus. The use of the representational power of the first-order predicate calculus to express specifications for problem solving by PROLOG has made it of immense importance to computer science in general, and to artificial intelligence in particular. The benefits of using first-order predicate calculus for a programming language include a clear syntax and well- defined semantics.

PROLOG has proved to be a useful tool for investigating experimental programming issues such as, automatic code generation, program verification and design of high-level specification language. PROLOG and other such logic based languages support a declarative style of programming rather than a procedural one. A declarative style of programming puts emphasis on constructing a program in terms of descriptions of the constraints of a problem, whereas, the procedural style of programming means writing a program as sequence of instructions for implementing an algorithm.

A detailed overview of programming using PROLOG is given in subsequent paragraphs.

7.2.1 Representation of Facts

In logic programming the facts can be manipulated to draw some conclusion. For purpose of processing knowledge, facts are represented in some convenient form. Prolog uses simple ways to represent these facts. It has following elements for fact representation:

7.2.1.1 *Integer and Real*

Any numerical value can be represented using 'domain' integer or real. An integer value represents a whole number and is a string of digits. The range of valid integer varies from machine to machine. The normal range is from -32768 to 32767. Examples of valid integers are-

101,   99,   -50,   1,   32767

The domain real represents fractional number. It has a value associated with a fractional part. It can be used to represent facts like percentage of marks, fees of a student, temperature of a day etc. the numbers can be represented in either normal number or in exponent notation. Thus a real number is represented in following format of digits-

- an optional leading + or − sign
- an optional decimal point followed by a sequence of digits representing fractional part
- an optional character 'e' representing exponent
- positive or negative maximum three digit indicating value of exponent

Examples of valid real numbers are-
    32777,   -53.54e-47,   0.101e4

7.2.1.2 *Variable or Symbol*

A variable can store some value. It is a sequence of letters uppercase and lower case, digits 0 to 9 and special character underscore.

The symbol value is written in double quote. Examples of symbol are-
Name,   Roll-number,   "Adwet",   father

7.2.1.3 *String*

It is sequence of character enclosed within double quotes. It can be used to store some sentence, phrase, paragraphs.

Examples of string are:
"my country is best"
"my name is Kumar Adwet"

In prolog, variables can be declared as of string type and it can store values of string type.

7.2.1.4 *Representing facts*

To represent the fact in prolog, some symbol is chosen which suitably represent the relation among various parts constituting the fact. For example, consider the following fact:
"my name is Adwet"

To represent this fact, the possible symbol may be my-name, the data corresponding to this will be Adwet. Thus it will be represented as
my-name (Adwet)

The symbol name (i.e. my-name) can be anything (e.g. name or x or p) but it is customary to take meaningful name appropriate to facts. Representations of some facts are as follows:

	Fact	Representation
(a)	Gaurav is my friend	my friend (Gaurav)
(b)	Milind is adwet's father	father ("Milind", "Adwet")
(c)	Rabindranath Tagore is author of Gitanjali	author("Rabindranath Tagore", "Gitanjali")
(d)	John likes Bill	like (John, Bill)
(e)	Everyone likes Sue	likes (Everyone, Sue)
(f)	John likes Bill and John likes Sue	likes (John, Bill); likes (John, Sue)

there may be statements having multiple facts. These are represented using connectors between basic atomic facts. The connectors in prolog are represented as –

English	Prolog
and	,
or	;
only if	:-
not	not

A prolog program consists of a set of specifications describing some facts and relations corresponding to problem domain. The facts collectively referred as database for that problem. The prolog interpreter responds to questions about this set of specifications. Queries to database are patterns in the same logical syntax as the database entities. The prolog interpreter uses pattern directed search to find the answer.

7.2.1.5 Variables

A variable is a symbol that can store some data value. It is called as variable bound to that data. The symbol or variable name can be kept according to rules of identifier naming except that leading character of symbol must be upper case letter.

Examples of symbols are:

Name,   Age,   X,   Father_name,   Employee_name.

The variable can be bound variable or free variable. The bound variable can be assigned a data value. A free variable is one to which no value is assigned.

7.2.1.6 Queries

The queries or Goals are questions regarding given facts. The facts and rules are stored in database and prolog interpreter finds the answer to the goals.

e.g.   goal   :my_friend ("Gaurav")
        true

        goal   :my_friend ("Piyush") and my_friend ("Vertika")
        true

        goal   :my_friend (X)
        X= "Gaurav"
        X= "Piyush"
        X= "Vartika"

7.2.2 Basics of Programming

To write Prolog program, the facts and rules are specified in corresponding domain. Then queries may be asked in form of goal. Prolog is primarily an interpreted language. Some versions of Prolog run only in interpretive mode, while other allows partial or complete compilation of program or all of the set for faster execution. Prolog is interactive language.

Consider the following facts:
* Patna is capital of Bihar
* Lucknow is capital of Utter Pradesh
* Chandigarh is capital of Haryana
* Bihar, Utter Pradesh and Haryana are states of India
* India is a country

These will be represented as:
* capital ("Patna", "Bihar")
* capital ("Lucknow", "U.P.")
* capital ("Chandigarh", "Haryana")
* states ("Bihar", "U.P.", "Haryana")
* country ("India")

The symbol outside parenthesis is called *predicate name*.
Prolog allows defining the rules. For example R1, R2, R3 are rules.

R1: "If X is son of Y, then Y will be father of X"

this rule can be written as:
Son_of (X, Y) :- father_of (Y ,X)
R2: If X is son of Y, Y is son of Z then X is grandson of Z.
Can be written as:
son (X,Y), son (Y,Z) :- grandson (X,Z)

Similarly,
R3: X is a parent of Y, if X is either father of Y or X is mother of Y
Can be written as:

    parent (X,Y) :- father (X,Y)
    parent (X,Y) :- mother (X,Y)

In PROLOG , The task of program development is divided into two parts:
* creation of data file, and
* development of program file

The data file stores all facts and program file stores rules. One example of program for student information is as follows:

    / file name   student information
domain
    roll_number, class, = integer
    name, father name, = symbol
predicates { - - - body of program

            - - -

        }

7.2.2.1 I/O and String Manipulation

Prolog has inbuilt functions for giving input and taking output. The input statement is 'write'. Its general form is:

$$\text{Write } (x_1, x_2, \ldots\ldots, x_n)$$

Where x_i is variable (bound to some value) or it may be a constant. The value of x_i must be assigned before its use. e.g. assume a fact,

"Gaurav" is friend of "Adwet"

represented as:

friend ("Gaurav", "Adwet")

Now the goal

friend (x_1, x_2),
write $(x_1$ is friend of $x_2)$

will give the display,

Gaurav is friend of Adwet.

\n, \t, \integer value can be used in write statement to indicate start of new line, from the text tab position and the output of a character with decimal ASCII code equal to integer value.

The input statement is readint. The readint (X) will accept a sequence of character terminated by return or enter key. The variable X must be integer. To read real and character number statements are read real (X), read char (X). Free variable X must be of type read and character simultaneously.

The standard input and output devices are keyboard and screen. If required, the input can be given from files also.

The output can be taken in specific form also. For this purpose, the inbuilt predicate *writef* is used. It outputs the constants and bound arguments as per specifications with a format specification string. Writef (formatspecification string $x_1, x_2, ..., x_n$) results in formatted output as per the specifications within format specification string.

7.2.1.2 String Manipulation

An arbitrary number of characters enclosed within a pair of quotes constitute a string. Prolog provides a number of built in predicates for string manipulation, e.g.

        "My country is best"

        "My name is Kumar Adwet"

are strings.

    There are many operations that can be applied on the strings.

    Predicate str_len is used to find number of characters in a string.

    A string can be broken into two parts; one, leading character that can be found by predicate 'frontchar', and other, rest of string.

    To join two strings, predicate 'concat' is used. It accepts input as two strings and binds the result to a variable given as third argument.

    Predicate str_char is used for conversion of a string to char and vice versa.

    predicate str_int and str_real is used for conversion from string to integer and string to real.

    Predicate upper_lower is used to convert a string from upper case to lower case.

    Predicate file_str converts between the contents of a file to a string.

    Some examples of programs related to string are given below:

- what is length of a null string

  goal: str_len ("   ", N)

  N = 0

- goal: str_len ("My name is Adwet", N)

  N = 16

Example1:

Program to convert a given string into list of constituting characters.

```
domains
      list = char
predicates
      str_list (string, list, integer)
clauses
      str_list ("    ", [    ], o)
      str_list (st, [H|Tail], N) :-
                  frontchar (st, H, S1)
                  str_list (S1, Tail, N1),
                  N = N1+ 1,
                  str_list (St, N),
```

goal str_len ("Lotus", L, R)
    L = ['L','o', 't', 'u', 's'], R = 5

Example 2:

Program for counting occurrence of a specific word in a string.

```
predicates
        count_word (string, string, integer)
clauses
        count_word (_, "    ", o),
        count_word (X, string, count) :-
                front token (string, X, Reststring),
                count_word (X, Reststring, count1),
                count = count1 + 1
count_word (X, string, count) :-
                front token (string, Y, Reststring),
                not (X=Y)
                count_word (X, Reststring, count),
```

7.2.2.2 *Arithmetic and Relational Expression*

Prolog is basically developed for logic programming and it is not a procedural language. But it also allows the construction of arithmetic and relational expression. The programmer can create an arithmetic expression and can bind it to certain value using assignment operator.

An expression is created using operands and operator. Operands are constants such as, integer, real, character, symbol, string etc. or variables instantiated to values belonging to standard domains. The expression can be

```
Total = Total + 5,
Sum = 0
Value = 3/4 + 5/4
```

7.2.2.3 *Arithmetic Operator*

The operators provided by prolog to perform arithmetic operations are as follows:

Operator	Function
- or +	unary negation
mod,	remainder operation
div,	integer division
*, /	multiplication and division
+, -	addition and subtraction

The precedence of evaluation of these operators are from top to bottom (i.e. unary + or – highest precedence and addition or subtraction lowest precedence).

The evaluation of expression consisting of operator of same precedence is done from left to right. The precedence of operation evaluation can be changed by the use of paranthesis.

Examples of some expressions are:

X+1,   random (X) * N,   B * B- 4.0 * A * C,   Result = N*Res 1

In case of division, the answer is always of real type. The mathematical functions can be framed in form of rules also, e.g. following are valid mathematical expressions:

    add (A,B,C) :-

                C = A + B;
                write ©;
                nl.

    log (X) :-

                Y = log (X)
                write (Y)
                nl.

        exp (X) :-
                Y = exp (X),
                write (Y),
                nl.

        rand (N,X) :-
                rand (Y),
                Y = (N*N + N) * Y.

Some built in predicates to perform arithmetic manipulations are given in following table:

Name	Function	Meaning
abs	abs (X)	in case X is bound to –a, the value of abs (X) returns the value, a otherwise it returns normal value of a.
sin	sin (X)	calculate the sine of angle 'x'
cos	cos(X)	calculate the cosine of angle 'x'
tan	tan (X)	calculate the tangent of angle 'x'
arctan	arctan (X)	calculate the $\tan^{-1}$ of this value
exp	exp (X)	calculate exponentiation of X i.e. (e^x)
ln	ln (X)	calculate the natural log of X (i.e. $\log_e(X)$)
log	log (X)	calculate log of X base 10
sqrt	sqrt (X)	calculate square root of X
random	random(X)	results in binding of a real value to X in the range 0 to 1
round	round(X)	returns integer part of value bound to X

7.2.2.4 Relational Operator

A relational operator is applied in two operands. It gives the answer in true or false. A typical relational expression may look like:

$$e_1 \qquad op \qquad e_2$$

where e_1 and e_2 are either constants or variable bound to some values and op is a relational operator. The expression can be of type real, integer, character, string or symbol and op is relational operator. Various relational operators are:

Name	Meaning
>	greater than
>=	greater than or equal to
<	less than
<=	less than or equal to
=	equal to
<>	not equal to

Some examples of relational expressions are as follows:

$$N > 5, \qquad C >= \text{'a'}, \qquad X < \text{'Z'}$$

A relational expression can be goal or subgoal.

7.2.2.5 Cuts

While the analysis of some goal is to be performed, PROLOG requires backtracking. In the process of backtracking, if any subgoal corresponding to a goal is not satisfied, the rest of goals are not tried to be satisfied and prolog starts back from fresh trying another rule. Sometimes when rulebase is large after many steps the back tracking is required. This causes inefficiency in a program. To prevent backtracking whenever desired, prolog provides the facility of cuts.

Let a series to be summed like this:

$$\text{Rule 1:} \qquad \text{sum}(X) = X + \frac{X^2}{2} \text{ if } \quad X > 3$$

$$\text{Rule 2:} \qquad \text{sum}(X) = X - \frac{X^2}{2} \text{ if } \quad -3 < x < 3$$

$$\text{Rule 3:} \qquad \text{sum}(X) = 0 \qquad \text{if} \quad X = 3$$

These rules are mutually exclusive i.e. for any possible value of X, any one rule will hold and correspondingly the value of Sum will be calculated. Thus the program should be written in such a way that only one rule is instantiated. This can be done with the help of cuts. Cut is represented by symbol !. Thus using cuts, the above rules will be written as:

Rule 1:	sum (X,X) :-	X>3!
Rule 2:	sum (X, X) :-	X≥ -3!
Rule 3:	sum (X) :-	X<3

If the goal is given like sum (2, Ans), after comparing the value of X with 2, the rule 1 will be dropped and rule 2 will be instantiated.

7.2.2.6 Logical Operators

The logical operators are AND and OR. The symbol for AND is ' ,' and for OR is ;. This AND operation gives answer 'true' if both operand expressions are true, and 'false' if any one is false. The 'OR' operation gives answer 'true' if any one operand operation is true.

7.2.2.7 Lists

A list is a simple data structure which represents an ordered sequence of n numbers of elements. These elements of list are put in square brackets separated by commas. Elements of a list may be of any type i.e. integer, real, character, string or symbol.

Following are valid examples of lists:

[1, 2, 99, 10, 13, -15, 17]
[3.14159, 15p, 17.53, 3.0e10]
[Kanpur, Lucknow, Agra, Allahabad]
[violet, indigo, blue, green, yellow, orange, red]

Any list can be broken into two parts, 'head' and 'tail'. The first element is called 'head' and rest of the list is called 'tail'. The empty list is represented by [ ]. Thus, in general a list can be represented as:

[Head | Tail]

e.g.   [Kanpur | Lucknow, Agra, Allahabad]

The tail can further be decomposed into head and tail. Thus above list looks like:

[Kanpur | [Lucknow | Agra, Allahabad]]

Similarly, decomposing further, the list will be:

[Kanpur | [Lucknow, | [Agra | [Allahabad | [ ]]]]]

There are various operations that can be applied on list, like finding whether a particular element is present in a list or not, the length of list, appending two lists etc.

7.2.2.7 Membership of a list

Predicate 'membership' checks whether a particular element is present in a list or not. The predicate is defined as follows:

                member (X, [X | _])
                member (X, [_ | Tail]) :-
                            member (X, tail).

The algorithm for membership predicate works as follows:
Element E is a member of the list L if:
*   X is equal to the head of the list L, or
*   X is member of the tail of the list L.

Consider following list:
    [a, b, c, d, e, f, g, h]

    Goal: member (a, [ ])
    False
    Goal: member (X, [X, Y, Z])
    X = "X"
    X = "Y"
    X = "Z"

Here, in the successive execution of member function, first variable X will be bound to first element. In next execution, it will be bounded to second element and next time to third element and so on.

Predicate member is quite useful for many applications, e.g. three lists may be created. In one list name of states may be stored and in second, name of their capitals and in third, their languages may be stored. The values are stored in the same order, e.g., the first element of first list stores some state, the first element of second list stores capital of that state and first element of third list stores language spoken by the native of that state. These rules may be stored in clause section e.g.,

    Info (X, Y, Z) :-   member (X, ["Haryana", "Rajasthan", "Utter Pradesh"]
                            member (Y, ["Chandigarh", "Jaipur", "Lucknow"]
                            member (Z, ["Haryanvi", "Rajasthani", "Hindi"]

Within the predicate section we include the general form of this predicate, i.e.
Info (symbol, symbol, symbol)
Then, if we give a goal such as:
    Info (A, B, C)
the program gives answer:
    A = "Haryana"
    B = "Chandigarh"
    C = "Haryanvi"
In the next run,
    A = "Rajasthan"
    B = "Jaipur"
    C = "Rajasthani"
Similarly in the third run, other values will be given.

The prolog interpreter generates these solutions by simple pattern matching. The tree travel algorithm is called as "Depth first" because, to find the solution, the prolog interpreter goes as deep as possible before the search back tracks up to look for additional solutions. Thus, in above example, it binds variable X to "Haryana", Y to "Chandigarh" and Z to "Haryanvi". In successive runs, it binds the next head member to variable X, Y and Z in the same order.

7.2.2.7.2 Addition of two lists

Two lists can be joined or appended using 'append' predicate. The result is stored into third list, e.g.,

Goal: append(["Haryana", "Rajasthan", "Utter Pradesh"],
                      ["Madhya Pradesh", "Bihar", "Gujrat"])

stares =   ["Haryana", "Rajasthan", "Utter Pradesh", "Madhya Pradesh",
             "Bihar", "Gujrat"])

The append operation works as follows:
        append ([   ], L, L)
        append ([Head | Tail1], List2, [Head | Tail3]) :-
                append (Tail1, List2, Tail3).

i.e., if first argument is bound to an empty list, then the resultant list is the same as stored list; (i.e. append ([   ], L, L)) otherwise, when the first argument is bound to a non empty list then same has its Head and Tail.

7.2.2.7.3 Deletion from a list

To delete any element from a list, it is compared with the Head of the list, if it happens to be the same, then Tail of the list is copied in output parameter and the first element stands deleted, otherwise the Head is copied as such in the list and same predicate is operated on Tail of the list. Thus, predicate delete can be written as:
        Delete (X, [X | Tail], Tail)
        Delete (X, [Y | Tail], [Y | Z]) :-
                        Delete (X, Tail, Z).
Consider a list,
        list = [a, b, c]
    Goal: delete (a, [a, b, c], X)
            X = ["b", "c"]
Goal delete (X, [a, b, c], L)

        No solution

Goal delete (X, [X, Y, Z, X], [Y, X, Z])
        True

In the situation where all the occurrences of a desired object is to be deleted, the predicate would be like this:

```
            domain
                    list = symbol
            predicate
                    delete (symbol, list, list )
    clauses
            delete ( _, [   ], [   ]).
            delete (X, [X | Tail], Result) :-
                            delete (X, Tail, Result).
            delete (X, [Y | Tail], [Y | Result]) :-
                            not (X = Y),
                            delete (X, Tail, Result).
    Goal:  delete (X, [X, Y, X, Z], L)
           L = ("Y", "Z")
    Goal   delete (X, ["1", "2", "3"], A)
           A = ["1", "2", "3"]
```

A related application of list can be where every occurrence of a symbol is replaced by another given symbol. This predicate will first check the presence of first symbol in the input list then it will write second symbol at the same place.

The predicate for this will be as follows:

```
    predicates
            replace (symbol, symbol, list, list)
    clauses
            replace ( _, _, [   ], [   ])
            replace (X, Y, [Z | T1], [Z | T2]) :-
                            not (X = Z),
                            replace (X, Y, T1, T2).
```

The predicate requires two symbols, one which symbol is to be replaced and other by which it is to be replaced; and two lists, one input list and other output list.

The first clause means in case the input list is a null list, the output list is also null list. This serves as a terminating condition. The second clause results in binding of X to old value for the purpose of replacement and Y is bound to new value. Third and fourth argument looks at head and tail of the input list. Here, in case Head is same as X, it will be replaced by Y and Y is bound to Head of output list. If Head is not same as X, then X is bound to Head of output list.

7.2.3 Examples on Prolog

This section presents some examples on prolog programming.

Example 1. Write a prolog program to find length of an input list.

Answer:

```
        /* length of a list */
    domains
        symbolist = symbol *
        integerlist = integer *
    predicates
        length (symbolist, integer)
        length (integerlist, integer)
    clauses
        length ([   ], 0)
        length ([ _ | Tail], N) :-
                        length (Tail, N1).
                        N = 1 + N1
```

Explanation:

The first clause means that if the input list is a null list like resulting variable gets instantiated to zero and serves as the terminating condition. Second predicate invokes predicate length recursively on Tail, to find length of Tail, and adds one to find length of total length.

Example 2: Write a prolog program to count presence of a token string in a given input string.

Answer:

```
        predicate (string, string, integer)
    clauses
        number ( _, "    ", 0)
        number (X, string, count) :-
                        front token (string, X, rest string),
                        number (X, rest string, count1),
                        count = count + 1.
        Number (X, string, count)

                        :-
                        front token (string, Y, rest string),
                            not (X = Y)
                        number (X, rest string, count)
```

Explanation:

Here, clause 1 serves as a terminating condition. Clause 2 checks the first token. If it is same as the token to be searched, the count is incremented by 1 and Head of the string is removed. In third clause, if token is not equal to the word that is to be searched, the count is not incremented and next token is searched. It works as follows:

Goal: number ("Very", "He is very good boy", X)
           X = 1
Goal: number ("Very", "He is very very good boy", X)
           X = 2
Goal: number ("Very", "He is good boy", X)
           X = nil

Example 3: Consider two lists arranged in ascending order. Write a prolog code to merge in one ordered list.

Answer:

```
predicate
          merge (integer list, integer list, integer list,)
clauses
          merge ([   ], L, L).
          merge (L, [   ], L,).
     merge ( [X | Rest1], [Y | Rest2], [X | Rest3]) :-
                                              X < Y
          merge (Rest1, [Y | Rest2], Rest3).
     merge ([X | Rest1], [Y | Rest2], [Y | Rest3]) :-
                                              X > Y
          merge ([X | Rest1], Rest2, Rest3).
```

Explanation:

The first two clauses serve as terminating condition. If any one list is null, another list is copied into result list, otherwise the two input lists are replaced into head and tail. If head of first list (X) is less than head of second list Y, X is copied into third list. If head of first list X is greater than head of second list Y, Y is copied into third list. It works as follows:

```
Goal:  merge ([2, 6, 10, 13], [0, 5, 7, 9], L)
       L = [0, 2, 5, 6, 7, 9, 10, 13]
```

This program assumes that the input list stores integers. If they contain real or integer, they should be accordingly declared.

Example 4: Write a prolog program to find union of two sets.
Answer:

```
predicate
     union (integer list, integer list, integer list,)
clauses
     union ([   ], L, L).
     union ( [ H | Tail1], L2, [ H | Tail3]) :-
          member (H, L2),
```

```
            delete (H, L2, L3),
            union (Tail1, L3, Tail3).
union ([ H | Tail1], L2, [ H | Tail3]) :-
            not (member (H, L2)   ),
            union (Tail1, L2, Tail3).
```

Explanation:

The predicate assumes that the elements of the set are of integer type. The first clause serves as terminating condition. The second and third clause calls predicate delete and member. They should be included externally (by "include" statement). The second clause removes head from the first set and copies into third set, if that element is present in the set also, it is removed from there and union is called for tail of first set and the result set. If the head element is not a member of second set, it is copied into result set.

Example 5: Write a prolog program to find whether a given set is sub set of another set.

Answer:

```
predicates
        subset (integer list, integer list)
        member ([ Y | Tail], L) :- member (Y, L),
                            subset (Tail, L)
clauses
        subset ( [   ], _ ).
        subset ([ Y | Tail], L) :- member (Y,L),
                            subset (Tail, L).
        member (Y, [Y1, _ ]).
        member (Y, [ _ | Tail1]) :- member (Y, Tail ).
```

Explanation:

It is assumed that two sets store integer values. The first clause says that a null set is sub set of any set. Second set separates head of first list, checks it in L, if head (Y) i.e. Y is member of L, then presence of tail is checked in the set.

Example 6: Write a prolog program to ignore space characters from input.

Answer:

```
predicate
        ignore _ space
clauses
        ignore _ space :-
            read char ©,
            char _ int (C, N),
            N = 27,
```

exit.

;

N = 32

ignore _ space

;

write ©;

ignore _ space

***Example 7*:** Write a LISP program to solve *Tower of Hanoi* problem.
Answer:

The tower of Hanoi problem requires moving of disks from one tower to another
in such a way that
- one and only one disk is to be moved at one time
- A larger disk may never be placed on a smaller disk.

The prolog code is as follows:

```
        domains
    loc = a; b; c;
    predicates
            tower_of_hanoi ( integer)
            move ( integer, loc, loc, loc)
            output( loc, loc)
    clauses
            tower_of_hanoi ( N)  :- move ( N, a, b, c).
            move ( 1, A,  B,  _ ) :- output (A, B).
            move ( N, A,B,C) :-
            N  >= 2,
            N_1 = N – 1,
            move ( N_1, A,  C, B),
            output (A, B),
            move (N_1, C, B, A).
```

output (X, Y) :- write (" \n move on disk from ", X, " to " Y).
running this code will be as follows.

```
        Goal : tower_of_hanoi (4)
```

Move on disk from a to c
Move on disk from a to b
Move on disk from c to b
Move on disk from a to c
Move on disk from b to a
Move on disk from b to c

Move on disk from a to c
Move on disk from a to b
Move on disk from c to b
Move on disk from c to a
Move on disk from b to a
Move on disk from c to b
Move on disk from a to c
Move on disk from a to b
Move on disk from c to b

Example 8: Write a PROLOG code for reading in a character, and deciding if it is digit or an alphanumeric character.
Answer:

```
domain
                /* finding a character whether digit or alphanumeric

predicates
    alphanumeric ( char)
    alpha ( char)
    digit ( char)
    run1
    run

clauses
    run1:-
    readchar(X),
    alphanumeric (X).
    alphanumeric (X) :- char_int (X< 27), exit.
    alphanumeric (X) :- alpha(X) ; digit (X);
    write ( "\n character typed in is not an alphanumeric \ n")

    alpha (X) :- X>= 'a',
    X <= 'z',
    !,
    write ( "lowercase alphabet"), n1.
    alpha (X) :- <= 'z',
    !write ( uppercase alphabet"), n1.
    digit (X) :- X = '0',
    X<= '9',
    write ( "digit"),n1.
    run:- write ( "\n type in a character \n"),
    run1, run
```

Example 9: Write a PROLOG program to find maximum element of a list.
Answer:

```
                domains
                integerlist = integer*
        predicates
        max (integerlist, integer)
                clauses
                max([X],  X).
                max ( [ H ! Tail ], H ) :- max ( Tail, MaxTail), H > MaxTail.
                max ( H ! Tail], MaxTail) :- max( Tail, MaxTail),  H <= MaxTail.
```

running this program gives.
```
        Goal: max ( [ 89,  67,  111, 100], LIST)
        LIST = 111
```

Example 10 : Write a PROLOG code to convert a decimal number to binary.
Answer:

```
        predicates
                dec_to_bin ( integer, string)
                clauses
                dec_to_bin ( 0,  " ")
                dec_to_bin ( decimal , string_binary) :-
                        digit = decimal mod 2,
                         str_int (SI, digit),
                         I1 = Decimal div 2,
                         dec_to_bin ( I1, SR),
                          concat ( SR , SI, String_binary).
```
running this program gives:
```
        goal: dec_to_bin ( 256, Binary)
        Binary = 100000000
```

Example 11: Write a PROLOG code to check whether a given year is leap year or not.
Answer:

```
    predicates
        run
        check_year ( integer)
        clauses
        run:-
        write ( "type in the year"), n1,
        readint ( Y),
        check_year( Y),
        write ( " this is a leap year "), n1.
    run:- write ( " this is not a leap year" ), n1.
    check_year (Y) :-
```

                     X = Y mod 100,
                     X = 0,!
                     X = Y mod 400,
                     X = 0, !.
          check_year(Y) :-
                     X = Y mod 4,
                     X = 0.
          running this program gives
          check_year (1978).
          " this is not a leap year"

Example 12: Write a prolog code for finding the greatest common divisor of two positive integers.
Answer:

```
             /* filename is gcd.pro
        predicates
                gcd ( integer, integer, integer)
                clauses
                gcd( M, 0, M).
                gcd( M, N, Result) :-
                        Rem = M mod N,
                        gcd ( N, Rem, Result).
        running this program gives.
                gcd( 16, 14, Result)
                Result = 2
                gcd ( 24, 119, Answer)
        Answer = 1
```

Example 13: Write PROLOG code for finding the least common multiplier of given two positive integers.
 Answer:
     The least common multiple of two numbers is given by formula
          LCM = multiplication of the two numbers / greatest common divisor
     For finding the greatest common divisor, the program given above is included in this program.

```
         /*
         include " gcd.pro"
    predicates
            lcm (integer , integer, integer)
            clauses ( M, N, Result) :-  gcd ( M, N, Res1),
                        Result = M * N / Res 1.
```

running this code gives

```
lcm ( 16, 14, Result)
Result = 112.
lcm( 24, 119, Answer)
answer = 2856
```

7.3 PROGRAMMIMG IN LISP

Since its inception about 47 years back, LISP has been an important language for artificial intelligence programming. Originally, the LISP was designed for symbolic computing. With the passing of time and as per requirement of AI applications, it has been extended and modified repeatedly. PROLOG is a declarative language whose programs define relationships and constraints in problem domain, whereas; LISP programs describe the methodology to implement an algorithm. LISP is a functional language and is in a way, different from traditional imperative languages like FORTRAN or C++.

The syntax and semantics of LISP are derived from the mathematical theory of recursive functions. LISP is popular in the field of AI problem solving because it contains set of high-level tools for building data structure such as predicates, frames, networks and objects. LISP is used for implementing AI tools and models as well as for building and testing prototype systems.

Some salient features of LISP are as follows:

- LISP is highly recursive language. LISP functions may be defined in terms of themselves.
- Lisp is highly symbol oriented data structure: the basic data structures it allows are atoms and lists. Lists are objects composed of other lists and /or atoms which are primitive, indivisible data type. Lists in LISP are also known as s expression. the Lisp is a functional language and in this programs, functions, and data all are represented by lists. This gives LISP programs the capability of operating on other programs as if they were data.
- Lisp in interactive language. LISP has been routinely available as an interpreter on mainframe and minicomputer.
- LISP provides automatic dynamic storage allocation. Since a LISP program is a dynamic collection of shrinking and growing lists, the problem of storage allocation can be quite complex. But LISP systems provide automatic storage allocation with garbage collection to reclaim memory no longer needed by the program. Hence the programmer need not bother about the size of program.

A detailed overview of programming through LISP is presented in subsequent paragraphs.

7.3.1 Basic Lisp Syntax

The basic elements of the LISP programming are *symbolic expressions,* also known as s-expressions. In this, both programs and data are represented as s-expressions, an expression may be either an atom or a list. LISp atoms are the basic syntactic units of the language and include both numbers and symbols. Basic syntax of LISP constructs are as follows:

7.3.1.1 Atoms

The smallest indivisible element of LISP syntax is called as an atom. LISP supports several kinds of atoms including numbers, characters, symbols, hyphenated symbols, strings, and vectors. These may be constituted by:

$$* , -, +, / \ @, \$, \%, ^, \&, \_ , <, >, \sim.$$

Examples of valid LISP atoms are:

3.1416, 100, X, hyphenated – name, *some – global*

nil

Characters in LISP syntax are designated by a '#\' preceding the character and permit use of non control characters. Example include:

    #\a   : ASCII lower case a
    #\A   : ASCII upper case a
    #\(: ASCII parenthesis as a character
    #\ return   :   ASCII carriage return command
    #\tab   : ASCII tab command

Symbols are identifiers made from any combination of letters, numbers and special characters. Example of symbolic literal atoms include:

    x ,   Sanjeev,   T , NIL,   Suraksha,   My_country

7.3.1.2 String

LISP strings closely resemble strings of procedural languages and include any sequence of characters . examples of symbolic or literal atoms include:

    " how are you?"
    " so is this"
    " city , state and ZIP"

7.3.1.3 Vector

It is a data structure with an arbitrary number of components. Its structure resembles a list prefixed by a '#'. An example of vector is:

    # (a b c d e f)

Example of illegal atoms include:

)   {as it is a special LISP character}
    (3 4 2 5)   { it is a list and not a symbol }

This sentence has spaces   {it contain spaces, the *delimiter* (balnk) used by LISP.

LISP symbols may contain such special characters as +, *,   and ? , but may not contain the special LISP characters; \ !)(} {   ][@ and blank.

There are two special atoms which, LISP programmers encounter frequently. The first of these is the atom indicating 'true' or 'non zero'. This is the atom 't' which LISP refers to as # ! TRUE, e.g.,

> (= ? 5   5)

LISP respond

#!TRUE

It means the LISP has indicated it is true.

If following code is asked

> (= equal ?   4   6)

Here arguments 4 and 6 are not equal hence it would be

( )

It should be noted that it will not be "f or FALSE"

There is another special symbol, referred to as NIL, and in fact if we ask

(equal ? Nil ())

It replies

! TRUE

Other equality queries for the numerical comparison are

eq ?	: compares symbols
= ?	: compare numbers
eqv ?	: compares symbols or numbers
equal ?	: compares lists, vectors and arrays

7.3.1.4 Lists

A list is a sequence of either atoms or other lists separated by blanks and enclosed in parentheses. Formally lists are similar to sets, with the difference that lists are ordered and the same element can appear more than once in a list. It can be defined as

" A list is a sequence of atoms and / or other lists enclosed within parenthesis. A list may contain zero or more atoms or lists.

Examples of valid lists include:

(1 2 3 4)

(Adwet Vidushi Vishwant Prakhar)

(a (b c) (d (e f)))

(

()

Following are the examples of illegal lists:

(a b c d e f g

) a b c d e f (

((a b()

The elements of a list themselves may be list. This nesting may be arbitrarily deep and allows us to create symbol structures of any desired form and complexity. A list having no element i. e () is called as empty list. It plays a special role in the construction and manipulation of LISP data structures and is given the special name nil. Nil is the only expression that is considered to be both an atom and a list. Lists are extremely flexible tools for constructing representational structures. Lisp comment starts with a (semicolon) ;, and can be placed anywhere.

LISP provides several categories of functions used for computation. These are as follows:

7.3.1.5 Numerical Arithmetic

Addition:

This function performs addition of numbers
> (+ 5 10 15)
30

Subtraction:

It performs subtraction of two given numbers
> (- 20 27)
- 7

Multiplication:

It performs multiplication of numbers
> (* 1 2 3 4 5)
> 120

Division:

It performs division of two given numbers
(/ 75 5)
15

Absolute:

It takes the absolute value of the argument.
> abs (- 7)
> 7

7.3.1.6 Transcendental Functions

Exponential function:

This function calculates the exponential value of a number on base e.
> (exp 1)
2.7182818287459056

Exponentiation function:
It calculates the value of x to the power y.
> (exp 3 5)
243

Square root function:
This function calculates the value of square root of the argument.
> (sqrt 144)
12

Cosine function:
It calculates the value of cosine.
> (cos (3.141592654 4))
0.707106781114031

7.3.1.7 Relational Predicates

These functions perform the function of relational operators.

Equality test:
This performs the equality test on the list of argument.
>(= 8 9)
()

Less than or equal to:
It checks whether the first argument is less than or equal to second.
> (<= 18 24)
! TRUE

Greater than:
It checks whether the first argument is greater than second or not.
> (> 100   144)
( )

Max:
This returns the maximum of it's arguments:
> Max(45 64 125 120)
125

Min:
It returns the minimum of its arguments
> min(45 64 125 17)
17

7.3.1.8 List Manipulation

Besides arithmetic operations, LISP allows list manipulation functions. These are the functions to construct and combine lists, to access elements of lists, and to perform various tests on list elements. These are the functions which are used to manipulate the list. LISP's response is in capital letters.

```
> (list 1 2 3 4 5)
(1 2 3 4 5)
```

The function 'list' returns the list of elements supplied as arguments. Similarly, following outputs are reported by LISP evaluator:

```
> (nth 0 '(a b c d))
a
(nth 2 ( list 1 2 3 4 5))
3
> (nth 2 '((a 1) (b 2)(c 3)( d 4)))
(c 3)
> (length '(a b c d))
4
(member  7 '( 1 2 3 4  5))
nil
> ( null  ( ))
t
> (car '(one two three))
ONE
```

Function car returns the first element of a non-null list.

```
> (cdr ' (one two three))
(TWO THREE)
```

Function cdr returns the elements of the list except the first element. It is complementary of car.

```
> (cons 'a '(b c d))
(A B C D)
```

It is constructor function. It returns the joined list after performing car + cdr.

```
> (append ' (Taj is ) ( beautiful) )
(TAJ IS BEAUTIFUL)
```

Append concatenates the list. It takes any number of arguments.

```
> list; ( a b) ' ( c d )
((A B) (C D))
```

It returns a new list made from the arguments of list.

```
> reverse '(1 2 3 4))
(4 3 2 1)
```

This function returns a list in the reverse order.

```
> (length '(1 2 3 4))
4
```

This function computes the length of the list.

In LISP the lists are used to store program as well as data, e g. the lists

```
(*7 9)
(- (+ 3 4) 7)
```

may be interpreted as arithmetic expression in a prefix notation. Hence, (*79) represents the product of 7 and 9.

When LISP is invoked on the computer, the user enters an interactive dialogue with the LISP interpreter. The interpreter prints a prompt (or >), reads the user input, attempts to evaluate the input and, if successful, prints the result. For example:

```
> (* 7 9)
63
>
```

Here the user enters (* 7 9) and LISP interpreter responds with 63, the evaluated answer of this result. The LISP then prints another result and wait for more user input. This cycle is known as read –eval – print loop and is the heart of LISP interpreter. LISP expressions that may be meaningfully evaluated are called as forms. If the user enters an expression that may not be correctly evaluated, LISP prints an error message and allows the user to trace and correct the problem. See following examples:

```
> (+ 10 5)
15
> (+ 1 2 5 6)
14
> (- (+ 5 4) 9)
> 0
> (* (+ 5 5) (- 7 ( / 21 7)))
>40
> (= (+ 2 3) 5)
t
> (> (*5 6) (+ 4 5))
>t
> (a b c)
invalid function a
```

In evaluating a function, LISP first evaluates its arguments and then applies the function indicated by the first element of expression to the result of these evaluations. In the situations where arguments are themselves function expression. LISP applied this rule recursively to their evaluation. Thus, LISP allows nested function calls of arbitrary depth. The readers should note that by default LISP interpreter evaluates everything. LISP uses the convention that numbers always evaluate to themselves. If, for example 5 is typed to the LISP interpreter, it will give result 5. Symbols such as x may have a value bound to them. If a symbol is bound, the binding is returned when the symbol is evaluated. If the symbol is unbound it is an error to evaluate that symbol. A diagram evaluating the expressions (+ (*2 3) (*3 5)), is shown in following tree:

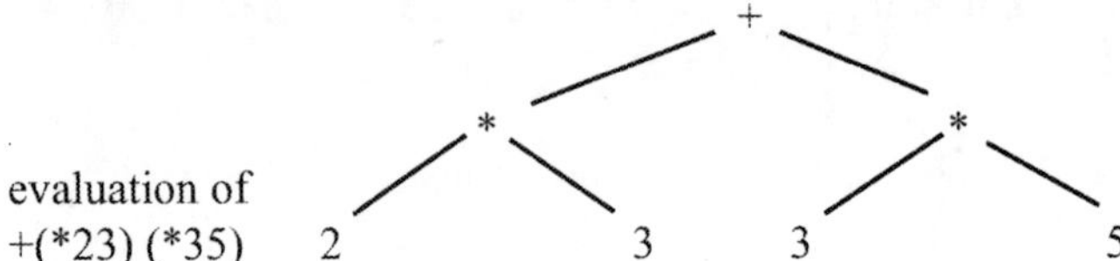

evaluation of
+(*23) (*35)

The expressions in LISP are in form of s-expression. Formally, an 's' expression is defined as follows:

- An atom is an s- expression
- If s1, s2, …..sn are s expressions, then also the list (s1, s2, ….sn)

A list is a nonatomic 's' expression. The form is an s expression that is intended to be evaluated. If, it is a list, the first element is treated as the function name and the subsequent elements are evaluated to obtain the function arguments.

The evaluation of an s expression is performed as follows:

If, the s expression is a number, return the value of the number

If, s expression is an atomic symbol, return the value bound to that symbol, if it is not bound it is an error.

If the s expression is a list, evaluate the second through the last arguments and apply the function indicated by first argument to the result.

LISP also provides certain built in list operations. These are as follows:

Concat – It is used either to join two lists or to decompose one list into two lists. Predicate concat takes three arguments concat (L1, L2, L3) where L1, L2, L3 are lists. It first merges L1 and L2 lists and then assign list L3 with this new list. It returns true if is unifies with L1& L2, e.g.,

Example 1:

    1?- concat ([c, a, t], [5], Result)
    Result = [c, a, t, 5]

Here result is a variable (You can recall that names starting with capital letter behave as variables) and here it appears as third argument (L3). So here lists [c, a, t] and [5] will be simply joined and unified in L3.

Example 2:

    1? – Concat (Root, [I, n, g], [I, u, m, p, I, n, g])
    Root = [I, u, m, p]

Here root is a variable, so to find value to this variable L2 (I, n, g) is compared with L3 (I, u, m, p, I, n, g). Comparison is right justified and variable root is assigned the value (I, u, m, p)

Example 3:

1?concat (Start, End, [L, O, T, U, S])

Here Start and End are two variable depending upon the value of one variable the second will be determined, i.e.

> If ,   Start = [ ]
> Then   End = [L, O, T, U, S]
> If Start = [L, O]
> Then End = [T, U, S]
> If Start = [L, O, T, U, S]
> Then End = [ ]

7.3.1.9 Input and Output statements

These statements are used to provide the input or take the output from LISP program. These are read, print, print1, princ, terpri, and format.

Read:

This is input statement. It takes no arguments. When it appears in the procedure, processing halts and waits for the input to be entered, e.g.,

> > (+ 15 read)
> 10
> 25
> >

note here that after evaluation of one expression LISP interpreter displays the prompt and waits for another s expression.

Print:

It takes one argument. It prints the argument as it is received and then returns the argument, e.g.,

> > print '(a b c)
> ABC
> ABC

Double printing here is because of the fact that print first prints its arguments and then returns it causing it to be printed by *read evaluate print* loop. This is true with strings also, e.g.

> > (print " hello India")
> " Hello India"
> hello India

princ:

It is similar to print except that it does not print quotation marks and allows multiple lines to be printed on the same line.

>   > (princ " hello India")
>   hello India " hello India"

terpri:

This function takes no arguments. It introduces a new line wherever it appears and then returns nil format. This function permits a cleaner output than is possible with just basic functions.

7.3.2 Control Structures in Lisp

The control structures in any language give facility to write programs. LISP also provides control structures. These structures are called as special forms. These control structures are as follows:

< *IF*> *structure*:
(If < cond> < coneseq> < alternative>)
where,
<cond> is a condition to be evaluated
<conseq> is evaluated and returned if cond = t
< alternative> is evaluated and returned if cond = ()

for instance
(if > 5 10) 'continue' stop)
returns
STOP

Consider another example
(cond ((<? 80386 68030)' less than)
((< ? 80386 68030) ' greater than)
(else ' is_ equal))
produces the output
GREATER_THAN

Do structure:

<DO> special form (iteration)
(do (<var 1> <initial> < step>....)
(<test> < exprl>   ...)
where
< var 1 > identifier which serves as counters
<initial> expression evaluated as initial value of var 1
<step 1> expression evaluated as next value of var 1
<test> expression evaluated first for each iteration:

if test evaluates to ().
Then all statements (stmts) evaluated
If test evaluates to t, then
Iteration is terminated
Expri evaluated in order
Do return the value of the last expression.

An example of the use of this iterative special form to print out the five integers and return the value of square of the sixth is shown:
```
> (do (I 1 (+ I 1)))
((> I 5 (* I I))
(display i)
(display " " ))
yields
1 2 3 4 5 36
```

Both init 1 and step1 are optional parameters; if they are missing var 1 is not updated and, rather than looping , the DO structure performs as an IF structure

7.3.2.1 Conditional Control Structure

LISP branching is based on function evaluation. Control function performs tests and depending upon the result, selectively evaluate alternative forms. function 'cond' is used to evaluate a conditional statement. it takes as argument a number of *condition – action – pair:* it's general form is shown below:

```
(cond ( < condition 1> < action 1>)
 ( < condition 2> < action 2>)
 ............
 (< condition  n> < action n>))
```

Conditions and actions may be arbitrary s-expressions, and each pair is enclosed in parenthesis. Function 'cond' does not evaluate all of it's arguments instead it evaluates the conditions in order until one of them returns a non nil value. When it occurs, it evaluates the associated action.

Consider following function to evaluate the absolute value:
```
(defun absolute_value (x)
        (cond (( <x 0 ) ( - x))
        ((>= x 0) x))
```

Following definition also calculates the absolute value:
```
(defun absolute _value (x)
        (cond (( <= x 0 ) ( - x))
        (t  x)))
```

It may be noted in the second definition, that the second condition is always true if the first one is false. In LISP the atom t corresponds to true. By convention, t always evaluates to itself: this causes the last action to be evaluated if all preceding conditions return nil.

Although any evaluable 's' expression is used as condition. Generally, these are in form of predicate. A predicate is simply a function that returns a value either true of false depending on whether or not its argument possesses some property. The most obvious examples of predicates are the s-expressions made from relational operator. These are shown in the following examples:

```
> (= 11 (+ 6 5))
t

> ( >= 19 4)
t
> ( <8 ( / 4 2))
nil
> ( oddp 3)
t
> ( minus p 6)
nil
> ( zerop 0)
t
> ( plusp 10)
t
> (plusp -2)
nil
```

Member predicate is used to check whether a particular element is a member of a list or not.

```
> (member  3 '(1 2 3 4 5 ))
(3 4 5)
```

LISP allows the use of logical connectives like *and, or, not* while creating an s expression. The functioning of '*and*' and '*or*' is based on conditional evaluation. Both of these functions can take any number of arguments. 'not', takes one argument and returns 'f' if its argument is nil, and nil otherwise. The evaluation of an 's' expression having the connectives is done from left to right. The evaluation stops when any one of the arguments evaluates to nil or the last argument has been evaluated. It therefore evaluates to non-nil only if all its arguments return non-nil. Similarly, the 'or' form evaluates its arguments only until a non-nil value is encountered, returning this value as result. See following examples:

```
> (and ( odd 2) ( print " third statement was evaluated"))
nil
```

> (and (oddp 3) (print " second statement was evaluated"))
second statement was evaluated

As mentioned earlier that the LISP is mainly based on list processing. It provides function for list processing. The basic functions for accessing the components of lists are 'car' and 'cdr'. 'car' takes a single argument, which must be a list, and returns the first elements of a list. 'cdr' also takes a single argument, which must be a list, and return that list with its first argument removed., e.g.,

```
>( car '( a b c ))
a
> (cdr ' ( a b c))
(b c)
> ( car ' (( a b ) ( c d)))
( a b)
> ( cdr '(( a b ) ( c  d)))
((c d ))
> ( car ( cdr ' ( a b c d )))
b
```

Besides these two functions, a more primitive list constructor is the function cons that takes two s-expressions as arguments, evaluates them, and returns a list whose car is the value of the first argument and whose cdr is the value of the second.

```
> ( cons 1 ' (2 3 4))
( 1 2 3 4)
> ( cons ' ( a b )' ( c d e))
(( a b ) c d e)
```

The following constructs are made with these operators:

```
> car ( cons 1' (2 3 4 )))
1
> cdr ( cons 1' ( 2 3 4)))
( 2 3 4)
```

The examples of programs based on the list manipulation is given in the last.

Nested lists: Normally the functions used to combine two lists are cons and append. But there is difference between two functions. if cons is called with two arguments , it makes the first of these a new first element of the second list. whereas append returns   a list whose elements are the elements of two arguments: see following example:

```
> ( cons ' (a b) ' ( 3 4 ))
(( a b ) c d)
>( append ' ( a b) ' ( c d))
( a b c d)
```

It should be noted that lists (a b c d) and ((a b) c d) are different.

The LISP is based on the theory of recursive functions. It provides a very powerful capacity of car / cdr recursion. The early LISP was the first example of a functional or applicative programming languages. An important aspect of purely functional languages is the lack of any side effect as a result of function execution. That means the value returned by a function call depends only on the function definition and the value of parameters of the call.

As mentioned earlier that the variables can be used in the function definition. In actual evaluation some numerical value of these variables need to be supplied. This is called as binding. The function 'set' is used to assign the actual value to variable, called binding the variable. 'set' takes two arguments . The first must evaluate to a symbol and the second may be an arbitrary s expression, e.g.

        > (set 'x 0)
        0

Set assigns the value 0 to the variable x.

LISP provides an alternative function, setq, for the same purpose. However, the difference is that it does not evaluate the first argument. See following example:

        > setq (x 0)
        0

there exists another function *let*. It allows a creation of local variable. the syntax of let expression is:

        (let (< local variable>) < expression>)

where the elements of (< local – variables>) are either symbolic atoms or pairs of the form:

        (< symbol> < expression>)

After the evaluation of bindings defined by set and let functions the expressions are evaluated in order within this environment. The following example shows functioning of let and setq.

        > (setq a 0)
        0
        > (let ((a 3) b)
          (setq b 4)
          (+ a b))
        7

        >a
        0
        >b
        error   (b is not bound at first level)

LISP is considered very powerful language because of it's capability of recursion. a recursion function calls itself successfully to reduce a problem to a sequence of simpler steps. Recursion requires a stopping condition and a recursive step.

list provide a very powerful method to represent a tree structure. the structural difference of two lists is given in following figure:

consider list (1 2 3 4) and ((1 2) 3 4)

Programming in LISP:

This section discusses how a new LISP program is created. common lisp includes a large number of built in functions., including:

- A full range of arithmetic functions, supporting integer, rational, real and complex arithmetic.
- a variety of looping and program control functions
- list manipulation and data structuring functions.
- input output functions
- forms for the control of function evaluation.
- functions for the control of the environment and operating system.

In LISP a new program is created by defining a new functions and using the built in functions. these new functions are defined using 'defun' . 'defun' is short form of DEfine FUNction. once a function is defined it can be used in the same fashion as function that are built into the language. for example , if a user is defining a function called **square** , that takes one argument and returns it's square. it will be written as follows. student should remember that for building the expression LISP uses a prefix notation. the expression of square is:

```
( defun square (x)
   (* xx))
```

The first argument to defun is the name of the function being defined, the second is a list of formal parameters for that function. the formal parameters must be symbolic atoms. the remaining arguments are zero or more 's' expressions, which constitute the body of the new function, the LISP code that actually defines it's behavior. Unlike most LISP functions defun does not evaluate it's arguments, instead it uses them as specifications to create a new functions. however, like all LISP functions , defun returns a value, although the value returned is simply the name of new function.

One important result of evaluating a defun is the side effect of creating a new function and adding to the new LISP environment. In above example square is defined as a function that takes one argument and returns the result of multiplying that argument by itself. once a function is defined it must be called by the same number of arguments and by numeric value of those argument called actual parameters. The parameters or 'arguments symbolic name', which are used for defining the function are called as " formal parameters" and the parameters used for invoking the function are called as formal parameters. when a function is called the actual parameters are bound to the formal parameters. the body of the function is then evaluated with these bindings. for example call (square 7) causes 7 to be bound to the formal parameter x in the body of the definition. when the body (*77) is evaluated , LISP first evaluates the arguments to the function. because x is bound to be 7 by this call, this leads to the evaluation of (*77) .

More concisely syntax of a defun expression is:

(defun < function name> (< formal parameters>) < function body>)

the formal parameters are enclosed in a list.

Example 1: Function to calculate Factorial of a number
The recursive step in factorial is the product of n and factorial (n – 1). The stopping condition is reached when n= 0

```
> defun factorial (n)
        ( cond  (( zerop n) ! ))
            ( t ( *n ( factorial ( -n !))))
FACTORIAL
    > factorial (8)
    >40320
```


Example 2. Calculate the value of hypotenuse in a right angle triangle.

In right angle triangle $c = \sqrt{a^2 + b^2}$
Where a and b are inputs.
The function hypotenuse is defined as follows:

```
> (define hypotenuse a b)
 ( sqrt ( + ( * a a ) ( * b b )))
```

the function is invoked by the call

```
> ( hypotenuse  3  4)
```

and it returns

5.

Example 3. Convert Fahrenheit to Celsius temperature.
The code conversion equation is given by

$$C = (5 / 9) * (F - 32)$$

The LISP code implementing this conversion is:

```
> define Far_to_cel_con  f)
        (( * -5 ( - f 32))  9)
```

invocation by function call

```
> (Far_to_cel_con  212)
```

yields the expected result
100.

Example 4. Fibonacci Sequence
The Fibonacci sequence is an interesting mathematical series generated by recursive definition:

Fibonacci (0) = 0
Fibonacci (1) = 1
 Fibonacci (n) = Fibonacci (n – 1) + Fibonacci (n – 2)
The function is defined as follows:

```
( define ( Fibonacci n ))
( cond (( = ? n 0) 0 ))
(( = ? n 1 ) 1)
( else ( + ( Fibonacci ( - n 1)))
( Fibonacci ( - n 2))
> (Fibonacci 10)
55    .
```

Example 5. Define a recursive function to find whether an element is a member of a list or not.

the function is defined as follows:

```
( defun member( element  input_list)
  ( cond (( null input_list) nil)
    (( equal element ( car input_list)) input_list)
    ( t ( member element ( cdr input_list)))))
```

running this function will be as follows:

```
> member 4' ( 1 2 3 4 5 6 ))
( 4 5 6)
> ( member 5'( a b c d))
nil
```

Example 6. Define a recursive function using car and cdr to calculate the length of a list.

The function to calculate length of a list will be as follows:

```
( defun length ( input_list)
( cond(( null input_list) 0)
( t ( + ( length( cdr input_list ))))
```

Example 7. Write a recursive LISP code to find n th element of a list.

```
defun ( n-th-element ( n input_list)
      ( cond (( zerop n) ( car  input_list))
             (t ( n-th-element ( - n 1) ( cdr input_list)))))
```

Example 8. Write a LISP code to calculate the roots of a quadratic equation:
consider the quadratic equation

$$ax^2 + bx + c = 0$$

it's roots are given as follows:

$$x = (-b \pm \sqrt{(b * b - 4\,a\,c)})\,/\,2\,a$$

the lisp code is as follows:

```
(defun quad_roots-1 ( a b c)
( setq temp ( sqrt ( - (*bb) ( * 4 a c))))
 ( list ( / list ( / ( + ( - b) temp) ( * 2 a ))
( / ( - ( - b) temp) ( * 2 a))))
```

Example 9: Write a lisp code to perform the breadth first search.

the function is written as follows:

```
defun breadth first()
( cond (( null *open*) nil)
(t (let(( state ( car *open* )))
( cond    (( equal state *goal * ) success)
( t ( setq * closed* ( cons state * closed*))
( setq * open* ( append ( cdr * open* )
( generate – descendants state * moves* )))
        ( breadth first)))))))
( defun run – breadth ( start goal)
( setq * open* ( list start))
( setq * closed* nil)
( setq * goal* goal)
( breadth –first))
```

here open list is tested. if it is nil, the algorithm returns nil. This indicates failure. otherwise it examines the first element of * open*. if this is equal to the goal the algorithm halts and return success. other wise it calls generate descendants to produce the children of current state, adds them to open and returns.

function generate descedants is defined as follows:

```
defun generate descendants ( state moves)
        (cond (( null moves  ) nil)
        ( t ( let (( child ( funcall ( car moves state))
        (rest ( generate _ descendants state( cdr moves))))
        (cond (( null child) rest)
        (( member child rest : test # ' equal ) rest)
        (( member child  * open*: test #' equal) rest)
        (( member child *closed* : test # ' equal) rest)
        ( t (cons child rest )))))))
```

7.4 SMALL TALK

It is a object oriented language which is used also used as AI programming language.

Some salient features of small talk are presented here.

Object:

The object is defined as package of information and descriptions of its manipulation. Hence object is a collection of data and procedures which belong together. while conventional languages cleanly distinguish between data and procedures, a small talk object consists of both the knowledgebase and procedures which operate on it.

Message: sending a message in Smalltalk is the equivalent of invoking a procedure or operator in conventional language. Computation is performed by sending messages to objects. The message includes a message selector and it's operands. The small talk equivalent of the LISP read evaluate print cycle is the specify – object – send –it- message, receive – result – object cycle.

Method: the small talk method is equivalent of a body of a conventional language subroutine or a procedure. it is a description of the sequence of actions to be taken when a message is received by an object. The message is made up of three parts:
- a message pattern
- temporary variable name
- list of expressions

Class: is the fundamental small talk data structure describing one or more similar object . a new object is always first described. this is done by creating a basic class template, a framework with slots which are filled in to create object. The slot names include class name, instance variable name, method. By filling a slot for a particular object with it's characteristics set of instance variable we create an instance of an object.

Inheritance: inheritance is popularly used in knowledge representation, in which ojects share all the attributes of their class and all classes of which they are subclasses.

Method dictionary: the method dictionary contains pairs of selectors and methods. when a message is sent to an object, the method dictionary for that class is scanned for the appropriate method to execute .

7.5 POP 11

It is general purpose programming language designed by Robbin Popplestone of Edinburg university. it was originally developed as a tool for artificial intelligence research and teaching. at present, it's use has spread to graphics, image processing, expert system design, and VLSI circuit design. this language is a combination of LISP, PROLOG, and provides a complete AI software development environment tool providing series of increment compilers and editors. the language behind POP is POPLOG. POPLOG provides an environment in which programs written in Pascal, Fortran, C, and POP11 can be integrated and linked dynamically.

let us discuss some salient features of POP in brief:

syntax: the POP 11 allows two types of expressions.

- expressions referring to objects:
- imperatived referring to actions.

the objectives include simple data types like numbers , words, strings, and lists. imperatives result in POP11 actions which may create objects, cpmpare, search store and print out objects.

e.g a simple imperative command to perform addition will be written as:

30 + 25 → ;;; This is a print arrow.
and POP 11 responds
** 100

the value is assigned to a variable as follows:

40 ? temp;

here value 40 is assigned to variable temp.

the commands are terminated by semicolon (like Pascal), and the arrow direction is reversed in case of assignment. commands are indicated but three semicolons on a, single line or multiline comments are enclosed by /*.......*/. variables and constants declaration in POP 11 closely resembles Pascal. to declare x, y, z as objects, we write:

var x, y, z ;

constants may be declared and assigned a single value only:

constant country:
' India' → City;

lists are assigned , using the [.....] list delimiters as:
var List1;
[a b c d e f] → List1;

the procedure definitions resemble those of LISP without parenthesis:

define shape (figure);
figure → figure →
end define ;

this function can be invoked to yield:
shape [circle]
**[circle]
**[circle]

in conclusion, this chapter presented a detailed theory on AI programming languages. there were other languages also developed for AI programming but they could not survive much. Several special purpose languages designed for building expert systems were also designed. But these are very specialized languages and their discussion is beyond the scope of this book.

EXERCISE

1.   Write a LISP program to find whether a given year is leap year or not.
2.   Write a LISP function that takes a list as its argument and returns the first top element of the list.
3.   Write a LISP function to find whether a given substring is present in a string or not.
4.   Draw cell structure of following list.
     (i) (ab)   (ii) (b)   (iii) (a(b))
     (iv) (12)   (v) (a b c)   (vi) ((a))
     (vii) (a(b c d))   (viii) (a(b c) d))
5.   Assume that variable 1st has value
     (a (b c) ((de)) (f))
     what is the value of (car (cdr (car (cdr 1st$_1$))))
6.   What are the values of following three LISP function calls
     (i) (list '(12) '(3))
     (ii) (cons '(12) '(3))
     (iii) (append '(12) '(3))
7.   Write a PROLOG program that answers questions about family members and relationships. Include predicates and rules which define sister, brother, father, mother, grandchild, grandfather and uncle. The program should be able to answer queries such as the following:
     ? – father (X, Bunty).
     ? – grandson (X, Y).
     ? – uncle (bill, sue).
     ? – mother (mary, X).

8

Reasoning with Uncertainty

8.1 INTRODUCTION

The AI problem solving techniques discussed earlier like predicate and propositional logic, search techniques etc. require defining the search space and are applicable in the situations where the total outcomes are discrete and concretely defined. They can be considered as events having certain (defined) situations. However, the real word is full of situations, where the available data and information is uncertain. These are termed as uncertain situations and the theory of Artificial Intelligence will not be complete if it is not able to handle such uncertainties.

Reasoning, in simple terms means deriving conclusion from the available set of data and information. For example, if the given information is:

- *King Dasharatha was father of Rama.*
- *Rama was father of Luv and Kush.*

From the given information, it can be concluded that King Dasharatha was grandfather of Luv and Kush. We could conclude this because we have knowledge that father of our father is called our grandfather. Also, we are called intelligent when we are able to draw conclusions like this. Hence, for a human being to be intelligent, it is necessary to have ability to reason. However, in real world, there are many situations where we are required to draw conclusions from incomplete and uncertain evidences. For example, if the available information is:

- *Birds can fly.*
- *Yamu is a bird.*

From this information, an obvious conclusion would be that Yamu could fly. However, this conclusion is based on the most likely characteristics of birds. We often draw conclusions based on assumptions we make that are inclined towards most likely characteristics of the situation or object under consideration and also, our beliefs about real world situations. If some information is withdrawn or some new information is added, them our assumptions and hence, our conclusions would change. For example, in the above mentioned case, if one more information is added that the said bird Yamu was an Ostrich, our conclusion would be exactly opposite of what had been earlier. Our aim is to understand that we have to deal with many such situations in every day life that are full of uncertainties. Such type of situations are called uncertain situations and reasoning with these situations is known as reasoning with uncertainty.

These uncertainties arise due to many factors. In fact, source of all uncertainties is real world. Our knowledge is based on real world phenomena and whatever uncertainties we encounter in our daily life are because of these real world phenomena. Some of the sources of uncertainties are mentioned below:

- Most of the knowledge we acquire is from beliefs and hypotheses. Whenever we draw some conclusion, it is based on the information derived from these beliefs. When we get some new information, or beliefs change, we face uncertainty.

- Another source of uncertainty is vagueness associated with natural language understanding. Sometimes, we make mistake in listening or referring something because of imprecision in natural language and that causes uncertainty. For example, two sentences *"stop, not let them go"* and *"stop not, let them go"* though, have same wordings, convey entirely different meanings to the listener or interpreter. It will definitely cause uncertainty in the mind and approach of listener or interpreter.

- Experimental errors are also source of uncertainty. Any conclusion drawn based on experiments will cause uncertainty if the equipments used or experimental procedure is faulty. For example, if a medical diagnosis is made on the basis of medical tests conducted in pathological laboratory which are not consistent because of fault in the equipments used, doctor will face uncertain situation in making correct diagnosis.

- Randomness in events also causes uncertainty. For example, there is a belief that clouds bring rains. There are heavy clouds in the sky and we are sure of rains. Suddenly, strong winds start blowing and cloud cover is removed and hence possibility of rains vanishes. Thus, we are never sure of rains howsoever thick cloud cover is witnessed in the sky.

- Uncertainties are caused by lack of evidences also. For example, during the trial of a culprit for a crime, judges often are uncertain whether a particular crime is committed by the culprit due to lake of evidences.

Whatever could be the source, uncertainties are part and parcel of our routine life and we are dealing with them successfully. Knowledge based or AI systems function within the domain of their limited knowledge base. The knowledge stored in the knowledge base is incomplete. Hence, AI systems, if at all have to show intelligence, would be required to deal with uncertain situations of real world. In this chapter, we discuss how to deal with uncertainties. In real world most of the situations keep on changing and are far more complex. The normal logical problem solving techniques using predicate and propositional logic can not work in these situations because the goal is concretely not defined and the propositional & predicate calculus can not handle uncertain situations. To handle such situations different AI techniques have been devised. As discussed earlier to solve any problem the task oriented knowledge is required to be represented. Similarly, to handle uncertain situation, the uncertain knowledge needs to be represented. Let us first understand how uncertain knowledge is represented.

8.2 REPRESENTING UNCERTAIN KNOWLEDGE

An uncertain situation requires representation of uncertain knowledge. Consider following examples of certain and uncertain events:

Certain events:
- India is a democratic country.
- Earth revolves around Sun.
- The states of a chess game.

Uncertain events:
- If it is cloudy, it will rain.
- If the weather is sunny, it will not rain.
- If a patient is vomiting, he is suffering from cholera.

The representation of uncertain knowledge requires attachment of an additional factor indicating the correctness of knowledge. This additional conceptual factor is called *"degree of belief"*. The value of this factor varies between 0 and 1. It can take any fractional value in this range. Thus, the uncertain situation is represented by attaching a degree of belief factor e.g. in medical diagnosis, we observe some symptoms in the patient, but if those symptoms are present, still it can not be guaranteed that a particular disease is present. Only with some degree of belief, it can be said that particular disease is present. The degree of belief is a conceptual factor indicating the degree of correctness of diagnosis. This belief factor is also related with probability theory. However, in the theory of probability, the total possible outcomes are defined, but in real world problems there may be situations where even total outcomes are not defined. But saying that it will rain with the degree of belief "0.8" means that with 80% belief we can say that it will rain, but it does not mean that we have 0.2 belief that it will not rain. Here mentioning degree of belief for rain does not indicate any thing about not raining. The degree of belief and degree of truth are different. A probability 0.8 means 80% truth in the event, but saying 80% degree of belief, does not mean 80% truthness of the event. It only indicates that user's belief in the correctness of the conclusion is 80%.

In representing uncertain knowledge, we define certain terms as follows:
- *Evidence*: it is the observations obtained in real world.
- *Belief*: it is any meaningful and coherent expression that can be represented. Hence it can be true or false. Belief represent just observer's view about any incidence. At the time of defining the fact, nothing can be said about the truthness of belief.
- *Hypothesis* : it is a justified belief that is supported by some evidence.

8.3 REASONING WITH UNCERTAIN KNOWLEDGE

We have tried to get an overview of what does it actually mean by reasoning with uncertainty. Before going into details of this very important aspect of human behavior that somehow would have to be incorporated in the knowledge-based systems to make them intelligent, we should and would try to understand the meaning and concept of reasoning.

AI means building intelligent systems to solve real world problems. Intelligent systems provide solutions on the basis of facts and rules stored in the knowledge base. These facts and rules are often incomplete and hence uncertain. AI systems are required to reason with this uncertain knowledge or information. Thus, reasoning is the process by which we use available knowledge, in whatever quantity or of whatever quality, to draw conclusions or to infer about a new event. A system can be intelligent only if it is able to solve or handle a new task. Without this ability, the AI system will simply be considered as "information system" giving answers based on look up table. The three basic types of reasoning methods are:
- Inductive reasoning
- Abductive reasoning
- Deductive reasoning

8.3.1 Inductive Reasoning

Inductive reasoning is based on the generalizations of the previous experiences about the problem, e.g., if we consider the situation:
- *He is studying in the eighth standard.*
- *The name of his school is D.A.V. Public School.*

If somebody asks us to guess about the school environment then because of our experience of studies in school and primary school, we can infer (or guess) about the presence of many things concerned with the environment of the said school, like:
- The school has classrooms, library, office, laboratories, and computer room.
- It has many students and teachers.
- It has a play ground, etc.

This is the example of induction that works on the principle of generalization of similar previous experiences. Inductive reasoning method is very useful in most of the AI applications and it is used in machine learning.

8.3.2 Abductive Reasoning

Abductive reasoning looks back through the chain of events to perform reasoning e.g. if a student "enters late in the class" and teacher "scolds him". To find the reason of teacher being angry with the student, one requires looking back in the chain of events that "teacher is punctual", "he does not like students entering late in the class", "student has entered late in the class" hence he is angry with the student. This reasoning is not very reliable and it is very well possible that he is angry with the student because he has not done the homework. Abduction, thus is an unsound rule of inference that means conclusion is not necessarily true for every interpretation made based of environment. Abduction can be used in the cases where the knowledge is "incomplete". With the given evidence it can provide the best "guess".

8.3.3 Deductive Reasoning

Deduction works on the standard logic. It is a kind of explicit reasoning, e.g. consider the situation that "if the switch is off", "bulb is not lightning". Here it is evident that if switch is off, it is certain that the bulb will not lighten. This is a case of deductive reasoning. Here the second conclusion is deduced from the first one. This situation in terms of logical representation can be represented as:

$$\text{"switch(off) ? not lightening (bulb)"}$$

In deductive reasoning the reverse is not true, e.g. if bulb is not lightening, then it might be possible that the bulb is fuse.

8.4 TECHNIQUES ADOPTED FOR DEALING WITH UNCERTAIN SITUATIONS

We have gone through logical reasoning methods where facts and rules help us to infer new information. These facts and rules are certain and consistent. Such type of reasoning allows us to store useful information in the database. For certain situations, where the knowledge base stores consistent information, all new knowledge that is added to it is bound to be consistent with the previous knowledge. Such type of reasoning is known as ***monotonic reasoning*** and in systems using this, the size of knowledge base always increases. In monotonic reasoning, whenever some conclusion is drawn as true, it remains true under all circumstances. We use this method in theorem proving. However, in real life, all inferences do not necessarily be considered correct under all circumstances. Whenever we make some conclusion, it is based on some belief. We predict and perform majority of actions relying on these beliefs. It is always a possibility that during the course of a particular action, some events might occur that enhance or reduce our faith on belief. For example, suppose you have decided to go for shopping on next Monday because it is not a holiday and you believe that there would be no rush because of this fact. Suddenly on Saturday, a weather forecast predicts rains on Monday. You change your mind and postpone the shopping for some other day. On Monday, though forecast fails and there are no signs of rains and you decide to go for shopping right then.

The example shows how our beliefs change with change in environment. Although these beliefs may not be changing frequently, such type of changes in beliefs are not uncommon in day-to-day life. A monotonic reasoning system, thus cannot work effectively in real life environment because of the following reasons:

1. Data and knowledge stored in the knowledge base or the information available is always incomplete.
2. Inference methods available are insufficient.
3. Circumstances change during the course of action for finding solutions and hence, the solutions.
4. Solutions are based on preconceived beliefs and assumptions have to be made for minimizing time to arrive at the correct solutions.

What does it mean in simple terms can be viewed as logical reasoning can not be a realistic presentation of real world. On the contrary, intelligent beings are required to make decisions and function in a world full of uncertainties. However, while reasoning with uncertain knowledge conclusion is drawn based on what is most likely to be true. Following approaches are followed for this type of reasoning:

*   *Nonmonotonic reasoning*: In this type of reasoning, the rules of inference are extended to make it possible to reason with incomplete information. The systems using this method show the property that at any given point of time, a statement is either believed to be true, believed to be not true or not believed to be true or not true.
*   *Probabilistic reasoning*: These are also known as statistical methods of reasoning. In these methods, the results are not in the form of TRUE or FALSE but some numeric value is assigned to them that is a measure of certainty of those events to be true under given circumstances. Some of the methods using probabilistic reasoning methods are:
    –   Bayesian belief networks
    –   Reasoning with certainty factors
    –   Dempster Shaffer theory
    –   Fuzzy reasoning

8.4.1 Non-monotonic Reasoning

The logics described earlier which give valid deductions are monotonic logics. In monotonic logic, addition of new axioms and facts are consistent with earlier stored knowledge and facts so knowledge grows monotonically but in uncertain situations addition of new axioms may contradict with earlier and might be required to be removed from the knowledge base and the size of knowledge base grows non-monotonically. As described in the above example of shopping, new facts contradict the earlier ones and remove the same from the database. This type of reasoning is called ***non-monotonic reasoning***. Consider following example:

Given the fact that X is an intelligent student and he scores good marks. Based on this information and the knowledge about an intelligent student which is generally true, you guess that X will be an obedient student. However, being intelligent and obedient are unrelated characteristics and obedience is a personal characteristics (i.e. an intelligent student may be in specific situation become arrogant). An intelligent student will be obedient is only a *belief* of listener, which may be wrong also. Hence if for specific instance of X, it is told that student is not obedient, this will contradict the general belief and to accommodate this fact in the knowledge base, the old knowledge will require modification.

Two general approaches used for nonmonotonic reasoning are:

- *Abduction*: It works on the principle of inferring some situation based on the current evidence and series of past events. When new contradictory evidence is encountered, the previous evidence is removed and new one is considered, e.g. if a patient has symptoms of vomiting, as per general belief the disease is diagnosed as Diarrhoea, but after more investigation it is found that the disease actually is dehydration and hence, the earlier information would be replaced by the new one.

- *Property inheritance:* It is another form of non-monotonic reasoning. It works on the principle that a subclass will inherit the characteristics of parent class unless otherwise told. In the situations where the subclass does not inherit properties of parent class, it is specifically mentioned. For example, we know that birds can fly and Ostrich is a bird. Hence, we would infer that Ostrich can fly but it is wrong because evidence contradict that. Hence, flying, though is inherited property of birds, special mention would be required about some birds that cannot fly.

While building expert systems, it is unreasonable to expect that it would be possible to acquire, code and store all the knowledge needed for a particular task. Normally, the initially stored knowledge would likely be incomplete, inconsistent and uncertain. Even if it is assumed that the initial knowledge be complete, valid and consistent, it would not remain same and true forever because of changing environment. Hence, traditional logical reasoning methods required extensions and modifications. Researchers have proposed many extensions and alterations that accommodate different forms of uncertainties and nonmonotony. Various methods used to deal with uncertain situations are discussed later on in this chapter.

Nonmonotonic systems face an important problem. This problem is the task of efficiently revising a set of conclusions in the light of changing beliefs. If, for example, we use the predicate **p** to infer **q**, then removing **p** because of change in beliefs would require removal of support for **q** as well as any conclusion that used **q**. It means, unless there is independent set of inferences supporting **q**, it must be retracted. Implementation of this retraction process would require recomputation of all conclusions each time a belief changes. To deal with this kind of problem, an AI system would require a support system that maintains the consistency of knowledge base. *Truth Maintenance Systems* are such type of support systems. Their concept, formation and functioning is described in detail in the following section.

8.4.1.1 Truth Maintenance Systems (TMS)

These are also called belief or revision maintenance systems. Truth maintenance is a mechanism for keeping track of dependencies and detecting inconsistencies. In the nonmonotonic systems, wherever the new knowledge is found to be inconsistent with the earlier knowledge, it uses its mechanism to correct and update the knowledge base with the true knowledge. Thus, main job of truth maintenance system is to maintain consistency of knowledge being used by the problem solver. As discussed earlier the general problem solver is used to solve any AI problem. Whenever it solves a problem, it generates new facts, which in certain situations may be contradictory to the previously stored knowledge. In such situations to store new facts and to maintain the consistency, the old knowledge needs to be removed. It will reduce the size of knowledge base. Consider again the example mentioned above:

"Generally, we consider an intelligent student scoring good marks would be an obedient student. Assume X is an intelligent student. By our belief, X should be an obedient student. However, in a specific circumstance, X is intelligent but very poor student and he requires earning his livelihood along with studies. He needs to study as well as to work to earn some money for feeding his family. In this situation, if his teacher asks him to perform some extra duty and he refuses it because of his engagement in his workplace, he would be treated as disobedient. This situation is the case when student is generally obedient but because of certain reason, he is behaving otherwise. If we consider that after few years, the situation has improved, his family members became self-supporting and his liabilities towards his family reduced. Now if teacher asks him to perform some extra work, he will perform and the earlier belief about the student's behavior will prove to be wrong. Again, consider a knowledgebase containing a sentence P, perhaps a default conclusion recorded by a forward chaining algorithm, or perhaps just an incorrect assertion and we want to execute TELL (KB, $\neg$P). To avoid the contradiction we must first execute RETRACT (KB, P). In normal situations, it is easy to do this retraction. But in the situations if some additional sentences were inferred from P and asserted in KB (like P $\rightarrow$ Q) it will require retracting all inferred sentences first. Which will be a problem.

The truth maintenance systems are also called *belief revision systems* because in large systems handling real world situations like "finding the presence of a mineral in Earth's crust", or "designing a complete weather forecasting system", or "designing a planning system for aerospace applications", these are used as supporting systems to inference engines. The main job of TMS is to maintain consistency of the knowledge being used by the problem solver and not to perform any inference functions. As stated earlier, it is not reasonable to expect that all the knowledge needed for a set of tasks could be acquired, validated and loaded into the system at the time of designing the same. Practically, at the time of initial designing of any system the available knowledge is very less, inconsistent and in very crude form. It remains full of redundancies, inconsistencies, and other sources of uncertainties. Moreover, the real world is ever changing. Hence, the facts obtained once about the real world may not remain true forever. Thus, the knowledgebase designed once based on the present facts needs to be updated with the changing situations. Beliefs that are valid today might require revision later and this task is performed by belief revision systems, the TMSs.

The traditional knowledge representation techniques like predicate and propositional logic can not accommodate the dynamic situations of present world. Hence, they require extensions. The extensions accommodate such types of real time forms of uncertainty and nonmonotony. Truth maintenance systems allow the revision in belief and accommodate the real world changing situations. These even allow the addition of contradictory situations. As is evident from the name, such systems are used only to maintain the consistency (i.e. the truth according to the latest situation) in the knowledge base. These systems are not reasoning systems. It is an additional system used with the reasoning system to provide it consistent and updated knowledge. It maintains the complete record of justifications of the reasoning and retractions. It is used in general problem solver along with inference engine and knowledge base for providing the solutions to AI problems.

The general problem solving system is shown in Fig. 8.1:

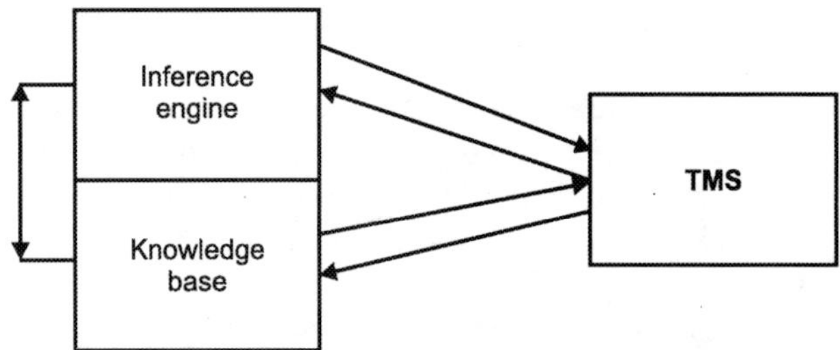

Fig. 8.1. diagram of general problem solver using TMS

This figure illustrates the role of TMS in the functioning of a general problem solver. The inference engine makes inferences based on current set of beliefs, while TMS maintains the set of currently active beliefs. After each inference, information is exchanged between inference engine and TMS. The inference engine tells the TMS about the deductions made and TMS tells it regarding current beliefs and reasons for failures. TMS thus maintains a consistent set of beliefs for the inference engine to rely upon even if new knowledge is added or removed in the knowledge-base. Some of the most sophisticated truth maintenance systems are:

- Justification based TMS
- Assumption based TMS
- Logic based TMS

We will consider the working of these TMSs in the following section:

8.4.1.1.1 Justification based TMS (JTMS):

Justification based TMS is one of the earliest truth maintenance systems created by Jon Doyle (1979). In JTMS each sentence in the knowledge base is annotated with a justification consisting of a set of sentences from which it was inferred e.g., if the knowledge base already contained $P \rightarrow Q$ then TELL (P) will cause Q to be added with the justification (P, $P \rightarrow Q$). Justifications are used to make retractions efficient. Now, If RECALL(P) is executed then JTMS will delete exactly those sentences for which P is a member of every justification. Hence if there is further more justification that (P, $PVR \rightarrow Q$) it would also be removed. The JTMS only marks the justifications for deletions; it does not actually delete the justification. It is done so because in future, the belief may change and again the earlier justification may be required. Hence, JTMS retains all the inference chains that it uses. As JTMS maintains one copy of justification at one time, it is called single context TMS.

As pointed out earlier, whenever beliefs are revised, it becomes necessary to re-compute support for items in a knowledge base. This can be done by storing justifications for each inference and then reconsidering support for conclusions in the wake of new beliefs. TMS thus records all the justifications for beliefs. Each statement having at least one valid justification is made a part of current belief set. Whenever a contradiction is encountered, the propositions or statements responsible for the contradiction are identified and an appropriate one is retracted. This in turn may result in other retractions and additions. This procedure used to perform this process adopted by JTMS is called *dependency-directed backtracking*.

JTMS performs three types of operations. First, the JTMS inspects the network of justifications. This inspection can be triggered by queries from the problem solver. These queries can be :Should proposition p be believed? Why to believe proposition p? What assumptions support proposition p? etc. If we elaborate this further, we would understand that problem solver asks for justification from the TMS for a particular change in the solution by asking series of questions. TMS would provide the justifications, store the new justifications based on changed environment and marks for removal of old justifications, if any.

The second function of JTMS is to modify the dependency network. These modifications are inspired by the information supplied by the problem solver. Modifications generally tend to modify knowledge base to make it consistent by adding new proposition, adding or removing already existing beliefs as per changing environment, adding contradictions and justifying the belief. Dependency network consists of a set of things that are used to draw a conclusion. Whenever there is a change in belief, problem solver interacts with the TMS and passes on the new information. TMS in tern modifies the deependency network to account for the change in situation by removing old beliefs with new ones, adding new information if any and so on so forth.

The third operation of JTMS is to update the network. This operation is required whenever there is a change in the dependency network, i.e. existing beliefs, assumptions etc. The update operation re-computes the labels of all propositions in a way that is consistent with the existing justifications. It means, JTMS maintains consistency with the already existing dependency network by updating operation.

As mentioned earlier, JTMS employs dependency-directed backtracking in performing the task for which it is designed. To understand this phenomenon, let us consider one example:

"We are required to draw conclusion about a situation p. We cannot infer about p directly and make an assumption q that if true, will support p. Hence, we assume q and infer about p. We continue our reasoning and based on p, conclude r and s. We continue further and without the support of p, r or s, draw results t and u. Finally, we discover that our earlier made assumption q was wrong. We would require backtracking the whole exercise."

Backtracking means going back from current state and exploring other possible alternatives for arriving at final decision point. This method is used in search-based problem solving systems. There can be two ways of backtracking in the example mentioned above. One way is to revisit the reasoning steps adopted in the reverse order in which they were made. This approach is called *chronological backtracking*. This method, though would systematically check all alternatives, is time consuming, inefficient and in very large space, becomes useless.

Another way to do backtracking is to go immediately back to the source of contradictory information. In context of the example under consideration, we would be required to go to the assumption q because it was q that was contradicted. From there we would go forward retracting p, r and s. We may at this time check whether r and s can be derived independently without support of p and q, because if they were derived originally by false assumption does not mean they cannot be derived using other supports. Finally, since t and u were derived without the support of p, r or s, we would not need to reconsider them. This type of approach is known as dependency-directed backtracking, perhaps, because the backtracking here is directed towards the dependencies (beliefs and assumptions) that are contradicted.

In order to apply dependency-directed backtracking in a reasoning system, we must take care of certain aspects, which are:

- We must associate justification with the conclusion because this justification gives an indication of the process used for deriving that particular conclusion. The justification must include all the facts, rules and assumptions used to infer conclusion. If some dependency is proved wrong and contradiction occurs, this justification would help us in retracting.
- When a contradiction occurs and justification for the same is available, we must provide a mechanism that locates the false assumptions, which led to contradictions, within that justification. By doing so, we would be able to identify and target the assumptions that led to contradictions by sparing other assumptions.
- We must retract the false assumptions.

- We must also create a mechanism to follow up the retracted assumptions and to retract any conclusion derived based on these false assumptions. However, all the retracted conclusions might not be false and they should be checked to ascertain whether they could be justified using other supports irrespective of false retracted assumptions.

We would now discuss a method to build dependency-directed backtracking system. As we have understood by now that JTMS is a system using dependency-directed backtracking approach. JTMS works with sets of nodes and justifications. Nodes denote beliefs and justifications support belief in nodes. Labels IN and OUT are associated with nodes which indicate the belief status of the associated node. We can reason about the support for any node (belief) by relating it to the INs and OUTs of the other nodes that makeup its justifications. To demonstrate the functioning of JTMS, we construct a simple dependency network. We would use a model operator M suggested by McDermott and Doyle (1980) which, if placed before a predicate, is read as *'is consistent with'*. For example,

$$\forall X \; student(X) \wedge M \; obedient(X) \rightarrow good\_student(X)$$
$$\forall Y \; lazy\_person(Y) \rightarrow not \; (good\_student(Y))$$
$$student(Adwet)$$

These propositions can be read as: for all X where X is a student, and if the fact that X is obedient is consistent with every other things we know, then X will be a good student. For all Y, Y is a student and is a lazy person and a lazy person is not a good student. Adwet is a student.

In simple words, it is a general belief that 'all the obedient students are good students', and unless this is proven wrong, Adwet, who is a student would be considered good student. However, if another belief that 'lazy students are not good students' is added to the network, and it is found that Adwet is lazy, the conclusion would have to be retracted.

We would now convert this set of propositions into a justification network. In a JTMS, each predicate representing a belief is associated with two other sets of beliefs. The first set labeled **IN** is the set of propositions that should be believed for the proposition to hold. The second, labeled **OUT** are propositions that are not to be believed for the proposition to hold. To represent the network in pictorial form, some notations shown in Figure 8.2 are used. Figure. 8.2(a) shows the way in which justifications are labeled. Figure. 8.2(b) depicts the combinations of propositions that support a conclusion. Figure. 8.3 represents the justification that supports good_student(Adwet).

With the information given in the network shown in the above Figure 8.2, the problem solver can reason that good_student(Adwet) is supported because the premise good_student(Adwet) is considered true and is consistent with the fact that obedient students are good students. Also, there is no evidence in this example that Adwet is not obedient.

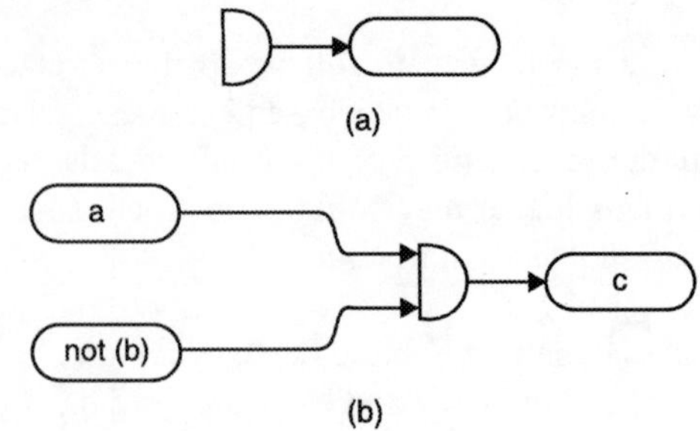

Fig. 8.2: (a) Labelling of Justification **(b)** Combination of propositions

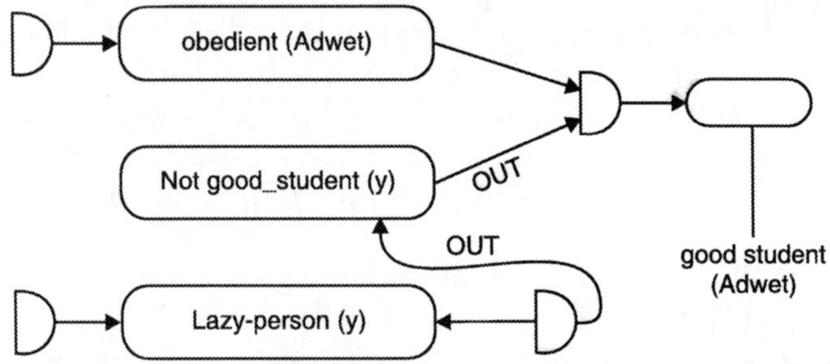

Fig. 8.3: Justification network of good_student(Adwet)

Suppose we now add a new belief lazy_person(Adwet) which will enable to derive not(obedient(Adwet)) using second proposition of the initially mentioned set of propositions. The belief good_student(Adwet) is no longer supported. The justifications for this new situation are shown in Fig. 8.3.

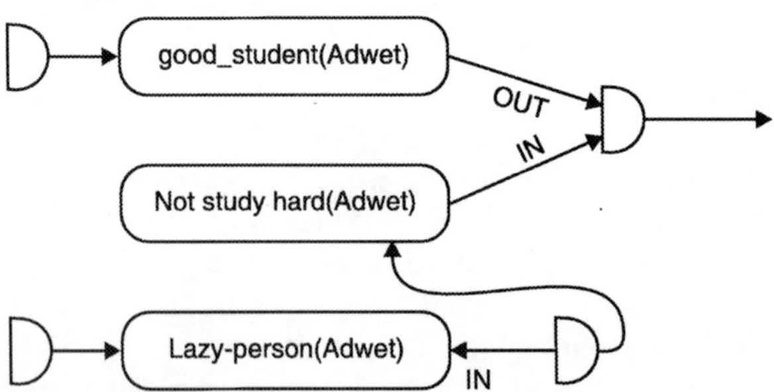

Fig. 8.4: Belief network of lazy_person(Adwet)

8.4.1.1.2 Assumption based TMS (ATMS)

This type of truth maintenance system maintains all the copies of a justification assuming their requirement later. This is unlike JTMS where at one time only one copy of justification is maintained. It is also known as multiple context truth maintenance systems. In practical situations sometimes, it is convenient to perform reasoning in the context of different hypothetical worlds, which may or may not resemble the way the world actually is. For example, in doing diagnosis, it is often worthwhile to assume that a certain fault has occurred and then make predictions based on assumption and see if they are backed up by evidences. This strategy is particularly useful if there are large numbers of hypothesis competing to account for the observations, with the possibility that a composite hypothesis may be required to cover all of them.

The term *assumption-based* was first introduced by deKleer. Assumption-based backtracking systems use labels of nodes as set of premises (assumptions) instead of IN and OUT as used in JTMS. In these systems, a distinction is made between premise nodes that hold universally and premise nodes that could be assumptions made by problem solver and might be retracted later. ATMS overcome some of the shortcomings of JTMS. One of the advantage of ATMS over JTMS is that former provide additional flexibility in dealing with multiple possible states of belief. The communication between ATMS and its problem solver is similar to that between JTMS and its problem solver with the aim of inspection, modifications and updating. The apparent difference is that with ATMS there is no longer a single state of belief but a sub set of potential supporting premises, whereas in JTMS there is a single state of belief and all the nodes are labeled IN. The goal of computation within ATMS is to compare results from different choices of premises to find minimum sets of promises sufficient for the support of each node. Presence of different belief sets enables ATMS to compare different existing solutions for the problem as well as to detect contradictions. ATMS thus are advantageous over JTMS in a way that they enable the problem solver to deal with multiple set of beliefs, however, they also have many disadvantages. Some of the shortcomings of ATMS are the inability to represent premise sets that are themselves nonmonotonic and their control over the problem solver.

8.4.1.1.3 *Logic based TMS (LTMS)*

It is also a single context TMS. It maintains a single copy of justification at one time. Nevertheless, it is logic based. In this, corresponding to logic, its contradiction is also asserted. Thus, solutions of the statements which involve finding of the contradiction of the statements are very easily handled by such systems. These systems are based on the work of McAllester.

8.5 PROBABILISTIC REASONING

So far, we have gone through reasoning techniques that consider a particular fact or belief as true, not true or not assumed in one way or other. Reasoning is a technique applied in solving real world problems. In this section, we would try to concentrate on the issue of using probability theory in the process of reasoning. In simple terms probability is defined as chances of a particular event to occur. By probability, we can also describe how combinations of events are able to influence one another. Though inception of theory of probability goes back to as early as middle ages of Greeks including Llull, Porphyry and Plato, it got final shape by the mathematicians of twentieth century only, including Fisher, Neyman and Pearson. The functioning of probability theory is described as follows:

We understand and record the frequency with which a particular event occurs and use this information to reason about the frequencies of occurrence of future events or combinations of events. For example, in throw of a dice, you get one number from 1 to 6 and if you record the frequency of getting 6 in suppose 20 numbers of throw, you can predict the chances of getting 6 in a throw in future.

There can be number of situations where probabilistic analysis would be appropriate. Real world problems can be divided into two categories: first kind of problems are those to which some degree of randomness is associated whereas second type of problems are those that could be solved using techniques described in last paragraphs. For example, cloud cover brings rain but there is always presence of many random factors that may spoil or enhance the possibility of rain and we cannot predict the outcome with certainty, however, we do have some knowledge of various possible results. Probabilistic analysis of randomness associated with such type of events can help us to reason in great deal.

In second kind of problems, the relevant environment is not random and it behaves normally until some kind of exception occurs. Although events in the world might not be truly random, it is often impossible to know and measure all causes and their interactions to predict events. For example, very high but fluctuating fever with shivering are the symptoms of malaria and unless deep investigation and medical tests negate the presence of malaria, we assume it so be. However, in such type of cases, sometimes difficulty arises in handling them because of the presence of many possible exceptions. Statistical measures may serve the purpose very well in solving such type of problems rather than enumerating all the possible exceptions. The statistical approach groups all exceptions to a relationship together and then uses this measure to describe how often an exception of any type might be expected to occur. For example, a statistical analysis of past diagnosis when high fever with shivering was observed in patients can tell how often the belief was justified and how many times exception of some form occurred. On the basis of this analysis, we can assign a mathematical value for ascertaining the chances of exception of any sort to occur.

Probabilistic reasoning is a method that can be used to strengthen knowledge representation techniques with statistical measures that describe levels of evidence and belief. In knowledge based problem solving, we often are required to reason with limited knowledge and incomplete information about a particular situation. Probabilistic reasoning techniques can be a logical guide in these situations. In this section, we would try to concentrate in Bayesian analysis and then a restricted form of Bayesian inference known as belief networks. Nevertheless, before that let us discuss more about theory of probability and probabilistic reasoning.

Probability of an uncertain event A is a measure of degree of likelihood of occurrence of that event. The set of all possible events is represented as S. Following are the basic axioms of probability theory that define the probability scale:

- $0 \leq P(A) \leq 1$ for any event $A \subseteq S$. It means all probabilities of occurrence of A are between 0 and 1.
- $P(S) = 1$, means certain outcome and $P(S) = 0$, means no outcome.
- For $E_i \cap E_j = \varnothing$ for all i not equal to j, $P(E_1 \cup E_2 \cup E_3 \cup .....) = P(E_1) + P(E_2) + P(E_3) + ...$

In the theory of AI, probabilistic reasoning is used when the problem outcomes are uncertain. In real world, the situations are different from mathematical probability application and our conclusions are based on available evidences and past experiences, which are normally incomplete. In most situations, we get only partial knowledge and using the partial knowledge one is supposed to guess about the outcomes.

For example, if you are asked to tell about the "activities going on inside the earth", you are supposed to make conclusions about the same on the basis of the observations from firstly, the upper portion of the earth and secondly, the related theories telling the geographical details of the inner portion of the earth. However, observations recorded from both the ways help only to make a guess about the result. Such type of conclusions which are based on imperfect knowledge and observations can not be guaranteed to be true. Similarly, in case of medical diagnosis, when a physician examines a patient's history, symptoms and test results provide some but not conclusive evidence of possible ailments. This knowledge gained by the physician's experience with the previous patients, improves the likelihood of predicting the patients unknown disease. But because of the facts which are not known, the predictions about the disease may be wrong. Further, the prediction about the weather forecast are based on the available knowledge about the behavior of whether with the changing parameters like temperature, pressure, humidity etc. As the physical relationships that govern these phenomenons are not fully understood hence, predictions are far from certain.

Probabilistic reasoning is the kind of problem solving technique that is applied when the normal first order predicate logic fails. For example, in case of medical diagnosis where the solution requires extensive knowledge about the problem, the normal logics are not sufficient to represent the knowledge because of following factors:

- Presence of too many antecedents or consequences makes the rule interpretation too hard.
- Medical science seldom gives the complete theory about any disease.
- The perfectly complete diagnosis about patient's details is not practically done.

The probabilistic inference is used for drawing conclusions in events like these. Consider a medical rule: "if a patient has toothache then he may have cavity".

This rule is correct up to a certain level. Because, it might be possible that toothache was due to some other reason. Moreover, not all cavities cause pain. Still in the theory of medical diagnosis, the cavities are major cause of pain. Now if the doctor is supposed to handle the situation of pain in tooth, he will observe the patient's symptoms, if cavity is found, he will diagnose this with some probability, e.g. he may say that it is 80% certain that he has toothache because of cavity. In case of uncertain events 80% probability does not indicate 80% truth ness of the diagnosis, it indicates doctor's 80% belief in the diagnosis. The real world events for the purpose of representation use propositional logic. For the representation two quantities are required, first quantity to which degree of belief is to be assigned and second, the value of degree of belief according to ones own experience and observations.

8.5.1 Bayesian Reasoning

Bayesian reasoning is a kind of probabilistic reasoning, introduced by Thomas Bayes in the eighteenth century that is based on formal probability theory and is used in several areas of research including pattern recognition and classification. Assuming a random sampling of events, Bayesian theory devises the calculation of complex probabilities from previously known results. Probability is of two types:

- *PRIOR PROBABILITY*: This probability is also popularly known as *unconditional probability*. It is probability assigned to an event in the absence of knowledge supporting its occurrence or absence, i.e. the probability of the event prior to any evidence supporting or negating the occurrence of that particular event. The prior probability of an event is represented as: P(event).

- *POSTERIOR PROBABILITY*: This type of probability is also known as conditional probability. It is the probability of an event after evidence, i.e. the probability when some evidences supporting or negating the outcome are known. Posterior probability is symbolized as: P (event | evidence).

To understand two types of probabilities, let us consider one example. There was a one-day international cricket match between India and Pakistan. If you were asked about the probability of India winning the match, the honest answer would be 50%. This probability would be called prior or unconditional probability because you were not aware of the evidences supporting or negating the chances of Indian team's win. Now, before asking the same question, if you were told about the team combination, ground condition, crowd support etc., you would increase or decrease the probability of Indian team winning the same match due to various known evidences supporting or negating the team's performance. This probability now would be called posterior probability.

Bayes Theorem is based on the theory of conditional probability. We would try to explain the concept by an example of medical diagnosis. Suppose **n** is the set of persons present in the domain under consideration out of which certain number of persons are sick and the set of patients is **p.** Out of total number of patients, certain numbers of persons have symptoms of a particular disease **d** and set of patients having symptoms of that particular disease is **s**. The unconditional probability of a persons having disease **d** is the number of people having some disease (i.e. number of patients) divided by the number of people in the domain of concern (total number of people examined). Since we do not have any other information available, all the sick persons having symptoms **s** of disease **d** or not, would be considered having that disease.

Hence,

Unconditional probability **P(d) = |p| / |n|**

Where,　　|p| = number of sick persons or number of patients

　　　　　|n| = total number of persons in the domain

Now, let us assume that we have some evidence in support of available symptoms and find that not all of the total persons having symptoms **s** of the disease **d** are actually having that disease. Hence, in this case,

d = set of persons actually having disease d

s = set of persons having symptoms of disease d

d ∩ **s** = set of persons actually having disease d and symptoms s both.

Thus, the conditional probability of persons having disease **d** with symptoms **s** or simply, probability of a person having disease **d** if he has symptom **s** would be number of persons actually having disease **d** divided by number of persons having symptoms **s** of disease **d,** and would be represented as:

P(d | s) = |d ∩ s| / | s |　　　　　　　　　　　　　　(1)

Where, |d ∩ s| = number of persons having disease **d** and symptoms **s** both

| s | = number of persons having symptoms **s**

To better understand the above mentioned probabilities, let us consider that total 1000 people are present in the domain out of which 100 persons are sick. Out of 100 patients, 60 persons had high fever that is symptom of malaria. Further investigations found that in fact, only 20 persons had malaria. Remaining, though had symptoms of malaria, actually had some other disease. Here,

|n| = 1000, |p| = 100, |s| = 60 and |d ∩ s| = 20

Thus, Unconditional probability of persons having malaria, P(d) = 100/1000

= 0.10.

And, conditional probability of persons having malaria with high fever,

P(d | s) = 20/60

= 0.33.

Also, please note that unconditional probability of the persons actually having malaria, would be number of persons actually having malaria divided by total number of persons in the domain. Thus,

$$P(d \cap s) = 20/1000$$
$$= 0.020,$$

and unconditional probability of patients having symptoms of disease d would be number of patients having symptoms s divided by total number of persons. Thus,

$$P(s) = 60/1000$$
$$= 0.060$$

Now, from above:

$$P(d \cap s) / P(s) = 0.02/0.06$$
$$= 0.33$$
$$= P(d \mid s)$$

That means, conditional probability of persons having disease **d** with symptoms **s** is unconditional probability of persons actually having disease **d** with symptoms **s** divided by unconditional probability of persons having symptoms **s** of that disease. Hence,

$$P(d \mid s) = P(d \cap s) / P(s) \tag{2}$$

Similarly, we can have an equivalent relationship for conditional probability of persons having symptoms **s** with disease **d** or probability of a person having symptom **s** if he has disease **d** as:

$$P(s \mid d) = P(d \cap s) / P(d) \tag{3}$$
$$\text{Or,} \qquad P(d \cap s) = P(s \mid d) * P(d) \tag{4}$$

Substituting this result in the equation for $P(d \mid s)$, we get:

$$P(d \mid s) = (P(s \mid d) * P(d)) / P(s) \tag{5}$$

This equation is known as Bayes theorem. The advantageous thing about Bayes theorem is that numbers on right-hand side of the equation for $P(d \mid s)$ are easily available compared to number on left-hand side of the equation. For example, it is easier to find the number of patients having high fever in case they have malaria because of limited size of domain, compared to number of patients who have malaria if they have high fever because high fever can be due to many diseases and size of domain of persons having high fever could be very large. Hence, greater degree of uncertainty is associated with this kind of situation. Whenever some reasoning needs to be done regarding this type of uncertain situation, the Bayes theorem can be applied with ease. To elaborate the theorem and to understand its applications, let us consider one example:

"Given is a domain of people out of which some are patients having Diarrhoea. It is known that Diarrhoea causes vomiting in patients and

probability of patient having vomiting if he has Diarrhoea is 0.70. The doctors have knowledge that prior probability of a patient having vomiting because of any reason is 0.05, and prior probability of having Diarrhoea is 0.00005. You are required to reason the probability of a patient having Diarrhoea if he has vomiting."

Given, disease d = Diarrhoea, symptom s = vomiting,
Prior probability of having symptom, $P(s) = 0.05$,
Prior probability of having disease, $P(d) = 0.00005$
Posterior probability of having symptom s (vomiting) in case patient has disease d (Diarrhoea), $P(s \mid d) = 0.70$.
Required is $P(d \mid s)$
From Bayes theorem, $P(d \mid s) = (0.70 * 0.00005)/0.05$
$$= 0.0007$$
From the above example, it is evident that though 7 out of 100 patients have vomiting if they have Diarrhoea, only 7 out of 10000 patients would have Diarrhoea if they have vomiting. This is because prior probability of having vomiting is much higher than prior probability of having Diarrhoea.

We have discussed above a particular case of medical diagnosis and use of Bayes theorem in reasoning about a disease, however, in real world there could be many situations where we would require to assess the chances of some belief or hypothesis to be true given some evidence in support of the same. Hence, we present here the most important finding of probability theory, the general form of Bayes theorem. Taking reference of the above discussion, the disease would now be called *hypothesis* (H) and symptom would be called *evidence* (E). Substituting these notations in the equation (5) mentioned above, we get:

$P(H|E) = P(E|H) * P(H)/ P(E)$ (6)

This is most simple view of Bayes theorem. It can be applied assuming real world phenomena as simple and straight forward as any thing. However, real world situations are complex and tedious where we have to deal with multiple hypotheses and multiple evidences. The key to using Bayes theorem as a basis for uncertain reasoning lies in the fact of recognizing what does it actually say. Specially, when we say $P(H|E)$, we are describing the conditional probability of H given that the only available evidence is E. If, however, there is also other relevant evidence available, that too must be considered. For example, let us consider following facts regarding a medical diagnosis case:

e_1 : patient has spots
e_2 : patient has measles
e_3 : patient has high fever

These are the three evidences about the symptoms of patient. Without any additional evidence the spots supports the presence of measles. It also supports presence of high fever. But suppose we already know that patient has measles then additional evidence of fever actually does not tell any additional thing about the disease, but it only supports (or enhances) the possibility of measles. We all know either spots alone or fever alone would constitute evidence in favor of measles. But if both are present, we would be required to take both in to account to determine total weight of the evidence. But, as spots and fever are dependent events, we can not just sum their effects, but we need to represent conditional probability that arises from their conjunction. Hence, the unconditional probability of evidence E, P(E) in the equation (6) above would be required to take in to account the multiple hypotheses and should be represented in the form of conditional probability of that evidence with respect to various hypotheses.

From definition of conditional probability, we know that probability of evidence E to support hypothesis H is represented as:

$$P(E|H) = P(E \cap H)/P(H) \qquad \text{(from equation 3 mentioned above)}$$

Or $\qquad P(E \cap H) = P(E|H)*P(H)$ $\hfill$ (7)

As said earlier, in real world situations, we normally have to deal with a set of exhaustive and mutually exclusive hypotheses say H_j (j = 1 to n, n is number of hypotheses). For example, let us consider a case of medical diagnosis again. We know that fever is caused by many diseases like, malaria, viral, measles etc. Hence, unconditional probability of fever in absence of any evidence will be sum of probabilities of fever caused because of any disease. If set of diseases is D_j (j=1 to n), then prior probability of symptom (fever in this case) P(s) will be:

$$P(s) = P(s \cap D_1) + P(s \cap D_2) + P(s \cap D_3) + \ldots\ldots$$

Or, $\quad P(s) = \sum_{J=1}^{n} P(s \cap D_j)$

Now if disease is hypothesis H and symptom is evidence E, then for any evidence E, we have:

$$\mathbf{P(E) = \sum_{J=1}^{n} P(E \cap H_j) = \sum_{J=1}^{n} P(E| H_j) * P(H_j)} \hfill \textbf{(8)}$$

(substituting the value of P(E∩H) from equation 7 mentioned above)

Now, if we generalize the Bayes theorem represented by equation (6) above, the probability of a hypothesis H_i if only evidence E is given and no other information is available would be:

$$\mathbf{P(H_i|E) = P(E|H_i) * P(H_i)/ P(E)}$$

Substituting the value of P(E) from equation (8):

$$P(H_i|E) = \frac{P(E|H_i) * P(H_i)}{\sum_{J=1}^{n} P(E|H_j) * P(H_j)}$$

This is generalized version of Bayes theorem, where:

$P(H_i|E)$: the probability that H_i is true given evidence E

$P(H_i)$: the probability that H_i is true overall

$P(E|H_i)$: the probability of observing E when H_i is true

n is the number of hypotheses.

The Bayes theorem was successfully applied in PROSPECTOR program developed by Duda (1979). This program was designed to guess the presence of minerals like copper, uranium, manganese etc. in the earth's crust. To perform this guess we examine geological evidence at a particular location to determine whether that has the presence of some symptoms. We must know in advance the probability of finding each of mineral and the probability of certain evidence being present when each particular mineral is found. This type of analysis is done to find out that whether it would be good to dig at a particular place. We can use Bayes formula to compute from the evidence we collect, how likely it is that the various minerals are present. Bayes theorem can be applied in various other problems of uncertain reasoning like this.

We can thus notice that Bayes theorem can help in reasoning specially when cases simply contain single disease and single symptom, because in these cases many numbers are not needed on the right-hand side in the equation of Bayes theorem. However, trouble starts when reasoning is required to be done about possible disease from among the set of multiple diseases and multiple symptoms. Let us consider multiple diseases d_m from the set of diseases D and multiple symptoms s_n from the set of symptoms S. In this case, we would require (m x n) posterior probabilities and (m + n) prior probabilities. (in case of single disease and single symptom, m = 1 and n = 1; hence we require one posterior and two prior probabilities; in all three values to compute desired result)

In actual real world situations, we hardly have single disease and single symptom. A doctor often has to consider multiple symptoms while examining a patient. The Bayes theorem in this case would look like:

$$P(d|s_1 \ \& \ s_2 \ \& ... \& \ s_n) = (P \ (s_1 \ \& \ s_2 \ \& ... \& \ s_n \ |d)) * P(d) / P \ (s_1 \ \& \ s_2 \ \& ... \& \ s_n)$$

As mentioned earlier, with one disease and single symptom, we need only (m x n) measurements. Now if symptoms are two, suppose s_i and s_j and a disease d, we need to know both the probabilities $P \ (s_i \ \& \ s_j \ |d)$ and $P(s_i \ \& \ s_j)$. If there are 3 symptoms say, s_i, s_j and s_k in S, the number of such pairs would be 6. [$P \ (s_i \ \& \ s_j \ |d)$, $P \ (s_j \ \& \ s_k \ |d)$, $P \ (s_k \ \& \ s_i \ |d)$, $P(s_i \ \& \ s_j)$, $P(s_j \ \& \ s_k)$, $P(s_k \ \& \ s_i)$] This number is equal to n! or n(n – 1). Hence, for n number of symptoms, there are n x (n - 1) possible pairs of probabilities. To get a rough estimate, let us take this value as approximately

n^2. Now, suppose there are m number of diseases in D and if we want to use Bayes theorem to calculate the probability of a patient having a particular disease out of possible m, if he has n number of symptoms, we would require about $(m \times n^2)$conditional probabilities + n^2 symptoms probabilities + m disease probabilities to complete the right-hand side of the Bayes theorem. Suppose a patient has four symptoms and he could have any of two diseases, we would need about $2 \times 4^2 + 4^2 + 2$, in all 50 probabilities to be collected to estimate the probability of patient having a particular disease. This could well be a difficult task. If still you do not find anything astonishing in this, think of a realistic medical system with 100 diseases and 1000 symptoms. In this situation, the number of probabilities to be known could be over 100,000,000.

However, we may get some relief. Out of all the symptoms, many would be independent. Independent symptoms mean symptoms that are not related. For example, in case of medical diagnosis, if a patient has symptoms of high fever and sore elbow then these two symptoms would be called independent because probability of having high fever is not affected by patient having sore elbow. Thus, these two symptoms would not be considered together for a particular disease. Only dependent symptoms would be considered. Even if ten percent of the domain symptoms are dependent, we still get about 10,000,000 number of probabilities to be considered for diagnosis in the above case.

As discussed above, we need to calculate joint probabilities also, when for a given evidence 'e' some new evidence 'E' is observed. Hence instead of P(H|E), we require P(H|E,e), represented as:

$$P(H|E,e) = P(H|E) \frac{P(e|E,H)}{P(e|E)}$$

In a complex world full of uncertainties, the size of the set of these joint probabilities required to compute this function grows as 2^n, if we consider different propositions amounting to n. This again becomes a huge task. From the above analysis, we must notice that suddenly, too simple looking things started turning too complex. Due to need of so many unconditional and conditional probabilities, Bayes theorem becomes intractable for this and several other reasons mentioned below:

- One needs too many probabilities to reason a single situation and knowledge acquisition becomes a really huge and substantial task. We require all the probabilities of relationships of evidences with various hypotheses as well as the probabilistic relationship between various evidences.
- We need to rebuild probability tables as and when new relationships between hypotheses and evidences are discovered. In many active research areas such as medical science, new discoveries happen continuously and since Bayesian statistics requires complete and up-dated probabilities, including joint probabilities, to get correct conclusions, we need to up-date database continuously.

- We require huge space to store all these probabilities. It is obvious looking in to the number of probabilities needed to calculate the desired probability.
- Since the number of probabilities required is surmountable, we need enormous time to calculate these.

These are some most noticeable intricacies faced in using Bayes theorem in routine real world problems. In spite of these difficulties, Bayesian statistics provides a viable and attractive alternative for developing reasoning systems required to deal with uncertain situations. Hence forth, many mechanisms have been developed on the basis of this very popular theorem. We would discuss some of those, Bayesian networks, certainty factors based systems, and Dempster Shafer Theory with a trace of fuzzy reasoning in the coming sections.

8.5.2 Bayesian Networks

As discussed in the previous section, due to combining effect of hypotheses and evidences, large number of probabilities are required to use Bayesian theorem. Clearly, the time and storage requirements for such huge number of data are among the drawbacks of Bayesian reasoning. Also, inferring with such large numbers of probabilities we would seldom be able to model human process of reasoning because human beings normally tend to single out only a few propositions which are known to be causally linked when reasoning with uncertain beliefs. For example, let us consider a real world problem faced by almost all of us, the problem with our car. Suppose we observe following evidences in a car:

    S   : the car has starting problem
    H   : the headlights are not functioning

The beliefs or hypotheses supporting these evidences can be:

    N   : there is no fuel in the car
    B   : the car battery is not properly charged
    F   : the headlight bulbs are fuse

If you are required to reason about the possible causes of the two evidences, you would try to find out the correlation between evidences and hypotheses as well as interdependence of hypotheses. Hence, you would need to calculate the joint probabilities or combined probabilities of all the variables. Combined probability of two events occurring together if they are independent is represented as:

$$P(A\&B) = P(A) * P(B)$$

But, if A and B are not independent, their combined probability will be
$$P(A\&B) = P(A) * P(B|A)$$

Hence, in the case of car example, the combined probability of all the five variable will be represented as:

$$P(S,H,N,B,F) = P(S)*P(H|S)*P(N|S,H)*P(B|S,H,N)*P(F|S,H,N,B)$$

As mentioned earlier, the number of joint probabilities in this case will be $2^5 = 32$. Of course, it is only a minor problem with just five parameters. A situation of reasonable size with say 50 or more parameters would require billions of probabilities.

Now, in a real and practical situation, if you face a car problem like the one mentioned above, you as a human being would use your heuristics and intuition to separate evidences and hypotheses that are not dependent. For example, we know that 'no fuel' hypothesis and 'non functional headlights' are independent events. Similarly, 'no start' and 'fuse bulb' are also independent events. However, 'no start', 'battery problem' and 'non functional headlights' are dependent events. Knowing the above facts, you can form a graph showing interdependence of various parameters as shown in the following figure:

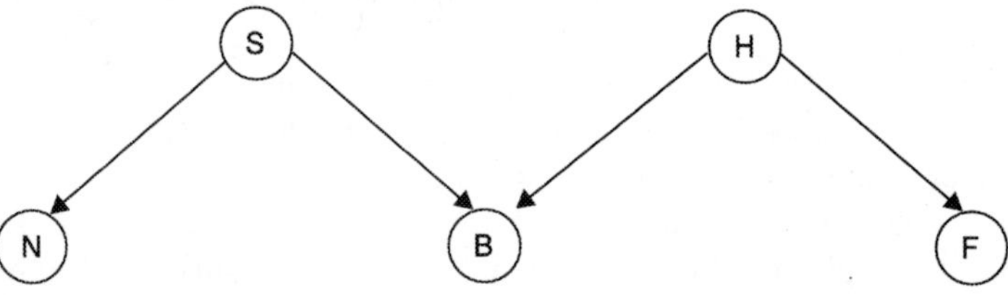

Fig. 8.5. Bayesian representation of car problem

In the above diagram, propositional variables are represented as nodes and the causal influences or dependencies among the nodes are represented by arcs. Such types of graphical presentations are known as *Bayesian networks* proposed by Pearl in 1988. Each node that precedes the corresponding nodes is called parent of the connected nodes. For example, node S is parent of nodes N and B in fig. 8.5.

Most important thing to note here is that Bayesian belief networks relax many constraints of the full Bayesian model. The modularity of problem domain often allows the relaxation of many of the dependent/independent constraints required for Bayes. In most reasoning situations, it is not necessary to build large joint probability tables in which the probabilities for all possible combinations of events and evidences are listed. Rather, human experts apply their inherent knowledge and select local phenomena to interact and obtain probabilities or influence measures that reflect only dependent events. Experts assume all other events either conditionally independent or that their correlations are small enough to be ignored.

Let us consider again the car problem example. If we can support the assumptions that the parameters are only dependent on the probabilities of their parents, the calculation of P(S,H,N,B,F) will become:

$$P(S,H,N,B,F) = P(S)*P(H)*P(N|S)*P(B|S,H)*P(F|H)$$

We have made many simplifications. To understand these, let us consider the P(N|S,H) from the previous equation. We have reduced it to P(N|S) in new equation. This reduction is based on the assumption that N and H, i.e. 'no fuel' and 'headlights not functioning' are independent events and fuel in the car has hardly any effect on the functioning of headlights. Similarly other probabilities have been reduced depending upon the correlations the events have with their parents. The probability distribution for P(S,H,N,B,F) will now have 20 parameters than 32. It might not seem to be a considerable change, but in realistic problems having large parameters, we might require only hundreds of parameters instead of billions after applying Bayesian network in place of full Bayes probability distribution approach.

Once belief network is constructed, an inference engine of an intelligent system can use it to maintain and propagate beliefs. If some new information is received, the effects of the same can be propagated throughout the network until equilibrium probabilities are reached. Pearl has proposed simplified methods for updating networks of this type by fusing and propagating the effects of new beliefs and evidences such that equilibrium is reached in time proportional to the longest path through the network. At equilibrium, all propositions will have consistent probabilities.

If we sum up and summarize what has been discussed above, we come up with following salient features:

Bayesian networks are a graphical representation of dependent events. In real world, the events are dependent on each other and one method to represent them is using a table having joint probabilities also called combined probability table. But if the entries are more, then these tables become unmanageable commodities containing billions of numbers. Bayesian networks are an easy graphical representation of real world dependent events. These have a directed acyclic graph, in which nodes represent the events or evidence and the arcs represent their dependence.

The basic properties of Bayesian network are as follows:

- Bayesian networks have a set of random discrete or continuous variables, generating the nodes of the network.
- They have a set of directed links or arrows connecting pair of nodes. If there is an arrow from node x to node y, x is said to be parent of y.
- Each node x_i has a conditional probability distribution $P(x_i \mid parent(x_i))$, which quantifies the effect of parent on the node.
- The graph has no directed cycles. It means Bayesian belief networks are representation of directed acyclic graphs (DAG), reason being, causal inference reasoning is not circular because an effect cannot circle back to cause itself. Causal inference reasoning assumes that influences of nodes are directed and presence of one node causes other events in the network, not itself.

The topology of graph indicates that node specifies the conditional independence relationships of the problem.

Thus, while constructing belief networks, we construct a directed acyclic graph that represents causality relationships among the variables. The idea of belief networks has been used for designing and developing many systems, particularly medical diagnosis systems such as CASNET (Weiss,1978) and INTERNIST/ CADUCEUS (Pople, 1982).

Let us consider one more example taken from Pearl (1988). This is known as water sprinkler-rain problem. This problem states that possibilities of grass being wet depends upon water from either rain or from sprinkler system. The water from rain or from sprinkler system depends upon season of the year. This correlation between various events is shown in Fig. 8.6.

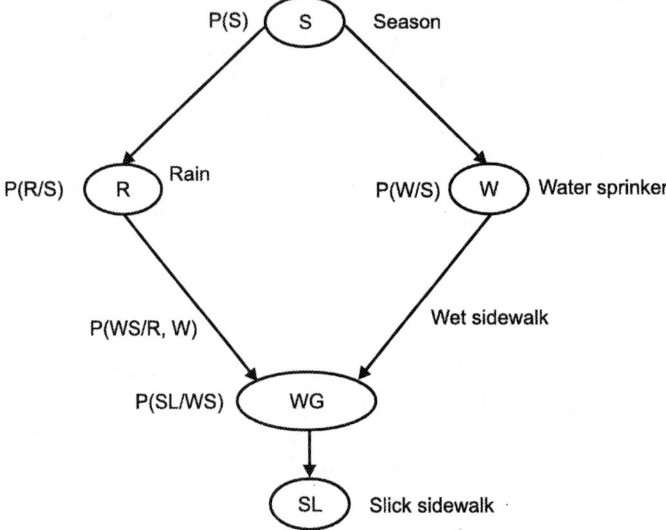

Fig. 8.6. Bayesian probabilistic network. Probability dependencies are located next to each node

In the above figure, we have expressed the probability relationship that each of the parameters has with its parents. Now, if we try to describe the probability of wet grass, we find that it is dependent on two parents, the rain and water sprinkler. The independent probabilities of rain and water sprinklers both affect the probability of grass becoming wet. Had two parents been independent, it would have been easy as was the case of car problem, but here, two parents are not mutually independent and depend up on season. For example in summer, there is always higher probability of rain and water sprinklers would also be used for sure hence, probability of wet grass would increase. Thus, in this situation, complete correlation of the two variables (rain and water sprinklers) along with their correlation with season must be considered. The calculation is exponential in the number of possible causes of wet grass (WG) and is shown in following combined probability Table:

We now would try to calculate first probability p in the above table when R and W are both true and we assume that season S is either hot or cold. The desired probability p would be given as follows:

p   = P(R=t & S=t) for all conditions of S
       = P(S=hot)*P(R=t| S=hot)*P(W=t| S=hot) +
         P(S=cold)*P(R=t| S=cold)*P(W=t| S=cold)

Table 8.1: The probability distribution for (WG) as a function of P(R) and P(W) given the effect of S.

	R	W	P	
	t	t	x	
	t	f		{S = hot
	f	t		{ S = cold
	f	f		

As is evident from the above derivation, the probability of grass being wet would depend upon joint probability of rain and water sprinklers. However, rain and sprinklers are not independent, but depend upon season. Hence P(R & S) would be conditional probability of rain and sprinklers and would be the sum of these probabilities for both the possibilities of season, i.e. hot and cold. This conditional probability has been derived using equation (2) mentioned in the previous section.

The DAG drawn above illustrates the causality relationships that occur among the nodes it contains. In order to use it as a basis for probabilistic reasoning, we need to have more information as well as a mechanism for computing the influence of any arbitrary node on any other. For example, suppose we have observed rain last night. Based on this observation, what would we conclude about the probability of this being a rainy season? The answer of this question requires the directed acyclic graph (DAG) as drawn above to be converted into undirected graph in which arcs can be used to transmit probabilities in either direction depending upon from where the evidence is coming. Similarly, we require mechanism to ensure that the probabilities are transmitted correctly. For example, we know that wet grass might be taken as evidence for rain and observation of rain is evidence of wet grass, but we must ensure that no cycle is traversed in such a way that if wet grass is take as evidence for rain, rain is then taken as evidence for wet grass.

For doing computations like the above, three types of algorithms are used. These are mentioned below:

- Clique triangulation method
- Message-passing method, and
- Other Stochastic algorithms.

First, we would discuss the clique triangulation approach proposed by Pearl in 1988. In this approach, we replace the constraint propagation of the DAG with an *acyclic clique tree* also known as *junction tree*. In clique triangulation method, explicit arcs are introduced between pairs of nodes that share a common descendent, for example, in the case of wet grass problem mentioned above, a link would be introduced between nodes R and W. This link helps us to assess the impact of observation W on the hypothesis R. We should understand that this assessment is important since wet grass could be evidence of either of R and W, but the evidence of WG and R can not be evidence for W because we already have evidence for wet grass in the form of rain. The clique tree on the basis of belief net work shown in the Fig. 8.7(a) is shown in the following Fig. 8.7(b):

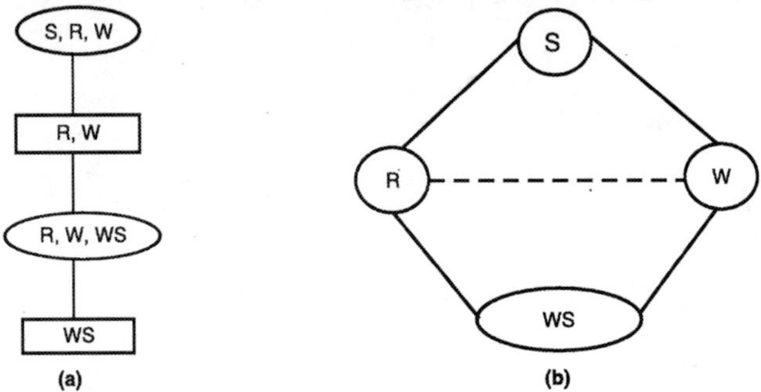

Fig. 8.7: A junction tree (a) for Bayesian probabilistic network (b)

In the above figure of junction tree, rectangular boxes reflect the variables that the cliques above and below it share. Also, the linking variable along with all its parents must be present in the clique. Thus, in developing a belief network, we must assess properly the number of parents a particular state has. Cliques overlap also, as shown in the fig. 8.7 (b), to pass information through the full clique tree. We would now understand the algorithm used to create a clique or junction tree from a belief network. The steps involved in the said algorithm are as follows:

- Make all directed links undirected for all nodes in the belief network.
- Draw links between all parents for any node. (for example, a link by dashed line has been marked between R and W in the above DAG for wet grass problem).
- Check the network and ensure that all the cycles have only three nodes. If not, add further links to reduce all the cycles having maximum three nodes. This process is called triangulation. However, this process is not required in the above example).
- Form the junction tree from the resulting triangulated structure. This is done by finding the maximal cliques. The variables in these cliques are put into junctions and the junction tree is created by connecting any two junctions that share at least one variable.

Second approach mentioned earlier is known as message-passing approach proposed by Pearl in 1988. this approach is based on the observation that to compute the probability of any node A, given known information about the other nodes of the network, we need following three things:

- The total support arriving at A from its parent nodes i.e. the causes of A.
- The total support arriving at A from its children i.e. following nodes which forms its symptoms.
- The conditional probability of A representing its relation with its parents to generate causes.

Several methods for propagating these messages and updating the probabilities at the nodes have been developed. The choice of suitable approach depends upon the structure of the network. Details of this approach and more information are available in Pearl (1988).

Finally, we have stochastic algorithms for updating belief networks. One such algorithm proposed by Chavez in 1989 transforms an arbitrary network into a Markov chain. Stochastic algorithms provide fast solutions but these might not produce absolutely correct results.

Belief networks though provide a handy tool for the purpose of probabilistic reasoning, they have many limitations from the view point of knowledge engineering and computational complexity both. These limitations have motivated research in hierarchical and composable Bayesian models. Further research in this field has developed many algorithms for building belief networks and propagating arguments as and when new evidence is acquired, like those mentioned above and proposed by Lauritzen and Spiegelhalter (1988), by Druzdel and Henrion (1993) and by Dechter (1996) who presented the bucket elimination algorithm as a unifying framework for probabilistic inference. However, the clique triangulation approach and message-passing approach are the two most used algorithms in the area for desired computations.

The area is new and open for further research specially in the field of developing stochastic algorithms due to importance of these algorithms in the field of AI, for example in problem solving using probabilistic agents, in the area of learning and natural language processing.

Consider one more example.

You have installed a burgler alarm in your house. The alarm responds to burglary, earthquake, two neighbours Vidushi and Mr. Girish. However to avoid the unnecessary confusion caused by neighbours , they have promised to ring on telephone after hearing the alarm. let us assume the following :

Probability of activating the alarm because of burglary P(B) :   .001

Probability of activating the alarm because of burglary P(B) :   .001

Probability of Vidushi's ringing the telephone on hearing the alarm : .9

Probability of Vidushi's ringing the telephone without hearing the alarm : .05

Probability of Mr. Girish ringing the telephone on hearing the alarm : .85

Probability of Mr Girish ringing the telephone without hearing the alarm: .01

This situation in terms of Bays network can be represented as shown in Fig. 8.8.

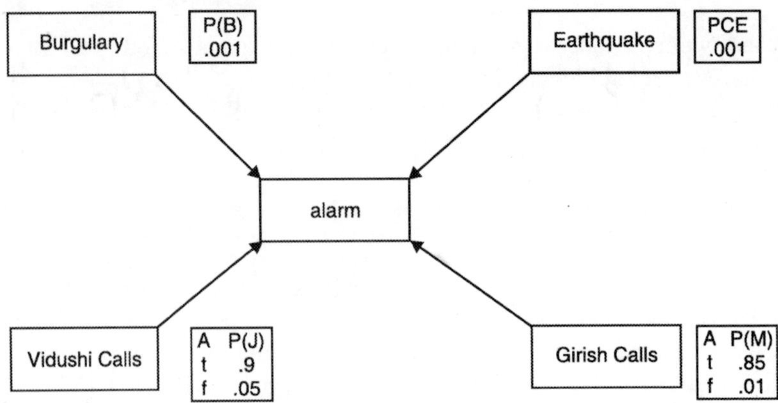

Fig. 8.8: Bayesian network representation of Burgulary network

Now , it can easily seen from the diagram that the cause of ringing the alarm is burglary, earthquake, and Vidushi, and Girish. Here it is assumed that as the neighbours are human being they can commit mistake also by ringing the telephone without hearing the alarm. Hence , while getting the information about the probabilities there can virtually be infinite set of conditional and joint probabilities. The real world is full of activities which are dependent on each other. The probability of occurring these activities independently is separately observed and their joint probabilities are separately observed. The conditional probabilities are represented in a table called as conditional probability table (CPT). This type of table is useful for discrete variables. Each row in a CPT contains the conditional probability of each node value for a conditioning case. A conditioning case is a possible combination of values for parent nodes. The summation of each row in the table should be 1. this is because the entries represents an exhaustive set of cases for the variable. In case of Boolean variable as the values it can take is only 0 or 1. the probability of an event not being true i.e. $\neg$P is simply 1- P . in general, a table for a Boolean variable with k Boolean parents contains 2^k independently specifiable probabilities. A node with no parent has only one row representing the prior probabilities of each possible value of variable.

8.5.3 Reasoning with certainty factor

As discussed earlier, in AI various approaches are devised to deal with uncertain situations. The logic-based approaches, in which the knowledge is represented in terms of prepositional and predicate logic, are cumbersome and computationally intractable for many applications, especially expert systems. As an alternative approach, expert system like PROSPECTOR used Bayesian techniques. But this approach also requires collections of independent assumptions, continuous updates of statistical data and numerous calculations. In case of large number of evidences, the calculation about probability, joint probability and conditional probability restricts the application of Bayesian network up to a certain extent. An alternative to these approaches was used at Stanford for development of early expert systems including MYCIN. One such approach is reasoning using certainty theory.

Certainty theory is different from probability theory. It is based on many real-life observations and few most important are presented below:

- The first is, that in traditional probability theory the sum of 'confidence for a relationship' and 'confidence against the same relationship' must add to one. However, a human expert might say in some situation that confidence for the relationship is 0.5 but his confidence against the same situation might be 0.2 or he might have no idea of the confidence against the situation. For example, in rainy season, if there is heavy cloud cover and you are asked about the probability of 'rain', your answer could be 80%. Now as per the probability theory, the probability of 'no rain' in this case would be 20%. However if you are asked about the probability of 'no rain', your answer might be 10% or you might have no any idea about the chances of 'no rain'. The aim is to understand that in real world situations, human beings reason about a given situation in such a way that their confidence for and confidence against the same situation are independent assessments i.e. they are not linked.

- A further observation that supports certainty theory is that the knowledge content of the rules is much more important than algebra for computing the confidences. This is because confidence measures, such as "it is probably true" "it is almost certainly true" or it is "highly true", that human experts attach to their conclusions are informal and are based on the heuristic knowledge of human beings acquired from experience. The weights human beings give to their results are not based on probabilistic analysis of the situation hence knowledge including heuristic knowledge about the given situation is more important compared to mathematics involved.

The Stanford certainty theory makes some simple assumptions for creating and assigning confidence measures for and against any given situation. The first assumption is to split 'confidence for' from 'confidence against' a relationship and treat them separately. This is because unlike in probability theory, in certainty theory, $P(A) \neq 1 - P(\text{not } A)$. We define these two confidences as follows:

Call MB (H|E)   the measure of belief of a hypothesis H given evidence E, means confidence for the hypothesis H in presence on evidence E.

Call MD (H|E)   the measure of disbelief of a hypothesis H given evidence E, means confidence against the hypothesis H in presence of evidence E.

Now, in the situation where measure of belief MB (H|E) = 0, means you do not have any belief for the hypothesis H. But, as discussed above, it would not mean that you have 100% disbelief or 100% belief against the same hypothesis for the same given evidence. Hence, MD(H|E) would be less than 1. Now, since you have no belief in the hypothesis hence you must be having some amount of disbelief or belief against H for given E, hence MD(H|E) would be more than 0.

Thus:

$$\text{For } MB(H|E) = 0,\ 1 > MD\ (H/E) > 0$$

Similarly,

$$\text{For } MD(H|E) = 0,\ 1 > MB\ (H/E) > 0$$

In actual problem, these two constraints restrict each other in the sense that a given piece of evidence is either for or against a particular hypothesis. This is an important difference between certainty theory and probability theory. This phenomenon can be understood further in such a way that in certainty theory, if an evidence works in favor of some hypothesis, it would have no effect in assessing the belief against the same hypothesis since two confidence measures are separated. While in probability theory, if some evidence is for the hypothesis, it will have its bearing in computing the confidence against the same hypothesis also and the measure against the hypothesis would be 1- measure for the hypothesis.

Hoping it has been understood well that in certainty theory, MB(H|E) and MD(H|E) are not linked and their assessment is done splitting the two confidences, the more is the value of MB(H|E) compared to MD(H|E), our confidence for the hypothesis would be more compared to confidence against the hypothesis. Similarly, it is for other way round. Now, if we want to know the effect of a given evidence E on a hypothesis H, we would find the values of two measures of belief and to know that E is working for or against H, one way could be to find the difference between two measures. More the value of difference, more would be the support of E for H, and vice versa. This difference of these two measures of belief is defined as certainty factor (CF). Hence,

$$CF\ (H|E) = MB(H|E) - MD(H|E)$$

The value of CF may vary between +1 and -1. As its value approaches +1, the evidence is stronger for a hypothesis, and as CF approaches -1, the confidence against the hypothesis gets stronger. CF =0 indicates that either little evidence exists for or against the hypothesis or that the evidence for and against the hypothesis is balanced.

In case of real world problems, the decision about the value of two measures of confidence and hence, certainty factor is a matter of opinion. Upon seeing particular evidence, the Experts decide the value of degree of belief in a certain hypothesis based on the heuristic knowledge. Hence, in actual problems, experts put a rule base and they agree on a CF to go with each rule. The CF reflects their confidence in the reliability of the rule. Real world problems are hardly so simple where there is single evidence and single hypothesis. We are required to deal with situations having multiple evidences and multiple hypotheses. Thus, we need to study the combined effect of evidences and hypotheses on certainty factor. In real world, we normally face following types of situations:

1. First, where we have to deal with multiple evidences supporting single hypothesis. Like in medical diagnosis where there remain multiple symptoms and the expert's opinion about the presence of a particular disease is based

upon the combined effect of all the symptoms. The presence of multiple symptoms may strengthen or weaken the belief (or certainty factor value) in a particular diagnosis. Hence, it is needed to study the effect of multiple events on certainty factor.

2. Similarly, sometime a given symptom can support different diseases, for example, if the symptom was 'headache', physician would have to conclude whether it is due to 'migraine' or simple 'fatigue'. Hence, assessment of multiple conclusions would be required to be done based on single evidence.

3. Finally, there is situation where rules are chained together in such a way that the uncertain outcome of one rule provides input to other.

MYCIN's formulae are applied for all the situations mentioned above. Let us first discuss the case where multiple evidences support a single hypothesis. The CF's of MYCIN's rules are provided by the experts who write the rules. These CF's need to be combined to reflect the operation of multiple pieces of evidence. Hence, in this case where several rules provide evidence that relates to a single hypothesis, the combining function should satisfy the property which states "since the order in which evidence is collected is arbitrary, the combining functions should be commutative and associative." In this situation, the measure of belief and disbelief of hypothesis H where two evidences E1 and E2 are compounded are defined as:

$$MB\,[H\,|E1\,\text{and}\,E2]\;=\;\begin{cases} 0 & \text{if MD }[H\,|E1\,\text{and}\,E2\,]= 1 \\[2mm] MB[H|E1] + MB[H|E2].(1-MB[H|E1]) & \text{otherwise} \end{cases}$$

MB[H|E1 and E2] is also denoted as MB[H, E1∧E2], Hence

$$MD\,[H\,|E1 \wedge E2]\;=\;\begin{cases} 0 & \text{if MB }[H\,|E1\wedge E2\,]= 1 \\[2mm] MD[H|E1] + MD[H|E2].(1-MD[H|E1]) & \text{otherwise} \end{cases}$$

The rules are simple to understand. The measure of belief is 0, if MD = 1, (i.e., if 100% disbelief is there) otherwise every supportive evidence of hypothesis will increase the degree of belief.

Consider an example of a medical diagnosis. Suppose we make observation e_1 in favor of a hypothesis h, with MB = 0.25. Then MD $[h_1, e_1] = 0$ and CF $[h_1, e_1] =$ 0.25. In another observation e_2 which also confirms h, with MB $[h_1, e_2] = 0.4$, then

$$MB\,[h|\,e_1\,\text{and}\,e_2] = 0.25 + 0.4 \times (1 - 0.25)$$
$$= 0.25 + 0.300$$
$$= 0.55$$

$$MD\,[h|\,e_1\,\text{and}\,e_2] = 0.0$$

$$CF\,[h|\,e_1\,\text{and}\,e_2] = 0.55$$

The combined value of CF is more than any of individual value of certainty factor. It shows that supportive evidence increases belief in a particular hypothesis.

In second situation, one evidence supports multiple hypotheses. The combination certainty factor can be calculated by finding the values of MB and MD for this situation where evidence e supports two hypotheses h_1 and h_2 by the formulae given as follows:

$$MB\ [h_1 \text{ and } h_2\,|e] \quad = \quad \min\ (MB\ [h_1\,|\,e],\ MB\ [h_2\,|\,e])$$
$$MD\ [h_1 \text{ and } h_2\,|\,e] \quad = \quad \min\ (MD\ [h_1\,|\,e],\ MD\ [h_2\,|\,e])$$

Similarly,

$$MB\ [h_1 \text{ or } h_2\,|\,e] \quad = \quad \max\ (MB\ [h_1\,|\,e],\ MB\ [h_2\,|\,e])$$
$$MD\ [h_1 \text{ or } h_2\,|\,e] \quad = \quad \max\ (MD\ [h_1\,|\,e],\ MD\ [h_2\,|\,e])$$

In third situation rules are chained, (that means output of one result is fed as input to another). This type of situation arises where we are not sure about the certainty of evidence. This happens when evidence is outcome of some laboratory result, which cannot be completely accurate. In such a case, the certainty factor of the hypothesis must take into account the strength with which evidence supports the hypothesis and the level of our confidence on the evidence. MYCIN provides a chaining rule which is based on the property "if uncertain inferences are chained together, then the result should be less certain than either of the inferences alone." This means, the CF of result would be less than the CF's of all the evidences chained together. The rule is defined as follows:

Let $MB'[h\,|\,e\,']$ be the measure of belief in h when we are absolutely sure about validity of evidence $e\,'$. Let e be the evidence that led us to believe in $e\,'$ (for example, 'high fever' is the evidence supporting 'malaria'. Now we are 100% sure about this fact and presence of high fever is supported by 'measurement of the temperature by thermometer'. Here, h is 'malaria', $e\,'$ is 'high fever' and e is 'measurement by thermometer'.) Now, if we are not sure about $e\,'$ then measure of belief in h due to presence of $e\,'$ would be defined as:

$$MB\ [h\,|\,e\,'] = MB'\,[h\,|\,e\,'] * \max\ (0,\ CF[e\,'\,|e])$$

It means, if some rule is initially defined with certain MB but we are not 100% sure about the certainty of evidence supporting rule and some more evidence is observed supporting previous evidence or the result of previous rule is fed as input for other rule, then certainty factor of both evidences will decide the final MB.

The methodology described above was used by MYCIN for calculation of certainty factors. The steps involved in calculation adopted by MYCIN are as follows:

- The certainty factor of the conjunction of several facts is taken as the minimum of the CF's of individual facts. If E1 and E2 are two events and their individual certainty factor are CF(E1) and CF(E2) then the certainty factor of their combination or conjunction is defined as:

$$CF\ (E1 \text{ and } E2) \quad = MIN\ (CF(E1),\ CF(E2))$$

For example, the given facts are (a) there is problem in ignition system with CF of 0.6 and (b) there is problem in fuel flow with CF of 0.7, then the CF of the combination of the two facts for their combined effect on the starting of car would be minimum of the two, i.e. 0.6.

- The certainty factor of the disjunction of several facts is taken as the maximum of the CF's of individual facts. As above, the CF of disjunction of E1 and E2 would be defined as:

CF (E1 or E2) $\qquad$ = MAX (CF(E1), CF(E2))

And the CF of the disjunction of the two facts in car problem mentioned above would be 0.7 for the effect of either of the two facts on the problem of starting of car.

- The CF of the final conclusion is obtained by the multiplication of the combined CF of all the facts with the CF of the rule. For example, if two facts are given as above in the car example, then the car will have problem in starting with CF of 0.5. Now, if we want to calculate the CF of rule means what will be the CF of starting problem due to the combined effect of two evidences, it will be:

$$CF = \text{Conjunction of CF's of facts} * \text{CF of rule}$$
$$= 0.6 * 0.5$$
$$= 0.30$$

- The CF of the final conclusion about a rule when the rule is supported by different sets facts is maximum of different conclusions obtained because of different sets of facts. For example,

> IF F1 (CF = 0.2) & F2 (CF = 0.4), THEN C (CF = 0.3), and
> IF F3 (CF = 0.5) & F4 (CF = 0.6), THEN C (CF = 0.8)

In this situation, conclusion C is supported by two sets of facts by two rules. In first rule, CF(C) based on facts F1 and F2 = MIN (CF(F1), CF(F2))* CF(C)

$$= 0.2*0.3$$
$$= 0.06$$

In second rule, CF(C) based on facts F3 and F4 = MIN (CF (F3), CF(F4))* CF (C)

$$= 0.5*0.8$$
$$= 0.4$$

Since both the rules have different sets of supporting facts, the CF (C) based on two rules would be MAX(0.06, 0.4) i.e. 0.4

Consider a specific situation in which E1 and E2 are two symptoms used for a medical diagnosis. If their individual certainty factors are CF (E1) = 0.65 and CF (E2) = 0.80, then,

> CF (E1 and E2) = 0.65, and
> CF (E1 or E2) = 0.80.

In case of multiple evidences like E1 and E2 and ......En, these values of degree of belief and disbelief regarding the presence of a particular diseases can be obtained by joining them on above parameters, e.g.,

If E1, E2 and E3 are three evidences. The certainty factors of E3 is given as CF (E3) = 0.9. Then,

$$
\begin{aligned}
\text{CF (E1 and E2) OR E3} \quad &= \text{MAX (MIN (CF(E1), CF(E2)), CF(E3))} \\
&= \text{MAX (MIN(0.65, 0.8), CF(E3))} \\
&= \text{MAX (0.65, 0.9)} \\
&= 0.9
\end{aligned}
$$

It can be interpreted as presence of evidence E3 exhibits maximum degree of belief in a particular hypothesis (as its individual certainty factor is 0.9) and along with other multiple evidences, if only this evidence is present, it will create a strong belief in the hypothesis.

Let us now consider actual MYCIN production rule and its working. The production rule in expert system MYCIN looks like:

R/:   IF:
- the strain of organism is gram positive, and
- the morphology of the organism is coccus, and
- the growth confirmation of organism is clumps,

THEN

It is a suggestive evidence (0.7) that the identity of organism is staphylococcus.

The interpretation of this rule is as follows:

"If the facts are 100% correct, then it is only 70% certain that the organism is staphylococcus."

Rules are stated to the user in this form. Actually, they are represented internally in an easy to manipulate LISP list structure. This rule will be represented as:

```
PREMISE: ($ AND (SAME   CNTXT   GRAM       GRAMPOS)
                (SAME   CNTXT   MORPH      COCCUS)
                (SAME   CNTXT   CONFORM   CLUMPS)
ACTION:  (CONCLUDE   CNTXT   IDENT   STAPHYLOCOCCUS
                TALLY 0.7)
```

Let us consider a real life example. Suppose the user is 100% sure about the first two antecedents of the MYCIN rule stated above, i.e. organism is showing gram positive and is also coccus. The system now poses the question:

MYCIN: Did the organism grow in clumps, chains or pairs?

User provides the answer:

User: Chains(0.6), Pairs(0.3), Clumps(- 0.4)

The answer implies that the organism grows in chains (CF=0.6), pairs (CF= 0.3) and clumps (CF= - 0.4). We want to calculate the CF of organism being streptococcus in presence of above three facts. The rule can be presented as:

IF:

      Organism grows in chains (CF(ch | e) = 0.6), or
      Organism grows in pairs (CF(p | e) = 0.3), or
      Organism grows in clumps (CF (cl |e) = - 0.4)

THEN:

      Find the CF of the organism is streptococcus (CF=0.7)

The combined CF of three facts CF(C)   = CF (ch or p or cl |e)
                                                = MAX (CF(ch|e), CF(p|e), CF(cl|e))
                                                = MAX (0.6, 0.3, - 0.4)
                                                = 0.6
New CF of conclusion   = CF(C)* 0.7
                                                  = 0.6 * 0.7
                                                    = 0.42

Hence, when we are not 100% certain about the facts, the CF of conclusion will decrease. As in the above example, since we are only 80% certain about the third antecedent, the CF of organism being streptococcus will decrease from original 0.7 to 0.42.

Like other approaches, certainty theory also has its advantages and disadvantages. As we understand by now, the certainty factors are human estimates of symptom/cause relationship and their probability measures. As in Bayesian theory, if p, q and r all influence s, we need to combine all the prior and posterior probabilities including P(s), P(s|p), P(s|q) and P(s|r) when we want to reason about s; while in certainty theory, we do not need so many values. Knowledge engineer would need to combine the effect of all the facts and assign a single value to the rule known as CF, i.e., in this case the problem will be presented in the form of a simple rule: IF p and q and r THEN s (CF). As long as we are certain about facts, CF will hold good, and whenever there is any change in the measure of belief of any or all of the facts, new CF would be calculated easily using MYCIN rules. It can be felt that this simple algebra better reflects how human experts combine and propagate beliefs compared to Bayesian approach.

In spite of having well conceivable advantages, certainty theory faced criticism for being *ad hoc*. Although certainty theory is defined in formal algebra, the meaning of certainty measures is not as precisely formulated as measures of probability theory. However, it should be noted that certainty theory does not attempt to produce an algebra for 'correct' reasoning. Rather, it is only a 'tool' that enables the expert system to combine confidences as it moves along with the problem on hands. It is ad hoc in the sense that confidence of human expert in his result is approximate, heuristic and informal. When MYCIN is run, the CF's are used in the heuristic search to give a priority for goals to be achieved and a cut off point when a goal need not be considered further. However, MYCIN proved to be a huge success in the calculation of certainty factors and in the process of uncertain reasoning. This success led to the development of EMYCIN (Empty MYCIN) as an expert system development tool for further expert system building projects.

In a database there will be multiple rules R1, R2,......Rn like this.

Consider the rules in a knowledge base

(P1 and P2) or P3 $\rightarrow$ R1(0.7) and R2(0.3),

where, P1, P2, P3 are premises and R1, R2 are the conclusions of the rule and CFs 0.7, 0.3 respectively.

These numbers are added to the rulebase. If any running program has produced P1, P2 and P3 with CFs as 0.5, 0.7, 0.2 then R1 and R2 may be added to collected case specific results with CFs calculated as:

$$CF\ (P1\ (0.5)\ and\ P2\ (0.7) = MIN\ (0.5, 0.7) = 0.5$$
$$CF\ (0.5,\ or\ P3\ (0.2) = MAX\ (0.5, 0.2) = 0.5$$

The CF of R1 is 0.7 in the rule hence R1 is added to the set of case specific knowledge with the associated CF of $(0.7 \times 0.4) = 0.28$.

The CF of R2 is 0.3 in the rule hence R2 is added to the set of case specific knowledge with the associated CF of $(0.3 \times 0.4) = 0.12$.

8.5.4 Reasoning with Fuzzy Sets

In the previous sections, we have discussed about the limitations of traditional logic based approach in reasoning with uncertain and incomplete knowledge. We have also discussed methods, which extend the expressive power of logics and apply various schemes of nonmonotonic reasoning. One noteworthy aspect of all the approaches discussed so far has been that they admit interpretations, which are either true or false. However, in real life situations, the use of two-valued logic is too limiting because it fails to represent vague or fuzzy concepts effectively. For example, consider the following statement:

"If the temperature is 40°C, the weather is called hot."

Now if a system is working on the basis of formal logic, if you ask some question to it, it will reply in 'yes' or 'no' based on the knowledge it has. The conversation is represented as follows:

IF

    The temperature is 40°C, is the weather hot?

THEN

    Yes (answer)

IF

    The temperature is 39°C, is the weather hot?

THEN

    No (answer)

It means, formal logic theory will not consider weather as hot if the temperature is even slightly below 40°C, whereas, in real life situation, if you ask the same question to a normal person, he may consider weather as hot even if the temperature is 38°C. What do we mean to say is that formal logics fail while dealing with real life situations because of the vagueness involved. Hence, we need to devise some other suitable mechanism to deal with such types of situations. Nevertheless, before that, let us understand more about traditional logic theory.

The traditional formal logic is based on two fundamental assumptions:

- For any element and a set belonging to some universe, the element is either a member of set or else it is a member of compliment of the set. It means the element will either be completely inside a set or completely outside the set. For example, if set of 'beauty' is given, a beautiful woman, if belongs to the set of 'beautiful women', it will not belong to the set of 'not beautiful women', of course, only logically.

- Second assumption is "law of excluded middle". This states that an element cannot belong to both a set and also to its complement. For example, logically, a woman cannot belong to both the sets of 'beautiful women' and 'not beautiful women' and also, she must belong to either of the two sets, means there cannot be a possibility of middle path i.e. woman cannot be somebody in between or in the middle of being beautiful and not beautiful.

To deal with real world vague situations, we present a different set theory called "fuzzy set theory" developed by Lotfi Zadeh in 1983. It violates the above mentioned two assumptions of formal logic. The invention of fuzzy theory is based on a real life example of its inventor Prof. Zadeh. One day he had a discussion with his friend about "whose wife was more beautiful". As beauty cannot be formally defined, it becomes a matter of individual's perception. After applying all the logic they could, they ultimately failed to find the answer of the question. This led Mr. Zadeh to develop some other technique which could deal such type of vague situations. Hence, to accommodate these varying opinions about vaguely defined quantities, he thought of the idea of fuzzy theory.

The motivation to fuzzy set theory is provided by the need to represent the meaning of propositions. The main claim of its developer is, though probability theory is enough for measuring randomness of information, it cannot represent the meaning of information. In the language representation and understanding, the problem is not with the representation of words but the problem lies with the vagueness and clarity of words and phrases. This is a crucial point for analyzing language structure and can also be important in creating a measure of confidence in production rules. Zadeh proposes *possibility theory* as a measure of vagueness just as probability theory measures randomness. Thus, fuzzy theory is most suitable for representing the events which are vaguely defined, e.g.,

- This building is very beautiful.
- Vidushi is very healthy.
- Exceptions to the rule are nearly impossible.
- Most Indians can hardly speak English.
- Girish and Gaurav are good friends.

In FOPL, there is no direct way to represent the facts mentioned above. It is not easy to represent vague parameters such as 'very beautiful', 'nearly impossible', 'hardly speak' and 'good friends'. An attempt has been made in fuzzy set theory to represent vague statements. This theory has been describes in the next section.

8.5.4.1 *Fuzzy set theory*

In standard set theory, an element either is a member of a set or is not. There is no middle situation. For example, if S is a set of prime numbers then 2, 11, 17, 29, ... are members of S, but 8, 27, horse and pencil are not members of S. To represent this, we use a characteristic function f of a set S, where fS(s) =1, if s $\in$ S; and 0, if s$\notin$ S. Thus f is defined on the universe U and for all s $\in$ U, f: U $\to$ {0, 1}.

Thus, in standard set theory, membership has only two values, either 1 or 0. We will now generalize the concept of a set by allowing it to assume values other than 0 and 1. For example, let us define imaginary set called fuzzy set with the characteristic function m which maps from U to a number in the real interval [0, 1], i.e. m:U ? [0, 1]. Thus, the we can define fuzzy set as follows:

> "Let S be a set and s is a member of that set. A fuzzy subset F of S is a set of ordered pairs {s, mF(s)}, for all s$\in$ S, where mF(s) is known as *'membership function'* having values in [0, 1], and which measures the *"degree"* or 'level of membership' to which s belongs to F".

A value of membership function as 1 represents that an element definitely belongs to a set, a value of 0 represents that it at all does not belong to the set. A value in between shows that s partially belongs to F. The belongingness of element varies according to degree of membership. A membership of 0.5 shows that an element belongs to a set with half degree.

It is important at this point to understand the difference between probability and characteristic function of fuzzy set. Probability of an event is the measure of degree of its uncertainty, likelihood or belief which is based on the frequency of occurrence of the event. Whereas the fuzzy characteristic function is a measure of the feasibility or ease of occurrence of an event. For example, if we say there are 80% chances of rain to-day. Then, if this was probability of the occurrence of rain, it would mean that during past, 80 times out of the 100, it had rains under the same circumstances. However, if it was fuzzy characteristic function, it would mean there is 80% *possibility* of rain under the given circumstances. Fuzzy function is the measure of the vagueness involved in the occurrence of rain. Although it has rained 80 times out of 100 in the past, still there is vagueness involved and one might reason 'it is very likely to rain' and hence the possibility of occurrence of rain would give better estimate compared to probability of the same.

Let us consider one example of fuzzy set represented in the following figure 8.9. Let S is a set of positive integers and F is a fuzzy subset of S, known as set of 'small integers'. Now various integer values can have a 'possibility distribution' defining their 'fuzzy membership' in the set of small integers. A fuzzy membership value of 1 will mean that the integer definitely belongs to the set of small integers. Any integer close to being small integer will also be a member of the set of small integers but with reduced membership value.

The graph indicates that up to value 2, the integers can be considered as small, and of the "set of small integers" they will be complete members. This complete membership is represented by "degree of membership as 1". However,

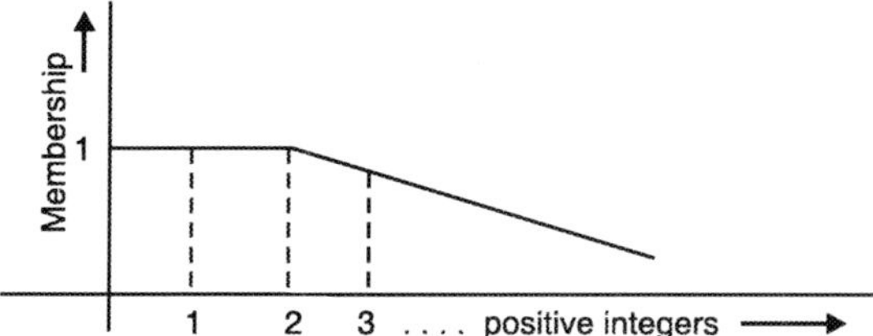

Fig. 8.9. The fuzzy set representation of small integers.

the integer 3 cannot be said as large integer and it does not completely belong to the set of small integers, so 3 is member of this set with reduced degree of membership. Similarly, as the integer value increases, it belongs to this set with reduced degree of membership. The possibility distribution or fuzzy membership value of various numbers may be represented as:

mF(1)   = 1.0,
mF(2)   = 1.0,
mF(3)   = 0.9,
mF(4)   = 0.8......
mF(60)   = 0.001, etc.

Actually, the degree of membership factor is created to represent vague situation e.g., if we say, "it is hot" and the temperature is 40^0 C then if the temperature is 39^0 C, it can not be said as cool. Similarly, at 41^0 C also it will be called as hot. Hence, the physical phenomenon like hot, cold, good, intelligent etc. are represented using set theory by associating "degree of membership". Temperature of 39^0 C will also be considered as member of the set of hot temperatures, but with reduced degree of membership.

Hence, to represent such type of vague situations multi valued logic is required. The traditional modal logic deals with two levels and 'yes' or 'no' type of situation and in multi valued logic, the degree of truth between yes or no is acknowledged. If at all a system has to act intelligently, it should be able to deal with the vague situations encountered during the process of finding solutions to real world problems, which more than often, are full of ambiguities. The causes due to which, ambiguities arise can be represented as follows:

- Ambiguities arise because of incomplete knowledge e.g., if a person does not know any language, he cannot understand it. Hence, ambiguity in understanding will arise because of lack of knowledge.
- Ambiguities also arise because of multi meaning words, e.g., English word 'bank' has several meanings such as 'piece of land adjacent to both ends of a river' or 'a financial organization' or 'a place where collected blood is stored' etc.
- The real world knowledge is imprecise. This includes ambiguity arising because of presence of noise or "inevitable errors".

- Fuzzy situations also cause ambiguity. There are situations, when we remain unable to properly define a variable. These refer to ambiguities caused due to individual's perception about the concept e.g., if asked, "how was the picture?", the reaction of different people may vary among 'very good', 'good' or 'not good' etc.

Let us consider one more example to understand the concept of fuzzy set and fuzzy membership function value. Suppose we have a set S of 'age' and a subset F of S as the set of 'middle age' defined as:

$$S = \{ \text{ age } \}; F \subseteq S \text{ such that } F = \{ s \}, 30 \le s \le 50$$

It means, age from 30 years to 50 years are members of F. Now if F is normal set, 29 years or 51 years will not be a member of F while, 35 years and 49 years will be very well the members of F. Kindly note that here boundaries are clearly defined as 30 years and 50 years. Anything outside the boundaries is out side the set also. This type of set is called *'crisp set',* which means *'concretely defined'*. Now in real life situation, if you are asked whether 29 years would be called middle age, the answer could very well be 'yes'. Hence, there cannot be a figure below which you can say with certainty that the age will not be 'middle age' or will be called 'lower age'. Similarly, there cannot be a figure of age above which you can say with full command and confidence that the age will not be middle age or it will be 'old age'. These types of situations where boundaries are not well defined are called fuzzy situations. The word fuzzy is opposite to crisp, which means *"not concretely defined"*. Hence, in real world situation, set F of middle age will be called fuzzy set. To deal with such situations, a *'membership characteristic function'* as defined and described earlier, has been introduced. Membership characteristic function is a measure of possibility of an element being member of a particular fuzzy set. A value ranging from 0 to 1, known as 'degree of membership' of an element is associated with every element depending upon the possibility of it being member of the given set. A value of 1 of degree of membership indicates that the element completely belongs to the set, and a value of 0 indicates that the element does not belong to the set. Hence, in case of example on hands, the age from 30 years to 50 years will have degree of membership as 1. Age of 29 years will also be a member of the set of middle age, but with reduced degree of membership, say 0.9. Let us now draw a possibility distribution of three age groups, lower age, middle age and old age as shown in the following figure 8.10.

From this possibility distribution graph, the age up to 18 years is lower age with degree of membership of 1. Age just above 18 years to 25 years is member of set of 'lower age' with reduced degree of membership. Age from 22 years to just below 30 years and from just above 50 years to 57 years is member of set of 'middle age' with reduced degree whereas age from 30 years to 50 years is middle age with degree of membership of 1. Similarly, age from 55 years to just below 65 years is old age with reduced degree, while age from 65 years and above is member

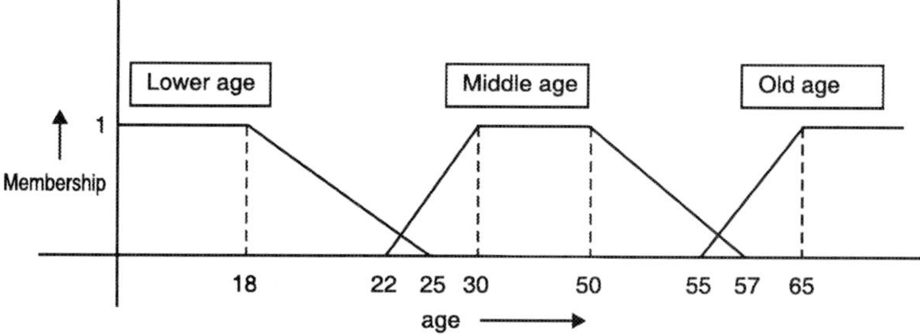

Fig. 8.10: A fuzzy set representation of lower age, middle age and old age
(Here, X-axis shows age and Y-axis shows 'yes (1)' or 'no (0)')

of set of 'old age' with degree of membership of 1. It should also be noted here that age from 22 years to 25 years is member of both the sets of lower age and middle age. Similarly, age from 55 years to 57 years is member of both the sets of middle age and old age.

The assumption about the middle age (i.e. crisply defined between 30 to 50 years) is appropriate from the viewpoint of computer representation. Computer being a machine works on the principle of mathematical modeling of any problem This mathematical modelling requires a quantitative and precise definition of the problem. The real world problems are not so precisely defined. Hence, it forces us to well define these imprecise students. Moreover, the real world phenomenon are analog or continuously changing. For the purpose of representation in numerical numbers they need to be converted to digital numbers. The process of digitization introduces some error. Hence, with the digital representation of analog quantities, the actual nature of physical phenomenon is slightly disturbed.

The membership function can be represented in terms of table. e.g dice numbers, the membership function of even numbers and large numbers is defined as it is interpreted as follows:

number 2 belongs to the set of even numbers with degree of membership μ_A (2) = 1; similarly number 5 belongs to the set of large numbers μ_B (5) with degree of membership 0.8,

From the above discussion, one thing, that is not only important but an essential ingredient of fuzzy reasoning mechanism has come out thick and fast and the name of that is "*membership characteristic function*". We have defined this function at the start and also tried to understand its use through couple of examples. Looking into the importance of membership characteristic function in fuzzy logic theory, we would like to devote some more time and space to it before dropping the curtain. The salient features of membership characteristics function are:

- It describes vague natural real world concepts.
- A fuzzy set admits the possibility of partial members with associated membership characteristic function value.
- The degree an object belonging to a fuzzy set is denoted by membership value between 0 and 1.

- A membership function associated with given fuzzy set maps input value to its appropriate membership value.

The fuzzy set theory is a mathematical theory to deal with ambiguities using quantified description in exact methods. The objects of fuzzy set theory are to deal with uncertainties. Hence, it is desirable for fuzzy set theory to have a sound mathematical base. In this, first the uncertainties are represented with membership function, then the function is manipulated in a method defined in fuzzy theory. We have also learnt how the possibility distribution graphs are drawn and a hint of combined possibilities. Fuzz set theory is , however not concerned with how these possibilities are created, but rather the rules for computing the combined possibilities over expressions that contain fuzzy variables. Thus, it is necessary to study rules for combining possibility measures for expressions containing fuzzy variables. The laws for the **or, and,** and **not** of these expressions are similar to those presented in Stanford certainty factor algebra. We are presenting now the operations involved in fuzzy sets and laws for combining possibility measures. These can be represented as follows:

- Operations on fuzzy sets
  - (i)   *Law of equality*:
    If A and B are two fuzzy sets such that $A, B \subseteq U$, then
    $A = B$ if and only if $mA(x) = mB(x)$ for all $x \in U$
  - (ii)   *Law of containment*:
    $A \subseteq B$ if and only if $mA(x) \leq mB(x)$ for all $x \in U$
  - (iii)   *Law of union*:
    $A \cup B$ is the smallest fuzzy sub set of which both A and B are subsets.
  - (iv)   *Law of intersection*:
    $A \cap B$ is the largest fuzzy subset, which is a subset of both A and B.
  - (v)   *Law of distribution*:
    $A \cup (B \cap C) = (A \cup B) \cap (A \cup C)$
    $A \cap (B \cup C) = (A \cap B) \cup (A \cap C)$
  - (vi)   *Law of association:*
    $(A \cup B) \cup C = A \cup (B \cup C)$
    $(A \cap B) \cap C = A \cap (B \cap C)$
  - (vii)   *Law of commutation:*
    $A \cup B = B \cup A$
    $A \cap B = B \cap A$
  - (viii) *Law of idempotency:*
    $A \cup A = A$
    $A \cap A = A$

- Operations on membership characteristic functions
  - (i)   *Law of union:*
    $m(A(x) \cup B(x))$ or $mA(x)\mathbf{or}B(x)$ $= \text{MAX } \{mA(x), mB(x)\}$
  - (ii)   *Law of intersection:*

$$m\ (A(x) \cap B(x))\ \text{or}\ m\ A(x)\mathbf{and}B\ (x) \qquad = \text{MIN}\ \{mA(x), mB(x)\}$$

(iii) *Law of negation:*

Negation of $mA(x) = 1 - mA(x)$

These are some of the operations used in fuzzy set theory. These operations are similar to those of normal set theory. However, there are some operations unique to fuzzy set theory. These are defined as follows:

- *Dilation*:

  If A is a fuzzy set such that $A \subseteq U$, for all $x \in A$, the dilation of A is defined as:

  $$DIL(A) = [mA(x)]^{1/2} \qquad \text{for all } x \in U.$$

- *Concentration*:

  The concentration of A is defined as:

  $$CON(A) = [mA(x)]^2 \qquad \text{for all } x \in U.$$

- *Normalization:*

  The normalization of A is defined as:

  $$NORM(A) = mA(x)\ /\ \text{MAX}\ \{mA(x)\}$$

These three operations are represented graphically in following figure 8.11.

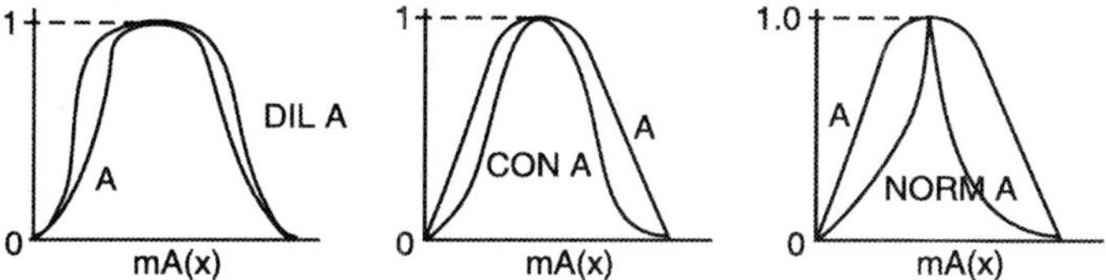

Fig. 8.11: Dilation, concentration and normalization of membership function, m

Form the above curves, it can be noted that dilation increases the degree of membership of all partial members x of a fuzzy set A by spreading out the characteristic function curve. The concentration is opposite of dilation, in the sense that it decreases the degree of membership of partial members x and hence, concentrates the characteristic function curve. Normalization is the process of normalizing all characteristic functions to the same base. These operations are used to manipulate the membership characteristic function according to the variation in fuzziness of a function. For example, if we have a fuzzy set of 'hot temperatures', we can represent this set in a possibility curve assigning various values of degree of membership to the elements according to possibility of these being the members of the set. Now, if we want to define 'very hot temperature', then all the members of the set of 'hot temperatures' will be the members of the set of 'very hot temperatures', but with modified degree of membership or to be precise, reduced degree of membership. Hence, the possibility curve or membership characteristic curve will be concentrated using law of concentration. This exercise has been shown in Fig. 8.12:

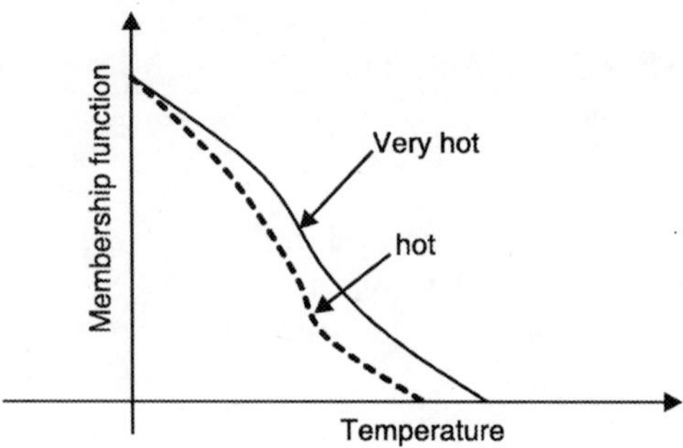

Fig. 8.12. Possibility curve of fuzzy sets of 'hot temperature' and 'very hot temperature'

We have tried to cover some of the important aspect of fuzzy logics in the above sections. Since its inception in 1965, much research has been conducted in the area of fuzzy set theory and fuzzy logic. As a result of this, the concept has been extended to various areas such as fuzzy arithmetic, fuzzy statistics, fuzzy random variables and fuzzy set functions. Initially, researchers were reluctant to acknowledge and accept fuzzy logic as a viable alternative to first order predicate logic. In spite of this, successful system employing fuzzy logic have been developed including development of fuzzy logic controlled commercial air-conditioner by Mitsubishi Heavy Industries of Japan, a fuzzy VLSI chip produced by Bell Telephone Laboratory of New Jersey etc.

The fuzzy theory has wide applications in the AI problem domain. the real world situations are very vague and can not be crisply defined. hence they are truly modeled using fuzzy theory. as far as reasoning with fuzzy theory is concerned , the rules which are imprecisely defined are represented using fuzzy sets and by applying the basic operators on them the inferences are drawn.

8.5.5 Dempster Shafer Theory

In earlier sections, we have discussed the probabilistic techniques of dealing with uncertainty. They consider individual propositions and assign a numeric estimate of the degree of belief to them. One of the limitations of these approaches is their use of a single quantity to measure what may be very complex situation. Quite often, uncertainty results from a combination of missing evidence, the limitations of heuristic rules and limitations of our own knowledge. There are some other serious drawbacks also, in using Bayesian approach as a model of uncertain reasoning. These are explained as follows:

- As said earlier, the probabilities are described as single numeric values. Since probabilities are based on past results under the same circumstances, the probability assigned to current event may well be the distortion of the precision that is actually available in the support of the event. For example, if we say that probability of rain is 0.8, by saying this, actually we mean, we have strong conviction that there is a chance of about 0.7 to 0.9 suppose, that it will rain.

- Another problem with traditional probability theory is that in this, there is no way to differentiate between uncertainty and ignorance. It means, in many situations, what we term as uncertainty, could be our ignorance because of lack of knowledge. These are two different concepts and hence, should be treated distinctly. For example, if your car is having 'starting trouble' and the reasons for that could be A='no fuel', B='battery problem' or C='wiring problem'. You have some evidence in support of problem in battery from some other source and hence, you would assign a measure of this belief P(B) = 0.8. Now, as per traditional probability theory, the probability of other reasons would be 0.2 and would be equally distributed between the remaining two causes. However, actually, in absence of knowledge about causes A and C, you might not be willing to assign equal measures of belief to A and C. In fact, we might have no knowledge to justify either the amount of uncertainty or the equal division of it between causes A and C because of our ignorance about A and C.
- Last but not the only remaining aspect of probability theory is, that in it, the measure in support of some belief and measure in support of disbelief are functionally opposite, i.e. if some belief A is assigned the probability P(A)= 0.4, then we must assign the probability P(not A) = 0.6, because as per traditional probability theory, P(A) + P(not A) = 1. However, in real life situations, many times the probabilities for the belief and for disbelief could well be equal.

As remedy to above-mentioned problems, a generalized theory has been proposed by Arthur Dempster in 1968 and was extended by his student Glenn Shafer in 1976. It is popularly known as Dempster-Shafer theory of evidence. The Dempster-Shafer theory is an alternative approach to deal with uncertainty. It is based on the opinion that separate probability measures may be assigned to all subjects of a universe of discourse rather than just to single member as is done in traditional probability theory. Thus, this theory considers sets of propositions and assigns to each of them an interval [Belief, plausibility] within which the degree of belief for each proposition must lie.

In Dempster-Shafer theory, we assume a universe of discourse or simply, a universal set U and a set corresponding to n propositions, out of which only one is true. We introduce here a parameter m known as *set function* or *basic probability assignment* or *probability density function*. It represents the measure of belief committed exactly to any subset A of U. A belief function, **bel**, corresponding to a specific set function m for the set A, is defined as the sum of beliefs committed to every subset of A by m. Thus, bel(A) is the measure of the total support or belief committed to A and *reflects the minimum value for its likelihood.* It is defined in terms of all belief assigned to A as well as to all proper subsets of A. Thus:

$$\text{bel}(A) = \sum_{B \subseteq A} m(B)$$

For example, if A, B, C, and D are mutually exclusive subsets of U, then belief function of any set of subsets of U, (A, B, D) will be:

$$Bel(\{A,B,D\}) = m(\{A,C,D\}) + m(\{A,C\}) + m(\{C,D\}) + m\{(A,D\}) + m(\{A\})$$
$$+ \ m(\{C\}) + m(\{D\})$$

Belief indicates the strength of evidence in support of a set of propositions. It varies between 0 (i.e. no evidence) to 1 (i.e. certainty).

Now, since bel(A) only partially describes the beliefs about A and hence, we need to assess our belief for notA, i.e. the doubts we have regarding A. In another way, belief for some proposition P, bel(P) is not equal to 1- bel(notP), hence for each value of bel(notP), there will be some value of 1- bel(notP) other than the value of bel(P) which will also create some support for P. This value measures the extent to which evidence in favor of notP will create an impact on evidence in favor of P, and is known as ***plausibility,*** **pl(P)**. Plausibility defines the *upper limit of belief in P*. Thus,

In Dempster-Shafer theory, plausibility of a proposition P, pl(P) is defined as:

$$\textbf{pl(P) = 1- \ bel (\ not \ (P))}$$

Plausibility also ranges between 0 and 1. We thus get two values bel(P) and pl(P) to define belief for P and the degree of belief or the belief interval is defined as [bel(P),pl(P)]. It is also referred to as the ***confidence*** in P, while the value of pl(P)-bel(P) is referred to as ***uncertainty*** in P.

If we have certain evidence in favor of not(P), then bel (not(P)) will be 1 and pl (P) will be 0. The only possible value of bel(P) will also be 0. Thus, degree of belief in this case will be denoted by interval [0,0]. It means, belief that the proposition is false. Because there is no belief in support of the proposition either directly because of lesser evidence in support of not(P) (there is certain evidence in support of not(P)), or indirectly because of lesser belief for not(P) giving some value of plausibility to create some belief for P. Given below are some of the belief interval values to understand the semantics involved in the phenomena:

[0, 1]	represents no belief in support of the proposition
[0, 0]	represents the belief that the proposition is false
[1, 1]	represents the belief that the proposition is true
[.4, 1]	represents partial belief in the proposition
[0, .7]	represents partial disbelief in the proposition
[.3, .8]	represents belief from evidence for and against proposition both

The belief, plausibility interval discussed above measures not only our level of belief in some propositions, but also the amount of information we have. Suppose we have two competing hypotheses h_1 and h_2 . When we have no information supporting either of the hypotheses, they both will have degree of belief in the range of [0, 1]. As evidence is gathered, this interval will shrink representing increased confidence for the hypotheses. If we have similar situation and apply Bayesian approach, we would probably begin by distributing prior probabilities equally between the two hypotheses in absence of any information. Thus, for each hypothesis, $P(h_i) = 0.5$. Now, note the difference between two approaches. Dempster-Shafer approach makes it clear that no evidence is available when we start and belief measure interval changes as soon as evidences arrive. The Bayesian approach, on the other hand may result in the same probability values even if we collect volumes of evidence. Thus, Dempster-Shafer approach can be very useful when we are required to make a decision based on the amount of evidence that has been collected.

As mentioned earlier, Dempster-Shafer theory addresses the problem of measuring certainty by making distinction between uncertainty and ignorance. In probability theory, we express the extent of our knowledge about an hypothesis h in single number, $P(h)$. But, the probability of occurrence of h could be influenced by many other factors about which we might not be aware. Hence, objection of these two gentlemen Dempster and Shafer to probability theory is that we cannot always know the supporting probabilities of h, and therefore, any value of probability assigned to h, $P(h)$ may not be justified.

The Dempster-Shafer theory is based on following two concepts:
- Obtaining the degree of belief for one question, from subjective probabilities for related questions.
- Using a rule for combining these degrees of belief when they are based on independent items of evidence.

These concepts are aimed, basically to cover the ignorance part in dealing with uncertain situations. To understand the mechanism of using above mentioned concepts, let us consider following example:

Suppose the subjective probability of reliability of a student in a particular context is 0.8. It means the probability that he is reliable is 0.8 and that he is unreliable is 0.2. Suppose the student tells that, he has 'not copied an assignment'. This statement is true if student is reliable, but it is not necessarily false if he is not reliable. Hence, unreliability of student creates no belief for the negation of the statement, i.e. that he has 'copied the assignment'. Therefore, student's testimony alone justifies a degree of belief of 0.8 in favor of the hypothesis, that he has 'not copied an assignment' and 0 against the hypothesis, that he has 'copied the same'. Belief of 0 for the proposition "copied the assignment" does not mean we are sure that student has copied the assignment, whereas, a probability of 0 would mean so. Because, we might be ignorant of other facts which could create some belief in favor of proposition 'copied the assignment'. It merely means that student's testimony gives me no reason to believe that he has copied the assignment.

The plausibility pl for this situation is:

$$pl(\text{assignment\_notcopied}) = 1 - bel(\text{not}(\text{assignment\_notcopied})) = 1 - 0.0$$
$$= 1$$

This means that my belief measure for student is [0.8, 1.0]. Note that still there is no evidence that the student has copied the assignment.

We now present another example to consider combination of various evidences arriving from different sources. Suppose you are going out of the town and have informed your neighbours John and Alisha. You have also told them to give intimation to you in case there is any unwanted happening in your house in your absence. Now, assume both of your neighbours inform you one day that there is a theft in your house. Assume probabilities of John and Alisha being reliable are 0.8 and 0.7 respectively. Hence, the probabilities of they being not reliable are 0.2 and 0.3 respectively. Also, assume that testimony of john and Alisha about your house is independent of each other and they have separate reasons to believe that there is a theft in your house. The probability that both John and Alisha are reliable is the product of their respective probabilities, i.e. 0.56, because events are independent. The probability that they both are not reliable is 0.06. The probability that at least one out of the two is reliable is $1 - 0.06 = 0.94$. Now, since both of your neighbours told that there is a theft in your house and the probability that at least one out of the two is reliable is 0.94, you would assign degree of belief of [0.94, 1] to the event that there is a theft in your house.

Now suppose John and Alisha disagree that there is a theft in your house. John says that there was, but Alisha says there was not any theft. In this case, because of the differing information provided by them, both cannot be correct and at the same time, both cannot be reliable. Either both are not reliable or only one is reliable. The prior probability that only John is reliable is $0.8 * (1 - 0.7) = 0.24$ (multiplication of the probabilities of John is reliable and Alisha is not reliable). Similarly, prior probability that Alisha is reliable but John is not is $0.7 * (1 - 0.8) = 0.14$; and that both are not reliable is $0.2 * 0.3 = 0.06$. Hence probability that at least one of your two neighbours is not reliable is $(0.24 + 0.14 + 0.0.06) = 0.44$. From this, we can calculate the conditional probability that only John is reliable and hence, that there was a theft in your house as $0.24/0.44 = 0.556$. Similarly, conditional probability that only Alisha is right and that there was no theft in your house as $0.14/0.44 = 0.318$. Now, note the probability that at least one of your neighbours is reliable is sum of probabilities of both being reliable, only John being reliable and only Alisha being reliable, i.e. $0.56 + 0.24 + 0.14 = 0.94$, same what was calculated earlier. Here, when it was reported that there was a theft in your house, there were three possibilities supporting this proposition, first, both the reporters are reliable, second, only John is reliable and third, only Alisha is reliable. The belief 0.94 was the sum of these possible supporting hypothetical beliefs. Thus, we have shown here Dempster rule to combine beliefs.

Next, we present Dempster's rule for combining beliefs when evidence arrives from different sources. We are given an exhaustive set U of mutually exclusive hypotheses. Suppose Z is defined as set of various subsets of U and our aim is to assign some measure of belief m called set function to various subsets of U. In fact, in this type of situation, all evidence is not supportive of all elements of U directly, rather evidence supports different subsets Z of U. Also, since we have assumed that elements of U, i.e. hypotheses are mutually exclusive, evidence in favor of some might have an effect on our belief for others. In Bayesian approach, we address this situation by considering all the possible conditional probabilities, however, in Dempster-Shafer approach, we handle this situation by directly manipulating the sets of hypotheses. Let there are n sources of evidence and the amount of belief assigned to subset Z is $m_n(Z)$. We have Dempster's rule for this situation as:

$$m_n(Z) = \frac{\Sigma_{X \cap Y = Z}\, m_{n-2}(X)\, m_{n-1}(Y)}{1 - \Sigma_{X \cap Y = \phi}\, m_{n-2}(X)\, m_{n-1}(Y)}$$

where, X and Y are two subsets, the co-occurrence of which supports Z.

Let us consider one example to understand phenomenon mentioned above. Suppose U is the set containing following hypotheses:

C : Patient has cold
F : Patient has flu
H : Patient has headache
M : Patient has meningitis

As already mentioned above, any evidence will support subsets of U instead of individual hypothesis. For example, suppose a first evidence of fever supports a subset {C,F,M} with a belief measure of 0.6. We call this first belief m_1. If this is only set of hypothesis, $m_1\{C,F,M\} = 0.6$ and hence $m_1(U) = 0.4$ which will account for the belief of other remaining subsets of a set of hypotheses of U. Note here that 0.4 is not the belief of the compliment of {C,F,M} but that of remaining subsets of hypotheses of U.

Now if we acquire some new evidence during our diagnosis, suppose that patient has extreme nausea supporting the subset of hypothesis {C,F,H} with belief measure of 0.7. Let us call this belief as m_2. We have thus, $m_2\{C,F,H\} = 0.7$ and $m_2(U) = 0.3$. We now use Dempster's rule to combine these two beliefs coming from different evidences supporting subsets of a universal set of hypotheses U. Let m_1 assigns a nonzero value to X which is the subset of set U and m_2 assigns a nonzero value to Y, which is another subset of U.

We now create a combination belief m_3 due to effect of m_1 and m_2 defined on subset Z of U using Dempster's rule. Note that here $X \cap Y \neq \phi$, hence denominator of the above equation is 1. The belief measure of m_3 for various possible combinations of X and Y is shown in following table:

Table 8.2: Belief distribution for m_3 using Dempster's rule

m_1	m_2	m_3
$m_1\{C,F,M\}= 0.6$	$m_2\{C,F,H\}= 0.8$	$m_3\{C,F\}= 0.42$
$m_1\{U\}= 0.4$	$m_2\{C,F,H\}= 0.8$	$m_3\{C,F,H\}= 0.28$
$m_1\{C,F,M\}= 0.6$	$m_2\{U\}= 0.3$	$m_3\{C,F,M\}= 0.18$
$m_1\{U\}= 0.4$	$m_2\{U\}= 0.3$	$m_3\{U\}= 0.12$

Note that the sum of all the values of m_3 is 1.0, which means total belief derived by the combination has been distributed among the various intersections of Z and remaining part of U. From the values derived above, we can refer that belief in support of subset containing cold and flu because of two evidences is 0.42. Also note that initially, we assumed the belief measure of 0.8 for the sub set {C,F,H} because of new evidence. This new evidence is not supporting M hence final belief for the subset {C,F,M} which contains M has been reduced from initial 0.6 to 0.18. Similarly, since both the evidences are supporting C and F, hence belief of the subset {C,F} because of the combined effect of two available evidences is maximum.

We now extend this example to cover the empty belief sets. Suppose we acquire new evidence resulting from laboratory tests and as associated with meningitis. We now have say, m_4 {M} = 0.8 and hence, $m_4(U) = 0.2$. We will use Dempster's rule to combine m_3 with m_4 to get m_5. The results of numerator of above equation for combining beliefs are shown in following table: (Note here that for many X to which m_3 assigns nonzero value and Y, to which m_4 assigns nonzero value, $X \cap Y$ = f, hence denominator in this case will not be 1).

Table 8.3: Combining m_3 and m_4 to get m_5 using Dempster's rule

m_3	m_4	m_5
m_3{C,F}= 0.42	m_4{M}= 0.8	m_5{}= 0.336
m_3{U}= 0.12	m_4{M}= 0.8	m_5{M}= 0.096
m_3{C,F}= 0.42	m_4{U}= 0.2	m_5{C,F}= 0.084
m_3{U}= 0.12	m_4{U}= 0.2	m_5{U}= 0.024
m_3{C,F,H}= 0.28	m_4{M}= 0.8	m_5{}= 0.224
m_3{C,F,M}= 0.18	m_4{M}= 0.8	m_5{M}= 0.144
m_3{C,F,H}= 0.28	m_4{U}= 0.2	m_5{C,F,H}= 0.056
m_3{C,F,M}= 0.18	m_4{U}= 0.2	m_5{C,F,M}= 0.036

The belief measure for M, m_5{M} is produced by the intersection of two different pairs of sets and hence, the total m_5{M}= 0.24. Now the intersection of two sets produce empty set {} and total m_5{}= 0.336 + 0.224 = 0.56. Thus, the denominator of Dempster's equation = 1 − 0.56 = 0.44. Hence, the combined belief function for m_5 will be values given in above table 8.3 divided by 0.44. These values are calculated as:

m_5{M}= 0.545	m_5{C,F}= 0.191	m_5{}= 0.56
m_5{C,F,H}= 0.128	m_5{C,F,M}= 0.082	m_5{U}= 0.055

Note again that, since third evidence is supporting M, our diagnostic results again take a turn. The belief of the subset {C,F} decreases from 0.42 to 0.191. One thing which might seem to be little surprising is that belief for null set {} is very high. This could be because of the fact that evidences are conflicting in nature.

We have shown several features of Dempster-Shafer reasoning approach. However, when there are large hypothesis sets and as well as complex sets of evidences, the calculations for belief sets becomes cumbersome. However, amount of calculation is considerably less than that involved in formal Bayesian approach.

8.6 DEFAULT REASONING

One method to handle uncertainty is using non monotonic reasoning. In real world where the knowledge is incomplete the uncertainty arises. Human being deal with the problem of uncertainties because of incomplete knowledge by making default assumptions. The reasoning based on this assumption is called default reasoning. It is a form of non monotonic reasoning. The theory of default reasoning is developed by renter. A default is expressed as

$$\frac{a(x) : mb1\ (x) \ldots\ldots mbn(x)}{c(x)}$$

where $a(x)$ is the statement mentioning precondition of $c(x)$, M is consistency operator and $bi(x)$ are conditions which should be consistent with KB e.g. if x is Indian citizen and x is above 1 years age (i.e. major) then infer that x can vote.

This would be represented as :

$$\frac{Citizen(x):\ major\ (x)\ :\ vote\ (x)}{Vote\ (x)}$$

Default theories consists of a set of axioms and default inference rules. Theorems derivable from default system follow first order logic and assumptions from default rules. These default rules are useful in hierarchical KB's.

8.7 CLOSED WORLD ASSUMPTION

As is evident from the ongoing discussion that dealing with uncertain situation is really difficult. The situations when the total possibilities are not given makes the judging about the outcomes of that event very critical. Hence different reasoning methods were devised for reasoning with such situations. Closed world assumption is a kind of minimalist reasoning suggested by Reiter (1978). It is another form of assumption wrt. Incomplete knowledge. It is applicable in the situations where most of the facts are known. The closed world assumption says, if a proposition can not be proven it is false. That means in the starting if any statement (or fact) is not given assume it false, then try to prove the assumption as false, hence it will prove the starting statement is true. Moreover failure to prove a given statement False results in assuming that statement F true. Consider following example:

If the knowledge about birds properties says that "normally" birds fly. Here this knowledge is general knowledge about birds , which very well can be false in specific situation like penguin (as penguin does not fly). Hence it can be said that it is incomplete knowledge. But the closed world assumption will consider the statement true (i.e every bird flies) unless the opposite of it (that specific situation where bird can not fly) as false.

It can be represented as:

∀–X bird (X) ^ not (abnormal (X)) → flies (X)

This definition is given for bird, but the definition of predicate abnormal will accommodate the specific situation where birds can not fly. Like the bird is not a penguin, or it does not have broken wing, or it is not dead. The specification of the predicate abnormal is potentially undecidable.

The closed world assumption is used for the situations that provide ways of describing things that are generally true. These are based on the concept of " minimal model". A model is called minimal if there are no other models in which fewer things are true. The idea behind using minimal model as a basis for nonmonotonic reasoning about the world is assuming that there are many fewer true statements than false ones. Therefore , if something is true and relevant, it has been entered into our knowledge base. New statements , only if they can be proved as true will be entered in the knowledge base to maintain consistency.

8.8 DECISION THEORY

The presence of uncertainly changes the way how decision should be taken. In normal course goal is given and such action is taken which moves the system towards the goal. But in uncertain situation (e.g. the goal is mentioned with 90% probability) it can not be decided whether an action move system towards the goal or not. To make choice about actions, action must have preferences between different possible outcomes. To mention the goodness of action, a "utility value" is attached with every preference. This utility theory along with the probability theory gives rise to rational decisions called decision theory. Thus decision theory

$$\text{Decision theory } = \text{utility theory} + \text{probability theory}$$

the basic idea of decision theory is that a rule is rational if and only if it chooses the action that yield the highest expected value of utility averaged over all the outcomes of the action. this is called the principle of maximum expected utility (MEU).

The further discussion on decision theory is beyond the scope of this book.

8.9 SOLVED EXAMPLES

Example 1:   *Is it possible to compute P(A|¬B) when you are only given P(A), P(B|A) and P(B)?*

Solution: We have P(A|¬B) or P(A|notB) = P(A&¬B) /P(¬B)   ....(1)
And P(B|A) = P(B&A)/P(A)   ....(2)
If B is a given event then B and ØB will be mutually exclusive,

hence probability of any independent event A can be expressed as:

$$P(A) = P(A\&B) + P(A\&\neg B) \qquad \ldots\ldots(3)$$

Also, $P(A\&B) = P(B\&A)$

Hence, $P(A) = P(B|A) * P(A) + P(A\&\neg B) \qquad \ldots\ldots(4)$

[putting the value of P(A&B) from equation (2) in equation (3)]
From equation (4), we can calculate the value of $P(A\&\neg B)$ and we have, $P(\neg B) = 1 - P(B)$. These values will make it possible to calculate $P(A|\neg B)$. Hence, by known values, it is possible to calculate $P(A|\neg B)$.

Example 2:   *There are three villages V_1, V_2 and V_3 where 30%, 40% and 50% villagers are patients. It is also give that out of the patients, 2%, 3% and 4% in respective villages are having malaria. If one patient is picked at random and is found having malaria, find the probability of this patient belonging to village V_1, V_2 or V_3?*

Solution: Let E_1, E_2, and E_3 define the events that a patient picked at random belongs to village V_1, V_2 or V_3. Let M represent patient is having malaria. Thus, probability of picked patient belonging to respective villages are:

$P(E_1) = 0.3, P(E_2) = 0.4$ and $P(E_3) = 0.5$

Now, probability of picking a patient having malaria from village V_1

$$P(M| E_1) = 0.02 \quad \text{(given)}$$
$$\text{Similarly, } P(M| E_2) = 0.03, \text{ and}$$
$$P(M| E_3) = 0.04$$

We have to find probability of picked patient having malaria belonging to village V_1 , i.e.,

$$P(E_1|M) = \frac{P(M| E_1) * P(E_1)}{\sum_{i=1}^{3} P(M| E_i) * P(E_i)}$$

$$= [0.02*0.3]/[(0.02*0.3) + (0.03*0.4) + (0.04*0.5)]$$
$$= 0.006/0.038$$
$$= 0.158$$

Similarly,

$$P(E_2|M) = [0.03*0.4]/[0.038]$$
$$= 0.315$$
$$P(E_3|M) = 1- [P(E_1|M)+ P(E_2|M)]$$
$$= 1- [0.158 + 0.315]$$
$$= 0.528$$

Hence, probabilities of a patient picked at random belonging to villages V_1, V_2 or V_3 are 0.158, 0.315 and 0.528 respectively.

(Note that probability is highest for the village having maximum number of patients having malaria.)

Example 3:   *Write the joint distribution of x_1, x_2, x_3, x_4, x_5, and x_6 as a product of the chain conditional probabilities for the following casual network:*

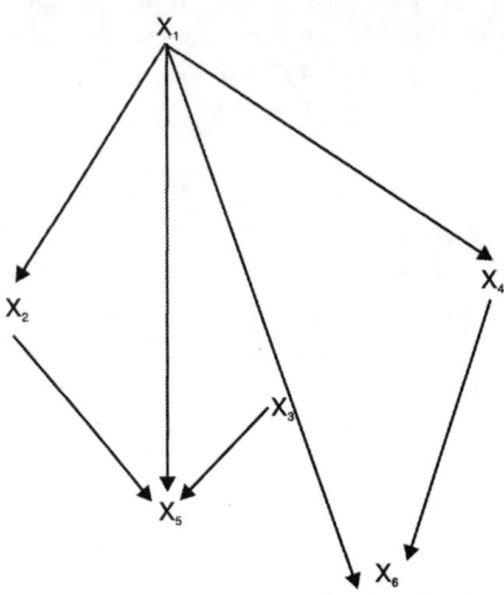

Solution: The joint probability of given variables is denoted as follows:

$$P(x_1,\ x_2,\ x_3,\ x_4,\ x_5,\ x_6) = P(x_1)*P(x_2|x_1)*P(x_3)*P(x_4|x_1)*P(x_5|x_1,x_2,x_3)*P(x_6|x_1,x_4)$$

(Refer section 4.2.2 of this chapter)

Example 4:   *There is a problem of excessive oil consumption in your car. There could be two causes for this: oil leakage and worn piston rings. There is general estimate that oil leakage is common in 15% of cars and problem of worn piston rings is common in 30% cars. However, 40% cars have heavy oil consumption due to oil leakage while 50% cars have the same due to worn piston rings. Find most likely cause of heavy oil consumption in your car?*

Solution: We are given unconditional probabilities of car having oil leakage say $P(L) = 0.15$ and that of worn piston rings, $P(R) = 0.3$. Also given are conditional probability of heavy oil consumption due to oil leakage, say $P(O|L) = 0.4$ and that due to worn piston rings, $P(O|R) = 0.5$. We have to find the conditional probabilities of oil leakage causing heavy oil consumption and worn piston rings causing heavy oil consumption, i.e., $P(L|O)$ and $P(R|O)$. Let us assume that unconditional probability of car having heavy oil consumption, $P(O) = 0.8$.

We have from Bayes theorem,

$$P(L|O) = P(O|L)*P(L)/P(O)$$
$$= 0.4*0.15/0.8$$
$$= 0.086$$

Similarly,

$$P(R|O) = P(O|R)*P(R)/P(O)$$
$$= 0.5*0.3/0.8$$
$$= 0.214$$

Since, $P(R|O)$ is greater than $P(L|O)$, the likely cause of heavy oil consumption is worn piston rings.

Example 5: *In a database, a rule is defined as:*
(P1 and P2) or P3 ? R1(0.8) and R2(0.3),
where, P1, P2, P3 are premises and R1, R2 are the conclusions of the rule with CFs 0.8, 0.3 respectively. If any running program has produced P1, P2 and P3 with CFs as 0.5, 0.8, 0.2 respectively, find the CF of results on the basis of premises?

Solution:

Let us first calculate the combined CF of premises using rules of conjunction and disjunction as follows:

CF (P1 (0.5) and P2 (0.8)) = MIN (0.5, 0.8) = 0.5
CF (0.5 or P3 (0.2)) = MAX (0.5, 0.2) = 0.5

The CF of R1 is 0.8 in the rule hence CF of R1 based on premises will be:
(0.8 x 0.5) = 0.35.
Similarly, the CF of R2 on the basis of premises will be:
(0.3 x 0.5) = 0.15.

Example 6: *Using MYCIN's rules for inexact reasoning, compute CF, MB and MD of h_1 when three given observations are:*
$$CF(h_1,o_1) = 0.5$$
$$CF(h_1,o_2) = 0.3$$
$$CF(h_1,o_3) = -0.2$$

Solution:

Note that this is the case when different evidences support the same hypothesis.

Given, $CF(h_1,o_1)$ = 0.5, means $MB(h_1,o_1) = 0.2$ and $MD(h_1,o_1) = 0$.

Similarly, $MB(h_1,o_2)$ = 0.3 and $MD(h_1,o_2) = 0$, and $MB(h_1,o_3) = 0$ and $MD(h_1,o_3) = 0.2$

The combined measure of belief for hypothesis, $MB(h_1, o_1$ and o_2 and $o_3)$ can be calculated using MYCIN's rule as under:

$$MB(h_1, o_1 \text{ and } o_2) = MB(h_1, o_1) + MB(h_1, o_2) *[1 - MB(h_1, o_1)]$$
$$= 0.5 + 0.3[1 - 0.5]$$
$$= 0.65$$
$$MB(h_1, o_1 \text{ and } o_2 \text{ and } o_3) = 0.65 + 0 *[1 - 0.65]$$
$$= \mathbf{0.65}$$

Similarly, measure of belief against hypothesis, $MD(h_1, o_1$ and o_2 and $o_3)$ can be calculated as under:

$$MD(h_1, o_1 \text{ and } o_2) = MD(h_1, o_1) + MD(h_1, o_2) *[1 - MD(h_1, o_1)]$$
$$= 0 + 0[1 - 0]$$
$$= 0$$
$$MD(h_1, o_1 \text{ and } o_2 \text{ and } o_3) = 0 + 0.2*[1 - 0]$$
$$= \mathbf{0.2}$$

$$CF(h_1, o_1 \text{ and } o_2 \text{ and } o_3) = MB(h_1, o_1 \text{ and } o_2 \text{ and } o_3) - MD(h_1, o_1 \text{ and } o_2 \text{ and } o_3)$$
$$= 0.65 - 0.2$$
$$= \mathbf{0.45}$$

Example 7: *It is rainy season and there is heavy cloud cover. The prediction is:*

"There are 80% chances of rain to-day." However, there is uncertainty regarding the type of cloud cover. Some expert tells he is confident that there are 90% chances of these types of clouds bringing rains. Using Dempster's approach, find the uncertainty associated with the above prediction?

Solution: Given probability of rain, $P(R) = 0.8$, hence $P(notR) = 0.2$.
The confidence associated with the evidence, i.e. clouds is 0.9, hence
Belief for rain, $bel(R) = 0.8*0.9 = 0.72$, and
$bel(notR) = 0.2*0.9 = 0.18$.
Thus, plausibility of rain, $pl(R) = 1 - bel(notR)$
$$= 1 - 0.18 = 0.82$$
The belief interval is [0.82, 0.72]
Hence, uncertainty associated with the prediction $= pl(R) - bel(R)$
$$= 0.82 - 0.72$$
$$= 0.10$$
Hence, uncertainty associated with the prediction $= 10\%$

Example 8:   *There is a phone call that a bomb has been planted in some government building. Police identifies four terrorist groups T1, T2, T3 and T4, which could be behind the crime. As per police record, groups T1 and T3 are most likely to commit the crime and a degree of belief of 0.6 has been associated with this combination. Further evidence show that group T3 cannot be responsible for the act hence a degree of belief of 0.8 is associated for remaining three groups, T1, T2 and T4. Find the value of belief associated with various possibilities by using Dempster's rule?*

Solution: Let U is the universal set of terrorist groups. X and Y are two subsets of U such that. X = {T1, T3} and Y = {T1, T2, T4}. We are given,

m_1{T1, T3}= 0.6 and m_2{T1, T2, T4}= 0.8. Hence, m_1{U}= 0.4 and m_2{U}= 0.3. We have to find out combined belief of m_1 and m_2 which we denote as m_3. Since, no intersection of X and Y has empty, hence denominator of Dempster's rule will be 1. The numerator is calculated and is shown in following table:

m_1	m_2	m_3
m_1{T1, T3}= 0.6	m_2{T1, T2, T4}= 0.8	m_3{T1} = 0.42
m_1{U}= 0.4	m_2{T1, T2, T4}= 0.8	m_3{T1,T2, T4} = 0.28
m_1{T1, T3}= 0.6	m_2{U}= 0.3	m_3{T1, T3} = 0.18
m_1{U}= 0.4	m_2{U}= 0.3	m_3{U} = 0.12

From above combined degrees of belief, terrorist group T1 is most likely to have committed the crime.

EXERCISES

1. Consider two coins P1 and P2. These are tossed together. Calculate the probability that head turn up on both coins.
2. What is meant by complimentary outcomes and what is the relationship between the probabilities of two events.
3. Identify three application domains where reasoning under conditions of uncertainty is necessary. Pick one of these areas and design six inference rules.

   Given the following rules in a back chaining expert system application

   $A \wedge \neg B \Rightarrow C(0.9)$

$C \vee D \Rightarrow E$ (0.85)

$F \Rightarrow A$(0.6)

$G \Rightarrow D$(0.8)

The system can conclude following facts with confidence

F(0.9)

B(-0.8)

G (0.8)

Use the Stanford certainty factor algebra to determine E and its confidence.

4. Create a Bayesian belief diagram for automated automobile fault analysis application.

5. Explain the applications of fuzzy set theory. Where it is applied?

9
Natural Language Processing

9.1 INTRODUCTION

Natural languages are the languages naturally evolved and used by human beings for communication purposes, for example, Hindi, English, French, German are natural languages. Natural Language processing or NLP (also called Computational Linguistics) is the scientific study of languages from a computational perspective. In NLP, the techniques are developed which aim the computer to understand the commands given in natural language and perform according to it. At present, to work with computer, the input is required to be given in formal languages. The formal languages are, those languages which are specifically developed to communicate with computer and are understood by machine, e g. FORTRAN, Pascal, etc. Obviously, to communicate with computer, the study of these formal languages is required. Understanding these languages is cumbersome and requires additional efforts to understand them. Hence, it limits their applications in computer. As compared to this, the communication in natural language will facilitate the functioning and communication with computer easily and in user friendly way.

Natural language Processing is significant area of artificial intelligence because a computer would be considered intelligent if it can understand the commands gives in natural language instead of C, FORTRAN, and PASCAL. Hence, with the ability of computers to understand natural language, it becomes much easier to communicate with computers. Also the natural language processing can be applied as productivity tool in application ranging from summarization of news to translate from one language to another. Though, the surface level processing of natural languages seems to be easy, the deep level processing of natural languages, understanding of implicit messages and intensions of speaker are extremely difficult avenues.

Before presenting the theories of natural language processing, certain examples of natural language sentences are mentioned below which illustrate the complexity of their analysis:

(i) *"It is the dog that worried the cat, that killed the rat, that ate the malt, that lay in the house, that Jack built."*

                                      - Mother Goose, The house that Jack Built

(ii) *"Then you should say what you mean", the march here went on.*
"I do" Alice hastily replied" at least, at least I mean what I say – that's the same thing, you know"

"not the same thing a bit" said the Hatter.
"you might as well say that "I see what I eat" is the same thing as "I eat what I see"

- Lewis Caroll, Alice in wonderland

(iii) *"When I use a world" Humpty – Dumpty said in a rather scornful tone, "it means just what I chose it to mean- neither more or less"*

- Lewis Caroll, Alice in wonderland

(iv) *How many legs does a dog have if you call its tail a leg?*
Four.
Calling a tail a leg doesn't make it one.

- Attributed to Abraham Lincon

(v) *Gracie "oh yeah.... And then Mrs. And Mr. Jones were having matrimonial trouble and my brother was hired to watch Mrs. Jones.*
George: Well I imagine she was a very attractive woman.
Gracie: she was. My brother watched her day and night for six months.
George: Well, what happened?
Gracie: She finally got a divorce.
George: Mrs. Jones?
Gracie: No, My brother's wife.

- George burns and Gracie Allen in the salesgirl

(vi) *"The procedure is quite simple. First you arrange things into different groups depending upon their makeup. Of course, one pile may be sufficient depending upon how much there is to do. If you have to do somewhere else due to lack of facilities that is the next step. Otherwise, you are pretty well set. It is important not to overdo any particular endeavor. That is it is better to do few things at once than too many.*

- Jatin D Brand ford and Mercis K Jatinson

(vii) *"A paragraph said to have no theme, used in experiments. Subjects found it very hard to comprehend or recall until it was given a theme by adding the heading washing machines."*

- Anonymous

(viii) *"I think sir, you can care for the advice of an old man, sir, you will find it a very good practice always to verify your references sir"*

- Martin Joseph Routh

9.2 BRIEF HISTORY OF NLP

The natural language processing is comparatively a new area. This section describes briefly various development phases of Natural language processing.

9.2.1 Foundational Insights: (1940 - 1950)

In this period, work mainly confined itself to two foundational paradigms; namely the automation and the use of probabilistic models. The automation started in 1950s with Turing's model of algorithmic computation. Turing's work led first to the development of Mc Culloch Pitts neurons, which made a simplified model of neuron as a kind of computing element that could be described in terms of propositional logic, and then to the work of Kleene on finite automation and regular expression. Shannon applied probabilistic models of discrete Markov processes to automate the language processing. Drawing the idea of finite Markov process from Shannon's work, Chomsky, first considered finite state machines as a way to characterize a grammar and defined a finite state language as a language generated by a finite state grammar. These early models led to the field of formal language theory, which used algebra and set theory to define formal languages as sequences of symbols. This includes the context free grammars, first defined by Chomsky for natural languages but independently discovered by Backus and Naur in their description of the ALGOL programming language.

9.2.2 Second Era: (1957-1970)

In the second era, language processing had split very clearly into two paradigms: symbolic and stochastic. The symbolic work took off from two lines of work. The first was the work of Chomsky, and the other on formal language theory and generative syntax through the late 1950s to early 1960s, and the work of many linguists and computer scientists on parsing algorithms, initially using top down and bottom up approaches and then via dynamic programming. One of the earliest complete parsing systems developed based on this approach was Transformations and Discourse Analysis Project. The second line of research was the new field of Artificial Intelligence. In an AI workshop held in 1959, the early Natural language systems were discussed. These were simple systems that worked in a single domain mainly by a combination of pattern matching and keyword search with simple heuristics for reasoning and question answering. By the late 60s more formal logical systems had been developed. The 1960s also saw the rise of the first serious testable models of human language processing based on 'transformational grammar', as well as on the 'on line corpora'. The Brown corpus of American English was a collection of 1 million samples from 500 written texts from different genres, (newspapers, novels, non-fiction, academic etc.) which was assembled at Brown University in 1963-64.

9.2.3 Third Era: (1970-1993)

The next period saw an explosion in research in language processing. The SHRDLU's success showed that the parsing was well enough understood to begin to focus on semantics and discourse models. Roger Shank and his colleagues built a series of language understanding programs that focused on human conceptual knowledge such as scripts, plans and goals, and human memory organization.

The logic-based and natural language understanding paradigms were unified on systems that used predicate logic as a semantic representation. LUNAR is an example of such system.

A discourse-modeling paradigm has been focused on four key areas of discourse analysis. Grosz and her colleagues introduced the concept of study of substructure in discourse and of discourse focus.

9.2.4 Fourth Era: (1993-till date)

In this era, use of probabilistic and data driven models became quite standard throughout natural language processing. Algorithms of parsing, part-of-speech tagging, reference resolution and discourse processing, all began to incorporate probabilities and employ evaluation strategies borrowed from speech recognition and information retrieval. Also, the technological innovations in hardware such as the increase in speed and memory of computers, had allowed commercial exploitation of a number of sub areas of speech and language processing, in particular speech recognition and spelling and grammar checking. Moreover, the rise of web applications in the recent past has added a new dimension of emphasis on the need for language based information retrieval and information extraction.

9.3 SIGNIFICANCE OF NATURAL LANGUAGE PROCESSING

Natural language processing has emerged as an interdisciplinary area. It is a combination of computational linguistics and Artificial Intelligence. The natural language processing uses the tools of Artificial Intelligence such as: algorithms, data structures, formal models for representing knowledge, models of reasoning processes etc. The goal of natural language processing is to specify a language comprehension and production theory to such a level of detail that a person is able to write a computer program which can understand and produce natural language. Typical sub-areas of the field include the specification of Parsing algorithms and the study of their computational properties, the construction of knowledge representation formalisms that can support the semantic analysis of the sentence, and the modeling of the reasoning processes that account for the analysis of context affects and interpretation of sentences.

While the goals of the computational approach overlap those of theoretical linguists and AI workers, the tools that are used in both differ remarkably. Theoretical linguists are primarily interested in producing a structural description of natural languages. They usually do not consider the details of the way that actual sentences are processed or the way that actual sentences might be generated from structural description. A major constraint on linguistic theories is that the theories should hold true in general across different languages. Thus, theoretical linguists attempt to characterize the general organizing principles, which underlie all human languages and spend less time and effort examining any particular language. The goal of theoretical linguistics is a formal specification of linguistic structure. However, from engineering point of view, the term language processing typically refers to the analysis and design of techniques, which are used for understanding the languages with the help of computer. The rapid advancements in technology particularly information technology made use of computer practically inevitable in all areas. Earlier computers were used as a computing device but with the advent and incorporation of newer techniques of 'Artificial Intelligence', this is becoming intelligent device and is even replacing 'humans' for some applications. To give a feel of human expert, computer is needed to interact with the user in natural languages. For this purpose a significant amount of R&D work is now being done on Natural Language Processing. There are two primary motivations for this. First, the technological motivation to build intelligent computer system, such as natural language interfaces to databases, automatic machine translation system, text analysis system and speech understanding system. Secondly, the linguistic or cognitive science motivation, which is to gain a better understanding of how human beings communicate using natural languages. Of the two, the intelligent computer system with natural language interface to data bases and automatic machine translation system to analyze the speech understanding is more important.

Research in Natural Language Processing has increased enormously in recent years. Adding to many of its catalytic factors like the increase in the Internet and web applications has opened an entirely new world of applications for natural language interface. The following scenario illustrates some elementary applications:

- A Canadian computer accepts daily weather data and generates weather reports, which are passed to the public in English and French.
- The Bable fish translation system handles over 1000000 translation requests a day from the Alta vista search engine site.

Natural language processing could also cope up with information overload. The various sources of information like printed sources, television, radio and human conversation give lot of information to us daily. But because of limited capacity of mind we do not remember all of these. This wastage of information can be stopped if we collect the information properly, organize it and put in the data-base or knowledge base system.

Datable management systems or knowledge base systems are repository of good amount of information, but they require special language known as query language to obtain information from database. A good system would be, if the interaction with database is possible in natural language. To interact with the database in natural languages, computer is required to have knowledge of basic alphabet, lexicon, grammar, words formation, sentence formation rules of that language. Besides this, to interpret the sentence properly an environment consisting of other things like general knowledge, common sense knowledge, domain specific knowledge is also required. A natural language interface is shown below in Fig. 9.1.

The general aims of NLP understanding are:

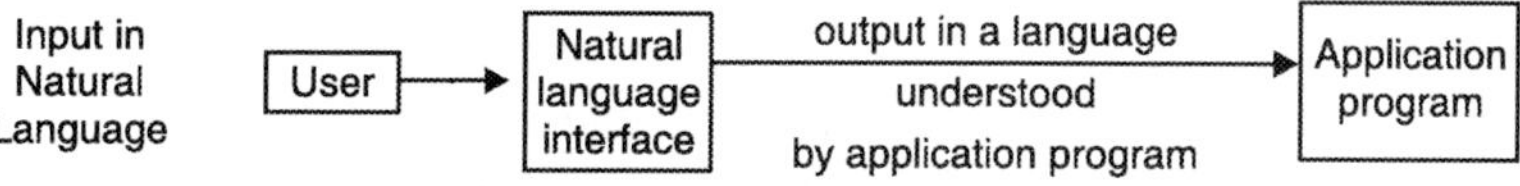

Fig. 9.1: Block diagram of NLP system

(i) *The theoretical investigation of human language*: It explores the details of language from computer implementation point of view.

(ii) *More natural man machine communication*: This aims at producing practical automated system.

Another area of language processing is called machine translation. Machine translation is the field that deals with translating a piece of text from one human language to another with the aim of high-speed conversion and accuracy. Natural Language Processing is more than simple machine translation. In addition to simple machine translation, it aims at full understanding of text, checking syntactic and semantic validity of linguistic input and using the real world knowledge to understand the participant's goals and beliefs and also, speech acts. Natural language processing has wide applications in data base front ends, grammar development environments with intelligent text processing and articulate expert systems.

9.4 EARLY NLP SYSTEMS

In early 1960s, few isolated NLP systems were developed. However, all of these provide very little theoretical basis to the field of NLP. Most of the NLP programs were intended to carry out some task other than Parsing (For example problem–solving, question- answering) and accordingly they did not perform any true parsing of their input sentences. In fact, most of them were characterized with only a keyword based analysis and often intended to employ crude searches for keywords or patterns in the input string. Some of such NLP systems are as follows:

9.4.1 ELIZA System

This system was developed in 1966-1967 by Weizenbaum at MIT. The ELIZA is a famous program that mimics a Rogerian psychotherapist. This program is one of the most popular Artificial Intelligence programs of all time since it carried the keyword based analysis approach to an absurd (but impressive) extreme. Although, it has no understanding of the conversation, it is able to give the appearance of intelligence by repeating back earlier assertions that contain keywords in the form of questions. It carries on a conversation with a user via a terminal, about any topic that the human choose, and never seems lost for a response. Some examples of interaction with ELIZA are as follows:

USER	:	Men are all alike.
ELIZA	:	In what way?
USER	:	They are always bugging us about something or the other.
ELIZA	:	Can you think of a specific example?
USER	:	Well, my boyfriend made me come here.
ELIZA	:	Your boyfriend made you come here.
USER	:	He says I am depressed much of the time.
ELIZA	:	I am sorry to hear that you are depressed.
USER	:	It is true. I am unhappy.

ELIZA	:	Do you think coming here will help you not to be unhappy?
USER	:	I need some help, that much seems certain.
ELIZA	:	What would it mean to you if you got some help?

The program was based on very simple tricks, and its responses were of two kinds:

- Stock phrases (For example, "in what way")
- Standard patterns with fragments of a previous input sentence inserted into them (For example "I am sorry to hear that ....?, tell me more about...."), with the adjustments (For example "changing my to your").

These techniques produced an amazing level of fluency, but the program primarily lacked in understanding.

9.4.2 LUNAR System

One of the largest and most successful question–answering systems using AI techniques was LUNAR developed in 1970. This system had a separate syntax analyzer and a semantic interpreter. Its Parser was written in ATN form, and it used to build a Chomskian deep structure for an input sentence. The semantic rules were designed to operate on this tree–structure, building database queries, which reflected the meaning of the question or command, which had been parsed. These queries were executable commands in a special procedural database language.

The system was used in various tests, and responded successfully to queries such as:

(i)   What is the average concentration of iron in ilmenite?
(ii) Give me the modal analysis of those samples for all phases.
(iii) How many rocks have greater than 50 ppm nickel?
(iv) Of the type 'A' rocks which is the oldest?

Although this program mainly had to deal with queries about its stored information concerning moon rock samples, and was not a general-purpose natural language front–end, still the system was quite impressive in its performance.

9.4.3 SHRDLU System

In 1970, the SHRDLU program had an overwhelming effect on research in NLP. This was a dialogue system which could converse with a human user about simple tabletop world containing building blocks. The program had a (very crude) simulation of a hand and eye, which it could use within the simulated blocks world.

The program contained a syntactic parser, written using a special purpose high level language called *programmer*. SHRDLU's syntax trees were a combination of deep and surface structure and they were lavishly labeled with syntactic features, some of which furnished information about the deep position of constituents such as 'wh' phrases. The syntax tree acted on various semantic

specialists (LISP Procedures) to construct semantic structures. These structures
are represented as expressions or commands in another special purpose
programming language, 'Micro – Planner'. The system evaluated the pieces of
Micro planner program in the computational environment of the BLOCKS
database, and constituted the response to the original input sentence. The
arrangement allowed conversational exchanges such the following:

USER	:	Pick up a big red block.
SHRDLU	:	OK.
USER	:	Grasp the pyramid.
SHRDLU	:	I don't understand which pyramid you mean.
USER	:	What does the box contain?
SHRDLU	:	The blue pyramid and the blue block.
USER	:	What is the pyramid supported by?
SHRDLU	:	The box.
USER	:	How many blocks are in the box?
SHRDLU	:	Four of them.

SHRDLU's main features are:

(i)   It contains a syntactic parser with a fairly wide coverage which builds
surface structures that are not simply of trivial category labeling.

(ii) It attempts to explore the idea of procedural semantics in an implementation.

(iii) It performs the integration of many components, all exemplifying the
contemporary level of performance into a whole system.

9.4.4 Practical Front Ends

Besides the special purpose task oriented NLP systems, front-ends interfaces to
databases are also important NLP applications. Any computer system that has to
be used by people who are not computer programmers will find it easier to use, if
it can converse reasonably fluent in natural language like English. Various dialogue
interfaces have been constructed throughout the past years and generally, these
posses following characteristics:

(i)   The fact that a restricted subject matter was involved, allows various
simplifying assumptions in the grammars.

(ii) The need of a practical working system was given more importance than
the desire to explore theoretical aspects of language.

(iii) The output performance given by it (sentence generation) often looked
impressive but was dependent on the use of stored phrases, rather than
subtle sentence generation.

Woods suggested that the attempt to solve problems of Natural Language
Understanding from engineering point of view might throw light on theoretical
issues in a quite profound way. If a grammatical technique is devised simply to
cover the data in an elegant fashion (as in linguistics) then it has no *explanatory*
value. It has the peculiar form and because of this, the linguist prefers it to use for

describing things. On the other hand, a solution designed with efficiency in mind (as in engineering) requires covering the data elegantly to offer certain functional explanation. Leaving aside the question of explanation, there is the interesting point that a long-term engineering approach might benefit from the adoption of some of the methodological criteria applied by theoretical linguists. A conventional grammarian set against this background may seek to construct descriptions which are general in nature (in the sense of covering a wide range of data) and elegant (in the sense of internal coherence and simplicity) as far as possible. If a computer program for understanding English sentences is made to be robust and extensible, these qualities are highly desirable. In fact, generality and elegance are guidelines for good programming. More so, when the subject is concerned with grammatical interpretations, the goals of linguist and the long-term interests of the engineers become pertinent in order to contain the above feature.

However, when the task is to design a system, which uses natural language as a medium of communication, the task of the computer becomes enormously difficult due to logical weaknesses of the man-machine communication. Natural Language is a highly imprecise system, which tends to be used with great effectiveness by humans, not only because humans have evolved with a distinct biological basis for language processing but also because of the large amount of reasoning and world- knowledge which humans alone bring to bear on problems such as disambiguation, filling of unspecified details etc. Unless the machine with which we are conversing is intelligent enough to perform these tasks at a level equal to human level in these various supporting areas, the communication would be quite confusing. Stylized notations (For example. programming languages, query languages) may not be quite as friendly as English, but at least they tend to make it easier to be sure of getting across precisely what we mean.

9.4.5 General NLP System

A wholly general NLP system, which include all the facilities used in the above types of programs has the overall structure as shown below in Fig. 9.2.

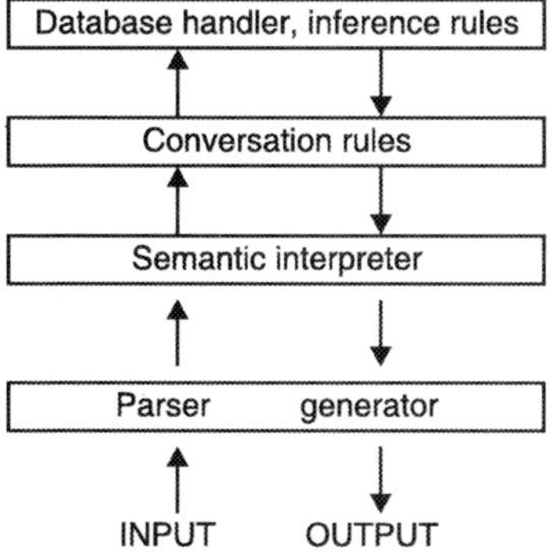

Fig. 9.2: A general NLP system

In normal NLP system, the input is given in natural language. This input is given to parser and it generalizes a syntactic structure (in the form of a parse tree) of sentence. Then semantic interpreter captures its semantic details and generates a more deep structure of it. The conversation rules accept this deep structure of sentence and make it compatible for the database storage point of view. The database handler works on it to generate a processed form from the storage point of view. These steps indicate the input side processing of natural language sentence. The reverse process is followed in natural language generation.

9.5 ROLE OF KNOWLEDGE IN NATURAL LANGUAGE PROCESSING

Language processing mainly relies on formal models or representation of knowledge related with language at the levels of phonology, phonetics, morphology, syntax, semantics, pragmatics and discourse. A large umber of formal methodologies including finite state machine, formal rules, logic and probability theory are used to capture this knowledge.

The main difference between data processing and language processing applications is the use of knowledge in the later case. The knowledge regarding various linguistic structures can be separated into following categories:

(i)   Phonetics and phonology- knowledge of linguistic sound.

(ii) Morphology- knowledge of meaningful components of the words.

(iii) Syntax- knowledge about the structural relationship about the words.

(iv) Semantics- knowledge of meaning of words.

(v)   Pragmatics- knowledge of how language is used to accomplish goals.

(vi) Discourse- knowledge of joining of linguistic units larger than a single utterance.

A very critical problem in natural languages is the ambiguity, which is their inherent weakness, because ambiguity refers to more than one meaning. In the theory of computational linguistics, several types of ambiguities are defined. Here we present only those types of ambiguities, which are normally found in the practical AI based systems:

(i)   *Lexical ambiguity*: When one word can have several different meanings, the resulting ambiguity is called lexical. To resolve this ambiguity additional knowledge regarding words is used according to context. For example, consider the following sentences:

1.   Withdraw some money from the *bank*.

2.   Do not go near the *bank* of the river.

      Here, word *bank* has two entirely different meanings in the context of its use.

(ii) *Syntactic ambiguity*: Sometimes, sentences can be parsed in more than one way, that is, phrases can be put together differently. This ambiguity is resolved by using commonsense knowledge about the task. For example, consider the following sentences:

1.   I saw the boy with the telescope.

2.   I saw the boy with the telescope.

These two sentences could have entirely different meanings depending upon the interpreter. The first sentence can be referred as 'you saw the boy using a telescope', while the second sentence can be referred as 'you saw the boy having a telescope with him'.

(iii) ***Referential ambiguity***: The use of pronoun and other anaphora can cause referential ambiguity. The anaphora are replacement words that are used in place of noun in later part of discourse. The discourse is a term, which indicates multiple coherent sentences. Process for solving referential ambiguity involves complex reasoning on the part of both speaker and the hearer. The contextual knowledge, knowledge regarding the belief system of the speaker and the hearer, commonsense knowledge about the particular task are used to resolve such ambiguity. For example, consider the following sentence:

"John saw a beautiful Chevrolet Spark at the Showroom. He showed it to Bob. He bought it".

In this example, 'he' can refer to 'John' and 'Bob' and 'it' can refer to 'Chevrolet Spark' or 'showroom'.

(iv) ***Pragmatic ambiguity***: This ambiguity underlies in meaning of the sentence. This arises because of different intensions of speaker. For example if an employee reaches office at 9.30 a.m. (whereas office starts at 9.00 a.m.) and boss asks him "what is the time?", the answer might be 9.30 a.m., but the intension of the boss is to make him realize that he was late. To resolve this ambiguity, the commonsense knowledge and contextual knowledge is required.

9.6 ENGLISH GRAMMAR

This section discusses some of the basics of English Language, which are relevant for the understanding of language analysis. Every Language defines certain basic alphabets, words, word categories and language formation rules called grammar rules. These categories are made according to their role in part of speech. From the language analysis point of view, the style of language must be concretely defined to design a working parser for that language. Though there is no hard and fast rule to name the formal categories, but it is customary to give various parts of speech their traditional names. The set of grammatical categories (like noun, verb etc.) which are taught in English literature are very informal and are not precisely defined as formal grammar. In addition to this, there are many more distinctions that have to be made in a real parser.

Hence, it is evident that for language processing using computer, the grammar writer should very clearly understand the basic word categories of any language, types of words and other constituents of the language and the process in which they interact with each other.

In linguistic analysis, Chomsky has done pioneer work in 1960s. He has formally defined various grammars, types of grammars, features and characteristics of grammars. These are described in detail later in this chapter. As a result of Chomsky's work on transformational generative grammar, a vast amount of fairly descriptive linguistic analysis is carried out, and as a result of it, a large repository of terminology has grown up, which augments informal set of old fashioned terms. Now let us describe elementary terminology of English grammar.

9.6.1 Fundamental Terminology of English Grammar

The well-accepted English grammar terminology is as follows:

(i)   **Noun**: Traditionally, noun is considered as a naming word. Formally, it is defined as "*the name of a person place or thing*". However, noun can also be abstract things like "snow", "unicorn", "sideboard" or "measles", which directly might not be representing a person, place or thing, but represent a phenomenon.

(ii) **Noun phrase**: These are phrases, which can act as a complete subject or object and do the work of noun, e.g., consider a sentence, "most of the first three coaches were destroyed". Here, "most of the three coaches" is noun phrase. Similarly, consider following sentences:

1.   The boy wants something.

2.   The boy wants to go home.

Here, in the first sentence, '*something*' is noun and is object of the verb '*wants*'. Similarly, the group of words '*to go home*' is the object of verb '*wants*' in the second sentence. Hence, this group of words does the work of noun in sentence no.2. The group of words 'to go home' is thus a 'noun phrase'.

(iii) **Proper Noun**: The proper noun names some specific items contrary to the common noun, which names some generic class. Usually, proper noun operates as a full noun phrase without the need of determiner, (for example we do not write "A Ram" or "An Ram". Ram itself is a complete word". But some proper names ("The Eiffel tower" or "The Taj") seem to need a determiner.

(iv) **Article**: These are words 'the', 'a' and 'an', which are placed before noun.

(v) **Verb**: These represent action. However, some verbs describe passive forms of doing. Examples of such verbs are, "run", "know", "be", "have".

(vi) **Auxiliary verb**: These are the words which behave differently and which can be put in a sequence at the front of a verb phrase. Example of auxiliary verb are; "be", "have", "do", "can", "will", "may" "might", "could", "must", "shall", "should" etc.

(vii)**Preposition**: These are words, which are attached before a noun or pronoun to establish its relation with other noun or pronoun of the same sentence, for example, consider the following sentences:

1.   The book is **on** the table.

2.   The boy ran **into** the house.

In the above sentences, words 'on' and 'into' are used before the nouns 'table' and 'house' to establish their relation with other nouns 'book' and 'boy' of the respective sentences. Other examples of preposition are 'to', 'from', 'within', 'in', 'about', 'before', 'for', 'by' etc.

(viii) **Adverb**: An adverb is a word that modifies the quality of anything except noun, pronoun and interjection, e.g., consider the following sentences and the use of adverb in these:

1. He *writes* **correctly**. (modifies verb)
2. You are a **very** *good* boy. (modifies adjective)
3. The crow flew **just** *over* my head.(modifies preposition)
   Sometimes, an adverb modifies the quality of even the complete sentence or phrase. For example, consider the following sentences:
4. **Probably** *you are wrong*. (modifies complete sentence)
5. I will not read **all** *through this book*. (modifies a phrase)

(ix) **Adjective**: It is a word, which specifies quality of noun. It is describing word. It can be attached to a noun to modify its meaning or it can be used to assert some attribute of the subject of sentence, e.g., blue, large, fake, main etc.

(x) **Verb phrase**: A verb along with its object constitutes a verb phrase, e.g. **she gave** flower to the teacher.

9.7 PHASES OF NATURAL LANGUAGE PROCESSING

The analysis of Natural Language is broken into various broad levels such as phonological, morphological, lexical, syntactic, semantic, pragmatic and discourse analysis. These are described in the following sub-sections.

9.7.1 Phonological Analysis

Phonology is analysis of spoken language. Therefore, it deals with speech recognition and generation. The core task of speech recognition and generation system is to take an acoustic waveform as input and produce as output, a string of words. The phonology is a part of natural language analysis, which deals with it. The area of computational linguistics that deals with speech analysis is computational phonology.

9.7.2 Morphological Analysis

It is the most elementary phase of NLP. It deals with the word formations. In this phase, individual words are analyzed according to their components called **"morphemes"**. In addition, non-word token such as punctuation etc. are separated from words. Morpheme is the basic grammatical building block that makes words.

The study of word structure is referred to as morphology. In natural language processing, it is done in morphological analysis. The task of breaking a word into its morpheme is called morphological parsing. A morpheme is defined as minimal meaningful unit in a language, which cannot be further broken into smaller units. So for example, word 'fox' consists of a single morpheme, as it can not be further resolved into smaller units. Whereas word 'cats' consists of two morphemes the morpheme 'cat' and morpheme 's' indicating plurality. Here we define term meaningful. Though cat can be broken in 'c' and 'at', But these do not relate with word 'cat' in any sense. Thus word 'cat' will be dealt as minimum meaningful unit. Morphemes are traditionally divided into two types, (i) "free morphemes ", that are able to act as words in isolation (e g. "think", "permanent", "local") and (ii) "bound morphemes", that can operate only as part of other words. (e.g. "is" 'ing' etc.) The morpheme, which forms the central part of word, is also called "stem". In English, a word can be made up of one or more morphemes, e.g.,

Word ——-Think   → stem "think"
Word ——-Localize   → stem "local", suffix "ize"
Word ——- Denationalize   → prefix "de", stem "nation", suffix "al", "ize".

The computational tool to perform morphological parsing is finite state transducer. A transducer performs it by mapping between two sets of symbols, and a finite state transducer does it with finite automaton. A transducer normally consists of four parts: **recognizer, generator, translator**, and **relator**. The output of transducer becomes a set of morphemes.

9.7.3 Lexical Analysis

In this phase of Natural Language analysis, validity of words according to lexicon is checked. Lexicon stands for dictionary. It is a collection of all possible valid words of the language along with their meaning. In NLP, the first stage of processing input text is to scan each word in the sentence and compute (or look up) all the relevant linguistic information about that word. The lexicon provides the necessary rules and data for carrying out the first stage analysis.

The details of words, like their type (noun, verb & adverb, and other details of nouns & verb etc.) are Checked.

9.7.4 Syntactic Analysis

Syntax refers to the study of formal relationships between words of sentences. In this phase the validity of a sentence according to grammar rules is checked. To perform the syntactic analysis, the knowledge of grammar and parsing technique is required. The grammar is formal specification of rules allowable in the language, and parsing is a method of analyzing a sentence to determine its structure according to grammar. The most common grammar for natural languages is the *context free grammar* (CFG) also called *phrase structure grammar* and *definite clause grammar*. These grammars are described in detail in a separate section.

Syntactic analysis is done using parsing. Two basic parsing techniques are: *top-down parsing* and *bottom- up parsing*. These are discussed in detail somewhere later in the chapter.

9.7.5 Semantic Analysis

Semantics deals with the meaning of Natural Language Sentences. In this phase, meaning of the sentence is understood. If computers wish to communicate by means of Natural language, a computational representation of these sentences (called knowledge representation) is required to capture the meaning. Natural Language semantics consists of two major features:
(i) How to represent the meanings in a way that allows all the necessary manipulations. (particularly inference)

(ii) How to relate these representations to that part of linguistic model which deals with structure. (the grammar or syntax) To a large extent, the aim of both semantics and knowledge representation is to formalize what people know about words and sentences; and what they know about meanings of natural language words, phrases etc. These are also connected with the knowledge about the world. For example, to model a natural language utterance, which discusses time and duration, we need a representation of time which reflects the way people talk about time and the way people think about the time. There are two main approaches to find computationally usable theory of meaning for natural language. Some of these approaches are discussed later in this chapter.

9.7.6 Pragmatic and Discourse Analysis

Pragmatics is the study of relation between language and context of use. Context of use includes such things as the identities of the people and objects. Hence, pragmatics includes analysis of how language is used to refer to pupil and things. Contextual environment includes the discourse context. In this phase of NLP, the main intension of speaker behind a message is understood. The discourse is a collection of sentence, but arbitrary collection of multiple sentences does not make discourse. In discourse, the sentences must be coherent. Collection of well-formed and individually interpretable sentences often forms the coherent discourse. During discourse analysis, understanding of referents is required. Referents are used in the later part of discourse, in place of nouns introduced in the earlier part of discourse.

Natural languages offer many ways to refer to entities. Each form of sentence helps hearer about how it should be processed with respect to the discourse model and set of beliefs about the word are replacement words. The discourse interpretation requires that one should build an evolving representation of discourse state called discourse model that contains representation of entities and relationship between entities. Some methodologies of pragmatic and discourse analysis are described later in the chapter.

9.8 PARSING TECHNIQUES

As discussed earlier, to extract the meaning of sentence, it needs to be analyzed. The analysis normally consists of two stages: (i) syntactic analysis, and (ii) semantic analysis. This process is indicated in the Fig. 9.3.

During language analysis, the parser generates basic syntactic structure of the sentence. This stage uses grammatical information to perform some structural preprocessing on the input. It performs the task of applying grammar rules and

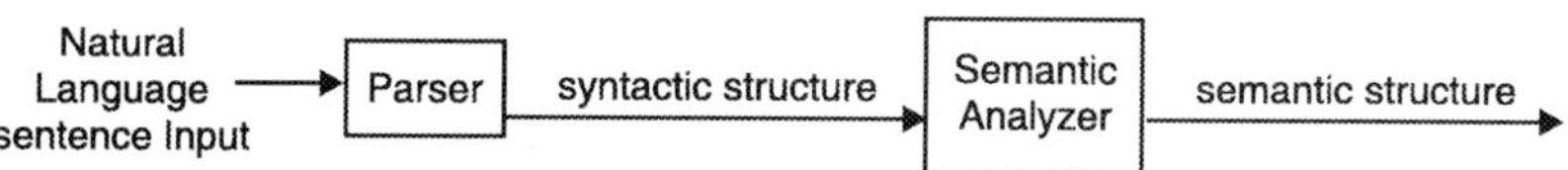

Fig 9.3: The process of natural language understanding

computes syntactic representation of the meaning. This preprocessing stage is called *parsing*. The parsing performs grouping and labeling of parts of a sentence in a way that displays their relationships to each other in a useful way. It checks the validity of a sentence according to grammar rules. However, it cannot check the semantic validity of a sentence. Hence, a sentence, if grammatically correct, and semantically incorrect will be considered as correct after first phase. The basic parsing technique is shown in Fig 9.4.

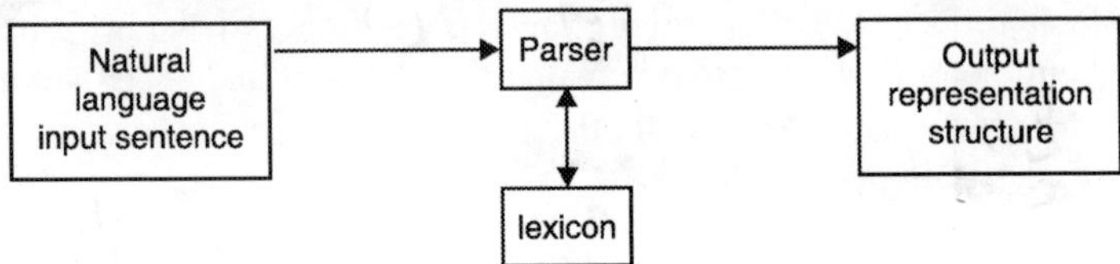

Fig 9.4: Basic parsing technique

The parser is a computer program, which accepts the natural language sentence as input and generates a output structure suitable for analysis. The lexicon is a dictionary of words, where each word contains some syntactic, some semantic and possibly some pragmatic information. The entry in the lexicon will contain a root word 'head' and its various derivatives. Some typical entries of lexicon are shown in Table 9.1 below:

Table 9.1: Typical entries of lexicon

Word	Type	Features
A	determiner	{3s}
Be	verb	Trans: intransitive
Boy	noun	{3s}
Can	noun	{1s, 2s, 3s, 1p, 2p, 3p}
	Verb	trans: intransitive
....		
....		
.....		
Orange	adjective	
	noun	{3s}
	determiner	
The	determiner	{3s, 3p}
To	preposition	
We	pronoun	{ 1p}
		case subjective

Here, the abbreviations 1s, 2s, 3s stand for first person singular, second person singular, etc. There may be situations where one word has more than one type, like 'can' is both noun and verb and word 'orange' is both adjective and a noun.

For general purpose NLP package, the lexicon stores a large number of words. The organization and entries of lexicon will vary from one implementation to another, but they are usually made up of variable length data structure like list or records arranged in alphabetical order. Access to the words may be done by any of 'indexing', 'binary searches', 'hashing' or by combination of these methods. A lexicon may also be partitioned to contain a base lexicon set of general frequently used words and domain specific components of words.

The next phase of Semantic analyzer applies various computational techniques and generates the meaning of a sentence. Hence, the semantic analysis will find out, whether a sentence is really meaningful.

The parsing can be considered as a typical AI search problem, in which:
- the initial state is input sequence of words,
- the goal state is a complete tree representing the whole sentence structure,
- the production rules are the grammar rules, and
- the choices in search space are what consist of selecting which rule to apply to which constituent. In syntactic parsing, the parser can be viewed as searching through the space of all possible parse trees to find the correct parse tree for the considered sentence.

The parsing techniques are of two types:
1. Top down parsing.
2. Bottom up parsing.

9.8.1 Top Down Parsing

Top down parsing begins with starting symbol (i.e. sentence) and proceeds by breaking the sentence into its constituent words. In top down parsing, words of sentence are replaced by their categories like noun phrase (NP), pronoun, verb phrase (VP) etc. These symbols like (NP, VP) are rewritten as per grammar rules. Finally, terminal symbols are replaced by language words. Let us consider one example to illustrate the concept of parsing.

Example 1: Write top down parse for the sentence "*Jatin ate the apple*" and construct top down parsing tree for the same.

Answer: The top down parse of the above sentence is presented below:

S	→	NP VP	(Replace S by its linguistic constituents NPVP)
	→	Name VP	(Replace NP by Name)
	→	Jatin VP	(Replace constituent category name by terminal value)
	→	Jatin Verb NP	(Replace VP by constituent category)
	→	Jatin ate NP	(Replace verb by terminal value)
	→	Jatin ate ART noun	(Replace NP by category)
	→	Jatin ate the noun	(Replace ART by terminal value)
	→	Jatin ate the apple	(Replace noun by terminal value)

The top down parse tree of the above sentence in shown in Fig. 9.5.

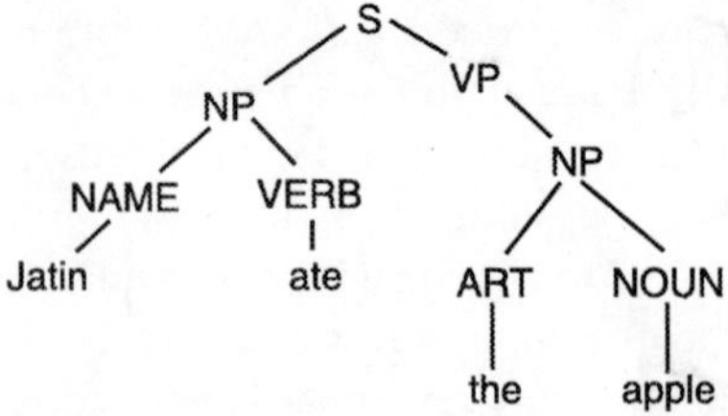

Fig. 9.5: Parse tree of "Jatin ate the apple"

9.8.2 Bottom up Parsing

The bottom up parsing is the earliest known parsing algorithm. It was first suggested by Yngve (1955) and is used in the shift reduce parser, common for computer languages. In bottom up parsing, the starting is done from sentence and the words of sentence are replaced by their relevant categories. Then, these categories are rewritten according to grammar rule. The bottom up parse for sentence "*Jatin ate the apple*" would be as follows:

→	Jatin ate the apple	
→	Name ate the apple	(replace Jatin)
→	Name verb the apple	(replace ate)
→	Name verb art apple	(replace the)
→	NP verb art apple	(replace Name)
→	NP verb NP	(replace Noun phrase)
→	NP VP	(replace verb NP)
→	S	(replace NP VP)

The parse tree (also called syntax tree) of the above sentence is shown in Fig. 9.6.

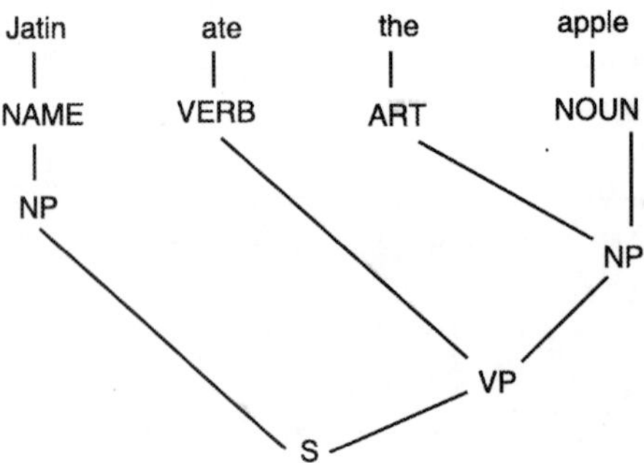

Fig. 9.6: Parse tree of sentence "Jatin ate the apple"

As said earlier, in syntactic analysis the meaning of the sentence is not checked. Hence, if we consider the sentence, *"Jatin ate the cat"*, it would also have the same parse tree. (only apple will be replaced by cat) This sentence might be semantically wrong, but it will be declared as syntactically correct.

9.8.3 Comparison of Top Down and Bottom up Parsing

Each of the two approaches, i.e. top down and bottom up parsing, has its own advantages and disadvantages. The top down strategy never wastes time in exploring trees that cannot result in S, since it begins by just generating those trees. That means, it never explores sub trees that cannot find a place in some S rooted tree. Unlike this, in bottom up strategy, trees that have no hope of leading to an S, or fitting in with any of their neighbor are generated with wild abandon, e.g., in the sentence "Book that flight", if the parser replaces 'book' by word category noun and generates the tree, the same would be a waste.

The top down approach has its own inefficiencies. While it does not waste time with trees that do not lead to an S, it does spend considerable effort on S tree that are not consistent with input. This weakness of these trees could possibly be used in parsing this sentence. This weakness in top down parser arises from the fact that they can generate trees before examining the input. Bottom up parsers on the other hand never suggest trees that are not at least locally grounded in actual input. The ambiguity resolution is most frequent problem in parser. A sentence is known structurally ambiguous if the grammar assigns it more than one possible parse. This problem is relatively less encountered in bottom up parsing.

Neither of these approaches adequately exploits the constraints presented by the grammar and the input word.

9.8.4 Bidirectional Parsing

The parsing approaches discussed above perform the parsing from either top or bottom. There are number of ways of combining the best features of top down and bottom up parsing into a single algorithm. One method is bidirectional parsing. The parsers based on this start the parsing from both directions simultaneously. It means, they parse the sentence simultaneously from 'left to right' and from 'right to left'.

9.8.5 Deterministic Parsing

The deterministic and nondeterministic parsers are transition network based parsers. A deterministic parsing is one, which permits only one choice for each word category. That means, there is only one replacement possibility for every word. Thus, each arc will have a different test condition. Parser based on this principle cannot do backtracking, and if the incorrect test choice is accepted from some state, the parser will fail. This situation may arise when one word satisfies more than one word categories, such as noun and verb or adjective and verb. However, such types of situations are generally not affordable and the deterministic parser has this shortcoming. Hence, this situation is dealt by making sure that a parser takes the correct choice by using look ahead mechanism in the parsers. Still, the design and implementation of deterministic parser is easy. The deterministic network is shown in Fig. 9.7.

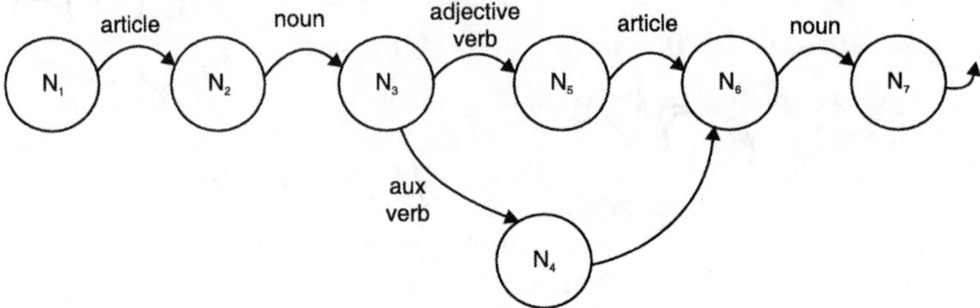

Fig. 9.7: The deterministic network

9.8.6 Non-Deterministic Parsing

The non-deterministic parsing allows different arcs to be labeled with the same test. Thus, they can uniquely make the choice about the next arc to be taken. A non-deterministic network is shown in Fig. 9.8.

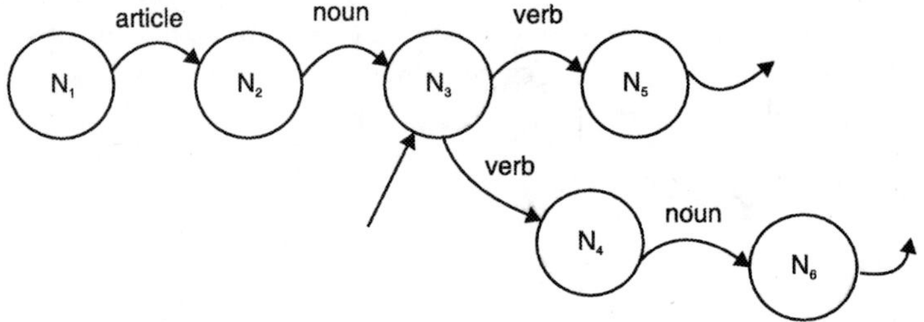

Fig. 9.8: A non-deterministic network

In nondeterministic parser, the next test from any state may not be uniquely determined by the state and the current input word. The parser must guess at the proper constituents and then backtrack if guess is proven to be wrong. This will require saving more than one potential structure during parts of network travel.

Consider the example of parsing the sentence "the strong bear the loads". If the parser chose to recognize 'strong' as an adjective and 'bear' as noun, the parse would fail since there is no verb following bear. A non-deterministic parser on the other hand, would simply recover from backtracking when failure was detected, and then would take another arc, which accepted 'strong' as 'noun'.

Example 2:	Develop a parse tree structure for the sentence "Jatin slept on the bench", using following rules:	
S	$\rightarrow$	NP VP
NP	$\rightarrow$	N
NP	$\rightarrow$	DET N
VP	$\rightarrow$	V PP
PP	$\rightarrow$	PREP NP
N	$\rightarrow$	Jatin : Bench
V	$\rightarrow$	Slept
DET	$\rightarrow$	the
PREP	$\rightarrow$	on

Answer: The parse tree is shown in Fig. 9.9.

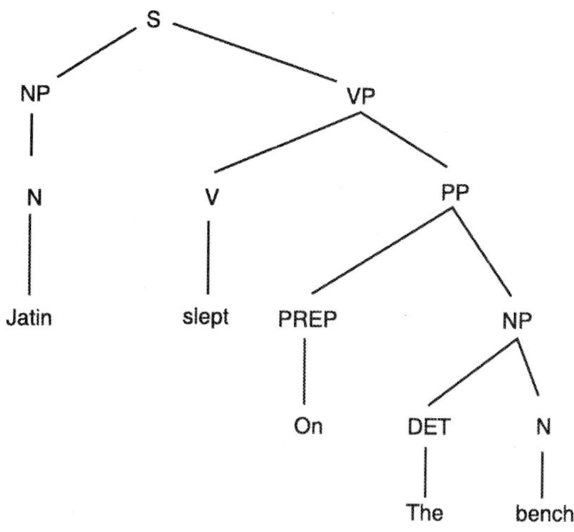

Fig. 9.9: Parse tree for the given sentence

Example 3:	For each of the following sentences show the parse tree. The grammar is given as:	
S	$\rightarrow$	NP VP
NP	$\rightarrow$	the NP1
NP	$\rightarrow$	PRO
NP	$\rightarrow$	PN
NP	$\rightarrow$	NP1! PREP NP
NP1	$\rightarrow$	ADJS N! NVP
PREP NP	$\rightarrow$	preposition NP

ADJS	→	e! ADJS
VP	→	v
VP	→	V NP
N	→	file! printer! movie! story
PN	→	Beena! Jatin
PRO	→	I
Preposition	→	with !to
ADJ	→	short !long !fast
V	→	printed !created ! went

(i) Jatin went to movie with Beena.

(ii) I heard the story listening to the radio.

Answer: The parse tree for the first sentence is shown in the Fig. 9.10, and that for the second sentence in Fig. 9.11.

(i) Jatin went to movie with Beena

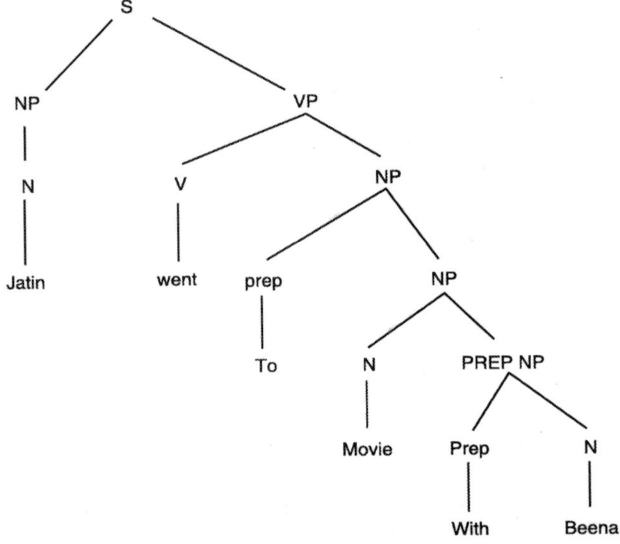

Fig. 9.10: Parse tree for sentence (i)

(ii) I heard the story listening to the radio.

9.9 TRANSITION NETWORKS

Transition networks are other methods to represent the sentence information. One way to specify the information necessary to parse a sentence is to indicate what steps to take as each symbol is processed, including tests on the input symbol and

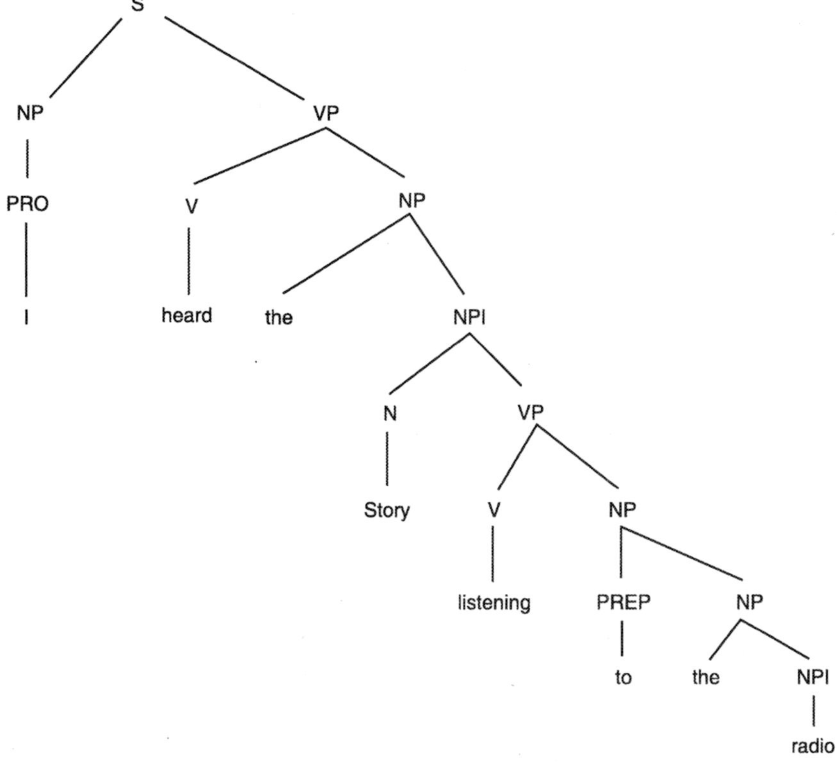

Fig. 9.11: Parse tree for sentence (ii)

action to carry out in the various possible cases. That means, some form of flow chart can be made for parsing a sentence, such parsing grammar could be represented in form of a graph with each node corresponding to a situation that might occur during parsing, and the outgoing edges from each node indicating the available options. The tail end of each arc would be connected to another node representing new situation created by taking that options.

A graphic representation of a labeled network that represents the syntactic structure of sentence is called a transition network. It consists of **node** and **labeled arcs**. The nodes represent various states and arcs represent transition from certain states to final state. Starting at a given node, one can traverse an arc if the current word in the sentence is in the category on the arc. If an arc is followed, the current word is updated to the next word. A sentence is accepted by transition network, if there is a path from the start node to a final node with arc accounting for every word in a sentence. An example transition network is shown in Fig. 9.12.

Again, consider a grammar rule $A \rightarrow BCD$, which means that A derives to B, then C and then D. Its transition diagram is shown in Fig. 9.13.

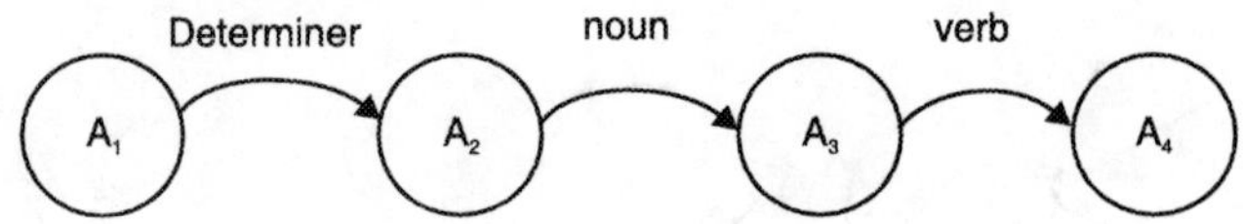

Fig. 9.12: A transition network

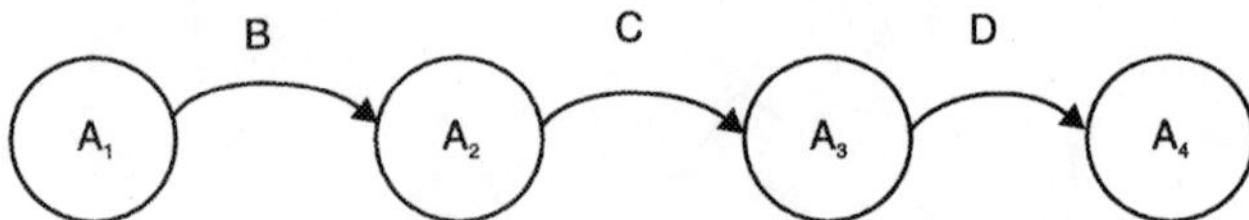

Fig. 9.13: A transition network of grammar rule A → BCD

A is the starting or initial state, A2, A3, are intermediate states and A4 is final state, B, C, & D are the constructs on which transition is possible. Parsing through transition network is done as follows. Starting at a node, one can traverse an arc if the current word in the sentence is in the category of arcs. If an arc is followed, the current word is updated to the next word. A phrase is a valid phrase if there is a path from the node of NP to pop arc accounting for every word in a sentence. For example, starting with A, as transition on B is allowed, network moves to states A2. Similarly after taking the transitions on C and D, network moves to A3 and A4, which is a final state.

The transition network is a good method to represent grammar and do parsing. They are easy to implement but they can accept only simple type of sentences and they are not powerful enough to recognize the variety of sentences, a human natural language can create. In the situations where the representation methodologies restrict the acceptability of actual natural sentences, the basic concept of natural language analysis is somewhat diluted. The transition networks discussed above fail to recognize the languages generated by context free grammar. Hence, some extensions in the transition networks is required.

9.9.1 Recursive Transition Network (RTN)

It is a modified version of transition network. It allows arc labels that refer to other networks rather than word category. The natural languages allow variety of sentence formation rules. For the understanding point of view, they require powerful transition networks. The simple networks are not powerful enough to recognize variety of sentences. To be honest, they fail to recognize all languages that can be generated by context free grammar. Hence, some additions are required in normal transition networks to accommodate complex features associated with natural languages.

A recursive transition network (RTN) is a transition network, which permits arc labels to refer to other networks. As the name indicates, they can also recursively refers to themselves. In addition to this, they can refer back to the referring network

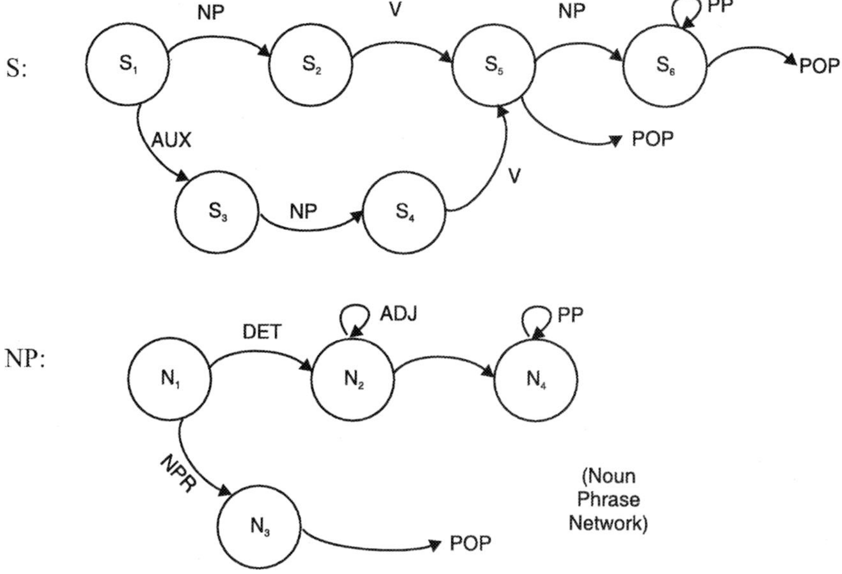

Fig. 9.14: An RTN network

rather than just permitting the word category used previously. The RTN described by William Woods (1970) is illustrated in Fig. 9.14.

Here, the arc category NP itself is a network. If forms starting state S1, the AUX is obtained, then main network will reach into S3, and if NP category is taken then the whole NP network will be popped.

The network is normally traversed in a clockwise order. Thus in the top level RTN, the NP arc will be called first. If this arc fails, then arc labeled AUX will be tested.

While traversing a network, a record is maintained of the word position, and return nodes would be used as return points when control has been transferred to a lower level network. During a network traversal, a parse can fail if following two conditions are obtained:

(i)   The end of input sentence (a period) has been reached, when the task from the last node is not a terminal (POP) value.

(ii) If a word in the input sentence fail to satisfy any of the available arc tests from some node in the network.

To extend the number of sentences accepted by RTN, backtracking can be allowed whenever failure occurs. This requires that states having alternative transitions be remembered until the parse progresses past possible failure points. In this way, if failure occurs at some point, the interpreter can backtrack and try alternative path. The disadvantage with this approach is that parts of a sentence may be parsed more than one time resulting in excessive computations.

9.9.2 Augmented Trasition Netwrok (ATN)

An ATN is a modified transition network. It is an extension of RTN. The normal transition networks discussed so far are not very useful for language understanding. Based on the grammatical rules, they can only accept or reject the input sentence, whereas the real understanding of natural language requires capturing of additional features of sentence. The ATN uses a top down parsing procedure to gather various types of information to be later used for understanding system. It produces the data structure suitable for further processing and capable of storing semantic details also. It was first used in LUNAR system. In ATN, the arc (that is transition) itself can be a RTN. It uses all the same notation and processing conventions as RTN grammar but each arc can have (in addition to a basic category test), a further arbitrary test and an arbitrary action. These extra tests store additional information of a sentence like tense etc. For example, a simple noun phrase could be described by the network of Fig. 9.15.

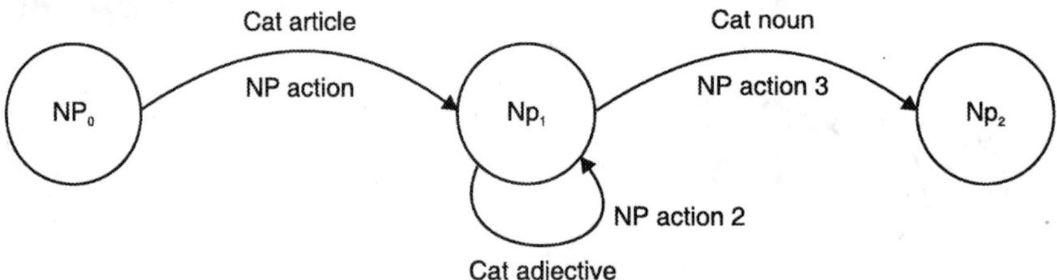

Fig. 9.15: The ATN network

Here, the circled points in the network are the "states" and the connecting lines are the "arcs". The interpretation of the networks is as follows.

"At state NP0 if next word is article, perform NP action1, and move on to state NP1. At state NP1, if the next word is CAT adjective, then perform NP action2 and return to state NP1. If next word is CAT noun, perform NP action1 and return to state NP1 if next word is CAT noun, perform action NP3 and Move to state NP2. In an ATN grammar, the arc can be of category "push" which indicates an invocation of another network. For example, the following network shown in Fig. 9.16 specifies that a noun phrase should be sought first then a verb phrase.

Here, noun phase and verb phrase of separate networks, thus the ATN grammar, should contain other networks labeled "Nouns phrases" and "verb phrases", which should be scanned by the parser while carrying out push arcs.

Both context free grammar and transition networks have deficiency that they can only accept or reject the sentence. They can not produce an analysis of the structure of the sentence. The graphical representation of ATN is shown in the following Fig. 9.17.

The ATN, besides simple parsing, collects the sentence features for further analysis. The additional features that can be captured by the ATN are; subject NP,

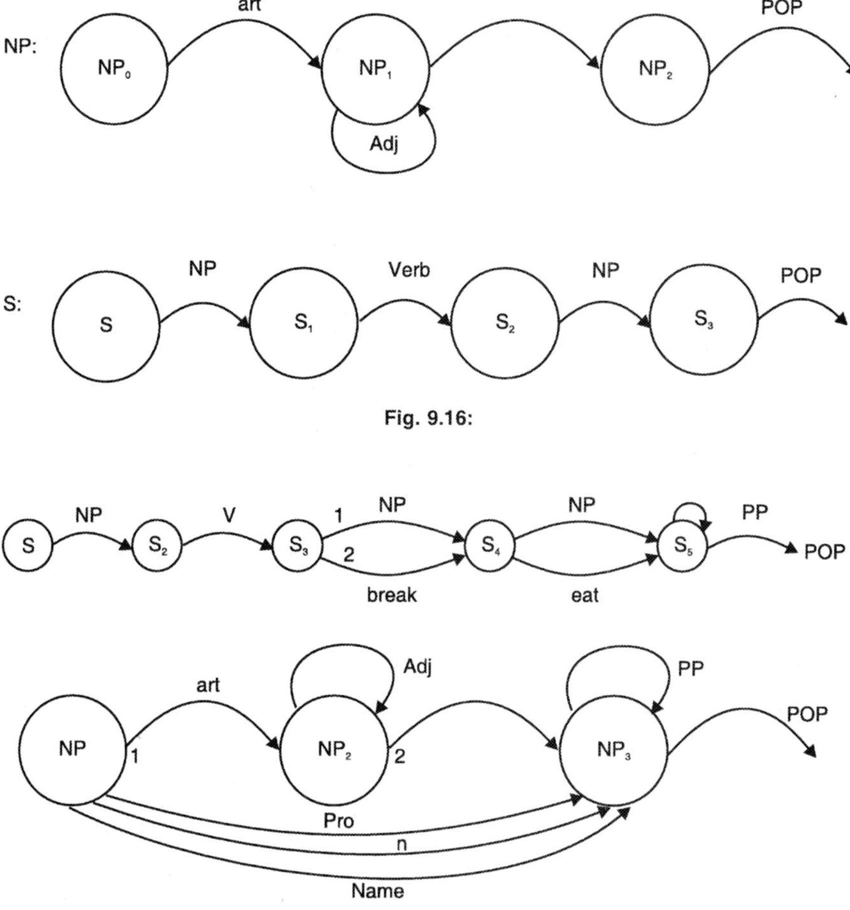

Fig. 9.16:

Fig. 9.17: The ATN structure

the object NP, the subject verb agreement, the mood (declarative or interrogative), tense and so on. This means that additional tests must be performed to determine the possible semantics a sentence may have. Without these additional tests, much ambiguity will still be present and incorrect or meaningless sentences might be accepted.

The ATN represents sentence structure using a slot filler representation, which reflects more of the functional role of phrases in a sentence. For example, one noun phrase may be identified as '**syntactic subject**' (SUBJ) of a sentence and another as the **syntactic object of the verb** (OBJ). Within noun phrases, parsing will also identify the determiner structure, adjectives, the head noun etc. The sentence "Mita found a flower" may be represented as shown in Fig. 9.18:

(S **SUBJ** (NP **NAME** Mita)
MAIN – **V** found
TENSE PAST
OBJ (NP **DET** a
HEAD flower))

Fig. 9.18: Representation of sentence in ATN

The ATN maintains the information by having '**registers**' (DET, ADJS, HEAD, and NUM). Registers are set by actions that can be specified on the arcs. When the arc is followed, the specified action associated with it is executed. Each time when a new network is pushed, a new set of empty registers are created and the whole network is popped and then that register disappears. The ATN can capture various features of English for analysis. These features are discussed as follows:

(i) *Subject Verb Agreement*:

According to English grammar, there should be **number** agreement between subject and verb. The other dimension along which a subject and verb must agree is the **person.** Person is explicitly indicated in English pronoun system. It consists of first person (I, we), second person (you), and third person (he, she, it, they etc.). All nonpronominal subjects are considered to be the third person.

(ii) *Auxiliary Verb Agreement*:

Another area where features provide a significantly cleaner analysis is the verb group. Verb group is a sequence of verbs consisting of zero or more auxiliaries followed by the main verb, such as follows:

(a) I <u>can see</u> the house.
(b) I <u>will have seen</u> the house.
(c) I <u>was watching</u> the movie.
(d) I <u>should have been watching</u> the movie.
(e) I <u>will be seen</u> at the house.

(iii) *Verb Complements*:

The complement structure of a verb includes the NPs and the clauses that immediately follow the verb. **Intransitive verbs** allow no NP, whereas **transitive verbs** allow one NP to follow (i.e. object).

9.10 HUMAN PARSING

How do people parse? The study of human parsing (also called human sentence processing), is relatively a new area and we do not have a complete answer to these questions. However, in the last 20 years, we have learnt a lot about human parsing. These results are relatively recent and there is still a disagreement over the correct way to model human parsing techniques.

An important component of human parsing is ambiguity resolution. How can human beings create two parse structures of the same sentence to resolve the ambiguity? It has been observed that in natural languages, though almost every sentence is ambiguous in one way or the other, people rarely notice these ambiguities. Instead, they only seem to see one interpretation of the sentence. Researches have shown that human sentence processor is sensitive to 'lexical sub-categorization preferences'. Consider following examples:

(i) ***The woman kept the dog on the beach.***

Possible Interpretations	Number of persons voting for the same
(a) The women kept the dogs, which were on the beach.	5%
(b) The women kept them (the dogs) on the beach.	95%

(ii) ***The women discussed the dogs on the beach.***

(a) The women discussed the dogs, which were on the beach.	90%
(b) The women discussed them (the dogs) while on the beach.	10%

Here (i) and (ii) are sentences and (a) and (b) are their interpretations performed by number of listeners. Here the proposition phrase '*on the beach*' could attach either to a noun phrase '*the dogs*' or verb phrase. People were asked to read the sentence and check off a box indicating which of the two interpretations they got first. The possible results are indicated in front of each interpretation. These results indicate that subjects preferred VP attachment with 'keep' and NP attachment with 'discuss'. This suggests that 'keep' has a sub categorization preferences for a VP with tree constituents (VP $\rightarrow$ V NP PP)while, 'discuss' has a categorization preference for a VP with two constituents (VP $\rightarrow$ V NP), although both verbs still allow both sub categorizations.

The ambiguity resolution is the most problematic task of human parsing. Much of the most recent ambiguity resolution research relies on a specific class of temporarily ambiguous sentences called **garden path** sentences. These sentences first described by Bever(1970) are sentences, which are cleverly constructed to have three properties that combine to make them very difficult for people to parse. These are as follows:

(i)   They are **temporarily ambiguous.** The whole sentence is unambiguous, but its initial portion is ambiguous.

(ii) One of the two or more parses in the initial portion is somehow preferable to the human parsing mechanism.

(iii) But the un-preferred parse is the correct one for the sentence.

The result of these three properties is that people are "led down the garden path" towards the incorrect parse, and then are confused when they realize it's the wrong one.

See parse trees given by Bever (1970) Fig. 9.19.

These sentences are so hard to parse that reader often needs to be shown the correct structure.

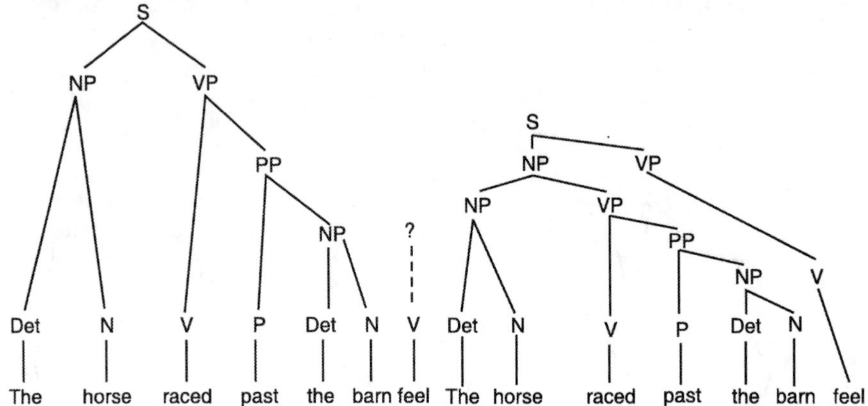

Fig. 9.19: The horse raced past the barn fell

Besides the grammatical knowledge, human parsing is affected by other factors like **resource constraint** (such as memory limitations), thematic structure (such as whether a verb expects a semantic *agent* or *patient*), semantic discourse and other contextual constraints. While there is general agreement about the knowledge sources used by human sentence processor, there is less agreement about the *time course* of knowledge use. Researches have shown that an initial interpretation of human parsing is built using purely syntactic knowledge and semantic, thematic and discourse knowledge is used only after it. This view is termed as **'modularist'** approach. Though, there are various approaches developed to understand the human parsing, but it has been generally agreed based on garden path sentences and other on line sentence processing experiments that the human parser operate probabilistically and uses probabilistic grammatical knowledge such as sub categorization information.

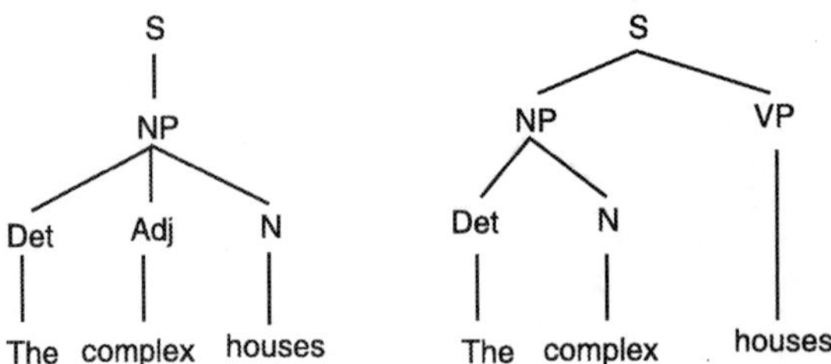

Fig. 9.20: Partial parse of sentence: the complex houses married and single students and their families

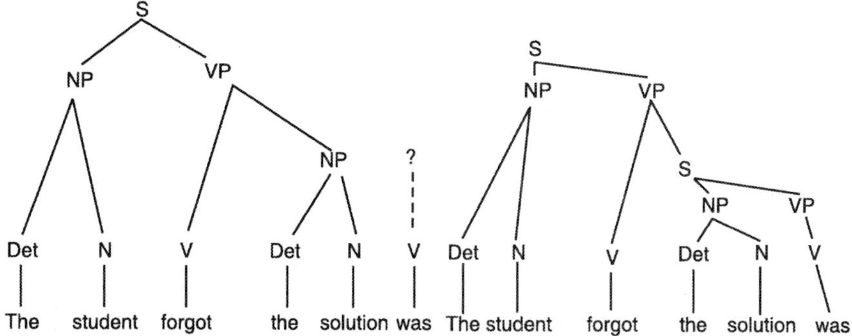

Fig. 9.21: The student forgot the solution was in the back of the book

9.11 APPROACHES TO SEMANTIC ANALYSIS

In the earlier section, we have discussed basic purpose of semantic analysis. This section discusses some elementary approaches to semantic analysis. It is already mentioned that semantics deals with the meaning of the sentence. The creation of rich and accurate meaning representation necessarily involves a wide range of knowledge sources and inference techniques. Among the sources of knowledge that are typically used are the meaning of words, the meaning associated with grammatical structures, knowledge about the structure of discourse, knowledge about the context in which the sentence is occurring.

9.11.1 Syntax Driven Semantic Analysis Approach

This is elementary approach of semantic analysis. However, this approach is fairly limited in its scope. It assigns meaning representation to input, based solely on the static knowledge from the lexicon and the grammar. In this approach, the representation of input natural language sentence is context independent and inference free. Meaning representation in this type corresponds to the notion of a literal meaning. The basic concept behind this approach is that the meaning of a sentence can be composed from the meaning of its parts. Though this idea is not very effective in finding out the meaning because of the fact that the sentence is composed of words, and according to this principle, to find out the meaning of sentence, the basic word meaning will play prime role, but it does not include the ordering of words, and relations between the words in the sentence.

9.11.2 Lexical Semantic Approach

This approach makes the use of semantic grammar. With this approach, input sentences are transformed through the domain dependent semantic rewrite rules, which create the target knowledge structures. Another informal lexical semantic approach uses conceptual dependency theory. Conceptual dependency structures provide a form of linked knowledge that can be used in larger structures such as scenes and scripts. The conceptual dependency theory is described in detail in another chapter.

9.11.3 Compositional Semantic Approach

In compositional semantic approach, the meaning of an expression is derived from the meaning of the parts of that expression. The target knowledge structures constructed in this approach are typically logical expressions, such as the formulas of FOPL. The LUNAR system developed by Woods (1979) uses this approach. The input string is first parsed using an ATN, from which, a syntactic tree is generated as output. This becomes input to a semantic interpreter, which interprets the meaning of the syntactic tree and creates the semantic representation. For example, suppose the following declaration is submitted to LUNAR

"Sample 37 contains silicon"

This would be parsed and the tree structure of Fig. 9.22 would be available as an output from ATN:

```
(S DCL
    (NP (N(Sample 37))))
    (AUX (TESE (PRESENT)))
    (VP (V (contain))
    (NP (N (silicon))))
```

Fig. 9.22: An ATN structure

Using this structure, the semantic interpreter would produce the predicate clause,

(CONTAIN sample 37 silicon)

which would have the expected FOPL meaning.

9.12 COMPUTATIONAL GRAMMAR

This section presents a detailed analysis of computational grammar from the viewpoint of natural language processing. Grammar is declarative description of a language. The linguists define various types of grammars. From the viewpoint of natural language analysis, the Chomsky hierarchy of language is most widely accepted for large categorization of grammars. The Chomsky hierarchy of grammar is given below:

  (i) Recursively enumerable set or type 0 grammar.

 (ii) Context sensitive language or type1 grammar.

(iii) Indexed languages or indexed grammar.

 (iv) Context free languages or type 2 grammar.

  (v) Finite state languages or types 3 grammar.

The Chomsky hierarchy represents the basic dimension of '*grammar power*' whose lowest level is type 3 class of languages and highest level is type 0 class of languages, also called 'recursively enumerable sets'. Chomsky differentiated languages as *context free* or *context sensitive*. The language in which, meaning of sentence is same in all context, are called context free language. Normally in natural languages, the meaning of a sentence depends upon the context. The same English sentence said in different context conveys different messages. Such grammars are context sensitive grammars.

9.12.1 Context Free Grammar

Grammar in which each production has exactly one terminal symbol in its left hand side and at least one symbol at right hand side is called context free grammar. It is simplest form of grammar. It consists of:
  (i) *Non terminals-* These are syntactic symbols, which can be further replaced by some symbols.
  (ii) *Terminals* - These are syntactic symbols that cannot be further replaced by any symbol.
  (iii) *Starting Symbol* -This is generally written as S. It indicates starting of a sentence.
  (iv) *Production rules-* These indicate how a syntactic label may be decomposed into a sequence of other symbols.

According to any grammar, a sentence is considered as syntactically valid, if starting with symbol S and according to rewrite production rules, a string consisting of all terminals can be generated. It is customary to write a grammar by its production rules. The non-terminals are written in capital letters and terminals are written in small letters e.g.

S	$\rightarrow$	NPVP
NP	$\rightarrow$	Art N
VP	$\rightarrow$	VNP
Art	$\rightarrow$	a
N	$\rightarrow$	Dog
N	$\rightarrow$	Biscuits
V	$\rightarrow$	Ate

9.12.2 Transformational Grammar

Transformational grammars are based on transformational rules designed for context sensitive situations. The transformational grammars specify legal structures of language by giving rules that generate them. The transformational grammars use context free rules to represent the "deep structure" (or meaning of the sentence). A basic sentence (complete with tree structure) built by context free rules is called a deep structure. The deep structure is represented as parse tree that not only consists of terminals and non-terminals, but also includes a set of symbols

representing additional features like number, tense and other context sensitive features. In general, the transformational rules perform following functions:
(i) Put features on constituents.
(ii) Move constituents.
(iii) Add constituents.
(iv) Delete constituents.

In the language analysis, after the application of transformational rules to a deep structure, a legal English structure called "surface structure" is generated as shown in Fig. 9.23.

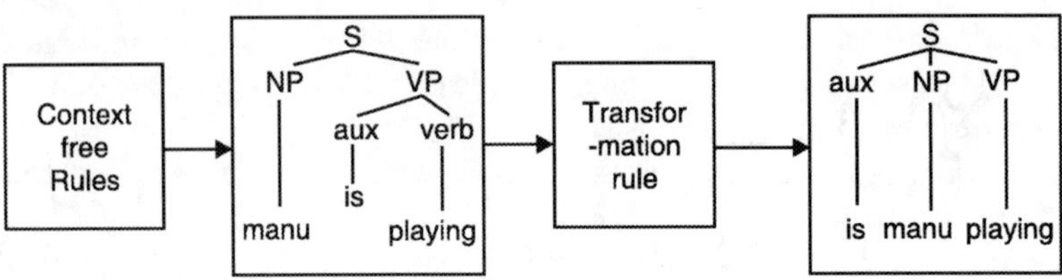

Fig. 9.23: Surface structure generation

Some of the important transformational rules are described as follows:
(i) ***Aux inversion***: This rule converts a normal imperative sentence to interrogative sentence. It can be represented as shown in figure 9.24.

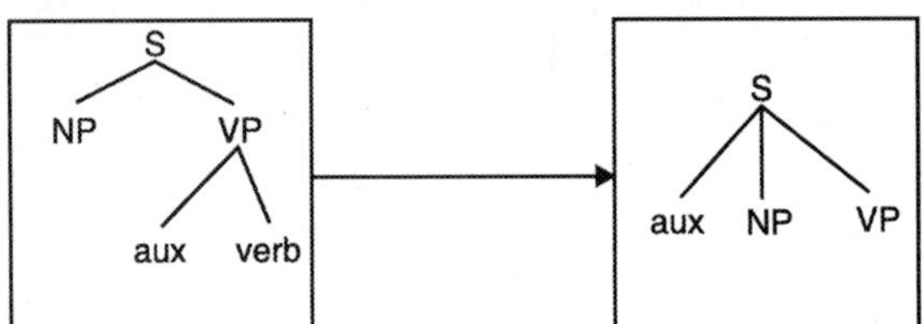

Fig. 9.24: Aux conversion

This transformational rule indicates that the sequence 'np' (noun phrase) 'aux' (auxiliary verb like is am, are etc.) and 'verb' (action like eating playing etc) can be replaced by sequence "auxiliary verb, noun phrase and verb phrase". This is clear from following sentence:

"Adwet is playing" is transformed as "is Adwet playing".

(ii) ***Reflexivization***: Pronouns like himself, herself and themselves etc. are called reflexive pronouns. Consider following sentences:

Milind washed himself.
Milind washed him.

In the first sentence the referent (i.e. to whom, verb 'washed' indicates) is Milind and in second, the referent is other than Milind. That means, the two sentences differs in the sense that in the first sentence referent is same for object and agent, and in second it is not. The Reflexivization rule accommodates this feature by adding subscript with noun phrase.

The use of i in NPi indicates that the two noun phrases refer to same individual.

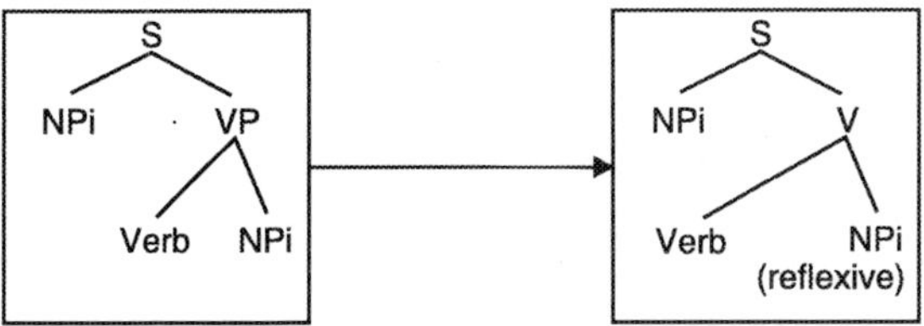

Fig. 9.25: Reflexivization rule

(iii) ***Imperatives***: This rule is applicable on imperative sentences. Consider the sentence,

"Buy a   loaf or bread".

This sentence does not have an explicit agent. The agent "you" is assumed here (that means the sentence basically means "you buy a bread". For this reason, the imperative is also called *"you deletion"*. From the language point of view, it means that the sentence structure consisting of sequence of NPVP (e.g. you go to market) can be replaced by sentence starting with VP (i.e. go to market). This is clear from Fig. 9.26:

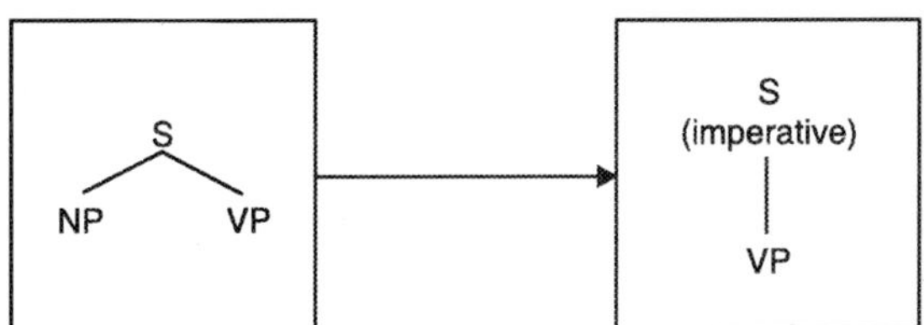

Fig. 9.26: 'You' deletion rule

(iv) ***Passive***: This rule is derived to capture the relation between active and passive sentences. Consider following sentences:

He hit Piyush.
Piyush was hit by him.

Here, the first sentence is said in active voice and the second sentence is said in passive voice. In the second sentence, we had to change "he" of the first sentence to "him" in the second sentence. Now consider another set of sentences.

He loves his Mother.
His mother loves him.

Here the use of him in second sentence indicates object role. It effectively means that it is required to distinguish between nominative case and accusative case. In natural languages, the objects are related with the cases. The active to passive transformation rules is shown in Fig. 9.27.

This rule says that to generate a passive structure of a sentence, the noun phrases should be interchanged (replace Np1, by Np2) and the verb is replaced by sequence "be verb by"

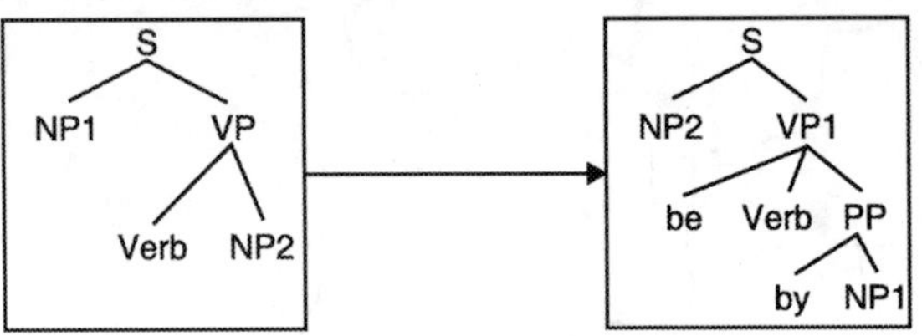

Fig. 9.27: Active to Passive movement

(v) ***Dative movement***: This rule is designed for the sentences having two agents. Consider following sentences:

Gaurav gave a gift to his friend. → Gaurav gave his friend a gift.

Adwet told Vartika a story → Adwet told a story to Vartika.

Here, in each sentence there are two objects (like gift and friend, Vartika and story). These objects are called direct (i.e.,gift) and indirect (i.e., friend) objects. Indirect object is also called secondary agent or a noun phrase in dative case. Some verbs do not allow dative movement. This is illustrated in the following example:

Mini set the words to music → Mini set music the words.

Here, the second sentence is not correct. Thus, these two sentences are not equivalent.

9.12.3 Unification Grammars

Unification grammars are designed for semantic analysis. The unification of two or more feature sets is the smallest feature set which has both or all of them as subsets and has no inconsistent feature value. The unification is possible only if two feature sets have compatible values. (For example, the unification is not possible if, *tense* = *present* in one and *tense* = *past* in another). The rule of unification grammar states that if two items are to be equated, it effectively corresponds to the unification of these items. The unification can be seen as a way of merging descriptions to create a shared value. This is shown in Fig. 9.28.

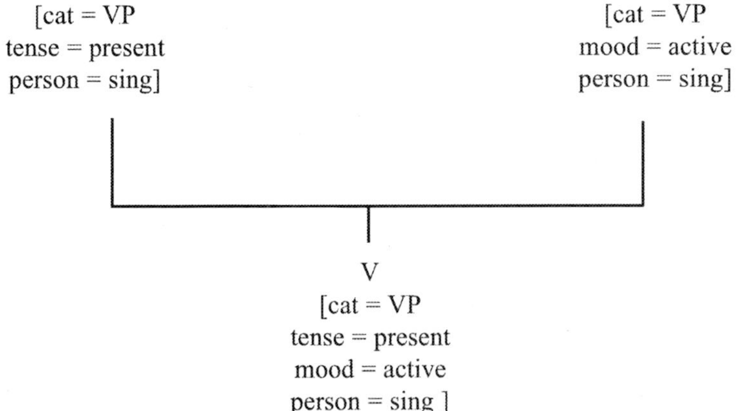

Fig. 9.28: The unification grammar

With the use of unification grammars, the sentences whose semantic meaning are same, (i.e. they share the same semantic features) can be joined. Thus, a different syntactic version, however, similar semantic version of a sentence, can be generated.

9.12.4 Fillmor's Grammar

The Fillmore's grammar was developed by Fillmore (1969). It is also called *"case grammar"*. In some traditional natural language grammars such as Latin, the noun and noun phrase are classified according to 'case', which they had in sentence. A case is basically a role which a particular word performs in the sentence. In a language like Latin, words change their form (inflect) to indicate their case, e.g.,
(a) Puer puellar florem donat. (means, the boy gives the girl the flower)
(b) Puero puellar florem donat. (means, the girl gives the boy the flower)

Here the meaning of both the sentences is just opposite and at the sentence structure level, there is change of only one word. This shows that the role (or case) in which a subject appears, significantly influences the meaning of the sentences. Hence, in some languages the case inflections can convey information, which in other languages might be conveyed by the order of the words.

In 1969, Fillmore gave the concept of *"deep case"* to accommodate this phenomenon of case. He suggested that each verb should have a case frame. Case frame lists all types of possibilities that can be associated with a verb, for example, verb 'give' represents activity of giving, which essentially requires some 'agent' who will give, some recipient who will receive, and some object or thing which is given. Thus, case frame of 'give' will accommodate these three constituents:

Case frame   :   'give' [Agent, Recipient, Object]

Sentence	:	*'Prakhar' gave 'Vidushi' a book* will be represented as:
Verb	:	give
Agent	:	Prakhar
Recipient	:	Vidushi
Object	:	book.

This representational scheme has various advantages. The different surface forms, which contain same information about respective roles of different participants can be represented in the same way. For example, the following sentences have same semantic meaning:

(i) "Prakhar gave a book to Vidushi."
(ii) "A book was given by Prakhar to Vidushi."

These will have same representation as above. Case grammars are designed to combine syntactic and semantic interpretations. Sometime, sentences of same syntactic structure have very much different semantics, e.g., consider following sentences:

Cook Cooked for dinner.
Cake Cooked for dinner.

Here the meaning of first sentence is that cook prepared 'the dinner', and that of second sentence is, that 'cake' is prepared for dinner. There syntactic structures are same, but semantic structures should be different. Figure 9.29 illustrates this difference.

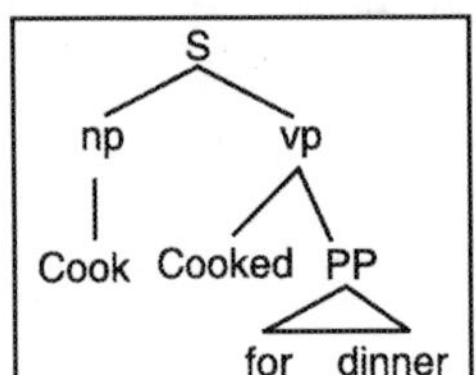

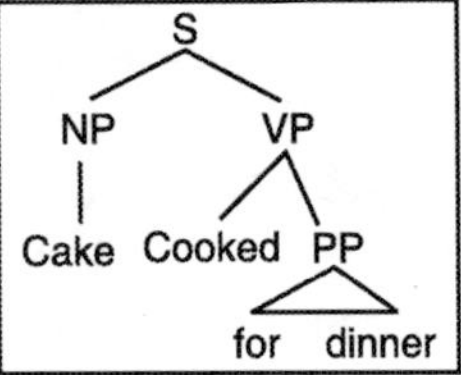

Fig. 9.29: The different syntactic structures of sentences 'Cook Cooked for dinner' and 'Cake Cooked for dinner'.

Their case grammar representation is:
(cooked (agent cook)
(occasion dinner))
(cooked (object cake)
(occasion dinner))

In these representations, semantic role of "cook" and "cake" are made explicit. Some other cases used in languages are:

Agent (A)	:	Some animate (or living object) who will perform the action.
Object (O)	:	Things on which action is performed.

Instrument (I)   :   A thing with which some action is caused.
Dative (D)   :   Some animate, who is affected by the action.
Locative (L)   :   Place where event has taken place.
Source (S)   :   Place from where action movement has started.
Goal (G)   :   Place at which the movement (action) has stopped.
Beneficiary(B)   :   Animate who has got the benefit of action.
Time (F)   :   Time at which action is performed.

The syntactic structure, which is built by parser, is called "surface structure". This surface structure helps in understanding the formation of a sentence according to grammar rules. To interpret the meaning, (or semantics) various grammars like Fillmore's grammar were developed, which make the deep structure of sentence. In language, there are sentences that represent some event, e.g., consider following sentences:

(i)   It is raining.

(ii) He has eaten the cake in birthday.

(iii) The weather is pleasant outside.

To understand the meaning conveyed by these sentences, some additional knowledge of context is must. This additional context knowledge is called "*domain knowledge*".

In Natural Language Understanding packages, the domain knowledge is added by the system builder.

To capture the information regarding event and concepts conveyed by a natural Language sentence, "conceptual dependency" theory was developed by shank [1974]. The conceptual dependencies are described in other chapter in detail. It defines various primetime conceptualization, which a sentence may have.

9.12.5 Definite Clause Grammar (DCG)

It is a widely used form of grammar based on unification. It is closely linked with PROLOG, a programming language. In this grammar, rules are written as PROLOG clauses and the PROLOG interpreter is used to perform top down depth first parsing. DCG uses a unification on the basic principle of "Resolution" theorem proving. Category labels in DCG are complex structures, but they are logical terms in the sense of first order logic. In this a '**functor**' (some atomic constant) followed by zero or more '**parameters**' (variable names, or other terms), (For example, np, np(sing), vp(past, plural, active), s(np(_N), vp(_N)) are valid category labels. The rules in DCG are similar to CFG rules using terms instead of atomic category labels (for example, s(Num) $\rightarrow$ np(Num), vp (Num), is a valid rule). From computational viewpoint, parsers can be designed, which are guaranteed to compute correct results for any given DCG.

9.12.6 Generalized Phrase Structure Grammar (GPSG)

GPSG is a grammar that produces a linguistic theory, which is quite general and rigorously defined. It covers both syntax and semantics in a compatible and non-trivial manner. The main attributes of GPSG are given below:

  (i) *Features*: A syntactic category consists of a set of features. The features are properties with a specified value (For example. [Tense PAST]).

 (ii) *Variables*: Variable is defined as property, which ranges across feature values. A rule in the rule base of practical system may have a variable appearing in multiple positions. The variable of the rule can take the feature values from the defined range.

(iii) *Partly Specified Categories*: Rules are made to refer to syntactic categories by giving a subset of the features involved. The rules are then applied to any one of the categories, which contain those feature values (together with other if required). Hence, by classifying all verbs as [-N, +V], and the auxiliary verbs as also having the feature value [+AUX], are taken care in the rules, which refer to all verbs ([-N, +V]), all auxiliaries ([+AUX]) or to all non auxiliaries ([-AUX]).

 (iv) *Bar levels*: Various syntactic categories are observed as being closely related in the sense that some are projections of the others. This gives certain additional features, which are reflected in their grammatical category. The bar levels captures these additional features. (For example. [+N, -V] for nouns, etc.)

  (v) *Concurrence and defaults*: These are rules, which define valid syntactic categories in terms of feature values.

 (vi) *Heads*: One traditional linguistic notion, which GPSG incorporates is, that within a construction (i.e. within a structure described by a rule), there is one constituent which is dominant on the other. This is called the **head** of that construction.

(vii) *Meta rules*: Similarities between rules are sometimes handled by defining meta rules (rules about rules) which state that if there is a rule of a particular shape in the grammar, then there must also be another related rule of a particular shape. The relationship between active and passive voice sentences in English is handled by Meta rules.

9.13 NATURAL LANGUAGE GENERATION

Natural Language Generation (NLG) is the process of constructing natural language outputs from non-linguistic input. It is reverse of natural language analyses. Relatively, there has been less study of this area within artificial intelligence. Historically, since 1990s, there has been growing thrust in the research related with this area. The over all process of natural language generation is shown in Fig. 9.30.

Thus, it is clear that the generation maps internal representation of natural language to a readable text format. In this process, the issues are almost same as

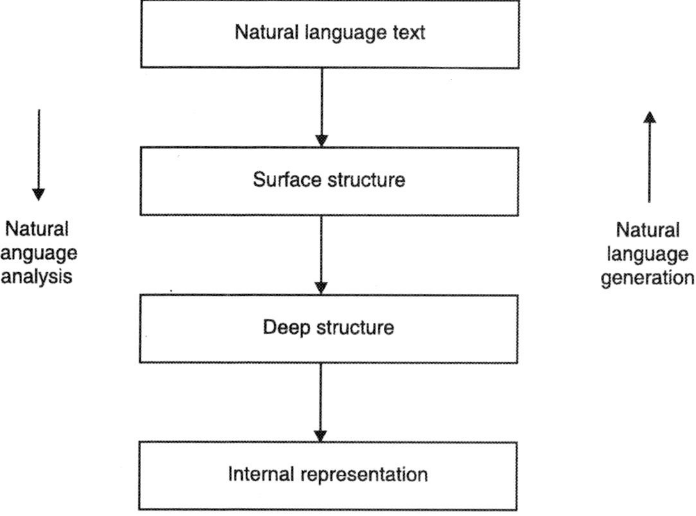

Fig. 9.30: Natural language generation

discussed in natural language understanding (NLU), but NLG has following two differences from NLU:

(i) ***Nature of input***: The generation process varies widely from one application to another. Which means, the natural language generation is more complicated task as compared to NLU. The nature of practical systems existing in the world differs widely. Here, one application system may be related with the discussion of a complex set of numeric tables, whereas the other may be a medical diagnosis system, or it may be a aerospace application and so on. As a result, the generation system must extract the information necessary to devise the generation process.

(ii) The dictionary (lexicon) representation of NLU and NLG widely differs. For analysis purpose, the contents in the dictionary need to store details for the purpose of ambiguity resolution. Thus, NLU is categorized as a process of hypothesis management in which, the linguistic input is sequentially scanned as the system considers alternative interpretations. The non linguistic representation input to a NLG system is relatively unambiguous, well specified and well formed. The NLG system concentrates mainly on choice. Generation system must make selection between following choices:

(i) **Lexical selection** - The system should select appropriate word from the lexicon according to the concept.

(ii) **Content selection** - The system must choose the appropriate content to express from a potentially over specified input. That means, according to application it should select the environment.

(iii) **Sentence structure** - After selecting the different words, the system must choose appropriate phrase and clause to frame sentence. Then the system must determine how to refer to the object being discussed.

(iv) Referring expressions - The system should determine how to refer to objects being discussed.

(v) Discourse structure - A complete message generally consists of multiple sentences (called discourse) which must have a coherent structure. The NLG system should be able to generate this discourse.

(vi) Conceptualization - In the process of conceptualization, a general framework corresponding to the application is decided. Then from lexicon, appropriate words describing these concepts are chosen. Once all the words have been chosen, these are converted to sentences and then surface realizer converts these to the natural language out put.

9.13.1 Components of Natural Language Generator

The natural language generator is a system used for generating natural language sentences. It has two basic components:

1. Discourse planner: it performs following functions:

(i)   It accepts the input and decides the communication goals.

(ii)   It takes various decisions about content selections.

(iii) It plans the discourse.

2. Surface Realiser: It receives fully specified discourse plan and generates individual sentences as generated by its lexical and grammatical resources. It may generate multisentence output according to plan of input. In brief, the surface realizer handles the issues of decision making in sentence generation including content selection, lexical selection, referring expressions and discourse structure planning.

The reference architecture of NLG system is given in Fig. 9.31:

9.14 SPEECH RECOGNITION

Speech recognition is the task of identifying a sequence of words uttered by a speaker through acoustic signals. The speech is a dominant modality for communication between humans and this method of communication was evolved before the evolution of written form of communication (i.e., script). The speech understanding is the identification of meaning of the utterance. Though speech recognition is a complete topic in its own aspect, here we would like to discuss it in brief.

Unlike in text, in speech there might exist noise and artifacts introduced by the digitization process. During digitization of sound (or acoustic signal) there can be changes (distortions) in the signal. These may create different pronunciation, or there may be situations where different words sound the same, for these reasons the speech recognition becomes a complicated task and the theory of probabilistic inferencing is more applied in this field. From the viewpoint of speech

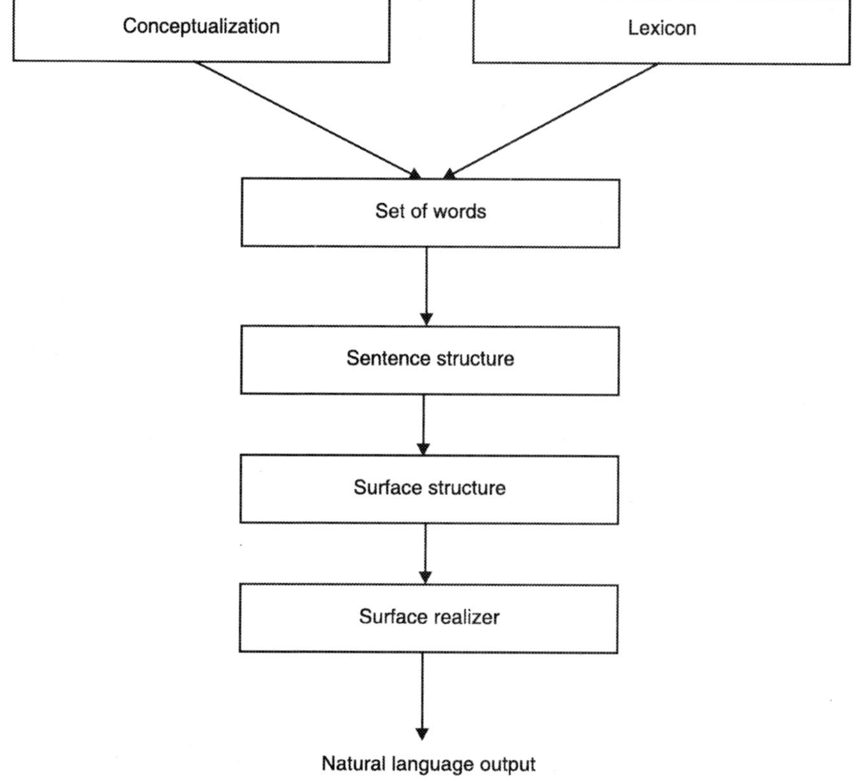

Fig. 9.31: The Natural language Generator

understanding, the 'word' is considered as random variable ranging over all possible sequences of words that might have occurred and 'signal' is defined as 'acoustic sequence'. Hence, the words we utter during conversation are acoustic signals. The probabilistic inference says that the most likely interpretation of an utterance is the value of words that maintains highest probability of words/signal (represented as P (words/signal)). Whenever we develop a model based on the analysis of word and corresponding acoustic signal, (i.e., P (words/signal)), it is called acoustic model. Where, P (words) is called language model. Thus, in language model, word 'ceiling' and 'sealing' will be different, but in acoustic model they will be considered same. For speech understanding, the acoustic model is developed. It is based on the theories of phonology. Phonology is the study of how language sounds. The basic terminology of speech recognition is defined by following terms:

(i) **Phoneme**: A phoneme is the smallest unit of sound that has a distinct meaning to speaker of a particular language.

(ii) **Word**: In speech understanding, each word is considered as distinct probability distribution $P(x|word)$, where, x specifies the phone state of that word.

(iii) ***Sentence***: Sentence is a continuous collection of words. In sentence, understanding the recognition of individual words is done and also the markings at the end of words (called segmentation) is to be understood. Hence, segmentation is the problem of deciding where one word ends and next begins.

(iv) ***Speech recognizer***: It is the system developed for recognition of speech. It has components to develop various models used for understanding like word pronunciation model, phone model, language processing algorithms used to extract spectral features from acoustic signals. The further description of speech recognition theory is beyond the scope of this book.

9.15 CONCLUSION

In this chapter we have discussed many aspects of natural language analysis, natural language understanding and natural language generation. However, it should be noted that natural language understanding is very complex phenomenon and understanding the real intension of speaker behind a message is virtually impossible. There are complexities involved at utterance level, sentence formation level and above all at intension level. As far as the development of computational techniques for this purpose are concerned, the natural language analysis has reached at advanced stage and techniques have been developed for syntactic and semantic level analysis. Nevertheless, the natural language understanding and natural language generation are still in early stage of research, and lot of work is required to be done to develop a system, which can exhibit the real capabilities of understanding natural languages. Frankly speaking, one group of AI critics even go on to say that a real natural language understanding system exhibiting capabilities equivalent to human being can never be developed. They support their claim by saying that how can a computer can understand those intensions which even human beings find difficult to understand.

However, our aim is not to emphasize what can not be done or is almost impossible to achieve, but our endeavor is intended to build an intelligent system which does not operate using specified computer programming languages, but is able to converse in natural languages, the same way we humans do. Looking in to the advancements made in the recent past and the pace of the research and developments taking place, we should hope for the best and must look forward to converse with our computer the same way we do with our nears and dears!

EXERCISES

1. Define natural language and natural language processing?
2. What are major advantages of NLP?
3. Explain various types of ambiguities encountered in natural languages. Give example of each type of ambiguity.
4. Identify the type of ambiguity in each of the following sentences:
    (i)   He was not sure that he has taken a drink.

    (ii)   Vidushi broke her glasses.

   (iii)   I saw the boy with the telescope.

5. Differentiate between natural language processing and natural language generation?

6. Give various interpretations of each of the following sentences. Mention the ambiguity / incorrectness, if present in them.

    (i)   Colorless green ideas sleep furiously.

    (ii)   Fruit flies like a banana.

   (iii)   George Washington was the fifth president of USA.

7. Indicate the type of ambiguity in following sentences.

    (i)   The picture is angry.

    (ii)   The picture is empty.

   (iii)   The English ruled INDIA for a long time

   (iv)   Kishan went out to a restaurant last night. He ordered pizza. When he was going to pay for it, he noticed that he was running out of money. Did Kishan eat pizza?

8. What is morpheme? What is its role in the language?

9. Consider the sentences "Flying Planes are dangerous" and "flying plane is dangerous". give various interpretations of these sentences.

10. The Dog's world grammar is defined as follows:

    1.   sentence « noun_phrase verb_phrase

    2.   noun_phrase « noun

    3.   noun_phrase « art noun

    4.   verb_phrase « verb verb_phrase

    5.   verb_phrase « verb noun_phrase

    6.   article« a

    7.   article « the

    9.   noun « man

   10.   noun « dog

   11.   verb « like

   12.   verb « bites

According to this grammar analyze following sentences:

    (i)   the dog bites the dog.

    (ii)   the big dog bites the man

   (iii)   Emma likes the boy.

   (iv)   the man likes.

    (v)   Bite the man.

        In case, you find some sentences illegal, what changes do you suggest in grammar to incorporate those sentences.

   11.   Give an example how a parser segregates a sentence?

   12.   generate a parse tree of following sentence:

        (i) The man likes the dog.

        (ii) The dog bites the man.

11. Generate the parse tree of following sentence. Choose the required language construct like noun / verb / adjective / adverb yourself.
    (i)   Reasoning is an art and not a science.
    (ii)   To err is human, to forgive divine.
12. Generate a parse tree of the following sentences
    (i)   Piyush wanted to go to market with Ganesh.
    (ii)   I heard the story listening to the radio.
    (iii) I heard the kids listening to the radio.
    (iv)   All books and magazines that deal with controversial topics have been removed from the syllabus.
13. Explain the role of generator in NLP ?
14. Explain how NLP can be used as a grammar analyzer?
15. In the following paragraph, find to which noun, each of the pronoun refers to:
    " Jatin went to a Mall, the sales person asked him how could he help him. He said, he wanted a red shirt. The salesman found one and he tried it on. He paid for it and left."
16. Write an ATN grammar which recognizes verb phrases involving auxiliary verbs. The grammar should handle phrases like "went", " should have gone", " had been going", "would have been going", " would go", " would have gone".
17. Draw the case structure representation of following sentences.
    (i)   The aeroplane flew above the clouds.
    (ii)   Girish flew to Mumbai.
    (iii) The co-pilot flew the plane.
18. How the semantic details can be incorporated in the sentence analysis using case grammar and conceptual dependency. In what ways the two are similar, in what ways they are dissimilar. Compare the two approaches taking following example
    " Jatin broke the window with the hammer"
19. What is meant by case sensitive grammar. Generate a grammar to incorporate the sentence
    " man should not bite dogs, although dog can either like or bite man".
20. Consider a sentence " someone walked slowly to the supermarket" and the following lexicon
    pronoun → someone
    Adv → slowly
    Det → the
    V → walked
    Prep → to
    Noun → supermarket
    Which of the following grammar combined with the lexicon, generates the given sentences. Show the corresponding parse trees.

Grammar 1 :
S → NP VP
NP → Pronoun / Article noun
VP → VP PP / VP Adv / Verb
VP → Verb
PP → Prep NP
NP → Noun

Grammar 2 :
S → NP VP
NP → Pronoun / noun
VP → art NP / Verb Vmod
Vmod → Adv Vmod / Adv
Adv → PP
PP → Prep NP

Grammar 3 :
S → NP VP
P → Pronoun / article NP / Verb Adv
Adv → PP
P → Prep NP
P → Noun

10

Machine Learning, Planning, Understanding

PART—I

10.1 LEARNING: AN INTRODUCTION

Human beings are blessed with several unique characteristics. If you remember, many of these had been identified and listed by Alan Turing and are mentioned in Chapter 1. Learning is also one out of many such types of characteristics that enables humans to acquire new things and to adapt to new situations. Learning is an incessant process. It is done by viewing, listening, interacting with others, studying etc. and also, by experience. Learning helps us in not only acquiring new knowledge but also in refining and updating the knowledge already possessed. It helps us in correcting our mistakes once committed and makes us capable not only to repeat our performance but also to enhance the level of perfection in our performance. Learning provides us power to handle new problems on the basis of similar problems tackled some other time. In all, learning is a unique skill possessed by us that infuses in us power to reason, capability to deal with new situations and in one sense, enables us to act intelligently.

We are intelligent because we possess knowledge of the world. Learning plays a vital role in acquiring this knowledge by human beings. If man is an intelligent machine, apart from having other skills in his possession, he has ability to learn. That means, any machine if at all has to be intelligent, it needs to possess skill of learning. Thus, making a machine intelligent would require making it to learn and hence, machine learning becomes a necessary and challenging assignment apart from being interesting.

However, language understanding and learning are two out of the most vital human skills that are most difficult to computerize. A machine cannot be called intelligent, if it does not have power of learning. Hence, an intelligent machine should be able to learn new things and to adapt to new situations rather than simply doing things as they are told to be done. Over the years, these two areas of language understanding and learning have functioned as goal challenges and touchstones for the scientists and engineers working in the field of AI. Learning is important for practical applications of Artificial Intelligence. Feigenbaum and McCorduck have termed learning as the

'Knowledge Engineering bottleneck' acting as the major obstacle in the wide spread use of intelligent systems.

As stated earlier, nature has provided us so many surprising but indispensable characteristics that make a human being unique among other species present around us. Some of these features are inborn; others are developed unknowingly and automatically along with the growth of our body. We possess them, feel them, recognize them, refine them and also, use them, but we hardly know them. If we are trying to build them, it is necessary for us to first get acquainted with them, and in the process, first step is to define them. It has always been difficult to define these abstract characteristics and the same is true for learning also. We know how to learn, but we do not know the mechanism involved in the process of learning. The general model of learning is described in a Fig. 10.1. There can be numerous aspects to define learning; however, we adopt the definition proposed by one of the ancestors of AI, Hebert Simon. Simon has defined learning as:

"any changes in a system that allows it to perform better the second time on repetition of the same task or on another task drawn from the same population"

Here the input program is any general program executed for solution of a problem. The results are reported as output, but results are also stored back to acquire knowledge for future use. It means, in case similar problem is required to be solved next time, the results can automatically be taken from previously acquired knowledge.

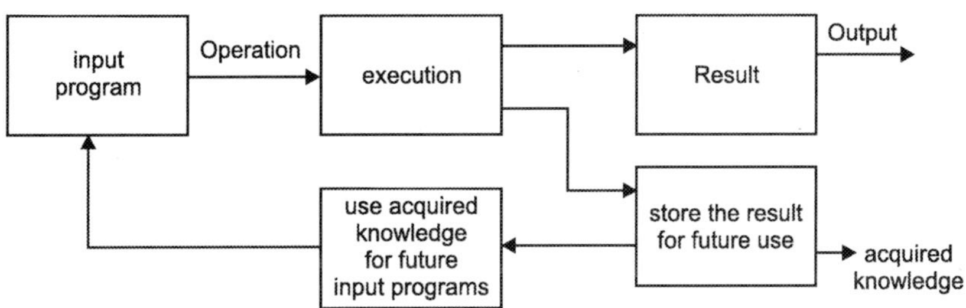

Fig. 10.1: A general learning system

Learning involves generalization from experience. Computer system is said to have learning if it is able to not only do the "repetition of same task" more effectively, but also the similar tasks of the related domain. It covers a wide range of phenomenon. One is knowledge acquisition. It refers to the situation in which computer executes one program and remembers the process for future use. Another is skill refinement, which means ability because of that by doing some task repeatedly people tend to solve the task in lesser time. Thus, by practice skill tends to get refined. The salient features of learning are:

(i) *Skill refinement*: Term skill refinement refers to the situation of improving the skill by performing same task again and again. Human beings also become more accustomed to perform a task more efficiently and perfectly by handling it multiple times. Similar should be applicable to machines. If machines are able to improve their skills with the handling of task, they can be said having skill of learning.

(ii) ***Knowledge acquisition***: The improvement in the skill is because we have a tendency to remember the experience or gain some knowledge by handling the task. This is known as knowledge acquisition. Any machine liable to be called possessing learning capabilities should have tendency and ability to acquire knowledge. Process of knowledge acquisition proceeds in two steps:

In first step the initial knowledge base construction is done. In this step, initial facts regarding some tasks are fed. The second step is refinement of knowledge. In this step, additional knowledge that refines the knowledge base is fed.

10.2 TYPES OF LEARNING

Human beings learn by various ways and methods. In this section we would discuss various types of learning methods in context of machines. Some of these learning methods are:

 (i) Learning through memorization (rote learning)
 (ii) Learning by taking advice (direct instruction)
(iii) Learning by Induction
(iv) Learning by deduction
 (v) Learning by analogy

10.2.1 Rote Learning

It is the most elementary form of learning. In this, the data of a particular task is simply stored (or memorized), e.g., if a game is played, the winning sequence of moves will simply be remembered by the players involved, and next time, instead of selecting a move arbitrarily from all possible moves, they will select a move from among the "winning moves". Hence, by repeatedly remembering the winning situation, the choice of move becomes improved. This technique is also called caching. It is similar to learning by studying in case of human beings. From computational aspect, whenever computer executes some program, it stores the computed values for further use, it will save the computational time in future and later programs will be executed with a faster pace compared to previous ones. This is called data caching. When programs involve extensive computations, requiring more time for computations, then using normal strategy of computations becomes more expensive in terms of time, and data caching saves significant amount of time. Caching is used in many AI programs to produce some surprising performance improvements. One good example of this is Samual's (1963) checkers program. It was designed to store the chess moves played by its creator and thus used to learn the game. It learned to play checkers to such a good extent that ultimately it was able to beat its own creator.

Being elementary in form, the rote learning cannot be used in sophisticated applications. However, this method does possess few capabilities that can be used in complex learning systems. One of these capabilities is, that this method enables the machine to acquire and store organized information. This information can be used as and when repetition of some task is performed because it is always faster to use stored information instead of recollecting it. Though, this method can be of immense use in solving complex problems for saving precious time, it fails when complexities increase in stored information itself and it becomes difficult to access right information at right time. In this situation, we need techniques that are more sophisticated.

The second advantage of this method is that we can get generalized information stored in the database using this kind of learning. The capacity of a system to store information can be unlimited and as long as it keeps on learning, it would keep on adding more and more information. Ultimately, the information and data stored would become unmanageable. Hence, to keep the information stored in the database to manageable limit, it is necessary to generalize the information. This aim can be fulfilled in case of rote learning. If a system is learning by storing the information, it can manage it.

As stated earlier, this is not one of the best methods of learning and in practice, the AI applications use more sophisticated techniques of learning.

10.2.2 Learning by Taking Advice

Out of the many ways to learn, learning by taking advice is one way. In normal life span, human beings use this method quite often. Rather, we learn most of the things in our early life by this method only. Right from our parents, relatives to our teachers, when we start going to school, give us valuable advice as and when required and we learn almost all the initial things and acquire all of the early knowledge through learning by taking advice from others.

We all know that computers have nothing of their own. They function on the basis of the program fed on them. Computer programs are written by programmers. When a programmer writes a computer program, he or she gives many instructions to computer to follow, the same way a teacher gives instructions to his or her students. A computer follows the instructions given by the programmer. Hence, a kind of learning takes place when computer runs a particular program by taking advice from the creator of the program.

Let us consider one example where this form of learning takes place. There is a program known as FOO, described by Mostow(1983), which plays a popular cards game called *"hearts"*. This program takes the advice of the programmer for deciding the moves. Hearts is a game played by four players where each player avoids to score and the player who scores 100 points first, looses the game. There are 26 points at stake in a round and there are thirteen deals in each round. Queen of spade bears 13 points and all the 13 cards of hearts bear 1 point each. However, if a player scores all the 26 points in a round, he scores zero and his all the opponents score 26 points. A programmer would give many instructions or advices to the computer like:

1. A general advice as 'do not take points'.
2. If a deal has a card bearing point, drop the lowest card to loose the deal.
3. If you do not have the card of the category of the deal, drop the queen of the spade if you have it.
4. If luckily in a deal, you get cards so that you can score all the 26 points, do that.

There can be several such types of advices given by the programmer, following those, a computer only plays the game, but also, it defeats you in more rounds than you can anticipate.

10.2.3 Learning by Induction

It is similarity based learning. In this, large number of examples are given and machines learns to perform similar actions in similar situations. In case of human beings also, this form of learning is used frequently. When we are children, our teacher tells us so many things by giving examples. Suppose there are two fruits, one is green apple and other a peas. As an adult, we are able to make a difference easily, however, for a child, it might not be easy to differentiate between above two fruits. In such situations, various examples of both the fruits are given to teach the difference.

Similarly, in our daily life we see many examples of birds flying. Also, there are examples that when there are clouds in the sky, it rains. Based on these examples we formulate certain rules like, 'all birds can fly' and 'clouds bring rain'. When we formulate such types of rules and use them to draw conclusions in given situations, we learn the things by induction. Induction means 'the inferring of general laws from particular instances'. Thus, inductive learning means, generalization of knowledge gathered from real world examples and use of the same for solving other similar problems. Our conclusions drawn on the basis of rules formed from learning by examples, however, this might not always be true, as, generally birds can fly but if the bird in question is an ostrich, our conclusion would be wrong. In spite of that, these rules and the conclusions drawn based on them are very useful. Thus, learning by induction or inductive learning is a method which generalize the rules of past. The production rules in general can be summarized as, "in situation? do action."

The action may be internal action or an inference. Generally, in this, the left hand side is said to be concept and right hand side, the rule. The inductive learning can be represented as:

Situation1	$\rightarrow$	action1
Situation2	$\rightarrow$	action2
Situation n	$\rightarrow$	action n
Situation future	$\rightarrow$	action future

It means, if the knowledge of first 'n' situations and corresponding actions is available, it can give an idea about future action for future situation, e.g., if we say,

Object1 is swan	$\rightarrow$	object1 is white
Object2 is swan	$\rightarrow$	object 2 is white
Object n is swan	$\rightarrow$	object n is white
?x is swan	$\rightarrow$	?x is white

In general, in many AI applications, we create a rule base. The rule base consists of "IF–THEN" type of structures. These are nothing, but the "Situation-Action" sequence. The induction learning method, while solving a particular task using this rule base remembers this "situation – action" sequence and in future, given the similar situation, automatically takes the similar action.

To match the situation, the program follows a matching procedure. The matching procedure should be able to identify the object (e.g. swan) defined in the left part of the rule. Without this matching, the rule can never be invoked. For identification of the object, various classes of the objects are defined. This is, typically called classification.

The salient activities performed in the classification are:

(i) Abstraction of dominant features, relevant to the application. In this, a mathematical function, often called scoring function is created by giving proper weights to these features like,

$$f = w_1 s_1 + w_2 s_2 + \ldots\ldots\ldots + w_n s_n$$

where, s_1, s_2,........ s_n are the salient features and w_1, w_2,..... w_n are their weights according to their significance, e.g., if the task is to judge the student's overall performance, the features s_1, s_2,....... s_n can be marks obtained, personal hygiene, sports participation, obedience, communication skills etc. and w_1, w_2,..... w_n will be associated weights. The values of weights can vary according to application, e.g., from the task of "clearing the exam" the weight w_1 will get the highest value, whereas, in a debate competition, weight w_5 (associated with communication skill) will get more value.

(ii) Isolation of set of features that are relevant to given application. These features are then grouped in to a structure. For example, if the task is to identify various fruits, the features of each fruit such as size, shape, colour, taste etc. can be stored as a structure. Now, a sub-set of this structure is defined as class.

(iii) Creation of a relevant storage structure to store these identified parameters. The choice of data structure is a critical aspect from the computational viewpoint. As discussed earlier, the nature of AI problems are widely different. Accordingly, the type of knowledge required for their solution is different. Hence, the data structure also varies according to that.

10.2.3.1 *Generalization and Specialization*

There are many techniques, which are necessary for applying inductive learning methods. Inductive learning requires an estimate to be made of larger class after observing only few examples of that class. For example, after observing only few crows, by inductive learning we make a guess or an estimate that all the crows are black. This is called the process of generalization.

Specialization is opposite of generalization. Specialization is required when learning algorithm over-generalizes in the search of target concept. For example, after observing clouds and occurrence of rain because of these, we may formulate a general rule that clouds bring rain. But, there are instances when even heavy clouds do not cause rains. Thus, we have to use specialization to restrict the generalization of the observations so that the rule is applicable only to special types of clouds, which cause the rains most of the times.

Generally, any rule consists of variables and constants. Variables are used for generalization, whereas constants are used for specialization. For example, consider the following sentences:

Sparrow can fly.
Parrot can fly.
Crow can fly.

From these observations, a rule is formulated as:
Birds can fly.

Here, 'sparrow', 'parrot' and 'crow' are constants and are used in specialized rules, whereas, 'birds' is variable, and is used in generalized rule. Hence, one method to specialize a rule is to change variables in to constants. Other methods to specialize are adding a conjunct, removing a disjunct and taking out exceptions from any description. These methods are used as and when required and are useful tools for constructing knowledge structures.

Similarly, there are methods for generalization. These are discussed as follows:

Changing constants to variables

This method can be understood from the above mentioned example, where constants like 'sparrow', 'parrot' and 'crow' are changed in to variable 'birds' to form a generalized rule as 'birds can fly.' In the process of generalization, the learning programs must follow a definite direction and order of search, as well as should use the available training data and heuristics to search efficiently. For example, suppose a learning program is given following training input data:

$$size(obj1, small) \land color(obj1, white) \land shape\ (obj1, round)$$

the learner will take this input as candidate concept and will classify this as the only positive instance seen. If the algorithm is given another positive instance, like:

$$size(obj2, large) \land color(obj2, white) \land shape\ (obj2, round),$$

the learner would generalize the two candidate concepts by replacing constants with variables and will form a rule as:

$$size(X, Y) \wedge color(X, white) \wedge shape(X, round)$$

Dropping conditions

By dropping one or more conditions from the description, we may generalize the same, e.g., S is a set such that S= {all the white balls}. If we drop the condition 'white' then the set S will be {all the balls}, and hence, it will represent more general description of the objects under consideration.

Climbing a generalization tree

If we are able to represent the classes of objects in the form of a tree maintaining a hierarchy, we can achieve generalization by simply climbing the tree to a node, which is higher and hence, gives a more general description of the object class. For example, a tree is shown in the following Fig. 10.2, in which, if we move up, say from electrons, we get more general class description of matter.

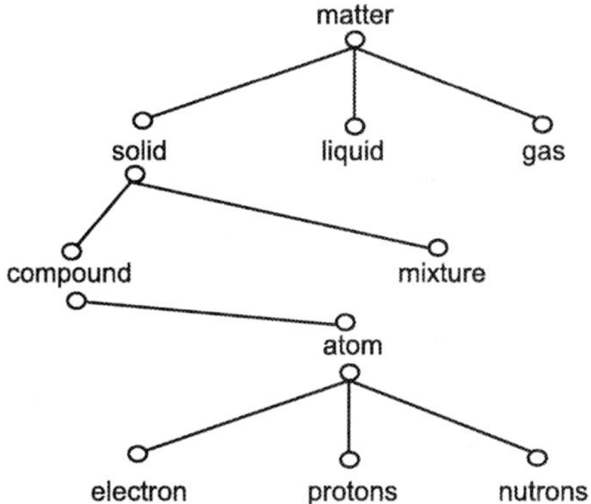

Fig 10.2: Generalization tree

Adding an alternative

In this method of generalization, an alternative is added to the possible objects and in this way, the resulting description becomes more general. For example, in one of the examples mentioned above, if we add one more class of objects as S = {set of all white balls and all red balls}, then the description becomes more general.

Closing an interval

It is method of performing more restricted form of generalization than changing constants in to variables. When the given domain of descriptor is ordered, i.e. $(x_1 < x_2 < x_3 < \ldots\ldots x_n)$ and few values lie in a small interval, we can generalize the values to a closed interval. For example, if two instances are given as, $X = x_i$ and

$X = x_j$, where $x_i < x_j$, we can make a generalization as $X = \{ x_i \ldots\ldots x_j \}$. That means, X can have any value in the interval x_i to x_j.

There are many other methods of generalization, which are not used frequently.

10.2.3.2 Winston's Learning Program

In the field of learning by induction, Winston has done a pioneer work. His program is called Winston's learning program. The Winston's learning program and other related concepts are discussed in this section.

The Empiricist Algorithm

The empiricist algorithm is based on getting the empirical data about the application and based on the analysis of this large amount of data, learning is performed. The large amount of data creates a context about the application. This context is considered as general knowledge or commonsense knowledge about the application. The situations where general knowledge is available with the system, the new instances may weaken or strengthen its antecedent. An antecedent is stronger, if it says more about the incident, e.g. suppose a robot has inferred the rule "(ins ?x feline) should (pet ?x)" (means, if x is an instance of feline then x can be considered as pet) from observation of several house cats. Now if robot uses this rule "when ?x is a tiger" and interprets the tiger as pet, it will cause severe problems. This experience tends to disconfirm the rule. When a rule is disconfirmed, the proper response is usually not to discard it but to specialize (or typecast) it, so that it applies to fewer situations, e.g., in above example, to define the tiger, the rule can be further specialized as "if a feline has size bigger than 1 feet, it can not be considered as pet. (Or, here actual characteristics of tiger can be added, which differentiates it from cat) Accordingly, the program must find a way to distinguish situations involving felines, in which petting was rewarded from those in which it was punished. This can be done like "(inst ?x feline) (size ?x small) – should (pet ?x)". Here, adding a conjunct to the antecedent of the rule strengthens it so that it is satisfied in fewer situations. An empiricist algorithm automatically generates a specialized rule if it is not applicable in present form. In general care also, the machine should be able to generate a specialized rule in the situation when the selected rule is not applicable in present form.

By summarizing the above discussion, we realize that the problem is to find a pattern, or concept definition that applies to one set of situations and does not apply to another; or to generalize from the positive instances to a general pattern but not up to the extent so that it includes any of the negative instances.

Many programs have been written using this method. Winston conducted one of the most important studies, among all. The rule it learned had conclusions of the form (inst ?x category). Where category was some class objects that could be built out of blocks as "arch". That means it learned the concept of arch. It was tested by giving many related objects some of which were arches and some were not. Following arch and non-arch descriptions were given to it in the form of predicate calculus:

Description of arch

(on a1 a2) (on a1 a3)   (not touch a2 a3)
(parts a {a1 a2 a3})
(inst a1 brick) (inst a2 brick) (inst a3 brick)
(inst a arch)

A typical arch described as above is shown in the following Fig. 10.3.

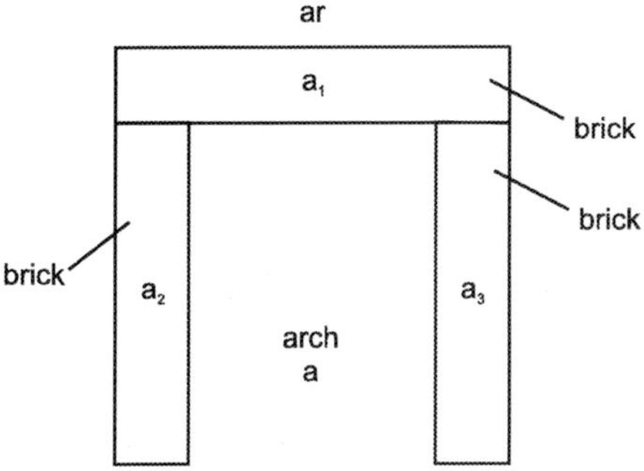

Fig. 10.3: Arch 'a' with brick-top

Description of non- arch

Assume b1, b2, b3 are objects of non-arch category placed in the following configuration:

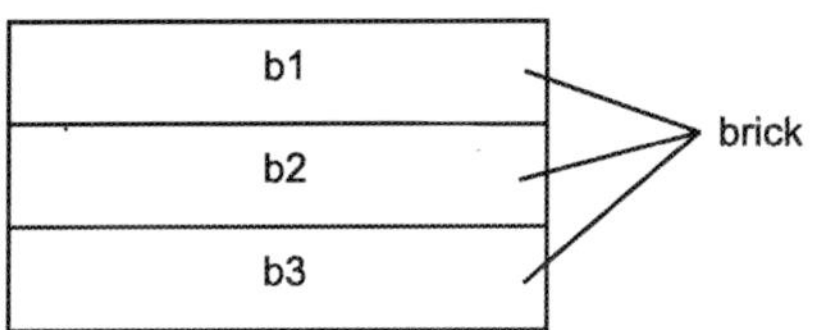

Fig. 10.4: A non-arch

Its description is:
(on b1 b2) (on b2 b3)
(parts b { b1 b2 b3})
(inst b1 brick) (inst b2 brick) (inst b3 brick)
(non (inst b arch)

Winston's program refines candidate descriptions given as above through generalization and specialization. Generalization changes the graph to let it accommodate new examples. Suppose, a new example with following description is added to algorithm:

(on a1 a2) (on a1 a3)   (not touch a2 a3)
(parts a {a1 a2 a3})
(inst a1 pyramid) (inst a2 brick) (inst a3 brick)
(inst a arch)

The Fig. 10.5 of arch generated based on above description is shown below:

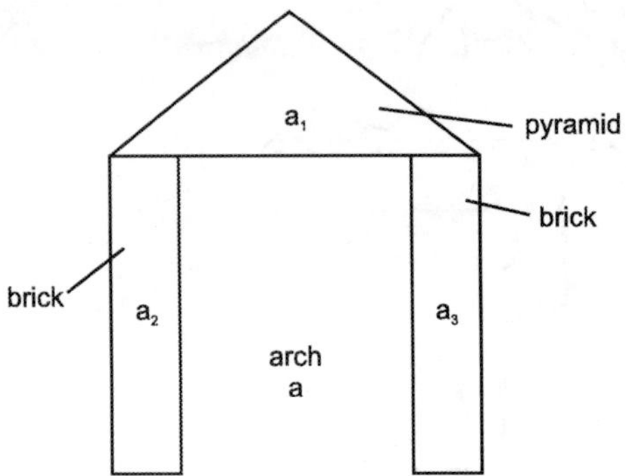

Fig. 10.5: Arch 'a' with pyramid-top

Now, when a learning program gets two examples of arches described and shown above, it matches these graphs and detects the differences between them. The graph matches all the components except the top elements. In first case, the top element is a brick and in second case, it is a pyramid. In this situation, the program generalizes the graph by replacing the constants by variable. Thus, the constants brick and pyramid are replaced by the variable 'polygon'. The generalized description becomes:

(on a1 a2) (on a1 a3)   (not touch a2 a3)
(parts a {a1 a2 a3})
(inst a1 polygon) (inst a2 brick) (inst a3 brick)
(inst a arch)

Notice one aspect in the above descriptions of the candidates. If we remove the condition (not touch a2 a3), we might get a arch shown in the following Fig 10.6:

This type of situation is called *near miss*. When a near miss is encountered, or an example is introduced that differs from the target concept (which is arch in this case), the program uses specialization to exclude the example and uses 'not touch' link to exclude the near miss.

These operations, generalization by replacing links with a more general concept and specialization by adding links, define a space of possible concepts. Winston's program performs a hill-climbing search on the concept space, which is guided by the examples given to the program. The order of the examples is very important in this case, because the program does not back-track, hence, a bad ordering may

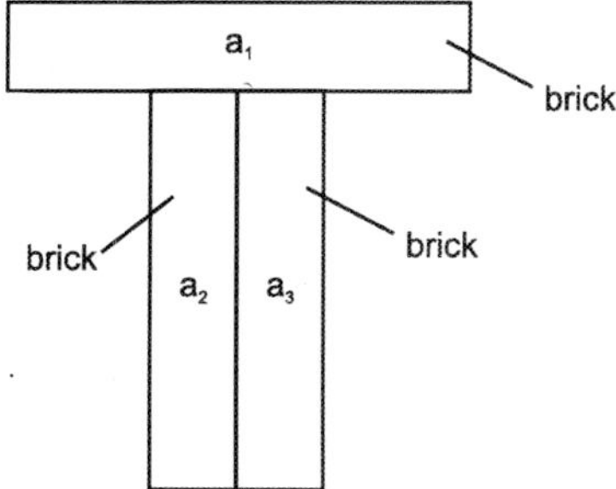

Fig. 10.6: A graph showing near-miss

result in the dead ends in search space. Training examples, i.e., the examples fed in the learning program must be presented in such a way so that they assist the program to learn the desired concept, in a similar fashion as a teacher organizes lessons for students to learn. The quality of training examples is also important for graph to perform matching. Efficient matching requires that there should not be too much dissimilarity among the graphs. We would learn about the concept of matching in the following section.

Winston's program was given enough positive and negative instances of the concept like 'arch'. The program learned from this and was able to infer its definition shown below:

if and   (part $?x$ {$?x_1$, $?x_2$, $?x_3$})
           (on $?x_1$ $?x_2$)
           (on $?x_1$ $?x_3$)
           (not (touch $?x_2$ $?x_3$))
       (inst $?x$ arch)

Winston's program, in spite of being an early example in the field of inductive learning, presents the features and problems that are shared by majority of machine learning techniques.

Matching

Matching describes a relationship between abstract pattern and concrete one. Variants of empiricist algorithms are generated by exploring different ways of processing parts of following Fig. 10.7.

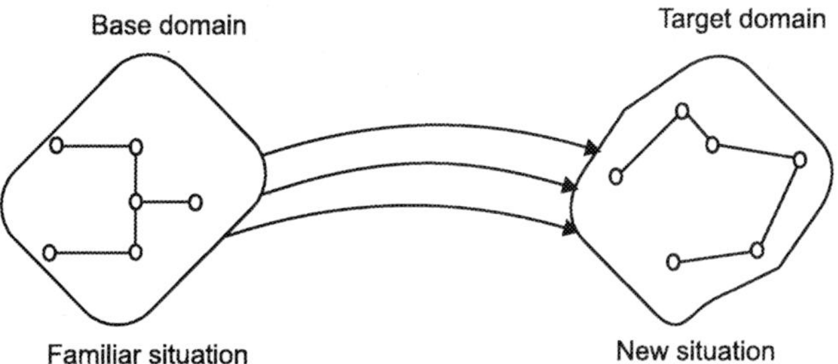

Fig. 10.7:

Deriving a relationship from general situation to individual situation is called abstraction mapping. Deriving an individual pattern from general pattern is instantiation, in which variables are replaced with constants.

A matching algorithm derives all set of input conjuncts. It looks for the conjuncts, which have maximum matching in all objects and report that as answer. Let us take an example.

Suppose that f = {(colour   ? x red); (size   ? x large), (shape   ? x cube)} and suppose s includes following data

(color ob1 red)   (color ob2 green)   (color ob3 blue)
(size ob1 small)   (size ob2 large)   (size ob3 small)
(shape ob1 sphere)   (shape ob2 cube)   (shape ob3 cube)

According to the given query the best match has {x = ob2} with just one difference i.e. (color ob2 red), there will be two miss matches i.e. (size ob1 large) and (shape ob1 cube). Thus in such problems minimum mismatch is reported.

10.2.4 Symbol Based Learning

The symbol based learning considers the basic representation of knowledge as elementary symbols. It consists of three basic operations:

1. ***Specification of data and goal:*** One of the primary ways to characterize learning problems is based on two basic components, i.e. (i) goals of learner, and (ii) the given data. Accordingly, there are two basic approaches of learning algorithms. One is data intensive approach and other is goal intensive approach. The data intensive approach is based on the collection of more number of negative and positive examples of target class and thus performing learning using solution of these data; and goal intensive approach is based on starting with general concept about a phenomenon and inferring from simple training example. The explanation based learning falls in later category.

    We can also characterize a learning algorithm by the goal or target. The goal of many learning algorithms is a concept, or general description of a class of object. Learning algorithms may acquire problem solving heuristics or other forms of procedural knowledge. The properties and qualities of training data are also one dimension along which we specify learning tasks. The data may come from outside environment or it may be generated by program itself. Out of the total data, some data may be redundant or in an organized form, or it may be less then required, needing more data acquisition.

2. ***Representation of learned knowledge***: Machine learning programs make use of all representations discussed here, e.g. programs that learn to classify objects represent these concepts as in predicate calculus form or they may use a structured representation such as frames or objects.

    In learning problems, the concepts are represented as conjunctive sentences containing variable, e.g. two instances of ball may be represented as size (obj1, small), color (obj1, red), shape(obj1, round) and size (obj2, large), color (obj2, red), shape(obj2, round).

The general concept of "ball" could be defined as:

$$\text{Size } (x, y), \text{ color } (x, z), \text{ shape } (x, \text{round})$$

Where variable 'x' indicates the object 'ball', 'y' indicates its size and 'z' indicates its color. The shape of a ball is bound to be round, hence shape does not have variable. It has constant as 'round'. To draw a conclusion whether given object is ball, if object's description matches (or unifies) with this description, it can be declared as ball.

3. ***Set of operations***: After going through the training session, the learner should generate a heuristic rule or plan objecting its goal. This requires the ability to manipulate representations. Typical operations include generalizing or specializing symbolic expressions, adjusting the weights in a neural network or otherwise modifying the program's representation.

The generalizations are created by replacing the constants with variables, e.g. the description of a ball

$$\text{size } (z, \text{small}), \text{ color } (z, \text{blue}), \text{ shape } (z, \text{round})$$

will declare object "z, a small blue ball". The description of a ball of any size and any color would be:

$$\text{size } (z, ?), \text{ color } (z, ?), \text{ shape } (z, \text{round})$$

10.2.5 Identification Trees

"Identification" is important learning method. It is a tree representation of any problem indicating all possibilities. That means it is a kind of decision tree. The identification trees can be created for medical diagnoses, property, geological surveys etc.

Consider a situation where, many students of a class were examined on certain parameters. The aim was to test the overall performance of the students. Thus, the aim is finding the student requiring extra coaching. The observations are listed in the following Table 10.1:

Table 10.1: Observations about various students

Name	Marks	Hygiene	Health	confidence	Result
Adwet	90%	excellent	good	excellent	☞
Milind	92%	excellent	excellent	good	☞
Gaurav	90%	good	poor	average	♦
Piyush	85%	average	good	good	♦
Vartika	60%	good	excellent	average	♦

The identification tree would be like the one shown below:

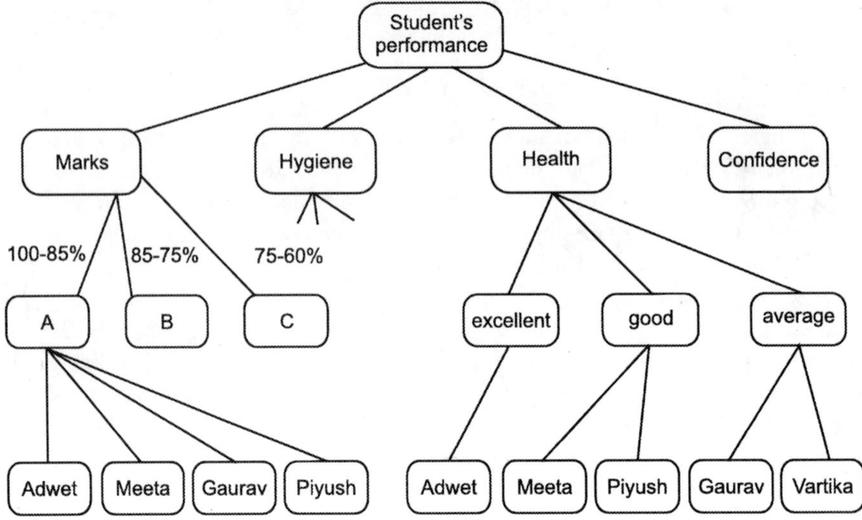

Fig. 10.8: Identification tree

These identification trees represent the data like a railroad switch yard. Each unknown object is directed down one branch or another at each test according to its property knowledge. To be effective, the newly acquired knowledge should be integrated with existing knowledge in some meaningful way so that nontrivial inferences can be drawn from the resultant body of knowledge. The knowledge should be accurate, non redundant, consistent, and computable.

10.2.6 Explanation Based Learning

As discussed above, there are primarily two approaches of learning, i.e. data intensive approach and knowledge intensive approach. In the data intensive approach (like rote leaning), the main emphasis is given on data. Large number of positive and negative examples are given to the machine and based on the outcomes of these examples, the machine learns. The explanation based learning is knowledge intensive approach. It is a kind of analogical learning. It is also called situation based learning. In this, more emphasis is given on knowledge. There are certain applications where instead of data, the knowledge plays more important role, e.g. chess playing, medical diagnosis. In such types of applications, a critical situation is handled and machine is given the example to handle this situation. This is explanation based learning. Here, one example in form of a knowledge solution or past experience is sufficient for learning a new solution.

e.g. consider the following configuration in game of chess:

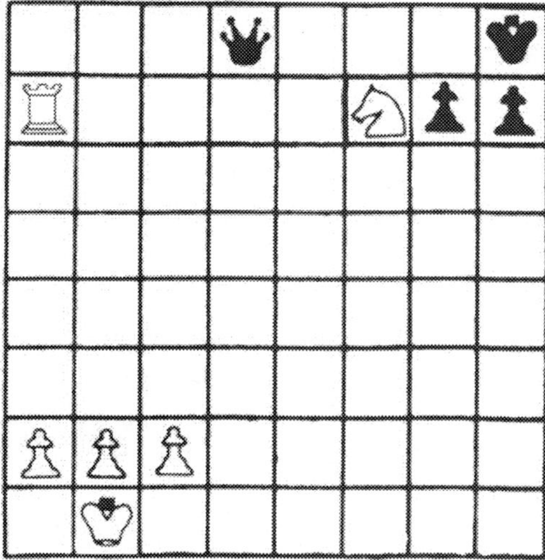

Fig. 10.9: Configuration of chess game in fork position

Here, the white knight is attacking the black king and black queen both. Black is bound to save his king, therefore the queen is bound to be captured. This situation is called fork position. This situation can be generalized as, if any piece of opponent attacks both king and any other piece, the other piece is bound to be captured. Hence, it is very critical situation. In the chess game, one cannot become a good player if he is not able to handle such types of critical situations. Moreover, there will not be dozens of such type of critical situations, but one situation will be enough for loosing a game. Handling one such situation will be enough for learning to handle this. Such type of learning is based on knowledge. The chess player may have plenty of domain specific knowledge that can be brought to bear. That knowledge can be used to identify critical aspects of training example. In case of fork, the double simultaneous attack is important rather than the positions of pieces.

Hence, in general, we can say that in case of explanation based learning, the emphasis is given to learn more by taking the critical examples, rather than by having more examples. In this, one positive training example is given to machine in order to perform the learning. In explanation based learning, the learned knowledge is valid knowledge. It is obtained by performing a deductive reasoning process on a set of facts. In EBL while solving a problem its salient features are abstracted. These features are given below:

(i)   Formal statement about goal

(ii) Minimum one training example

(iii) Domain theory that relates to the concept and training example

(iv) Criteria for applying an operator.

This information is stored in the knowledge base. While solving a new problem using this method, a matching is performed of new problem details with existing problem details. If partial matching occurs, that solution is taken from the knowledge base and modified according to new problem.

Just to summarize what has been discussed so far, we can say that an EBL program attempts to learn from a single example by explaining why is it an example of target concept. When program formalizes the explanation, it generalizes this explanation and stores for further use. The system thus learns and its performance improves through knowledge acquired in this fashion.

There are number of benefits offered by explanation based learning. These are presented as follows:

1. Training examples often contain irrelevant information. The domain-theory of explanation based learning enables the learner to select the relevant aspects of the training examples.
2. There can be many possible generalizations of a given example. Most of these generalizations are either useless or wrong with respect to the goal space. EBL forms generalizations that are relevant to the specific goals and are almost guaranteed to be logically consistent with the domain theory.
3. EBL allows learning from a single training instance.
4. Construction of an explanation enables the learner to hypothesize unstated relationships between its goals and its experience.

Winston's system was an analogical learning system developed for exhibiting the natural language understanding. Using relationship and acts of action in one story, it was designed to understand it. Based on the understanding, it was able to comprehend other similar stories having similarities among relationships and motives of second group of characters. It was able to learn through analogical reasoning process.

The salient features of Winston's learning system are:

(i) It used frame based representation for storing knowledge. Slots within the frames were given special meaning such as 'AKO (A Kind Of)', 'appear-in', etc. Individual frames are linked together.
(ii) If the system was given similar situation, it was able to recall similar previous situation. According to current situation, analogous previous situations were retrieved from memory. Memory used hierarchical indexing scheme.
(iii) Similarity matching procedure was adopted in the best of known situations during the reminding process. For recall candidate, similarity matching score is computed. This score is computed for all pairing between two frames and the pairing having the highest score is selected as proper analogue.

The explanation based learning is a form of deductive learning where the learner develops a logical explanation of how the positive training example defines a concept. In this, in first step, explanation of first concept is formulated using training example and domain theory and then, it is generalized by regression formulae.

10.2.7 Transformational Analogy

Learning with this approach is based on the concept of "Means Ends Analysis" of problem solving. In this approach, problem solutions are indexed and stored for later retrieval. The solutions are stored in form of initial state, goal state and sequence of actions. The method is called transformational analogy, because when the same sequence of operators are applied on same set of initial and final states, it results in the same transformations (i.e., problem solution). A new problem is first matched against potentially relevant known problem solution using similarity measurement. In transformational analogy, the main emphasis is given on transforming a set of states and not on the derivation process.

10.2.8 Society Based Learning

The society Based learning describes the learning by human being from the interactions with the society. A very important and relevant theory called "the game of life" was given by mathematician John Hortron Conway and appeared in Scientific American (1970). The game of life is a simple example of a model of computation called cellular automata. Cellular automata are families of simple finite state machines that exhibit interesting and emergent behaviors through their interactions in population.

10.2.8.1 The game of life

The game of life is basically developed to explain the evolution of life in AI terminology. The life game is explained below:

Consider the simple two dimensional grid (called 'game board of life') as shown in following Fig. 10.10. Here the shaded regions indicates the set of neighbours for the "game of life".

Here, we have one black square surrounded with its eight nearest neighbours indicated by gray shaded cells on the board. The board is transformed over time-periods, where the state of each square at time t+1 is a function of its own present state and its immediate neighbours present state. Following three rules drive evolution in the game.

1. If any square whether occupied or not has exactly three of its nearest neighbours occupied, it will be occupied in the next time period.
2. If any occupied square has exactly two of its nearest neighbours occupied, it will be occupied in the next time period.
3. For all other situations, the square will not be occupied at the next time period.

One interesting interpretation of these rules is, for each generation or time period, life at any location will survive or not, will depend upon its own as well

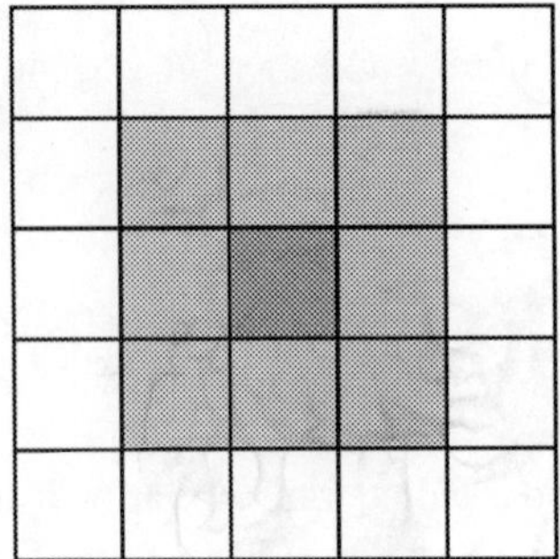

Fig. 10.10: The game board of life

as its neighbours life during the previous generation. In the grid, the life at any location is represented by 1. That means, too dense a population of surrounding neighbours (more than three) or too sparse a neighboring (less than two) at any time period will not allow life for the next generation. It gives the concept of "Artificial Life". Artificial life is defined as "life made by human effort rather than by nature". Thus, any board pattern where a cell is surrounded by exactly three shaded cells, will survive in the next time cycle.

This is shown in the following Fig. 10.11.

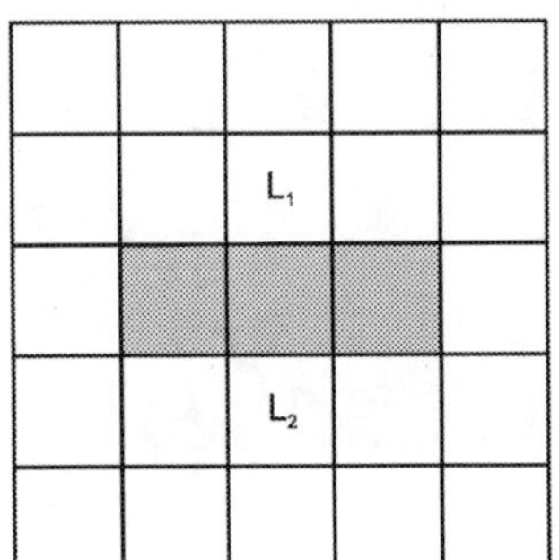

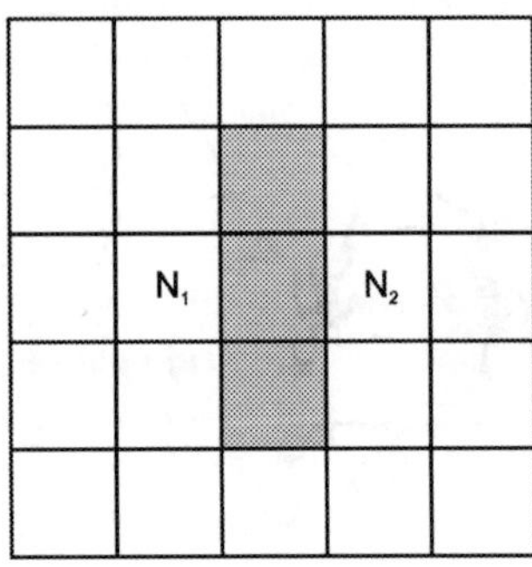

Fig. 10.11a: A set of neighbours indicating presence of life in next cycle

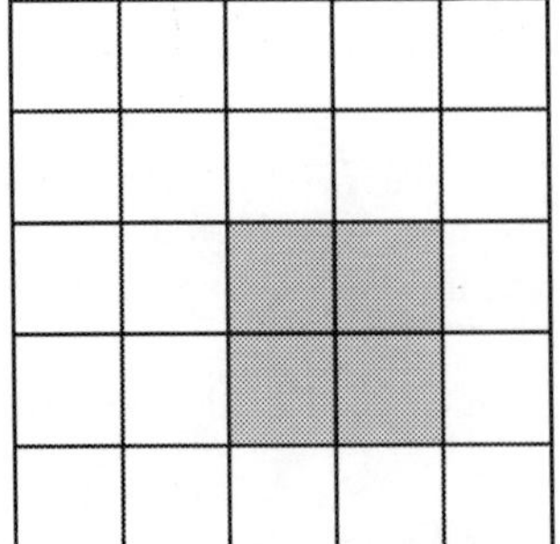

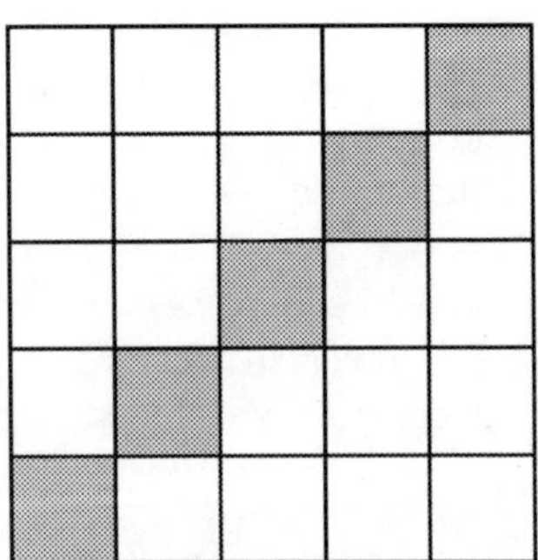

Fig. 10.11b: A set of neighbours indicating no presence of life in next cycle

Here, exactly two squares indicated by L1 and L2 have three neighbours, at the next life cycle it will survive and produce state N1 and N2. Hence, population appearing in this cellular configuration will survive, whereas in following patterns as the neighboring states of A1, A2 and B1, B2 has two neighbours, they will not survive.

10.3 GENETIC ALGORITHM

It is an example of biological learning. It is based on analyzing how the evolution of human beings took place. Natural evolution procedures are generally analyzed in genetic algorithms. Genetic algorithms are based on the ideas that are analogous in some ways to individual mating, chromosome crossover, gene mutation, fitness and natural selection.

In biological system, each cell contains a nucleus, which in turn contains chromosomes. Earlier, in nineteenth century, chromosomes were identified as custodians of the trait determining factors, traditionally called genes. Genes are wrapped along chromosomes like cars on a railroad section.

Genetic algorithms are method of breeding computer programs and solutions to optimization or search problems by means of simulated evolution process loosely based on natural selection, crossover and mutation are repeatedly applied to a population of binary strings, which represent potential solutions. A typical genetic algorithm requires two things to be defined:

(i)   A genetic representation of the solution domain
(ii) A fitness function to evaluate the solution domain.

In genetic based learning, the standard method equates fitness with relative quantity. In general, the fitness of a chromosome is the probability that the chromosome survives to the next generation. Accordingly we need a formula that relates the fitness of ith chrosomoe "f_i", a probability ranging from 0 to 1. To the quality of corresponding object qi, a number ranging from 1 to 9.

The following formula in which the sum is over all candidates, is one possibility

$$Fi = qi / Ej\ Qj$$

Henceforth, the use of this formula is referred to as standard method for fitness computation.

The rank method links fitness to quality rank

The standard method for determining fitness provides you with no way to influence selection. One alternative is to use the rank method, which not only offers a way of controlling the bias towards the best chromosome, but also eliminates implicit biases, introduced by unfortunate choices of the measurement scale, that might otherwise do harm.

Basically, the rank method ignores quality measurements, as those measurements serve to rank the candidates from the highest quality to the lowest quality. Then the fitness of highest quality candidate among the ranked candidate is some fixed constant P. If the best candidate, the one ranked number 1 is not selected, then the next best candidate, the one ranked number 2 is selected with fitness P. This selection process continues until a candidate is selected or there is only one left. In which case, that last candidate is selected.

PART—II

10.4 PLANNING

Various actions are required to solve a problem, either big or small. If a given problem is attempted for its appropriate solution, the likely actions to be taken, if decided and applied in a logical sequence, would find the solution easily and timely. For this, we need to do 'planning' before starting the process to find the solution. The planning we are going to discuss, is similar to the planning we do before say, constructing our house or before starting a journey. For constructing a house, number of actions take place. These actions have to be selected and taken in a definite sequence for the smooth running and completion of the task, otherwise, the things might turn haphazard. A good planning could take care of the types and sequence of actions to be applied. Thus, *planning is finding a sequence of actions that will achieve a goal.*

In chapter 2 & 3 we have discussed the basic problem formulation of AI and the solution finding techniques using state space representation and search techniques. The state space represents complete solution prospect and the search starts with the initial condition, applies the valid operators on current states and finds the path to reach up to goal state. The search technique can be blind or informed. The blind search techniques are useful for small scale problems. Though informed search techniques reduce the search space to a large extent, but still for very big problems, finding the total state space and using search techniques for finding a solution becomes tiresome.

For more complicated problem domain it becomes important to be able to work on small pieces of problem separately and then to combine the partial solution at the end into a complete problem situation. If we do not do this, the number of the states of components of a problem becomes too large to handle in the amount of time available.

The state definition of a problem like 8-puzzle is easy. However, if we consider the problem of guiding a robot around an ordinary house, the state description demands description of every object in the house. This makes the problem very complex. A given action on the part of robot will change only a small part of total state. If the robot pushes a chair across the room, then relative location of chair and other objects will change. However, location of other object relative to each other will not change.

The problem definition may be made easier by describing only those parts of problem, which are dynamic. Thus, the decomposition can make the solution of hard problems easier. The AO* algorithm provides a way of doing this when it is possible to decompose the original problems into completely separate sub problems. This type of breaking problems into multiple sub problems is normally possible in large range of problems. However, there are certain problems where it does not work. Simon (1981) has called such problems as "nearly decomposable" by which, we mean that they can be divided into sub problems that have only a small amount of interaction, e.g., if we want to move all the furniture out of a room, the problem can be broken into smaller problems of moving small pieces of furniture out of room. Within each of these sub problems considerations such as drawers can be addressed separately for each piece of furniture. However, if there were shelf behind the sofa, then we must move the sofa, before we can move the shelf. Hence, shelf and sofa can be viewed as a single object. To solve such nearly decomposable problems, we would like a method that enables us to work on each sub problems separately, using techniques such as the ones we have already studied, and then to record potential interaction among sub problem and to handle them appropriately.

The methods to solve problem using the technique of decomposition is "planning". The planning refers to the process of computing several steps of the problem solving procedure before executing any of them. Here, it must be noted that there is a difference in "planning the action" and "performing the action". The planning refers to checking out the sequence of action required to fulfill the task, and performing means actually doing those activities. In solving the 8-puzzle, it cannot actually push any title around. So when we talk about the computer solution of 8-puzzle problem, what we are really doing is outlining the way, the computer might generate a plan for solving it. For problems like 8-puzzle, the distinction between planning and doing is important. Nevertheless, in the problems where backtracking is not allowed or the path once followed cannot be undone, this planning is very important. In some problems, though, real world steps may be irrevocable, computer simulation of those steps is not. So we can circumvent the constraint of real world by looking for a complete solution in a simulated world in which, backtracking is allowed.

10.4.1 Components of Planning System

The basic components of a problem solving system follows the steps mentioned below:

  (i) Select best rule to apply based on the best available heuristic information.

  (ii) Apply chosen rule to compute new problem state that arises from its application.

  (iii) Stop, if goal has been achieved.

  (iv) Detect dead ends, so that they can be abandoned and the system's efforts proceed in more fruitful direction.

In big and complicated problems, instead of these activities following action is also performed:

(v) Detect, when almost correct solution is found and employ special techniques to make it totally correct.

10.4.2 Terminology of Block World Planning System

The technique of planning was applied to handle block world problem. The block world domain is defined as follows:

There is a flat surface on which blocks can be placed. There are number of square blocks all of the same size. They can be stacked one upon another. There is a robot arm that can manipulate the block. The available operators are:

(i) UNSTACK (A, B) – Pickup block A from its current position which is on block B. The arm must be empty and block A must have no blocks on top of it.

(ii) STACK (A, B) – Place block A on block B. The arm must already be holding A and the surface of B must be clear.

(iii) PICKUP (A) – Pickup block A from the table and hold it. The arm must be empty and there must be nothing on top of block A.

(iv) PUTDOWN (A) – Put block A down on the table. The arm must have been holding block A.

There are certain initial states on which the conditions are applicable (Known as preconditions). These states are listed as follows:

ON (A,B)	-	Block A is on Block B
ONTABLE (A)	-	Block A is on the table
CLEAR (A)	-	there is nothing on top of Block A
HOLDING (A)	-	the arm is holding block A
ARMEMPTY	-	the arm is holding nothing.

The FOPL statements corresponding to this block world are:

$[\exists x: \text{HOLDING}(x)] \rightarrow \neg \text{ARMEMPTY}$ (i.e. if the arm is holding anything, then it is not empty)

$\forall x: \text{ONTABLE}(x) \rightarrow \neg \exists y: \text{ON}(x, y)$ (i.e. if a block is on the table, then it is not on another block)

$\forall x: [\neg \exists y: \text{ON}(y, x)] \rightarrow \text{CLEAR}(x)$ (i.e. any block is clear, if no block is on it)

The basic description of block world is as shown in Fig. 10.12:

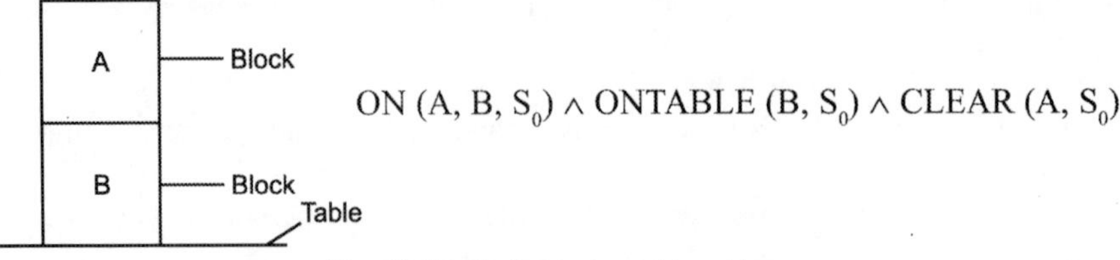

$$\text{ON}(A, B, S_0) \wedge \text{ONTABLE}(B, S_0) \wedge \text{CLEAR}(A, S_0)$$

Fig. 10.12: Basic block world problem

There are STRIPS operators devised for block world. These are as follows:

STACK (x, y)
        P : CLEAR (y) $\wedge$ HOLDING (x)
        D : CLEAR (y) $\wedge$ HOLDING (x)
        A : ARMEMPTY $\wedge$ ON (x, y)
UNSTACK (x, y)
        P : ON (x, y) $\wedge$ CLEAR (x) $\wedge$ ARMEMPTY
        D : ON (x, y) $\wedge$ ARMEMPTY
        A : HOLDING (x) $\wedge$ CLEAR (y)
PICKUP (x)
        P : CLEAR (x) $\wedge$ ONTABLE (x) $\wedge$ ARMEMPTY
        D : ONTABLE (x) $\wedge$ ARMEMPTY
        A : HOLDING (x)
PUTDOWN (x)
        P : HOLDING (x)
        D: HOLDING (x)
        A: ONTABLE (x) $\wedge$ ARMEMPTY

Here P stands for precondition list, D stands for deletion list and A stands for addition list. It means, to apply an operator the existing state should match with the precondition, and after applying the operator, the delete conditions should be removed from the list and the "add conditions" should be added to the list, e.g., in order for an arm to pickup a block, the block must have no other block on the top of it. After it is picked up, it still has no block on top of it.

Similarly, once robot PUTDOWN block x, it should initially hold it, and after putting down its arm will be empty and the block will be on the table.

The components of planning system are implemented as follows:

(1) *Selection of rule* – the most widely used technique for selection of a operator is first to isolate set of difference between desired goal state and current state, then identify rules that are relevant to reducing those differences. If multiple rules are applicable then heuristic information is used to select most appropriate rule.

(2) *Applying rule* – in second step, the selected rule is applied. If the rule is directly applicable on the current state it is applied, otherwise first certain other rule, which brings the current state, to a state where present rule is applicable, is chosen.

10.4.3 Identifying a Solution

It is must for planning system to be able to identify the solution. For simple problem solving systems, this question is easily answered by a straightforward match of state description. However, if entire states are not represented explicitly, but rather are described by a set of relevant properties, then this problem becomes more complex. For any problem representational scheme, it must be possible to reason with representation to discover whether one matches another. There can be multiple representational schemes that could be used to describe problem state. Then any one scheme can be used to describe problem state. However, the corresponding reasoning mechanism should be used to discover when a solution has been found.

One good problem representation technique, which is used in many planning systems is predicate logic. It provides a deductive mechanism, which is found to be an attractive option for finding the goal.

Identification of dead ends in search of solution is typical aspect. While finding the solution it may be possible that a dead end is encountered. The dead end is the problem state where there are no applicable operators left and the solution is not reached. As planning system is searching for a sequence of operators to solve a particular problem, it must be able to detect a dead end while it is exploring a path for a solution.

If the search process is reasoning forward from the initial state, it can abandon any path that leads to a state from which the goal state cannot be reached, e.g., suppose we have fixed a supply of paint colored red, white and pink. We want to paint a room so that it has light red walls and white ceiling. We can produce light red paint by adding some white paint to the red colored paint. However, then white paint will not be left for ceiling. So, the approach of mixing the red and white paints together should be abandoned. We should also abandon paths that appear to be leading no closer to a solution than the place from which they started.

Similarly, a backward moving search can be dropped because either it is sure that the initial state cannot be reached or because little progress is being made. In the backward reasoning each goal is decomposed into subgoals. Each of them, in turn, may lead to a set of additional subgoals. Sometimes it is easy to detect that there is no way that all the subgoals in a given set can be satisfied at once, e.g., the robot arm can not be both empty and holding a block. Any path that is attempting to make both goals true simultaneously can be pruned immediately. Other paths also can be pruned if they do not make any progress.

10.4.3.1 *Performing fine tuning on the solution*

The solution finding strategies discussed so far, work on the belief that problems are completely decomposable and they proceed to solve the subproblems separately. A slightly better approach of problem solution is to look at the situation that results when the sequence of operations corresponding to the proposed solution is executed, and to compare that situation with the desired goal. This difference is obtained and an operator is selected to reduce this difference. This solution finding strategy is based on the principle of finding an almost correct solution in least number of steps; and then fine-tune the solution to obtain correct and complete solution.

10.4.4 Goal Stack Planning

One of the earliest techniques of solving compound goals was used in STRIPS. It was basically developed for block world and it generates a plan for moving block for achieving a specific goal. In this method, the problem solver makes use of single action that contains both goals and operators that have been proposed to satisfy these goals. The problem solver relies on database that describes current situation, and the set of situations described as PRECONDITION, ADD and DELETE lists.

The functioning of goal stack planning is explained through following block world example.

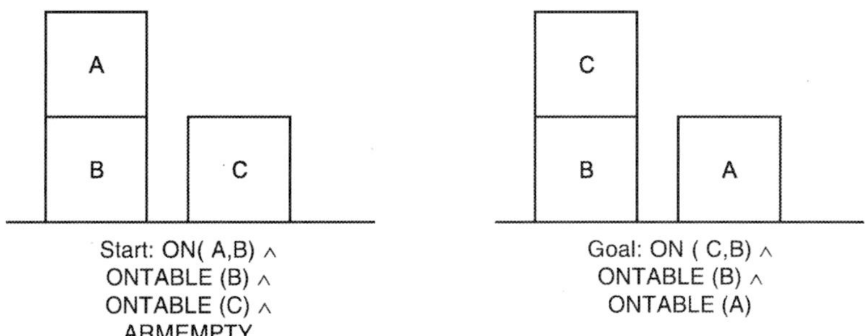

Consider following block world configuration of start and goal state.
Let us start with the goal state and try to satisfy these conditions one by one:
ON (C, B) ∧ ONTABLE (B) ∧ ONTABLE (A)
Let us put these conditions in a stack form
ON (C, B)
ONTABLE (B)
ONTABLE (A)

Out of these conditions to be satisfied, check in start state which conditions are already satisfied. ONTABLE (B) is satisfied. The conditions which need to be satisfied are:
ON (C, B) and ONTABLE (A)
Let us start satisfying these goals one by one:
(i)   To fulfill goal ONTABLE (A), choose operator
UNSTACK (A, B)

The preconditions to apply this operator are,
ON (A, B) ∧ CLEAR (A) ∧ ARMEMPTY
(Recall these are the above mentioned preconditions for UNSTACK(x, y), with appropriate replacement done for x and y)
In start state all these conditions are true, hence UNSTACK (A, B) is applicable. Thus, it is applied. The postconditions generated after the application of this operator are:
HOLDING (A) ∧ CLEAR (B)

(ii) to fulfill goal ONTABLE(A), the appropriate operator is
PUTDOWN (A)

The precondition for this is:
HOLDING (A)
This is satisfied, so this operator is applied. After these two steps, the sequence of operators to be applied are UNSTACK (A, B), PUTDOWN (A) and generated conditions are ONTABLE(A) $\wedge$ ARMEMPTY and goal ONTABLE(A) is satisfied.
(iii) Next goal is ON(C, B)
To meet this goal, operator is STACK(C, B), which requires preconditions
CLEAR (B) $\wedge$ HOLDING (C)
Seeing in the start state, CLEAR(B) is satisfied, but holding (C) is not yet true.
To satisfy this, the operator PICKUP(C) is applied first. It generates postconditions as HOLDING (C). Now STACK(C, B) is applicable and goal ON(C,B) is fulfilled.
As all the goal have been fulfilled, we have generated the required plan as:
UNSTACK (A, B)
PUTDOWN (A)
PICKUP(C)
STACK(C, B)

The goal stack planning attacks problem involving conjoined goals by solving the goals one at a time. A plan generated in this manner contains the sequence of operators for attaining the first goal, followed by a complete sequence for the second goal. Though goal stack method works well for small problems but for large problems goal interactions create trouble. In goal interaction the operators used to solve one subproblems may interfere with the solution to the previous subproblems. It makes finding the solution difficult. The goal stack planning generates the solution as a linear sequence of sub-plans, hence it falls in the category of linear planning. Another problem solving technique is nonlinear planning. In this, an intertwined solution of nonlinear sequence of action is generated for goals. The nonlinear planning tries fulfilling different subgoals simultaneously.

PART-III

10.5 UNDERSTANDING

Understanding means transforming some text, speech or picture from one form to another where the second representation has been chosen to correspond to a set of available actions that could be performed. In the process of understanding, a mapping is designed so that for each state generated in previous phase an appropriate action can be taken. The level of understanding varies according to the contextual knowledge of recipient. It should be noted here that the success and failure of an understanding program can rarely be measured in absolute sense, but must instead be measured with respect to particular task to be performed. Human beings perform understanding from all five senses. Computer understanding has so far been applied primarily to images, speech and typed languages.

10.5.1 The Complexities of Understanding

Following features make understanding very complex:
1. Understanding about the target representation is tough. The process of understanding requires taking some action to generate target representation. For this process, complete knowledge about target is required.
2. The types of mapping can be one-one, many-one, one-many or many-many. The decision about these is difficult.
3. Identification about level of interaction of the components of source representation is difficult.
4. The presence of noise in the electrical representation of quantities makes it difficult to understand.

Consider following sentence:

"I want to read all about last prime ministerial election."

To perform the understanding about this sentence, the representation should capture the semantically prime components of this sentence and they are "election" and "prime minister". Hence, the representation should be translated as:

(SEARCH KEYWORDS = ELECTION AND PRIMEMINISTER)

However, suppose the English sentence represents some feeling or abstract phenomenon, e.g. consider following sentence:

"Vishwant told Meeta, he would not go to market with her.
Her feelings were hurt."

The result of understanding this story could be represented using the conceptual dependency structure. Here, the second sentence conveys feelings of the subject, i.e. Meeta. This requires a very complex representation. All the things being equal, constructing such a complex representation is more difficult than constructing a simple one, as more information must be extracted from the input sentences. Extracting that information would require the use of additional knowledge about the world described by the sentences.

10.5.2 Mapping

This section discusses various mappings used in the process of understanding. As stated earlier, understanding is the process of mapping an input form to a different and more useful one. The mapping can be one to one, one to many, many to one and many to many. Out of these, the simplest mapping is one to one. In this, each different statement maps to a single target representation that is different from that arising from any other statement. Practically the understanding is possible only for mathematical type of expressions or language having strict formal format. In such a language, the representation of A:= B + C * D would be as shown in following Fig. 10.13:

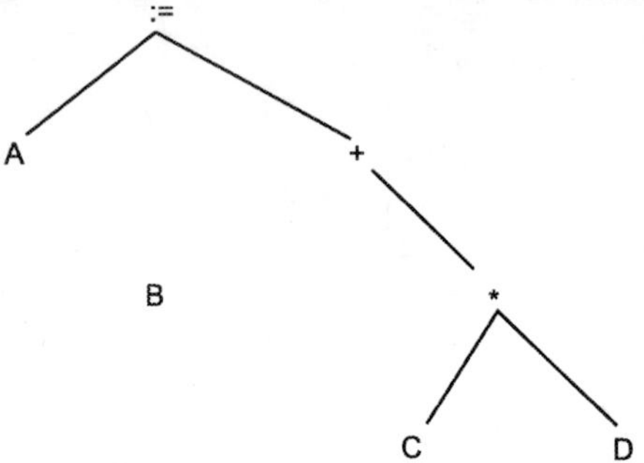

Fig. 10.13: mapping of A:= B+C*D

This representation is practically not applicable in most of the situations. One reason of this is that in many domains, inputs must be interpreted not absolutely but relatively with respect to some reference point, e.g., when images are being interpreted, their size and perspective will change as a function of viewing position. Hence, a single object would look different in different images, e.g.,

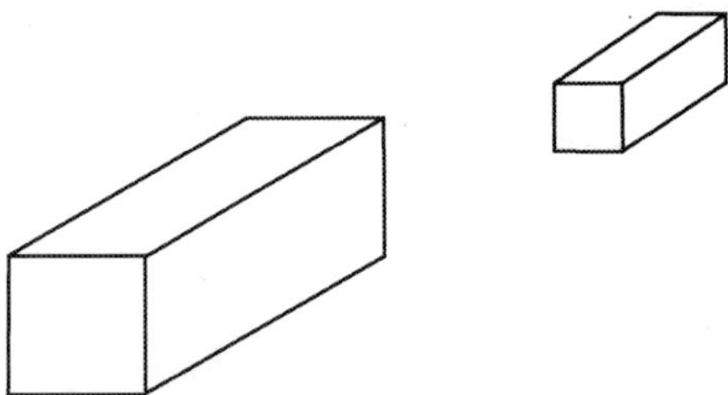

Fig.10.14: Same drawings looking different from different distances

If distance of two objects is different from viewing position, they will appear as different. The similar situation occurs in the text also. E.g. in English, word 'tall' specifies one height range in the phrase 'a tall Giraffe' and a different height range in other phrase 'a tall poodle'.

A second reason that many to one mapping are frequent is, that free variation is often allowed, either because of physical limitation of the system that produces the input, or because such variation simply makes the task of generating the inputs manageable. Both of these factors explain why natural languages require many to one mapping. As is known to every body, no two people speak identically. In fact, even the same person does not say a given word in the same way every time. The analysis of concentration of energy in a sound is done in a spectrogram. Practically it has been observed that the spectrogram of different utterance of same word are different.

In written language also, we find many-to-one mapping such as the following one occurring in English front end to a key word data retrieval system. Consider following three sentences:

(i)   Tell me about the last prime ministerial elections.

(ii) I would like to see all the stories of the last prime ministerial elections.

(iii) I am interested in last prime ministerial elections.

In all the above sentences, the search may be done using following:

(SEARCH KEYBOARD = ELECTION & PRIME MINISTER)

Mapping of kind many-to-one requires that understanding system know about all the ways that a target representation can be expressed in source language. Thus, they typically require a structural analysis of the input rather than a simple exact pattern match.

Unlike this, one-to-many mapping requires a great deal of domain knowledge besides input in order to make the correct choice among the available target representation. See following sentences and their representation:

(i)   They are flying air planes.

It may have following representations:

(a) (They are

(flying air planes))

(b) (They (are flying)

air planes)

similarly sentence " They are flying planning tools" may be represented as

(a) (They are

(flying planning tools))

(b) (They (are flying)

planning tools)

Though this sentence is ambiguous in isolation, it would usually not be interpreted as being ambiguous by a human listener in specific context. Clues, both from previous sentences and from physical context in which sentence occurs usually makes one of these interpretations appear to be correct. The analysis of such sentences requires the identification of how to encode this contextual information and how to exploit it while processing each new sentence.

10.5.3 Noise in the Input

Understanding is the process of interpreting an input and assigning it, its meaning. In many understanding situations, the input to which meaning should be assigned is not always the input that is present to the listener. Because of the complex environment in which understanding occurs, other things often interfere with the basic input before it reaches to the listener. In speech and image understanding, this problem is common. These undesired elements are called noise. Thus, it is required to separate the speech component from background noise in order to understand the speech. In case of typed languages, the noise occurs in the form of typing errors.

10.5.4 Understanding as Constraint Satisfaction

From AI viewpoint, understanding can be framed as constraint satisfaction problem. The number of interpretations that can be assigned to individual components of an input as large and number of combinations of these components is enormous. However, the deep analysis reveals that because of many constraints, many combinations usually cannot occur. These constraints can be exploited in the understanding process to reduce complexity.

The problem formation of understanding from AI viewpoint can be done in following steps:
1. Find out the constraints by analyzing the problem.
2. Solve the problem by applying a constraint satisfaction algorithm that effectively uses the constraints from steps 1 to control the search.

10.5.4.1 Waltz algorithm

This algorithm is primarily developed for labeling line drawings. This algorithm models the problem as constraint satisfaction. On a superficial analysis, many understanding tasks appear critically complex. The number of interpretations that can be assigned to individual component of an input is large and number of combinations of those components is enormous. But a closer analysis severals that many combinations can not actually occur. These natural constraints are exploited and only remaining constraints are left to be fulfilled.

Important steps in the use of problem solving are:
(i) Analyze the problem domain to determine the constraints
(ii) Solve the problem by applying constraint satisfaction algorithm.
  Consider the following Fig. 10.15.
  To make the line image of this picture, we need to identify each of the lines in the figure as representing either:
(i) *An obscuring edge*: A boundary between objects or between objects and background.
(ii) *A concave edge*: An edge between two faces that form an acute angle when viewed from outside the object.
(iii) *A convex edge*: An edge between two faces that form an obtuse angle when viewed from out side the object.

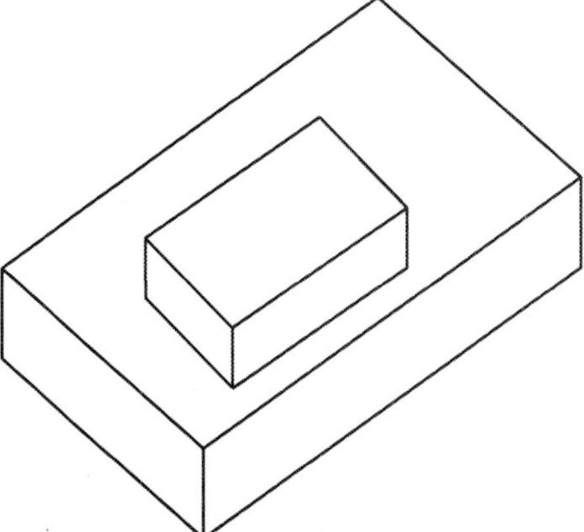

Fig.10.15: A line understanding process

In real world, objects can be more complicated and they can have other edge types such as cracks between coplanar faces and shadow edges between shadow and background. For analyzing these figures, this analysis method is extended. For convenience of understanding, we restrict our discussion to trihedral vertices, i.e. vertices, which have exactly three planes meeting together.

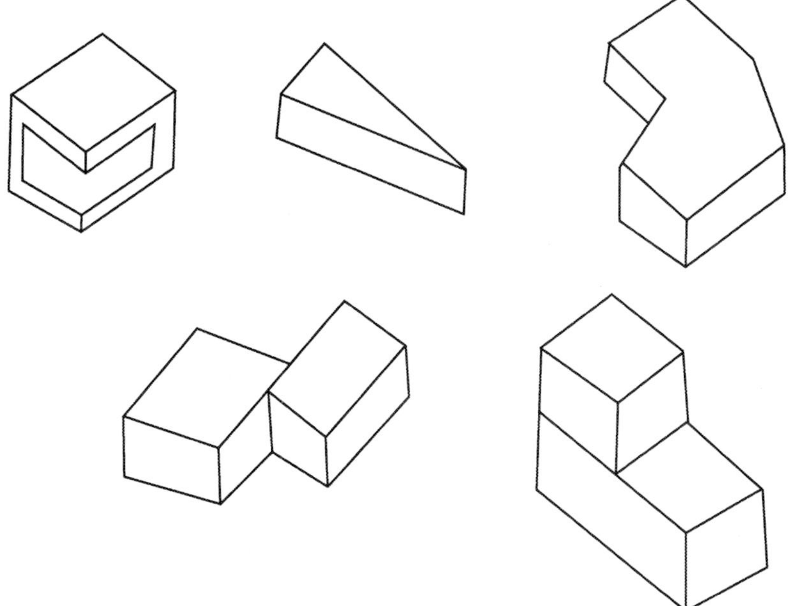

Fig. 10.16: Some trihedral figures

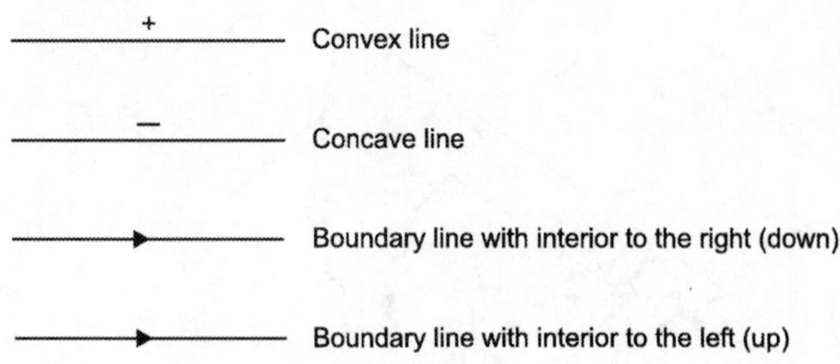

Fig. 10.17: Some nontrihedral figures

These are shown in following Fig. 10.16.

To analyze these objects, conventional line labeling conventions are shown below:

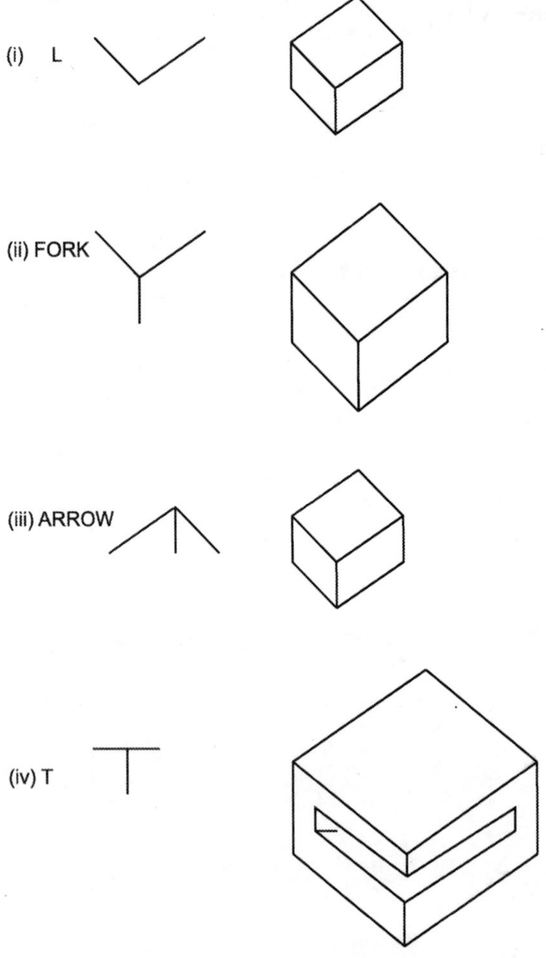

Fig. 10.18: Line labeling Conventions

Now once the labeling is done, to understand the figure, the constraints are formulated. The constraints are formulated as follows:

As there are four line types, we can calculate the number of ways of labeling a figure composed of N lines is 4^N. Out of these lines, how can we find the correct one? The critical observation here is that every line must meet other lines at a vertex at each of its ends. For the considered trihedral figures, there are only four configurations that describe all possible vertices.

For identifying the figure, all lines which meet at angle 90 degree should be chosen. To do this, first the maximum number of ways that each of the four types of lines might combine with other lines at vertex is judged. Similarly other constraints about the planes, edges and angles are identified. After determining all constraints, the figure is understood by combining the constraints.

EXERCISES

1. Why is learning considered as important component of intelligence? Give example to support your answer.
2. Consider the behavior of Winston's learning mechanism on the following sets of pieces.

    step

    small box   big box

    create a semantic net representation of three or four examples of near misses and show the development of concept.
3. Differentiate between deductive, inductive and Abductive learning giving at least one example of each.
4. Create a simple table of examples in some domain like classifying animals by species and trace the construction of a decision tree by the IDB3 algorithm.
5. With the help of suitable example, prove that property inheritance and abduction are examples of nonmonotonic reasoning.
6. There exists a new concept of neuro dynamic programming in the field of reinforced learning. Study this and prepare a study paper on it.
7. Analyze Samuel's checkers playing program from a reinforced learning perspective. Can you offer your own suggestions in this regard?
8. Consider following tree
    A depth first search tree is shown below. During node traversed, it was detected that controversy occurs at node F. Trace the path of
    (i) Chronological backtracking
    (ii) Dependency directed backtracking
    which path should be followed? Comment?

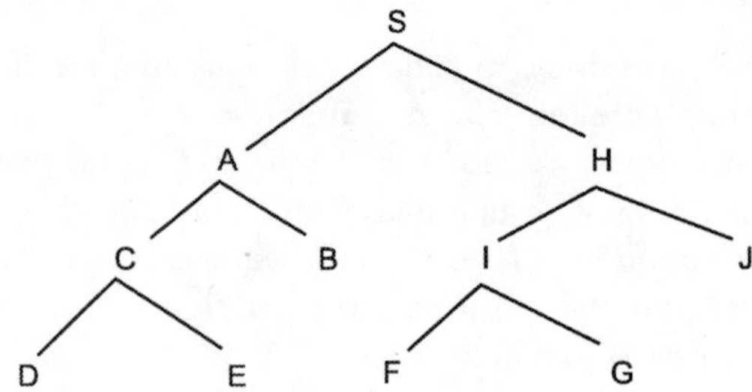

9. Explain the functioning of truth maintenance system.
10. Explain machine learning. Differentiate between the following.
    (i) Supervised learning and inductive learning
    (ii) Classification and regression
11. What are the differences between training set and test set. How they are important for learning.
12. What are decision trees? And how do they learn. How does the decision tree learn differently from decision list.
13. There are two terms called "expressiveness of the hypothesis learning" and "ease of learning". Do you find any relationship between the two?
14. What is meant by cumulative learning? How does the prior knowledge improve the learning ability of learning agent. Give an example in support of your answer.
15. With the help of suitable example, explain how the explanation based learning makes use of principle of induction.
16. "ILP" can be done with a top down approach of refining a very general rule through a bottom up approach of inverting a deductive process. Justify the statement.

11

Applications of AI

In this chapter, we discuss some major applications of AI apart from the expert systems. These are neural networks, pattern recognition, and computer vision. The expert systems are dealt in detail in the next chapter.

PART-I

11.1 NEURAL NETWORKS

The area of Artificial intelligence aims at developing the machines capable of exhibiting the intelligence matching those of human beings. The development of 'artificial neural networks' or simply 'neural networks' is an endeavor in this direction. The neural networks are developed on the principle of human brain functioning, hence these are based on the working of biological neuron. The artificial neural network based systems have wide applications in real world problem solution techniques. In real world, the natural objects like people and animals are much better and faster at recognizing images than the most advanced computers. However, the computer outperforms the natural objects in doing the calculations and arithmetic operations. Hence, if a machine can be developed having qualities of both natural objects and computer, it will actually become superior to human beings. Advances have been made in developing and applying such systems for solving problems, which are considered intractable or difficult for traditional computation methodologies. Neural networks can supplement the enormous processing power of Von Neumann digital computer with the ability to make sensible decisions to learn by ordinary experience.

To begin with, we would discuss the history of the development of neural networks.

11.1.1 History of Neural Networks

The initial development of neural networks started in 1943, with the evolution of formal model of an elementary computing neuron by Mc Culloch and Pitts. This model included all necessary elements to perform logic operations and hence, it was used as basic 'arithmetic logic computing element'; but because of the then existing state-of-art technology of "vacuum tubes", its implementation could not be done.

In 1949, Donald Hebb first proposed a learning scheme for updating Neurons connection that is now called '*Hebbian learning rule*'. He stated that the information can be stored in connections, and postulated the learning technique that had a profound impact on future developments in this field.

During the 1950s, by the developments of implementation technology of computers, the first neuro-computer was built by Minsky. It adapted connections automatically. During this stage, Frank Rosenblatt invented the neuron like element called '*perceptron*' in 1958. It was a trainable machine capable of learning to classify certain patterns by modifying connections to threshold.

In 1960s, Bernard Widrow & Marcian Hoff developed a powerful device called ADALINE. (ADAptive LINEar combiner) It was a machine exhibiting good amount of learning. The learning rule it adopted, was later called Widrow–Hoff learning rule. The rule minimized the summed square error during training, involving pattern classification. The applications to ADALINE and its extension as MADALINE (Many ADALINE) included pattern recognition, weather forecasting and adaptive control.

The neural networks of present era were developed after 1970s. During the period from 1965 to 1984, the research in associative memory was perused by Tuevo Kohonam in Finland. 1977 onwards, James A Anderson's unsupervised learning networks were developed for future mapping of regular array of domains. During the period from 1982 until 1986, a large amount of research work was conducted. In 1982, John Hopfield introduced recurrent neural network architecture for associative memories.

Beginning from 1986–87 till date, many new neural network research programs have been initiated. The present intensity of research in neuro computing discipline can be measured by quickly growing number of conferences and journals devoted to this field.

Hence, it is clear that, the Artificial Neural Networks (ANN) are the computational systems inspired by biological neuron. However, the correspondence between ANN and real neural network is still weak. Vast discrepancies exist between both the architectures and capabilities of artificial and natural neural networks. Knowledge about the human brain functioning is so limited that no models have been successful in duplicating the performance of human brain. Therefore, the brain has been and still is only metaphor for a wide variety of neural network configurations that have been developed.

Let us first discuss the basic functioning of biological neuron.

11.1.2 Biological Neuron

In human brain, the elementary nerve cell called a 'neuron' is the fundamental building block of biological neural networks. Its schematic diagram is shown in following Fig. 11.1.

A biological neuron has three major regions:

(i) **Soma**: It is the cell body.

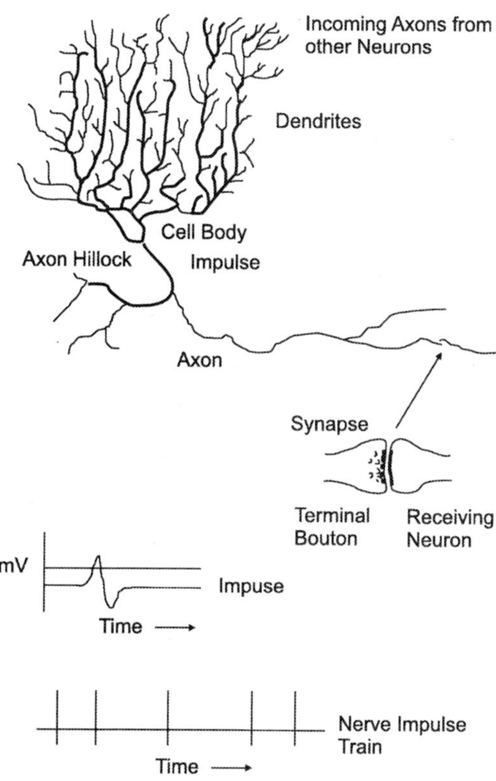

Fig. 11.1: Biological Neuron

(ii) ***Axon***: It is the long cylindrical connection that carries impulses from the neurons.

(iii) ***The dendrites***: It is the fine bush of thin fibers around the neuron's body.

In biological neuron, Dendrites receive information from the neurons through axons–long fibers that serve as a transmission line. The end part of an axon splits into a fine arborization. Each branch of it terminates into a small end bulb, almost touching the dendrites of neighboring neurons. The axon-dendrite contact organ is called synapse. At this point of synapse, the neuron introduces its signal to the neighboring neuron. The signal between synapse and dendrite remains in form of electrical impulse.

The neuron is able to respond to the total of its inputs aggregated within a short time interval called 'period of latent summation'. The neuron's response is generated if the total potential of its membrane works as a shell. It aggregates the magnitude of incoming signal over some duration.

A human brain consists of approximately 10^{11} computing elements or neurons. They communicate through a connection network of axons and synapses having a density of approximately 10^4 synapses per neuron. In brain the information is processed, evaluated, and compared with the stored information in the central nervous system. The commands are generated here, as and when required and these are transmitted to the motor. The neurons operate in a chemical environment that is even more important in terms of actual brain behavior. Hence, the brain can be considered as a densely connected switching network conditioned largely by biochemical processes. In actual human brain, the vast neural network has an elaborate structure with very complex interconnections. The input to the network is provided by sensory receptors. The stimuli conveys information into the network of neurons. As a result of information processing in the central nervous system, the effectors are controlled and give human responses in the form of diverse actions. The actual neural network has an elaborate structure with very complex interconnections. Thus, a model of brain can be considered as a three- stage system consisting of :

(i)   Receptors
(ii) Neural network
(iii) Effectors, in control of the organism and its act.

The following Fig. 11.2 shows the information flow between these components.

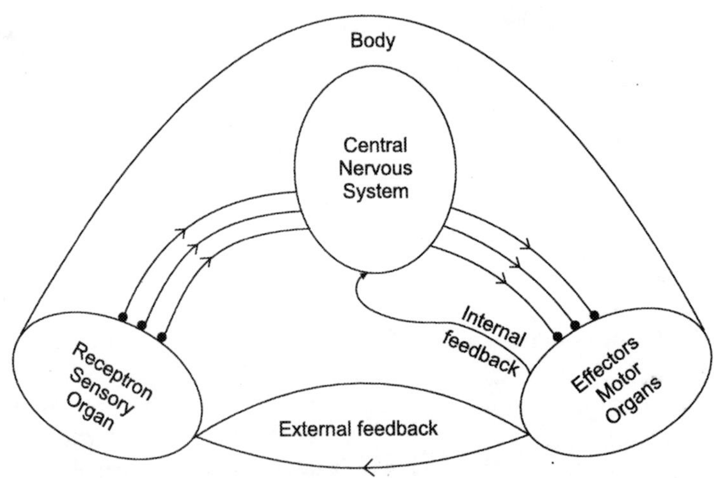

Fig. 11.2: Information flow among components of brain

11.1.3 McCulloch – Pitts Neuron Model

This model shows highly simplified version of biological neuron. It is represented in following Fig. 11.3.

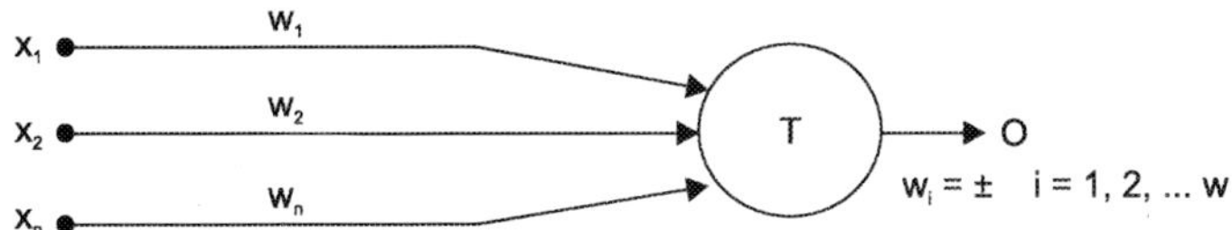

Fig. 11.3: McCulloch-Pitts Neuron Model

Here, the inputs x_i, for $i = 1,2,\ldots,n$, are the inputs to the network. They can take value 0 or 1 depending upon the absence or presence of the input impulse at instant k.

The neuron's output signal is generated as 'O'. The firing rule of this model is defined as:

$$O^{k+1} = 1, \text{ if } \sum_{i=1}^{n} w_i x^k_i \geq T$$

$$O^{k+1} = 0, \text{ if } \sum_{i=1}^{n} w_i x^k_i < T$$

where, $k = 0, 1, 2\ldots$ are discreet time instant and w_i is the weight connecting i^{th} input with neuron's membrane. It is assumed that,

(i)   There exists a unity delay between instants k and k+1

(ii) The $w_i = +1$ for excitatory synapses, $w_i = -1$ for inhibitory synapses; and T is the neuron's threshold value.

This neuron model is able to perform basic logic operations NOT, OR, AND and memory cell, if its weights are properly adjusted.

The basic NOT, OR, and AND gate formations are shown in following Fig. 11.4.

As the normal computer hardware consists of basic logic gates and memory cell, the digital computer of arbitrary complexity can be constructed using an artificial neural network consisting of these as basic building block.

11.1.4 Neuron Node

Neuron node is the processing element created from basic neuron. The basic neuron node consists of a neuron-processing node and a set of weighted inputs.

The basic neuron node is shown in the following Fig. 11.5.

Hence, every neuron model consists of a processing element with weighted synaptic input and single output. The signal flow is unidirectional. The neuron signal output is given as follows:

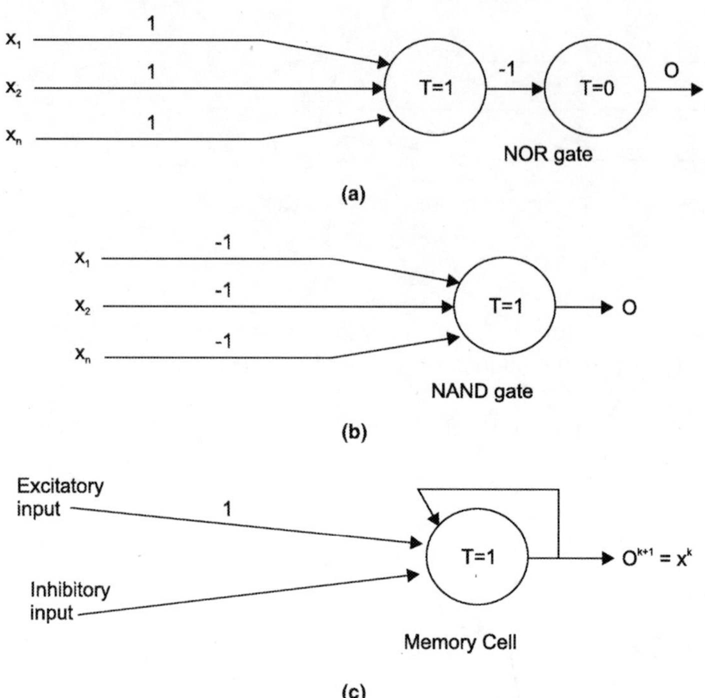

Fig. 11.4: The logic gate formation using neural network

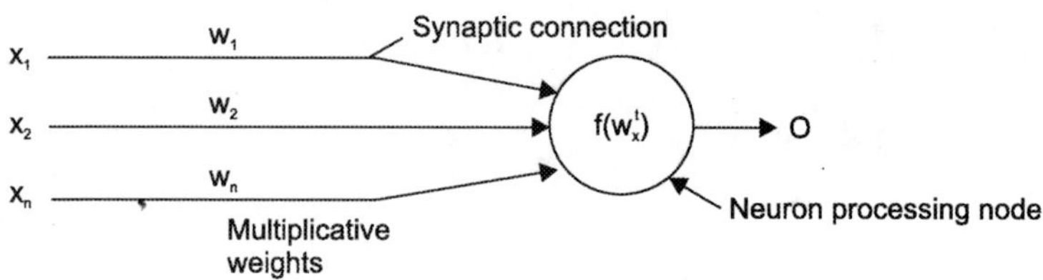

Fig. 11.5: Basic neuron node

$$F(w_x) \text{ or } f\left(\sum_{i=1}^{n} w_i * x_i\right) \qquad \dots(1)$$

Where, w is the weight factor defined as:

$$w = \begin{bmatrix} w_1 \\ w_2 \\ w_3 \\ \cdot \\ w_n \end{bmatrix}$$

and X is the input vector defined as:

$$X = \begin{bmatrix} x_1 \\ x_2 \\ x_3 \\ . \\ x_n \end{bmatrix}$$

Function $f(w_x)$ is activation function.

Its domain is the set of activation values, known as 'net' of the neuron model. Variable net is defined as scalar product of weight and input vector:

$$Net = [w]\, x \qquad\qquad ....(2)$$

The basic neuron shown in the above diagram is defined by equations (1) and (2).

11.1.5 Neuron Model for Artificial Neural Networks

The neuron model for Artificial Neural Networks (ANN) is an extension of Mc Culloch model developed for actual systems. The Mc Culloch model is a mathematically developed model, which makes use of drastic simplifications. The basic biological neuron functioning based artificial neural networks is able to acquire, store and utilize experimental knowledge. This definition of neuron is based on its capabilities. The neuron network can also be defined as interconnection of neurons with weighted inputs and weighted outputs to other neurons including themselves. It allows binary 0, 1 states only, and it operate under discrete time assumptions. Further, it assumes synchrony of operation of all neurons in a larger network.

11.1.6 Feedforward ANN

The feedforward neural network is one that does not have any connection from output to input. It is a network consisting of m neural nodes, m inputs and n outputs. All inputs with variable weights are connected with every other node. A single layer feedforward network has one layer of nodes, whereas a multilayer feedforward network has multiple layers of nodes.

The input and output of a single layer neural network is given below:

$$X = \begin{bmatrix} x_1 \\ x_2 \\ x_3 \\ . \\ x_n \end{bmatrix}$$

$$O = \begin{bmatrix} o_1 \\ o_2 \\ o_3 \\ . \\ o_n \end{bmatrix}$$

The inputs can be weighted also. Weight w_{ij} connects the ith neuron with j^{th} input. The first subscript denotes the index of source.

The activation values of ith neuron are given as follows:

$$Net_i = \Sigma\, w_{ij} * x_{ij} \qquad \text{(for i=1 to n and j = 1 to m)}$$

The output is given by,

$$O_i = f\,(w_i^t\, x), \qquad \text{(for i = 1 to m)}$$

Where, weight vector w_i contains weight leading toward the ith output node. It is defined as:

$$W = [w_{i1}\ \ w_{i2}\ \ \ldots\ldots\ldots\ldots w_{in}\,]^t$$

The basic input-output connection of feedforward ANN is shown in Fig. 11.6.

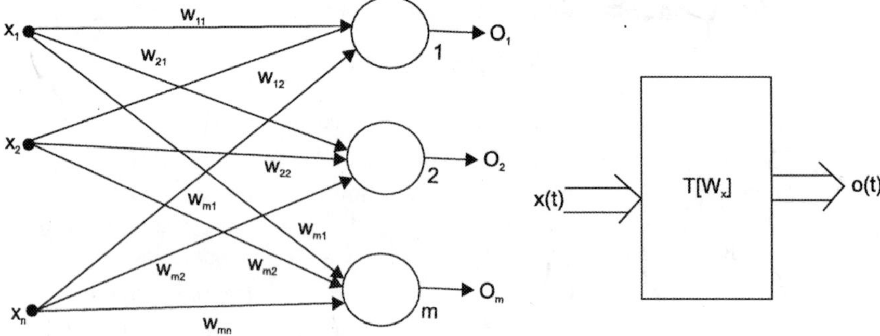

Fig. 11.6: Basic input-output connection of feedforward ANN

In terms of matrix notation, the output-space and input-space relationship is represented as:

$$O = \Gamma|\ wx|$$

Where, w is weight matrix. It is also called connection matrix. It is given as:

$$W = \begin{bmatrix} W_{11} & W_{12} & \ldots\ldots W_{1n} \\ \ldots\ldots\ldots & & \\ W_{m1} & W_{m2} & W_{mn} \end{bmatrix}$$

and,

$$G = \begin{bmatrix} f(1) & 0 & 0 & 0 \\ 0 & f(1) & 0 & 0 \\ 0 & 0 & f(1) & 0 \\ 0 & 0 & 0 & f(1) \end{bmatrix}$$

Γ is a nonlinear matrix operator, mapping input space x to output space o. The nonlinear activation function f(1) in the diagonal of the matrix operator, operates component wise on activation values of each neuron. Each activation value is a scalar product of an input with respective weight vector. Each activation value is a scalar product of an input with respective weight vector.

11.1.7 Feedback ANN

The feedback network has a connection from output to input besides the normal connection of input to output. It is shown in following Fig. 11.7.

The interconnection scheme of discrete time feedback network is shown in following Fig. 11.8.

In this network the output of instant 't' is feedback at the input at instant 't + Δ'. Here Δ is the delay. The delay is introduced by delay element in feedback

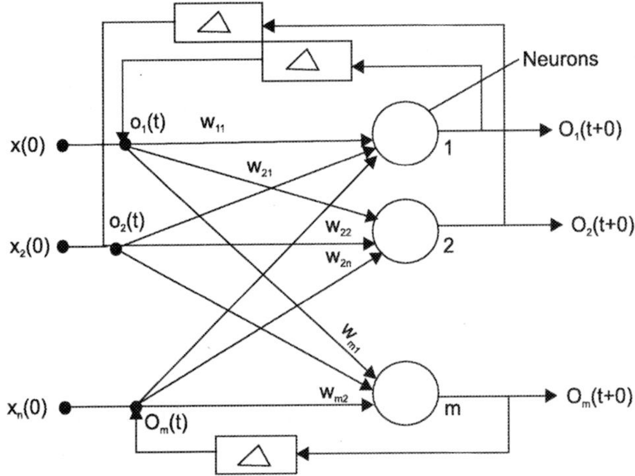

Fig. 11.7: Basic input output connection of feedback ANN

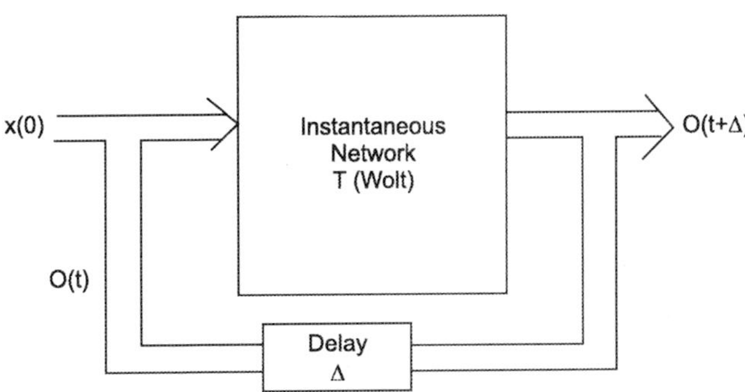

Fig. 11.8: A single layer discrete time feedback network

loop. This delay corresponds to the refractory period of an elementary biological neuron model. The output of feedback network is given below:

$$O\,(t + \Delta) = \Gamma\,[w\,O(t)]$$

Here, input vector $X(t)$ is needed to only initialize this network, so that $o(0) = x(0)$ (that means, at $t = 0$, the output is equal to input). The input is then removed, and the system remains autonomous for $t > 0$. There are two categories of single layer feedback network:

(i) **Discrete time system**: in this system, time is considered as discrete variable and network performance is observed at discrete time instants Δ, 2Δ, $3\Delta,\ldots\ldots$. Here, Δ is the unit delay. For a discrete time artificial neural system, the output is given by:

$$O^{k+1} = \Gamma\,[w\,O^k], \qquad \text{for } k = 1,2,3\ldots.$$

Where, k is the instant number.

(ii) **Continuous time system**: in this system, time is considered as continuous variable and network performance is continuously monitored at $t = 1,2,3,\ldots$ instants. It can be seen that a continuous time network can be obtained by replacing delay elements of discrete time system with suitable continuous time lag producing component.

11.1.8 Neural Processing

In this section, we would discuss how the pattern matching can be done using neural networks. Assume initially there are certain patterns stored in the neural network. If the network is presented with a pattern similar to a member of stored set, it may associate the input to the closest stored pattern. The process of matching a input pattern with the closest stored pattern is called '*autoassoication*'. It is shown in Fig. 11.9.

Now, if a degraded or distorted input is given to the neural network, the neural network is able to match with the stored patterns. This distorted input

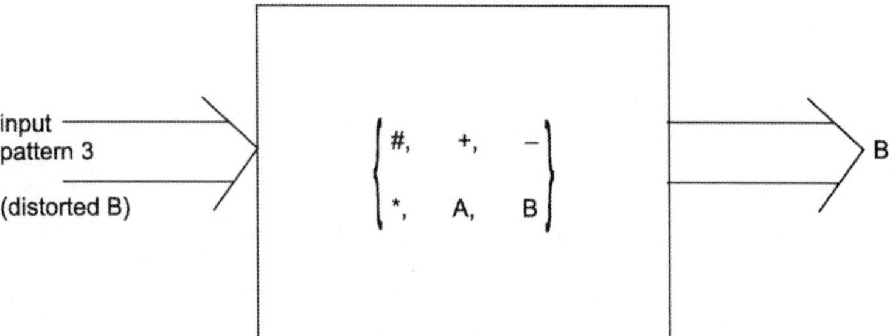

Fig. 11.9: The autoassoication in neural network

behaves as a cue for retrieval of its original pattern and the best matching figure is presented as output.

Association of input pattern can also be stored in form of a heteroassociation variant. In this, the association between a pair of heterogeneous patterns are identified. In heterogeneous pattern storage, corresponding to one pattern, other similar patterns are also stored. The input is matched against one pattern but similar other patterns are also reported as output. The heteroassociation is shown in Fig. 11.10.

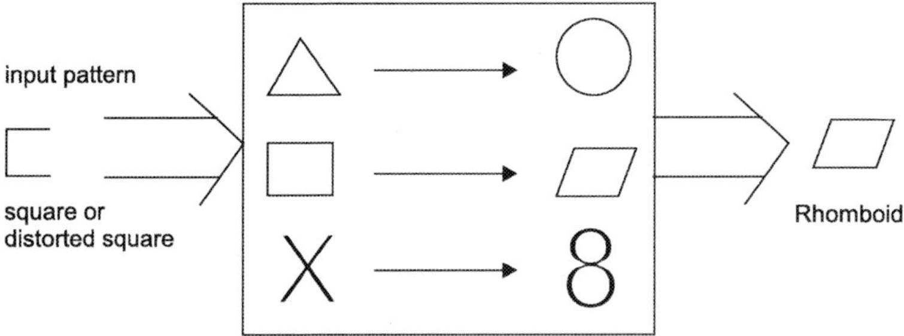

Fig. 11.10: Heteroassociation in neural network

Another form of neural computation is classification. In this, a pattern is divided into many small classes or categories and these are stored in neural network. In response to an input pattern from the set, the classifier is supposed to recall the information regarding class membership of input pattern. Typically, classes are expressed by discrete valued output vector, and thus output neurons of classifiers would employ binary activation function. The classification based computing is shown in following Fig. 11.11:

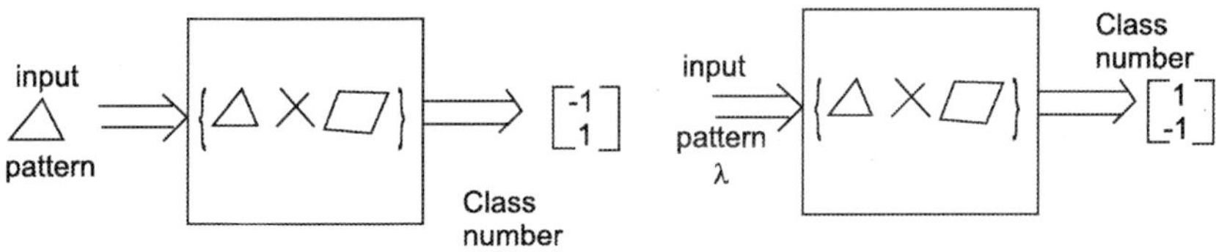

Fig. 11.11: A classification based neural computing

The classification is a special case of heteroassociation. In this, the association is between input pattern and second member of heteroassociative pair, which is supposed to indicate the input's class member. The neural processing of understanding a class of object that does not exactly match with stored pattern is called recognition. When the class membership for one of the patterns in the set is recalled, recognition becomes identical to classification.

Neural networks exhibit very good characteristics of generalization. The ability to generalize means they can sensibly interpolate and extrapolate the input patterns.

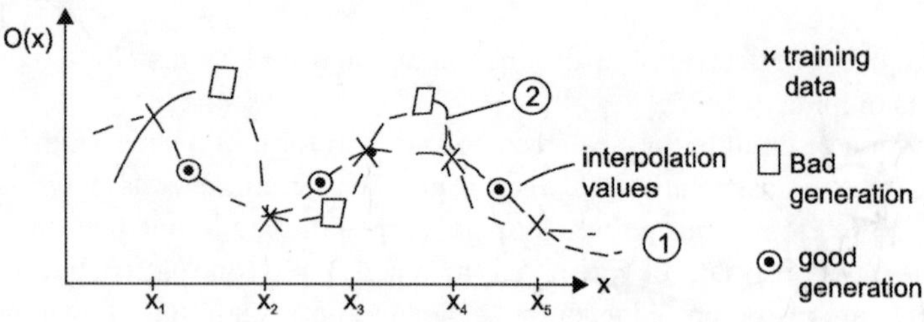

Fig. 11.12: The interpolation by neural network

It can generate the new patterns in this way. The generalization is shown in following Fig. 11.12.

Here, it is assumed that the network has been trained using data x1 – x5. The points between training points X are generated itself by neural networks. In many cases, neural networks provide input-output mappings with good generalization capability. As these can generalize, it can be said that neural networks exhibit learning. Data, which is internally generated, is stored as a result of learning. Various learning methods are described in next section.

11.1.9 Types of Activation Function

While training the neural net, various types of activation functions are used. These activation functions are described below.

11.1.9.1 Threshold function

This type of activation function is defined as follows:

$$f(v) = \begin{cases} 1, & \text{if } v \geq 0 \\ 0, & \text{if } v < 0 \end{cases}$$

This threshold function is also referred as Heaviside function. Correspondingly, the output of neuron k employing such a threshold function is expressed as:

$$y_k = \begin{cases} 1, & \text{if } v_k \geq 0 \\ 0, & \text{if } v_k < 0 \end{cases}$$

where, v_k is the induced local field of neuron; it is given by:

$$v_k = \sum_{j=1}^{m} w_{kj} + b_k$$

$$F(v) = \begin{cases} 1, & v \geq +\frac{1}{2} \\ v, & +\frac{1}{2} \geq v \geq -\frac{1}{2} \\ 0, & v \leq -\frac{1}{2} \end{cases}$$

The threshold function is shown in following Fig. 11.13.

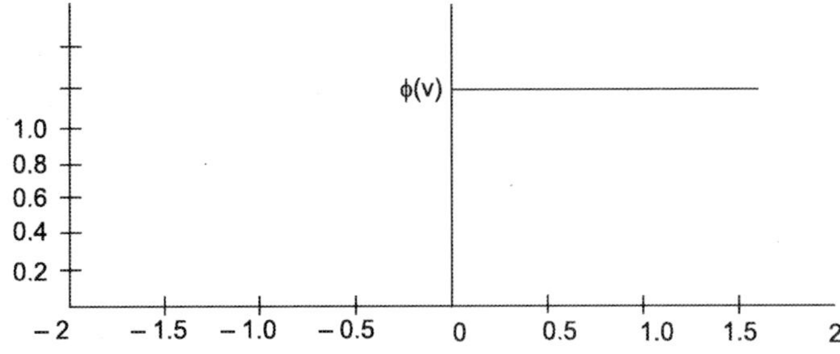

Fig. 11.13: Threshold function

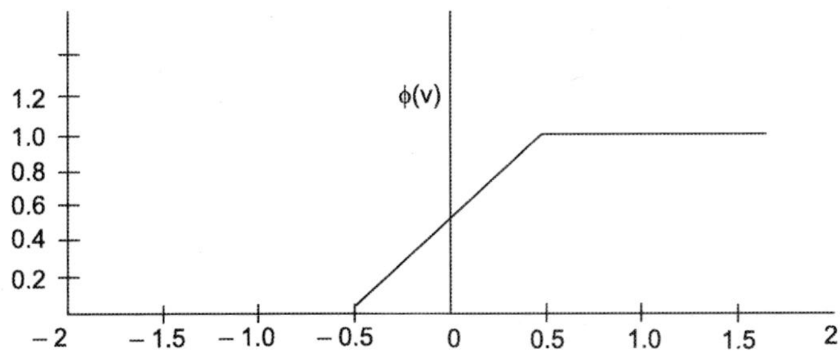

Fig. 11.14: Piecewise linear function

11.1.9.2 Piecewise Linear Function

Piecewise linear function are combinations of various linear functions, where the choice of linear function depends upon the relevant regions of the input space.

11.1.9.3 Sigmoid function

It is most common form of activation function used for construction of artificial neural networks. It is shown in following Fig. 11.15.

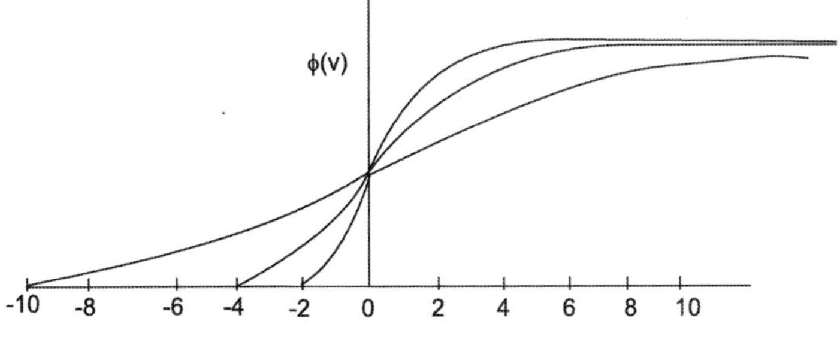

Fig. 11.15: Sigmoid function

It is a function, which maintains a graceful balance between linear and non-linear behavior. An example of sigmoid function is given below:

$$F(x) = 1/ (1+ \exp (-av))$$

11.1.10 Characteristics of Neural Network Systems

ANN architectures are very different from conventional computer architectures. In conventional computers, it is possible to correlate discrete information with memory cells, e.g., a social security number could be stored as ASCII code in a contiguous group of memory cells. By examining the pattern of this contiguous group, the other social security numbers could be directly constructed.

ANNs are modeled on the basis of current brain theories, in which information is represented by weights. However, there is no correlation between a specific weight and a specific item of stored information.

The salient features of ANNs are:
 (i) Storage is fault tolerant. Portions of the net can be removed and there will be only a small degradation in the quality of stored data. This is because of distributed storage of data.
 (ii) The quality of stored image degrades gracefully in proportion of the amount of net removed. The storage and quality features are also characteristics of holograms.
(iii) Data are naturally stored in the form of associative memory. An associative memory is one in which partial data are sufficient to recall the complete stored information. This contrasts with conventional memory, in which data are recalled by specifying address of that data.
(iv) Nets can extrapolate and intrapolate from their stored information. The nets can also be trained. Training teaches the net to look for significant features or relationships of data.

These characteristics make ANNS attractive for Robot spacecraft, oilfield equipment, underwater devices, process control and other applications that need to function for long time in hostile environment.

11.1.11 Stochastic Model of Neuron

The neuron models described above are deterministic in the sense that their input-output behavior is precisely defined for all inputs. However, the human brain is nondeterministic and its output cannot be so precisely defined. The stochastic model of neuron is based on probabilistic approach. In this, the firing of neuron (i.e. switching from on state to off-state and vice versa) and its being in state $+1$ or -1 is guided by certain probability. Thus, in stochastic model of neuron the state of neuron x is given as:

$$X = \begin{array}{l} +1, \text{ with probability } P(v) \\ -1, \text{ with probability } 1 - P(v) \end{array}$$

A standard choice for P(v) is the sigmoid shaped function:

$$P(v) = 1 / (1 + \exp(-v/T))$$

Where, T is the pseudotemperature, which is used to control the noise level and therefore the uncertainty in firing. It should be noted that T is not a physical temperature, be it a biological or an artificial neural network, but T is a parameter which controls the thermal fluctuations representing the effects of synaptic noise. When T becomes 0 (that means a noiseless environment), the neuron model becomes deterministic and it reduced to McCulloch –Pitts model.

11.1.12 Learning in Neural Network

This section discusses various learning methods of neural networks.

11.1.12.1 Reinforced learning

In reinforced learning, the input-output mapping is performed through continued interaction with the environment in order to minimize a scalar index of performance.

The features of reinforced learning based network are as follows:
  (i) The network is presented with a sample output from the training set.
  (ii) The network computes what it thinks should be sample output.
  (iii) The network is supplied with a real valued judgment.
  (iv) The network adjusts its weights and the process repeats.

The reinforced learning is shown in following Fig. 11.16.

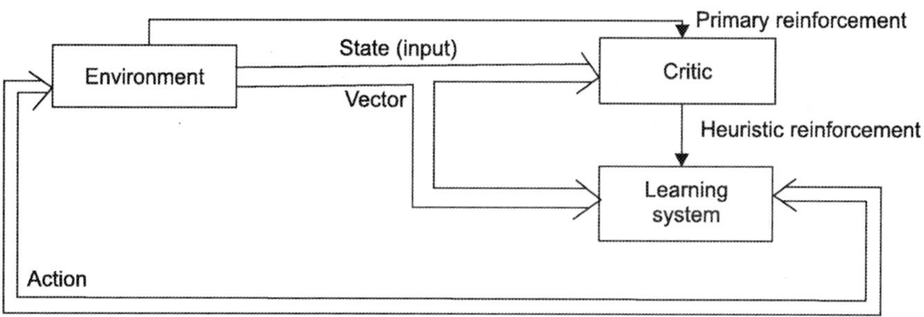

Fig. 11.16: Reinforced learning

This learning system has one signal called heuristic reinforced signal, both of which are scalar inputs. The system learns under delayed reinforcement, which means that the system observes a temporal sequence of stimuli. The stimuli received from the environment results in the generation of heuristic reinforced signal. The goal of learning is to minimize a 'cost-to-go' function. The environment provides state vector to critic. The cost-to-go function is defined as the expectation of the cumulative cost of actions taken over a sequence of steps instead of simply the intermediate cost. The function of learning machine, which constitutes the second component of the system, is to discover these actions and to feed them back to the environment.

There are two problems associated with reinforced learning:

(i) There is no teacher to provide a desired response at each step of the learning process.

(ii) It has a temporal credit assignment problem. This occurs because of delay incurred in the generation of primary reinforcement signal. This means, the learning machine must be able to assign credit and blame. Individually to each action in sequence of time steps which led to the final outcome, while the primary reinforcement may evaluate only the outcome.

In spite of the above problems, the reinforced learning is very appealing. It provides the basis for the system to interact with its environment, thereby developing the ability to learn to perform a prescribed task solely on the basis of the outcomes of its experience, which results from the interaction.

11.1.12.2 Unsupervised learning

In unsupervised learning or self organizing learning, no external agent is present to provide supervision. As there is no teacher (or supervisor) required, it is called unsupervised learning. In this type of learning, a set of input data is given to the network and it is allowed to analyze it and discover regularities and relationships between the different parts of the input.

The data for unsupervised learning is shown in the following Table 11.1.

Table 11.1: Data for unsupervised learning

Features	Has sea	population >1crore	is-capital	has river	has hills	has industries
City						
Delhi	0	1	1	1	0	0
Bombay	1	1	1	1	0	1
Calcutta	1	1	1	1	0	0
Nagpur	0	0	0	1	0	0
Shimla	0	0	1	0	1	0
Faridabad	0	0	0	1	0	1
Ahmedabad	0	1	1	1	0	1
Chennai	1	1	1	0	0	0
Jammu	0	0	1	1	1	1
Jaipur	0	0	1	0	0	0

In this type of learning, the data is analyzed and some classification is performed according to their feature set. For example, in above data set, the cities can be grouped into metropolitan cities and non-metropolitan cities based on their feature value 'population > 1 crore', similarly the cities can be grouped as hill station or non-hill station based on their feature 'has-hill'.

Hence, in this method, learning is made possible through the input set and its features, e.g., in above data, if we try to group the cities on the feature value 'having technical university', then, this grouping cannot be performed, because this feature is not provided in the input data set.

To perform unsupervised learning, we may use a competitive learning rule, e.g., we may use a neural network, which consists of two layers, i.e.,

(i) an input layer, and

(ii) a competitive layer. The input layer receives the input data. The competitive layer consists of neurons, which compete with each other for the opportunity to respond to features contained in the input data.

11.1.12.3 Hebbian Learning

An explanation of learning by neuron was given by Hebb. Hebb's postulate of learning is the oldest and the most famous of all learning rules. It is named in the honour of neuropsychologist Hebb (1949). He has described this learning rule for biological neuron and later it was extended for neural networks. In Hebbian learning, the neuron's efficiency in triggering another neuron increases with firing. Firing means that a neuron emits an electrochemical impulse that can stimulate other neurons connected to it. The Hebbian learning of neural network is based on following two basic rules:

(1) If two neurons on either side of a synapse (connections) are activated simultaneously, then the strength of that synapse is selectively increased.

(2) If two neurons on either side of a synapse are activated asynchronously, then that synapse is selectively weakened or eliminated.

A synapse exhibiting these characteristics is called *Hebbian Synapse*. The hebbian synapse is a synapse which uses a time dependent, highly local, and strongly interactive mechanism to increase synaptic efficiency as a function of correlations between the presynaptic and postsynaptic activities.

Further discussion on this topic is beyond the scope of this book.

PART-II

11.2 PATTERN RECOGNITION

God has given human beings an excellent capability to recognize and identify objects. Once a picture is shown to human beings, next time by seeing only a part of picture, they are able to identify the complete picture. Similarly, if we hear a song once, then next time by hearing only part of it, we identify the song. In human, the idea of identifying some concept or object is broadly termed as *Cognition*. The abstract level of cognition is performed at the level of:

(i) *ideas,* e.g. terrorism, electromagnetic radiation, rain etc.

(ii) *concepts,* e.g. beauty, generosity, complexity, and

(iii) *procedures* like making a journey, or performing some dance, etc.

In technical terms, the ability of identifying a complete object just by seeing or listening a pattern of it, is known as '*Pattern Recognition*'. Naturally, developing the ability of pattern recognition in machine would be a wonderful idea. Defining technically, *the pattern recognition is a process whereby computer programs are used to recognize various forms of inputs like visual or speech patterns.* This field is normally studied in the area of machine learning. As such, the techniques adopted for pattern recognition is a collection of methods used for supervised learning. In fact, recognizing some object means establishing a close match between new stimulus and previously stored stimulus patterns. Pattern recognition is the area of AI, which is much motivated by activities of animates. In the animates, the ability of sensing and pattern recognition is manifested at both conscious and unconscious levels. Primarily the animates exhibit following types of sensing:

(i) **Visual Recognition**: By this, they identify objects like home, office, school, restaurants, faces of people, handwriting and printed words.

(ii) **Aural Sensing**: By this, they identify familiar voices, songs, pieces of music, and other sounds.

(iii) **Touch Sensing**: By this, they identify physical objects such as pens, cups etc.

Human's skill of cognition motivated the development of certain procedures resulting in 'pattern recognition' in computers. An impressive amount of research has been done in this area and they have given excellent results. Systems have now been developed to readily perform character and speech recognition, fingerprint and photograph recognition, graphical pattern identification, and detection of explosive and hostile threats.

Object Classification is also closely related to recognition. The ability to classify or group objects according to some commonly shared features is a form of class of recognition. Classification is essential for decision making, learning and many other cognitive acts. Hence, Pattern recognition aims to classify data (patterns) based on either *a priori* knowledge or on statistical information extracted from the patterns. The patterns to be classified are usually groups of measurements or observations, defining points in an appropriate multidimensional space.

A complete pattern recognition system consists of:

(i) *a sensor* that gathers the observations to be classified or described;

(ii) *a feature extraction mechanism* that computes numeric or symbolic information from the observations;

(iii) *a classification or description scheme* that does the actual job of classifying or describing observations, relying on the extracted features and,

(iv) *a matching rule generator.*

These are described in detail in the next section. The classification or description scheme is usually based on the availability of a set of patterns that have already been classified or described. This set of pattern is termed as the training set and the resulting learning strategy is characterized as supervised learning. Learning can also be unsupervised, in the sense that the system is not given *a priori* labelling of patterns, instead it establishes the classes based on the statistical regularities of the patterns.

Typical applications of pattern matching are automatic speech recognition, classification of text into several categories (e.g. spam / non-spam email messages), the automatic recognition of handwritten postal codes on postal envelopes, or the automatic recognition of images of human faces. The last two examples form the subtopic image analysis of pattern recognition that deals with digital images as input to pattern recognition systems.

Pattern recognition becomes more complex when templates are used to generate variants. For example, in English, it has been identified that sentences frequently follow the "N-VP" (noun - verb phrase) pattern. This type of templates make the analysis and processing of pattern recognition easier, but identifying such templates is practically difficult. A good amount of observation on the English sentences is required to detect the pattern. Pattern recognition is studied in many fields, including psychology, ecology, and computer science.

11.2.1 Pattern Recognition Process

The pattern recognition process has following four components:
 (i) Sensor
 (ii) Feature selection
(iii) Matching
 (iv) Classification rules

The block diagram of a pattern recognition system is shown in Fig. 11.17.

The sensory objects provide the stimuli. It has been observed that more prominent attributes like size, shape, color and texture produce strongest stimuli. These inputs are used to generate a pattern in the form of the input vector X. The

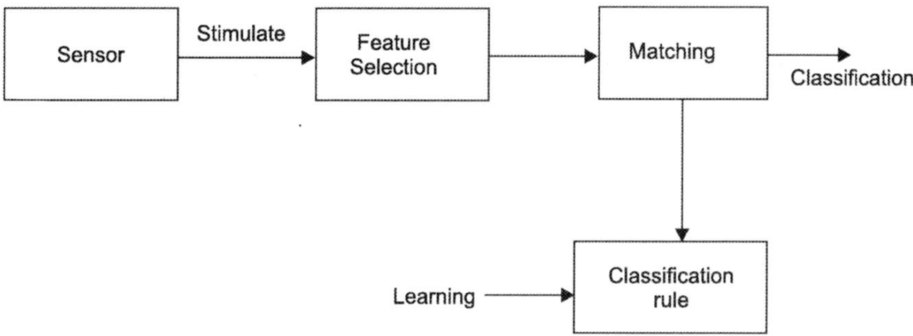

Fig. 11.17: Pattern Recognition Process

vector X is generated by some grammar, classification tree, a description graph, or some other means of representation.

The feature selection selects salient features, performs specific grouping or clustering of the objects, consistent with some goals associated with object classification. This subset represents the reduction in attribute classification process.

In next step of pattern recognition process, with the help of these selected attribute values, class characterization models are learnt by forming generalized phototype description. These models are stored for subsequent recognition.

In the last step of pattern recognition process, the recognition of familiar objects is achieved through applications of previously learned rules, and by comparing and matching of object features with the stored models, refinements and adjustments can be performed continually thereafter to improve the quality and speed of recognition.

The pattern recognition is performed using two basic approaches:
 (i) Syntactic approach
 (ii) Decision theoretic approach

11.2.1.1 Syntactic (or structural) Approach

It works on the principle of structural interrelationships of features. This approach is based on uniqueness of "syntactic structure" among the object classes. A wide range of algorithms can be applied for pattern recognition, from very simple Bayesian classifiers to much more powerful neural networks. This approach defines a grammar in terms of object description instead of alphabets. Its vocabulary is based on shape primitives. It is shown in the Fig. 11.18.

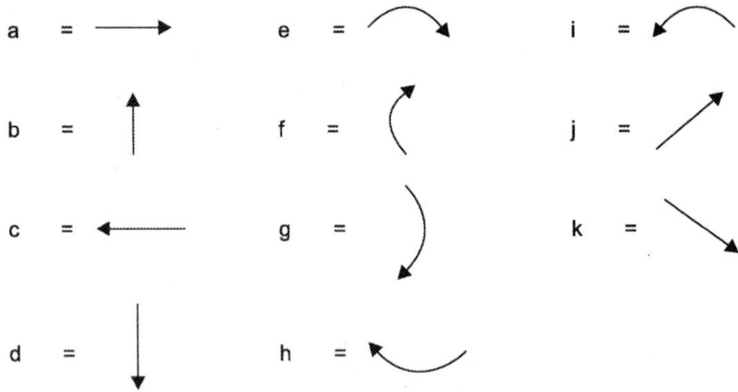

Fig. 11.18: Basic primitive shapes

The objects are defined in terms of this grammar as shown in Fig. 11.19.

Using syntactic analysis, the classification is achieved by assigning an object to class C_i when the string describing it, has been generated by the grammar G_i. It means that, the string be recognized as a member of the language $L(G_i)$.

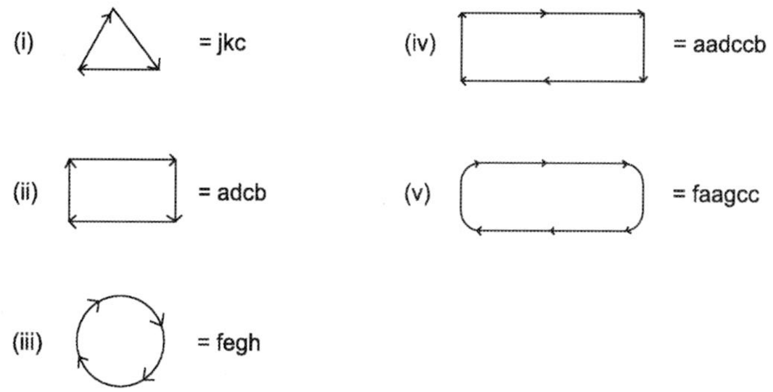

(i)   = jkc   (iv)   = aadccb

(ii)   = adcb   (v)   = faagcc

(iii)   = fegh

Fig. 11.19: Syntactic charecterisation of objects

When the patterns are noisy or subject to random fluctuations, ambiguities may occur since patterns belonging to different classes may appear to be the same. In such cases, stochastic or fuzzy grammars may be used. Classification for these cases may be made on the basis of least cost to transform an input string into a valid recognizable string, by the degree of class set inclusion.

11.2.1.2 Decision Theoretic (or Statistical) Approach

Statistical pattern recognition is based on statistical characterizations of patterns, assuming that the patterns are generated by a probabilistic system. It uses a decision function to classify objects. A decision function maps pattern Vector X into decision region of D. Formally, the problem of pattern recognition may be formulated as follows:

1. Given a universe of objects, say OBJECT = $\{ob_1, ob_2, \ldots\ldots\ldots ob_n\}$, let each object ob_j has k observable attributes and relations expressible as a vector $V = (v_1, v_2, \ldots\ldots v_n)$.

2. For the data given in step 1, perform the following:
    (a) Find subset of $m \le k$ of v_i say $X = (x_1, x_2, \ldots\ldots x_m)$ whose values uniquely characterize the o_i,
    (b) Find $c \ge$ groupings or classifications of the o_i, which exhibit high intraclass and low interclass similarities such that a decision function $d(X)$ can be found with partitions D into 'c' disjoint regions. The regions are used to classify each o_i as belonging to at the most one of the 'c' classes.

To execute the steps of (a) and (b), it effectively requires, (i) mapping from measurement space M to feature space F and then, (ii) a maping from F to the classification or decision space D. i.e. transformation $M \rightarrow F \rightarrow D$ is required. The measurement space is defined as the "set of all measurements" and, feature space is defined as "set of all feature attributes".

It has been practically observed that in the situations, where there are two classes of pattern vectors say C_1 and C_2, the values of the object's pattern vectors may tend to cluster into two disjoint groups. The object's class is determined by weighted linear decision function d(X). It is given by following equation:

$$d(X) = w_1 x_1 + w_2 x_2 + w_3 x_3$$

here, 'w' are the weight factors and 'x' are attribute values. The linear decision function is shown in the Fig. 11.20.

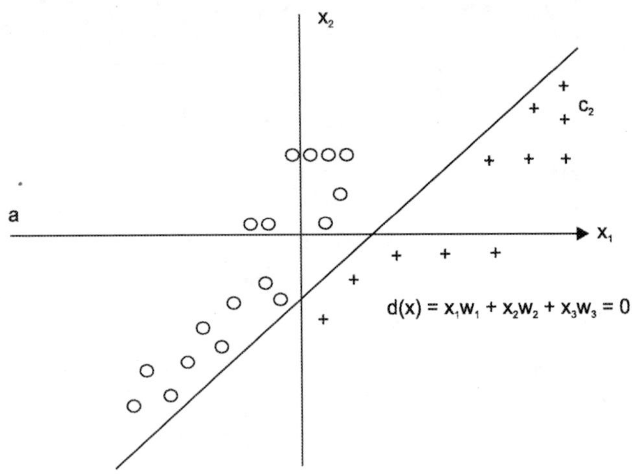

Fig. 11.20: A linear decision function

The constants w_is are the weights that are adjudged to find a separating line for the classes. When a function d is used, an object is classified as belonging to C_1, if its pattern vector is such that d(X)< 0, and as belonging to class C_2, when d(X)> 0. The classification is indeterminate, so any of the classes may be selected.

When the class reference vector's prototype R_j for j = 1,2, ...c, are available, the decision function can be defined in terms of the distances of X from the reference vectors. Thus the distance,

$$d_i(X) = (X - R_i)' (X - R_i)$$

could be computed for each class C_i , and class C_k would then be chosen when d_k = min {C_i}.

The decision function approach of pattern recognition is an example of deterministic recognition, as x_is are deterministic varaibles. In the situations where the attribute values are affected by noise or other random fluctuations, it may be more appropriate to determine probabilistic decision function. In probabilistic decision function, the attribute vectors X are treated as random variables and the decision functions are defined as measures of likelihood of class inclusions.

11.2.2 Learning Classification Patterns

Before a system can recognize objects, it must process knowledge of the characteristic features of those objects. It means, the special feature rules must be stored in the system. In case of linear decision function, the weights that define class boundaries must be predefined or learned. The pattern recognition is an example of supervised learning. It is accomplished by training examples to the learning unit. The examples are labeled beforehand with their correct identities or class. The attribute values and object labels are used by the learning component to inductively extract and determine pattern criteria from each class. This knowledge is used to adjust parameters in decision functions or grammars rewrite rules.

PART-III

11.3 COMPUTER VISION

Vision is another remarkable human sensing capability. Through the visual system, we are able to acquire information about our environment. The human visual organ acquire the information at phenomenal rate and with an excellent resolution. The human eye has the resolution of the order of 25×10^6 parts per square centimeter, whereas the TV camera has the resolution of 500 parts per square centimeter. Thus human beings have the resolution, which is several orders of magnitude more than that of TV camera. Besides this, the human beings receive and acquire images with perfect ease and virtually in an effortless manner. Vision in organic system is the process of sensing a pattern of light energy and developing an interpretation of those patterns.

To imitate this capability of human beings, the computer should be made to understand the patterns or images using some sort of direct sensing capabilities. Computer vision is the area of developing the theories and methodologies, which can directly sense some images. Computer vision is one way for a computer system to reach beyond the supplied data and capture the images about the real world. There are many important applications of computer vision. These are in the following fields:

(i) *Manufacturing*: In this field, the image understanding is used for part's inspection, control and assembly, sorting, dispensing, locating and packaging of programs.

(ii) *Medical*: In this field, it is used for screening, tomographic, ultrasound, and other medical images.

(iii) *Defense*: In the area of defense, it has wide applications. The image understanding is used for (a) photo reconnaissance, analysis and scene interpretation (b) target detection, identification and tracking (c) weapons guidance (d) remote and local site monitoring.

(iv) *Robotics*: In this area, image understanding is used for guidance of welders, and spray paint nozzles, autonomous guidance of land.

(v) *Business*: In this area, the image understanding is used for visual document readers, design tools for engineers, and architects.

(vi) *Space Research*: The image understanding and remote sensing is specially useful in the area of space research. There, it is used for discovery and interpretation of astronomical images, terrestrial image mapping, and interpretation for plant disease, mineral deposits, insect infestations and soil erosion.

Computer vision is used for image understanding. Now we will describe the process of image understanding in brief. The image understanding involve the techniques of image acquisition, their processing, their classification, their recognition and performing various types of manipulations on those images. Different scientists have given various other definitions of computer vision. Some of these are presented herewith:

> *"Computer vision is the enterprise of automating and integrating a wide range of processes and visual perception."*

- Ballard and Brown (1982)

> *"Computer vision is more than recognition, it is the low level processing and operations on purely image processing algorithms, and again subsume image processing of image".*

- Boyle and Thomas (1988)

Niblock(1986) describes image processing as the computer processing of pictures. It includes many techniques of image processing, but is broader than it, in the sense that it is concerned with a complete **"visually capable machine"**.

11.3.1 Human Vision Processing

In human beings, the sensory organ involved in the vision process is eye. Sensing the pattern of light energy and developing an interpretation of those patterns. The human process of visual interpretation is shown in the Fig. 11.21.

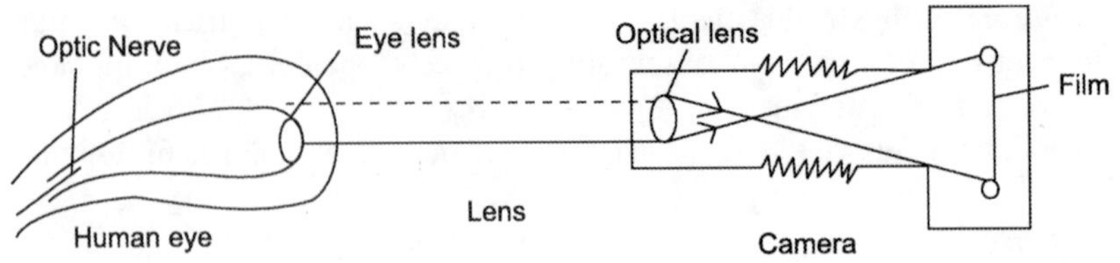

Fig. 11.21: Human vision processing

In human beings, the light from illuminated object is collected by the transparent lens of eye. It is focused and projected onto the retina, which excites the light sensitive organs. When excited, the sensors send impulses through the optic nerve to the visual cortex where the images are interpreted and recognized.

In computer vision system, almost all these processes are simulated. A typical computer vision system follows following steps:

(i) Capturing and sensing of image formation. In this step, the basic image to be viewed is sensed and then digitized.

(ii) The image is broken into segments and wave shaping type of local level processing is applied on it.

(iii) Semantic understanding of the image is performed.

The vision processing has many similarities with the natural language processing. The image sensor corresponds to the speech recognition process of natural language processing. The low and intermediate level of processing corresponds to the syntactic and semantic level of language processing and high level processing in both cases, corresponds to the development of high level knowledge structures.

Block diagram of vision process is shown in the Fig. 11.22.

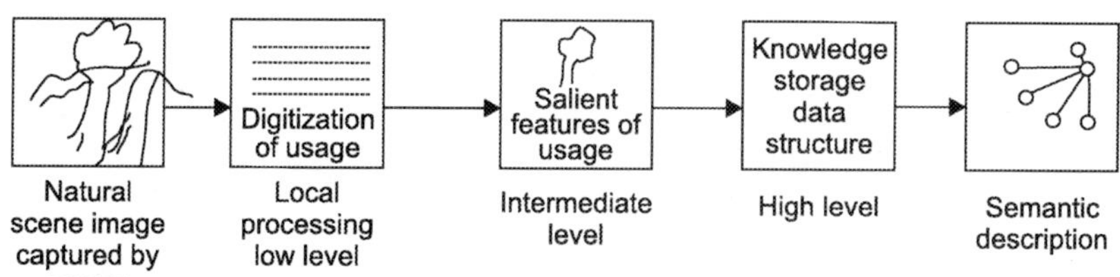

Fig. 11.22: Block Diagram of vision process

The basic input to the vision process is a two dimensional image collected from light sensitive surface. After scanning, the image is formed in terms of continuously varying voltage patterns. These scanned images are digitized. That means, first the image is sampled. In the process of sampling, the value of voltage is taken at discrete time interval and for different pixels. These samples for discrete pixels are converted into numbers. The number corresponds to the grey level intensity for black and white images. For color images, the intensity value is comprised of three separate arrays of numbers, one for the intensity of each of the basic colors, i.e., red, green, and blue.

After digitization, some low level processing is done on this digitalized image. This is smoothing of neighbouring points to reduce noise, finding outlines of object or edge elements, performing the threshold analysis and determining the texture, color and other object feature. These initial processing steps are one, which are used to locate object boundaries and other structures within the image.

The second stage is intermediate level processing. The functions performed in this stage are connecting, filling in, combining boundaries, determining regions, and assigning descriptive labels to objects. This stage builds higher level structures from the lower level elements of the first stage.

The last step is higher level image processing. It consists of identifying the important objects in the image and their conversion in the well formed knowledge structures.

Now, let us discuss these steps in detail:

11.3.1.1 Digitization

For use in the computer the images must be represented in the form, which the machine can read. In the process of digitization, the analog video image is converted into a digital image. The digital image is basically a stream of numbers, each corresponds to the small region of image. The number is a measure of the light intensity of the pixel. It is called a grey level. Following Fig. 11.23 shows the digitized image.

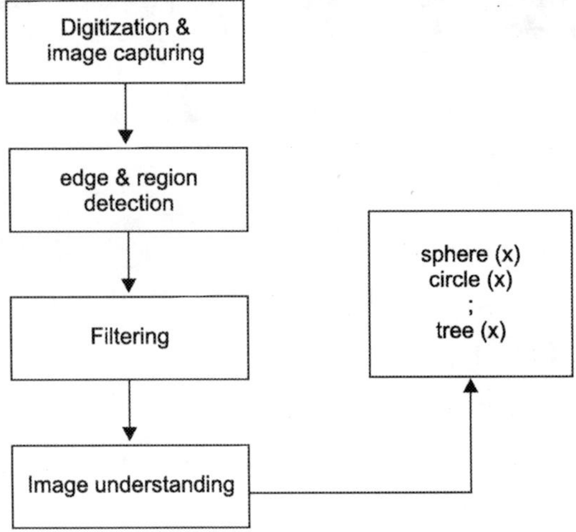

Fig. 11.23: A digitisation & under standing of image

The conversion to grey scale is performed by simple algorithm. It converts the images into small parts called pixels and simply assigns a number to that part, based on their darkness. The blurring of edges, and other effects conspires to make the grey scale image inaccurate. In some cameras, the pixel is rectangular rather than square. This concept is based on the aspect ratio. The relationship between darkness and grey scale recorded may not be linear.

After the image is converted into grey levels, a thresholding is performed to select key features of it. In this process, all the pixels whose grey level has crossed certain value are selected.

The detection of edges of the images plays an important part. The edge detection in image formation is also performed by thresholding. It is used to perform the sharpening of the object by enhancing some portions and reducing others. Like noise and some unwanted features. In real world there are certain objects, which have general low level intensity; and certain objects whose general level of intensity is more. The thresholding is used to distinguish these objects. In such situations several threshold levels may be necessary, because, otherwise the low level intensity objects may be lost because of high threshold value, and unwanted background will be picked up and enhanced by low threshold levels. Thresholding at several levels may be the best way to determine the different regions of the image when it is necessary to compensate for variations in illuminating of poor contrast.

In image capturing, first the histogram is produced. The histogram records the frequency of occurrence of different intensity levels within the image. An analysis of histogram reveals where concentration of different intensity levels occur. From this knowledge the best choice of threshold (T) values are identified, e.g., a histogram with two or more clear separations between intensity levels that have a relatively high frequencies of occurrence will suggest the best threshold levels for object identification and separation. A histogram is shown in the following Fig. 11.24.

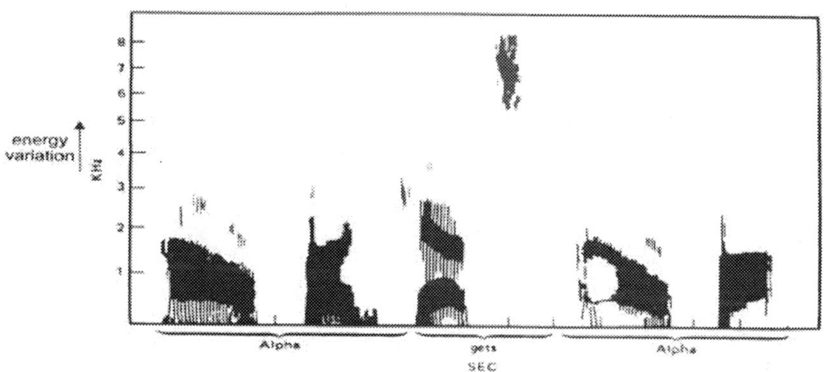

Fig. 11.24: Histogram of an image

11.3.1.2 Digital filtering

This process falls in the category of wave shaping or signal processing. The digital filters are used to perform some further processing on the digitized image. As mentioned earlier, we have the problem of noise, blurring, and lightening effects. Various signal processing techniques, which make image interpretation difficult can be applied to the image in order to remove some of the effects of noise or enhance other features, such as edges. There are various types of filtering techniques for performing this task. Some of them are described below:

Smoothing

This is a form of digital filtering. It is used to reduce the noise and other unwanted features and to enhance certain other image features. It gives some sort of smoothing effect to the image. It eliminates the spikes and flattens widely fluctuating intensity values. Popular smoothing techniques are local averaging, the use of modeling techniques, parametric form filtering.

In local averaging method of smoothing, each pixel in the array is replaced by weighted average of pixel and its neighbouring values. It is done using filter masks, which use some configuration of neighbouring pixel values to compute a smooth replacement value. For example, average of eight neighbouring pixel values is taken, and whatever is the outcome, all the pixels intensities are replaced by this average intensity value. The effect of smoothing in terms of image quality becomes loss of brightness or fast intensity variations, and in terms of image storage, is reduces amount of data. The degree of smoothing and hence blurring, can be controlled with the use of appropriate weighting values in the mask. Weighted smoothing of this type over a region is known as convolution. Local boundary detection is the process of finding a boundary or edge or delimiter between two regions. An edge shows up relatively thin line or arc between two otherwise contrast regions. This is discussed in next section.

Many filters can be applied for smoothing. The *Gaussian filter* is one such filter. The Gaussain filter is a special smoothing filter based on the bell shaped Gaussian curve, well known in the statistics as normal distribution. We imagine a window of infinite size, where the weights w(x, y) assigned to the pixel at position x, y from the centre are given as:

$$w(x, y) = 1 / \sqrt{\pi \sigma^2} = \exp [(x^2 + y^2)]$$

where, the constant σ is a measure of the spread of the window, i.e., how much the image will be smeared by the filter. A small value of sigma will mean that the weights in the filter will be small for distant pixels, whereas a large value allows more distant pixels to effect the new value of current pixel. If noise effects, groups of pixels together, then large value of sigma is used.

11.3.2 Edge Detection

It is the prime function to be performed in computer vision. Normally, an image appears smooth and continuous hence, detecting an edge is a difficult task. Regions belongings to the same object are usually distinguishable by one or more features, which are relatively homogeneous throughout, such as color, texture, three dimensional flow or intensity. The edges represent the discontinuities in one or more aspects. The edges form a key part of human visual understanding. This is clear from the fact that human beings can guess about a picture by just seeing few lines of a two or three diemnsional image. Edge detection primarily consists of two steps:

(i) In first step, potential edge pixels are identified by looking at their grey level compared with surrounding pixels.

(ii) In second step, individual edge pixels are traced to form the edge lines. Some of the edges may form the closed curves, while others will terminate or form a junction with other edge.

The discountinuities are identified by rate of change in intensity in horizontal or vertical direction. The difference function which identifies rate of change is defined as follows:

$$D_x = f(x,y) - f(x-n,y)$$
$$D_y = f(x,y) - f(x, y-n)$$

Where, n is a small integer greater than or equal to 1.

In an image, wherever edges are there, values of Dx and Dy will vary sharply, whereas in homogeneous region, they will vary smoothly. The rate of change of gradient can also be useful in finding local edges.

We can use gradient operator to perform edge detection by identifying areas with high gradients. There are various gradient operators used. These are robert's operator, Soble's operator and laplacian operator.

11.3.2.1 Edge following

After identifying the pixels, which may be present on the object edges, in next step those pixels are arranged together to make lines. That is to identify which group of pixels make an edge. In the process of edge following, the edges that make a line are identified.

In the process of 'edge following', the following activities are performed:

(i)   Select any potential edge pixel, which has not already been used.

(ii) Choose one direction to follows first.

(iii) Find any adjoining pixel in the right general direction.

(iv) If the orientation of the pixel is not too different then accept it.

(v)   In a situation when adjoining pixel is not found, scan those one or two pixels away.

(vi) If an acceptable pixel has been found, repeat from (iii), otherwise repeat the process in another direction.

11.3.2.2 Region detection

In image understanding, the identification of region detection is also important. The region is defined as a connected group of pixels whose intensity is almost the same. Region detection aims to identify the main shapes in an image. In the process of region detection following steps are performed:

(i) Identification of the identical pixels and grouping them together.

(ii) Estimating the boundaries between these regions, if the difference is more than a threshold, merging the regions.

11.3.3 Texture and Color

Texture is repeated pattern of elementary shapes occurring on an object's surface. Texture may be regular and periodic and random or partially periodic. The texture can cause problems in all types of image analysis, but region growing has some special problems. If the image is unprocessed then a textures surface will have pixels of many different intensities. It may lead to many small island regions within each large region. The identification of pixel is normally based on statistical analysis of small groups of pixels, the application of pattern matching, the use of fourier transform, or modeling with special functions called fractals. Discussion of these are beyond the scope of the chapter.

11.3.4 Reconstruction of an Image

After the edges and regions are identified, the image is reconstructed. For this purpose, various hidden features of image need to be inferred about the objects. We can use constraint satisfaction algorithms to determine what possible objects can be constructed from the lines given. These lines are categorized into concave lines, convex lines and obscuring edges. An obscuring edge occurs where a part of one object lies in front of another object or in front of different parts of an object. To mark these edges + or – signs are used. The convention is to use a '+' to label a convex edge and '–' to label a concave image and 'arrow' for obscuring edge. Some line configurations are shown in the following Fig. 11.25.

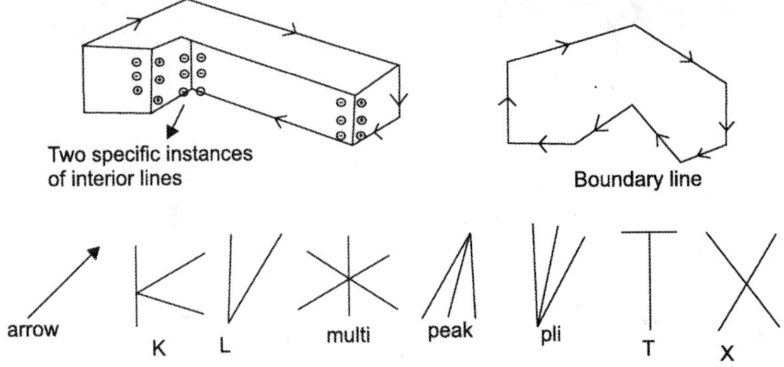

Fig. 11.25: Some line configurations

In this chapter, we have presented elementary concepts of image understanding. Actually, it is a big topic in itself. And lot of work is going on in this area. Students are advised to go through other reference material for more studies.

11.3.5 The Waltz Algorithm

The Waltz algorithm is used for image reconstruction. In the process of image reconstruction, after identifying the constraints, these are applied to analyze the problem. The Waltz algorithm works as follows:

(i) Find the line at the border of scene boundary and label them. These can be found by finding an outline, such that no vertices are outside it. This is done first to perform the process of identification of related constraints propagation.

(ii) Number the vertices of the figure to be analyzed. These will correspond to order in which the vertices will be visited during the labeling process. For deciding on a numbering, following steps are followed:

(a) Start at any vertex on boundary of figure. As boundary lines are known, the vertex involving them are more highly constrained then interior boundaries.

(b) Move from vertex along the boundary to an adjacent unnumbered vertex and continue until all boundary vertices have been numbered.

(c) Number interior vertices by moving from a numbered vertex to some adjacent unnumbered one.

(iii) Visit each vertex V in order and attempt to label it by performing the following:

(a) Using the set of possible vertex labeling

(b) Eliminate some of labeling on the basis of local constraints. To do this, examine each vertex A, that is adjacent to V and that has already been visited. Check to see that for each proposed labeling for V, there is a way to label the line between V and A in such a way that at least one of the labeling listed for A is still possible. Eliminate from V's list any labeling for which this is not the case.

(c) Label the labeling to constrain the labeling at vertices adjacent to V.

This algorithm would always find the unique correct figure labeling if one exists. For ambiguous figures, the algorithm will terminate. The usefulness of the algorithm increases as size of domain increases.

EXERCISES

1. Draw the diagram of neural network which computes the XOR function of two inputs.

2. Draw a feedforward 3-2-3-2 network (show how a connection is allowed from a node layer I to node layer i+1). How many hidden layers does this network has?

3. Consider the image of a house. Digitize this image. Then, threshold this image at each of the following levels: 1, 5, 8. Record your results on squared or graph paper marking each square which exceeds the threshold.

4. Differentiate between Syntactic approach and Decision theoretic approach of pattern recognition.

5. Explain the pattern recognition process with the help of suitable diagram.

6. Explain the computer vision process with the help of suitable diagram.

7. What is the difference between a standard disjunction and an internal disjunction.

8. Given the following histogram, what are the most likely threshold points.

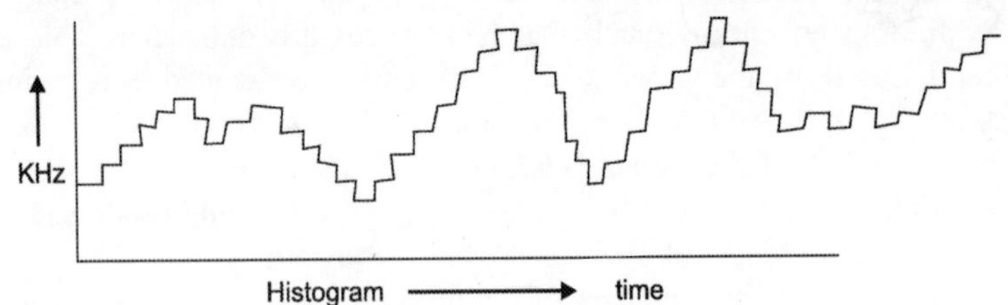

9. How much memory is required to produce and compare five different binary images each of with a different threshold level. A secure system resolution 1024x1024. Can the binary images be compressed in some way to reduce memory requirements.

10. Consider a situation in which CPU takes 300 nanosecond to per form memory/register transfer and 600 nanoseconds to perform basic arithmetic operations. Estimate the time required to produce a binary image for a system with a resolution of 256x256 pixels.

11. Explain the functioning of fixed increment perception learning algorithm. Invent a three feature linearly separable classification problem on which to test your program.

12. Compare symbolic AI with connections AI. Explain what problems can be categorizes under two headings.

13. What are the salient features of hebbian learning. How it is different than competitive learning.

14. List various applications of feedforward and feedback neural network systems.

15. Study and list some other neural network activation function, which are not explained in the chapter.

12
Expert Systems

12.1 INTRODUCTION

Fifty years back, when AI was born, its prime areas of concern were game playing, planning and problem solving. During that era, it would have been hard to imagine that thirty years later, AI would become backbone of problem solving techniques and its role would become vital in the areas of medical diagnosis, geology, mining and engineering etc. and in tern would form the basis of modern development and economic growth. Today, the most important areas of AI are centered around knowledge engineering in general, and expert systems in particular.

Considerable amount of success that expert systems have gained in the areas mentioned above during the past few years has led to substantial amount of interest in variety of fields such as battle plan management, optimal routing, fault diagnosis, optimal portfolio selection etc.

12.2 EXPERTS AND EXPERT SYSTEMS

An *expert* is a person who has specialization and expertise in a particular field. It means, an expert has knowledge and skills which most of other people do not have. An expert can solve a problem much easily and much efficiently than others who can not solve that problem, e.g., an eye surgeon will operate and solve the problem related to eye in a much professional and efficient way compared to a normal person, only because an eye surgeon is an expert in his field.

An *expert system* is also "something" which acts as an expert of a particular field just like human expert. Early researchers have defined that "something" as "an intelligent computer program". It means an expert system is nothing but a computer program that acts intelligently and solves the problems in the same manner in which a human expert will.

12.3 SUCCESSIVE DEVELOPMENT OF EXPERT SYSTEMS

A trace of developing problem solving tool is found way back in 1940s in the works related to post production rules. Subsequently in late 1950s and early 1960s, a number of programs were written with the aim of problem solving. One of the earliest programs known as DENDRAL was written and developed at Stanford in the late 1960s by a team of Ed Feigenbaum, Bruce Buchanan and Joshua Lederberg to interpret the output of a mass spectrometer as accurately as expert chemists. The basic function of DENDRAL was to infer the structure of organic molecules from their chemical formulae and mass spectrographic information about the chemical bonds present in the molecules. Since number of organic molecules is very large, the number of possible structures of these molecules is also huge. DENDRAL handles the problem of this large search space by applying the heuristic knowledge of expert chemists. DENDRAL's method proved to be very effective in finding the correct structure out of the possible millions after only a few trials. The impact of DENDRAL was vital and many systems were developed later on for use in chemical and pharmaceutical laboratories.

Next major development was in the field of medical diagnosis. Feigenbaum, Buchanan and Edward Shortliffe, again at Stanford in the mid 1970s developed a system called MYCIN to diagnose blood infections. Whereas DENDRAL was first program to use knowledge to achieve expert level performance, MYCIN established the methodology for developing expert systems and many other contemporary systems were built based on the same methodology. Details of these expert systems will be dealt with in subsequent paragraphs of this chapter.

Other examples of expert systems are PROSPECTOR, a program for determining the probable location and type of ore deposits based on geological information about a site; the INTERNIST, a program for performing diagnosis in the area of internal medicine; XCON, a system for configuring VAX computers; CLIPS, STEAMER, LITHO, TIMM etc.

Since 1960s, when a fully functional expert system was first built up till now, the development and use of expert systems has been through a long journey. Now a days, expert systems are used to solve problems in many areas such as medicine, education, business, design, geology, engineering and others successfully. Lot of work is still going on and lot of research is to be done to fulfill unaccomplished task.

12.4 AN OVERVIEW OF EXPERT SYSTEMS

A doctor is able to diagnose and cure a disease because he possesses knowledge about medicines. Similarly, a geologist is able to discover mineral deposits because he possesses deep knowledge about geology. Doctors and geologists are called experts of their respective areas. It means experts possess deep knowledge about their area. They acquire this knowledge from books, magazines, journals etc. and through experience they gain from working over the years in a particular field. Hence, it should be understood that *knowledge* is basic and most important factor responsible for making a person expert of a particular field. The knowledge of a specific field possessed by an expert of that field is called *domain- knowledge*. The job of experts is to solve any problem related to their area of interest. The information related to the problem is called problem area or *domain*. For solving any problem, first step is to identify the domain of problem to be solved. After this, the problem is passed to an expert who possesses required amount of knowledge or expertise about that particular domain. Expert knowledge is a combination of theoretical understanding of a problem and a collection of heuristic problem solving techniques. An expert applies both of these for solving a particular problem.

Expert systems are also built with the aim to get work from them similar to that of human experts. It means, expert systems are meant to solve real world problems. Hence, any expert system would primarily require deep knowledge of a particular area. This knowledge is acquired from human experts and coding of the same is done into a form that is applicable by a computer to solve a problem of a particular domain. Hence, a major feature of expert systems has been their reliance on the knowledge of human experts for problem solving strategies of the system. The most challenging job before knowledge engineers had been to acquire and represent sufficient amount of knowledge for constructing an expert system. A simple method of acquiring knowledge and building an expert system is illustrated in fig. 12.1. An expert provides the necessary knowledge of the problem domain through a general discussion of his/her problem solving techniques and by demonstrating those skills by a set of sample problems. The knowledge engineer then codes this knowledge explicitly in knowledge base and uses the same for developing a computer program that is both effective and intelligent in its behavior. Once such a program is developed, its expertise is refined by giving to it example problems for solving, getting comments of the human experts about the results produced and getting modifications done to the expert's knowledge as suggested by human experts. This process is repeated until the program achieves desired level of performance in solving the problems.

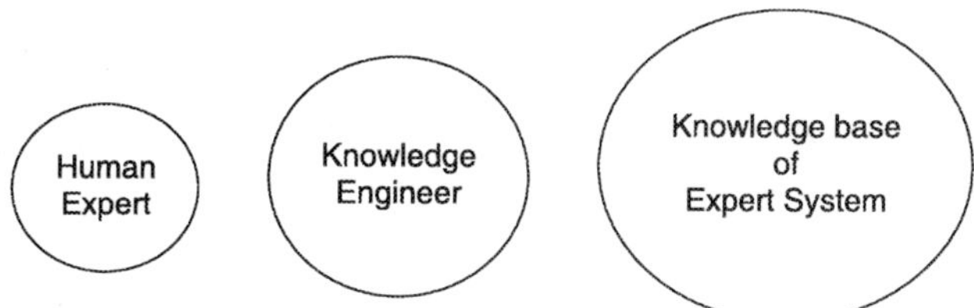

Fig. 12.1: Process of acquiring knowledge

After understanding what has been written until now, we should try to define expert system. An expert system basically, is a computer program that acts intelligently like a human expert and performs the task of designing, diagnosing, analyzing, monitoring, advising and scheduling etc. Professor Edward Feigenbaum of Stanford University has defined an expert system as *"an intelligent computer program that uses knowledge and inference procedures to solve problems that are difficult enough to require significant human expertise for their solutions."* Hence, an expert system is a computer program that *emulates* the decision-making ability and problem solving capability of a human expert.

Although human experts have obvious advantages over the expert systems, the benefits and support they provide for solving real world problems is undoubtedly awesome. It is also necessary to mention that in many aspects, expert systems perform in a better way in comparison to human experts. Though a general-purpose problem solver is still a dream of knowledge engineers, expert systems function well in their restricted domain.

12.5 HUMAN EXPERTS V/S EXPERT SYSTEMS

As mentioned earlier, human experts have distinct advantages over expert systems. On the other hand, expert systems have advantages over human experts also in more than one aspect. We will now try to focus on these issues in detail in the subsequent paragraphs.

12.5.1 Advantages of Human Experts Over Expert Systems

Although modern technology has facilitated development of expert systems that compete well with the expertise of human experts, it would be a mistake to overestimate the ability of expert systems while comparing those with human experts. Human experts still have advantages over the machines in some specific areas, as mentioned below:

- *Depth of knowledge base*- human experts not only possesses deep knowledge of the problem domain, but also are able to apply heuristic knowledge and common sense as and when required. On the other hand expert systems find difficulty in capturing deep knowledge. Their functioning depends upon the knowledge base they possess and that limitation of knowledge affects the output they provide of a particular problem. They also lack in application of common sense knowledge, e.g., MYCIN does not possess any knowledge about human physiology. It does not know anything about the function of spinal chord. A famous legendary saying is that once MYCIN asked whether the patient was pregnant during selection of drugs for treatment of meningitis, even though it was told that the patient was a male. This might be a joke in its true sense, such incidents indicate towards the narrowness of knowledge of expert systems. A human expert will hardly commit such type of mistake.

- *Ability to provide explanations*- human experts are not only able to provide best possible solution of a problem in hand, but also are able to explain why is the solution most appropriate and about the approach applied to find the solution of a particular problem. Expert systems are not able to explain the above facts because of the lack of deep knowledge they possess.

- *Flexibility and robustness*- if humans are encountered with a problem that is difficult for them to solve immediately, they can wait and find some strategy to solve the problem. Expert systems cannot do so. Whatever result they will produce today, the same they will provide ever after.

- *Learning from experience*- human experts keep on adding to their knowledge by experience they acquire over the years without any extra effort and they are able to use that enhanced knowledge in dealing with the problems that may come before them later on. Whereas expert systems once built will not learn anything from experience and their performance will remain same unless modifications are done to their program.

In spite of the limitations of expert systems mentioned above, they have proved their worth in a number of applications. Because of this fact, development of expert systems is a burning area of research and their use in almost all the areas is increasing day-by-day.

12.5.2 Advantages of Expert Systems Over Human Experts

Although it is hard to eliminate human experts, expert systems have taken over them in many areas because of the ease, efficiency and economy in using expert systems for solving intricate problems. Some of the advantages expert systems possess over the humans are mentioned below:

- *Easy availability-* expert system once developed is easily available to any computer. One expert system can be used at different places at the same time. Thus, expert systems are tools of mass production. Human experts are not easily available and they have limitations of working hours. In addition, one expert can deal with one problem at a time at single place.
- *Economy-* use of expert systems is much more economical compared to humans.
- *Permanence-* the expertise of expert systems is forever. Human experts may quit or die, but expert systems will last indefinitely.
- *Multiple expertise-* multiple expert systems can be used to work simultaneously on one problem and the combined expertise may exceed that of a single human expert. It is difficult to use multiple humans to work on a single problem at a time.
- *Fast response-* expert systems respond faster than humans depending upon the hardware and software used in developing them. It is beneficial to use expert systems where fast response is required in some emergency situations.
- *Steady and unemotional-* expert systems do not have emotions, hence their results are unaffected by circumstances. On the other hand, results produced by human experts are sometimes affected by emotions and may not be ideal solutions of the problem. Also, the efficiency of the expert systems remains same irrespective of the duration of their use, while human experts get fatigued and their working efficiency tends to decrease with time. Expert systems are steady and will provide same result of the same problem every time, whereas human experts may come out with different results of the same problem some other time.
- *Intelligent tutor-* expert systems can act as tutor to someone who is interested in learning the reasoning and approach used in solving a particular problem by using the system for various examples. This facility is not available with human experts.

- *Intelligent database-* expert systems can be used to access a database and the same can be used for some other purpose, whereas it is impossible to read the heart and mind of a human expert.
- *Refined knowledge base-* the knowledge base of expert systems is built by acquiring the knowledge from humans. The implicit knowledge present in human's mind is converted into explicit knowledge before entering into knowledge base of an expert systems and this knowledge can be checked and refined before doing so. Hence, quality of knowledge possessed by expert systems is improved. Knowledge possessed by human experts on the other hand, cannot be explored by others and hence cannot be refined or corrected if need be.

We may, thus conclude the above discussion with the understanding that expert systems are vital tools in the area of problem solving. No matter they use the knowledge extracted from the human experts, their performance in more than one ways comes out smarter and better compared to human experts. That is why; expert systems are built to deal with wide range of problems in domains such as medicines, engineering, geology, computer science, mathematics, business, defense and education.

12.6 CHARACTERISTICS OF AN EXPERT SYSTEM

Expert systems are constructed to assist and replace human experts from intricate problem domains for achieving efficiency and economy in problem solving techniques. Hence, it is necessary for expert systems to possess expertise or we may call in straight terms, characteristics similar, if not better than those of human experts. An expert system normally should possess following features:

- The performance of an expert system must match that of human experts. The solution provided by the system of a given problem should be of high quality. This should differentiate the expert system from other computer programs, mathematical modeling or computer animation.
- The response time of the system should be adequate. The system should produce results in reasonable amount of time comparable or better than that of human experts. A system that takes considerably more amount of time, even if produces better quality results, would not be preferable. Requirement of time-bound performance is more in case of real-time systems.
- The system must be able to solve the problem by use of more and more heuristic knowledge. This ability makes them comparable with human experts.
- It should be able to deal with subject matter with realistic complexity that normally requires considerable amount of human expertise.
- The expert system must exhibit high-level performance in terms of speed and reliability in order to be a useful tool. It should not be prone to crashes and should be able to give steady and consistent performance.

- It must be capable of explaining and justifying solutions or recommendations in order to convince the user that its reasoning is correct.
- A system can store huge amount of knowledge. Hence, it should possess desired level of flexibility so that addition, correction, deletion and modification to the knowledge base can be done as and when required to improve the performance of the system.
- System asks many questions to the user for finding the correct path to reach required solution. It should be able to justify the questions it is asking because unnecessary discourse of the system with the user would make the process lengthy, time consuming and may develop complicacies that may affect the final out come.

If an expert system possesses above-mentioned characteristics, it is almost certain that it will perform well and compete with the performance of human experts. The aim of knowledge engineers should be to take care that the system is built having more and more of these characteristics.

Because of the extensive use of knowledge. The expert systems can be considered as extension of knowledge base systems. According to the formal definition of knowledge base systems, These are the systems that perform the task by applying rule of thumb to a symbolic representation of knowledge. These simply posses knowledge in coded or rule base form. Thus, a program talking about 'weather' will be knowledge base system and whereas a system having knowledge about meteorology, which is able to perform weather forecast will be an expert system.

12.7 EXPERT SYSTEM ARCHITECTURE

As mentioned earlier, an expert system should possess certain characteristics so that it might be able to produce desired quality of out put with ease. For imparting required character in an expert system, knowledge engineers design various components which work together to perform different functions. Following figure 12.2 shows architecture of a typical expert system.

An expert system has following modular diagram:

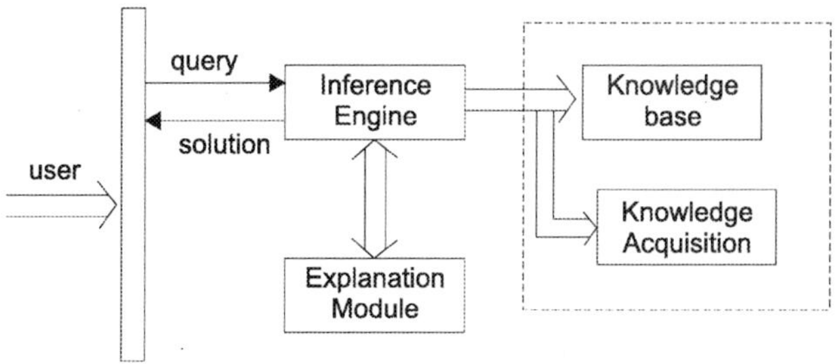

Fig. 12.2: Expert system architecture

- User interface
- Explanation system
- Knowledge base
- Inference engine
- Knowledge base editor
- Knowledge acquisition facilities

These components of an expert system are discussed in detail in following section.

12.7.1 User Interface

User interacts with the system through a user interface. It acts as a bridge between user and expert system. This module accepts the user queries and submits those to expert system. The user normally consults the expert system for following reasons:

- To get answer of his queries.
- To get explanation about the solution for psychological satisfaction.

The user interface module is designed in such a way that at user level it accepts the query in a language understandable by the user and transforms it in appropriate form, which is understandable by expert system. To make the expert system user friendly, the user interface interacts with the user in natural language. Presenting a real world problem to the system for a solution is what is meant by having a consultation. The user interface provides as much facilities as possible such as menus, graphical interface, etc., to make the dialog user friendly and lively.

12.7.2 Explanation System

The explanation facilities allow the program to explain its reasoning to the user. The credibility of expert system will be established only when it is able to explain how and why a particular conclusion is drawn. This explanation increases the belief of user in the expert system. The explanation of how and why has emerged in a comparatively new field of AI called as *"human computer interaction"*. This field is a mixture of AI, engineering, and psychology. The contribution of expert system researchers to this date has been to place a high priority upon the accountability of consultation programs and to show how explanation of programs behavior can be systematically related to the chains of reasoning employed by such systems while explaining the way in which a particular solution has been obtained. The expert in this mode tells all the rules which are applied.

The explanation of expert system behaviors are significant because:

- Users of the system need to be satisfied that program conclusions are correct for their particular problems.
- To give a feedback to knowledge engineer, so that they can satisfy themselves that the knowledge is applied properly.

- Domain expert need to see a trace of the way in which their knowledge is being applied in order to judge whether knowledge elicitation is proceeding successfully.
- Managers of expert system technology, who may end up being responsible for program decision, need to convince themselves that a system module is working properly.

12.7.3 Knowledge Base

Knowledge base is the heart of an expert system. It is repository of knowledge in the expert system. The expert system uses this knowledge to answer the queries or to give a consultation to the user. The knowledge base is a core module of any expert system. The knowledge can be of various types like commonsense knowledge, task oriented knowledge, domain specific knowledge etc. This module of expert system stores task oriented knowledge. The capabilities of expert system are dependent on the amount of knowledge it contains. We require lot of knowledge to build an effective knowledge base. This knowledge is acquired from various sources by applying knowledge acquisition techniques. Knowledge acquisition is full-flagged area of research in the domain of AI. We discuss some of the important aspects of knowledge acquisition here.

12.7.3.1 Knowledge Acquisition

As mentioned earlier, knowledge is gathered from various sources. The process of gathering the knowledge is called knowledge acquisition. It is shown in Fig. 12.3 one of the simple and most common method of acquiring knowledge from human experts is *interview method*. This process of knowledge acquisition is accomplished by interacting and interviewing the human experts of that domain. The job is performed by knowledge engineers. The knowledge acquisition is itself a skilled job. The person interviewing the expert should also have some basic knowledge of the concerned field to find out what to ask. The gathered knowledge is then encoded

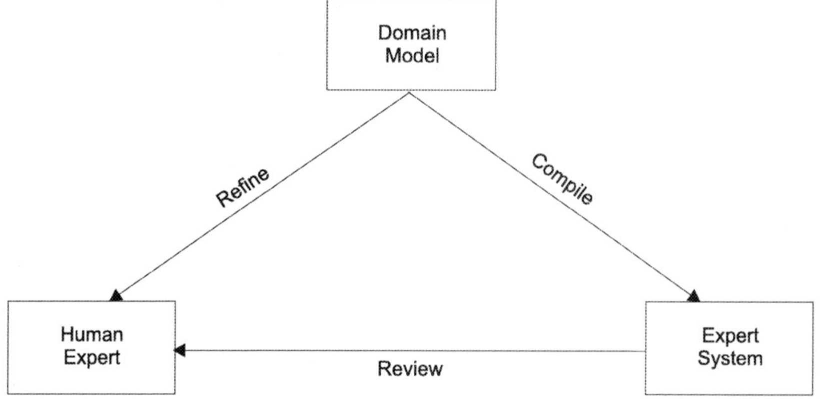

Fig. 12.3: Knowledge acquisition in expert system

in a format suitable for storage in computer memory. This encoding task is performed by a computer specialist. Thus, designing of a knowledge base is vital component as far as construction of expert system is concerned. It is estimated by various studies that consulting experts produces two to five units of knowledge (i.e. rule of thumb) per day. This low output has lead researchers to treat knowledge acquisition as a "bottleneck" in the development of expert systems. Some critical problems which have been encountered during knowledge acquisition are discussed below:

- Expert areas have their own jargon and it is often difficult for the experts themselves to communicate their knowledge in communicable language. Expressing the complicated concepts on a paper is difficult, as these concepts are rarely straightforward and normally do not follow any precise mathematical or logical pattern, e.g., a military strategist may talk about "aggressive posture" of a foreign power without being able to clearly define exactly what distinguishes such a posture from a non-threatening one.

- In real world, there are many application domains where facts also have conceptual aspects. The conceptual aspects regarding facts cannot be characterized precisely in terms of mathematical theory or deterministic model e.g. a financial expert through his experience or heuristics may know that certain events cause the stock market to go up and down, but the exact mechanism that mediate these effects and the magnitude of these effects themselves, can not be identified or predicted with certainty. Thus any mathematical model is not applicable on it. In such type of applications, Statistical models are used to make general, long-term prediction.

- Human experts posses knowledge which they generally acquire over their entire lifetime from various sources. Thus the human knowledge, even in relatively narrow domain, is often set in broader context that involves a good deal of commonsense knowledge about the everyday world, e.g. in case of a legal expert involved in litigation, it is difficult to delineate the amount and nature of general knowledge needed to deal with an arbitrary case.

To overcome the difficulties of interview method of knowledge acquisition, other alternative methods have been evolved. One such method is *automated knowledge elicitation*. In this method, an expert's knowledge is transferred to a computer program as a side effect of a person machine dialogue. Another method is evolved in the area of machine learning. It involves the idea that computing system could perhaps learn to solve the problems in much the same way as humans do. We would discuss few of the important methods of knowledge acquisition here for understanding the concepts involved in their theory and application.

Knowledge acquisition methods adopted by expert systems

Different expert systems have adopted different methods for knowledge acquisition. These are mentioned as follows:

Knowledge acquisition by interview:

This method was adopted in expert system COMPASS. COMPASS is an expert system, which examines error messages derived from switch's self test routine. It looks for open circuit, short circuit, time lag etc.

The knowledge acquisition cycle in COMPASS (from Preran 1990) is shown in Figure. 12.4:

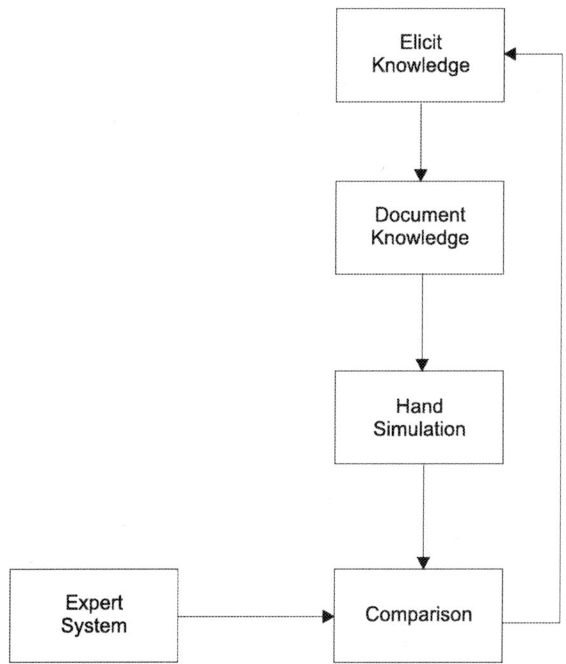

Fig. 12.4: Knowledge acquisition cycle

The knowledge acquisition cycle performs following steps during its functioning:

- acquires knowledge from expert
- documents the acquired knowledge
- tests the new knowledge, as follows:
    - employs an expert to analyze the new set of data
    - analyzes the same data in the form of documented knowledge
    - compares the results of expert opinion
    - if the results differ, then finds the rules that generated the discrepancy and again starts from top to acquire new knowledge.

Knowledge base knowledge acquisition:

This is another method of knowledge acquisition. The working of expert system have given feedback regarding deficiencies in knowledge acquisition. Attempts to use expert systems for tutoring purposes have lead to a deeper understanding about kind of knowledge that experts employ in problem solving and the attempts to build generic expert system tools like EMYCIN have given the feedback that it is difficult to encode the knowledge from some arbitrary domain into frame or production rule format.

Such feedback required researchers to examine the role of domain knowledge and domain inference more closely. The method of knowledge based knowledge acquisition is developed to automate the process of knowledge acquisition. In other words, the knowledge acquisition program needs some knowledge of domain or problem area in order to acquire new knowledge effectively. Similar to the situation where knowledge engineers need to have some knowledge of a domain before they can communicate effectively with an expert.

The knowledge that is needed in order to acquire more knowledge is viewed as form of meta knowledge.

Besides these discussed approaches of knowledge acquisition, some latest approaches include:
*   Problem oriented knowledge acquisition strategies.
*   Unsupervised machine learning of rules by induction over a set of examples.

Other important aspect in the area of development of expert systems is knowledge representation. Though knowledge representation has been dealt with in detail in other sections, we discuss some aspects of it in context of expert systems in this chapter hereunder.

12.7.3.2 Knowledge Representation

In reference to expert systems, knowledge representation is, mostly concerned with finding ways in which large bodies of useful information   can be formally described for the purpose of symbolic computation. That means the knowledge can be represented in some unambiguous language notation, which has well defined syntax governing the form of expression in the language, and a well-defined semantics, which reveals the meaning of such expression by virtue of their form.

AI researchers have expanded a good deal of effort in constructing representation language, i.e. computer languages that are oriented toward organizing descriptions of objects and ideas rather than stating sequences of instructions or storing simple data elements. The knowledge representation should have characteristics of logical completeness, heuristic power, and notational convenience. These are explained below:
*   *logical completeness*-it means, representation should be capable of making the complete description of the concepts e.g., it is not possible to represent the idea that every drug has some side effects unless one is able to

differentiate between the designation of a particular drug and a particular side effect. Accordingly, one cannot make a generalized statement about the concept that " for any drug ,there is an undesirable side effect associated with it."

- *Heuristic power-* means that though the representation should have a good expressive way, simultaneously, there must be some way of using the representation to solve the problems in a short straightforward manner. Normally, the more expressive the language is, in terms of the number of semantic distinctions that it can make, the more difficult it is to control the process of drawing inferences during problem solving. Much formalism that is appreciated by practitioners may seem quite restricted in terms of their powers of expression. Yet they frequently gain in heuristic power consequently, i.e. bringing right knowledge at right time becomes easy. Knowing which areas of knowledge are more relevant to which problems is what that differentiates an expert from an amateur.
- *Notational convenience-* as the coding of vast amount of knowledge is required, the notations chosen for coding should be easy to read and write, and it should be possible to understand the meaning without knowing how it will be interpreted.

There are various ways of representing the knowledge in knowledge base. The most commonly used knowledge representation (KR) structure is in the form of "IF- THEN – ELSE" type of structure. It states that a conclusion or an action is sure to take place, if the situation on IF parts arises. A rule is said to be triggered or fired, if condition of IF part is satisfied. An example of rule may appear as follows:

Rule 1
    IF   the marks secured by the student is less than 50
    THEN declare him as failed.
Rule 2
    IF   the car does not start
    AND there is petrol in the car
    AND fuse is working properly
THEN there would be fault in fuel flow.
Rule 3
    IF material quality is poor
    OR the negligence on human part
    OR the quality check is not proper
THEN the output quality of product will be poor.

These rules simply indicate that each production rule is a fragment of AND / OR tree used for problem reduction.

In AI applications there are situations where one can not be certain about some conclusion e.g. to analyze the disease of the patient, even if one has matched all the symptoms, still one can not be hundred percent sure about the disease. These are called as uncertain events, which are also guided by 'beliefs' besides normal symptoms.

To accommodate the situation of uncertainty, one additional parameter called *'certainty factor'* is associated with the production rule. The certainty factors are the numerical estimates of the belief in the conclusion where all the conditions are known with total certainty.

12.8 INFERENCE ENGINE

The expert systems can be used either to answer some query given by user or to give some expert advice or consultation. For performing either of the above tasks, inference engine has to act. Inference engine is the module, which finds an answer from the knowledge base. It applies the knowledge to find the solution of the problem. In general, inference engine makes inferences by deciding which rules are satisfied by facts, decides the priorities of the satisfied rules and executes the rule with the highest priority. It is also called *rule interpreter*, as the knowledge is normally stored in terms of rules.

The inference engine performs following tasks:

*   It matches the IF condition of a rule with given input condition, if match occurs then triggers that rule and similarly triggers many rules to reach at conclusion.
*   Adds the previously drawn conclusion to knowledge base as inferred facts for future use.
*   The major task of inference engine is to trace its way through collection of rules to arrive at some answer according to users query. The technique of drawing the conclusion is called as inferencing.

The inferencing can be of two types:
*   Forward chaining
*   Backward chaining

12.8.1 Forward Chaining

In forward chaining, the given condition (fact) is matched with the left part of a rule (called as antecedent). When the antecedent conditions are met, the rule is fired. That means the rule is replaced by right hand side of the rule. It now becomes the new fact to be matched with antecedent part of another rule. Forward chaining is also called as data driven search or antecedent search. This chaining method is explained below:

Consider the set of facts F1, F2, F3....., F6 and set of consequents C1, C2,C3...C5. The production rules are assumed to be as follows:
*   IF F1 and F2 then C1
*   IF F3 and C1 then C3
*   IF F6 then C3

- If F2 and C3 then C4
- IF C4 then C5
- IF C2 then C3
- IF C5 then C6

Let us assume that the input is, facts F1 and F3 are true, and the query is that whether consequent C6 is true or not. The system will proceed as follows:

Apply rule no.	Rule states	inferred fact
1	applied	C1
2	applied	C3
3	not required	
4	applied	C4
5	applied	C5
6	not required	
7	applied	C6

Thus, through firing of rules 1,2,4,5,7 the inferred fact becomes C6, which is proved to be true.

This is the case of simple rules and limited in number. However, in actual expert systems the rules are large in number and multiple conditions in IF clause exist. The inferencing requires checking all possibilities in order to reach at source conclusion. In forward chaining the given facts behave as starting states and the conclusions which are to be drawn behave as goal states. Situations where the starting states are more than goal states, the forward inferencing method is used.

12.8.2 Backward chaining

This is the reverse process of forward chaining. In this, rule interpreter starts with matching "THEN" part of the rule and if match occurs, it is replaced by "IF" condition. Here the rule interpreter starts with goal state and proceeds towards start state, thus backward chaining is also called as *goal driven search*.

In the above example, if user specifies that C6 has to be proved. Let us assume that F2 and F3 are true again. The inferencing using backward chaining would proceed as follows:

	rule applied	condition matched	inferred
C6 (given as true)	7		C5
C5	6,5	condition matched	C2, C4
C4	4	condition matched	C2 and A2
C3	3	condition matched	A3
C2	2	condition matched	A3, C1
C1	1	condition matched	A1, A2

With this sequence of steps, A1 is proved to be true.

12.9 KNOWLEDGE BASE EDITOR

The function of knowledge base editor is to help the programmer to locate the deficiencies in the performance of the program and to correct those. This is done by often accessing the information provided by the explanation system. They also assist in addition of new knowledge to knowledge base, help make correct rule syntax and perform consistency checks on the updated knowledge base.

12.10 KNOWLEDGE ACQUISITION FACILITIES

Knowledge acquisition facilities impart methods and tools in an expert system that make it capable to acquire knowledge automatically by the user while using it instead of requiring the knowledge to be coded by knowledge engineer before entering into knowledge base. These facilities make the system capable of enhancing its knowledge while in use and thus help in improving the performance of the system.

Components described above are the normal ones an expert system is supposed to possess. Besides these normal features of the expert systems, they are also designed to have metaknowledge. The metaknowledge is knowledge about knowledge. It is knowing what one knows and knowing when and how to use it.

Though expert systems are designed to perform the function of an expert, still those have some limitations. Because the knowledge used for making the knowledge base of an expert system is acquired from human experts, it becomes difficult to acquire type of knowledge that even human beings cannot describe or express in some communicable form. For example, we all perform the task of speech recognition extremely well, but none of us have much idea how we actually do it. Thus, acquiring such type of knowledge and making expert systems for such type of applications is not practical and hence not very successful. Moreover, there is a limit up to which a skill can be mechanized, e.g in the following applications , it is difficult to code the knowledge.,

- In robotic and computer vision If a task involves complex sensory motor skills beyond the scope of current technology,.
- If the task involves commonsense reasoning.

It is interesting to note that there is a big difference in the kind of knowledge required to become an expert in some field with the kind of knowledge that one needs just to get the work done.

After learning the components an expert system needs to possess for making it suitable for solving problems, we may now concentrate on process of designing expert systems.

12.11 DESIGN OF EXPERT SYSTEMS

In this section, we would present general guidelines for building a practical expert system suitable for solving real world problems. As we understand by now, the real function of an expert system is to provide a quality tool in the hands of users so that they are able to deal with the problems before them in cost effective manner and within the stipulated time frame. At the same time, it is also important that the process of designing of an expert system should be less tedious, economical and time-effective. Expert systems can be developed to solve any problem, but it is advisable to assess the development process on the parameters mentioned above so that precious time of experts, efforts and money is not wasted in futile exercises.

In general, following stages are involved in the development of an expert system:

- Selection of problem
- Decision about appropriate tools
- Development of prototype
- Testing of prototype
- Development of final system

12.11.1 Selection of Problem

As the development of expert systems involves substantial amount of human efforts and money, attempts should be made to analyze a problem before going for the development of expert system to solve it. Researchers have developed guidelines to assess whether a problem is appropriate for expert system solution. There guidelines are mentioned below:

- The solution of a problem by using expert system should justify the cost and efforts involved in building the same. Many expert systems have been built and are successfully performing in the areas of business, defense, mineral exploration and medicines where there is large scope of saving money, time and human life.
- In remote areas where visit to site by human experts if required, involves lot of expenses and time, expert systems can be used to save these. For example, in geological mining and exploration sites, which are situated at far remote places, a site visit by human experts requires huge investment in terms of time and money and hence use of expert systems at such locations should be encouraged.
- The problem domain should not require use of commonsense knowledge because, it is always difficult to code such type of knowledge for use by expert systems.
- If a problem can be solved using traditional techniques, use of expert system technology should be avoided because, we are generally more familiar with traditional methods and use of unconventional methods might only complicate the situation instead of easing it.
- As we know, the knowledge used by expert systems is derived from the knowledge and experience of human experts hence, before taking any problem in hands, it should be ascertained that human experts are available having expertise in the problem domain and also, they are willing to share their knowledge and expertise.

- The solution of a problem neither should require special adroitness nor perception which, human experts may possess and use in finding the solution of a particular problem. For example, robots and vision systems, though use expert system technology, lack in sophistication and flexibility of human beings. Hence, they need improvement so that these can be used in wider areas and can be a viable replacement of human experts.

Apart from the considerations mentioned above, some other aspects to be taken care of before selecting a problem for expert system solution are:

- *Assessment of payoff-* payoff is the return of the investment made in the form of manpower, resources, time and money employed in the development of the system. A proper assessment of the return should be made. The return can be in the form of money, increase in efficiency or any other advantage.
- *Assessment of development cost-* cost is a major and most important factor in the development of expert systems. Total cost of building a system involves cost of manpower, resources, time devoted, hardware and software. Apart from these, investment might have to be made in training of persons if necessary trained personnel are not available.
- *Assessment of maintenance cost-* every system requires periodic maintenance. The cost of maintenance of a system is very important because it adds to the expenditure incurred in running the same. The systems having very high maintenance cost are not desirable as it eats up a major portion of the monitory benefits derived after the use of expert system for solving a problem. Hence, assessment of maintenance cost should be made before going for the development of an expert system.

12.12 TYPES OF EXPERT SYSTEMS

As stated earlier, we would describe in detail, the structure and functioning of two out of the several most famous expert systems available.

12.12.1 Dendral

Dendral is the expert system developed for inferring process of structure elucidation of chemical compounds. This project began at Stanford University in 1965. DENDRAL is concerned with the interpretation of data obtained from a device called *"mass spectrometer"*. In the field of structure elucidation of compounds chemical expertise is needed in two major aspects:

- Domain specific knowledge is needed for reading and interpreting the output of X-ray crystallography, ultraviolet spectroscopy, infrared spectroscopy, and NMR spectroscopy.
- Extensive domain specific knowledge is essential during assembly process.

The control process employed by DENDRAL is of the kind, "generate and test". The search starts at an arbitrary initial state and by employing a generator, generates a set of states.

The normal procedure to obtain the structure of organic compound is given below:

- First, the basic testing of compounds is done in order to identify major groups. This is done by X- ray crystallography, infrared analysis, ultraviolet analysis, and nuclear magnetic resonance. The results available from these tests indicate their groups like alcohol, acetone, aldehydes etc.
- Once the groups are available, the chemists assemble these according to specific rules.
- After that, when a set of compounds and their structures are available, specialized tests are carried out to confirm the structure.

12.12.1.1 Control Process of Dendral

As mentioned earlier, the control process employed by DENDRAL is to 'generate and test'. In 'generate and test procedure' (like state space search), starting with arbitrary initial state and by employing a generator, all possibilities regarding presence of compounds is generated. On these possibilities a series of tests are carried out to eliminate unwanted states.

In DENDRAL instead of generating all possibilities, some planning is done and single possibility is generated. The procedure is known as "plan – generate – test". The planning program provides constraints for 'generate and test' modules.

CONGEN (CONstraints GENerator) is a DENDRAL program which constructs complete chemical structures by manipulating symbols that stand for atoms and molecules. It receives as its input, a molecular formula, together with a set of constraints which serve to restrict the possible interconnections among atoms. As output, it generates a list of all possible ways of assembling the atoms into molecular structure with imposing the given constraints.

DENDRAL has programs to rule out some hypothesis knowledge of mass spectrometry to make testable predictions about candidate molecules. The program "MSPRUNE" eliminates undesired elements.

12.12.1.2 Knowledge Base of DENDRAL

The knowledge base of DENDRAL basically consists of huge knowledge about organic chemistry. The entire knowledge about organic chemistry is coded in the form of production rules. One such rule is given below:

IF there are two peaks at mass units m1 and m2
           AND x1 + x2 = molecular weight + 28
           AND at least one of x1 or x2 is high
THEN Ketone group is present.

12.12.1.3 Working of DENDRAL

During functioning of DENDRAL, in the starting compound testing is planned. It is fed into programs and various groups are identified. The planner's production rule MSPRUNE is used to prune the number of alternate structures in the compound. The major task of MSPRUNE is to generate a hypothetical spectrum for structure. To perform this task it requires knowledge about characteristics spectra of all organic groups. This knowledge is coded in production rule format. A module called as MSRANK ranks the candidates into various groups. This subsystem has the knowledge of spectrometry to rank candidate structure

12.12.2 Mycin

MYCIN is one of the oldest and successful expert system used for diagnosing bacterial infectious diseases. It was developed at Stanford University in 1976 to help physicians in identifying which bacteria has been the cause for the infection and to suggest the appropriate remedial measures.

MYCIN was developed for domain "treatment of blood infections". It presupposes no specialized medical knowledge on the part of the user. Still, as is true for any expert system, having some basic knowledge about the application is crucial to understand the functioning of the program. There have been many extensions, revisions, and abstractions of MYCIN, but the basic version of MYCIN remained same. The organization of MYCIN is shown in the following figure 12.5. (from Buchanam and Shortliffe, 1984).

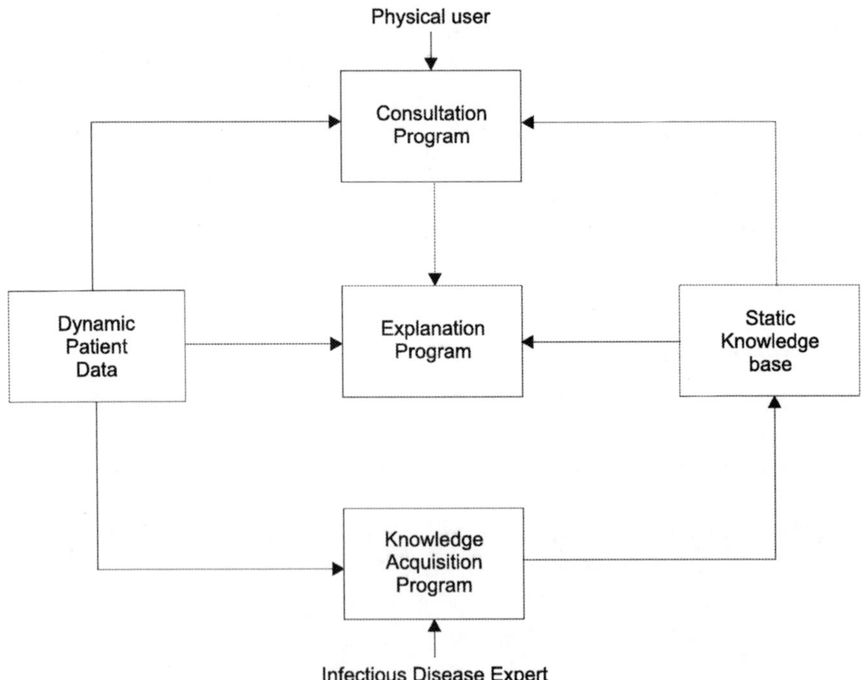

Fig. 12.5: Basic MYCIN organization (courtsy Buchnam and slortlife 1984)

MYCIN, basically has five components.

- *Knowledge base*, which contains features and judgmental knowledge about the domain.
- *Dynamic patient database* that contains the information regarding the patient
- *A consultation program*, which interacts with the user, asks questions, draws conclusions and gives advice about a particular case based on patient's data and the static knowledge.
- *The explanation program* that directly does not answers any questions and only justifies the advice given by expert system using static knowledge and by tracing the program execution.
- *Knowledge acquisition program* for adding new rule and changing existing one.

MYCIN was basically developed for treating blood infections. The treatment of blood infection, was done by suggesting any drug having antimicrobial agent able to kill bacteria. The selection of therapy for arterial infection is considered as a four-step decision making process:

- Deciding if the patient has significant infection
- Determining the possible organisms involved
- Selecting a set of drugs that might be appropriate
- Choosing the most appropriate drug

In MYCIN to gather the input, some samples are taken from the site of infection. These are sent to a microbiology laboratory for culture test. Culture test is an attempt to grow organism by putting the sample in a suitable medium. In blood infection, early evidence of growth may allow a report of morphological or staining characteristics of the organism.

MYCIN was basically developed to assist a physician, who is not expert in the field of antibiotics for the treatment of blood infections.

12.12.2.1 Knowledge Base of MYCIN

MYCIN's knowledge base is organized around a set of rules of the form mentioned below:

"*IF condition 1 and ....condition n are true then draw conclusion 1 and...... conclusion n*".

A typical MYCIN rule for inferring a class of an organism may appear as follows:

IF

      The stain of the organism is *gramneg*

      AND the morphology of the organism is rod

      AND the aerobicity of the organism is aerobic

THEN

> there is strongly suggestive evidence (0.8) that the class of the organism
> is *enterobacteriaceae.*

The rule is interpreted as follows:

"If an isolated organism appears rod shaped, stains in a certain way, and grows in the presence of oxygen, then it is highly likely to be in the class enterobacteriaceae. The number (0.8) is called certainty factor, which indicates how certain the conclusion is, if given conditions are satisfied. Actually, in nature there are events about which we cannot draw conclusions with certainty, e.g., in the areas of weather forecasting, medical diagnostics, mineral exploration etc., it is always difficult to conclude with certainty regarding some result. To deal with such applications, a factor indicating measure of belief called as certainty factor is associated. The value of certainty factor indicates the amount of truth ness of conclusion. The importance of degree of certainty is more or less as follows.

"If condition1 holds with certainty x1 ….. and condition m holds with certainty xm then draw conclusion 1 with certainty y1 and conclusion n with certainty yn".

Here the *certainty* associated with each conclusion is a function of *combined certainties* of the conditions and the tally, which is meant to reflect the degree of confidence in application of the rule.

In addition to rules, the knowledge base also stores facts and definitions in following forms:

- *Simple list,* e.g. the list of all organisms known to the system.
- *Knowledge tables* that contain record of clinical parameters and the values they take under various circumstances, e.g. the structural shape or morphology of every bacterium known to the system.
- *A classification system* for the clinical parameters according to the context in which that apply.

In MYCIN, information regarding patient is stored in the form of 'context tree'. Following figure 12.6 shows a context tree representation of a particular patient:

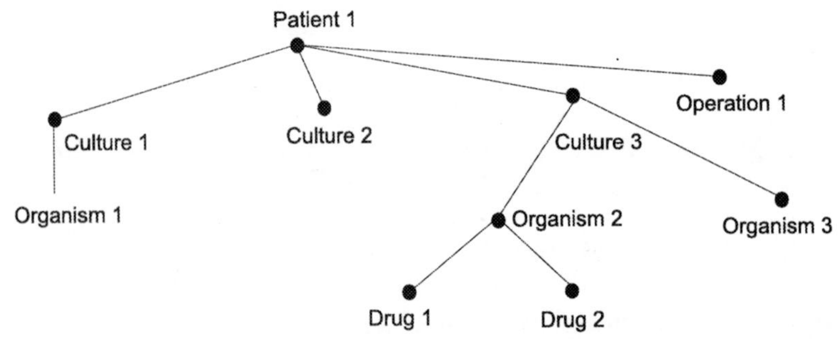

Fig. 12.6: Context tree of MYCIN (Buchnam 1984)

Above figure represents data of patient1, with three cultures and a recent operative procedure that may need to be taken into account.

Suppose we have following data stored in a record structure attached with node for organism1

Gram	=	(Gramneg 1.0)
MORPH	=	(Rod 0.8) (COCCUS 0.2)
AIR	=	(AEROBIC 0.6)

i.e.

- The gram stain of ORGANISM -1 is surely negative.
- It has a rod morphology with certainty 0.8 and COCCUS morphology with certainty 0.2.
- Organism-1 is aerobic (grows in air) with certainty 0.6.

If above mentioned rule is applied, here all three conditions are satisfied with the data. The certainty of individual events is 1.0, 0.8 and 0.6 and the certainty of their conjunction will be minimum of their individual constrains. Hence, it will be 0.6.

Thus, in this case we draw a conclusion that class of the organism is enterobacteriaceae with a degree of certainty = 0.6 x 0.8 = 0.48. Here, 0.6 is certainty factor of conjoined condition and 0.8 is CF of role. Thus,

$$CF(action)= CF (premise) \times CF (rule)$$

12.12.2.2 Control Structure of MYCIN

MYCIN adopts a high-level approach for the task of consultation, which is mentioned below:

IF
- there is an organism which requires therapy
- consultation has been given to any other organism requiring therapy
THEN

compile list of possible therapies and determines best one.

The symptoms of patient are matched with premise and if matching occurs, the rule is fired. To find out whether some rule is applicable or not, MYCIN first finds out, if there is indeed an organism present which is associated with significant disease. This information is obtained directly by user or via chain of inferences. The consultation is *search through a tree of goals*. The top goal is at root of the tree, and then it is divided into sub-goals. MYCIN's control structure uses AND/ OR tree.

12.12.2.3 Explanation Facility of MYCIN

MYCIN has facilities to answer queries of type "why" and "how". "Why" questions can be asked at any time from the system. When it is asked, the system first responds with action part of the rule. It displays the premises already instantiated followed by premises likely to be "how" question tells the reasoning process of how the answer was arrived at.

12.12.2.4 Working of MYCIN

MYCIN program was designed to diagnose and then prescribe treatment for an infectious disease in particular. The problem is, first to decide what bacterium is causing the disease or what are the most likely possibilities and second, based upon that decision to decide what antibiotic to give the patient to cure it. The information given by patient includes details of patient and disease plus more specialized things derived from laboratory tests. To perform their tests, culture is done. A small amount of material from infected part is placed on a sterile medium, if bacteria grows it tends to suggest that there is an infection.

In actual disease finding, there may be situations where multiple answers are found. To find out the actual output , in such situations the order in which facts and rules appears is checked . It corresponds to depth first search. In the above examples the goals were regarding single condition. Similarly, goals can be given for two or more conditions which must be satisfied simultaneously, e.g.,

$$1? - \text{number (x. singular). Noun (x)}$$
$$X = \text{dog}$$

It means, find the value of x such that x is a noun and number of x is singular.

12.13 DOMAIN EXPLORATION

The expert system is designed to work in a specific domain. Thus they store knowledge related with specific domain. A random collection of names, dates, places and old proverbs is not the kind of knowledge that provides basis of expertise. Knowledge implies organization and integration, in that different pieces of knowledge relate to each other.

While acquiring the knowledge for expert system the domain exploration is done. It is the process of performing in-depth study about application domain. Domain exploration is basically a knowledge acquisition method.

In order to gain knowledge of a domain whether it be a game like chess or a substantive field of technical expertise, there exist certain presupposition and prerequisites that one must fulfill, e.g. in the game playing one must understand that he has to win. Then in a particular game like chess, one must understand what a game is, how it is played and what the conditions of winning etc are. This type of background knowledge is called as deep knowledge in the expert system literature and opposite to it, there exist shallow knowledge, which consists of adhoc linking of stimulus and response.

Hence a chess program which simply chooses legal moves at random has no deep knowledge of the game, whereas a program which knows various board positions and values of pieces has some deep knowledge. Similarly a medical

transcription program will have shallow knowledge , if it simply Matches the symptoms and it will have deep knowledge, if it also produces coherent explanation of all the symptoms in terms of some small number of commonly occurring disorders.

Normally to build an expert systems, the domain knowledge is acquired and stored in the knowledge base as background knowledge. Then while handling the application, the expert system gathers more knowledge. OPAL is a knowledge elicitation program that has knowledge of domain of cancer therapy. it use domain knowledge to translate the information acquired from user to gain further knowledge. This combination of incremental knowledge acquisition , followed by knowledge compilation is a preferred methodology of building the expert system.. that is why it is said that expert system has learning.

12.14 EXPERT SYSTEM SHELLS

It is an interpreter that could be used to create a new expert system by adding new knowledge corresponding to new problem domain. The shells provide greater feasibility in representing knowledge and in reasoning.

EXERCISES

1. Why is it important that an expert system be able to explain the why and how question related to a problem solving session.
2. Describe and compare different types of problems solved by DENDRAL, & MYCIN.
3. Identify and describe two good application areas for expert systems within a university environment.
4. What are various knowledge representatives techniques used in expert system.
5. With the help of block diagram explain the expert system architecture.

References

1. Barnett, J., K. Knight, I. Mani and E.A. Rich. 1990. Knowledge and natural language processing, *Communications of the ACM* 33(8).
2. Barr, A., E.A. Feigenbaum and P.R. Cohen. 1981. *The Handbook of Artificial Intelligence*. Los Altos, CA: Morgan Kaufmann.
3. Baudet, G.M. 1978. On the branching factor of the alpha-beta pruning algorithm. *Artificial Intelligence* 10(2): 173–199.
4. Beal, D.F. 1990. A generalised quiescence search algorithm. *Artificial Intelligence* 43(1).
5. Bledsoe, W.W. 1997. Non-resolution theorem proving. *Artificial Intelligence* 9(1).
6. Block, H.D. 1962. The perceptron: A model for brain functioning. *Reviews of Modern Physics* 34(1): 123–135.
7. Bobrow, D.G. and T. Winograd. 1977. An overview of KRL, a knowledge representation language. *Cognitive Science* 1(1).
8. Bond, A.H. and L. Gasser, eds. 1988. *Readings in Distributed Artificial Intelligence*. San Mateo, CA: Morgan Kaufmann.
9. Brachman, R.J. 1979. On the epistemological status of semantic networks. In *associative Networks* ed. N.V. Findler. New York: Academic Press.
10. Brachman, R.J., V.P. Gilbert and H.J. Levesque. 1985. An essential hybrid reasoning system: Knowledge and symbol level accounts of KRYPTON. In *Proceedings IJCAI-85*
11. Brachman, R.J. and H.J. Levesque, eds. 1985. *Readings in Knowledge Representation*. Les Altos, CA: Morgan Kaufmann.
12. Brachman, R.J. and J. Schmolze. 1985. An overview of the KL-ONE knowledge representation system. *Cognitive Science* 9(2).
13. Brady, M. 1985. Artificial intelligence and robotics. *Artificial Intelligence* 26(1).
14. Bratka, L. 1986. *Prolog Programming for Artificial Intelligence*. Reading MA: Addison-Wesley.
15. Brooks, R.A. 1986. A robust layered control system for a mobile robot. *IEEE Journal of Robotics and Automation* RA-2(1).
16. Brownston, L., R. Farell, E. Kant and N. Martin. 1985. *Programming Expert Systems in OPS5: An Introductionto Rule-Based Programming*. Reading, MA: Addison-Wesley.

17. Bruce, B. 1975. Case systems for natural language. *Artificial Intelligence* (6(4): 327–360.

18. Burton, R.R. 1976. *Semantic Grammer: An Engineering Technique for Constructing Natural Language Understanding Systems.* Tech. Rep. 3453, Bolt Beranek and Newman, Boston, MA.

19. Carbonel, J.G. 1983. Learning by analogy. In *Machine Learning. An Artificial Intelligence Approach*, ed. R.S. Michalski, J.G. Carbonell and T.M. Mitchell. Palo Alto, CA: Tioga Press.

20. Carbonell, J.G. 1986. Derivational analogy: A theory of reconstructive problem solving and expertise acquisition. In *Machine Learning, Volume II*, ed. R.S. Michalski, J.G. Carbonell, and T.M. Mitchell. Los Altos, CA: Morgan Kaufmann.

21. Chandy, K. and J. Misra. 1989. *Parallel Program Design: A Foundation.* Reading, MA: Addison-Wesley.

22. Chang, C.L. and R.C. Lee. 1973. *Symbolic Logic and Mechanical Theorem Proving.* New York: Academic Press.

23. Charniak, E. and D. McDermott. 1985. *Introduction to Artificial Intelligence.* Reading, MA: Addison-Wesley.

24. Cheeseman, P., M. Self, J. Kelly, W. Taylor, D. Freeman and J. Stutz. 1988j. bayesian Classification. In *Proceedings AAAI-88.*

25. Chomsky, N. 1957. *Syntactic Structures.* The Hague: Mouton.

26. Chomsky, N. 1981. *Lectures on Government and Binding.* Dordrecht, Holland: Foris.

27. Church, K. and R. Patil. 1982. Coping with syntactic ambiguity or how to put the block in the box on the table. *Journal of Computational Linguistics* 8: 139–149.

28. Clark, D.A. 1990. Numerical and symbolic approaches to uncertainty management in AI. *Artificial Intelligence Review* 4: 109–146.

29. Clark, K.L. and S. Gregory. 1986. Parlog: Parallel programming in logic. *ACM Transactions on Programming Languages and Systems* 8(1).

30. Clocksin, W.F. and C.S. Mellish. 1984. *Programming in Prolog, 2nd ed.* New York: Springer-Verlag.

31. Colby, K. 1975. *Artificial Paranoia.* New York: Pergamon Press.

32. Corkill, D.D., K.Q. Gallagher and P.M. Johnson. 1987. Achieving flexibility, efficiency, and generality in blackboard architectures. In *Proceedings AAAI-87.*

33. Culingford, R.E. 1986. *Natural Language Processing: A Knowledge Engineering Approach.* Totowa, NJ: Rowman and Allanheld.

34. Davis, M and H. Putnam. 1960. A computing procedure for quantification theory. *Journal of the ACM* 7: 201–215.

35. Davis, R. 1982. Applications of meta level knowledge to the construction, maintenance and use of large knowledge bases. In *Knowledge-Based Systems in Artificial Intelligence*, ed. R. Davis and D.B. Lenat. New York: McGraw-Hill.

36. deJong, K. 1988. Learning with genetic algorithms: An overview: *Machine Learning* 3: 121–138.

37. Dempster, A.P. 1968. A generalization of bayestian inference. *Journal of the Royal Statistical Society. Series B* 30: 205–247.

38. Dijkstra, E. 1972. Notes on structured programming. In *Structured Programming*, ed. O.-J. Dahl, E.W. Dijkstra and C.A.R. Hoare. New York: Academic Press.

39. Dijkstra, E. 1976. *A Discipline of Programming*. Englewood Cliffs, N.J.: Prentice-Hall.

40. Doyle, J. 1979. A truth maintenance system. *Artificial Intelligence* 12(3).

41. Duda, R.O., P.E. Hart, K. Konolige and R. Reboh. 1979. *A Computer-Based Consultant for Mineral Exploration*. Tech. rep., SRI International.

42. Englemore, R. and T. Morgan, eds. 1989. *Blackboard Systems*. Reading, MA: Addison-Wesley.

43. Erman, L.D., P.E. London and S.F. Fickas. 1981. The design and an example use of Hearsay III. In *Proceedings IJCAI-81*.

44. Etherington, D.W. 1988. *Reasoning with Incomplete Information*. Los altos, CA: Morgan Kaufmann.

45. Fahlman, S.E. and G.E. Hinton. 1987. Connectionist architectures for artificial intelligence. *IEEE Computer* 20(1): 100–109.

46. Feigenbaum, E.A. and J.A. Feldman, eds. 1963. *Computer and Thought*. New York: McGraw-Hill.

47. Fikes, R.E. and N.J. Nilsson. 1971. STRIPS: A new approach to the application of theorem proving to problem solving. *Artificial Intelligence*. 2(3–4): 189–208.

48. Fillmore, C. 1968. The case for case. In *Universals in Linguistic Theory*, ed. E. Bach and R.T. Harms. New York: Holt.

49. Findler, N.V. ed. 1979. *Associative Networks: Representation and Use of Knowledge by Computer*. New York: Academic Press.

50. Gasser, L., C. Braganza and N. Herman. 1987. Implementing distributed artificial intelligence systems using MACE. In *Proceedings of the Third IEEE Conference on Artificial Intelligence Applications*, 315–320. (Reprinted in *Reading in Distributed Artificial Intelligence* (1988), ed. A.H. Bond and L. Gasser, published by Morgan Kaufmann, san Mateo, CA.

51. Gazdar, G. 1982. Phrase structure grammar. In *The Nature of Syntactic Representation*, ed. P. Jacobson and G.K. Pullum, 131–186. Dordrecht, Holland: D. Reidel.

52. Gazdar, G., E. Klein, G.K. Pullum and I. Sag. 1985. *Generalized Phrase Structure Grammar*. Cambridge, MA: Harvard University Press.

53. Gelemter, H., J.R. Hansen and D.W. Loveland. 1963. Empirical explorations of the geometry theorem proving machine. In *Computers and Thought*, ed. E.A. Feigenbaum and J. Feldman. New York: McGraw-Hill.

54. Genesereth, M and N. Nilson. 1987. *Logical Foundations of Artificial Intelligence*. Los altos, CA: Morgan Kaufmann.

55. Ginsberg, M.L. ed. 1987. *Reading in Nonmonotonic Reasoning*. Los Altos, CA: Morgan Kaufmann.

56. Gleitman, H. 1981. *Psychology*. New York: W.W. Norton.

57. Goldberg, D. 1989. *Genetic Algorithms in Search, Optimization and Maching Learning*. Reading, MA: Addison-Wesley.

58. Green, C. 1969. Application of theorem proving to problem solving. In *Proceedings IJCAI-69*.

59. Grosz, B.J. K. Spark Jones and B.L. Webber. 1986. *Readings in Natural Language Processing*. Los Altos, CA: Morgan Kaufmann.

60. Gupta, A. 1985. *Parallelism in Production Systems*. PhD thesis, Carnegie Mellon University, Pittsburgh, PA.

61. Hall, R. 1989. Computational approaches to analogical reasoning. *Artificial Intelligence* 39(1).

62. Halpern, J.Y. 1989. An analysis of first-order logics of probability. In *Proceedings IJCAI-89*.

63. Hanks, S. and D. McDermott. 1986. Default reasoning, nonmonotonic logics, and the frame problem. In *Proceedings AAAI-86*. (Reprinted in *Readings in Nonmonotonic Reasoning* (1987), ed. M. Ginsberg, published by Morgan Kaufmann, Los Altos, CA: pp. 390-395).

64. Hansson, O. and A. Mayer. 1989. Heuristic search as evidential reasoning. In *Proceedings of the Fifth Workshop on Uncertainty in AI*.

65. Harmon, P. and D. King. 1985. *Artificial Intelligence in Business*. New York: Wiley.

66. Hart, P.E., N.J. Nilsson and B. Raphael. 1968. A formal basis for the heuristic determination of minimum cost paths. *IEEE Transactions on SSC* 4: 100–109.

67. Hayes-Roth, B. and M. Hewett. 1989. BB1: An implementation of the blackboard control architecture. In *Blackboard Systems*, ed. R. Englemore and T. Morgan, 297–314. Reading, MA: Addison-Wesley.

68. Hendrix, G.G. 1977. Expanding the utility of semantic networks through partitioning. In *Proceedings IJCAI-77*.

69. Hendrix, G.G. and W.H. Lewis. 1981. Transportable natural-language interfaces to databases. In *Proceedings of the 19th Annual Meeting of the Association for Computational Linguistics*.

70. Hintikka, J. 1962. *Knowledge and Belief*. Ithaca, NY: Cornell University Press.

71. Hirsh, H. 1990. Learning from data with bounded inconsistency. In *Proceedings of the Seventh International Conference on Machine Learning*, 32–39.

72. Hirst, G. 1987. *Semantic Interpretation against Ambiguity*. New York: Cambridge University Press.

73. Hoare, C.A.R. 1985. *Communicating Sequential Processes*. Englewood Cliffs, NJ: Prentice-Hall.

74. Horn, B. 1986. *Robot Vision*. Cambridge, MA: MIT Press.

75. Huhns, M.N. ed. 1987. *Distributed Artificial Intelligence*. London: Pitman. (Available from Morgan Kaufmann, San Mateo, CA).

76. IBM speech recognition group. 1985. A real-time, isolated-word, speech recognition system for dictation transcription. In *IEEE International Conference on Acoustics. Speech and Signal Processing*.

77. ICOT. 1984. *International Conference on Fifth Generation Computer Systems*. Amsterdam: North-Holland.

78. Jagannathan, V., R. Dodhiawala and L.S. Baum, eds. 1989. *Blackboard Architectures and Applications*. Boston: Academic Press.

79   Jordon, M.I. 1988. Supervised learning and systems with excess degrees of freedom. In proceedings of the 1988 Connectionist Models Summer School, 62-75. San Mateo, CA: Morgan Kaufmann.

80. Joshi, A.K., B.L. Webber, and I. A. Sag, eds. 1981. elements of Discourse Understanding. Cambridge: Cambridge University Press.

81. Kanal, L.N. and J.F. Lemmer, eds. 1986. Uncertainty in Artificial Intelligence. New York. North-Holland.

82. Kandel, E.R. and J.H. Schwartz. 1985. Principles of Neural Science, 2ed. New York: Elsevier.

83. Kasif, S. 1986,. On the parallel complexity of some constraint satisfaction problems. In Proceedings AAAI-86.

84. Kautz., H. 1986. Constraint propagation algorithms for temporal reasoning. In Proceedings AAAI-86, 377-382.

85. Keams, M. and L.G. Valiant. 1989. Cryptographic limitations on learning Boolean formulae and finite automata. In Proceedings of the ACM Symposium on the Theory of Computing.

86. King M. 1983. Parsing Natural Language. New York: Academic Press.

87. Knuth, D.E. and R.W. Moore. 1975. An analysis of alpha-beta pruning. Artificial Intelligence 6(4).

88. Korf, R. 1985a. Depth-first iterative-deepening: An optimal admissible tree search. Artificial Intelligence 27(1).

89. Kumar, V., K. Ramesh, and V. Rao. 1988. Parallel best-first search of state-space graphs: A summary of results. In Proceedings AAAI-88.

90. Laffey, T.J., P.A. Cox, J. L. Schmidt, S.M. Kao, and J.YL Read. 1988. Real-time knowledge-based systems. AI Magazine 9(1):27-45.

91. Laird, J.E., P.S. Rosenbloom, and A. Newell. 1986. Chunking in Soar: The anatomy of a general learning mechanism. Machine Learning 1(1).

92. Lakoff, G. and M. Johnson. 1980. Metaphors We Live By. Chicago: university of Chicago Press.

93. Lauritzen, S.L. and D. J. Spiegelhalter, 1988. Local computations with probabilities on graphical structures and their applications to expert systems. Journal of the Royal Statistical Society. Series B 50(19):157-224.

94. Lenat. D.B. 1982. AM: An artificial intelligence approach to discovery in mathematics as heuristic search. In Knowledge-Based Systems in Artificial Intelligence, ed. R. Davis and D.B. Lenat. New York: McGraw-Hill.

95. Lenat, D.B. 1983a. Eurisko: A program that learns new heuristics and domain concepts. The nature of heuristics III: Program design and results. Artificial Intelligence 21(1-2).

96. Lenat, D.B. and R. V. Guha. 1990. Building Large Knowledge-Based Systems. Reading, MA: Addison-Wesley.

97. Levy, D.N. L. 1988. Computer Games. New York: Springer-Verlag.

98. Lindsay. R.K. 1963. Inferential memory as the basis of machines which understand natural language. In Computer and Thought, ed. E.A. Feigenbaum and J. Feldman. New York: McGraw-Hill.

99. Lytinen, S. 1986, Dynamically combining syntax and semantics in natural language processing in Proceedings AAAI-86.

100. Man, D. 1982. Vision: A computational investigation into the human representation and processing of visual information. Sac Francisco: W.H. Freeman.

101. McCarthy, J. 1986. Applications of circumscription to formalizing commonsense knowledge. Artificial Intelligence 28(1):89-116. (Reprinted in Readings in Nommonotonic Reasoning (1987), ed. M Ginsberg, Published Morgan Kaufmann, Los Altos, CA, pp. 153-166).

102. McCarthy, J. and Patrick J. Hayes. 1969. Some philosophical problems from the standpoint of artificial intelligence. In Machine Intelligence 4, ed. B. Meltzer and D. Michie. Edinburgh: Edinburgh University Press.

103. McCorduck, P. 1979. Machines Whgo Think. San Francisco: Freeman.

104. McDermott, J. 1982. R1: A rule-based configurer of computer systems. Artificial Intelligence 19(1):39-88.

105. McDonald, D.D. and L. Bolc. 1988. Natural Language Generation Systems. New York: Springer-Verlag.

106. McKeown, K.R. and W.R. Swartout. 1987. Language generation and explanation. In Annual Review of Computer Science, Volume 2. Palo Alto: Annual Reviews.

107. Minsky, M. 1975. A framework for representing knowledge. In the psychology of Computer Vision, ed. P. Winston. New York: McGraw-Hill.

108. Minisky, M. 1985/ The Society of Mind. New York: Simon & Schuster, Inc.

109. Minsky, M. and O. G. Selfridge. 1961. Learning in neural nets. In Proceedings of the Fourth London Symposium on Information Theory. New York: Academic Press.

110. Minton, S. 1988. Learning's Search Control Knowledge: An Explanation-Based Approach. Boston, MA: Kluwer.

111. Mitchell, T. M. 1978. Version Spaces: An Approach to Concept Learning, PhD thesis, Stanford University, Stanford, CA.

112. Newell, A.,J. C. Shaw, and H. A. Simon. 1963. Empirical explorations with the logic theory machine: A case study in heuristics. In Computers and Thought, ed. E. A. Feigenbaum and J. Feldman. New York: McGraw-hill.

113. Newell, A and H.A. Simon. 1963. GPS, a program that simulates human thought. In Computers and Thought, ed. E.A. Feigenbaum and J. Feldman. New York: McGraw-Hill.

114. Newell, A. and H.A. Simon. 1972. Human Problem Solving. Englewood Cliffs, NJ: prentice-Hall.

115. Newell, A. and H.A. Simon. 1976. Computer Science as empirical inquiry: Symbols and search. Communications of the ACM 19(3):113-126.

116. Nilsson, N.J. 1980. Principles of Artificial Intelligence. Palo Alto, CA: Morgan Kaufmann.

117. Nilsson, N.J. 1986. Probabilistic logic. Artificial Intelligence 28(1):71-87.

118. Nirenburg, S. 1987. Machine Translation: Theoretical and Methodological Issues. Cambridge. England: Cambridge University Press.

119. Norman, D.A. 1981. Perspectives on Cognitive Science. Norwood, NJ: Ablex.

120. Pearl, J. 1988. Probabilistic Reasoning in Intelligent Systems. Palo Alto: Morgan Kaufmann.

121. Pereira, F.C. N and D. H. D. Warren. 1980. Definite clause grammars for language analysis a survey of the formalism and a comparison with augmented transition networks. Artificial Intelligence 13(3): 231-278.

122. Pelya, G. 1957. How to Solve It. Princeton, NJ: Princeton University Press.

123. Pople, H.E. 1982. Heuristic methods for imposing structure on ill structured problems: The structuring of medical diagnosis. In Artifical Intelligence in Medicine, ed. P. Szolvits, 119-185. Colorado: Westview Press.

124. Quillian, R. 1968. Semantic memory. In Semantic Information Processing, ed. M. Minsky. Cambridge, MA: MIT press.

125. Quillian, R. 1969. The teachable language comprehender. Communications of the ACM 12:459-475.

126. Rauch-Hindin, W.B. 1986. Artificial Intelligence in Business, Science, and Industry: Volume I-Fundamentals, Volume II-Applications. Englewoods Cliffs, NJ: prentice-Hall.

127. Reiter, R. 1980. A logic for default reasoning. Artificial Intelligence 13(1-2).

128. muel, A.L. 1963. Some studies in machine learning using the game of checkers. In Computers and Thought, ed. E.A. Feigenbaum and J. Feldman. New York: McGraw-Hill.

129. R.C. 1973. Identification of conceptualizations underlying natural language. In Computer Models of Thought and Language, ed. R.C. Schank and K.M. Colby. San Francisco: Freeman.

130. Schank, R.C. 1975. Conceptual Information Processing. Amsterdam: North-Holland.

131. Schank, R. C. 1977. Dynamic Memory: A Theory of Reminding and Learning in Computers and People. New York: Cambridge University Press.

132. Schank, R.C. and R.P. Abelson. 1977. Scripts, Plans, Goals, and Understanding. Hillsdale, NJ: Erlbaum.

133. Schank, R.C. and J.G. Carbonell. 1979. Re: The Gettysburg Address: Representing social and political acts. In Associative Networks: Representation and Use of Knowledge by Computers, ed. N. Findler, New York: Academic Press.

134. Schank, R.C. and K. Colby, 1973. Computer Models of Thought and Language. San Francisco: Freeman.

135. Schank, R.C. and C. Owens. 1987. Ten Problems in Artificial Intelligence. Tech. Rep. 514. Computer Science Department, Yale University, New Haven, CT.

136. Searle, J.R. 1969. Speech Acts. Cambridge: Cambridge University Press.

137. Searle, J.R. 1975. Indirect speech acts. In Syntax and Semantics 3: Speech Acts, ed. P. Cole and J. Morgan. New York: Academic Press.

138. Shafer, G. 1976. A Mathematical Theory of Evidence. Princeton, NJ: Princeton University Press.

139. Shafer, G. and J. Pearl, eds. 1990. Readings in Uncertain Reasoning. Los Altos, CA: Morgar Kaufmann.

140. Shannon, C.E. 1950. Programming a computer for playing chess. *Philosophical Magazine [Series 7]* 41: 256–275.

141. Shieber, S.M. 1986. *An Introduction to Unification-Based Approaches to Grammar.* CSLI Lecture Notes, distributed by University of Chicago Press.

142. Shortliffe, E.H. and B.G. Buchanan. 1975. A model of inexact reasoning in medicine. *Mathematical Biosciences* 23: 351–379.

143. Sidner, C. 1985. Plan parsing for intended response recognition in discourse. *Computational Intelligence* 1(1): 1–10.

144. Simmons, Reid and T.M. Mitchell. 1989. A task control architecture for mobile robots. In *AAAI Spring Symposium on Robot Navigation.*

145. Simmons, Robert F. 1973. Semantic networks: Their computation and use for understanding English sentences. In *Computer Models of Thought and Language,* ed. R.C. Schank and K.M. Colby. San Francisco: Freeman.

146. Simon, H.A. 1957. *Models of Man.* New York: Wiley.

147. Simon, H.A. 1981. *The Sciences of the artificial, 2nd ed.* Cambridge, MA: MIT Press.

148. Simon, H.A. 1983. Why should machines learn? In *Machine Learning, An Artificial Intelligence Approach,* ed. R.S. Michalski, J.G. Carbonell and T.M. Mitchell. Palo Alto, CA: Tioga Press.

149. Simon, H.A. and L. Siklossy. 1972. *Representation and Meaning.* Englewood Cliffs, NJ: Prentice-Hall.

150. Sowa, J.F. 1984. *Conceptual Structures.* Reading, MA: Addison-Wesley.

151. Stefik, M. 1981b. Planing with constraints (MOLGEN: Part 1). *Artificial Intelligence* 16(2): 111–139.

152. Sussman, G.J. 1975. *A Computer Model of Skill Acquisition.* Cambridge, MA: MIT Press.

153. Thomason, R. ed. 1974. *Formal Philosophy: Selected Papers of Richard Montague.* New Haven, CT: Yale University Press.

154. Touretzky, D. 1989b. Connectionism and compositional semantics. In *Advances in Connectionist and Neural Computational Theory,* ed. J.A. Barnden and J.B. Pollack. Norwood, NJ: Ablex.

155. Turing, A. 1963. Computing machinery and intelligence. In *Computers and Thought,* ed. E.A. Feigenbaum and J. Feldman. New York: McGraw-Hill.

156. Weizenbaum, J. 1966. ELIZA–a computer program for the study of natural language communication between man and machine. *Communications of the ACM* 9(1): 36–44.

157. Weld, D.S. and J. de Kleer, eds. 1988. *Reading in Qualitative Reasoning about Physical Systems*. Palo Alto, cA: Morgan Kaufmann.

158. Wilensky, R. 1986. *Common LISP craft*. New York: W.W. Norton.

159. Wilks, Y.A. 1972. *Grammar, Meaning and the Machine Analysis of Language*. London: Routledge and Kegan Paul.

160. Wilks, Y.A. 1975a. Preference semantics. In *Formal Semantics of Natural Language*, ed. E.L. Keenan. Cambridge: Cambridge University Press.

161. Wilks, Y.A. 1975b. A preferential, pattern-seeking semantics for natural language. *Artificial Intelligence* 6(1).

162. Wilson, G.V. and G.S. Pawley, 1988. On the stability of the travelling salesman problem algorithm of Hopfield and Tank. *Biological Cybernetics* 5(1): 63–70.

163. Winograd, T. 197. On primitives, prototypes, and other semantic anomalies. In *Proceedings of the Second Workshop on Theoretical Issues in Natural Language Processing (TINLAP 2)*.

164. Winograd, T. 1983. *Language as a Cognitive Process: Syntax*. Reading, MA: Addison-Wisley.

165. Winograd, T. and F. Flores. 1986. *Understanding Computers and Cognition: A New Foundation for Design*. Norwood, NJ: Ablex.

166. Winston, P.H. 1975. Learning structural descriptions from examples. In *The Psychology of Computer Vision,* ed. P.H. Winston. New York: McGraw-Hill.

167. Winston, P.H. 1984. *Artificial Intelligence*. Reading, MA: Addison-Wesley.

168. Winston, P.H. and B. Horn. 1989. *LISP*, Reading, MA: Addison-Wesley.

169. Woods, W.A. 1970. Transition network grammars for natural language analysis. *Communications of the ACM* 13(10): 591–606.

170. Woods, W.A. 1973. Progress in natural language understanding: An application to Lunar geology. In *Proceedings of the AFIPS conference 42*. AFIPS Press.

171. Woods, W.A. 1975. What's in a link: Foundations for semantic networks. In *Representation and Understanding*, ed. D.G. Bobrow and A. Collins. New York: Academic Press.

172. Zadeh, L.A. 1979. A theory of approximate reasoning. In *machine Intelligence 9*, ed. J. Hayes, D. Michie and L.I. Mikulich, 149–194. New York: Halstead Press.

Index